Life Care Planning *and* Case Management Handbook

Edited by

Roger O. Weed, Ph.D.
Georgia State University
Atlanta, Georgia

CRC PRESS
Boca Raton London New York Washington, D.C.

Library of Congress Cataloging-in-Publication Data

Life care planning and case management handbook / edited by Roger O. Weed.
p. cm.
Includes bibliographical references and index.
ISBN 1-57444-075-6 (alk. paper)
1. Life care planning—Handbooks, manuals, etc. I. Weed, Roger O.
RM930.7.L54 1998
362.1′6—dc21 98-9288
CIP

Direct all inquiries to CRC Press LLC, 2000 N.W. Corporate Blvd., Boca Raton, Florida 33431.

Visit the CRC Press Web site at www.crcpress.com

International Standard Book Number 1-57444-075-6
Library of Congress Card Number 98-9288
Printed in the United States of America 2 3 4 5 6 7 8 9 0
Printed on acid-free paper

INTRODUCTION

Life care planning has become an industry unto itself. Conceptually, the process, methods, and standards associated with future care build upon the foundation of appropriate and coordinated medical and ancillary care for people who have experienced significant medical adversity. A combined definition of Intelicus' Annual Life Care Planning Conference and the American Academy of Nurse Life Care Planners agreed upon at the Forensic Section Meeting, NARPPS annual Conference, Colorado Springs, Colorado, April 3, 1998 is as follows:

DEFINITION

A Life Care Plan is a dynamic document based upon published standards of practice, comprehensive assessment, data analysis and research, which provides an organized, concise plan for current and future needs with associated costs, for individuals who have experienced catastrophic injury or have chronic health care needs.

PURPOSE

This book is intended to bring together the many concepts regarding developing life care plans into one publication, as well as offer current state-of-the-art thought, beliefs and procedures. It is the editor's view that this highly specialized health care industry offers a valuable contribution to managed care and quality of life issues for persons with catastrophic disabilities. Having a solid foundation from which to practice will advance the entire industry. The intended audience for the book is anyone who has a role in planning for complex medical care. Families, clients, medical professionals, allied health care professionals, and representatives of the legal profession are included. It seems that life care planning is ideal for managed care, if the focus is on quality of care while maximizing the purchasing power of available resources.

BOOK STRUCTURE

The book is presented in four sections. The first chapter represents an overview of the history as well as the current practice of life care planning with a view toward the future. Section I, comprised of Chapters 2 through 11, spotlights various professions commonly associated with developing a life care plan. The professional roles are outlined and suggestions for planning are offered for those unfamiliar with the various specialties. Each author was asked to provide an overview of their area of specialty as well as identify specific life care planning issues and topics. Obviously, not all contributors who possibly could be participants are included. For example, dietitian, recreational therapist, music therapist, and various medical specialties which are considered either too closely aligned to the others or not routinely part of the team are not included in the book.

Section II focuses on selected disabilities for which life care planning has been utilized. Certainly, current practice seems to encompass mostly injury-related disabilities, but the field is slowly expanding into disease and emotional disabilities if the required care is complicated or complex. Two examples are HIV and transplantation care plans. The chapter on audiology, located in Section I, necessarily includes topics relating to a specific disability which overlap with the section on selected disabilities.

Section III, Forensic Considerations, is included in the book given that life care planning was first introduced through the legal profession. And although future care planning is much broader in contemporary times, the legal roots are still obvious. This section represents a highly specialized civil litigation enterprise that has different rules in which most people, outside of the legal profession, are not familiar. The section includes basic concepts and perspectives from both plaintiff and defense attorneys. A unique contribution is the inclusion of the story of a father and a caregiver in a case where the life care plan was instrumental in settling litigation. Most people cannot fully appreciate what it must be like to have a family member involved in a traumatic injury and have to deal with major medical decisions as well as legal issues. Therefore, this chapter is included to offer some insight into these areas.

The fourth and final section is General Issues, and it covers important topics which are not easily aligned with other areas. Ethical issues transcend all categories and probably are the basis for the longevity of the life care planning industry. Ethical life care planners who adhere to a code of conduct will assure the future. Technology also transcends all categories and has immensely impacted the efficiency and professionalism of completing the life care plan. This industry has dramatically changed in the last one to two years and presents a major challenge for life care planners to keep abreast of new technology. Life care planning certification is the logical step in assuring minimum qualifications although many persons who call themselves "life care planners" are not certified or educated in this particular area. Hopefully, voluntary use of qualified life care planners will encourage others to pursue this specialized training. The last chapter of the book focuses on what all credible life care planners seek: resources. Networking among life care planners clearly reveals the tremendous thirst for data that can be used for planning. Some sources are well known, while others are obscure. The sources listed represent a significant amount of work and sharing of knowledge.

Finally, references are included for each chapter. This will allow readers, who need more information than could be included in a chapter, the ability to further research topics. It is my hope that this publication will advance the industry another notch and the information will assist all who read it by improving their knowledge and profession.

Roger O. Weed, Ph.D., CRC, CLCP, LPC, CDMS, CCM, FNRCA

THE EDITOR

Roger O. Weed, Ph.D., CRC, CLCP, LPC, CDMS, CCM, FNRCA is a graduate rehabilitation counseling coordinator and associate professor at Georgia State University. He is a Licensed Professional Counselor, Certified Life Care Planner, Certified Rehabilitation Counselor, Certified Disability Management Specialist, Certified Case Manager, and Fellow of the National Rehabilitation Counseling Association. He has authored or co-authored more than 70 rehabilitation books, articles, and book chapters. He has been honored with several awards for his work including the 1991 *Outstanding Educator* by the National Association of Rehabilitation Professionals in the Private Sector, the 1993 *National Professional Services Award* from the American Rehabilitation Counseling Association. He also is listed in the 1997 and 1998 edition of *Who's Who in America* and the 1998 edition of *Who's Who in the World.*

He is also past president of the National Association of Rehabilitation Professionals in the Private Sector (NARPPS) and maintains a nation-wide private consulting practice specializing in catastrophic rehabilitation and rehabilitation professional training. In addition, he holds adjunct faculty status with the Center for Rehabilitation Technology at the Georgia Institute of Technology and courtesy faculty with the University of Florida.

CONTRIBUTORS

Raymond L. Arrona
QuestCom, Rasar Management Services, Inc.
Smyrna, Georgia

Debra E. Berens
Rehabilitation Consultant
Atlanta, Georgia

Terry L. Blackwell
Department of Rehabilitation Counseling
Louisiana State University Medical Center
New Orleans, Louisiana

Richard Paul Bonfiglio
Medical Director
HealthSouth
Harmarville Rehabilitation Hospital
Pittsburgh, Pennsylvania

Melissa A. Brown
Department of Physical Medicine and Rehabilitation
University of Texas Southwestern Medical Center
Dallas, Texas

Everett G. Dillman
President
International Business Planners, Inc.
El Paso, Texas

Tyron C. Elliott, Esq.
The Elliott Law Firm
Manchester, Georgia

Randall W. Evans
President
Learning Services Corporation
Durham, North Carolina

Vic S. Gladstone
American Speech-Language-Hearing Association
Rockville, Maryland

Susan Riddick-Grisham
Care Coordination Consultant
Orinda, California

Lee D. Gunn, IV, Esq.
Gunn, Ogden and Sullivan, P.A.
Tampa, Florida

Tracy Raffles Gunn
Attorney
Fowler, White, Gillen, Boggs, Villareal, and Banker, P.A.
Tampa, Florida

Phala A. Helm
Department of Physical Medicine and Rehabilitation
University of Texas Southwestern Medical Center
Dallas, Texas

Anna N. Herrington
Rehabilitation Counselor
Atlanta, Georgia

Larry Higdon
American Speech-Language-Hearing Association
Austin, Texas

Julie A. Kitchen
Paul M. Deutsch & Associates
Orlando, Florida

Gloria Lane
Medical Case Manager
Arlington, Texas

V. Robert May, III
Executive Director
Commission on Disability Examiner Certification
Midlothian, Virginia

Ileana Seoane McCaigue
Occupational Therapist
Suwannee, Georgia

Robert H. Meier, III
Director of Medical Rehabilitation
O'Hara Regional Center for Rehabilitation
Denver, Colorado

Art Peddle
HealthSouth Corporation
Norcross, Georgia

Anne Sluis Powers
Department of Family Medicine and Psychiatry
University of Nevada School of Medicine
Reno, Nevada

Randall L. Thomas
National Center for Life Care Planning
Madison, Mississippi

Mamie Walters
QuestCom, Rasar Management Services, Inc.
Smyrna, Georgia

Thomas M. Ward
Physiatrist
Little Rock, Arkansas

Carolyn W. Watkins
Assistive Technology and Speech/Language Pathology
Watkins and Associates, P.C.
Atlanta, Georgia

Roger O. Weed
Georgia State University
Atlanta, Georgia

Terry Winkler
Ozark Area Rehabilitation Services
Springfield, Missouri

James A. Young
Department of Physical Medicine and Rehabilitation
Michael Reese Hospital and Medical Center
Chicago, Illinois

ABOUT THE CONTRIBUTORS

Raymond L. Arrona began his career in 1967 as an independent contractor with Wear-Ever Aluminum, Inc., Alcoa Aluminum's first subsidiary, which marketed Wear-Ever Cookware and Cutco Cutlery. He quickly achieved one of the company's coveted positions as Division Manager and relocated from Arizona to Georgia in 1976 where he was President and CEO until 1997 of RASAR Management Services, Inc./dba Vector Marketing, which represents the Cutco Cutlery product. He also operated as Vector's Southern Zone Division Manager for the states of Georgia and South Carolina. In late 1997, he joined a startup company QuestCom which develops web sites for businesses.

Mr. Arrona experienced every father's nightmare when his daughter, Anita, was tragically injured in an accident caused by a drunk driver. "The impact of Anita's accident has been far reaching in all areas of my family's life including the personal, financial, spiritual, educational, judicial, professional, and friendship levels. No emotion has been immune from the effects of that tragic day. It is my wish that by telling Anita's story, it will in some way help others through similar situations, or assist in allowing life care planners gain insight into our family as we continue to deal with this life changing event."

Debra E. Berens, M.S., CRC, CCM is a rehabilitation consultant in private practice in Atlanta, Georgia. She has extensive experience as a vocational rehabilitation counselor and case manager in the areas of workers' compensation, short- and long-term disability, Veterans Affairs job placement programs, Social Security, general liability and personal injury, and was vocational supervisor for an international health care management company. She currently practices as a rehabilitation consultant for the life care planning of persons with catastrophic injuries and has achieved the postgraduate certificate in Life Care Planning for Advanced Catastrophic Case Management. Ms. Berens is also serving a 5-year term as Commissioner on the National Commission on Rehabilitation Counselor Certification (CRCC) and is president of the Private Rehabilitation Suppliers of Georgia professional organization, the state chapter of the National Association of Rehabilitation Professionals in the Private Sector (NARPPS).

Terry L. Blackwell, Ed.D., CRC is Clinical Associate Professor of Rehabilitation Counseling, School of Allied Health Professions, Department of Rehabilitation Counseling, Louisiana State University Medical Center, New Orleans, Louisiana. Prior to his appointment as a clinical associate professor at Louisiana State

University Medical Center, Dr. Blackwell was in private practice in Montana and worked throughout the U.S. specializing in catastrophic rehabilitation and life care planning, consultation, and training. Dr. Blackwell sits on the editorial boards of several rehabilitation journals and has authored or co-authored a number of books and articles in the areas of job analysis, forensic rehabilitation, ethics, and life care planning.

Richard Paul Bonfiglio, M.D. is the medical director of HEALTHSOUTH Harmarville Rehabilitation Hospital in Pittsburgh, Pennsylvania. He is board certified by the American Board of Physical Medicine and Rehabilitation and the American Board of Independent Medical Examiners (ABIME). Dr. Bonfiglio has previously served as the medical director of several nationally recognized rehabilitation facilities including the Lake Erie Institute of Rehabilitation and the Bryn Mawr Rehabilitation Hospital. He has also maintained close acedemic ties, including having served as Residency Program Director at the Schwab Rehabilitation Center.

Dr. Bonfiglio's clinical practice within the field of physical medicine and rehabilitation has included providing care to children and adults with traumatic brain injuries, spinal cord injuries, amputations, and acute and chronic pain proglems. He is an internationally recognized speaker on various rehabilitation topics.

Dr. Bonfiglio has been involved for years in the review and critical analysis of Life Care Plans. His interests include the development of a strong medical foundation to enhance the accuracy and reliability of these plans. He is also an expert in life expectancy determinations for individuals following catastrophic illnesses and injuries. He has been on the faculty of the Rehabilitation Training Institute for life care planning since its inception.

Dr. Bonfiglio has sustained a strong clinical practice within the field of physical medicine and rehabilitation, providing care to children with a variety of physical and cognitive impairments, children and adults with traumatic brain injuries, spinal cord injuries, amputations, and acute and chronic pain problems.

Dr. Bonfiglio has been involved for years in the review and critical analysis of Life Care Plans. His interests include the development of a strong medical foundation to enhance the accuracy and reliability of these plans. He is also an expert in life expectancy determinations for individuals following catastrophic illnesses and injuries.

Melissa A. Brown, M.S., CRC is a Faculty Associate in the Department of Physical Medicine and Rehabilitation at the University of Texas Southwestern Medical Center at Dallas, and vocational rehabilitation counselor. She serves as medical case manager for the Physical Medicine and Rehabilitation Department's clinical practice and is the consulting vocational rehabilitation counselor for the North Texas Burn Rehabilitation Model System.

Everett G. Dillman, Ph.D., an educator and business consultant, is President of International Business Planners, Inc. Dr. Dillman has been active in governmental, business and financial circles in the Southwest for over thirty years. During this period he has served on the advisory board of the Lubbock Division of the Small Business Administration as well as on the board of directors of several profit and civic organizations. Dr. Dillman has served on the Board of Directors of the

National Association of Forensic Economists and on the Steering Committee for Forensic Rehabilitation of the National Association of Rehabilitation Professionals in the Private Sector. He has published extensively in both the vocational and economic areas.

Tyron C. Elliott, J.D. is a practicing trial lawyer with over 30 years of experience. His practice focuses on the area of neurolaw, which deals with brain and spinal cord injuries. Mr. Elliott primarily represents persons who have received traumatic injuries. He is an adjunct professor at Emory University School of Medicine in Atlanta, where he lectures on legal-medical issues. He is also an advocate member of the American Board of Trial Advocates and has given lectures and programs throughout the U.S., Canada and Mexico. Mr. Elliott is the executive editor of the *Neurolaw Letter* and has contributed several articles on brain injury and related litigation.

Randall W. Evans, Ph.D., A.B.P.P. is President and CEO of Learning Services Corporation, a national provider of neurorehabilitation and supported living services. A practicing neuropsychologist for over fifteen years, Dr. Evans has published extensively in the areas of neuropsychology, neuropharmacology, and neurorehabilitation. Dr. Evans is also a Surveyor for the Commission on Accreditation of Rehabilitation Facilities and he also serves as a Clinical Associate Professor of Psychiatry at the University of North Carolina School of Medicine at Chapel Hill. Dr. Evans is one of the first rehabilitation professionals in the U.S. to receive Diplomate status from the American Board of Rehabilitation Psychology.

Vic S. Gladstone, Ph.D., CCC (Audiology) is Associate Director for Audiology for the American Speech-Language-Hearing Association in Rockville, Maryland. He obtained his B.S. in speech pathology and audiology and his M.S. in audiology from Penn State University, and his Ph.D. in audiology from the University of Maryland. For 28 years, Dr. Gladstone was a Professor and Director of Audiology at Towson University in metropolitan Baltimore. While at Towson, he initiated the graduate audiology program and directed the audiology clinic. Dr. Gladstone has participated in numerous consultative activities including providing direct clinical services to children and their families and in industrial environments.

Susan Riddick-Grisham, R.N., CCM, CLCP maintains a private consulting practice specializing in care coordination for individuals with catastrophic injuries and life care planning. She has authored or co-authored several publications in the area of life care planning. A popular trainer, Ms. Riddick-Grisham has presented educational programs on case management, life care planning, and medical legal consultation.

Lee D. Gunn, IV, J.D. is a graduate of the University of Florida where he received degrees in business administration as well as law. Since graduating in 1982, Mr. Gunn has practiced in the area of personal injury defense and is currently with the law firm of Gunn, Ogdon & Sullivan, P.A., in Tampa, Florida. The firm specializes in personal injury defense, medical malpractice, life, health and disability, construction defect litigation, and insurance law. He was also the author of an article on the defense perspective in life care planning, published in a National Association for Rehabilitation Professionals in the Private Sector journal in 1994.

Tracy Raffles Gunn is an associate in the Tampa Casualty Department. She received her B.A. from the University of South Florida in 1990 and her J.D. summa cum laude from Stetson University College of Law, where she served on the Executive Board of the Stetson Law Review and was named outstanding graduate. She specializes in civil appeals and insurance coverage litigation, and has published several articles on insurance coverage issues.

Anna N. Herrington, M.S. is a graduate of the rehabilitation counselor training program and a counseling psychology doctoral student at Georgia State University in Atlanta, Georgia.

Phala A. Helm, M.D. is Professor and past Chairperson of the Department of Physical Medicine and Rehabilitation at the University of Texas Southwestern Medical Center at Dallas and is internationally known for her work in burn rehabilitation. She is the Director and Principal Investigator for the NIDRR funded North Texas Burn Rehabilitation Model System, establishing state-of-the-art treatment standards and outcome measures for burn rehabilitation management.

Larry Higdon, M.S., CCC (Audiology) is Vice President for Professional Practices in Audiology of the American Speech-Language-Hearing Association (ASHA) and is owner/audiologist of a private practice in Austin, Texas. His practice includes both direct service delivery and legislative consulting services, in which he is a lobbyist on behalf of various health and educational organizations, including the Texas Speech-Language-Hearing Association (TSHA). Prior to entering private practice full time, Larry served on the faculty of The University of Texas-Pan American, where he also served one year as interim program director, and at Southwest Texas State University. At each institution he was the director of clinical services, a product of his previous experience as a practitioner and administrator of hospital and community clinic programs. He has served as liaison to the Texas Education Agency, Department of Health, Department of Human Services, Medicaid, Texas Insurance Council, and the hearing aid dealers association.

Active in state and national professional organizations, he is a former president of TSHA, and is the immediate past-president of the Texas Speech and Hearing Foundation. He is Chair of the TSHA Publications Board and Managing Editor of the *Texas Journal of Audiology and Speech-Language Pathology* (*TEJAS*). As an ASHA member he has served as chair of numerous committees and boards (Long Range Strategic Planning, Honors, Public Policy Advocacy, Clinical Fellowship Year) and has been very active in the standards programs of ASHA.

Mr. Higdon is a Fellow of ASHA, and has received the Honors of TSHA and their highest leadership recognition award, the Jack L. Bangs Award.

Julie A. Kitchen, B.S., CLCP, CCM, CDMS is a certified case manager, life care planner, and disability management specialist who has been working in the development of life care plans for individuals with catastrophically injuries for over 15 years. She has authored or co-authored several monographs, chapters, and articles pertaining to injuries and long-term case management.

Gloria Lane, R.N., CCM is a registered nurse and certified case manager with more than 30 years experience. She also has achieved the University of Florida's certificate in life care planning. She has worked for several health care organizations including Kaiser Permanente where she was transplant coordinator (1992–1995) for the Texas region. She is currently an independent medical case manager in Arlington, Texas.

V. Robert May III, Ph.D., CDE II received his doctorate in rehabilitation from Southern Illinois University-Carbondale, and is currently the Executive Director of the National Association of Disability Evaluating Professionals (NADEP) and Executive Administrator of the Commission on Disability Examiner Certification (CDEC). He teaches functional capacity evaluation and impairment rating protocol in major metropolitan cities around the country as a member of the NADEP faculty and is currently adjunct professor in the Department of Rehabilitation, Rehabilitation Institute, Southern Illinois University. He maintains an outpatient industrial therapy center and a work capacity evaluation practice in two health clubs in Richmond, Virginia. His local therapy business trades as May Rehab and Therapy Services, which offers physical/aquatic therapy services, strength and conditioning training, and work disability/functional capacity evaluations. He has consulted with the Coca Cola Bottling Company, Overnite Transportation, Inc., and the Washington, D.C. Metropolitan Transit Authority regarding analyzing their jobs to ensure compliance with the Americans with Disabilities Act of 1990. Dr. May has lectured around the country on measuring work function, and has authored over 50 peer-reviewed journal articles and book chapters on industrial rehabilitation and Federal/State legislation governing occupational medicine practices. He holds certifications in rehabilitation counseling as a national certified counselor, certified rehabilitation counselor, and in impairment rating and functional capacity evaluation as a Certified Disability Examiner, Category II.

Ileana Seoane McCaigue, OTR/L, CDRS has been a practicing certified and licensed occupational therapist since 1977 when she graduated from the Medical College of Georgia in Augusta. She has worked in management and in direct care with patients of all ages and disabilities ranging from the neonatal intensive care unit to the nursing home. Her specialty interests and focus of treatment has been with adolescents and adults with acquired brain injuries, neurological disorders, and/or learning disabilities, especially in relation to adaptive driver rehabilitation. She is also a certified driver rehabilitation specialist and has been involved in driver rehabilitation since 1979. Ms. McCaigue has testified as an expert witness regarding issues related to transportation and home modification needs. She also assists in the development of life care plans in relation to these functional areas.

Robert H. Meier, III, M.D. is a physiatrist who has provided rehabilitative care for 27 years for persons with an amputation. For 8 years, he was Director of the Amputee Center at TIRR in Houston, Texas. For 11 years, he was the Director of the Amputee Center at the University of Colorado Health Sciences Center in Denver, Colorado. Dr. Meier is now Director of Medical Rehabilitation at the O'Hara Regional Center for Rehabilitation in Denver, Colorado, a subacute center for catastrophic disabling conditions. He also continues an interdisciplinary rehabilitation program for persons with amputations. In addition, he is a regular faculty member for the Intelicus training program on life care planning and an internationally known speaker on topics such as amputation, chronic pain, and neurological medical management. Dr. Meier is past President of the American Congress of Rehabilitation Medicine.

Art Peddle, PT graduated from Georgia State University with a B.S. degree in physical therapy and from David Lipscomb College with a B.A. degree in psychology. He has had very extensive experience in the field of physical therapy and in multiple disciplines specializing in the areas of industrial occupational medicine, orthopedic physical therapy, sports medicine physical therapy, and neurophysical therapy. He has worked in rehabilitation centers, hospitals, and private practice. His experience has included life care planning and consultation for a variety of physical therapy situations. He presently works with HealthSouth Corporation in Norcross, Georgia. He is a member of the APTA.

Anne Sluis Powers, Ph.D., R.N. is an assistant professor of clinical medicine in the Department of Family Medicine and Psychiatry at University of Nevada School of Medicine in Reno. Dr. Powers is a licensed psychologist and registered nurse who has co-authored five books regarding life care planning. She provides services clinically to medical patients and those with catastrophic injuries and illnesses.

Randall L. Thomas, Ph.D. is President of The National Center for Life Care Planning and has 28 years of experience in rehabilitation. He is a licensed psychologist, national board certified counselor, certified life care planner, certified rehabilitation counselor, and Diplomate of The American Board of Vocational Experts. He is associated with TecSolutions, a software development company for care management and life care planning activities. He has provided expert testimony in the field of rehabilitation and life care planning in numerous states throughout the U. S. He has authored or co-authored numerous articles in the fields of rehabilitation and case management/life care planning software. He is active in the training and education of life care planning. He has served on the Mississippi Board of Psychological Examiners as a member and executive secretary and has also served as a member of the Mississippi Worker's Compensation Advisory Counsel. He is a member of numerous national organizations and has served as president of the Mississippi chapter of NARRPS.

Mamie Walters, CNHP pursued a career in music theory and composition until 1981 when she became co-owner and successfully operated a cutlery distributorship for six years. During this period she met Ray Arrona, who was with Vector Marketing Corporation. Her busines acumen lead to a national promotion as Senior Assistant to the Executive Vice President of Sales and Marketing for the Southern Zone with Vector. In March 1994, this position ended and Ms. Walters pursued her education full time. In January, 1995, she began working as private hire for Ray Arrona, natural and legal guardian of Anita Arrona. Ms. Walters is a Certified Natural Health Professional and is currently enrolled and active in the Doctor of Naturopathy Program. She is also a member of the American Naturopathic Practitioners Association, and EarthSave International.

Thomas M. Ward, M.D. is a board-certified physiatrist in private practice in Little Rock, Arkansas. He graduated from the University of Kansas Medical School in 1985 and completed his internship in internal medicine at the University of California in Los Angeles and his residency in physical medicine and rehabilitation at the University of Minnesota. He belongs to several professional organizations and treats a wide range of disorders including chronic pain, brain injury, stroke, spinal cord injury, multiple sclerosis, pediatric cerebral palsy, and others.

Carolyn W. Watkins, Ph.D., CCC owns and operates a private practice in assistive technology in Atlanta, Georgia. Her practice includes assistive technology for all ages, as well as educational consulting, forensics and life care planning, and catastrophic health care of acquired brain injury, trach- and ventilator-dependent patients, and mediation and legal consulting. Dr. Watkins testifies as an expert witness in assistive technology for all ages, is the past Chair of the Georgia Board of Examiners for Speech Pathology and Audiology, and is the past Chair of Division 12 of ASHA, the AAC Division. She is active in multiple professional organizations and has taught and consulted in Russia, eastern Europe, and Hong Kong, China.

Terry Winkler, M.D., CLCP is a board-certified physiatrist (PM&R) physician in private practice in Springfield, Missouri. He is past Medical Director of Cox Hospital Rehabilitation Programs and Medical Director of Springfield Park Care Sub-Acute Rehabilitation Program and Curative Rehabilitation Center. Dr. Winkler serves on committees reviewing grants regarding spinal cord injury research for Paralyzed Veterans of America and the National Institute of Disability Rehabilitation Research. Dr. Winkler has several publications regarding Life Care Planning and has written a college text on rehab record systems. He specializes in Traumatic/Acquired Brain Injury, Spinal Cord Injury, Amputations, and Life Care Planning. Dr. Winkler holds an academic appointment as Clinical Associate Faculty at the University of Florida, Gainesville and LSU Medical Center, Department of Rehabilitation, New Orleans. Dr. Winkler's undergraduate training was at Louisiana Tech University and his residency in physical medicine and rehabilitation in Little Rock, Arkansas. Past honors include the America Award, Alumnus of the Year at Louisiana Tech University, "Who's Who Among Young Americans," and the Jean Claude Belot Award for Academic Achievement from Harvard University. In addition to his active medical practice, Dr. Winkler is a Certified Life Care Planner.

James A. Young, M.D. is a board-certified physiatrist and neurologist and board-certified in electrodiagnostic medicine in private practice in Chicago, Illinois. He received his medical degree from Indiana University in 1979, completed his residency in neurology in 1985, and his residency in physical medicine and rehabilitation in 1988. He is licensed in Illinois, Wisconsin, California, and Indiana. He is medical director of the Department of Physical Medicine and Rehabilitation at Michael Reese Hospital and Medical Center in Chicago. Dr. Young has taught medical courses relating to life care planning, is a faculty member of the University of Florida's certificate program in life care planning, and has spoken frequently on various medical topics including brain injury, headaches, coma, neurobehavior management, and neurologic complications of brain injury.

ACKNOWLEDGMENTS

There are a number of people who have contributed to helping this book become a reality. Certainly, first to be recognized are the contributors, who represent a major powerhouse of knowledgeable "movers and shakers" in the life care planning field from a wide range of specialties. My department chair, Dr. Richard (Pete) Smith, supported this venture with Georgia State University doctoral students Katie Baird and Anna Herrington, who have spent many hours contacting authors and assisting with editing chapters. Debbie Toole, with the fastest fingers on the planet, helped compose several publications and was invaluable with preparing manuscripts. Dennis McClellan, one of the original supporters of starting a national training program for life care planners, turned to publishing with St. Lucie/CRC Press and arranged for the release of this book.

I also think it is time to recognize others who have been instrumental in my career. Of course, my parents have primary credit for my existence as well as urging me to "break the mold" of local tradition by continuing my education. I was raised in a very small town where high school graduates commonly went to work in the timber industry. In fact, one of my peers could not understand why I would go to college when I could make almost as much money as a college graduate right out of high school! At the time, I did not have a good answer for him. However, he is now "between jobs" due to the massive turn-down in the local economy which is based almost entirely on wood products and logging.

Another individual who has always been a cheerleader is my good friend Sig Jokiel. He has encouraged me through many stressful life changes and business ventures. Also, at a time when I was strongly considering launching a private for-profit business, a local bank president, Bob Richards, agreed to go to lunch with me so I could "pick his brain." He donated several hours of time with wise suggestions, sound advice, and major emotional encouragement over many months as I developed my own rehabilitation business. (And he paid for the lunch!)

With a thriving business, my thoughts turned to enhancing my education. Dr. Todd Risley, who at the time was with the University of Kansas, told me he believed that I had doctoral potential. He invited me to apply to the University of Kansas where I slowly — very slowly — completed Ph.D. courses. It became evident that I would need to sell my business and pursue education full time if I were to graduate before retirement age. By then, Dr. Risley had moved to a university with no doctoral program, so I began searching for another educational source. When I sold my business in 1984 to pursue the Ph.D., Dr. Timothy Field, at the University of Georgia, agreed to be my major advisor. I can truly report that Dr. Field has been a major positive factor in my professional life. He has opened doors, been supportive beyond the call of duty, and shown me new horizons. Dr. Paul Deutsch, one of the original authors on life care planning, also inspired me to contribute to the development of literature and standards in this specialized industry. Last but certainly not least, my wife, Paula, has always encouraged me to do professionally whatever I wanted. This support resulted in many moves and job changes for her and she has never wavered. All in all, I believe that many people have observed more capability in me than I saw in myself. Through good fortune, outstanding resources, and a lot of assistance, this text comes to fruition.

R.O.W.

CONTENTS

SECTION II: SELECTED DISABILITIES: TOPICS AND ISSUES

SECTION III: FORENSIC CONSIDERATIONS

SECTION IV: GENERAL ISSUES

1

LIFE CARE PLANNING: PAST, PRESENT, AND FUTURE

Roger O. Weed

INTRODUCTION

Life care planning has become a major buzzword in the field of professional rehabilitation. Many people who have little knowledge about published concepts in life care planning are using the term *life care plans* in order to generate business. I recall reading a deposition from a Ph.D. level "life care planner" who, when asked by the opposing attorney about resources in life care planning, revealed that it was his opinion there were no written resources or training programs in life care planning. This discourse occurred in 1996, after there already existed a national certification in life care planning!

Clearly, life care plans have emerged as the standard by which other plans are to be measured with regard to the management of catastrophic impairments. The published methods, concepts, and procedures are an effective means to determine the road map of care as well as to identify reasonable costs associated with any impairment. However, not everyone is demonstrating quality practice; many do not know of existing standards of practice; and many professionals are resisting standardization of the concept. Perhaps it is helpful to review this emerging industry as a foundation for this book.

The Past

The original issuance of life care plans appeared in a legal publication, *Damages in Tort Actions* (Deutsch & Raffa, 1981), which established the guidelines for determining damages in civil litigation cases. By 1985 the life care plan was introduced to the health care industry in *Guide to Rehabilitation* (Deutsch & Sawyer, 1985). One of the first rehabilitation professional training programs was organized by Dr. Paul Deutsch and offered on September 16-17, 1986, in Hilton Head, South Carolina, where more than 100 rehabilitation professionals from throughout the United States assembled to begin the process of learning standards for life care plans. Initially the training comprised approximately two days to introduce rehabilitation professionals to the overall concepts and the format that was published in *Guide to Rehabilitation*. It also became evident that many people

1-57444-075-6/99/$0.00+$.50

were practicing life care planning in a variety of ways, some of which appeared to be contrary to the intended goals and purposes of ethical rehabilitation practice. In addition, as previously mentioned, many people were using the words "life care planning" as it became more popular, but had little or no awareness of the appropriate uses or practices associated with this emerging industry.

In the fall of 1992 five rehabilitation professionals, Richard Bonfiglio, MD; Paul Deutsch, Ph.D.; Julie Kitchen, CDMS; Susan Riddick, RN; and Roger Weed, Ph.D., met to discuss the apparent problems associated with the life care planning industry. Concerned that fragmentation and poor standardization would result in the overall decline of the industry, they decided to develop a concentrated training program consisting of eight 2½ day "tracks" representing the various aspects of life care planning.

Track I was a basic overview of life care planning process methods, standards, and formats. Track II was designed to include the vocational aspects of clients whose life care plans appropriately included work-related opinions. Track III addressed effective case management strategies within the complex medical environment. Track IV outlined the various forensic rehabilitation issues to which many rehabilitation professionals, willingly or unwillingly, are subjected. Track V focused specifically on spinal cord injury issues and Track VI identified brain injury issues. Track VII was an overview of the long-term care issues for other physical and emotional disabilities as well as some disease processes. Track VIII was organized to focus more explicitly on business and ethical practices including the use of technology in life care planning.

Following this process, a management company (Rehabilitation Training Institute) was contracted to set up training programs throughout the United States. Before the first flyers were fully distributed, the first of the organized tracks (scheduled for November 1993) was filled. Two introductory courses were developed — one on the West Coast and the other on the East Coast. It appeared obvious that there were a number of rehabilitation professionals who were interested in pursuing continuing education related to life care planning, and several participants requested official recognition for their educational efforts. Dr. Horace Sawyer of the University of Florida was approached and he agreed to pursue an official certificate of completion through the University of Florida's Continuing Education Department. A private–public partnership between the Rehabilitation Training Institute and the University of Florida was formed and named Intelicus. The five founders have donated the program content to Intelicus and, although some continue as faculty, they no longer have control over the content or management. Over the years these courses have been adjusted to focus on the roles and responsibilities that more specifically identify with life care planners based on participant comments and research. There are currently six modules with a provision for home study included.

Although the certificate underscored the value of obtaining education specific to this specialized industry, it did not provide the assurance of ethical practice or the professional identity that was desired by people who had invested thousands of dollars and much of their time in the training process. Several certification boards were contacted, with three indicating an interest in leading the way to certification. Eventually the Commission on Disability Examiner Certification based in Richmond, Virginia, and directed by V. Robert May, Ph.D. assumed the responsibility and the first certifications were offered in the spring of 1996. (For information regarding the requirements for certification see Chapter 26.)

It should be noted that Intelicus is not the only route for obtaining the necessary education to qualify to sit for certification. Professionals or organizations seeking to support the life care planning credential can develop programs that meet the Board's criteria.

Finally, life care plans have historically been subject to intense scrutiny in a variety of rehabilitation fields including managed care, workers' compensation claims, civil litigation, mediation, reserve setting for insurance companies, and federal vaccine injury fund cases.

The Present

At present the life care planning industry continues to grow, change, and modify the scope of practice associated with catastrophic case management. Although life care planning principles can be used in almost any aspect of care management, it is particularly useful in complex medical cases since the principles and methods that have been developed:

- reduce errors and omissions,
- allow fewer clients to "drop through the cracks," and
- reduce the failure to take into account various aspects that have an effect on the ultimate outcome of the client's medical care (Weed & Riddick, 1992; Weed, 1995a).

Complex case management has become a specialty in its own right and, indeed, there is the certified case manager designation that has emerged as another buzzword. Good case managers, professionals who are able to work consistently in a complex and often adversarial system, are very valuable professionals.

Sometimes arguments are raised that life care planners should be people with nursing backgrounds only (Weed, 1989). In addition, one recent article proposed that only professionals with at least a doctorate should be considered qualified to develop life care plans (Weed, 1997). However, in the view of the organizers of the national life care planning training program, it is the expectation that various professionals are qualified to practice in areas of their knowledge, skills, and abilities. For example, a rehabilitation nurse who has recently graduated from nursing school is ill prepared to handle catastrophic cases. On the other hand, a masters level vocational counselor who has spent several years working specifically in spinal cord injury rehabilitation may be extremely qualified to developed life care plans for that population. In addition, it is expected that life care planning members are part of a team and it is further expected that team members will practice within their knowledge area. Historically it has been common for vocational counselors and rehabilitation nurses to work together to develop vocational and medical rehabilitation plans (Riddick & Weed, 1996).

In current practice, many organizations and hospitals have adopted life care planning procedures for discharge planning (Riddick & Weed, 1996; Weed & Riddick, 1992). There are also allied health professionals (such as occupational therapists, physical therapists, speech/language pathologists, nurses, dietitians, counselors, psychologists, dentists, audiologists, etc.) who develop projected care based on the published formats used in life care planning. Although it is important that the various participants in the training have a rehabilitation education and relevant certification in their area of specialty before engaging in the life care planning process, this by itself is certainly not enough; additional education and experience are necessary (Weed, 1989; Weed, 1997). In order to identify some of the basic methodologies used in the industry and to underscore the relevance of the chapters included in this book, a review of the current standards is appropriate. Life care planning includes various topics that assure the effectiveness of the overall plan. Items included are explained in Table 1.1.

Once it is determined that a life care plan is appropriate, the location of a qualified life care planner is necessary. Certainly individuals who have completed the certificate program through the University of Florida and others who have achieved the national board certified life care planner designation should be qualified. There are other people who have had extensive experience who may supplant the need for a "designated" life care planner. Questions regarding the planner's qualifications, which include education, work experience, life care planning experience, research knowledge and experience, certifications in legitimate rehabilitation areas, and, in the area of civil litigation, forensic experience would be relevant (Table 1.2). It may also be important to determine the consultant's awareness of life care planning with regard to their expertise or knowledge about the certified life care planning designation, courses completed on life care planning, references and publications relevant to life care planning, and their knowledge of professionals who have been "movers and shakers" in the life care planning field.

It is relevant to determine the consultant's commitment to the profession by inquiring as to which organizations they participate in. Many professionals pay dues to associations but do not participate in professional development, committees, or other profession-enhancing activities. It is also pertinent to determine if the professional has contributed time and effort by either volunteering to work with clients, speaking on relevant issues, holding office with professional organizations, or writing for publications. Receiving awards, honors, or peer recognition is also pertinent.

Other questions to ask may include the consultant's industry experience. If the practitioner is expected to work in personal injury litigation, then experience in this arena seems appropriate. Other specialty industries exist and the rules differ, such that it is often extremely important to ensure that their experience covers these specialized fields (Weed, 1994; Weed, 1996).

Having an example life care plan may be appropriate to determine if the prospective professional establishes a medical foundation for their opinions and uses checklists and forms for other health professionals in the specific area of expertise. In general, it is expected that a physician be involved in the plan's medical opinions. Miscellaneous information may help determine if the consultant has a current Vita that outlines their experiences, as well as any history of ethics or malpractice complaints.

Table 1.1 Life Care Plan Checklist

Projected Evaluations: Have you planned for different types of non-physician **evaluations** (for example, physical therapy, speech therapy, recreational therapy, occupational therapy, music therapy, dietary assessment, audiology, vision screening, swallow studies, etc.)?

Projected Therapeutic Modalities: What therapies will be needed (based on the evaluations above)? Will a case manager help control costs and reduce complications? Is a behavior management or rehab psychologist, pastoral counseling, and/or family education appropriate?

Diagnostic Testing/Educational Assessment: What testing is necessary and at what ages? Vocational evaluation? Neuropsychological? Educational levels? Educational consultant to maximize 94-142?

Wheelchair Needs: What types and configuration of wheelchairs will the client require — power? shower? manual? specialty? ventilator? reclining? quad pegs? recreational?

Wheelchair Accessories and Maintenance: Has each chair been listed separately for maintenance and accessories (bags, cushions, trays, etc.)? Have you considered the client's activity level?

Aids for Independent Functioning: What can this individual use to help himself or herself? environmental controls? adaptive aids? omni-reachers?

Orthotics/Prosthetics: Will the client need braces? Have you planned for replacement and maintenance?

Home Furnishings and Accessories: Will the client need a specialty bed? portable ramps? Hoyer or other lift?

Drug/Supply Needs: Have prescription and nonprescription drugs been listed, including size, quantity, and rate at which to be consumed? All supplies such as bladder and bowel program, skin care, etc.?

Home Care/Facility Care: Is it possible for the client to live at home? How about specialty programs such as yearly camps? What level of care will he or she require?

Future Medical Care — Routine: Is there a need for an annual evaluation? Which medical specialties? orthopedics? urology? internist? vision? dental? lab?

Transportation: Are hand controls sufficient or is a specialty van needed? Can local transportation companies be used?

Health and Strength Maintenance: What specialty recreation is needed? blow darts? adapted games? rowcycle? annual dues for specialty magazines? (Specialty wheelchairs should be placed on wheelchair page.)

Architectural Renovations: Have you considered ramps, hallways, kitchen, fire protection, alternative heating/cooling, floor coverings, bath, attendant room, equipment storage, etc.?

Potential Complications: Have you included a list of potential complications likely to occur such as skin breakdown, infections, psychological trauma, contractures, etc.?

Future Medical Care/Surgical Intervention or Aggressive Treatment: Are there plans for aggressive treatment? Or additional surgeries such as plastic surgery?

Orthopedic Equipment Needs: Are walkers, standing tables, tilt tables, body support equipment needed?

Vocational/Educational Plan: What are the costs of vocational counseling, job coaching, tuition, fees, books, supplies, technology, etc.?

Table 1.2 Checklist for Selecting a Life Care Planner

✓ Professional's **qualifications**?

- **Education,** including degrees and continuing education? If doctorate, was the university accredited? (Some have "mail order" or degrees from "universities" that are less than stellar.)
- **Work** experience?
- **Life Care Planning** experience?
- **Research** knowledge and experience?
- **Certifications or Licenses**? Generally accepted rehabilitation certifications include **CLCP** (Certified Life Care Planner), **CRC** (Certified Rehabilitation Counselor), **CDMS** (Certified Disability Management Specialist), **CVE** (Certified Vocational Evaluator), **CRRN** (Certified Rehabilitation Registered Nurse), **CCM** (Certified Case Manager), Diplomat or Fellow **ABVE** (American Board of Vocational Experts).
- **Forensic experience** (if appropriate)? Familiar with the rules pertaining to experts? Have they testified? Do they have a list of cases in which they testified at deposition or trial for the previous 4 years? Plaintiff/Defense ratio?

✓ Prospective consultant's **awareness** of Life Care Planning?

- Are they a Board **Certified** Life Care Planner?
- Have they achieved the **Certificate** in Life Care Planning offered through the University of Florida?
- Have they completed **courses** offered by a noted program on Life Care Planning (e.g., Rehabilitation Training Institute, Intellicus, University of Florida, NARPPS, et al.)
- Can they cite Life Care Planning **references**?
- Do they know some of the **professionals** associated with Life Care Planning publications and training? (e.g., Terry Blackwell, Richard Bonfiglio, Stuart Cody, Paul Deutsch, Julie Kitchen, Robert Meier, Anne Sluis-Powers, Sue Riddick-Grisham, Horace Sawyer, Connie Sunday, Randall Thomas, Roger Weed, Terry Winkler, Jim Young)

✓ **Commitment** to the profession?

- What professional and disability specific **organization**(s) do they belong to? (Are these "legitimate" or fringe organizations such as a for-profit owned by an individual or group with little recognition or substance?)
- Do they **participate** in professional development?
- Have they **contributed** their time and effort by volunteering services to clients in need, speaking, holding office with professional organizations, writing articles, chapters, or books?
- Have they received **awards, honors, peer recognition**?

✓ **Industry** experience?

- Workers' compensation or Federal Office of Workers' Compensation Programs?
- Personal injury?
- Social Security?
- State rehabilitation?
- Longshore workers?
- Jones Act?
- Federal Employees Liability Act (FELA)?
- Long-term and short-term disability?
- Specialize in a particular disability?

Table 1.2 (continued) Checklist for Selecting a Life Care Planner

✓ **Medical foundation** for opinions established?
- Use established published **checklists** and **forms**?
- Routinely consult with a **physician** as part of the team?
- Include other **health professionals** as appropriate (e.g., OT, PT, SLT, RT, Audiology, Neuropsych, etc.)?

✓ **Other**
- What and how do they **bill** for their services? Do they charge different rates for interview, records review, deposition, or trial?
- Do they have a current curriculum **vita**?
- History of **ethics** complaints or **arrests**?

Step-by-Step Procedures

Assuming that the rehabilitation professional is qualified to project the lifetime care plan and is knowledgeable in the topics to be covered, the next step is to begin the process of the life care plan (Table 1.3). First, of course, the referral must be made to the life care planner and basic information including time frames, billing agreements, retainer information, and information release topics must be discussed (Weed & Field, 1994). Second, it is important to obtain as complete a copy of the medical records as possible, including nurses' notes, physician's orders, ambulance report, emergency records, consultant reports, admission and discharge reports, and laboratory and radiographic reports.

It may also be useful to obtain additional information from the client or family in the form of depositions, interrogatories, or other records. Employment records, tax records, and school records are usually helpful if there are vocational issues to be included in the report. If the client is a young child with no educational or medical "history," then it would be of value to survey in extensive detail the family history, including mother and father, aunts and uncles, and grandparents. In some situations, siblings may have school and other history that may be useful. Occasionally videotapes of the client prior to the injury or day-in-the life videos may be compiled by the attorney and can be useful, particularly in civil litigation defense cases or insurance consulting where the client is not readily accessible to the consultant.

An initial interview should occur at the client's residence (whether facility or home) and appropriate people should be invited to the interview, which may include parents, spouse, siblings, or caregivers. In general, initial interviews will last from three to five hours. When the professional attends the interview it is important to use interview forms or checklists that will help structure the interview and ensure that topics appropriate to be discussed are covered. There may be supplemental forms for pediatric cases, brain injury, assistive technology, activities of daily living, and others. It is useful to obtain a copy of the life care plan checklist to educate the client and/or family members as to the purpose of the life care plan. It is recommended that a camera or video recorder be used to record the living situation, medications, supplies, and equipment used for the

Table 1.3 Step-by-Step Procedure for Life Care Planning

1. Case Intake: When you talked with the referral source, did you record the basic referral information? Time frames discussed? Financial/billing agreement? Retainer received (if appropriate)? Arrange for information release?
2. Medical Records: Did you request a **complete** copy of the medical records? Nurses' notes? Doctor's orders? Ambulance report? Emergency room records? Consultants' reports? Admission and discharge reports? Lab/X-ray/etc.?
3. Supporting Documentation: Are there depositions of the client, family, or treatment team that may be useful? "Day in the life of" videotapes? And if vocational issues to be included in report — School records (including test scores)? Vocational and employment records? Tax returns?
4. Initial Interview Arrangements: Is the interview to be held at the client's residence? Have you arranged for all appropriate people to attend the initial interview (spouse, parents, siblings)? Did you allow 3 to 5 hours for the initial interview?
5. Initial Interview Materials: Do you have the initial interview form for each topic to be covered? Supplemental form for pediatric cases, CP, TBI, SCI as needed? Do you have a copy of the life care plan checklist? Example plan to show the client? Copy of appropriate Life Care Plan step-by-step booklet? Camera or video camcorder to record living situation, medications, supplies, equipment, and other documentation useful for developing a plan?
6. Consulting with Therapeutic Team Members: Have you consulted with and solicited treatment recommendations from appropriate therapeutic team members?
7. Preparing Preliminary Life Care Plan Opinions: Do you have information that can be used to project future care costs? Frequency of service or treatment? Duration? Base cost? Source of information? Vendors?
8. Filling in the Holes: Do you need additional medical or other evaluations to complete the plan? Have you obtained the approval to retain services of additional sources from the referral source? Have you composed a letter outlining the "right" questions to assure you are soliciting the needed information?
9. Researching Costs and Sources: Have you contacted local sources for costs of treatment, medications, supplies, equipment? Or do you have catalogs or flyers? For children, are there services that might be covered, in part, through the school system?
10. Finalizing the Life Care Plan: Did you confirm your projections with the client and/or family? Treatment team members? Can the economist project the costs based on the plan? Do you need to coordinate with a vocational expert?
11. Last But Not Least: Have you distributed the plan to all appropriate parties (client, referral source, attorney, economist, if there is one)?

client. For example, a home may need to be modified and photographs are useful for documentation.

In general, it is useful to consult with the therapeutic team members if possible. As noted above, there may be personal injury litigation defense cases or insurance consulting where this is not possible. It is also reasonable to retain the services of a physician or other individuals as appropriate when treatment team members are not available to discuss the case or the caregivers are not specialized. Also some treating physicians are not experts in the particular disability or are reluctant to provide recommendations, in which case it may be appropriate to arrange for specialty evaluations by other medical professionals.

Once a preliminary life care plan opinion is arranged it should include frequency of the service or treatment, cost, duration of the treatment, source of information, and perhaps vendors for the services or products listed.

It is not uncommon for basic evaluations to reveal various holes that may require additional medical or other evaluations to be appropriate. For example, a neuropsychologist may be required in brain injury cases. It is important that the consultant compose a list of questions that will assist the evaluator in addressing questions that are specific to the life care plan (Blackwell, Sluis-Powers, & Weed, 1994). For example, neuropsychologists may do an outstanding job in writing reports and listing the results of tests but may be less than adequate in identifying functional limitations that result from the disability, as well as revealing specific treatment options with costs so that a projection of its estimated value can be determined.

Once a life care plan has been completed it is common for the planner to research the costs of treatment, medications, supplies, and equipment. There are occasions where catalogs will provide the necessary resource, particularly for products that are commonly available through mail order or for locations where the services or products are limited. In some states, depending on the jurisdiction (e.g., civil litigation, workers' compensation, long-term disability, etc.), there may be a need to identify collateral sources. A common collateral source is a "free" service often offered through the school systems for qualified students. There may also be special rules regarding the costs associated with products. One state, for example, requires that costs of products and service for workers' compensation insurance cases be only a certain percentage above Medicare/Medicaid reimbursement schedules.

Once the life care plan is approaching finalization, it may be appropriate to consult with the client and/or family to determine that historical information is accurate and that the topics included in the life care plan are appropriate. Once the life care plan is complete it is the responsibility of the life care planner to distribute the life care plan to appropriate resources. The life care planner should be mindful of the rules within the industry to avoid distribution of a plan to inappropriate sources. In the case of civil litigation, the attorney who retains the consultant's service determines the appropriate recipient(s).

The Future

The future of life care planning seems bright indeed! Since the life care plan first emerged in the rehabilitation literature in 1985, the concept has grown immensely to represent the most effective case management method within the industry, particularly with regard to complex medically challenging cases. As this book goes to press, many of the topics that were considered "future" for life care planning just a few years ago have already become the present (Deutsch, 1994). Life care planning in the areas of reserve setting for insurance companies, managed care organizations, workers' compensation, personal injury, facility discharge planning, and government funded vaccine injury programs have strongly endorsed the concept. In civil injury litigation, the Daubert Ruling (1993) will continue to alter how some professionals develop life care plans by encouraging the practice of using a consistent, researched, and critiqued methods of developing opinions (see Chapter 20 for more information).

It is predicted that areas of mediation, facility-based life care planning, special needs trusts for children, divorces, and assisting families with financial and estate planning will increase. For example, in a divorce case where the settlement was based somewhat on the cost of a persistent vegetative state client living at home, the "soon-to-be" ex-wife was aware that the child's father planned to place the client in a facility because it was less expensive and therefore would reduce his obligation for child support. The care planner was initially asked to identify a reasonable care plan.

In addition, based on participants in recent training programs, more allied experts (occupational therapists, physical therapists, and speech and language pathologists) will participate individually and as a member of a team. Health maintenance organizations will use this procedure to assist with the projection of costs for their catastrophically impaired patient population. Managed care is a current phenomenon that has special application to life care planning. If the goal is to "manage care," then using life care planning procedures is a viable option. The design is an excellent method to avoid errors and omissions. Unfortunately, the term *managed care* often really means, *managed costs*. If the health maintenance organizations truly wish to enhance care outcomes for their patients, then we will observe many case management professionals involved in training programs focused on life care planning. At least one nationwide case management firm has adopted the basic life care planning procedure to work with insurance companies for catastrophic injuries in an attempt to assist them with overall rehabilitation planning and projection of costs. Structured settlement companies use the life care plan to develop proposals for settlements and estate planning. Facility and hospital discharge planners will use the method for more effective patient and family education as well as for assurance of comprehensive care.

CONCLUSION

Life care planning has emerged as an effective method for the prediction of future care costs. The industry continues to grow and develop new horizons. It is of specific importance that a coordinated effort with standardized approaches be promoted in order that the industry as a whole progresses and becomes more effective. As more professionals, including allied health professionals, become involved in this process, the industry will mature and develop more effective outcome measurements. Currently, at least two universities are developing doctoral programs to endorse or encompass life care planning procedures and methods. In civil litigation, defense attorneys have increasingly turned to rehabilitation professionals to consult on life care planning issues. It is now incumbent on the rehabilitation professional to assure that services offered are consistent with the standards of the industry. Building on the work of others, rather than reinventing the wheel, will assist in achieving this goal.

REFERENCES

Blackwell, T., Kitchen, J., & Thomas, R. (1997). **Life Care Planning for the Spinal Cord Injured**. Athens, GA: E & F Vocational Services.

Blackwell, T., Sluis-Powers, A., & Weed, R. (1994). **Case Management for the Brain Injured** (foreword by James S. Brady). Athens, GA: E & F Vocational Services.

Blackwell, T., Weed, R., & Sluis-Powers, A. (1994). **Case Management for the Spinal Cord Injured**. Athens, GA: E & F Vocational Services.

Deutsch, P. (1994). Life care planning: Into the future. **Journal of Private Sector Rehabilitation, 9(2 & 3),** 79-84.

Deutsch, P. & Raffa, F. (1981). **Damages in Tort Action**, Vols. 8 & 9. New York: Matthew Bender.

Deutsch, P. & Sawyer, H. (1985). **Guide to Rehabilitation**. New York: Ahab Press.

Deutsch, P., Weed, R., Kitchen, J., & Sluis, A. (1989a). **Life Care Plans for the Head Injured: A Step by Step Guide**. Athens, GA: Elliott & Fitzpatrick.

Deutsch, P., Weed, R., Kitchen, J., & Sluis, A. (1989b). **Life Care Plans for the Spinal Cord Injured: A Step by Step Guide**. Athens, GA: Elliott & Fitzpatrick.

Kitchen, J., Cody, L., & Deutsch, P. (1989). **Life Care Plans for the Brain Damaged Baby: A Step by Step Guide.** Orlando, FL: Paul M. Deutsch Press.

Riddick, S. & Weed, R. (1996). The Life Care Planning process for managing catastrophically impaired patients. **Case Studies in Nursing Case Management,** 61-91. Gaithersburg, MD: Aspen.

Weed, R. (1989). Life care planning questions and answers. **Life Care Facts, 1**, 5-6.

Weed, R. (1994). Life Care Plans: Expanding the horizons. **Journal of Private Sector Rehabilitation, 9(2 & 3),** 47-50.

Weed, R. (1995a). Life Care Plans as a managed care tool. **Medical Interface, 8(2)**, 111-118.

Weed, R. (1995b). Objectivity in Life Care Planning. **Inside Life Care Planning, 1(1)**, 1-5.

Weed, R. (1996). Life care planning and earnings capacity analysis for brain injured clients involved in personal injury litigation utilizing the RAPEL method. **Journal of NeuroRehabilitation, 7(2),** 119-135.

Weed, R. (1997). Comments regarding "Life Care Planning for young children with brain injuries." **The Neurolaw Letter, 6(5),** 112.

Weed, R. & Field, T. (1994). **The Rehabilitation Consultant's Handbook, 2nd Ed.** Athens, GA: Elliott & Fitzpatrick.

Weed, R. & Riddick, S. (1992). Life Care Plans as a case management tool. **The Individual Case Manager Journal, 3(1),** 26-35.

Weed, R. & Sluis, A. (1990). **Life Care Plans for the Amputee: A Step by Step Guide.** Boca Raton, FL: CRC Press.

I

THE ROLES OF LIFE CARE PLAN TEAM MEMBERS

2

THE ROLE OF THE PHYSIATRIST IN LIFE CARE PLANNING

Richard Paul Bonfiglio

INTRODUCTION

Following a catastrophic injury or illness, individuals will usually have lifetime medical, rehabilitative, and daily care needs (Braddom, 1996). An appropriate life care plan delineates these needs. Such a plan serves not only as "road map" that can guide the provision of ongoing medical and rehabilitative services, but also as a litigation tool (Cooper & Vernon, 1996; Romano, 1996). A sound medical foundation for the life care plan that addresses the individual medical situation, family considerations, premorbid condition, and desired outcomes significantly enhances the usefulness of the life care plan.

Physiatrists have unique training and experience that can aid in the medical foundation of such a plan. Their unique specialty in practicing rehabilitation medicine is based on a functional approach to patient evaluation and management. Additionally, the team approach, which is the norm in rehabilitation medicine, is essential in life care planning implementation.

With regard to civil litigation, many plaintiff attorneys now devote a greater effort to establishing the extent of damage related to individuals who have suffered catastrophic personal injuries or illnesses. Attorneys are using expert witnesses to identify ongoing care needs and delineate wage losses (Romano, 1996). Furthermore, as efforts to limit awards for pain and suffering grow, establishment of actual losses and ongoing medical and rehabilitative needs becomes increasingly important. A physiatrist can help define these ongoing needs.

Life Care Planning Implications

Ensuring the availability of appropriate ongoing medical, rehabilitative, and daily care needs has been bolstered by the development of the science of life care planning. However, the foundation for such plans is often highly contingent on the non-physician plan developer's experience and the treating physician's impressions. Both the life care planner and the treating physician may have only limited

1-57444-075-6/99/$0.00+$.50

Table 2.1 Recommendations for Selection of a Physiatrist

- Completion of residency from a recognized leading program
- Board certification in Physical Medicine & Rehabilitation
- Training or experience in applicable area of subspecialization (like traumatic brain injury or spinal cord injury)
- Previous publications and national presentations, especially on related topics
- Academic appointment
- Recognition by rehabilitation peers
- Comfort with litigation process
- Reputation for objective, thorough assessment and ethical practice
- Experience with testimony and litigation
- Significant clinical experience

experience with catastrophically injured individuals, especially for persons with spinal cord injuries and traumatic brain injuries. Some recommended services may not be the most appropriate for such patients. The life care plan presented may not recognize all of the unique needs of the injured individual. The recommended services, equipment, and supplies may also not be adequate over the injured individual's lifetime. The recommended services, may not allow for recent or reasonably anticipated future developments in medical and rehabilitative care, including technological and service delivery advances. Also, all of the potential patient medical complications may not be identified.

Choosing the Right Physiatrist

Physiatrists are physicians specializing in Physical Medicine and Rehabilitation (DeLisa, et al., 1993; Downey, et al., 1994; Fletcjer, 1992; Sinaki, et al., 1993). Based on their training and experience in providing medical and rehabilitative services to individuals with various disabilities, physiatrists are uniquely qualified to provide a strong foundation for life care planning. They are, by their training, experienced in dealing with individuals with injuries or illnesses who have catastrophic functional problems. Additionally, physiatrists are used to looking at the long-term needs of their patients.

Rehabilitation care is often essential in maximizing the abilities of individuals with significant disabilities. Rehabilitation physicians generally direct the provision of such services in rehabilitation settings. Relying on these physicians to help develop a long-term plan is a natural extension of their usual practice.

However, physiatrists tend to be optimists. Obtaining realistic information and projections requires selecting a physiatric expert appropriately. Civil litigation can place additional demands on the selection of an appropriate physiatrist. The checklist in Table 2.1 can help with the selection of a physiatrist as an expert witness in a case for an individual with a catastrophic injury and resultant significant disability.

Initial contact with the physiatrist should help establish the physician's accessibility, availability, and ability to articulate the key issues in establishing the extent of the injured individual's ongoing needs. Physicians who seem to avoid the attorney's or life care planner's contact, generally make inadequate witnesses. Review of the physician's past testimony, especially regarding comparable cases, may be useful in delineating the physician's opinion regarding key areas.

Role of the Physiatrist

Since the physiatrist may be called on to make projections regarding the patient's life expectancy and that serve as the basis for life long care needs, thoroughness in patient evaluations and medical record review is essential. A request for a sample report is appropriate for judging the physician's examination and documentation adequacy. Physiatrists are usually team-oriented because of the nature of the profession. Physiatrists should be identified who consider the life care planner to be part of the patient's care team.

In civil litigation, hopefully, the involved physiatrist can be educated about the need for financial settlement to facilitate the provision of needed ongoing medical and rehabilitative services for the injured individual. The physiatrist should be able to educate a jury about all aspects of the involved individual's disabling condition and its implications. The disabling condition often results not only in physical or cognitive limitations, but also in emotional and psychological complications. The additional energy requirements and time of performing tasks with a disability often take a toll on patients.

An individual's disability can also affect the family and change the existing family dynamics. These changes may add to the emotional pressure on the disabled individual.

Rehabilitation physicians can also play a key role in a team evaluation of an individual with catastrophic injuries or illness. Evaluations that include measurement of the patient's functional abilities by various team members including physical, occupational, and speech therapists, psychologists, and rehabilitation nurses are becoming more common. These evaluations serve as a stronger foundation for life care planning development. Physicians in complementary areas of specialization include:

- neurologists
- psychiatrists
- neurosurgeons
- orthopedists and
- urological surgeons.

Others may also be involved. The physiatrist can play a key role in coordinating these evaluations and developing a holistic approach to the resulting clinical impressions and recommendations.

Common Patient Scenarios*

Individuals Status Post Spinal Cord Injury (SCI)

Rehabilitation evaluation after a spinal cord injury is particularly important because of the alteration in physiology that accompanies a spinal cord injury. Virtually every organ system is affected. As an example, blood pressure maintenance is significantly affected by higher-level spinal cord injuries secondary to the loss of central connections for the autonomic nervous system. During the early period

* For more details, see separate chapters on selected disabilities.

after spinal cord injury, especially during "spinal shock," hypotension is common. During the early rehabilitation process, orthostatic hypotension can interfere with progress. Orthostatic measures like support stockings and an abdominal binder are important treatment measures. Even during the long course, accommodations may be needed, especially with position changes. Conversely, impaired autonomic control can also lead to autonomic dysreflexia or hyperreflexia for individuals with higher-level spinal cord injuries, especially above thoracic level six (T-6). Sensations that in an individual with an intact spinal cord would lead to noxious stimulation can trigger this response. Common triggers are bladder overdistention, excessive skin pressure, constipation, and sunburn. Initial treatment should include elimination of the precipitating factor and changing position, especially elevating the individual's head. Medication management may also be needed especially when the condition recurs frequently. If this condition is left untreated, life-threatening blood pressure elevations can occur.

Management of the spinal cord injured individual's neurogenic bladder is also very important. Periodic urological evaluations should be included in all life care plans for spinal cord injured individuals. Additionally, periodic urologic diagnostic testing is needed. At a minimum this should include regular bladder and renal ultrasound testing, urine cultures, and cystometrograms. Additional tests that may be needed include intravenous pyelograms and laboratory testing including electrolytes, BUN, and creatinine.

There are many other alterations in physiology after a spinal cord injury that result in conditions like spasticity and impaired thermal regulation. Additionally, there are numerous possible secondary complications like osteoporosis, contracture, heterotopic ossification, pressure ulcer, urinary tract stone, and a perforated abdominal viscus. Evaluating the likelihood or presence of these conditions in an individual case can be done by a physiatrist.

Traumatic Brain Injury (TBI)

Traumatic brain injuries can range from "mild" to those leading to a persistent vegetative state. Although extensive medical and daily care is required for anyone in a persistent vegetative state, the provision of services still should be specific to the individual's needs and can be influenced by many factors, including the family support system, available community resources, and architectural considerations.

Individuals with severe traumatic brain injuries usually require ongoing medical, rehabilitative, and daily care services (Rosenthal, et al., 1990). A physiatrist can help to outline the needed care. This medical foundation can aid the life care planner in establishing the most medically appropriate plan. Maximizing the injured individual's functional improvement is important. Anticipating potential future complications is also needed.

Even for an individual diagnosed as having a mild traumatic brain injury, the functional implications may be very significant. Neuropsychological testing to delineate the extent of these functional effects is important. A physiatrist can help to translate these functional limitations to life care planning effects.

Chronic Pain

Many individuals develop chronic pain because of trauma or illness. Establishing the etiology and relating it to a specific event can be difficult. Additionally, delineating the extent of pain and its functional implications can be problematic. Because of the experience of physiatrists in looking at functional implications of disease and disability, they can be helpful in establishing such links. Chronic pain is also a frequent sequela of spinal cord and brain injuries.

Amputation

A physiatrist can help determine the appropriate prosthetic device for an individual after an amputation. Recognizing the functional implications of an amputation and appropriate prosthetic and adaptive equipment is also within the experience of physiatrists. Many amputees have residual vascular and/or pain problems. Management of these problems facilitates functional improvements.

Life Expectancy Determinations

Provision of adequate funding for lifetime medical, rehabilitative, and daily care needs is dependent on an accurate prediction of life expectancy. Unfortunately, there is no medical literature for catastrophically injured individuals that projects life expectancy *based on the level of care* that is typically outlined in a life care plan. Additionally, the medical literature addressing life expectancy for those with catastrophic injuries or illnesses leading to brain or spinal cord injury has many other flaws. Additionally, such population studies do not address the unique situation of any particular patient. Therefore, an estimate provided by an experienced physiatrist can better predict life expectancy. However, such determinations require a thorough review of available medical records, especially to identify the already existing medical conditions and secondary complications that have already occurred. The physiatrist can help determine which complications can be prevented or treated with the services outlined in the life care plan and which are likely to occur despite good medical and rehabilitative care. The physiatrist can provide an opinion on the effect of the patient's underlying condition and secondary complications on life expectancy.

Example Case

Each entry in the life care plan requires certain data. Each recommendation must include the medical specialty, start date, stop date, frequency of service, and duration. A base or procedure cost is added that will allow an economist to estimate the total value of the services or procedures. To provide an example, in the table that follows are a *few* entries associated with the care of a 73-year-old woman with C5-6 tetraplegia, which is within the domain of the physiatrist.

Testimony

Physiatrists can provide the medical foundation for plaintiff life care plans. Since physiatrists recognize the unique needs of patients with disabilities as a regular part of the practice of physical medicine and rehabilitation, they are particularly valuable expert witnesses (Cooper & Vernon, 1996; Romano, 1996). They are equally capable of evaluating plaintiff-generated life care plans for medical accuracy and necessity. Determining whether recommended services are medically

*Recommendation**	*Dates*	*Frequency*	*Expected Cost*
Outpatient spinal cord injury reevaluation to include MD, RN, OT, PT, RT, Dietary	1997 to life expectancy	1 time per year	$850–1,200 each
IVP or renal ultrasound, CBC, UA, and others as needed	1997 to life expectancy	1 time per year	Included in yearly evaluation
Physiatrist	1997 to life expectancy	4 times per year	$156 per visit
Urologist	1997 to life expectancy	2 times per year	$120–150 per visit
KUB	1997 to life expectancy	1 time per year	$65.77 each
Orthopedist	1997 to life expectancy	1 time per year	$100–125 per visit

* Partial plan only. Illustration of physician related minimum needed data.

necessary and appropriate is important to the defense. Physiatrists can also provide testimony regarding the medical basis for life expectancy determinations.

CONCLUSIONS

Medical recommendations are a fundamental part of the life care plan and the physician, especially the physiatrist, is critical to the foundation of medical opinions. The appropriate physician expert in Physical Medicine and Rehabilitation can provide opinions regarding (Council on Ethical and Judicial Affairs, 1997):

- nature and extent of individual patient's disability and residual abilities
- patient's disease and disability past and future natural history
- potential future medical complications
- medical basis of vocational potential
- delineation of individual's functional limitations, including physical, cognitive, emotional, and fatigue aspects
- medical basis of needed equipment, supplies, home modifications, transportation needs, nursing, therapy, and other care services
- life expectancy

In civil litigation, the use of a physiatrist to bolster the life care planning process can facilitate the jury's deliberations regarding adequacy of awards. Such decisions are particularly important when the injured individual requires regular ongoing lifetime care.

Additionally, the physiatrist can help with implementing life care plans by determining the timing and extent of provision of specific services. Maximizing functional gains should be a focus of rehabilitation and future planning. Finally, the physiatrist can serve as an essential member of the team in the overall life care planning process and its implementation.

REFERENCES

Braddom, R. L. (1996). **Physical Medicine & Rehabilitation**. Philadelphia: W.B. Saunders.

Cooper, J. & Vernon, S. (1996). **Disability and the Law**. London: Jessica Kingsley Publishers.

Council on Ethical and Judicial Affairs. (1997). **American Medical Association: Code of Medical Ethics**. Chicago: American Medical Association.

Culver, C. M. (1990). **Ethics at the Bedside**. Hanover, NH: University Press of New England.

DeLisa, J. A., et al. (1993). **Rehabilitation Medicine Principles and Practice** (2nd ed.). Philadelphia: J.B. Lippincott.

Downey, J. A., et al. (1994). **The Physiologic Basis of Rehabilitation Medicine** (2nd ed.). Stoneham, MA: Butterworth-Heinemann.

Fletcjer, C. F., et al. (1992). **Rehabilitation Medicine: Contemporary Clinical Perspectives**. Philadelphia: Lea & Febiger.

Romano, J. L. (1996). **Legal Rights of the Catastrophically Ill and Injured**. Norristown, PA: Rosenstein & Romano.

Rosenthal, M., et al. (1990). **Rehabilitation of the Adult and Child with Traumatic Brain Injury** (2nd ed.). Philadelphia: F.A. Davis.

Sinaki, M. et al. (1993). **Basic Clinical Rehabilitation Medicine** (2nd ed.). St. Louis, MO: Mosby.

3

THE ROLE OF THE NURSE CASE MANAGER IN LIFE CARE PLANNING

Susan Riddick-Grisham & Roger O. Weed

INTRODUCTION

The National Coalition for the Advancement of Case Management defines case management as a collaborative process that promotes quality care and effective outcomes that enhance the physical, psychological, and vocational health of individuals. It includes assessing, planning, implementing, coordinating, and evaluating health-related services (St. Coeur, 1996). Life care plans have been successfully used for case management purposes for more than ten years (Weed & Riddick, 1992). The format can serve as the framework or road map to guide case managers as they navigate through the health care delivery system to provide services to patients, families, and payers. By using the basic skills that all nurses develop as part of their formal professional education (i.e., assessment, planning, intervention, monitoring, and evaluation of the patient), and by understanding the clinical and rehabilitation issues related to a catastrophic injury or chronic illness, the nurse case manager can fill an important and integral role in the development and management of the life care plans.

Integration of Care Management, Financial Management, and Information

There are several precursors to the current case management movement. Following World War II, insurance companies hired nurses and social workers to manage the physical, emotional, and social needs of severely disabled veterans (Blancett & Flarey, 1996). Case management grew as it was widely used in the management of individuals with mental illness. Employers and insurance companies, faced with escalating claim costs, court awards, and rising health care costs, used case management services to assess a claim, set goals and timetables to project costs, all to ensure effective use of their dollars spent.

Today case management continues to play a pivotal role in the evolving health care system by decreasing fragmentation and duplication of services, increasing communication and collaboration among all members of the care management

1-57444-075-6/99/$0.00+$.50

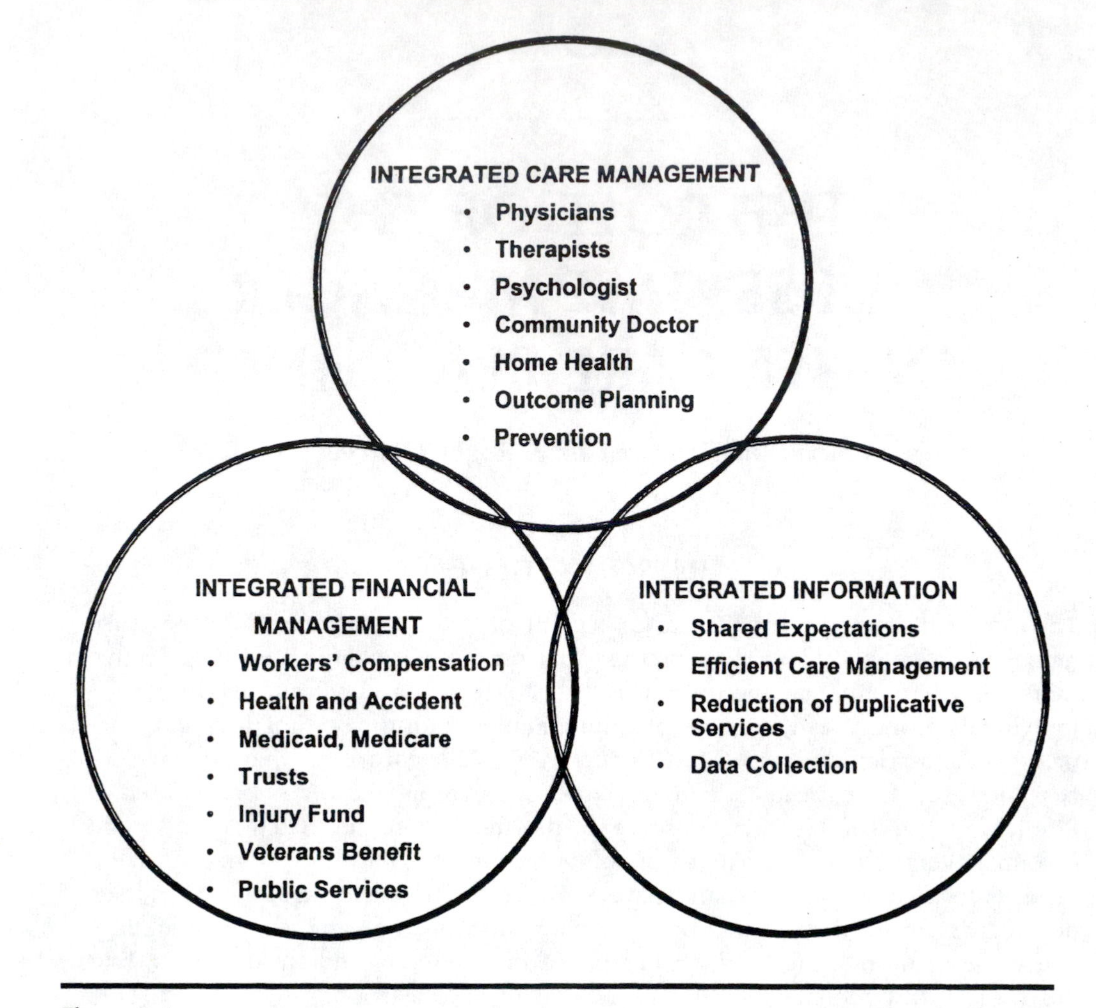

Figure 3.1

team, using available health care dollars efficiently, and achieving measurable and durable outcomes (Riddick & Weed, 1996).

In catastrophic injuries such as spinal cord injury, acquired brain injury, burns or multiple trauma, and in chronic illnesses such as diabetes and cancer, case management is most successful when the process is initiated as early as possible following the incident or diagnosis. The life care planning process is uniquely designed to assist those nurse case managers who work with these types of long-term, high-cost cases.

The life care planning process is the means by which the nurse case manager can develop a consistent, well-organized approach to the management of these cases. A comprehensive and thorough life care plan (LCP) is designed to allow for an integrated continuum of care addressing the need for the integration of information, care management, and the finance mechanisms, as illustrated by Figure 3.1.

Care and treatment of the catastrophically injured or chronically ill patient often involves multiple treatment providers in a number of treatment settings all with their own treatment protocols and outcomes. The nurse case manager is frequently the member of the care team who manages the patient across settings. The life care plan is the planning and management tool that, when utilized will allow all clinicians from all sites to be involved in the planning so that the care management plan is integrated and client or patient specific.

Life care plans are frequently used in the legal arena to illustrate the lifetime cost of care for an individual. Coverage for these complex cases can come from one or more of the following sources (Papastrat, 1992):

- Workers' Compensation (insurer, state fund or residual pool, or self-insured employer)
- accident and health plan (indemnity insurer, health maintenance organization (HMO), preferred provider organization (PPO), or self-insured employer)
- legal suits (product liability cases, third-party negligence, and terms of policy cases)
- auto liability
- government fund (CHAMPUS, Veterans Administration, Defense Department, Medicare, Medicaid, Social Security, or state victims' fund)
- reinsurance

The life care plan can be used to identify overall lifetime cost to medically treat and manage the catastrophically injured or chronically ill patient. It is important to integrate the various finance mechanisms available to the patient into the LCP, allowing for optimal use of the health care dollar.

As stated earlier, care and treatment of these patients often involves multiple providers at multiple sites. Often key pieces of information are not shared from provider to provider. Families and community services providers often feel uninformed, uninvolved, or powerless. It is not unusual to see duplicative services being provided by different provider settings. The life care plan can be used to ensure that information is being tracked and integrated. The nurse case manager, as the "implementer" of the life care plan, can act as the liaison of the information, dispensing it to the appropriate individuals (the patient, the family, the care management team, and the funding source) at the appropriate times, so the patient's care is managed efficiently.

The Role of the Nurse Case Manager

Case management in its broadest terms reflects the phases of the nursing process; it is the process in action (Blancett & Flarey, 1996). There are a variety of roles in which the nurse case manager can participate, including the creation and implementation of a life care plan.

Although a nursing education in itself provides a nurse with some of the basic skills used in the life care planning process, a higher level of knowledge and expertise is required to address the complex issues involved in life care planning.

Each nurse must make his or her own decision on the role they wish to participate in based on the following:

1. Individual degree of clinical knowledge of the disability
2. Understanding of the rehabilitation process and its involvement with other allied health professions
3. Knowledge of clinical research and data collection systems and resource availability and usage
4. Basic personal skills including organization, self-confidence, and a high level of professionalism.

Providing Support Services

The nurse case manager may choose a role that is more supportive in nature. Often, the nurse is retained or hired by the life care planner to provide support services that include medical records review and abstracting, medical research, and investigation into services that could be utilized in the development of an individual life care plan. Additional support services could include some of the traditional services provided within the case management process such as:

- obtaining vendor quotes
- obtaining contractor bids for home or vehicle modification
- procuring services, and
- patient and family education

St. Coeur (1996) provides an extensive overview of case management protocols in brain injury and spinal injury cases, as well as other types of cases, that is a useful resource for nurse case managers in life care planning.

There are times when the scope of the nurse case manager's role occurs only after the completion of the life care plan, when the financing mechanism is in place to allow for implementation of the plan. The actual life care plan then serves as the blueprint to guide the case management process and to provide an integrated continuum of care.

Providing Legal Services

Nurse case managers with life care planning experience are often hired by medical malpractice or personal injury attorneys to act as consultants to assist them in many areas, including performing medical records reviews, medical research, identification of experts, and case management. Many attorneys will rely on the nurse case manager to provide case management services for their clients to direct them to appropriate care providers. An attorney may also ask the nurse case manager to review a life care plan for accuracy, omissions, and errors. Table 3.1 outlines many of the services a knowledgeable nurse case manager can offer. It is essential that the nurse case manager clearly understand his or her role in providing consultative services so that they do not mistakenly get involved in providing opinions that are outside their area of expertise.

Table 3.1 Medical-Legal Consultation Checklist

☑ **Medical Records Analysis**
Organize and tab; define in layman's terms; describe number of operative procedures and invasive procedures; use of pain medication; special consultations; number of days in ICU or other special placements; complications experienced; physician names and specialty; discharge disposition.

☑ **Medical Research**
Relevant articles and books; med-line; software; networking; define content, highlight, organize, and educate attorney.

☑ **Experts**
Location of appropriate experts; coordination of referral to expert; securing services of appropriate experts including liability, causation, and damage experts.

☑ **Deposition: Review and Summarization**
Development of deposition questions and attendance at deposition. Review and summarize deposition to highlight damage and treatment issues.

☑ **Case Management**
Assessment of medical condition; coordination of medical care and physician referral; coordination of information with attorney, client/family, physician to physician.

☑ **Attendance at Medical Exam**
Documentation of physician/client interview and assessment.

☑ **Demonstrative Evidence**
Overheads; charts; graphs; photos; videotape; medical illustration and medical equipment; arrange for day-in-the-life and script; help develop settlement brochures.

☑ **Life Care Plan/Life Care Plan Review**
Development of a life care plan that identifies appropriate and reasonable care for individuals who have sustained catastrophic injury or chronic illness; review of existing life care plan for overlap and duplication of services; check costs for regional accuracy; assess planner's potential for bias; check math calculations; review for effective rehabilitation and potential to avoid complications; assure all appropriate topics are included in plan.

☑ **Vocational Issues**
Identify vocational experts and coordinate evaluation; discuss issues related to placeability, earnings capacity, rehabilitation plan, vocational handicaps, work life expectancy, and related issues.

As indicated above, a major role for the nurse consultant is reviewing and consulting in medical records review (Table 3.2). Obtaining a full copy of the records is only a beginning of the tedious process of organizing them for meaningful use. Determining the primary and occasionally secondary diagnosis, hospitalization days, operative procedures, and complications can have an effect on the needed care. Identifying the caregivers, including consultants, will reveal treatment goals and directions. Medications will help confirm diagnoses as well as reveal related services such as lab work. When writing reports or summarizing medical records, it is useful for the nurse to simplify medical language so the reader can interpret the information. The nurse probably will be effective as a consultant by reviewing and commenting on reports or life care plans by others. Although most nurses are not qualified to render opinions about vocational issues, he or she should be able to recognize the need for this topic and basic information about what should be included and how to tell if a quality product has been rendered.

Table 3.2 Checklist for a Comprehensive Medical Records Analysis

- ☑ **Primary/Secondary Diagnoses:** Have you thoroughly reviewed the records to identify primary and other diagnoses?
- ☑ **Hospitalization Days:** List all hospitals and treatment programs. Summarize the dates and days in each. Include the number of days in specialized care such as ICU or rehabilitation.
- ☑ **Operative Procedures:** What operations were performed, on what date, by whom, and what was the surgeon's specialty area (orthopedics, neurosurgery, plastic, ophthalmology, etc.)? What kind of anesthesia was used (local or general)? How long was the operation? Were there any complications?
- ☑ **Medications:** What medications were administered? Why were they administered (infections, pain, bowel or bladder program, blood loss, anxiety, etc.) ? Include the name, dosage, route of administration (oral, IV, IM, sublingual, catheter). Note any abnormal reactions and long-term effects.
- ☑ **Treatment Team:** Identify all treating physicians by name, specialty, address, and telephone.
- ☑ **Consultations:** Have you identified all consultations during treatment (e.g., endocrinology, infectious disease, pulmonology, radiology, urology, cosmetic, etc.)?
- ☑ **Invasive Procedures:** Note Foley catheters, intravenous, g-tube feeds, etc. Include length of required treatment and how much.
- ☑ **Post Hospitalization Treatment:** What post-acute programs or treatment programs were included? Day treatment? Home care? Include dates, purpose, and outcomes.
- ☑ **Complications:** List complications and dates. For example, septic shock, chronic infections such as urinary and respiratory, contractures, skin breakdown, adverse reactions to medications, psychological, etc. Include future risk factors such as bone non-union, traumatic arthritis, etc.
- ☑ **Report Writing:** Have you explained the medical records so that your reader can understand them (e.g., decubitus = skin breakdown; debride = clean the wound, etc.)?
- ☑ **Recommendations:** Have you offered recommendations so your client and/or account will receive appropriate and cost effective services? Should additional evaluations or treatment be offered? What effect does the incident have on the client's ultimate functioning or work?

For the nurse case manager who is also interested in providing expert services, additional training and professional development is recommended. Being an expert witness requires being available for testimony, either in deposition or in a courtroom, to render professional opinions regarding an individual life care plan. Basic understanding of the litigation process and the role of the expert witness is essential. This area of practice can be stressful and demanding. It requires that one be very well organized and an effective communicator. In summary, as with many occupations, there are traits that will enhance the life care planning nurse's desirability (Table 3.3).

Professional Development

The qualifications of Professional Rehabilitation Practitioners depend on specialty and academic preparation (Weed & Field, 1994). Professional nurses are bound to practice within the definition of the Nurse Practice Act for the individual states

Table 3.3 Desirable Traits for the Nurse Life Care Planner

- Know inpatient medical-surgical or acute rehabilitation services
- Have emergency medical experience
- Possess verbal and analytical reasoning skills
- Have the ability to communicate with variety of cultural, educational, and experiential backgrounds
- Possess problem solving, negotiation, and conflict resolution skills
- Be computer literate for research and communication
- Have knowledge of professional resources and access
- Have the ability to critically analyze literature
- Understand the scope and limitations of medical and allied health fields
- Have pharmacology knowledge
- Know normal laboratory values
- Know of drug actions/interactions
- Know pathophysiology of different disabilities
- Have basic abnormal psychology knowledge
- Know the effects of trauma on coping and psychological functioning
- Deal effectively with stress
- Pay attention to details
- Be well organized
- Document the work in the file
- Maintain meticulous files
- See the "big picture"
- Have self-confidence
- Be objective and professional
- Stay within area of expertise

where they are practicing. Additionally, the nurse case manager is held to the case management practice standards and certification code of ethics stated by the organizations that they have joined or certifications they have obtained. Such organizations could include:

- The National Association of Rehabilitation Professionals in the Private Sector (NARPPS)
- The Case Management Society of America (CMSA)
- The Association of Rehabilitation Nurses (ARN)
- American Association of Legal Nurse Consultants (AALNC)

The certifications could include:

- CCM (Certified Case Manager)
- CDMS (Certified Disability Management Specialist)
- CRRN (Certified Rehabilitation Registered Nurse)

Each of these organizations provides opportunities for continued educational and professional growth in the areas of catastrophic care management and life care planning. Recently a new organization, The American Academy of Nurse Life Care Planners, has announced continued education opportunities for nurse life care planners. (Note: At press time this organization was in the planning process to become an international association of life care planning and not exclusively nurses.) Additionally, many of the Level 1 trauma centers and facilities that treat individuals who have sustained catastrophic injuries provide ongoing educational opportunities.

In addition, a certificate program in life care planning is offered by the University of Florida and The Rehabilitation Training Institute (known as Intelicus). This program provides 120 hours of continuing education specifically for life care planning. Intelicus is currently the only coordinated education program that will qualify the nurse professional to sit for the national life care planner certification exam.

CONCLUSION

The nurse case manager plays a pivotal role in the ongoing management of the catastrophically injured or chronically ill patient. Management is focused not only on the quality and consistency of the care and treatment but also on the appropriate use of financial resources and the sharing of information across sites and services. The life care plan can serve as the road map that will guide case management activities throughout the care continuum.

Depending on the skill level and desire, the nurse case manager can participate in both the development and the implementation of the life care plan. A sound understanding of the life care planning process, along with extensive knowledge of the clinical aspects of the presenting catastrophic injury or illness, can prepare one to work in this challenging and rewarding area of practice.

REFERENCES

Blancett, S. & Flarey, D. (1996). Case studies in nurse case management. **Health Care Delivery in a World of Managed Care, 1,** 1-5.

Papastrat, L. (1992). Outcome & value following brain injury: A financial provider's perspective. **The Journal of Head Trauma Rehabilitation, 7 (4),** 13.

Riddick, S. & Weed, R. (1996). The Life Care Planning process for managing catastrophically impaired patients. **Case Studies in Nursing Case Management**, 61-91. Gaithersburg, MD: Aspen.

St. Coeur, M. (1996). **Case Management Practice Guidelines** (Vol. 3, p. 3). St. Louis: Mosby.

Weed, R. & Field, T. (1994). **Rehabilitation Consultants Handbook** (Rev. ed., p. 154). Athens, GA: Elliott & Fitzpatrick.

Weed, R. & Riddick, S. (1992). Life care plans as a case management tool. **Individual Case Manager, 3(1),** 26-35.

4

THE ROLE OF THE VOCATIONAL COUNSELOR IN LIFE CARE PLANNING

Debra E. Berens & Roger O. Weed

INTRODUCTION

The *Dictionary of Occupational Titles* (DOT), 4th ed., (1991), defines vocational counselor as one who "counsels handicapped individuals to provide vocational rehabilitation services." Such services generally include interviewing and evaluating clients, conferring with medical and professional personnel and analyzing records to determine type and degree of disability, developing and assisting clients throughout the rehabilitation plan (or program), and aiding clients in outlining and obtaining appropriate medical and social services. The DOT further states that vocational counselors may specialize in a type of disability (e.g., spinal cord injury, traumatic brain injury, amputation, burn, visual impairment, hearing impairment, chronic pain, etc.). The role of the vocational counselor in life care planning expands this definition and is specific to persons who are catastrophically impaired and have limited access to the labor market. This role has become more defined since the early 1980s, when life care planning was first introduced into the literature (Deutsch & Raffa, 1981). In today's climate, vocational counselors serve as an instrumental member of the rehabilitation team to coordinate assessments in an effort to measure a person's aptitude, achievement levels, and transferable work skills. These assessments help determine one's potential for future work activity, such as a sheltered workshop or supported employment or, in cases where work activity is not a realistic goal, to achieve their highest level of productivity or independent living. The essential premise underlying vocational rehabilitation is that involvement in work or some productive, meaningful activity is the goal of one's rehabilitation program (Marme & Skord, 1993). And if return to work or productive activity is appropriate, then the steps to achieve that goal must be included in the life care plan.

Vocational counselors who work within the life care planning arena generally are rehabilitation professionals with a minimum of a Masters' degree in rehabilitation counseling, hold one or more national certifications in the field of rehabilitation, and have extensive training and experience in the areas of evaluation and

1-57444-075-6/99/$0.00+$.50

assessment, catastrophic case management, transferable work skills, earnings capacity analysis, and job placement (Weed & Field, 1994). Vocational counselors can be credentialed in a number of areas, most notably CRC (Certified Rehabilitation Counselor), CDMS (Certified Disability Management Specialist), CCM (Certified Case Manager), CVE (Certified Vocational Evaluator), ABVE (American Board of Vocational Experts), and, most recently, CLCP (Certified Life Care Planner). "Credentials" can also be obtained from other organizations that, on the surface, appear to be based more on profit making than on advancing the role and function of the rehabilitation professional. While some of these credentials may be valuable, the authors strongly encourage those professionals interested in pursuing further credentials to thoroughly research the history of the organization and scrutinize the validity of the offer.

Vocational Counselor as Team Member

Vocational counselors with advanced degrees and appropriate credentials are properly trained, qualified, and fully prepared to complete life care plans. They can be found working in a variety of fields, including workers' compensation, personal injury, health or disability insurance/managed care, federal Office of Workers' Compensation Programs, and state vocational rehabilitation agencies. Additionally, many facilities (for example, specialty "centers of excellence" such as Shepherd Center in Atlanta, Georgia) employ vocational counselors to assist in the evaluation and, when appropriate, transition of a client into other services for return to work assistance or to achieve their highest productivity.

Vocational counselors must be knowledgeable and stay within the accepted standards and guidelines of the particular jurisdiction for which they are preparing the life care plan. For instance, in the workers' compensation arena, the vocational counselor must usually work within the established definitions of disability and return to work hierarchy (see Weed & Field, 1994, Chapter 3). This also includes the "odd lot" doctrine that has been defined by case law as "any work that the client may be able to perform which would be of limited quantity, dependability or quality, and for which there is no reasonably stable market for their labor activities" (Clark v. Aqua Air Industries, 1983; Gil Crease v. J. A. Jones Construction Company, 1982). In comparison, vocational counselors within the disability insurance arena, such as long term disability/short term disability (LTD/STD), will be expected to provide information on the status of the client's "any/own occupation" as well as the client's vocational potential and the cost of future vocational/educational needs. Similarly, the vocational counselor within the personal injury arena will need to determine if the client has vocational potential and to what degree. They will also need to provide information on the cost of the client's expected future vocational/educational needs in an effort to identify vocational damages associated with the injury or disability.

Regardless of the specific jurisdiction, vocational counselors in life care planning must be able to determine first if a client can work and, if so, what work can they perform? This determination would include providing information not only on the types of vocational activity a client can be expected to perform, but also the cost, frequency, and duration or replacement of any training or assistance (such as job coach, vocational counseling, rehabilitation technology, modified or custom-designed work station, supported employment, tuition/books, and/or other specialized education programs) that may be required to reach the goal (Weed & Riddick, 1992). Depending on the type of disability, the vocational counselor will work with a variety of medical and allied health professionals in determining one's vocational potential and providing information for the life care plan.

Professionals such as physicians and medical specialists, physical therapists, occupational therapists, speech/language pathologists, recreation therapists, nurses, psychologists, neuropsychologists, audiologists, counselors, or other mental health professionals, and, in the case of school-age clients, school personnel, all work with the vocational counselor to provide information for the life care plan. Generally, team members whose primary responsibilities are for cognitive and psychosocial remediation interact more with vocational counselors than do other team members, and interactions are more effective when focused on adaptive work behaviors such as ability to relate with co-workers and supervisors (Sbordone & Long, 1996). In many cases, the nurse case manager for a patient with catastrophic injuries will be the primary person for the life care plan and the vocational counselor must work in conjunction with the nurse to gather and disseminate vocationally relevant information (see Chapter 3). It is common for the vocational counselor to rely on the client's primary physician, typically a physiatrist or specialist in physical medicine and rehabilitation (PM&R), in determining a client's functional level and potential to perform vocational activity. In appropriate cases, the vocational counselor may request a functional capacity evaluation (FCE), which may also be known as a physical capacity evaluation or functional capacity assessment, to objectively delineate a client's physical functioning. The FCE provides objective, "hard" data regarding the client's ability to perform various physical demands (lifting, standing, walking, sitting, pushing/pulling, etc.) and this is usually conducted in a facility that specializes in occupational health information. The FCE provides a snapshot view of a client's abilities on one particular day (evaluation may be conducted over two days), and, given the outcome of the testing, the client's work capacity from a physical standpoint is determined. Additional factors that the vocational counselor must take into consideration in assessing a client's physical capacities is the client's ability to perform work activity over time (endurance), subjective complaints, test validity/reliability, and secondary gain issues. In summary, the FCE is just one of many pieces of information used by the vocational counselor in assessing a client's vocational potential.

It is the responsibility of the vocational counselor to maintain a vocational focus on issues related to the life care plan. Most important, the counselor needs to work with the team to establish a medical and/or psychological foundation to support a client's work potential. A case in which the authors recently consulted illustrates the need to establish a medical foundation. The case involved a 50-year-old iron-metal construction worker who fell 70 to 90 feet from scaffolding and received multiple orthopedic injuries. The nurse case manager assigned to the case referred the client for a vocational evaluation to determine his work potential. Results from the vocational evaluation coupled with the client's reported high motivation to return to work seemed to suggest that he had the capacity to return to work in some area related to his previous work experience. The vocational counselor then proceeded to conduct a labor market survey to identify actual jobs in his area. Although on the surface it appeared that the case was progressing appropriately (at least from the case manager's perspective), it was learned through contacts with the client's treating physician that it was his opinion the client was permanently and totally disabled from work. Indeed, the client even applied for and was approved for Social Security Disability Insurance (SSDI) benefits, which further confirmed he was permanently and totally disabled. The physician furthermore indicated that his recommendations with regard to the client's vocational potential had not been solicited by the case manager. In fact, the physician was unaware that a vocational rehabilitation plan had been developed to return the client to work, and he obviously did not support the plan. This is a clear example of the importance of interacting with a client's medical care providers to establish a foundation to support the vocational plan.

Vocational Assessment/Evaluation

The terms *vocational assessment* and *vocational evaluation* have been used over the years in rehabilitation literature to generally describe the process of gathering data and determining a person's potential for work activity. Botterbusch (1987) defines vocational assessment as "more limited in scope" than vocational evaluation and cites the Vocational Evaluation and Work Adjustment Association (1983) definition of vocational evaluation, which "incorporates medical, psychological, social, vocational, educational, cultural, and economic data (p. 191)." In Siefker (1992), it is noted that the two phrases "do not describe a significantly different process and can be considered synonymous" (p. 1). For purposes of this chapter, the phrases will be used interchangeably to describe the comprehensive evaluation of a client's biographical and social history, education and work history, medical and other pertinent records (employment/personnel records, school records, parent's school records in pediatric cases, etc.), psychological/neuropsychological records, and actual vocational test results in determining vocational potential.

In compiling data for the life care plan, it is within the role of the vocational counselor to recommend and obtain a formal vocational assessment/evaluation, particularly in the case of a client who:

- is of working age (generally age 16–60)
- has no or unclear vocational goal
- has no work history or a series of short, sporadic jobs
- has not been determined permanently and totally disabled (i.e., is thought to have some vocational potential)

For clients who are catastrophically injured, it is important for the vocational evaluation to be as specific as possible and to take into account the client's personality traits, interests, aptitudes, and physical capabilities so as to adequately identify appropriate vocational options. In their book *Counseling the Able Disabled* (1986), Deneen and Hessellund describe 10 of the most common reasons for vocational testing. Below is a modified version of the list that is felt to be most relevant to life care planning:

1. Provide information about a person's interests, mental and physical abilities, and temperament with respect to work.
2. Support, clarify, and document impressions gained during interviews.
3. Discover job interests and potential vocational objectives.
4. Objectively and accurately describe the client's likes, dislikes, needs, and abilities rather than rely solely on verbal interview information.
5. Observe and evaluate the client's physical stamina, endurance, agility, and ability as related to work performance.
6. Evaluate the degree to which a particular impairment is a physical disability or handicap.

Vocational assessments can vary depending on the particular jurisdiction in which the case is involved. For example, vocational evaluations performed for workers' compensation usually do not include personality testing in determining suitable employment. These evaluations generally focus on interests, aptitudes, and physical capacities as well as the client's demonstrated work history. It is the authors' opinion that vocational evaluations that do not contain personality testing should be closely scrutinized as to why such assessment tools are not included. Is it an oversight on the part of the evaluator? Is the evaluator not qualified to administer personality tests? Or is there a deliberate attempt not to define personality traits, which may have a positive or negative effect on the client's vocational potential?

When referring for a vocational evaluation, the vocational counselor must review the evaluator's credentials and specify which areas to evaluate. (Also see the section on referring for neuropsychological testing later in this chapter.) The vocational counselor should be concerned not only with the expertise and experience of the evaluator, but also with the technical or scientific aspects of a particular assessment tool and the way in which the test results will be used (Kapes & Mastie, 1988; Siefker, 1992). In developing a life care plan, the vocational counselor must be able to translate results from the vocational evaluation into requirements for the life care plan. Such requirements may include cost for training, transportation, tuition, specialized or adaptive equipment, and maintenance and replacement schedules of needed equipment (Siefker, 1992). For example, the authors were involved in identifying the costs associated with completing a Master's degree and pursuing a Ph.D. for a triple amputee who was a teacher at the time of his electrocution injury. Not only were costs included in the life care plan for education requirements, but also costs of transportation, prosthetic devices, maintenance and replacement, clothing allowance (due to increased wear and tear on garments as result of prosthetic use), and computer and other assistive technology needed to assist the client in attaining his vocational goal of education administrator. This case example also demonstrates that a client's ability to achieve a vocational goal is closely related to other life care plan issues such as ability to perform ADLs (activities of daily living), accessible housing and transportation, psychological adjustment to disability, home/attendant care, wheelchair or mobility needs, and others. This case also provides an example of the inclusive approach the vocational counselor must use in conducting a comprehensive assessment of the client and interrelating realistic vocational goals with all other aspects of the client's care.

Table 4.1 Selected Issues Related to Vocational Assessment

Speeded, Timed, and Untimed Tests	Speeded and timed tests may be biased against physically impaired clients. Untimed tests may not reveal how competitive a client may be.
Individual vs. Group Tests	Usually the group test is offered for economic reasons and is more general. Individually administered tests allow for examiner comment regarding effort and behavioral observation.
Short "Screening" vs. In-depth Testing	Vocational evaluators often use short tests for achievement, intelligence, aptitude, and interest screening. Tests such as the WRAT-R, Self-Directed Search, General Aptitude Test Battery (GATB), Slosson Intelligence Test, and others are not as precise as more detailed tests. Many evaluators are not qualified to administer more precise tests.
Tests vs. On-the-Job Evaluation	In order of general priority for best assessment: ■ on-the-job with an employer ■ on-the-job based on general standard by professional evaluator ■ work sample ■ individually administered test ■ group test
Leaving Out Personality Factors	It is common in workers' compensation to leave out interest and personality factors when developing an opinion. Basic information with regard to interests, work values, and personality as it relates to work is recommended.

In addition to having a comprehensive evaluation performed, the vocational counselor must be sensitive to how the specific tests are administered, for example: group vs. individual; time, speeded, or untimed; paper and pencil vs. computer administered vs. work sample; short vs. long form; normed vs. nonnormed; and objective vs. subjective, to name a few (Table 4.1). In general, group tests are not as specific as individual tests (Anastasi, 1982; Siefker, 1992), and speeded or timed tests are usually biased against catastrophically impaired persons. In clients who are motorically and/or cognitively impaired, tests that are timed may reveal a lower score than is intellectually indicated given that the score is based on speed rather than ability. Additionally, situational or job specific tests that evaluate a person's ability for work activity in an actual work environment are more favorable and yield more accurate results than a work sample assessment in which job tasks are simulated. Some authors suggest that a client's vocational potential can be most effectively determined when the workplace is used as the primary site of all rehabilitation activity. They further indicate that no other location can be compared to the workplace for face validity and actual job activities (Sbordone & Long, 1996).

Much has been written on the various vocational assessment tools given to persons with a disability (see *A Counselor's Guide to Career Assessment Instruments*, 1988; *Vocational Assessment & Evaluation Systems: A Comparison*, 1987; and *Vocational Evaluation in the Private Sector*, 1992). The following list is provided to give an overview of some of the more common or well-known tools used in the vocational assessment/evaluation of persons who are catastrophically impaired. The reader is referred to the publications referenced above for a description of each test and information regarding its usefulness for specific populations of persons with a disability.

Intelligence:

- Wechsler Intelligence Scales–Revised (the standard of the industry)
- Stanford-Binet Scales
- Slosson Intelligence Test (brief and very general)
- Raven Progressive Matrices (reasoning)

Personality:

- Minnesota Multiphasic Personality Inventory–2 (MMPI–2). Also in Spanish.
- 16 Personality Factors (16 PF)
- Myers-Briggs Type Indicator (MBTI)
- Temperament and Values Inventory (TVI)
- Personality Assessment Inventory (PAI)
- Rorschach Inkblot Test

Interest:

- Strong-Campbell Interest Inventory
- Career Assessment Inventory (CAI)
- Self-Directed Search (SDS)
- Kuder Occupational Interest Inventory

Aptitude:

- General Aptitude Test Battery (GATB)
- Apticom
- Armed Services Vocational Aptitude Battery (ASVAB)
- Differential Aptitude Tests (DAT)
- McCarron Dial System
- Crawford Small Parts Dexterity
- Hester Evaluation System
- Jewish Employment Vocational Services Work Sample System (JEVS)
- Purdue Pegboard

Achievement:

- Wide Range Achievement Test–Revised (WRAT-R)
- Woodcock-Johnson Psychoeducational Battery
- Peabody Individual Achievement Test
- Basic Occupational Literacy Test (BOLT)

Work Sample:

- VALPAR
- TOWER

Assessment of Physical Functioning:

- Vineland Social Maturity Scale
- PULSES (Physical condition, Upper limb, Lower limb, Sensory, Excretory, Support factors)
- Barthel Inventory of Self-Care Skills

In conjunction with objective test results, the vocational counselor must take into consideration behavioral observations made during the client interview and test session. Behavioral observations are an integral part of the vocational assessment process and should always be interpreted with the actual test results and client's history (Siefker, 1992). The qualified vocational evaluator is attuned to behavioral issues that may affect test results (e.g., pain behaviors, visual/hearing difficulties, need for medication or rest breaks, cultural issues and/or language barriers, and environmental issues, such as is the room too hot or cold? Is it early or late in the day?). Likewise, the client's behavior may reveal areas of concern or discrepancy that may warrant further investigation (e.g., Was the client late for the testing session? What are the nonverbal behaviors? Is their appearance and grooming appropriate?). Behavior is a valid indication of how one will respond in certain situations, whether it is in a work environment or social/community setting.

In addition to behavioral observations, information about a client's abilities and skills obtained through educational and work experience may be more valid than test results (Siefker, 1992). For this reason, a transferable skills analysis is an essential component of the vocational evaluation and to determine a client's vocational potential. Simply described, a transferable skills analysis gives a profile of the worker traits required of a specific occupation. It is used primarily for clients with a documented work history and takes into consideration one's work experience and residual functional capacities to determine appropriate vocational options. The DOT and *Classification of Jobs* (COJ) are necessary to compile a transferable skills analysis. See the vocational resources section later in this chapter for a description of these and other publications.

Neuropsychological Evaluations in Return to Work Prediction

Neuropsychological evaluations are performed on clients following a brain injury or disease and are essential in identifying the relationships that exist between one's brain and behavior or, more specifically, between one's actions and abilities and their higher-level cognitive processes (Gabel, Oster, & Butnik, 1986). It is within the role of the vocational counselor to refer a client for a neuropsychological evaluation in cases where there is documented or suspected brain injury. According to Gabel, Oster, & Butnik, referral to a neuropsychologist is appropriate to assess problems of a more long-standing nature and includes areas such as visual, auditory, or tactile processing difficulties; constructional apraxia (copying designs or free drawing); abstract reasoning or concept formation; receptive or expressive language deficits; attention/concentration deficits; and short- or long-term memory problems. Neuropsychological testing is valuable not only to assess a client's current behavioral and learning problems (i.e., to establish a functional baseline), but also to establish prognosis, monitor and document changes over time, and assist in the planning of the rehabilitation program.

Historically, the focus of neuropsychological testing has been on the determination of brain damage and its location. Presently, there is a growing interest within neuropsychology to focus on the client's capacity to function in everyday life. The prediction of work behavior is the second most frequent reason for referral to neuropsychological evaluations. However, such evaluations are somewhat limited by a lack of norms based on specific job types and specific client population and more work is needed in this area (Sbordone & Long, 1996).

Neuropsychologists and vocational counselors generally share the goal of assisting the client's transition to an active and productive life. Vocationally speaking, neurospsychological evaluations should assist the vocational counselor in identifying the client's vocational capabilities and behaviors and in planning for their successful entrance into an appropriate work environment or at minimum to achieve their highest level of functioning/productivity (Sbordone & Long, 1996). For this reason, neurospsychological evaluations are helpful for both adult and children or pediatric clients and, as with vocational evaluations, must be as specific as possible.

For purposes of life care planning, results from neuropsychological evaluations must relate specifically to the client's function and ability and also provide recommendations for future care needs. Problems in thinking and reasoning, information processing speed, attention/concentration, and long- or short-term memory are vocational barriers that need to be accurately assessed (Sbordone & Long, 1996). Additionally, psychosocial and interpersonal relationship skills need to be assessed such that "there is an obvious need for strong communication and collaboration between vocational counselors and neuropsychologists in the interest of maximizing return to work" (p. 370).

Neuropsychological testing helps determine how much assistance is needed in the home, on the job, at school, and within the community. When referring for a neuropsychological evaluation, it is prudent for the vocational counselor to know to whom he or she is making the referral and the credentials of the neuropsychologist. Experience has shown that the most qualified neuropsychologist not only has a Ph.D. in clinical psychology and is Board certified as a neuropsychologist, but also has experience in evaluating persons across all levels of severity of brain injury and has also demonstrated a commonsense approach to evaluation and test interpretation.

Once a referral is made to a neuropsychologist, it is recommended that the vocational counselor provide specific questions to the neuropsychologist, which, when answered, would provide information needed specifically for the life care plan. The effects of brain trauma can be found in any or all aspects of one's life, including interpersonal, vocational, educational, recreational, and activities of daily living. It is the role of the neuropsychologist to evaluate the long-term or lifelong effects of brain injury on the client's ability to function (Weed, 1994). Suggested questions specifically pertinent for the life care planning process are listed in Table 4.2. Vocational counselors should ask neuropsychologists to answer the questions as part of the evaluation for life care planning.

As stated previously, neuropsychological evaluations are useful in both adult and pediatric cases. The interested reader is referred to the book *Neuropsychological Assessment* (Lezak, 1995, 3rd ed.) for detailed information on neuropsychological evaluations. According to Lezak (1976), the basic neuropsychological battery contains both individually administered tests and paper and pencil tests that are self-administered. The individually administered tests can take up to three hours and the paper and pencil tests can take from three to six hours, depending on the extent of the client's impairment(s). The paper and pencil tests should not be timed; however the individually administered tests are timed. Especially in the

Table 4.2 Neuropsychologist Questions

In addition to the standard evaluation report, add the following as appropriate.

1. Please describe, in layman terms, the damage to the brain.
2. Please describe the effects of the accident on the client's ability to function.
3. Please provide an opinion on the following topics:
   a. Intelligence level? (include pre- vs. post-incident if able)
   b. Personality style with regard to the workplace and home?
   c. Stamina level?
   d. Functional limitations and assets?
   e. Ability for education/training?
   f. Vocational implications — style of learning?
   g. Level of insight into present functioning?
   h. Ability to compensate for deficits?
   i. Ability to initiate action?
   j. Memory impairments (short-term, long-term, auditory, visual, etc.)?
   k. Ability to identify and correct errors?
   l. Recommendations for compensation strategies?
   m. Need for companion or attendant care?
4. What is the proposed treatment plan?
   a. Counseling? (individual and family)
   b. Cognitive therapy?
   c. Reevaluations?
   d. Referral to others (e.g., physicians)?
   e. Other?
5. How much and how long? (Include the cost per session or hour and reevaluations.)

case of pediatric clients, neuropsychological evaluations are often given over two sittings in order to avoid fatigue factors. Again, the vocational counselor is cautioned to be sure the neuropsychologist provides a comprehensive evaluation that is sensitive to the client's particular needs and provides information that is relevant for life care planning. Similar to vocational evaluations, neuropsychological evaluations are not done with a single test but instead are a compilation of data based on test results and interpretation and behavioral observations. It is recommended, and good practice, for the vocational counselor to establish a mechanism to meet or speak directly with the neuropsychologist to discuss test results and get their input for life care planning.

For purposes of this chapter, a brief overview of some of the more common evaluation tools for each age group is given. For additional information, the reader is referred to Chapter 6.

Pediatric: Neuropsychological Evaluations

Pediatric cases present many unique challenges for the life care planner. One challenge is that there is little, if any, history on which to rely, and practitioners are hesitant to make future care predictions. For this reason, neuropsychological evaluations are particularly helpful in children to help qualify and quantify the impact of a child's brain injury on their functioning and/or behavior. Although there are many assessment tools to evaluate pediatric clients, the Halstead-Reitan and Luria-Nebraska batteries have become the most frequently used in the neuropsychological assessment of children (Gabel, Oster, & Butnik, 1986).

According to Gabel, Oster, & Butnik (1986), perhaps the greatest usefulness of the Halstead-Reitan batteries is the establishment of objective baseline data that can clarify a child's strengths and weaknesses and be helpful in outlining educational strategies and programs to enhance their capabilities. In comparison, the Luria-Nebraska Children's Neuropsychological Test Battery can be administered to children ages 8 to 12 years and focuses on functional systems involved in brain–behavior relationships. A third common assessment battery for children is the Kaufman Assessment Battery for Children (K-ABC), (1983) which is individually administered to children ages 2½ to 12½ years old and measures intelligence and achievement. Last, a useful tool to assess infants who have experienced brain trauma from age 2 months to 30 months is the Bayley Scales of Infant Development (1969). The scales are considered to be the best measure of infant development and provide valuable data regarding early mental and motor development and developmental delay. Other scales of infant developmental attainment are the Cattelle Scales of Infant Development and the Vineland Adaptive Behavior Scales (1984).

Adult: Neuropsychological Evaluations

Whereas there are numerous neuropsychological assessment tools from which to choose when evaluating children for life care planning, there are significantly more tests for adult assessments. Below is a brief list of some of the more common neuropsychological tools for adults and areas they evaluate. For more information and description on the listed tests, the reader is referred to Lees-Haley, *Last Minute Guide to Psychological and Neuropsychological Testing* (1993).

- Wechsler Adult Intelligence Scale–Revised (WAIS–R) (intelligence)
- Wisconsin Card Sorting Test (executive or higher order functions)
- Boston Naming Test (language)
- Rey Auditory Verbal Learning (memory)
- Weschler Memory Scale–Revised (WMS–R) (memory)
- Stroop Color Test (mental control)
- Serial 7s or Serial 3s (attention)
- Benton Visual Retention Test (visual memory)
- Gates-MacGinitie Reading Tests (reading academic skills)
- Hooper Visual Organization Test (visual perception)
- Woodcock-Johnson (academic)
- Haptic Intelligence Test (intelligence). Used for clients with visual impairment.
- Leiter Intelligence Test (intelligence). Used for clients with hearing impairment.
- Hisky-Nebraska Aptitude Test (aptitude). Used for clients with hearing impairment.

In summary, neuropsychological evaluations are essential in the field of life care planning to assess both the near- and long-term effects of brain damage on one's functioning and/or developmental levels. Information obtained through neuropsychological testing is crucial in developing the appropriate future care planning of a client with a traumatic brain injury. Inasmuch as neuropsychological evaluations are vital to life care planning, test results for young children are very variable. Generally, IQ test results are not considered of substantial value until the child reaches school age. Additionally, it is generally preferable to rely on a school child's standardized achievement test scores than actual grades as a true measure of their achievement. In referring a client for neuropsychological testing, the vocational counselor should ensure that the evaluator reviews all available medical and academic records and that the evaluation includes developmental assessments in addition to the more standardized test batteries. It is common to include in the life care plan provisions for neuropsychological reevaluations at specific life stages in the client's development or at specific time intervals throughout one's life expectancy in order to assess and monitor the client's functioning abilities. This also applies to the assessment of aging on brain injury or neurological impairment.

Wage Loss and Earnings Capacity Analysis

In addition to contributing information on a client's vocational and educational outlook with regard to life care planning, the vocational counselor also may be asked to assess the client's loss of earnings capacity. According to one source, future medical care and loss of earnings capacity are directly related to the education and experience of most vocational counselors. The vocational counselor can offer valuable input in three critical areas: lost capacity to earn an income, loss of opportunity to be employed (loss of access to the labor market), and cost of future medical care (Weed & Field, 1994). The first and second areas will be described in this chapter. The third area, establishing the cost of future medical care, is referenced throughout this book and will not be covered specifically in this section. Also, refer to Table 4.3 for a summary of the necessary details associated with vocational aspects appropriate for the life care plan.

With regard to lost earnings capacity, it is first necessary to establish the client's wages at the time of injury. This can be fairly simple for a client who was working at the time of injury in a job that is considered representative of his or her earnings potential. In pediatric cases or for young clients who may have been working but had not yet established a clear vocational identity, the process can be more challenging. The issue of identifying earnings capacity can be divided into four client populations:

1. Clients injured at birth or in the neonatal period
2. Clients injured before they reach school age (and have no academic grades or standardized test scores)
3. Clients injured before establishing a career identity
4. Clients injured after having an established work history representative of their vocational potential

Table 4.3 Life Care Planning Questions Regarding Vocational Needs

- First determine if vocational aspects have been considered or are already underway (e.g., already initiated by insurance company or attorney).
- What interview information have you obtained from the client (e.g., work skills, leisure activities, education, work, functional ability)?
- Have you obtained copies of relevant medical records?
- Have you obtained work-related information (such as tax returns, job evaluations, school and test records, training history, and treating MD comments)?
- Does the client need testing before determining vocational potential (e.g., vocational evaluation, psychological, neuropsychological or physical capacities testing)? Also, is the evaluation a "quality" and "valid" appraisal?
- If there is work potential, is there a need for justifying a plan by performing a labor market survey? (If LMS, what method is used? e.g., direct contact with employers vs. statistics or publications.)
- What is the client's expected income, including benefits? (If personal injury litigation, then pre- vs. postinjury *capacity*.)
- If there is an apparent market for the client's labor, is there a need for a job analysis? (And if an analysis was completed, was it done according to the Americans with Disabilities Act guidelines?)
- What are the estimated costs of the vocational plan?
    - Counseling, career guidance? (When does it start/stop, frequency and cost? e.g., 30 hrs. over 6 months at $65/hr.)
    - Job placement, job coaching, or supported employment costs?
    - Tuition or training, books, supplies? (Include dates for expected costs, e.g., Technical training 2 years @ $400/yr. for 1997–1999.)
    - Rehabilitation or assistive technology, accommodations or aides, costs for work, education, and/or training (e.g., computer, printer, work station, tools, tape recorder, attendant care, transportation — include costs and replacement schedules)?
- What effect, if any, does the injury have on worklife expectancy (e.g., delayed entry into work force, less than full-time, earlier retirement, expected increased turnover, or time off for medical follow-up or treatment)?

Clearly, there are differences in the way the vocational counselor considers information based on the age of the client at the time of injury. Table 4.4 outlines some considerations to make in establishing a foundation for earnings capacity in all four age groups.

The listed factors can be a good predictor or give a "reasonable approximation" of what the client could have done prior to the injury (preinjury earnings or capacity). Obviously, the more history and documentation there is, the better and more accurate a foundation can be established with regard to earnings capacity.

The vocational counselor must determine the level of the client's functioning both before the injury (preinjury) as well as after the injury (postinjury) as it relates to the types of jobs the client could hold now or in the future. In general, wage loss refers to the amount of money (wages) lost by the client as a result of the injury and is based on his or her actual past work history. Earnings capacity, on the other hand, refers to the loss of future earnings related to what would be considered a reasonable estimation of the client's work potential (capacity) (Weed & Field, 1994).

Table 4.4 Establishing a Foundation for Earnings Capacity

Client Age	*Factors to Consider*
0–1 year of age	Review of family history (i.e., parents, older siblings, aunts/uncles, and grandparents) to include education and work records as a way to establish family patterns.
2–5 years of age	Same as above plus day care records/observations, church school observations, preschool records, pediatrician records, family videotapes, baby books if well-maintained by parents, developmental records, neuropsychological evaluations, or other relevant records.
6–18 years of age	Review of family history, school records including standardized test scores, academic grades, honors, disciplinary records, extracurricular activities, pediatrician records, neuropsychological testing, vocational testing, or other relevant records.
18+ years of age	Review of employment/personnel records, school records, tax records, military records, community/civic involvement, neuropsychological testing, vocational testing, or other relevant information.

In some cases, it may be possible to determine that a client is permanently and totally disabled from the workforce based on his or her work history and type of injury. Such an example includes the case of a 58-year-old career truck driver who was involved in a motor vehicle accident and is a C4 quadriplegic. Although it may be arguable that the client could possibly be employed as a dispatcher or in some other related job in the trucking industry, it is not likely given his advanced age and the fact that he would require extensive job modification and rehabilitation technology, as well as an employer willing to make the modifications and employ the injured client. In such cases, the actual earnings of the client would be the basis on which to project wage loss.

In other cases, it may be more appropriate to identify a client's pre- vs. postinjury earnings capacity in categories of jobs rather than specific job titles. For example, in cases where the client is a child or young adult with no clearly established work history, the vocational counselor can identify categories of jobs that are representative of types of workers (such as skilled or unskilled) and can then identify certain jobs that fall under those categories (such as lawyer or laborer) to determine the client's earnings capacity.

To determine wage loss or loss of earnings capacity, the vocational counselor essentially evaluates the client's preinjury and postinjury employability (defined in Weed & Field, 1994, as possessing the skills, abilities, and traits necessary to perform a job) and compares the two. Once the counselor has evaluated the difference in pre- and postinjury earnings capacity, the economist then calculates the total amount of lost earnings capacity over the client's worklife expectancy (Siefker, 1992). See Chapter 11 on the Role of the Economist in Life Care Planning for further information.

There are many factors and approaches to consider when determining future wage loss and earnings capacity analysis. Of the many approaches, the RAPEL method considers most of the factors (Weed & Field, 1994). The RAPEL method, developed by Weed, (1994), offers a comprehensive approach to determining earnings capacity analysis. (See Chapter 20 for additional information). The approach incorporates a rehabilitation plan (or life care plan for the more catastrophically impaired), information with regard to the client's access to the labor market (employability), information with regard to their placeability (defined as the likelihood that the client could successfully be placed in a job), earnings capacity, and labor force participation or work life expectancy. Generally, if there is a reduction in the client's life expectancy given his or her injury, there also will be a reduction in the work life expectancy. The experienced vocational counselor would express this reduction in a percentage of loss or number of years lost in the labor market. For more information on the topic of wage loss/earnings capacity analysis, the reader is referred to Dillman (1987) and Chapter 11 in the book.

Labor Market Survey and Job Analysis

The labor market survey is designed to reveal current information about a specific job market. Questions include:

1. "Do jobs of a particular nature exist in the economy?"
2. "If these jobs exist, are they available locally?"
3. "If available locally, are these jobs open to my client?"
4. "What do these jobs pay (including benefits)?"

Part of the opinion regarding to an adult client's earnings capacity may be related to the current labor market. Obviously, a pediatric case would not include a specific employer-by-employer analysis; however, data that is collected by the government with regard to the future outlook of an occupation may be included. See Table 4.5 for common topics included in the labor market survey.

It should be noted that the way in which the consultant asks questions could skew the results toward a desired direction. In a recent case, a plaintiff's expert revealed that a client who had chronic pain was unemployable and used as partial justification the results of a labor market survey. She reported that the survey revealed that the client would not be an acceptable candidate for sedentary jobs that were directly in line with her work history. Following the deposition, the defense expert contacted the same employers and distinctly different information was provided. Probably the consultant asked questions in a way that solicited support for her conclusions. In another case, contact with the employers listed in another consultant's notes revealed that no employer on the list recalled being contacted with regard to a labor market survey.

Once a prospective job is located, it may be appropriate to conduct a job analysis. The analysis is designed to determine if job traits match the worker's traits and therefore represent a reasonable probability of employment. There are specific guidelines that the consultant must follow in order to make sure that they are conducting the analysis according to published standards. Indeed, one successful malpractice lawsuit resulted when a nurse completed a "job analysis" that consisted of less than one page. The topics covered in the analysis did not follow published standards. In fact, it appeared as if the nurse was unaware that the government and others have published on this topic.

Table 4.5 Labor Market Survey Checklist

Introduction (include the following identifying information for report)
- Name
- Age
- Date of injury
- Type of injury & medical limitations
- Work experience
- Education
- Other historical information
- Vocational test results

Method(s) Used (What method(s) was (were) used to obtain the information? Suggest starting with residual employability profile by VDARE for worker traits.)

Personal contacts (as appropriate) with:
- Personal network
- Yellow pages
- City Directory or Haynes Directory
- Chamber of Commerce
- Professional and trade associations
- Job service
- Vocational rehabilitation
- Other

Publications
- Wage rates for selected occupations (state)
- Occupational supply and demand (state Dept. of Industry and Trade or Labor)
- State career information systems (or similar)
- Manufacturing directory (SIC codes)
- Bureau of Labor Statistics; e.g., Area Wage Survey (federal)
- Census Bureau (federal)
- Job Service microfiche/posted jobs (state)
- Classified ads or job flyers
- Identified discreet jobs related to client's experience
- Labor Market Access Analysis (LMA 1991 computer program)
- Other

Results
- Employer's contacted — approximately 10
- Job(s) available
- Wages & benefits (holidays, vacation, sick, medical, dental, personal leave, etc.)
- Training/education needed
- Willingness to work with disabled
- Accessibility/architectural barriers
- Other

Conclusions (The professional's opinion)
- Placeability
- Expected income
- Other related comments

It is important that the life care planner, who may not be a vocational expert, be aware that when they work with the vocational aspects of the plan, the vocational expert must provide a proper foundation for their opinion. For more information, the reader is encouraged to review these topics in the *Rehabilitation*

Consultant's Handbook (Weed & Field, 1994) or the *Revised Handbook for Analyzing Jobs* (USDOL, 1991c).

Vocational Resources

The vocational counselor has many resources available to assist in assessing a client's vocational potential and make appropriate recommendations for the life care plan. Below are listed a few of the more valuable reference materials used by the vocational counselor:

- *Dictionary of Occupational Titles (DOT)*, 4th ed. (1991). Contains definitions of 12,741 job titles and descriptions of jobs found in the national economy. Data compiled by the U.S. Department of Labor. Now available in revised format on CD-ROM (Field & Field, 1995). This publication is expected to be eliminated when the O-net (see below) is activated on the world wide web.
- *Classification of Jobs (COJ)* (1992). Contains worker trait profiles of the 72 U.S. Department of Labor worker traits for each of the 12,741 DOT job titles. The worker traits are assigned a code and rated.
- *The Enhanced Guide for Occupational Exploration (GOE)* (1991). Provides descriptions of all jobs organized within related job clusters and includes information pertaining to academic and physical requirements, work environment, salary and outlook, typical duties, skills and abilities required, and where to obtain additional information.
- *The Revised Handbook for Analyzing Jobs (RHAJ)* (1991). Gives descriptions on how to examine individual jobs to determine suitability for a client.
- *Job Analysis and the ADA: A Step-by-Step Guide* (1992). This is another option for a comprehensive guide for determining the suitability of a job for clients with disabilities.
- *Occupational Outlook Handbook (OOH)* (1991). Clusters jobs by occupation and gives information with regard to employment potential, labor market trends, salary, requirements, and training needed to enter the occupation.

The above-listed resources use data compiled by the federal government with many published by the government. In addition to the ones listed, there are other state, regional, and local publications specific to occupations found in certain geographic areas.

Computer resources available to the vocational counselor include:

- LifeStep for Windows Job Matching System by LegalTech, 800-255-6945.
- Labor Market Access (CMA '92) computer job matching program available through Elliott & Fitzpatrick, 800-843-4977.
- Passport to Data on CD-ROM (includes the DOT, COJ, OOH, and RHAJ) available through Elliott & Fitzpatrick, 800-843-4977.
- CAPCO telephonic system of ordering job search and transferable skills information, 800-541-5006.

- O-net, the on-line replacement to the DOT, is located on the world wide web at http:/www.doleta.gov/programs/onet.
- For other Internet and web sites, see Chapter 25 on technology resources.

CONCLUSION

This chapter is designed to outline some of the factors that a life care planner may encounter if a client is expected to work. If the life care planner does not have the expertise to develop opinions in this specialized area, it may be reasonable to obtain services of a vocational expert. It is important to determine whether the vocational expert includes the appropriate areas, as described in this chapter, and has sufficient expertise to develop reasonable opinions. Some of the topics included in this chapter are designed to assist the non-vocational expert with an overview so that appropriate questions can be asked in order to enhance the ultimate care plan, reduce overlap or duplication in services, and facilitate the client's return to employment and/or achievement of their highest level of functioning.

REFERENCES

Anastasi, A. (1982). **Psychological Testing** (5th ed.). New York: Macmillan.

Blackwell, T., Conrad, D. & Weed, R. (1992). **Job Analysis and the ADA: A Step-by-Step Guide**. Athens, GA: E & F Vocational Services.

Botterbusch, K.F. (1987). **Vocational Assessment and Evaluation Systems: A Comparison**. Menomonie, WI: University of Wisconsin Materials Development Center.

Clark v. Aqua Air Industries, 435 So. 2d 492 (1983).

Crease, G. v. J.A. Jones Construction Company, 425 So. 2d 274 (LA App. 1982).

Deneen, L. & Hessellund, T. (1986). **Counseling the Able Disabled**. San Francisco: Rehab Publications.

Deutsch, P. & Raffa, F. (1981). **Damages in Tort Actions,** Vol. 8. New York: Matthew Bender.

Dillman, E. (1987). The necessary economic and vocational interface in personal injury cases. **Journal of Private Sector Rehabilitation, 2(3),** 121-142.

Field, J.E. & Field, T.F. (1980, 1984, 1988, 1992). **Classification of Jobs.** Athens, GA: Elliott & Fitzpatrick.

Field, J.E. & Field, T.F. (1995). **Passport to Data** [computer program]. Athens, GA: Elliott & Fitzpatrick.

Gabel, S., Oster, G., & Butnik, S. (1986). **Understanding Psychological Testing in Children**. New York: Plenum Publishing.

Kapes, J. & Mastie, M. (Eds.). (1988). **A Counselor's Guide to Career Assessment Instruments**. (2nd ed.). Alexandria, VA: National Career Development Association.

Lees-Haley, P. (1993). **The Last Minute Guide to Psychological and Neuropsychological Testing: A Quick Reference for Attorneys and Claims Professionals**. Athens, GA: Elliott & Fitzpatrick.

Lezak, M.D. (1976, 1983, 1995). **Neuropsychological Assessment**. (3rd ed.). New York: Oxford University Press.

Marme, M. & Skord, K. (1993). Counseling strategies to enhance the vocational rehabilitation of persons after traumatic brain injury. **Journal of Applied Rehabilitation Counseling, 24(1),** 19-25.

Sbordone, R.J. & Long, C.J. (Eds.). (1996). **Ecological Validity of Neuropsychological Testing**. Delray Beach: St. Lucie Press.

Siefker, J.M. (Ed.). (1992). **Vocational Evaluation in Private Sector Rehabilitation**. Menomonie, WI: University of Wisconsin Materials Development Center.

U.S. Department of Labor. (1991a). **Dictionary of Occupational Titles**. Washington, D.C.

U.S. Department of Labor. (1991b). **Enhanced Guide for Occupational Exploration.** Washington, D.C.

U.S. Department of Labor. (1991c). **Revised Handbook for Analyzing Jobs.** Washington, D.C.

U.S. Department of Labor. (1991d). **Occupational Outlook Handbook.** Washington, D.C.

Weed, R. (1994). Evaluating the earnings capacity of clients with mild to moderate acquired brain injury. In C. Simkins (Ed.), **Guide to Understanding, Evaluating and Presenting Cases Involving Traumatic Brain Injury for Plaintiff Lawyers, Defense Lawyers and Insurance Representatives**. Washington, D.C.: National Head Injury Foundation.

Weed, R. & Field, T. (1994). **Rehabilitation Consultant's Handbook.** (2nd ed.). Athens, GA: Elliott & Fitzpatrick.

Weed, R. & Riddick, S. (1992). Life Care Plans as a case management tool. **The Individual Case Manager Journal, 3(1),** 26-35.

5

THE ROLE OF THE PSYCHOLOGIST IN LIFE CARE PLANNING

Anne Sluis Powers

INTRODUCTION

As a member of the interdisciplinary rehabilitation team, the psychologist can play numerous roles. This chapter will consider the roles of inpatient and outpatient psychological services, as well as the ways a psychologist can work with individuals with disabilities, their support systems, and the rehabilitation team (also see Chapter 6 which discusses the role of the neuropsychologist). Several different topics will be considered: (1) choosing a psychologist, (2) psychological issues common to rehabilitation, (3) the psychologist's role in assessment and diagnosis, (4) psychological testing, and (5) types of psychological treatment.

Choosing a Psychologist

The following is an overview of the psychological training and preparation of the licensed psychologist. Though psychologists may vary in theoretical orientation, their academic requirements are consistent with the requirements of the American Psychological Association. Rehabilitation professionals should be well informed of the psychologist's credentials when selecting one and, in order to make the most appropriate referrals, should be aware of their theoretical orientation.

- A licensed psychologist almost always has a doctoral degree from an accredited university program or professional school that has been approved by the American Psychological Association (or deemed equivalent, in some select cases). Psychologists are required to complete a 1900 hour predoctoral internship in an approved program, followed by a minimum of one-year full-time equivalent post-doctoral internship supervised by a licensed psychologist.
- The candidate petitions the state board of psychological examiners for the right to take the written examination in professional psychology, which must be passed within state-legislated parameters. Then the candidate takes

1-57444-075-6/99/$0.00+$.50

an oral examination based on legal and ethical issues for the state in which she or he intends to practice. Successful passage of both examinations allows licensure within that state. It is only then that the person may use the title "psychologist." Use of the title without proper licensure constitutes a violation of legal statutes and ethical principles.

- Psychologists practice within the scope of their training and experience, and this may vary widely. It will be important for those engaged in life care planning to ascertain whether or not a psychologist has specific personal and/or professional experience in working with rehabilitation clients and their families. It may be helpful to choose a psychologist who has subspecialized in health, medical, or rehabilitation psychology or who has additional training as a registered nurse or rehabilitation counselor.

The following is a brief description of widely accepted theoretical orientations used by practicing psychologists. It is important that the rehabilitation professional understand the theoretical perspective of the psychologist when choosing the rehabilitation team referral.

- **Psychoanalytic psychologists** follow the theory and principles established by Sigmund Freud, including examination of early childhood and familial relationships, along with conflicts presumed to originate in early developmental stages.
- **Psychodynamic psychologists** incorporate the theories of those following Freud (Alfred Adler, Harry Stack Sullivan, Karen Horney, Erik Erikson, and others). These psychologists also focus on aspects of relationships presumed to originate in infancy and childhood.
- **Developmental psychologists** examine how individuals seem to be developing relative to their age-related peers, which may be useful following catastrophic events occurring before adulthood.
- **Behavioral psychologists** analyze environmental and personal factors that can be identified and altered in the interest of improving the incidence and frequency of desirable behaviors and decreasing the amount of problematic behaviors in an individual.
- **Cognitive-behavioral psychologists** incorporate behavioral principles and also consider the roles of thoughts and feelings in acquiring and maintaining certain behaviors. Both behavioral and cognitive-behavioral psychologists can help develop systematic behavior change programs.
- **Health psychologists** tend to adhere to the systems approach: no part of a system operates exclusive of others. Therefore, they adhere to the biopsychosocial model. In the rehabilitation process health psychologists work with a multidisciplinary team of health professionals (e.g., physicians, nurses, physical therapists, occupational therapists, case manager) to determine the treatment plan and its implementation.
- **Industrial psychologists** analyze work environments to enhance productivity through the human element. Considerations include management style; environmental considerations such as work site layout, music, and color; employee assistance programs; policy development, attention to group dynamics and other factors.

It will be important to choose a psychologist who is able to work well with an interdisciplinary team and who understands the roles of the various rehabilitation professionals. The psychologist should be properly licensed to eliminate concerns of credibility, and their orientation, when appropriate, should be relevant to the client's situation from a biopsychosocial-spiritual perspective, addressing the client's needs holistically.

Psychological Issues Common to Rehabilitation

The Family

Emotional Issues: Initially following catastrophic injury or the diagnosis of a life-threatening illness, the issue facing the client and family is that of mere survival. Will the person live or die? For family members, the initial reaction is usually one of panic. As this response subsides, feelings of disorientation and loss of control are common. It may be very difficult to concentrate, and family members may become confused by what they perceive to be different types of information coming from different sources. Feelings of disequilibrium continue for quite some time in many families, with members feeling "in control" one day and quite "out of control" the next. Behaviors that can signal these reactions include anger over both significant and seemingly trivial issues, concrete or very literal thinking, efforts to participate in the loved one's care in ways that are inappropriate, and neglect of other significant areas of one's life.

Functional Issues: Once it seems apparent that the client will survive the initial crisis, the focus will shift toward issues of functional abilities and quality of life. Will the client be able to talk, eat, walk, and care for themselves, return to normal family roles and responsibilities, return to school, or earn a living? Different levels of anxiety are associated with the different stages of stabilization and rehabilitation. Family members need a forum for discussing some of these concerns that are private and separate from the client, in addition to being involved in family therapy with their loved one. They may need assistance with relaxation strategies, help with prioritizing things, or to find as much information as possible to make good decisions.

Denial: Denial is a defense mechanism that is initially protective, keeping families from feeling overwhelmed by the enormity of a catastrophic event. However, denial of the facts prevents the family from dealing with real issues and consequences that must eventually be addressed. The rehabilitation team treads a fine line, wanting to support optimism and hopefulness, while presenting data about deficits and limitations that may endure. Encourage family members to focus one day at a time without letting expectations for the future affect the client's immediate needs. Gently asking family members "How does he seem to you?" or asking them to describe how their loved one did things prior to the illness or injury may allow an assessment of the family's degree of denial or acceptance.

Letting go of denial may lead to expressions, directly or indirectly, of anger. Anger may be expressed toward the client, toward others perceived as responsible for the injury or illness, medical care providers, the legal system, family members, God, or any number of others. Dealing with anger and frustration effectively may require the assistance of a mental health professional, who will suggest appropriate problem-solving strategies and may assist with various stress management techniques.

Other psychological concerns commonly seen in family members include:

- Fatigue
- Depression
- Sleep disturbance
- Criticisms from other family members and friends regarding care provided for the client
- Feelings of hopelessness, helplessness, and guilt
- Constriction of social activities and opportunities for social support
- Changes in the quality of the relationship with the injured or ill person

At this point, it is important for the rehabilitation team to remember how "family" may be defined. Certainly where issues of consent are concerned, legal statutes apply. We must not forget that the client's self-defined "family" may include those with whom no formal, legal ties exist. These relationships may, in fact, be closer than those within the biological family, including relationships with a significant other, close friends, stepfamily members, and so on. Some close relationships may have been defined within legal documents such as durable powers of attorney or living wills; the client's wishes should be respected and followed within the scope of the law. Extended family members should be supported with mental health services every bit as much as members of the client's biological family.

> It is important to note that psychological issues may surface and then reemerge over and over: developing a relationship with a caring provider that can endure over time, as the need arises, will be essential to a family's adjustment.

The Client

Rehabilitation clients can face tremendous challenges: physically, cognitively, emotionally, behaviorally, financially, and socially. Following traumatic brain injury, disordered and inappropriate features may emerge as a result of altered brain functioning (DeBoskey & Morin, 1985). For those with other kinds of injuries, it is important to remember that subtle brain injuries may have also occurred. Subtle or obvious problems may become apparent with regard to attention, concentration, memory, problem solving, insight, judgment, affective issues, pain management, and coping.

Problematic behaviors can include periods of the following:

- Agitation
- Irritability
- Outbursts of anger

- Inappropriate statements
- Inappropriate sexual behavior
- Egocentrism
- Concrete thinking
- Impulsivity
- Emotional lability
- Denial of deficits
- Suspicion or paranoia
- Anxiety
- Depression
- Apathy
- Obsessiveness
- Inertia
- Social immaturity
- Dependency
- Eating disorders

The Behavioral Psychology Approach

When a behavioral psychologist is asked to consult regarding these problematic areas, several things will occur. The psychologist will be interested in input from all members of the rehabilitation team in order to determine when problems occur and possible patterns in the problematic behavior. The client may be observed during therapies and quiet times for several days while the psychologist notes patterns of behavior. These behaviors will be charted on a 24-hour log and used as “baseline” data.

In general, behavioral interventions will be described specifically and the team will be asked to chart information about client responses. It is quite common for behavioral problems to actually increase for a short period of time when the behavioral program is instituted. The psychologist will look for decreases in the frequency, intensity, and/or duration of problem behaviors over time. Do not become concerned if the behavioral program does not instantly solve behavioral issues: modifications are commonly required and consistency in application is essential.

The following describes how a behavioral psychologist might work to assist the client in resolving problems.

- The psychologist may be able to **identify patterns of events** that precede the problem behavior. For example, a client may become agitated when a specific family member visits. Perhaps that family member is doing something that contributes to the problem. In other cases, clients become agitated when the stimulation level in the environment becomes excessive, when they become tired, or when they are uncomfortable.
- The psychologist will also try to **identify the impact or effect,** of the client’s behavior. For example, if an inappropriate behavior is followed by an event that the client perceives as reinforcing (e.g., getting to stop doing a painful physical therapy exercise when he yells, or being given a milkshake as a distraction), the probability is that the inappropriate behavior will

continue or even worsen with time. The psychologist will recommend different ways of responding to inappropriate behaviors that will lessen the likelihood of recurrence. It will be of utmost importance for the entire team to follow the behavioral plan consistently.

- Rehabilitation team members are in a unique position of being able to **model** ways of interacting with clients. Family members may be at a loss as how to respond to angry outbursts or episodes of poor social judgment. The team can show family members how to simplify language when speaking to someone who cannot think abstractly, how to distract a client who is focusing inappropriately, how to ignore certain behaviors in order to eliminate the reinforcing power of attention, and so forth.
- As a client's level of awareness and insight improves, it will be important to **involve the client** in the setting of behavioral goals. Explaining treatment rationales and getting the client to take responsibility for her own behavioral problem will increase her investment in the process and, ultimately, in the success of the program. Clients can keep track of progress on charts, in memory logs, or other creative ways that measure successes over time.

The Process of Adjustment to Disability

As insight improves, adjustment concerns become central. Individuals follow very similar patterns of adjustment to disability. Cohn (1961) has described a five-stage process of adjustment. The first stage is **shock**, wherein denial or minimization is common. In the second stage, **expectancy for recovery**, the client may admit to current deficits but continues to expect a quick and complete recovery. As the extent of the disability becomes apparent, **mourning** occurs. Depression, suicidal ideation, suicidal attempts, and disengagement from or active resistance to the therapy process are common during this stage and should be identified. During the fourth stage, **defense**, the adjustment process begins. The person reaches a critical point where either denial or moves toward independence tend to occur. The final stage, **adjustment**, occurs when the client has a realistic appraisal of the disability and begins to focus on moving forward with life.

Post-Traumatic Stress Disorder

When traumatic injuries have occurred, post-traumatic stress disorder (PTSD) can result. According to the American Psychological Association (1994) in the Diagnostic and Statistical Manual for Mental Disorders, Fourth Edition (DSM-IV) criteria, PTSD follows from exposure to "an extreme traumatic stressor ... that involves actual or threatened death or serious injury" (p. 424) to the self or someone else, or finding out about such an event experienced by a loved one. The person's response must involve "intense fear, helplessness, or horror; a persistent avoidance of stimuli associated with the trauma; a numbing of general responsiveness; and persistent symptoms of increased arousal" (DSM-IV, p. 424). The symptoms must be present for over one month and cause clinically significant distress or impairment in daily functioning (DSM-IV, 1994). The epidemiology of post-traumatic stress disorder varies, with 50% to 80% of those experiencing a devastating disaster going on to develop symptoms of the disorder (Kaplan & Sadock, 1991). The likelihood of developing PTSD correlates positively with the severity of the stressor.

Therapeutic Strategies

Early intervention programs are now being used to encourage clients to talk about their traumatic experiences in a supportive context. Behavior therapy, cognitive therapy, hypnosis, and some experimental approaches have been used. Group therapy can be particularly effective when members of the group have shared similar precipitating events. Family therapy is often useful because of the high incidence of marital disruption caused by PTSD symptoms. Drug therapy may be indicated in clients who are seriously affected and are not responding optimally to other therapeutic interventions. Hospitalization may be required during periods of severe symptoms or when there is a risk of suicidal or violent behavior.

> It is important to note that clients adjust to disability in highly individual ways. The stages of adjustment within the individual can vary as well. Often, personal stressors will arise that can lead to a revisiting of adjustment issues (e.g., changes in a personal relationship may lead to further examination of the impact of the disability). It may be quite helpful for the client to have a relationship with a psychologist who can be available, repeatedly if needed, for periods of brief therapy.

The Psychologist's Role in Assessment and Diagnosis

Psychologists are asked frequently to contribute to the initial assessment of a rehabilitation client. Generally, psychologists enter the picture in the rehabilitation facility, rather than during the acute hospitalization. In complex cases, however, it may be helpful to have psychological input during the transitional phase between acute hospitalization and rehabilitation placement.

The psychologist may address the following factors:

- Medical diagnosis
- Preexisting conditions (medical conditions, mental health issues)
- Premorbid health beliefs and behaviors (religious beliefs about health care, degree of compliance with medical treatment in the past, health-related practices, quality of prior relationships with health care providers, use of alternative medicine, degree of faith in Western medicine, etc.)
- Educational background
- Employment history (job titles and stability of employment)
- Medications, including side effects and interactions
- Functional limitations
- Physical rehabilitation potential, from a team perspective
- Premorbid personality characteristics
- Marital status and stability of primary relationship
- Role within family prior to injury or illness (e.g., wage-earner status, parenting responsibilities, household management tasks, financial obligations, relationship with extended family)

- Financial resources
- Extent of social support network
- Substance use and abuse history
- Abuse history (physical, emotional, sexual)
- Legal history
- Coping resources and compensatory strategies
- Community resources
- Adjustment, including stage of adaptation to disability
- Affective status (depression, anxiety, anger, etc.)
- Suicidal potential and lethality
- Insight
- Judgment
- Potential for post-traumatic stress disorder
- Compliance with treatment
- Initiative and motivation
- Passivity vs. proactivity
- Beliefs about outcomes
- Role of spirituality, past and present

Following a psychological evaluation, the team should be able to "see" who the client was prior to the injury or onset of illness, how the event has impacted the client and his or her support system in the present, and what changes can be anticipated in the future.

Psychological Testing

A number of psychological instruments can provide valuable information when planning care for a rehabilitation client. This section will identify some psychological tests that may be given, along with descriptions of the types of data they will generate.

Behavioral Assessment of Pain Questionnaire (BAP)

This 390-item questionnaire investigates issues related to the management of chronic pain (Lewandowski & Tearnan, 1993). Answers reveal the client's perception of pain and its severity, health care use patterns, degree of physical activity and activity avoidance behaviors, spousal influences on pain and wellness, physician influences on pain and wellness, perceived quality of the physician-patient relationship, nonproductive pain beliefs, coping strategies used, mood, and use of medications. Treatment recommendations are generated for managing the physician-patient relationship, reducing pain behaviors, examining pain beliefs, and addressing use of drugs and other substances. A post-treatment questionnaire is available for outcome evaluation.

Beck Anxiety Inventory (BAI)

Twenty-one physical and emotional symptoms are listed in this questionnaire. The client rates whether symptoms experienced within the past week are absent or are mild, moderate, or severe in intensity. Scores indicate whether symptoms of anxiety are within normal range or range from mild to severe. The physical symptoms within the inventory must be evaluated with medical diagnoses in mind: many may be manifestations of disease processes rather than symptoms of anxiety, though the severity of symptoms may be affected by anxiety as well.

Beck Depression Inventory (BDI)

The inventory contains twenty-one sets of statements related to depressing thoughts, feelings, and behaviors. The client circles the statement that most accurately describes symptoms during the past week. Scores indicate whether symptoms of depression are within normal range or range from mild to severe. Suicidal ideation, intent, and plan are assessed by one set of statements within the inventory.

Beck Suicide Inventory (BSI)

This inventory contains twenty-one sets of statements related to suicidal ideation, intent, and plan. The client circles the statement that most accurately describes symptoms experienced during the past week. Scores indicate the degree of suicide ideation. It is important to use clinical data, in addition to a suicide inventory, when assessing suicidal thinking or lethality.

Coping Resources Inventory for Stress (CRIS)

CRIS measures perceived coping resourcefulness based on transactional models of stress (Curlette, Aycock, Matheny, Pugh, & Taylor, 1992). According to these models, stress is the outcome of a perceived imbalance between demands and coping resources. CRIS scales measure self-disclosure, self-directedness, confidence, acceptance, social support, financial freedom, physical health, physical fitness, stress monitoring, tension control, structuring abilities, problem-solving, cognitive restructuring, functional beliefs, and social ease. An overall Coping Resources Effectiveness score is computed, along with primary and composite scales, wellness-inhibiting items, and validity keys.

Geriatric Depression Scale (GDS)

This scale asks thirty "yes/no" questions about thoughts, feelings, and activities related to depression in older adults. Scores range from "normal" to "severe."

Millon Behavioral Health Inventory (MBHI)

This 150-item true/false questionnaire is designed to assess psychological characteristics of patients receiving general medical care or evaluation. It contains twenty scales that provide data regarding coping factors related to the physical health care of adult medical patients. It can help identify possible psychological or psychosomatic complications, and may help predict responses to illness or medical treatment. The inventory takes about 20 minutes to complete and assumes an eighth-grade reading level. The MBHI report generates hypotheses that must be used as one facet of a total patient evaluation.

Millon Clinical Multiaxial Inventory-III (MCMI-III)

This self-report instrument contains 175 true/false items designed to assess personality disorders and clinical syndromes described in the Diagnostic and Statistical Manual–IV (DSM–IV). It can assist the clinician in developing individualized treatment plans and help identify potential barriers or obstacles to treatment. The MCMI–III assumes an eighth-grade reading level.

Minnesota Multiphasic Personality Inventory-A (MMPI-A)

This inventory is an empirically based test of psychopathology, derived specifically for adolescents. It is used primarily to aid in problem identification, diagnosis, and treatment planning in a variety of settings, including hospitals, clinics, school counseling programs, private practice, and correctional facilities. There are 478 true/false items. Administration times takes up to an hour and assumes a sixth-grade reading level. Family problems, eating disorders, and chemical dependency issues are addressed.

Minnesota Multiphasic Personality Inventory-2 (MMPI-2)

This inventory is the restandardized version of the original MMPI, an empirically based test of adult psychopathology. It is used to measure objectively psychopathology across a broad range of client settings where social or personal adjustment problems are acknowledged or suspected. The MMPI-2 can aid in identifying appropriate treatment strategies and potential difficulties with treatment. The inventory contains 567 true/false test items and assumes a reading level of sixth grade.

The MMPI-2 is an extremely sophisticated psychological assessment instrument and it is beyond the scope of this chapter to present the test in detail. However, the test yields several validity indexes that measure a client's degree of psychological sophistication and any attempts to fake psychological health or to present a more deviant picture. Ten basic clinical scales measure symptomatic and characterological symptoms and numerous subscales assess subtle and obvious aspects of psychological functioning. The consistency of responses and attentiveness while taking the test are also assessed.

State-Trait Anxiety Inventory (STAI)

Charles Spielberger developed this inventory to measure the anxiety level of individuals. It consists of two 20-item self-report scales designed to assess anxiety-proneness and the current level of anxiety. The test is appropriate for those with a seventh-grade education or higher and requires approximately 15 minutes to administer.

Wechsler Adult Intelligence Scale-Revised (WAIS-R)

This test is based upon a definition of intelligence as "… the aggregate or global capacity of the individual to act purposefully, to think rationally, and to deal effectively with his environment" (Wechsler, 1944). The eleven subtests classify verbal intelligence and performance intelligence. The interested reader is referred to Lees-Haley (1993) for further description of subtest content and interpretation. The test is of value for determining intellectual functioning for occupational, educational, and neuropsychological purposes.

Wechsler Intelligence Scale for Children-Revised (WISC-R)

Wechsler (1944) applied the same definition of intelligence as noted above under the category of "WAIS-R" to the development of a measure of intellectual functioning in children aged 6 years 0 months to 16 years 11 months. Twelve subtests classify verbal intelligence and performance intelligence. The WISC-R is often administered as part of a neuropsychological test battery (Lees-Haley, 1993).

Wide Range Achievement Test-R (WRAT-R)

This is a norm-referenced test designed to measure current arithmetic, reading, and spelling skills. Results provide grade equivalents, standard scores, and percentile rankings for an individual. The spelling and arithmetic subtests can be administered individually or in groups. The reading subtest is individually administered. Jastak and Wilkinson (1984) report greater test-retest reliability on the reading and spelling subtests than on the arithmetic subtest.

Types of Psychological Treatment

Different psychotherapeutic approaches have been used with success with those who have had a catastrophic injury or illness. Often an appropriate mixture of therapeutic approaches is needed to provide the client with the maximum benefit. When completing a life care plan, it will be important to include therapeutic modalities that will address the patient's changing needs over time, and to allow some flexibility so that the patient may enter and exit therapy as life experiences occur.

- **Individual therapy** allows the person to explore issues of a personal nature in a protected and private manner. The individual will need time and privacy to explore the feelings of loss related to the disability or illness. Having a confidential relationship with one therapist over time will facilitate disclosure and allow the therapist and client to develop individualized approaches to treatment issues. The therapist can help the client deal with personal feelings about relationships, manage the fluctuating emotions that emerge, develop plans for behavioral change, "troubleshoot" potential problem areas, and work on reintegration goals. In many instances, individual therapy can offer the client that opportunity to practice new skills and to bounce ideas off of a caring, neutral party in ways that are potentially less threatening than doing so with a relative or friend.

Individual therapy should be requested approximately three times per week during the rehabilitation facility phase. Once the individual is stabilized and participating in outpatient therapies, weekly visits for the first three to six months is appropriate. Check with the psychologist regarding issues specific to the individual that may require more intensive monitoring (e.g., suicidality).

- **Biofeedback** is a helpful modality for many clients as well, particularly those dealing with psychophysiological problems such as hypertension, muscle tension disorders, pain problems, and stress disorders. Biofeedback techniques help the client learn more about his or her individual responses to stressors and ways that they can learn to intervene directly, often without using medications or other medical interventions. Physical and occupational therapists have found biofeedback to be a helpful adjunct in neuromuscular reeducation programs.

  When adding biofeedback therapy to the life care plan, request approximately twelve hour-long weekly sessions initially, in order to learn and apply the technique. Follow-up visits can be scheduled every two weeks for two months, then once a month for two months. Check with your biofeedback referral source for their recommendations.
- **Hypnotherapy** is a somewhat controversial therapeutic technique that can be helpful for some clients. When practiced by a competent therapist, hypnotic techniques can help a client change behaviors they are already willing to change. For example, a person who wishes to quit smoking may find hypnotic suggestions regarding smoking cessation to be very powerful in encouraging abstinence. Hypnosis may also be a helpful stress management technique for some. Hypnotherapy is not useful, however, for helping clients accurately retrieve "suppressed memories."
- **Family therapy** is an extremely important therapeutic modality. A catastrophic injury or illness has profound effects on family functioning, and these effects need to be dealt with by involving the entire family. Changes in role behavior, role expectations, marital relationships, communication pathways, financial status, and family goals will require sensitive support and negotiation. When completing a life care plan, family therapy should be considered when major life transitions are encountered (e.g., child leaving home, death in the family, major illness diagnosed) by any family member. Family therapy sessions can provide a good forum for discussing quality of life issues, the development of living wills and advanced directives, and renegotiating family rules.
- **Group therapy** is helpful for many rehabilitation clients. Good cases can be made for including the client in group therapy designed specifically for one type of injury (e.g., spinal cord injuries only) and for more heterogeneous groups. An important consideration when selecting a group will be the members' functional communication level rather than functional physical level. Having a mixture of participants who are operating at different stages of adaptation to their disabilities can be helpful in providing newer members with hope and inspiration. A skilled group leader will

acknowledge the various stages of adaptation while sensitively encouraging the group to progress to a focus on abilities rather than disabilities, to hope rather than despair.

When completing a life care plan, include a group therapy modality on a regular basis (some groups meet weekly, others less often) for the first six months at least, if the client shows willingness to participate. Many groups become "leaderless" after this period of time, transitioning from professionally led to a self-help format.

- **Pain management** is an important subspecialty area that requires mention. Following catastrophic injury, pain problems are tied to the tissue damage that has occurred. Pain management strategies usually include the use of medications and, hopefully, relaxation techniques. As time passes, however, the client will need to reduce his or her reliance on potentially addictive pain medications and to increase independence in managing pain. A pain management specialist can help the client learn relaxation techniques, cognitive strategies, reactivation steps, and ways of dealing with the psychological components of pain.

If pain continues to be a focus of treatment after physical stabilization has occurred, consider a referral to a pain specialist. Pain is no longer merely a symptom: it has become a problem and needs to be addressed in an intensive manner.

CONCLUSION

This chapter has reviewed the ways in which a trained, experienced rehabilitation psychologist can participate as a member of the rehabilitation team. In rehabilitation, much attention is given to the preservation and restoration of functioning. Psychological issues can color the work of rehabilitation in subtle and obvious ways and should be carefully considered when planning for the client's care.

It is also important to remember that the relationship a psychologist establishes with a client can continue for many years following the catastrophic injury or diagnosis of illness. As a life care planning professional, you can ensure that your client receives the emotional and behavioral support needed to achieve his or her goals of functional independence.

REFERENCES

Anderson, R. M. (1994). **Practitioner's Guide to Clinical Neuropsychology**. New York: Plenum Press.

Archer, R. P. (1992). **MMPI-A: Assessing Adolescent Psychopathology**. Hillsdale, NJ: Lawrence Erlbaum Associates.

Altmaier, E. M. (1991). Research and practice roles for counseling psychologists in health care settings. **The Counseling Psychologist, 19,** 342-364.

Basmajian, J. V. (Ed.). (1989). **Biofeedback: Principles and Practice for Clinicians**. Baltimore: Williams & Wilkins.

Bellack, A. S., Hersen, M., & Kazdin, A. E. (Eds.). (1990). **International Handbook of Behavior Modification and Therapy** (2nd ed.). New York: Plenum Press.

Burns, D. D. (1980). **Feeling Good: The New Mood Therapy**. New York: William Morrow.

Cohn, N. (1961). Understanding the process of adjustment to disability. **Journal of Rehabilitation, 27(6)**, 16-22.

Curlette, W. L., Aycock, D. W., Matheny, K. B., Pugh, J. L., & Taylor, H. F. (1992). **Coping Resources Inventory for Stress Manual**. Atlanta, GA: Health Prisms.

Cushman, L. A. & Scherer, M. J. (Eds.). (1995). **Psychological Assessment in Medical Rehabilitation**. Washington, D.C.: American Psychological Association.

DeBoskey, D. S. & Morin, K. (1985). **A "How to Handle" Manual for Families of the Brain Injured**. Tampa, FL: Tampa General Rehabilitation Center.

Graham, J. R. (1993). **MMPI-2: Assessing Personality and Psychopathology** (2nd ed.). New York: Oxford University Press.

Greene, R. L. (1991). **The MMPI-2/MMPI: An Interpretive Manual**. Boston: Allyn and Bacon.

Grimm, B. H. & Beliberg, J. (1986). Psychological rehabilitation in traumatic brain injury. In S. B. Filskov and T. J. Boll (Eds.), **Handbook of Clinical Neuropsychology**, Vol. 2 (pp. 495-560). New York: Wiley-Interscience.

Hammond, D. C. (Ed.). (1990). **Handbook of Hypnotic Suggestions and Metaphors**. New York: W. W. Norton.

Hanson, R. W. & Gerber, K. E. (1990). **Coping with Chronic Pain: A Guide to Patient Self-Management**. New York: Guilford Press.

Jastak, S. & Wilkinson, G. (1984). **Wide Range Achievement Test-Revised Administration Manual**. Wilmington, DE: Jastak Associates.

Kaplan, H. I. & Sadock, B. J. (1991). **Synopsis of Psychiatry: Behavioral Sciences, Clinical Psychiatry** (6th ed.). Baltimore: Williams & Wilkins.

Karoly, P. & Jensen, M. P. (1987). **Multi-Method Assessment of Chronic Pain**. Oxford, U.K.: Pergamon Press.

Lees-Haley, P. R. (1993). **The Last-Minute Guide to Psychological and Neuropsychological Testing: A Quick Reference for Attorneys and Claims Professionals**. Athens, GA: Elliott & Fitzpatrick.

Lewandowski, M. J. & Tearnan, B. H. (1993). **Behavioral Assessment of Pain Questionnaire**. Reno, NV: Pendrake.

Lewinsohn, P. M., Antonuccio, D. O., Breckenridge, J. S., & Teri, L. (1984). **The Coping with Depression Course**. Eugene, OR: Castalia Publishing.

Lezak, M. D. (1988). Brain damage is a family affair. **Journal of Clinical and Experimental Psychology, 10**, 111-123.

Sohlberg, M. M. & Mateer, C. A. (1989). **Introduction to Cognitive Remediation: Theory and Practice**. New York: Guilford Press.

The Northern California Neurobehavioral Group, Inc. (1988). **The Neurobehavioral Cognitive Status Examination**. Fairfax, CA.

Wechsler, D. (1944). **The Measurement of Adult Intelligence** (3rd ed.). Baltimore: Williams & Wilkins.

6

THE ROLE OF THE NEUROPSYCHOLOGIST IN LIFE CARE PLANNING

Randall W. Evans

INTRODUCTION

Modern day clinical neuropsychology is roughly fifty to sixty years old, although the use of neuropsychological data has undergone considerable change within the last ten years or so. It could be safely argued that the primary use of neuropsychological test data until very recently was to assist in neurological diagnosis and localization of cognitive and mental functions to various brain regions. The pioneer works of Ward Halstead, Ralph Reitan, and Alexander Luria exemplified the early localization studies. Their work has since been built upon by such notable neuropsychologists and behavioral neurologists as Edith Kaplan, Arthur Benton, Frank Benson, Henry Hecaen, Antonio Damasio, Martin Alpert, and Nelson Butters, to name but a few. The contributions of these and others have established the field of clinical neuropsychology as a very respected clinical addition to related fields such as neurology, neuropsychiatry, gerontology, physiatry, neuropharmacology, and psychopathology.

The Focus of Neuropsychology

Until recently, most practicing neuropsychologists focused their efforts on determining and/or assisting neurological or neuropathological diagnoses, particularly as such diagnoses were applied to localization of brain dysfunction and extent of that dysfunction. Additionally, neuropsychologists are often asked to assist in the determination of whether brain dysfunction is thought to exist at all. The following populations are often the subjects of neuropsychological inquiry:

- Persons who have experienced neurological insults, for example, traumatic brain injury, stroke, anoxic events
- Persons undergoing dementia evaluations
- Persons suspected of developmental disabilities including autism, attention deficit disorder, learning disabilities, and other related disabilities

1-57444-075-6/99/$0.00+$.50

- Persons with neuropsychiatric disorders — Tourette's Syndrome, Korsakoff's Syndrome, conversion disorders, and other related syndromes
- Persons undergoing neuropharmacological interventions

Besides assessing persons in these categories some neuropsychologists, notably those employed in university-based medical centers, are involved in the uses of neuropsychological data in the broad study of brain and behavior relationships. Additionally, *research* neuropsychologists continually work to refine test construction and test development, in many respects in response to emerging neuroimaging developments. In these areas neuropsychological test data are used to cross validate and complement new imaging techniques.

During the last decade, neuropsychologists have turned their attention increasingly toward the use of neuropsychological data to predict short- and long-term outcomes in various patient populations. Initially, the interest in outcomes tended to focus on specific cognitive functions. For example, the relationship of current performance on memory tests to long-term memory functioning.

However, most of these studies did not focus on performance on neuropsychological test data as outcome predictors, failing to show how such performance related to more functional outcomes, such as a person's ability to return to work or to live independently. This lack of attention to what the industry refers to as "ecological validity" severely limits practical use of this rather sophisticated data.

Contributions to the Life Care Plan

With regard to the life care planning process, the contributions of the neuropsychologist are at least twofold. At a minimum, a neuropsychologist with significant experience with a given population or diagnostic group can contribute his or her experiential data base to the short- and long-term prognostic issues as reflected in the patient's neuropsychological test profile. This is somewhat analogous to the expert witness scenario. Additionally, the neuropsychologist can relate neuropsychological test performance to what is known in the literature as to how such performance relates to short- and long-term outcome, keeping in mind the importance of addressing the ecological validity of the projected outcome. With these two issues in mind this chapter will review:

- Commonly used neuropsychological inquiry approaches/test batteries
- Neuropsychological assessment literature as it relates to outcome prediction
- Common applications of neuropsychological data as they relate to the life care planning process
- A case example of neuropsychological data utilization in a life care plan
- A summary commentary regarding future contributions of the neuropsychologist to the life care planning process. As an example, this chapter will occasionally focus on the traumatic brain injury (TBI) population.

Neuropsychological Batteries in Current Use

This section will describe some of the more commonly used neuropsychological test batteries and the theoretical underpinnings underlying those approaches.

However, a brief discussion of the overall assumptions of neuropsychological assessment is in order.

Background Information

Ever since the French neurologist Broca discovered the anterior language center of the brain in 1865, medical practitioners have waged an aggressive campaign to articulate the relationships between distinct brain regions and human behavior. That campaign, well over a hundred years old, continues now with the support of sophisticated neuroimaging techniques as complementary tools. Modern day neuropsychology is concerned with the diagnosis and treatment of persons with, or suspected of having, various forms of brain dysfunction or brain damage. The "tools" of the neuropsychologist are well-normed test procedures, observation of patient function, detailed history taking, and an extensive working knowledge of those practitioners from Professor Broca and beyond. The neuropsychological exam is a dynamic process that must be flexible to the condition of the patient and to the very reason for the examination itself. There is a growing awareness in the field that whatever test strategy is used must address the day-to-day needs of the examinee. No longer is it appropriate to report neuropsychological performance in statistical terms. The performance of the patient on test procedures must be tied to the direct relevance of his or her ability to survive and prosper in today's world. Therefore, the neuropsychologist can have a healthy and meaningful contribution to the life care planning process.

Halstead-Reitan Neuropsychological Test Battery (HRB)

The most commonly used neuropsychological test "battery" is the Halstead-Reitan Battery (HRB), although most practitioners use supplementary measures based on patient status, diagnosis, data utilization need, and the referral question. Table 6.1 illustrates the tests used in the HRB together with the primary functions measured by each test.

These measures are basic to the HRB approach and it is almost always the case that the neuropsychologist will supplement this battery with additional tests relative to the issues raised above. Additionally, tests of emotional and personality functioning are usually included in a comprehensive evaluation. The test results are then analyzed from several perspectives. According to the HRB approach four "levels of inference" are used:

- **Level of performance.** This is a comparative analysis based on well-established norms whereby the person's actual performance is compared to a cutoff level, which reflects the probability of statistical variance. In the HRB approach, for example, a score below a statistical level determines the *probability* of brain dysfunction.
- **Pattern of performance.** This analytical approach attempts to take into account not only levels of performance but also that certain pathological conditions (i.e., a severe learning disability) usually show a *pattern* of deficit on the neuropsychological exam. This level-of-inference approach often takes years of experience by the examiner to refine as well as

Table 6.1 Halstead-Reitan Neuropsychological Test Battery

Test Name	*Primary Function(s) Measured*
Halstead Category Test	Concept formation, Reasoning, Learning, Judgment, Mental flexibility
Tactual Performance Test	Psychomotor coordination, tactile and kinesthetic Abilities, Incidental Memory (Spatial)
Seashore Rhythm Test	Auditory perception, Sustained attention and concentration
Speech Sounds Perception Test	Sustained attention and concentration, Language processing, Auditory-verbal perception
Trail Making Test	Visual scanning, Visual sequenceing, Speed of information processing
Wechsler Adult Intelligence Scale	Verbal and Performance intelligence
Sensory Perceptual Examination	Auditory, Visual, and Tactile discrimination
Aphasia Screening Test	Various apects of language ability and usage, Basic arithmetic abilities, Praxis skills
Finger Oscillation and Dynamometer	Simple motor speed and Grip strength

considerable experience with specific populations or specific diagnostic groups.

- **Pathognomonic signs.** This is a yes–no type of approach where the mere *presence* or *absence* of certain performance indicators suggests brain damage or brain dysfunction. For example, a clear sign of aphasia or neglect often constitute a pathognomonic sign strongly suggestive of brain dysfunction.
- **Right-left comparisions.** Certain tests measure performance of either the left or right side of the body (i.e., motor skills, perceptual skills) and therefore the examiner will look for *discrepancies* between the two sides. In this type of analysis, performance that is influenced by factors peripheral to the central nervous system must be taken into account.

These analytical approaches articulated by Halstead and Reitan decades ago are still quite pertinent today and can also be readily applied to other neuropsychological methods and batteries. There are several noteworthy advantages to the HRB approach, the most prominent of which is the extensive norms and research that accompany it. However, its prognostic utility is divided between good and poor. It is good from the perspective of predicting future psychometric performance. It is limited, however, in that it has not been adequately correlated to the neuropsychological performance of everyday life (i.e., ability to work, cook, manage money, and prioritize). Only in cases of very poor performance on the HRB can reliable inferences be made about ecologically valid performance issues. Finally, the HRB is limited in circumstances where frequent and repeated testing is necessary, as in pharmaceutical studies, because of limited alternate form availability.

Other Approaches

Approximately thirty years ago, A. R. Luria and Anne-Lise Christensen began publishing clinical and research observations that eventually led to the development of the **Luria-Nebraska Neuropsychological Battery**. This battery, while intending to measure many of the same motor, perceptual, and cognitive functions elicited by the HRB approach, has less of a following than the HRB. The Luria approach inherently places a premium on the importance of behavioral observations of the examinee in interpreting performance relevance, thereby limiting its use with psychometrists or those with limited patient experience. Additionally, most neuropsychologists would argue that an examiner using the Luria battery (vs. the HRB) must have a very firm grounding in neuropsychological theory as well as a considerable background in the history of the patient, further limiting its use to a smaller examiner base. The reader is referred to the works of Golden, Purisch, and Hammeke for additional information on the Luria approach to neuropsychological assessment. It should be noted that the Luria approach has never been routinely applied to issues of long-term outcome or ecological validity, except in cases of significant injury or significant impairment.

One of the more popular, flexible approaches to neuropsychological inquiry is the **Iowa-Benton Approach (IBA)**, which is tied to the exhaustive work of Arthur Benton and his colleagues. The IBA is considered a "hypothesis generating" approach. The IBA provides the examiners with a wide range of tools that can be customized to the functioning level of the patient and to the needs of the referral question(s). There is, however, a **core battery** to support this approach, which gives a broad sampling of the patient's performance and which can be referred to normative data sets. Benton believed that any approach to neuropsychological assessment should be viewed "in the same way as we view the physical or neurological examination, i.e., as a logical, sequential decision making process rather than the administration of a fixed battery of tests." For a more extensive review of neuropsychological test batteries see Lezak (1995).

Modern day neuropsychologists use a combination of proven assessment techniques (e.g., the HRB) and a compilation of newly devised and newly standardized approaches that are much more patient and referral-question focused than previous strategies. For example, test batteries and/or specific tests have been established for patients with specific diagnoses or impairment, including:

- Neurotoxic exposure
- HIV-positive exposure
- Acquired neurological injury
- Learning disabilities
- Developmental disabilities
- Neuropsychiatric disorders
- Dementia and other amnesic disorders

The current movement away from presence vs. absence of damage/dysfunction, with less focus on localization issues, will in this author's opinion, result in neuropsychological approaches that are more user friendly to the referring party,

Table 2 Neuropsychological Literature Relating to Global Outcome Measures: Traumatically Brain Injured Patients

Authors/Date	*Outcomes Measured*	*Population Studied*
Wehman, et al., 1995	Return to work	Severe TBI
Giacino & Zasler, 1995	Coma recovery	Severe TBI
Goldstein & Levin, 1995	Cognition & behavior	TBI > Age 50
Dikmen & Machamer, 1995	Neuropsychological & psychosocial levels	TBI patients (Lit. review)
Cifu, et al., 1997	Return to work	TBI patients (mixed)
Vogenthaler, et al., 1989	Return to work, independent living	TBI patients

as well as being more tightly focused on the clinical needs of the person under examination. In many respects, tailored evaluations, which are reinforced by valid norms, move in the desired direction toward ecologically valid interpretations of complex test findings. Again, the reader is referred to the expansive review of available neuropsychological test procedures presented by Lezak (1995).

Neuropsychological Inquiry and Outcome Prediction

As mentioned above, until recently most neuropsychological examinations focused on the identification of cognitive assets and deficits in persons who are suspected of cerebral dysfunction, compromise, or injury. Localization of lesions or dysfunction is becoming less important, except in rare circumstances, in these evaluations with the progress of neuroimaging procedures (e.g., MRI, PET, and SPECT). On the positive side, however, neuroimaging procedures used in combination with neuropsychological procedures will likely lead to exciting advances toward the understanding of brain and behavior relationships.

Essential to the life care planning process is the accuracy of predicting client need and the resources necessary to meet those projected needs. While some studies have addressed the predictive power of neuropsychological performance to patient outcome, most studies in the literature address the correlation between **current test performance** to **future test performance,** ignoring the social, vocational, or independent living competencies of the person examined as they relate to test performance. Therefore, much of the neuropsychological test literature is of minimal or no value to the life care planner, who inherently seeks information that has more global functional inferences.

Listed in Table 6.2 are references to important studies that address the relationship of neuropsychological test performance to outcomes that may be of interest to the life care planner. This list is not intended to be exhaustive; rather it is a starting point for further research.

These studies certainly can provide a benchmark for outcome prediction based on neuropsychological test performance. However, the notable shortcomings of such studies are twofold. First, neuropsychological data alone tell only part of the story — the cognitive and emotional one. Neuropsychological data often fall short when addressing the client's overall adaptation to loss or injury, nor do they usually address environmental management issues (i.e., ergonomic considerations) to compensate for cognitive losses and changes. Second, these studies do not offer long-term follow-up on the reliability and validity of predicted outcomes. The predictability/reliability issue is particularly important in cases of mild to moderate injury in which the issue of permanent loss or permanent inability to compensate is less certain. As the measured deficit becomes more severe, the reliability of predicted outcome usually increases. Several literature reviews have been published regarding short- and long-term outcomes following traumatic brain injury. The reader is referred to the references at the end of this chapter.

Global Measures Influencing Outcome Following TBI

There are certain accepted truths in the TBI literature relating to short- and long-term outcome following traumatic brain injury. These usually relate to mechanisms surrounding the injury and to certain injury factors. Laaksonen (1994) summarized these issues:

Mechanisms	*Factors*
1. Lesion or injury	Localization
	Size
	Speed of development
2. Individual factors of patient	General state of health, Age
	Degree of brain function dominance
	Intellectual capacity
	Motivation, interests, etc.
3. Factors re Therapy	Time of treatment after onset
	Therapeutic methods
	Therapy expertise
	Duration/Access to treatment

Many of these global influences can be gathered directly by the neuropsychologist (particularly the individual patient factors). The neuropsychological literature is filled with hundreds of studies addressing the influence of mechanism and patient factors, such as patient long-term functioning. The life care planner should have ready access to this literature and should be prepared to reference this literature as part of the life care plan.

Applications to the Life Care Planning Process

Thus far, most of the discussion in this chapter as to the role of the neuropsychologist in the life care planning process has focused on the relevance to neuropsychological test performance as related to short- and long-term outcome. While this is a very important contribution to the neuropsychologist's repertoire, experienced neuropsychologists also have considerable background in other areas of *clinical* neuropsychology, such as psychodiagnosis, counseling, crisis intervention, family and patient education. These areas must also be addressed in the life care planning process. In what may best be described as a consultative role in these areas outside of formal neuropsychological evaluations, the neuropsychologist can contribute to a life care plan with the following issues:

- Identification of client risk for developing various psychological conditions requiring intermittent or ongoing treatment.
- Identification of client need for periodic psychological or neuropsychological evaluations.
- Identification of compensatory mechanisms and resources that may reduce or alleviate handicap caused by the injury.
- Integration of allied health (occupational therapy, physical therapy, speech and language therapy, social work, vocational services) records and evaluations into a cohesive working plan to maximize the cognitive and emotional performance of the client.
- Expert witness testimony, particularly in relating neuropsychological data to long-term functioning.
- Integration of existing neuropsychological literature as supportive/related material to the neuropsychological performance estimates made in the life care plan.
- Participation in rehabilitation assessments and rehabilitation team conferences that integrate team findings into the life care plan.

In these areas, the neuropsychologist is used as an "on demand" consultant. His or her ability to assist the life care planner must be at a level where he or she can articulate existing rehabilitation and evaluative data into a cohesive and pragmatic story that takes into account current and anticipated databases and industry accepted practices. This integration, when articulated in the context of relevant neuropsychological research and applied literature, will result in a well-thought-out, well-designed, *empirically driven* contribution to the life care plan.

Beyond the Neuropsychological Evaluation

In the case of traumatic brain injury, it is the opinion of this author that the neuropsychologist must go well beyond the contributions of the neuropsychological evaluation to have the optimum impact in the life care planning process. Most neuropsychological evaluations are at risk to fall short of meeting the ultimate requirement of the life care plan: to make reliable predictions of functional outcome and the resources necessary and available to maintain the predicted functioning level. Neuropsychological evaluations, by definition, usually focus on describing the individual's functioning at the time of inquiry, with estimates as to how such functioning may change over time. While certain test performance levels may be statistically unlikely to change over the lifetime of the person, one's ability to adapt and compensate can change. The neuropsychologist ideally should be able to describe what conditions and circumstances need to exist for such changes to occur. In a similar vein the neuropsychologist, with input from other rehabilitation professionals, can project cognitive, emotional, and behavioral circumstances that can reduce the risk for exacerbation of existing handicaps or regression of same.

Case Study Illustration

A patient, M.C., was referred to this author by his life care planner. M.C., at the time of referral, was approximately nine months status after a severe brain injury sustained in an automobile accident. Until the injury, M.C. was a high functioning, fifty-two-year old sales executive, with a supportive wife and two adolescent children. There were no significant preinjury medical problems nor was there any history of familial neurological dysfunction or disease. M.C. had a college education and had recently been promoted in his job, secondary to exemplary performance. After the injury, M.C. received immediate medical intervention (within twenty minutes) by Emergency Medical Services (EMS) and was transported to a nearby neurotrauma center. His initial Rancho Los Amigos Level (RLAS) was III, indicative of a severe injury; additionally, his initial Glasgow Coma Score (GCS) was 5, again indicative of severe injury. His initial hospital course was uncomplicated and approximately one-week post injury his RLAS score had progressed to IV, and his GCS was 10. These early signs of improvement suggested a potentially good recovery. However, approximately ten days post injury, M.C. suffered an episode of status epilepticus (despite taking Dilantin prophilactically), and it was suspected that the patient suffered anoxic injury to the brain as well. Following this episode, the patient regressed to a RLAS III, a state that lasted for five days. Two months post injury the patient had stabilized at an RLAS V, at which time he started an extensive course of inpatient rehabilitation.

Following a three-month inpatient stay, which was complemented by an additional four months of outpatient treatment, the patient's life care planner was brought in to begin to assemble the life care plan (LCP). This author was asked to address the following referral questions:

- Determine the patient's current neuropsychological status and the likelihood for change within the next year.
- Determine a course of neuropsychological treatment, both short- and long-term.
- Determine the likelihood of whether the patient will be capable of competitive employment following his course of treatment.
- Determine what supports, if any, are likely to maintain or improve the patient's neuropsychological abilities once discharged to home.
- Determine the cognitive issues that will facilitate or limit the patient's ability to live independently (i.e., without the support of paid assistance).
- Provide relevant literature that supports the conclusions above.

These six questions could not have been better stated. That is, the life care planner insisted that the neuropsychologist integrate current test performance to issues that had ecological validity, such as the ability to return to work, the ability to live independently, durability of outcome, and the supports necessary to maintain outcome. With these referral questions well understood, the neuropsychologist proceeded with a flexible neuropsychological test battery (in this case the IBA) with certain additions that had literature relevant to the referral questions. The neuropsychological evaluation concluded with the following critical points:

- The patient's memory deficits were very severe and unlikely to change significantly, based upon the depth and chronicity of the memory impairment. Similarly, severe problems with initiation and persistence were likely to be lifelong. M.C.'s attention span was very short and he constantly needed redirection to all evaluation and treatment procedures.
- The patient's cognitive deficits were considered consistent not only with severe TBI, but also with cerebral anoxia.
- Treatment interventions would yield the highest probability of success if performed in very familiar surroundings (i.e., M.C.'s home) given the patient's inability to generalize.
- It was highly unlikely that the patient would ever be capable of competitive employment, although participation in a supported employment situation may prove some success.
- M.C., though in fairly good shape physically and medically, would likely require constant cueing from family members to complete his activities of daily living. Nonetheless, the patient should never be left alone for any extended period of time (greater than fifteen minutes), secondary to chronic inability to assess potential hazards in his environment.
- A follow-up neuropsychological evaluation was recommended at the eighteen-month anniversary of his injury in order to determine his neurometric status and to make additional recommendations for compensatory strategies.

The actual neuropsychological report contained dozens of test scores, percentiles, and other pertinent data. The summary statement, however, reflected the above-noted conclusions that were relevant to the LCP. The actual test data, combined with the extensive experience of the examiner, combined with detailed reference to the neuropsychological literature, supported the above-noted conclusions. Such integration is imperative for the outcome of a useful LCP.

CONCLUSION

Modern-day practices in neuropsychology can contribute significant value-added services to the life care planner in cases of neurological injury or disease. Traumatic brain injury was used as an example throughout this text. As is often the case, the experience base of both parties will have direct correlation to the reliability and validity of conclusions and recommendations made with the LCP. A critical element, however, of those contributions made by the neuropsychologist, needs to be determined at the time of the initial evaluation. It is very important that the life care planner clearly articulate that he or she desires that the neuropsychological data not only be integrated with data from other examinations, but also that the data be relevant to the global functioning issues addressed in the plan. If this expectation of data usage is not clarified, such issues are at risk of not being addressed, significantly lessening the contributions of the examination procedures. Supporting the conclusions with references to relevant research also strengthens the contributions of the neuropsychologist. Finally, it is incumbent that the neuropsychologist clarifies what factors in the person's environment (home, work, school, etc.) either support or serve as detriments to the patient's neuropsychological abilities. The neuropsychologist must recognize that the patient's world lies outside the examiner's office and that the patient is constantly faced with a dynamic set of conditions that must be managed within the context of disrupted cognitive, emotional, and behavioral conditions.

REFERENCES

Blackwell, T. L., Powers, A. S., & Weed, R. O. (1994). **Life Care Planning for Traumatic Brain Injury**. Athens, GA: Elliot & Fitzpatrick.

Christensen, A. L. & Uzzell, B. P. (1994). **Brain Injury and Neuropsychological Rehabilitation**. Hillsdale, New Jersey: Erlbaum Associates.

Cifu, D.X., Keyser-Marcus, L., Lopez, E., Weyman, P., Kreutzer, J., Englander, J., & High, W. (1997). Acute predictors of successful return to work 1 year after traumatic brain injury: A multicenter analysis. **Archives of Physical Medicine and Rehabilitation, 78**, 125-131.

Dikmen, S. & Machamer, J. E. (1995). Neurobehavioural outcomes and their determinants. **Journal of Head Trauma Rehabilitation, 10(1),** 74-86.

Evans, R. W. (1996). Commentary and an illustration on the use of outcome data in life care planning for persons with acquired neurological injuries. **NeuroRehabilitation, 7**, 157-162.

Giacino, J. T. & Zasler, N. D. (1995). Outcome after severe traumatic brain injury: Coma, the vegetative state, and the minimally responsive state. **Journal of Head Trauma Rehabilitation, 10(1)**, 40-56.

Goldstein, F. C. & Levin, H. S. (1995). Neurobehavioral outcome of traumatic brain injury in older adults: Initial findings. **Journal of Head Trauma Rehabilitation, 10(1)**, 57-73.

Laaksonen, R. (1994). Cognitive training methods in rehabilitation of memory. In A. L. Christensen & B. P. Uzzell (Eds.), **Brain Injury and Neuropsychological Rehabilitation** Hillsdale, New Jersey: Erlbaum Associates.

Levin, H. S., Benton, A. L., & Grossman, R. H. (1982). **Neurobehavioral Consequences of Closed Head Injury**. New York: Oxford University Press.

Lezak, M. D. (1995). **Neuropsychological Assessment** (3rd Ed.). New York: Oxford University Press.

Rizzo, M. & Tranel, D. (Eds.). (1996). **Head Injury and Postconcussive Syndrome.** New York: Livingstone Press.

Vogenthaler, D. R., Smith, K. R., & Goldfader, P. (1989). Head injury: A multivariate study, predicting long term productivity and independent living outcome. **Brain Injury, 3**, 369-385.

Wehman, P. H., West, M., Kregel, J., Sherron, P., & Kreutzer, J. (1995). Return to work for persons with traumatic brain injury: A data-based approach to program development. **Journal of Head Trauma Rehabilitation, 10**, 27-39.

7

THE ROLE OF THE OCCUPATIONAL THERAPIST IN LIFE CARE PLANNING

Ileana Seoane McCaigue

INTRODUCTION

The principal role of the occupational therapist in the life of an individual with a disability is to serve as an impartial facilitator, focusing on the potential functional abilities that he or she may be capable of performing with modifications as needed. When participating in the life care planning process, as whenever an evaluation is conducted, the occupational therapist assesses the person as a whole entity, with occupational performance areas ranging from activities of daily living to work activities and play or leisure skills.

Occupational therapy comes from the word occupation or "purposeful activity" (Hinojosa, Sabari & Pedretti, 1993). Occupational therapists use purposeful activities, therapeutic tasks, and exercises to achieve functional outcomes established for each person with a disability. Occupational therapy by definition as adopted and approved by the Representative Assembly of the American Occupational Therapy Association, Inc., is, "...the therapeutic use of self-care, work and play activities to increase independent function, enhance development, and prevent disability; may include adaptation of task or environment to achieve maximum independence and to enhance quality of life" (American Occupational Therapy Association, April 1986).

Qualifications of an Occupational Therapist

An occupational therapist (OT) or occupational therapy assistant (OTA) graduates from a university or college accredited by the Accreditation Council for Occupational Therapy Education of the American Occupational Therapy Association, Inc. An entry level OT must achieve a Bachelor of Science or basic Master of Science degree to be eligible to take a national certification examination. On passing this exam an OT is entitled to use the credentials OTR after his or her name to delineate themselves as a registered occupational therapist by the National Board for the Creditation of Occupational Therapy, Inc., (NBCOT, Inc.), formerly known

1-57444-075-6/99/$0.00+$.50

Table 7.1 Examples of Specializations within Occupational Therapy

Area of Specialty	*Initials*
Certified Hand Therapist	CHT
Certified Driver Rehabilitation Specialist	CDRS
Board Certified in Pediatrics	BCP
Board Certified in Neurorehabilitation	BCN
Certified Work Capacity Evaluator	CWCE

as the American Occupational Therapy Certification Board, Inc., (AOTCB, Inc.) until April of 1996 (Low, 1997). Occupational therapy assistants, upon graduating from a two-year program with an Associate of Science degree, also take a national examination to become certified as COTAs.

Under certain state regulations, some occupational therapists and occupational therapy assistants are required to apply for licensure in order to practice. Once licensure requirements are met, the OTR or COTA then may apply an "L" to their credentials as an OTR/L or COTA/L to designate his or her qualifications to practice in the state of his or her choice, and abide by the guidelines set therein. State licensure requires renewal by the respective qualifying state licensure board and varies as to the frequency per state, but is usually either annually or biannually. Licensure renewal generally requires a specified number of contact hours or continuing education credits to be met within the licensure period. National recertification by the NBCOT, Inc., is currently elective, with the certification period effective for five years beginning with renewals due March 1, 1997.

Additional specialty certifications are also available for occupational therapists with expertise in certain areas of practice (Table 7.1). Occupational therapists can qualify to sit for a certification examination in the clinical or practice areas of hand rehabilitation and merit the additional credentials of CHT or Certified Hand Therapist. In the area of driver rehabilitation, the credentials of CDRS can be added designating that therapist as a Certified Driver Rehabilitation Specialist upon passing this specialty examination. The practice areas of pediatrics and neurorehabilitation are two other clinical designations that can be achieved, applying the credentials of BCP for Board Certified in Pediatrics and BCN for Board Certified in Neurorehabilitation to identify the occupational therapist as a specialist in these areas. Certifications are also available, not necessarily via a certifying organization, but by programs offering extensive training courses. These include the area of work capacity evaluation by which an individual can earn the credentials of CWCE or Certified Work Capacity Evaluator. Additional specialty certifications, though too numerous to list, are available in almost every branch of occupational therapy practice from pediatrics to geriatrics.

Besides the basic Bachelor or Master of Science degrees, an OT can continue his or her education within the field of occupational therapy and pursue an advanced Master's degree or Doctorate in selected universities throughout the United States. Other countries have schools of occupational therapy; however, they are not accredited by the American Occupational Therapy Association. Upon entry into this country foreign therapists must pass a national registration examination qualifying them to have at least the same entry level skills that graduates from the accredited schools in America have acquired. They must then apply for certification and licensure, as would any new therapist. Supervision is then provided by the hiring facility for a designated period of time until they achieve status as a resident or return to their native country.

Occupational Therapy Areas of Overlap with Other Professions

Since occupational therapists practice in a multitude of settings ranging from the hospital environment and nursing homes to community based settings such as clients' homes, schools, and work sites, the settings often determine what role the occupational therapist plays within the treatment team. For example, when treating the client or patient who has difficulties with transfers from multiple surfaces in the home, the occupational therapist may be designated as the primary therapist to work on bathroom and car transfers. The physical therapist may be the primary therapist focusing on bed mobility and bed transfers. Though both disciplines are capable of performing these techniques given their training, these roles are delineated many times to avoid duplication of services or fees for service. Another example is that though the physical therapist is primarily responsible for ambulation and the client's status for mobility within their environment, the occupational therapist must also be aware of their status and how to ambulate them safely. This is necessary so that the occupational therapist can encourage the client to perform activities of daily living (ADLs), which will require mobility and transfers to and from varying surface heights, to achieve independence in their basic and higher-level self-care skills.

The schematic diagram in Figure 7.1 depicts ten professional fields or areas of practice with which the profession of occupational therapy interacts and/or overlaps. The primary professions that are most directly involved with the occupational therapist's treatment from a life care planning perspective are the life care planner, the physician, psychologist, speech/language pathologist, and physical therapist. Depending on the setting, nursing may also be involved with the OT in acute care with the rehabilitation counselor or the case manager for the overall care of that client. The occupational therapist must follow the guidelines for care based on the presenting problems, potential for return to prior level of functional abilities, availability of resources for the continuum of care outside the respective facility, and the client's own desire or motivation to progress with his or her rehabilitation. In the educational setting, the focus of care is on the development or habilitation of skills that are educationally driven, such as the self-care tasks of taking off and putting on a jacket, snapping fasteners, pulling pants up or down, handling a spoon or fork for feeding, drinking from a cup, toileting, and manipulating tools for drawing, coloring, painting, cutting, and writing while being able to sit to attend with appropriate behavior. Prevocational tasks are also emphasized since many children with multiple handicaps are often not able to continue in the higher levels of education and are placed out of high school in job settings suitable to their capabilities. The fields of overlap in these settings are with educators, school social workers, psychologists, speech/language pathologists, school nurses, physical therapists, and vocational specialists.

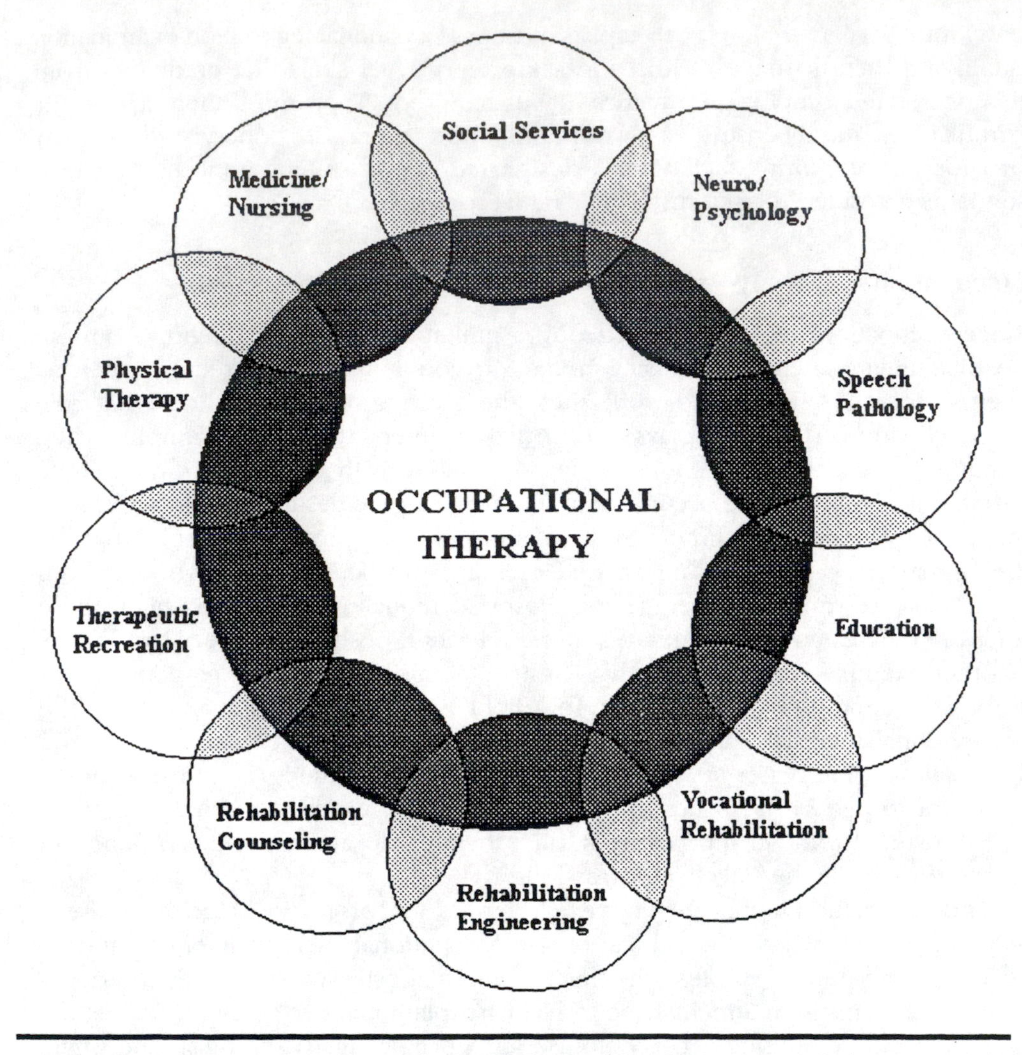

Figure 7.1 Schematic depiction of the interrelationship of Occupational Therapy among ten professions with which services are coordinated, depending on the providers' settings.

Some areas of common *overlap* covering the gamut of professionals with whom occupational therapists interact as part of a global plan of care for mutual clients are as follow:

- **Medicine/Nursing**: Review of medications and disease processes, determining medical stability in relation to rehabilitation potentials, case management, post-traumatic or post-surgical wound management, hand rehabilitation needs for possible surgical intervention, splinting or immobilization needs, range of motion maintenance, visual skills assessment, and developmental assessments.
- **Neuropsychology**: Individual and group dynamics, cognitive assessment and retraining, perceptual evaluation, and functional needs assessment, developmental assessments, psychosocial skills, community reentry skills, predriving skills assessment of potential to drive safely.

- **Physical Therapy**: Ambulation, functional mobility and positioning needs, transfers assessment and training, developmental assessments and treatment, accessibility needs, wound management, physical agent modalities and hand rehabilitation, prosthetics, physical capacities assessment for determining return to work potential and therapy needs to achieve goals.
- **Speech Pathology:** Dysphasia evaluation with resultant swallowing and feeding needs for treatment, augmentative communication needs assessment, visual and auditory perceptual skills assessment and treatment, cognitive assessment and retraining, oral motor evaluation and treatment.
- **Vocational Rehabilitation**: Evaluation and assessment of prevocational skills, determining potential to return to previous work capacity or other appropriate job possibilities, job site assessment and/or modifications needed, work related or transferable skills retraining needs and potential placements.
- **Rehabilitation Counseling**: Case management, determination of work or job skills status, accessibility issues, activities of daily living and driving status, life care planning.
- **Social Services**: Psychosocial factors affecting rehabilitation potential and/or abilities, medication and case management, funding sources, family and community resources, and risk management issues.
- **Therapeutic Recreation**: Assessment and therapeutic intervention for play/leisure skills specific to the client's interests; accessibility issues for community activities; assistive technology to adapt activities deemed as appropriate in relation to the clients' capabilities and leisure interests.
- **Rehabilitation Engineering**: Assistive technology design, fabrication, and implementation of low- and high-tech equipment and/or devices; accessibility issues and needs for home or environmental modifications; technology, positioning, and/or mobility equipment needs to enable transport to job sites.
- **Education:** School performance needs and capabilities, developmental assessments and remedial tasks, school-related self care skills, accessibility needs to maneuver in classroom and general school environment, prevocational training and modifications needed for job sites, assistive technology for low- and high-tech needs in the classroom, predriving skills and possible driving potential to determine vocational placement, cognitive training in compensatory strategies, handwriting training.

In every case or setting the occupational therapist must consider the innate desires of the adult or child with whom he or she is working. This should be considered as the main focus of the treatment plan, to engage that individual in his or her program, and enable him or her to achieve the goals outlined by the client and by the team of professionals involved with his or her care.

Common Terms Used in the Field of Occupational Therapy

The uniform terminology established for occupational therapy practitioners was revised for the third edition published in 1994 to replace the previous document adopted in 1989 (see Low, 1997). A Uniform Terminology Grid was originally developed by Dr. Winnie Dunn in 1988 (Table 7.2). (See Dunn, 1994). It was later revised and translated into the pictorial representation of the most current 1994

Table 7.2 Uniform Terminology Grid: Occupational Therapy

	Performance Areas																	
	Activities of Daily Living											Work Activities				Play or Leisure		
PERFORMANCE COMPONENTS	Grooming	Oral Hygiene	Bathing	Toilet Hygiene	Dressing	Feeding & Eating	Medication Routine	Socialization	Functional Communication	Functional Mobility	Sexual Expression	Home Management	Care of Others	Educational Activities	Vocational Activities	Activities	Play or Leisure Exploitation	Play or Leisure Performance
A. SENSORY/MOTOR COMPONENT 1. Sensory Integration a. Sensory Awareness																		
b. Sensory Processing (1) Tactile																		
(2) Proprioceptive																		
(3) Vestibular																		
(4) Visual																		
(5) Auditory																		
(6) Gustatory																		
(7) Olfactory																		
c. Perceptual Skills (1) Stereognosis																		
(2) Kinesthesia																		
(3) Body Scheme																		
(4) Right-Left Discrimination																		
(5) Form Constancy																		
(6) Position in Space																		
(7) Visual Closure																		
(8) Figure Ground																		
(9) Depth Perception																		
(10) Topographical Orientation																		
2. Neuromuscular a. Reflex																		
b. Range of Motion																		
c. Muscle Tone																		
d. Strength																		
e. Endurance																		
f. Postural Control																		
g. Soft Tissue Integrity																		
3. Motor a. Activity Tolerance																		
b. Gross Motor Coordination																		
c. Crossing the Midline																		
d. Laterality																		
e. Bilateral Integration																		
f. Praxis																		
g. Fine Motor Coordination/Dexterity																		
h. Visual-Motor Integration																		
i. Oral-Motor Control																		
B. COGNITIVE INTEGRATION & COMPONENTS 1. Level of Arousal																		
2. Orientation																		
3. Recognition																		
4. Attention Span																		

Table 7.2 (continued) Uniform Terminology Grid: Occupational Therapy

	Performance Areas																	
	Activities of Daily Living											Work Activities				Play or Leisure		
PERFORMANCE COMPONENTS	Grooming	Oral Hygiene	Bathing	Toilet Hygiene	Dressing	Feeding & Eating	Medication Routine	Socialization	Functional Communication	Functional Mobility	Sexual Expression	Home Management	Care of Others	Educational Activities	Vocational Activities	Activities	Play or Leisure Exploitation	Play or Leisure Performance
5. Memory a. Short-term																		
b. Long-term																		
c. Remote																		
d. Recent																		
6. Sequencing																		
7. Categorization																		
8. Conceptual Formation																		
9. Intellectual Operations in Space																		
10. Problem Solving																		
11. Generalization of Learning																		
12. Integration of Learning																		
13. Synthesis of Learning																		
C. PSYCHOLOGICAL SKILLS & PSYCHOLOGICAL COMPONENTS 1. Psychological a. Roles																		
b. Values																		
c. Interests																		
d. Initiation of Activity																		
e. Termination of Activity																		
f. Self-Concept																		
2. Social a. Social Conduct																		
b. Conversation																		
c. Self Expression																		
3. Self-Management a. Coping Skills																		
b. Time Management																		
c. Self-Control																		

uniform terminology definitions, which included the addition of performance contexts (not shown). Due to the extensive number of terms used in the evaluation, assessment, and treatment process, only those items that relate to the terms within the performance areas, performance components, and performance contexts are listed within this publication.

The Occupational Therapy Framework for Evaluation and Treatment

There are three critical aspects of performance in which occupational therapists are trained and instructed to evaluate when assessing the needs of each person with a presenting disability. These are skills or behaviors represented in the

performance areas of activities of daily living, work and productive activities, and play or leisure activities; the **performance components** of sensorimotor components, cognitive integration/cognitive components, and psychosocial skills/psychological components; and the **performance contexts** of the temporal aspects and the environment (Dunn & McGourty, 1989). Once these interrelated aspects are utilized to complete an evaluation of the person with a disability, the occupational therapist can assess the gestalt or global needs of the individual. A framework is then developed for intervention, and the therapist then gives a prognosis for that person's ability to achieve the functional outcomes established based on these factors (Dunn and McGourty, 1989).

Performance Areas

Performance areas are those activities of primary concern for the occupational therapist that cover the broad category of daily living skills that are considered typical for each person. Terms used within this domain are as follows:

Activities of Daily Living — Self-maintenance tasks.

- **Grooming:** Obtaining and using supplies; removing body hair (use of razors, tweezers, lotions, etc.); applying and removing cosmetics; washing, drying, combing, styling, and brushing hair; caring for nails (hands and feet), skin, ears, and eyes; and applying deodorant.
- **Oral Hygiene**: Obtaining and using supplies; cleaning mouth; brushing and flossing teeth; or removing, cleaning, and reinserting dental orthotics and prosthetics.
- **Bathing/Showering**: Obtaining and using supplies; soaping, rinsing, and drying body parts; maintaining bathing position; and transferring to and from bathing positions.
- **Toilet Hygiene**: Obtaining and using supplies; clothing management; maintaining toileting position; transferring to and from toileting position; cleaning body; and caring for menstrual and continence needs (including catheters, colostomies, and suppository management).
- **Personal Device Care**: Cleaning and maintaining personal care items, such as hearing aids, contact lenses, glasses, orthotics, prosthetics, adaptive equipment, and contraceptive and sexual devices.
- **Dressing:** Selecting clothing and accessories appropriate to time of day, weather, and occasion; obtaining clothing from storage area; dressing and undressing in a sequential fashion; fastening and adjusting clothing and shoes; and applying and removing personal devices, prostheses, or orthoses.
- **Feeding and Eating**: Setting up food; selecting and using appropriate utensils and tableware; bringing food or drink to mouth; cleaning face, hands, and clothing; sucking, masticating, coughing, and swallowing; and management of alternative methods of nourishment.
- **Medication Routine:** Obtaining medication, opening and closing containers, following prescribed schedules, taking correct quantities, reporting problems and adverse effects, and administering correct quantities by using prescribed methods.

- **Health Maintenance**: Developing and maintaining routines for illness prevention and wellness promotion, such as physical fitness, nutrition, and decreasing health risk behaviors.
- **Socialization**: Accessing opportunities and interacting with other people in appropriate contextual and cultural ways to meet emotional and physical needs.
- **Functional Communication**: Using equipment or systems to send and receive information, such as writing equipment, telephones, typewriters, computers, communication boards, call lights, emergency systems, Braille writers, telecommunication devices for the deaf, augmentative communication systems.
- **Functional Mobility**: Moving from one position or place to another, such as in-bed mobility, wheelchair mobility, transfers (wheelchair, bed, car, tub, toilet tub/shower, chair, floor). Performing functional ambulation and transporting objects.
- **Community Mobility**: Moving self in the community and using public or private transportation, such as driving, or accessing buses, taxicabs, or other public transportation systems.
- **Emergency Response**: Recognizing sudden, unexpected hazardous situations, and initiating action to reduce the threat to health and safety.
- **Sexual Expression**: Engaging in desired sexual and intimate activities.

Work and Productive Activities — Purposeful activities for self-development, social contribution, and livelihood. They include the following:

- **Home Management**: Obtaining and maintaining personal and household possessions and environment. This includes clothing care, cleaning, meal preparation and cleanup, shopping, money management, household maintenance, and safety procedures.
- **Care of Others:** Providing for children, spouse, parents, pets, or others, such as giving physical care, nurturing, communicating, and using age-appropriate activities.
- **Educational Activities**: Participating in a learning environment through school, community, or work-sponsored activities, such as exploring educational interests, attending to instruction, managing assignments, and contributing to group experiences.
- **Vocational Activities**: Participating in work-related activities. This includes vocational exploration, job acquisition, work or job performance, retirement planning, and volunteer participation.

Play or Leisure Activities — Intrinsically motivating activities for amusement, relaxation, spontaneous enjoyment, or self-expression. A list of these activities follows:

- **Play or Leisure Exploration**: Identifying interests, skills, opportunities, and appropriate play or leisure activities.
- **Play or Leisure Performance**: Planning and participating in play or leisure activities. Maintaining a balance of play or leisure activities with work and productive activities, and activities of daily living. Obtaining, using, and maintaining equipment and supplies.

Performance Components

Performance components are the fundamental human abilities that are required for successful engagement in performance areas. Terms within this framework area are as follows:

Sensorimotor components — The ability to receive input, process information, and produce output.

- **Sensory Information:**

  Sensory Awareness Receiving and differentiating sensory stimuli.
  Sensory Processing Interpreting sensory stimuli.

  1. **Tactile:** Interpreting light touch, pressure, temperature, pain, and vibration through skin contact/receptors.
  2. **Proprioceptive:** Interpreting stimuli originating in muscles, joints, and other internal tissues that give information about the position of one body part in relation to another.
  3. **Vestibular:** Interpreting stimuli from the inner ear receptors regarding head position and movement.
  4. **Visual:** Interpreting stimuli through the eyes, including peripheral vision and acuity, and awareness of color and pattern.
  5. **Auditory:** Interpreting and localizing sounds, and discriminating background sounds.
  6. **Gustatory:** Interpreting tastes.
  7. **Olfactory:** Interpreting odors.

  Perceptual Processing Organizing sensory input into meaningful patterns.

  1. **Stereognosis:** Identifying objects through proprioception, cognition, and the sense of touch.
  2. **Kinesthesia:** Identifying the excursion and direction of joint movement.
  3. **Pain response:** Interpreting noxious stimuli.
  4. **Body scheme:** Acquiring an internal awareness of the body and the relationships of body parts to each other.
  5. **Right–Left discrimination:** Differentiating one side from the other.
  6. **Form constancy:** Recognizing forms and objects as the same in various environments, positions, and sizes.
  7. **Position in Space:** Determining the spatial relationship of figures and objects to self or other forms and objects.
  8. **Visual-Closure:** Identifying forms or objects from incomplete presentations.
  9. **Figure ground:** Differentiating between foreground and background forms and objects.
  10. **Depth perception:** Determining the relative distance between objects, figures, or landmarks and the observer, and changes in planes of surfaces.
  11. **Spatial relationships:** Determining the position of objects relative to each other.
  12. **Topographical orientation:** Determining the location of objects and settings and the route to the location.

- **Neuromusculoskeletal Information:**

  Reflex Eliciting an involuntary muscle response by sensory input.

  Range of motion Moving body parts through an arc.

  Muscle tone Demonstrating a degree of tension or resistance in a muscle at rest and in response to stretch.

  Strength Demonstrating a degree of muscle power when movement is resisted, as with objects or gravity.

  Endurance Sustaining cardiac, pulmonary, and musculoskeletal exertion over time.

  Postural control Using righting and equilibrium adjustments to maintain balance during functional movements.

  Soft tissue integrity Maintaining anatomical and physiological condition of interstitial tissue and skin.

- **Motor Information:**

  Gross coordination Using large muscle groups for controlled, goal-directed movements.

  Crossing the midline Moving limbs and eyes across the midsagittal plane of the body.

  Laterality Using a preferred unilateral body part for activities requiring a high level of skill.

  Bilateral integration Coordinating both body sides during activity.

  Motor control Using the body in functional and versatile movement patterns.

  Praxis Conceiving and planning a new motor act in response to an environmental demand.

  Fine coordination/dexterity Using small muscle groups for controlled movements, particularly in object manipulation.

  Visual-motor integration Coordinating the interaction of information from the eyes with body movement during activity.

  Oral-motor control Coordinating oropharyngeal musculature for controlled movements.

Cognitive Integration and Cognitive Components — The ability to use higher brain functions. They include the following:

- **Level of arousal**: Demonstrating alertness and responsiveness to environmental stimuli.
- **Orientation**: Identifying person, place, time, and situation.
- **Recognition:** Identifying familiar faces, objects, and other previously presented materials.
- **Attention span:** Focusing on a task over time.
- **Initiation of activity:** Starting a physical or mental activity.
- **Termination of activity:** Stopping an activity at an appropriate time.
- **Memory:** Recalling information after brief or long periods of time.
- **Sequencing:** Placing information, concepts, and actions in order.
- **Categorization:** Identifying similarities of and differences among pieces of environmental information.

- **Concept formation:** Organizing a variety of information to form thoughts and ideas.
- **Spatial operations:** Mentally manipulating the position of objects in various relationships.
- **Problem solving:** Recognizing a problem, defining a problem, identifying alternative plans, selecting a plan, organizing steps in a plan, implementing a plan, and evaluating the outcome.
- **Learning:** Acquiring new concepts and behaviors.
- **Generalization:** Applying previously learned concepts and behaviors to a variety of new situations.

Psychosocial Skills and Psychological Components — The ability to interact in society and to process emotions.

- **Psychological Information**:
  Values Identifying ideas or beliefs that are important to self and others.
  Interests Identifying mental or physical activities that create pleasure and maintain attention.
  Self-concept Developing the value of the physical, emotional, and sexual self.
- **Social Information**:
  Role performance Identifying, maintaining, and balancing functions one assumes or acquires in society (e.g., worker, student, parent, friend, religious participant).
  Social conduct Interacting by using manners, personal space, eye contact, gestures, active listening, and self-expression appropriate to one's environment.
  Interpersonal skills Using verbal and nonverbal communication to interact in a variety of settings.
  Self-expression Using a variety of styles and skills to express thoughts, feelings, and needs.
- **Self-Management Information**:
  Coping skills Identifying and managing stress and related factors.
  Time management Planning and participating in a balance of self-care, work, leisure, and rest activities to promote satisfaction and health.
  Self-control Modifying one's own behavior in response to environmental needs, demands, constraints, personal aspirations, and feedback from others.

Performance Contexts

Situations or factors that influence an individual's engagement in desired and/or required performance areas. These are taken into consideration when determining the function and dysfunction in relation to performance areas and performance components, as well as in planning treatment intervention. Terminology used within this category is as follows:

Temporal Aspects

- **Chronological:** Individual's age.
- **Developmental:** Stage or phase of maturation.
- **Life cycle**: Place in important life phases, such as career cycle, parenting cycle, or educational process.
- **Disability status:** Place in continuum of disability, such as acuteness of injury, chronicity of disability, or terminal nature of illness.

Environment

- **Physical:** Non-human aspects of contexts that include the accessibility to and performance within environments having natural terrain, plants, animals, buildings, furniture, objects, tools, or devices.
- **Social**: Availability and expectations of significant individuals, such as spouse, friends, and caregivers; also includes larger social groups that are influential in establishing norms, role expectations, and social routines.
- **Cultural:** Customs, beliefs, activity patterns, behavior standards, and expectations accepted by the society of which the individual is a member. Includes political aspects, such as laws that affect access to resources and affirm personal rights; also includes opportunities for education, employment, and economic support.

Reprint permission granted for "Uniform Terminology, Third Edition" by the American Occupational Therapy Association, Inc., the original publisher and copyright holder. Portions of this document were reprinted for clarification of the terms listed on the previous grid as well as to explain the framework for practice.

SPECIFIC ISSUES WITH SPECIFIC POPULATIONS

Pediatrics: (Birth to 21 Years of Age)

Access to Services: To obtain occupational therapy services for children, several avenues of funding are possible. Services can be funded by either private pay, private health insurance, hospital grants, private foundation or corporate grant monies, federal Medicaid or via federal public laws affecting accessibility, education, and assistive technology needs. Since most families with special needs children are financially unable to bear the long-term costs of therapy and equipment needs privately, supplemental funding is a necessity. The following are some of the sources or options available to access occupational therapy services:

Private Health Insurance: With the advent of managed care and the establishment of health maintenance and preferred provider organizations, the insurance carriers often dictate the amount of services that they will cover via an internal case manager or insurance representative. Usually intervals of therapy services are funded on a short-term basis with a designated number of visits, requiring justification and rationalization by the external facility case manager and the therapist where services are being provided. If the guardian or parent has the standard health insurance option, therapy service coverage varies per each individual plan. It may be covered by the previously standard 80% to 90% reimbursement rate for fees for service or hourly rates with a standard deductible, or it may have to be appealed in order to be added to the plan as an addendum via the appeals process. However, in any of these scenarios, the fees are usually based on charges that are considered to be reasonable or usual and customary by the insurance carrier at sometimes discounted reimbursement rates for the service provider. Due to the lifetime cap usually placed on such policies, additional supplemental funding is often sought to meet the remainder of therapy needs over a longer period of the child's life.

Hospital Grants or Private Foundation and Corporate Funds: Many major hospitals have funds set aside either via fund-raising drives that involve community efforts or via donations made by physicians, private individuals, employees, or major companies. In order to qualify for these funds or for those through any private organization that offers assistance for charitable causes, the child's parent(s) or guardian(s) must complete a hospital application form from the social services department or the human resources division of an organization. They may then be referred to funds from United Way, the Kiwanis Club, the Lions Club, the Shriners, or other monies that have been set aside for specific patient populations in need of resources for medical assistance, which includes occupational therapy services since they are generally considered medically necessary to accomplish functional outcomes. (Please refer to the section, "Other Public and Private Sources of Funding," for a reference on how to obtain information regarding these grants and organization assistance programs.)

Medicaid: As part of the assistance offered by the federal government to individuals requiring medical assistance via Title XIX or Medicaid, each state has mandatory services it must provide, as well as optional services it can provide on a discretionary basis to its beneficiaries. Occupational therapy is listed as an "optional service" (Dunn & McGourty, 1989) which may be provided by each state, and which is funded at the same level of reimbursement as for the mandatory services if offered (e.g., at the 50% to 80% of the cost of the fee for service or procedure). Often the insurance carriers of the Medicaid funding will use the Medicare guidelines for reimbursement as a model. Therefore, as with Medicare and private insurance justifications, the occupational therapist and/or case manager for the service provider must seek prior approval for the services proposed to be provided based on an assessment of the child. The therapist and/or case manager must familiarize themselves with the Medicaid terminology in order to receive adequate and continued reimbursement for the child's ongoing treatment. The occupational therapist and/or case manager must also be knowledgeable regarding the appeals process and verbiage that will help to justify the services and/or equipment being denied.

One of the more difficult areas of occupational therapy to receive funding via Medicaid is in the recommendation of adaptive equipment or assistive technology needs of a child. Since assistive technology is not listed as a separate service under Medicaid regulations, the funding of technology has been identified through eight primary sources, one of which is occupational therapy services (Angelo & Lane, 1997).

In justifying any services or equipment, the occupational therapist must keep in mind that the functional limitations must be directly associated with the child's disability, that the services and/or equipment are warranted due to functional outcomes or goals that they will assist the child in achieving, and that this will ultimately improve the child's abilities, independence, and overall quality of life.

There are several waiver programs available through Medicaid. For those children with disabilities whose parents' income level exceeds the poverty range required for standard Medicaid eligibility, there is the Medicaid-Deeming Waiver Program (formerly known as Katie Beckett Program), which provides financial assistance for skilled medical and rehabilitation services. For additional information on the federal programs available for funding via Medicaid or other government assistance, individuals can contact the state Department of Family and Childrens' Services (DFACS) or the local state Medicaid Office for specific waiver program information.

Public Laws Affecting Education and Funding: Table 7.3 gives a comparison of requirements of disability statutes affecting public schools for the Americans with Disabilities Act (ADA, Title II), Section 504 of the Rehabilitation Act of 1973, and for the Individuals with Disabilities Education Act (IDEA), which took the place of Public Law 94-142 (The Education for All Handicapped Children Act) (Angelo & Lane, 1997). Specifics of these public laws will not be detailed; however, they impact on those services that will improve accessiblity for children to services, facilities, etc. (e.g., IDEA regarding identification of free and appropriate public education for children with disabilities).

Section 504 and the ADA require that those students with disabilities who do not qualify for special education services have access to all activities and programs offered within their schools in grades K through 12. For those students who qualify for special education services, the IDEA mandates that these children receive "free and appropriate public education" (Angelo & Lane, 1997) through the establishment of an Individualized Education Plan or IEP as part of due process within the public school system for children up to age 21. Since occupational therapy is listed as a related service under the IDEA, a child must first qualify for special education in order to receive occupational therapy funded by the provisions of the IDEA. The states' educational agencies set the specific guidelines for what qualifies children for special education services of varying categories (e.g., Orthopedically Impaired vs. Other Health Impaired, Speech Impaired, Specific Learning Disability, Autistic or Intellectually Disabled-Mildly, Moderately, Severely, or Profoundly). Therefore, reference should be made to the *Special Education Handbook* which each state should have printed for information on qualification guidelines to have a child receive special education, and possible related therapy, services.

Special education funds are limited to students who are eligible for special education and related services determined by an IEP. For students who are not eligible for special education services and in the event that occupational therapy services are required as an issue of access to education, determination of the extent of school responsibility is made under

Table 7.3 A Comparison of Requirements of Disability Statutes Affecting Public Schools

		AMERICANS WITH DISABILITIES ACT (Title II)	SECTION 504 OF THE REHABILITATION ACT OF 1973	INDIVIDUALS WITH DISABILITIES EDUCATION ACT
Who Must Comply?	Scope of Coverage	All Programs and Activities of State and Local Governments.	All Programs and Activities of Recipients of Federal Financial Assistance.	State and Local Education Agencies Funded Under the Individuals with Disabilities Education Act.
Who is Protected?	Definition of Disability	Non-categorical–Covers Persons with a Physical or Mental Impairment that Substantially Limits a Major Life Activity, Persons Who Have a Record of an Impairment that Substantially Limits a Major Life Activity, and Persons Who are Regarded as Having Such an Impairment.*	Non-categorical–Covers Persons with a Physical or Mental Impairment that Substantially Limits a Major Life Activity, Persons Who Have a Record of an Impairment that Substantially Limits a Major Life Activity, and Persons Who are Regarded as Having Such an Impairment.*	Categorical–Covers Specified Disabilities Only.
Oversight	Complaints	U.S. Department of Education, Office for Civil Rights.	U.S. Department of Education, Office for Civil Rights.	State Education Agency.
Planning for Compliance	Administrative Requirements	Requires Self-Evaluation. Requires Transition Plan if Structural Modifications are Needed if 50 or More Employees.	Requires Self-Evaluation. Requires Transition Plan if Structural Modifications are Needed.	Requires Triennial State Plan Submitted to Office of Special Education Programs.
	Designation of Responsible Employee	Requires ADA Coordinator if 50 or More Employees.	Requires Section 504 Coordinator if 15 or More Employees.	Not Required.
	Grievance Procedures	Required if 50 or More Employees.	Required if 15 or More Employees.	Not Required.
	Public Notice	Requires On-Going Notice of Nondiscrimination on the Basis of Disability.	Requires On-Going Notice of Nondiscrimination on the Basis of Disability.	Requires Notice to Parents of Child Find Activities.
Employment	Reasonable Accommodation	Required for Qualified Applicants or Employees with Disabilities, Unless Entity can Demonstrate Undue Hardship.	Required for Qualified Applicants or Employees with Disabilities, Unless Entity can Demonstrate Undue Hardship.	Not Required.
	Written Job Description	Advisable–Not Specifically Required.	Advisable–Not Specifically Required.	Not Required.
Facilities	Program Accessibility	Requires Services, Programs, and Activities in Existing Facilities to be Readily Accessible When Viewed in Their Entirety.	Requires Services, Programs, and Activities in Existing Facilities to be Readily Accessible When Viewed in Their Entirety.	Not Required.
	Facilities Accessibility	Requires Compliance with ADAAG or UFAS in New Construction or Alterations Begun On or After 1/26/92.	Requires Compliance with ANSI (R1971) in New Construction or Alterations Begun On or After 6/3/77; Compliance with UFAS On or After 1/18/91.	Not Required.
	Maintenance of Accessible Features	Required.	Not Required.	Not Required.
Communication Requirements	Auxiliary Aids and Services	Required for Persons with Visual, Hearing, and Speech Disabilities if Necessary to Provide Effective Communication.	No Requirement Specified. Obligation Exists to Provide Effective Communication.	Required Only if Written into the Student's Individualized Education Program.

*A student who is covered under the 2nd or 3rd prongs of the definition of individuals with disabilities, and who does not also have a physical or mental impairment that substantially limits a major life activity, is not entitled either to special education and/or related services or to regular education with related services. It is also important to note that protection under Title II and Section 504 is specifically afforded to qualified individuals with disabilities. Not every person with a disability is qualified.

page 1 of 2

"Not Required" means that there is no requirement in the statute or regulations relating to this specific issue.
"No Requirement Specified" means that the requirement is not specifically mentioned in the statute or regulations, but that other provisions of the regulations indicate an obligation exists.
"Advisable–Not Specifically Required" means that although the statute and regulations do not specifically require a certain action, such actions will assist school districts in complying with other provisions of the ADA and Section 504.

General Nondiscrimination Requirements for Public Schools	AMERICANS WITH DISABILITIES ACT (Title II)	SECTION 504 OF THE REHABILITATION ACT OF 1973	INDIVIDUALS WITH DISABILITIES EDUCATION ACT
Child Find	Requires Location and Identification of All Qualified Children with Disabilities Who are Not Receiving a Free Appropriate Public Education (K-12).*	Requires Location and Identification of All Qualified Children with Disabilities in Jurisdiction Who are Not Receiving a Free Appropriate Public Education (K-12).	Requires Location and Identification of All Children with Disabilities in Jurisdiction Birth to Twenty-One.
Parental Notice	Required.*	Required.	Required.
Free Appropriate Public Education (FAPE)	Required.*	Required.	Required.
Education Plan	Requires that the Student's Program be Described with Sufficient Specificity to Demonstrate that the Student's Needs have been Assessed on an Individual Basis (An Individualized Education Program Document is Not Specifically Required).*	Requires that the Student's Program be Described with Sufficient Specificity to Demonstrate that the Student's Needs have been Assessed on an Individual Basis (An Individualized Education Program Document is Not Specifically Required).	An Individualized Education Program Document (IEP) is Required.
Procedural Safeguards	Required. (Compliance with Requirements in IDEA will be Considered Compliance Under the ADA).*	Required. (Compliance with Requirements in IDEA will be Considered Compliance Under Section 504).	Required.
Evaluation Procedures	Required.*	Required.	Similar and Additional Requirements to those in Section 504 and Title II.
Placement Team	Requires Group, Including Individuals Knowledgeable About the Child, Meaning of Evaluation Data, and Placement Options.*	Requires Group, Including Individuals Knowledgeable About the Child, Meaning of Evaluation Data, and Placement Options.	Requires Group, Including Individuals Knowledgeable About the Child, Meaning of Evaluation data, and Placement Options.
Educational Setting	Requires Most Integrated Setting Appropriate.*	Requires Most Integrated Setting Appropriate.	Requires Least Restrictive Environment.
Non Academic Programs	Requires Equal Opportunity to Participate.*	Requires Equal Opportunity to Participate.	Requires Equal Opportunity to Participate.
Pre-School (ages 3-5 years)	Requires Equal Opportunity to Participate.*	Requires Equal Opportunity to Participate.	Requires a Free Appropriate Public Education.
Adult Education Programs	Requires Equal Opportunity to Participate.*	Requires Equal Opportunity to Participate.	Not Required.
Reasonable Modification	Requires Reasonable Modification of Policies, Practices, and Procedures of All Public Entities.	No Requirement Specified. General Obligation Exists to Make Reasonable Modification of Recipients' Policies, Practices, and Procedures.	Not Required.
Confidentiality	No Requirement for Students, but School Districts Must Maintain Employees' Medical Files Separate from Employees' Personnel Files to Ensure Against Unwarranted Disclosure of the Employees' Disability.	No Requirement for Students, but School Districts Must Maintain Employees' Medical Files Separate from Employees' Personnel Files to Ensure Against Unwarranted Disclosure of the Employees' Disability.	Requires Protection of Special Education Student Records and Conformance with Family Educational Rights and Privacy Act (FERPA).

*These Requirements are described in Subpart D of the U.S. Department of Education's Section 504 Regulation.
The U.S. Department of Justice interprets the general non-discrimination provisions in Title II to cover discriminatory conduct that is specifically prohibited under Subpart D of the Section 504 Regulation.

Funded by the National Institute on Disability and Rehabilitation Research of the U.S. Department of Education
Adaptive Environments Center, ADA National Access for Public Schools Project Schools Hotline 1-800-893-1225 January 1996

the provision of Section 504 through a 504 plan. However, it is important to note that unlike the provisions for implementation of the IDEA, there is no federal funding of services provided as a result of Section 504 procedures.

Other Public and Private Sources of Funding: In addition to the previously referenced sources of coverage for occupational therapy services and assistive technology, the Department of Human Resources within individual states may have reference materials regarding private and public sources of funding for persons with disabilities. In the state of Georgia, for instance, based on the Technology Related Assistance for Individuals with Disabilities Act of 1988 or Tech Act (Public Law 103-213, as amended in 1994) funded a project in 1991 via a federal grant through RESNA (Rehabilitation Engineering Society of North America) and NIDRR (National Institute of Disability and Rehabilitation Research) (Angelo & Lane, 1997). This project became known as "Tools for Life," Georgia's Assistive Technology Program, a service of the Georgia Department of Human Resources, Division of Rehabilitation Services. The manual produced by this program describes funding not only for therapy services and assistive technology, but for funding information in general over a wide area of coverage needs. Listed are twenty-eight public and sixty private sources of funding for persons with disabilities of all ages. To obtain a copy of the manual entitled, *Dollars and Sense: A Guide to Solving the Funding Puzzle and Getting Assistive Technology in Georgia* (Weeks, Kniskern, & Phillips, 1997), contact:

Georgia Division of Rehabilitation Services

"Tools for Life" Program
2 Peachtree Street, 35th Floor
Atlanta, Georgia 30303
800-497-8665 or 404-657-3084
TDD: 404-657-3085
Fax: 404-657-3086

Common Measures of Evaluation: Children are evaluated to determine if occupational therapy is needed to meet developmental milestones or functional goals being hindered by their disability. These assessments can be performed from clinical observations and/or testing materials that have been normed with standardized information for the child's specific age and/or gender. Table 7.4 is a partial list of evaluation and screening tools that have been used by occupational therapists in a variety of pediatric settings for assessing the treatment needs of children of varying ages.

Long-Term Considerations: When an occupational therapist evaluates a child for a life care plan, his or her professional assessment should consider not only the immediate needs within the settings in which the child currently participates, but those needs that the child may have later in life. This is determined from knowledge of the child's diagnosis and clinical predictors of cognition, longevity or expected life span, and presenting capabilities, which are determined as

Table 7.4 Partial Listing of Occupational Therapy Pediatric Screen Tools

- Activities of Daily Living Skills Inventory
- Battelle Developmental Inventory
- Bayley Scales of Infant Development-Second Edition
- Beery Developmental Test of Visual-Motor Integration (VMI) — Revised
- BRIGANCE Diagnostic Inventory of Early Development
- Bruininks-Oseretsky Test of Motor Skills
- Carolina Curriculum for Infants and Toddlers with Special Needs
- Clinical Observations–Ayres'
- De Gangi-Berk Test of Sensory Integration
- Denver Developmental Screening Test
- Detroit Tests of Learning Aptitude
- Developmental Programming of Infants and Young Children
- Developmental Test of Visual Perception, Second Edition
- Erhardt Hand Development Prehension Test
- Evaluation Tool of Children's Handwriting (ETCH)
- Fiorentino Reflex Testing
- First STEP Screening for Evaluating Preschoolers
- Functional muscle strength testing
- Grip and pinch strength measurements
- Hawaii Early Learning Profile (HELP)
- Hooper Visual Organization Test
- Jebsen Hand Function Test for Children
- Milano Comparetti Reflex Testing
- Miller Assessment of Preschoolers (MAP)
- Motor-Free Visual Perception Test-Revised
- Movement Assessment of Infants
- Neonatal Behavioral Assessment Scale (Brazelton)
- Peabody Developmental Motor Scales
- Pediatric Evaluation of Disability Inventory (PEDI)
- Purdue Pegboard
- Quality of Movement Checklist
- Range of Motion Measurements
- Sensory Integration and Praxis Tests (SIPT)
- Symbol Digit Modalities Test
- Test of Auditory Perceptual Skills (TAPS) — Revised
- Test of Sensory Function in Infants
- Test of Visual Motor Integration
- Test of Visual Motor Skills (TVMS) — Revised
- Test of Visual Perceptual Skills (TVPS)–Upper & Lower Levels — Revised
- Visual Skills Appraisal
- Wide Range Achievement Test — Revised (WRAT-R)
- Wilbarger Sensorimotor History

potentially realistic, given the presenting limitations. For example, a fifteen-year-old child has had an acquired brain injury of the left hemisphere since the age of seven years due to blunt trauma from a beating. He has the presenting problems of right-sided hemiplegia or paralysis with functional use of his right hand to assist the now dominant left hand, and is functionally ambulatory with an ankle foot orthosis (AFO). He exhibits distractibility with limited sustained attention, problems with visual convergence or merging visual focus on near objects, and a cognitive level of a mildly intellectually impaired person. His abilities include performing his basic self-care skills independently with minimal assistance for set-up of the activities (e.g., assistance to organize clothes in drawers for easy access and selection by color, item type, etc.). He is able to perform simple job tasks in a structured setting, can compute simple problems and math skills with use of a calculator, and can make simple change. He has the potential to live in a supported living setting given these skills. Considerations should be made as to whether he has the potential to be a safe and independent driver within familiar, local routes vs. extended distances; and whether or not, in consultation with a vocational counselor, he will be able to support himself via independent employment or supported employment options. Given that he probably has a normal life span expectancy, these are concerns that the occupational therapist needs to evaluate and assess with input from the parents, physician, rehabilitation team, educators, and school vocational placement counselors, among others, in order to fully assess his lifetime maximum functional potential.

Adults: (21 Years and Older)

Transportation — Driving Vs. Dependence: The ability to transport oneself independently is an issue of great consideration in an individual's access to gainful employment and community resources; therefore, much emphasis is placed on assessing a person's ability to drive with the limitations imposed by a disability. An occupational therapist who has received specialized education and training within the area of driving rehabilitation should be able to ascertain whether or not a person with a disability can independently and *safely* operate a car or van via extensive predriving clinical and road performance testing.

An occupational therapist can be certified to perform driving assessments and/or training via two channels. A CDI or Certified Driving Instructor's certificate, the same test taken by commercial driving school instructors, can be acquired after passing a test given by the state department of motor vehicles after establishing the facility as a driving school. In order to become certified as a Certified Driver Rehabilitation Specialist or CDRS, the occupational therapist must pass a certification examination administered by an independent testing agency contracted by the Association of Driver Educators for the Disabled or ADED. This certification examination encompasses a wide knowledge base of varying disabilities from orthopedic or spinal cord considerations to more abstract and less obvious problems of persons with mild to moderate acquired brain injuries and other neurological disorders. Before a determination of the potential to drive can be made, many factors must be assessed. These include, but are not limited to, the following:

- **Medical History/Medications**: An accurate medical history with a definitive diagnosis and list of current medications are imperative to review before assessing further predriving skills. Seizure status, medical precautions with regard to the diagnosis or presenting problems, psychiatric complications, and the stability of the medication routines are all critical factors that need to be addressed to accurately determine potential for driving.

- **Visual/Ocular Motor Skills**: Acuity at near and far distances, peripheral fields, tracking, convergence, quick localization, saccades, stereopsis or depth perception, desensitization to color, etc.
- **Visual Perceptual Skills**: Color perception, figure ground discrimination, spatial relations, form constancy, visual closure, and visual memory, etc.
- **Physical/Motor Skills**: Range of motion and strength in all available extremities; sensation for light touch, joint proprioception and kinesthetic awareness, temperature discrimination and any paresthesias or abnormal sensations; eye-hand and eye-foot reaction times bilaterally; gross and fine motor coordination, muscle tone, and the limitations imposed by weakness or spasticity; static and dynamic sitting balance; transfer skills; activity tolerance and endurance with effects of fatigue assessed; functional reach patterns, etc.
- **Cognitive/Perceptual Skills**: Anticipatory perception is critical to being able to formulate and execute defensive maneuvers, along with the judgment and perception of time distance in order to carry out the actions needed to avoid a collision. Processing speed is an integral factor in all of the above skills, as is the ability to compensate for reduced processing via other cognitive strategies (e.g., automatically allowing extra space to provide more time for reaction planning). Problem solving or reasoning skills based on situational cues, such as determining potential vs. actual road hazards and judgment of safety conditions, are critical skills needed to safely drive. This should be tested through controlled static and dynamic methods prior to exposing the person with a disability to a potentially risky road situation.

Once the history and skill areas have been evaluated, the information should be reviewed to determine if the person has met criteria considered to be indicators of safe, functional performance. Criteria are usually established by the facility or evaluator providing the service, and vary according to the norms chosen on selected tests or by the preference of the evaluator to road test all individuals with disabilities, vs. borderline to good candidates for safe performance. Prior to road testing, adaptive equipment or assistive technology may be prescribed by the occupational therapist with the vehicle equipment to be used matching the recommended set-up as closely as possible. Based on the predriving assessment, the type of vehicle to be used and the specific equipment needs are determined. Table 7.5 is a tool developed to assist the occupational therapist and case manager in determining whether a car or van is most likely to be needed to meet the client and his or her family's needs.

Should the person with the disability pass the road test, then a final assessment and determination is made of the adaptive equipment and driving restrictions that will be needed for safe and independent operation of the selected vehicle. The greatest cost is calculated to be for vehicular modifications, especially if the person has a disability that requires driving a van with high-tech needs (e.g., a person with a triple amputation or high-level quadriplegia). Tables 7.6 and 7.7 outline the possible adaptive equipment needs in a car for a client as a driver or for a

Table 7.5 Van vs. Automobile Selection

OCCUPATIONAL THERAPY
ADAPTIVE DRIVER REHABILITATION
VEHICLE SELECTION ASSESSMENT

Patient: ______________________ **Age:** ________ **Sex: M F** **Status: S M W D**

Diagnosis: ______________________________________ **Onset:** ________

Referred By: ____________________ **Phone:** (____) __________ **Referral Date:** __/__/__

Date of Evaluation: __/__/__ **Evaluator:** ______________________, ___OTR/L ___CDRS

Licensure Status: ___Current ___Temporary Permit ___Expired ___Pending Other: __________
Expiration Date: ___/___/___ Number: ______________Restrictions: __________

Driving Status: ___Pending Evaluation ___Cleared to Drive ___Unsafe/Inappropriate to Drive
___Status Uncertain ___Other: ____________________

••

QUESTIONNAIRE	YES	NO
1. Is the client wheelchair dependent for long distance/endurance mobility (traveling distances for work, school campus, shopping, etc.)?		
2. Is the client unable to independently transfer into or out of a car without fatigue or shortness of breath?		
3. If wheelchair dependent and able to transfer self into a car, is the client unable to maneuver self and wheelchair to fold and store the wheelchair behind the front seat?	(x2)	(x2)
4. Does the client live alone or is responsible for independent mobility/transportation needs?		
5. Do more than two passengers need to ride with the client for outings or other activities of daily living (shopping, laundromat, restaurant dining, etc.)?		
6. Is the client's illness or disability of a progressive nature where a wheelchair would be possibly needed during the next eight to ten years?	(x2)	(x2)
7. If ill, would the client possibly need to be transferred via wheelchair to a nearby physician and/or hospital? (Where the family member/friend would not be able to perform a stand/pivot or sliding board transfer with the client?)	(x2)	(x2)
8. Will the client's height, weight, size and/or disability make it physically straining over a short and/or long term to assist with transfers, possibly causing a resultant secondary injury to another individual?		
9. Will the client need to efficiently and expediently enter or exit his/her vehicle often during the course of his/her daily routines (work, school, etc.)?		
10. Is the client comfortable driving a vehicle larger than a standard car?		
RESPONSE TOTALS: **If the number in this column is GREATER, then a VAN would be the vehicle of preference.........→**		
If the number in THIS column is GREATER, then an AUTOMOBILE would be the vehicle of preference.........→		

ISM: 1/97

van with the person with the disability driving or riding as a passenger. In Table 7.6, some possible presenting problems and/or diagnoses are listed along the left-hand column. The headers list the major types of assistive technology that are currently available for car modification. Since the equipment is much more extensive for van modifications, Table 7.7 lists some of the possible presenting problems more typical for van drivers in the heading across the top of the pages,

Table 7.6 Adaptive Car Equipment — Client as Driver

Legend: X = Probable Need P = Possible Need *** If unable to adjust seating with 6-way power seat.**

DIAGNOSIS/ PROBLEMS	DOOR HANDLE OPENER	POWER STEERING	ADAPTIVE SIDE/PANA MIRRORS	LEFT SIDED HAND CONTROLS	RIGHT SIDED HAND CONTROLS	ADAPTIVE STEERING DEVICE	PARKING BRAKE EXTENSION	LEFT FOOT GAS PEDAL	FLOOR PEDAL EXTEN -SIONS	TURN SIGNAL ADAPTOR	GEAR SHIFT EXTENSION	CAR TOPPER	SEAT HARNESS	*SEAT CUSHION
1. HEMIANOPSIA, REDUCED PERIPHERAL VISION AND/OR NECK AROM			X											
2. PARAPLEGIA/ PARAPARESIS AND GREATER LEFT U.E. STRENGTH		X		X		X (Left)	X					P	P	P
3. PARAPARESIS AND GREATER RIGHT U.E. STRENGTH		X			X	X (Left)	X				X	P	P	P
4. RIGHT HEMIPLEGIA/PARESIS		X	P			X (Left)		X						P
5. LEFT HEMIPLEGIA/ PARESIS		X	P			X (Right)				X				P
6. DWARFISM (SHORT STATURE/LIMBS)	P	X	P			P	X		X			P	P	
7. ARTHRITIS AND REDUCED JOINT AROM (JRA, ETC.)	X	X	P			P	P		P					P
8. RIGHT L.E. AMPUTEE								X						P
9. LEFT L.E. AMPUTEE							X							P
10. BILATER L.E. AMPUTEE, LEFT U.E. - GREATER STRENGTH		X		X		X (Right)	X						P	
11. BILATER L.E. AMPUTEE, RIGHT U.E.- GREATER STRENGTH		X			X	X (Left)	X				X		P	
12. RIGHT U.E. AMPUTEE		X				X (Left)				P	X			
13. LEFT U.E. AMPUTEE		X				X (Right)				X				
14. TRIPLE AMPUTEE: BOTH L.E.s & RIGHT U.E. W/PROTHESIS & ABLE TO TRANSFER; UNABLE TO STORE WHEELCHAIR		X	P	X		X (Right)	X			P	X	P		P
15. TRIPLE AMPUTEE: BOTH L.E.s & LEFT U.E. W/PROSTHESIS & ABLE TO TRANSFER; UNABLE TO STORE WHEELCHAIR		X	P		X	X (Left)	X			X				
16. UPPER EXTREMITY WEAKNESS - ABLE TO TRANSFER, BUT NOT STORE WHEELCHAIR	P	X				P						X		

ISM: 1/97

Table 7.7 Adaptive Van Equipment

Legend: X= Probable Need P= Possible Need O= Option/Choice * = Bilateral U.E. Amputee ** = R or L U.E. Amputee

Adaptive Equipment/ Assistive Technology	Wheelchair Transfer to Driver's Seat	Client to Drive from Wheelchair	Wheelchair Driver with U.E. Weakness	W/C Driver with Limited U.E. AROM	Decreased Trunk/Neck Control	Transport Family in Rear of Van	Client Riding as a Passenger in W/C in Van
1. Electric Door Openers:	X	X	X	X	X	X	
A. Key Activated Toggle	X	P	P			X	
B. Magnetic Keyless	O	O	O	O	O		
C. Electronic Remote Control	O	O	O	O	O		
2. Wheelchair Lifts & Controls:							
A. Fully Automatic	X	X	X	X	X	X	O
B. Semi-Automatic							X
C. Folding Platform						X	O
D. Rotary Platform		O	O	O	O	O	O
3. Door Entry: Full Size Van	O	O	O	O	O	O	X
A. Raised Roof & Door	P	X	P	P	X	O	P
B. Lowered Fl oor in Center	P	X	X	X	X	O	P
C. Lowered Floor Driver's Side		X	X	X	X		
D. Entry/Courtesy Lighting	X	X	X	X	X	X	X
4. Door Entry: Mini Van Chrysler/Ford Lowered Floor (Size/Space Permitting)							
A. Fully Auto. Ramp & Doors	X	X	X	X	X	X	
B. Manual System for Opening							X
5. Driver Position:	X	X	X	X	X	P	
A. Removable Driver's Seat		X	X	X	X	X	
B. Auto. Wheelchair Tiedown		X	X	X	X	X	O
C. 3 Point Shoulder/Lap Belt	X	X	X	X	X	X	
D. Power Seat Base	X					X	
E. Power Mirrors	X	X	X	X	X	X	
F. Head Rest w/Touch Pad for Primary Controls	P	P	X	X	X	O	
6. Steering System:							
A. Standard Power Steering	P	P				P	
B. Low or Reduced Effort			X	X		X	
C. Zero Effort Steering Controls			P	P	X	O	
D. Tilt Wheel on Column	X	X	X	X	X	X	
E. Horizontal Steering		P	P	P	P	P	
F. Steering Column Extension	P	P	P	X	X	O	
G. Standard Wheel Size	X	P	P		P	O	

ISM: 1/97

Table 7.7 (continued) Adaptive Van Equipment

Adaptive Equipment/ Assistive Technology	Wheelchair Transfer to Driver's Seat	Client to Drive from Wheelchair	Wheelchair Driver with U.E. Weakness	W/C Driver with Limited U.E. AROM	Decreased Trunk/Neck Control	Transport Family in Rear of Van	Client Riding as a Passenger in W/C in Van
6. Steering System:							
H. Reduced Wheel Size		P	P	X	P	O	
I. Joystick (4-Way) Control		P	P (If Severe)	P (If Severe)	P	P	
7. Steering Devices:	X	X	X	X	X	X	
A. Spinner Knob	P	P	P	P		O	
B. Tri-Pin or V-Grip		P	P	P	P	O	
C. Palmar Clip		P	P	P		O	
D. Amputee Ring **							
E. Steering Disc (Floor) *							
8. Brake & Acceleration System:							
A. Standard Power Brakes	X	P					
B. Reduced Effort Brakes			P	P	P	P	P
C. Mechanical Hand Controls	X	P	P			P	
D. Electronic Gas/Brake(EGB)		P	P	P	P	P	
E. Parking Brake Extension	X	P				P	
F. Power Parking Brake	O	P	X	P	X	O	
9. Accessory Controls:							
A. Standard Primary & Secondary Controls	P						X
B. Electronic/Touch Pad for Secondary Controls		P	P	P	P	P	
C. MODIFIED PRIMARY CONTROLS: (Turn signals, Horn & Dimmer Switch, Wipers, Cruise Control Set)	P	P	P	P	X	O	
D. MODIFIED SECONDARY CONTROLS: (Windows & Locks, Headlights, Windshield Washers, Heat/AC, Cruise Control On)	P	P	X (If Severe)	X (If Severe)	X	O	
10. Miscellaneous:							
A. Passenger Wheelchair Tiedown System		P	P	P	P	P	X
B. Unoccupied Wheelchair Transport Lock	X						
C. Sliding Board Transfers	X						
D. Chest Restraint	P	P	P	P	X		P
E. Emergency Communication Device (Cellular Phone or C. B. Radio)	X	X	X	X	X	X	X
F. Dual (Back-up) Battery System	X	X	X	X	X	X	
G. Rear Heat/AC Systems	X	X	X	X	X	X	X

ISM 1/97

while the current available basic technology for vans are itemized vertically. In both tables equipment needs can be determined basically by matching the presenting problems with the types of equipment checked across the tables for those specific problems. Where there is a possible vs. probable need, the final decision on this equipment choice must be made with the clinical and road assessments completed to get an accurate picture of the client's needs. In preparing a life care plan where there may be projected or hypothetical needs in the future life span of the individual with a disability, the occupational therapist would want to give the life care planner a complete equipment list, including possible or optional items. In other words, if a client driving from a wheelchair has a ***possible need*** for a headrest with a touch pad for primary controls, this should be part of the itemized and projected costs for this client. This is especially applicable if he or she is a child at the time the life care plan is being developed, and has been assessed as having potential to be a driver in the future.

Liability or Responsibility: A point of great concern is when a person with a disability has a history of multiple accidents prior to the driving assessment and/or when the person does not demonstrate the ability to compensate for the limitations imposed by his or her disability and is considered to be unsafe to operate a motorized vehicle independently. This could occur during the predriving evaluation process, on completion of the road test, or after the person has been cleared to drive because of seizures or other changes in his or her physiological or emotional status. For liability purposes and as a matter of professional responsibility, any service provider who has concerns regarding a disabled individual's abilities to drive should make the treating team aware of his or her concerns, and should document this concern. Efforts should then be made to inform the person with the disability and his or her family of these concerns. Whether or not the physician, occupational therapist, case manager, or other health and rehabilitative care professional reports the person with the disability is a decision that is usually made according to the provider's facility procedures or to the degree of risk that the reporting person agrees to assume regarding this person's and the public's safety.

An occupational therapist performing a driving evaluation should routinely assess past driving history and performance as part of the intake information. The person being evaluated should be aware that the State Department of Motor Vehicles could be contacted to verify any prior record of accidents or restrictions as part of the driving assessment. If this person is found to be unsafe to begin or continue to drive independently or is recommended to drive under restricted conditions (e.g., low volume traffic areas on familiar routes during daytime good weather conditions), the occupational therapist usually sends a copy of the report to the State Department of Motor Vehicles (DMV), depending on the philosophy of the provider's facility and the regulations for that particular state regarding disabilities and driving status. There are states that require mandatory reporting of a person who sustains a disabling injury or illness by a physician and/or other medical personnel. However, other states do not require a person with a disability to be reported, and the assumption is made that anyone can report anyone who feels a citizen is unsafe to drive (e.g., either because of alcoholic or drug intake, a disability affecting physical abilities, or a psychiatric condition).

When an occupational therapist, case manager, psychologist, physician, or other service provider makes a report to recommend that a person with a disability be restricted from driving in some manner, then the individual's case is referred to the Medical Advisory Board of that state's Department of Motor Vehicles (DMV) or Public Safety. The Medical Advisory Board notifies the person with the disability of a licensure suspension pending review, and is then charged with the task of obtaining additional medical information to make the determination whether to reinstate licensure with or without recommended restrictions. Though the reporting person's information is regarded as confidential and can be requested to be anonymous, the person who was reported can have the DMV subpoenaed to provide the name of the person filing the charges through an attorney or the proper legal procedures. Therefore, it is in the best interest of the occupational therapist or service provider making the report to notify the person with the disability of his or her intent to report him or her to the DMV. He or she should also know that this referral is based on the information obtained from clinical data and/or road testing during the driving evaluation, or from the family and other service providers of incidents that have occurred since the person was cleared to drive, and that warrant concern regarding the individual's or the public's safety. To find out whether or not the state in which a client resides and in which he or she plans to drive has mandatory reporting requirements, contact the state's Department of Motor Vehicles or Department of Public Safety. To locate an occupational therapist and/or driver educator who has been certified to assess a client's potential to begin or return to safe and independent driving contact:

The Association of Driver Educators for the Disabled
P. O. Box 49
Edgerton, Wisconsin 53534
608-884-8833

Home Health Care

With the evolution of managed care and more controlled use of services by Medicare and private insurance carriers in the continuum of care, home health occupational therapy and rehabilitation services in general are being ordered more often by physicians with internal case managers' input for provision of treatment after the acute care phase of a disability or injury. Home health services are often implemented when the patient or person after an injury or disability will require a greater period of time to prepare for outpatient rehabilitation than is warranted in the specific policy of the insurance carrier or if there are no further pressing medical problems that would require continued hospitalization under Medicare guidelines. The home health recipient must be determined to be "homebound," unable to transport himself or herself by either driving, transferring independently into the passenger side of a vehicle, or independently calling and arranging for a taxi or transportation service of some type. The reasons that determine the person to be homebound must be of a medical and/or functional nature (e.g., wheelchair dependence with poor transfer and balance skills, oxygen dependency, poor endurance, bed mobility dependence, generalized weakness, visual or other sensory impairments, etc., that would impede independent mobility).

For occupational therapy and other rehabilitation services to be covered by Medicare, services must be considered medically necessary. A reasonable length of time and frequency of treatment sessions must be determined based on the number of limiting factors and presenting problems (e.g., bathroom doorways are too narrow for a wheelchair and there are no financial or community resources to widen door entries; sponge bathing is not feasible on a permanent basis since there is a good prognosis for return to independent ambulation with a walker or other aid).

Some of the areas that occupational therapists typically evaluate in assessing the total needs of a home health patient include, but are not limited to, the following:

- **Orientation/Cognition**: Awareness of person, place, date and event or situation; short- and long-term memory; judgment regarding personal safety; affect; presence or absence of mental confusion; following visual vs. verbal directions; ability to recall and repeat immediate information, and retention over a period of time, along with the ability to communicate functionally to indicate needs.
- **Psychosocial Status**: Emotional state during evaluation; ability to express feelings appropriately; social outlets or family and community resources; presence or absence of social isolation; insight into disability; degree of motivation or inner drive toward recovery and achievement of functional independence. Resources for community services following discharge may be recommended to assist with problems of chronic depression, emotional lability, etc. (e.g., adult day care, etc.).
- **Physical Status**: Vital signs at the time of assessment and/or treatment sessions, such as blood pressure and pulse (especially with any secondary problem of hypertension or when regular nursing visits are not mandated by orders, and any history of cardiovascular or cardiac conditions exists); range of motion or functional joint mobility for upper extremities specifically, and overall for the lower extremities as they affect self-care tasks; upper extremity strength, including hand grip and pinch measures; muscle tone, specifically for the presence or absence of spasticity and/or synergy patterns of arm use; active movements and overall coordination for gross and fine motor skills; hand dominance, and sensation or sensory deficits, including any paresthesias, ocular motor and visual skills; sitting and standing balance and activity work tolerance and endurance.
- **Perceptual Testing**: Motor-free visual perceptual skills, left-right discrimination abilities, body image or concept and self-esteem, the presence or absence of unilateral neglect, and other skills areas that could hinder self-care tasks.
- **Functional Abilities**: Activities of daily living skills for basic self-care (dressing, feeding, bathing, hair care, oral hygiene, shaving/makeup, transfers, bed mobility, and general ambulation status), as well as for higher self-care tasks such as homemaking (cooking, washing dishes, cleaning, laundry, bedmaking), reading, telling time, making change and money management, telephone skills, and potential to return to prior level of independent mobility or transportation before illness or injury.

- **Orthotics/Prosthetics**: Any splints, slings, anterior foot orthoses or other ambulation aid, prosthetic limb or other appliance, which was recommended and provided prior to return home; those positioning and/or facilitative appliances or supplies that should be recommended based on the initial home health visit for greater functional abilities and/or the prevention of deformity over a long period of time.
- **Assistive Devices and/or Adaptive Equipment Needs**: Any items that were provided or recommended and for which arrangements were made for delivery prior to discharge from the hospital (safety belt, bedside commode, hospital bed, wheelchair, rolling walker, hemi-walker, quad cane, reacher, dressing stick, long-handled shoehorn, and bath sponge, etc.); plus those items that will be needed to enable full or prior functional independence in the home (hand-held shower spray, tub transfer bench, leg lift and transfer loop, non-skid bath and floor mats, etc.).
- **Architectural Barriers**: If wheelchair or walker dependent, especially on a long-term basis, measurement of inside doorways into the bathroom and access to other areas of the home is critical with recommendations for feasible or reasonable modifications; access to resources to make modifications, especially for rampways or railings that may be needed to overcome exterior and/or interior steps; assessment of the exterior walkways for even surfaces, especially if broken concrete or asphalt, gravel, grass or dirt and significant surface irregularities are present.

Another key factor is determining the *prognosis* for achieving maximum functional potential in order to attain the outcomes or goals mutually developed by the therapist and the patient. Generally these goals are determined as close as possible to the functional levels exhibited prior to the injury or illness. However, it appears that the most important or key determinant of coverage is the ability to show continual and steady progress in order to further justify the utilization of skilled occupational therapy services or those services that cannot be carried out by a home health aide or other paraprofessional. Without the need for skilled intervention by a professional to carry out the activities directed to meet functional goals and the evidence of graded and steady progress, Medicare will scrutinize the therapy charges and often deny coverage. The billing facility can appeal these rulings through the established appeals process. If the appeal is denied, then a hearing can be requested and scheduled for an independent review of the Medicare carrier's decision to deny coverage. Chances for repeal of denials varies, but often have been favorable when terminology and wording have been simplified into less "rehab verbiage" and more functional, understandable language in order to clarify the procedures, the intent of treatment, and/or functional outcomes.

Aging and Geriatric Long-Term Care: If after receiving home health occupational therapy and other nursing or rehabilitative services in the home, the person with a disability is unable to live independently or reach a level of function appropriate for outpatient care, then supported living options need to be explored. There is funding assistance available through Medicaid known as the Medicaid Independent Care Waiver Program that offers financial resources for skilled nursing and rehabilitation services, as well as personal attendant care, with the goal of maintaining a person with a disability in the community rather than in a nursing home. Should an individual not be able to obtain placement in this program, then the alternatives would be to look at placement in a state funded or private nursing home, personal care home, or to acquire attendant care in the patient's home at the expense of the family or other private resources. There are also retirement communities that offer several levels of care, from monitoring or supervisory visits to skilled inpatient nursing services; however, these are usually very expensive and are paid for from private resources. At this level of independence, occupational therapy is usually available by private payment. However, if the person develops a medical condition that requires admission into the skilled nursing unit of that community or into a hospital that would make him or her eligible for Medicare coverage under Part A, he or she could then be eligible to receive occupational therapy and other skilled services under Medicare Part B. These services could be provided either in the skilled nursing facility or in the home, as long as the services were deemed medically necessary, and continued progress was shown toward achieving functional outcomes.

OCCUPATIONAL THERAPY IN LIFE CARE PLANNING

The Role of the Occupational Therapist as a Team Member

Unless the occupational therapist is the author of the life care plan, the role of the occupational therapist is to assist the life care planner in determining the activities of daily living, the work and play or leisure needs of a person with a disability throughout life expectancy. The areas of need would be assessed based on the framework for evaluation and treatment within the profession of occupational therapy outlined previously. This would include any assessment or intervention services, and assistive technology or adaptive equipment that would be needed to maintain the quality of life, as well the level of maximum functional independence. Once the global needs of the individual are determined, the occupational therapist could then assist in the cost determination for those services and/or equipment identified. Consideration must also be given to the duration expectancy of each item of equipment recommended (e.g., replacement of a tub transfer bench every six to eight years, depending on weight and other factors). This information would then be used to determine the overall cost of the life care plan for the individual with the disability with the occupational therapy component as one piece in the total life puzzle for that person.

CASE EXAMPLE:

EVALUATION AND IDENTIFICATION OF CONCERNS REQUIRING OCCUPATIONAL THERAPY

Mr. A is a six-foot-one-inch tall, fifty-year-old, married, black male weighing 220 pounds who sustained an on-the-job injury when he fell off a warehouse loading dock, causing primary trauma to his cervical or neck area. He experienced severe neck pain, plus headaches and muscle spasms of his neck, shoulders, and back. He ultimately underwent two cervical fusions after unsuccessful discectomies within a period of eighteen to twenty months after his original injury. Mr. A reported no history of hypertension or arthritis until after this work injury occurred. Radiologic studies verified the evidence of degenerative joint changes, especially in his cervical and shoulder regions (C3–T1 vertebral discs). He also complained of paresthesias in both his upper extremities with tingling, numbness, and cold sensations, greater toward his hands. Mr. A lives with his wife and two children, both dependent minors. His wife works full time during the day. Since he has been considered as having a catastrophic injury and unable to return to gainful employment due to the continued spasms, need for a permanent cervical collar, and other sensorimotor and functional limitations, he spends the day alone at home. He received six months of physical therapy on an outpatient basis; however, no home health services or occupational therapy was reportedly received by the client during his rehabilitation period.

An occupational therapy consult was recommended in order to provide information to complete a life care plan by an independent rehabilitation counselor. The occupational therapist was requested to assess Mr. A's activities of daily living skills, home environment safety issues, and status regarding safe and independent driving since he was driving to appointments with questionable safety, as reported by his case manager. A home visit was scheduled in order to assess Mr. A's needs with the following information obtained:

- **Medications:** At the time of the interview, Mr. A was taking six different types of medication for pain and spasms, edema, hypertension, and arthritis. He was unable to recall the names, frequency, or dosages for five of six prescriptions, and his blood pressure during the initial visit was 172/132, suggesting he was not taking them as scheduled. Side effects he reported as a result of these medications included dizziness, sleepiness, fatigue, and generalized weakness. He also reported a tendency to drop items if held in his hands for longer than a few seconds at or above shoulder level.
- **Orientation/Cognition/Perception**: Mr. A reported difficulty with sustained and focused attention, tending to shift focus rather quickly, and consequently he had problems with short-term memory and retention of information. He was oriented to the date and day by use of compensatory aids such as a calendar, and was cognizant of the occupational therapist's profession and purpose for the home visit. No problems were noted with ocular pursuits, left-right discrimination, or general visual perceptual abilities. Processing speed was, however, noted to be delayed for visual information, especially when compensatory trunk or torso motions were needed to compensate for an inability to rotate his neck due to the cervical collar. Mentation was found to be functional for general money management skills and telling time; however, Mr. A had difficulty following verbal and visual directions for more than two steps in a sequence, and reported difficulty with reading and phone use due to fatigue and spasms in his arms from elevating reading materials or the telephone for greater than thirty seconds at a time. Judgment regarding safety was assessed as questionable due to his continuing to drive long distances when unable to fully scan visually and rotate his trunk.
- **Physical Status**: On evaluation of active range of motion, muscle tone, and upper extremity strength, Mr. A was found to have limitations in his scapular and shoulder areas. This was estimated to be partially due to the need to keep the cervical collar in position at all times to prevent continuous and uncontrolled spasms posteriorly or toward the back of his neck into hyperextension. Shoulder motions, though limited, were found to be within functional limits,

except for external rotation of his upper arms bilaterally preventing him from reaching the back of his neck and top of his head without significant stress to his neck and back areas. No limitations were found for elbow, forearm, and hand motions; however, hand grip and pinch strength were very poor for a man of his large stature and above-average height (e.g., 18 pounds left hand grip with 9 pounds of lateral pinch, and 14 pounds for the dominant right hand grip strength with 6.5 pounds for lateral pinch).

Muscle tone at rest was palpated and found to be normal when no active movement was initiated; however, with any degree of assisted or independent motion, severe tremors and fasciculations of the upper arm and forearm muscles were noted in each limb. Muscle tone was normal for the lower extremities, as were range of motion and strength, except for the quadriceps and hamstrings muscle groups, with difficulty standing from a stooping or semi-squatting position observed.

Bilateral gross and fine motor coordination was observed to be slow and rather labored for rapid and alternating motions of the forearms, wrists, and fingers. Isolated finger movements were very slow, requiring visual compensation to complete. Ocular motor skills were found to be within normal limits for range of motion and speed of visual skills; however, Mr. A's hand skills moved at a much slower rate than did his eyes, making eye-hand skills delayed. This translated to his writing skills, being very crowded and illegible with irregular flow, hastening rather quickly when a tremor was building in his forearm musculature. With printing and number writing, his legibility improved due to the ability to make shorter, more controlled strokes, allowing small rest breaks for the hand-to-forearm motions.

Sensation was found to be impaired for stereognosis or discrimination of objects by touch only and joint awareness or position sense for the wrists and hands, but intact for sharp/dull discrimination, light touch, and hot/cold perception for the rest of the upper and lower extremities.

- **Activities of Daily Living/Functional Status**: The following areas of self-care were assessed:

  Dressing Skills Independently performed using Taylor sitting for socks, shoes, and shoe fasteners.

  Feeding Skills Independent for hand-to-mouth motions; however, required assistance to cut meat unless very tender, open containers if not easily removable, and use of a lightweight plastic mug with a handle to secure grip for drinking and avoid dropping or spillage.

  Hair Care Independent with compensatory positioning using trunk flexion to reach top of head with lateral trunk flexion to comb sides.

  Oral Hygiene Independent with electric toothbrush with minimal loosening of collar to allow rinsing.

  Shaving Independent with modified positioning. By leaning against the bathroom wall to block hyperextension, Mr. A could release the front half of the collar enough to shave by his sense of feel. Since there are sensory deficits in his wrists and hands, this seemed rather risky, especially without use of the wall mirror that was on the wall perpendicular to the head supporting wall.

Toilet Transfers Due to his height, Mr. A experienced neck, shoulder, and back pains when coming to stand from a standard height toilet without adaptation, though able to perform independently.

Tub Transfers and Bathing Able to perform without assistance; however, Mr. A uses poor judgment in his hand placements for supporting himself when stepping into and out of tub. He places one hand/arm on the sink counter that stands at near end of shoulder reach, while the other holds onto a towelbar to step. Once one foot is into tub, the edge of the tub tile is "grasped" though no grab bar or true edge is available. For bathing Mr. A uses a soft collar, which he states he loosens briefly to wash the neck and reports he is able to shower independently by supporting himself in standing with the tile wall while flexing or leaning his trunk laterally to reach leg and foot lifted up. This is another area of questionable judgment and safety to consider in making equipment recommendations.

Chair and Car Transfers Again Mr. A is able to perform these independently; however, with strain to his neck, shoulder, and back areas from low surfaces.

Mobility In bed Mr. A uses a tubular cervical pillow in the supine or face up position with the front half of the hard collar removed. He replaces the collar front to turn himself or to stand from this lying position. Ambulation is independent without assistive devices inside the home or on even, familiar surfaces; however, on uneven or outdoor grounds and surfaces, he prefers to use a straight cane to assist with balance. Stairs and steps are performed independently with the use of railings or for only one to two steps; however, if there are a number of steps and he is unfamiliar with their size and placement, he requires contact guard or supervision and cueing to maneuver them safely due to his inability to look down to see them accurately. Driving to familiar locations, though one requires highway driving of greater than thirty miles distance, is performed in his four-door sedan with automatic transmission, bucket seats, one driver's side view mirror, and the standard rearview mirror. This, again, is another area of concern for judgment regarding safety since Mr. A is unable to turn or rotate his trunk to either side more than forty to fifty degrees to compensate for his inability to move his head and neck to scan side to side before making decisions for intersection entries and exits.

Homemaking Skills Areas of concern in this higher-level skill area for daily tasks were for cooking with the use of knives for food preparation and the sensory deficits; stovetop cooking with an inability to see accurately to look into pots, skillets, etc., and oven cooking in an overhead oven due to his difficulty with elevating his arms more than just briefly to remove or place a hot item into or out of the cavity of the oven to place on a counter or table with questionable vision. The cleaning, bed making, and a majority of the laundry tasks were performed either by his daughters or his wife, though Mr. A did use a stool to sit to transfer clothing from the washer to the dryer. He attempted to carry a basket of clothes to and from the laundry to the rooms; however, he was unable to sustain the hold due to tingling and numbness in his arms and hands with sustained holding.

Money Management and Bill Paying This has always been done by Mrs. A; therefore, it was not an area of concern for writing skills needed. Because his signature is illegible most of the time and extensive writing is not feasible with standard pens or pencils, this is an area of concern for written expression of other sorts.

Assistive Technology for Assistive Devices or Adaptive Equipment No equipment or devices were available in the home nor provided from previous rehabilitation services provided as per report by Mr. A, verified by his wife and case manager.

- **Architectural Barriers**: From the driveway to the front porch, a series of two short steps of only five inches in height for one and four inches for the other exist with a railing along each side of the steps. At the front door another step measuring six and one half inches high was evident. Because of his familiarity with his entryways, Mr. A has had no observable or reportable problems with maneuvering these steps. There are no steps at the back and side entrances into the home, and the interior doorways and furniture set-up are adequate since he is not dependent on a walker or wheelchair to ambulate (though he does use a straight cane outside on uneven surfaces to assist with equilibrium or balance and righting reactions).
- **Avocational/Leisure Status**: Mr. A enjoys playing cards and reading, though he is unable to do these activities due to his inability to hold his arms elevated for long periods of time; attending or watching spectator sports such as attending games of baseball, basketball, and football; attending church services and activities, and participating in a support group via his psychologist's office for other persons with orthopedic disabilities.

Projection of Occupational Therapy Needs

It was determined that Mr. A would require a period of home health occupational therapy services for education and training on self-care, leisure, and safety issues. Equipment needs for provision of home-based services are as follow: (Costs presume one time only unless otherwise noted.)

1. A slantboard to reduce reading and writing strain by supporting the upper body, preferably on an elevated surface to have Mr. A's hand level with his eyes. In addition the use of lightweight clamps to hold reading materials and a ledge at the base of the slantboard is recommended. **Estimated cost:** $175.
2. A gooseneck extension for a phone holder or the provision of a speaker telephone. The gooseneck may be the preferred choice to enable private conversations as desired without having to hold the mouthpiece by hand. **Estimated cost:** $85.
3. Enlarged or built-up handles for writing, cooking, and other utensils or hand tools to reduce the grip strength needed for sustained holding and greater control. In addition a right-angle rocker cutting knife with a serrated edge and an adapted cutting board are recommended, along with the use of prism lenses to look downward for chopping or other food preparation tasks and stovetop cooking as well. **Estimated cost:** $30 for five rolls of

foam tubing to be added to handles. Replace every two to three years. Rocker knife estimated cost: $35, replaced every 15 years. Adapted cutting board estimated cost $55, replaced every 15 years. Prism lens estimated $70.

4. Use of dycem with the daily in-home tasks to secure items on counters, food trays, tables, or other surfaces. **Estimated cost:** $45 for a 16″ by 2 yards per roll every 10 years.
5. A reacher for use in the kitchen, bath, or cabinets and closets to obtain items out of reach, especially in overhead positions. **Estimated cost:** $75, replaced every 20 years.
6. A portable, folding cart on locking casters for carrying items throughout the home to enable ease of performance with laundry and meal preparation tasks especially. **Estimated cost:** $55, replaced every 20 years.
7. Nonskid material on bathmats and throw rugs (preferably eliminated), as well as a surface coating on the steps outside the home to avoid slipping and potential falls, especially when wet. **Estimated cost:** $85.
8. A wall grab bar to improve safety for standing transfers into and out of the tub area, as well as a shower seat with a back for washing in a safer seated position; long-handled bath sponge to wash the legs and back, and hand-held shower spray to enable safe rinsing. **Estimated costs:** Wall grab bar, $35; shower seat, $75; long handled bath sponge, $20 each, replaced every 2 years; hand held shower, $55, replaced every 15 years.
9. A portable elevated cushion for seating that would offer lumbar and cervical supports that could be used in the home and/or the car. **Estimated cost:** $85, replaced every 15 years.
10. Adaptive convex mirrors placed on *bilateral* sideview mirrors, a panoramic rearview mirror or Panamirror, and possible use of side/fender or windshield frame mirrors to aid with visual compensation for scanning, reaction/response time for unexpected obstacles in peripheral fields, and decision making regarding intersection crossings due to poor head/neck and limited trunk motions. (In addition the use of four-way stops or traffic lights at intersections, low volume local routes in good daytime weather, and driving during daily schedules when low medication side effects were expected once routine is stabilized are also recommended.) **Allowance for the above:** $225. May replace when the automobile is replaced.

Outpatient occupational therapy was recommended to assess Mr. A's predriving and road performance capabilities. This will help to determine his potential to drive safely and independently using compensatory strategies and adaptive equipment for vehicular modifications as needed. In addition, physical therapy (or conditioning in a community fitness program) and an exercise physiologist was also recommended in order to strengthen his leg musculature to assist with squatting and stooping motions, which would be needed to compensate for limited upper body abilities. (Service costs not calculated).

Frequency and Focus of Treatment

Home-based occupational therapy was projected to be needed at a frequency of three times a week for a period of four weeks, reducing to two times a week for six to eight additional weeks to cover all areas outlined for activities of daily living retraining, work simplification, and energy conservation education and training, upper extremity strengthening, education on compensatory positioning with the use of assistive devices and adaptive equipment, and home program instruction. Outpatient occupational therapy would be needed for approximately six sessions lasting from three to five hours for the initial evaluation, to one- to two-hour sessions for the remainder of the visits for further road testing and/or training with anticipated equipment needs. These are anticipated to be such items as bilateral adaptive side view convex and possible fender mirrors with a panoramic rear view mirror, and a steering knob at the 7:00 wheel position, along with an adaptive seat cushion and head/neck support to improve positioning and comfort. **Estimated costs for therapy:** $85 to $100 per session/visit for home health; **for driving services, estimated cost** is 15 hours at $125 per hour. **Estimated cost for devices:** $385.

Discontinuation of Occupational Therapy Services

Once Mr. A was found to be safe and reliable for following a medication schedule, and for the use of assistive technology and compensatory strategies in the home, he could be discharged from home health occupational therapy services. Prior to discharge, however, client and family education would be needed to suggest that he continue to be monitored regarding his medication routine and the effects this could have on his driving safety. If Mr. A follows the recommended driving protocols established via a structured adaptive driving program to drive at intervals between certain medications to prevent significant side effects impeding his skills, as well as driving within given restrictions of low volume, daytime good weather times on familiar local short-distance routes, then discharge from outpatient occupational therapy services can be recommended. However, annual screenings by occupational therapy for overall activities of daily living, including driving status and compliance, should be continued for a period of three to five years to ensure the client's, his family's, and the public's safety. Should any significant changes in medications, physiological, and/or psychological status occur, then the wife should have the ability to contact the physician to order occupational therapy follow-up regarding the client's judgment for safety, especially with regard to his driving skills.

Cost Estimates

Because fees for service or charges vary among facilities and the use of an appropriate facility will be primarily based on the location relative to the client's home, costs cannot be accurately estimated without performing a market survey of the facilities and services available within the immediate surrounding areas. Once a suitable home health agency and outpatient facility have been identified that provide the recommended occupational therapy services outlined previously, the hourly or program fees charged by each of these services can be multiplied by the number of hours projected via the assessment performed to predict a more accurate total cost for occupational therapy services needed.

CONCLUSION

Occupational therapy is a health and rehabilitative profession that can serve a vital role in the development of a life care plan for an individual with a disability caused by illness or injury. Through the occupational therapist's expertise in activity analyses, clinical and behavioral observations, as well as formal and informal testing methods, an accurate assessment of a person's functional abilities with regard to activities of daily living, work and play or leisure skills can be obtained. As a team member assessing the global needs of a child, adult, student, client, or patient, depending on the setting, the occupational therapist brings to the life care plan a unique perspective into the realm of purposeful activities. Occupational therapy generally focuses on the client's functional independence, and adaptive activity performance using assistive technology or task modifications, as needed, to achieve the desired outcomes. Occupational therapy can serve as the link to productive living — the link that enables the person with a disability to live a safe and independent life to the fullest of his or her potential with the quality he or she deserves.

ACKNOWLEDGMENTS

Special thanks and much appreciation are extended to Ryan and Lorena McCaigue for supporting their mother and her efforts in writing this chapter, and to Vivian and Phillip Gammell for their emotional support, technical expertise, and assistance in compiling the text. To Chris Bosonetto-Doane, M.S., OTR/L, Elizabeth Garrett, Ph.D., David Goudelock, MA, CRC, CDMS, CCM, CLCP, Vicki Sadler, M.Ed., CRC, CDMS, CCM, CLCP, Michael J. Weeks, and Ray Wight much gratitude is expressed for offering objective feedback to help the reader acquire a clearer understanding of the intent of this chapter, as well as professional support and encouragement to its author.

REFERENCES

American Occupational Therapy Association (April 1986). **Dictionary Definition of Occupational Therapy**. Adapted and approved by the Representative Assembly, April 1986, to fulfill resolution 596-83. (Available from AOTA, 4720 Montgomery Lane, P.O. Box 31220, Bethesda, MD 20824-1220).

Angelo, J. & Lane, S. (Eds.). (1997). **Assistive Technology for Rehabilitation Therapists.** Philadelphia: F.A. Davis 211-240.

Dunn, W., Foto, M., Hinojosa, J., Schell, B.A., Thomson, L.A., & Hertfelder, S. (1994). Uniform terminology — third edition: Application to practice. **The American Journal of Occupational Therapy, 48(11),** 1055-1059.

Dunn, W. & McGourty, L. (1989). Application of uniform terminology to practice. **The American Journal of Occupational Therapy, 43,** 817-831.

Hinojosa, J., Sabari, J., & Pedretti, L. (1993). Position paper: Purposeful activity. **The American Journal of Occupational Therapy, 47 (12),** 1081-1082.

Low, J.F. (1997). NBCOT and state regulatory agencies: Allies or adversaries? **The American Journal of Occupational Therapy, 51 (1),** 74-75.

Weeks, M.J., Kniskern, J., & Phillips, C.P. (Winter 1997). **Dollars and Sense: A Guide to Solving the Funding Puzzle and Getting Assistive Technology in Georgia.** Atlanta, GA: "Tools for Life" Program Publication.

8

THE ROLE OF THE PHYSICAL THERAPIST IN LIFE CARE PLANNING

Art Peddle

INTRODUCTION

Physical therapists serve as facilitators of health. They treat the patients with a broad range of potential inputs from other professionals, family, and friends. An open mindset to any given patient and situation is crucial to the enhancement and facilitation of health. The treatment of signs and symptoms, pain, irritation, lesions, catastrophic injury, and dysfunction are given viable solutions from the unique perspective of balanced deliverance of effective physical therapy skills with the positive participation by the patient. It is vitally important to create a synergistic application of physical therapy with the patient's willingness to be responsible toward maximizing their health and function. Cooperation with all professionals, financial supporters, family members, and friends contributes to the overall facilitation of health.

The Life Care Planning Process

In dealing with life care issues, there are fundamental questions and paradigms of thinking to be asked of the physical therapist and others involved in the care of the patient or client, such as:

- What was the level of health, function, and lifestyle before the injury, disease, lesion, or dysfunction?
- What level of health, function, lifestyle can be achieved given the present status of the patient and his or her physiological, social, psychological, financial, and spiritual environment?
- What are the ideal, hopeful goals and plans, balanced with the real goals and plans?

1-57444-075-6/99/$0.00+$.50

The physical therapist and all persons involved in life care planning should integrate their plans with the following concepts being interwoven in their healthcare delivery process:

- "Seek first to understand, before you are understood." (Covey, 1989, p. 239)
- "Walk a mile in my shoes." (Song performed by Joe South)
- "Do unto others as you would have them do unto you." (Bible, p. 7)

As we examine life care goals and priorities for the patient, we are building a foundation of true principles to develop our skilled delivery of physical therapy. Therefore, we return the patient, as much as possible, to full health and function with basic human dignity, rights, and privileges. If full health and function are not attainable, then at the very least we should create a plan, delivery, and environment of highest quality and dignity of life, minimizing suffering and creating a door of hope for tomorrow.

Again, the attitude for delivery is based on how we would want to be treated in any given situation. This attitude counteracts selfish goals and stirs physical therapists to strive for the best scenario and outcome, for the goal is quality of life. This way of life care planning requires commitment to the process. It includes active responsibility and participation of both the physical therapist and the patient.

The Evaluation

The physical therapist has the unique capability of providing a large spectrum of evaluative techniques as well as of evaluative protocol. The evaluation process is a multilevel process. Full detailed evaluation processes can occur or various levels may be specifically requested, as well as being appropriate.

In the general areas of medical studies and patient situations, a physical therapist is presented with a variety of evaluative techniques. These include the areas of orthopedics, neurology, soft tissue dysfunction, wound care, sports medicine, industrial medicine, and catastrophic injury to specific and/or multiple areas. The physical therapist can also specify evaluative techniques by age groups, including pediatric, youth, adult, and geriatric populations. Besides the areas of physical dysfunction and areas of given diagnostic diseases, lesions, or injury, a comparative evaluation and preparation for return to life evaluations can be delivered. Evaluations that involve return to life skills, including activities of daily living (ADL), function, work-related skills, sports-related skills, and overall total life skills can be set up with the appropriate parameters in order to be specific or holistic in nature.

The evaluation process involves consideration of the adaptability of the patient and/or the circumstances in which the patient is placed. Evaluations can involve specific areas of spine, extremities, and body systems, as well as specific areas of dysfunction and/or injury. General areas of consideration and evaluation involve the following.

Intake Interview

1. Review the existing medical history and subjective information.
2. Interview the patient. This involves a general subjective overview including verbal input by the patient, type of injury, surgical history, disease process, and dysfunction. Other areas involved in subjective information include present job situation, activity level before and after injury, previous types of physical therapy received, and medical care received.
3. Psychosocial questions and interview are considered as they relate to the present dysfunction. Other professionals may have covered psychosocial issues, but it is always appropriate to establish a base line of understanding of other involved issues in the patient's dysfunction.

General Evaluation Input

The subjective information and input obtained from the client is established as the base line for other evaluation considerations. Pain evaluations using standardized questionnaires, as well as various tests, have benefits for cross correlation and reliability of "subjective" information. This essential base line data of pain characteristics assists in leading the therapist toward establishing present dysfunction, as well as potential for further dysfunction and/or other complicating factors.

General characteristic complaints of pain are to be established, such as:

1. The location, duration, and frequency of the pain.
2. The specific qualities of the pain — constant, intermittent, diffused, localized, sharp, numb, burning, dull, tingling, radiating, quick, and/or sustained.
3. Examples of specific pain (e.g., night pain, pain upon arising in the morning, pain throughout the day).
4. Clarify the pain intensity by using a scale — 0 being no pain and 10 being acute pain.
5. Examples of activities that increase pain and activities that decrease pain (e.g., sitting, standing, walking, lying, bending, massage, ice, heat).
6. Is the pain getting better, worse, or remaining the same?
7. What is the maximum length of time patient can perform any particular function, such as sitting, standing, walking, and driving?

Pain questionnaires should also reveal relationships between how much function the patient can perform and at what level the pain occurs, such as how much can the patient lift and carry?

Objective Evaluation

Objective evaluation will analyze basic functional activities, such as the patient's gait; sitting, standing, rolling activities; and appropriate supportive devices.

Observation of the basic structure of the anatomy, weight-bearing capabilities, and appropriate body landmarks are an essential part of this examination. One should note appropriate posture, compared to the correct anatomical position, and specific noted deviations.

Other observations should include:

- Basic soft tissue evaluation,
- Appropriate understanding of joint position,
- Intervertebral movement,
- Normal joint movement,
- Range of motion (ROM), and
- Cardinal planes, diagonal planes, and as functional planes.

Special tests can target specific examination of any given extremity or body part. These tests rule out various complications and evaluate appropriate function and dysfunction.

Other appropriate evaluations include:

- A **neurological exam** would include basic reflexes as well as appropriate strength measuring, with manual muscle testing and sensory examination. It should be noted that during the evaluation any cross correlation with a basic generalized assessment can be made with more specific evaluations, including: functional aspects of a work capacity assessment (WCA), functional capacity assessment (FCA), isokinetic, neurological, and balance testing.
- **Joint mobility evaluations** include the normal ROM, correct anatomical position, appropriate accessory movements, and physiological movements.
- **Soft tissue evaluations** include palpation of tissue, noting restrictions, trigger points, pliability, plastic, and elastic responsiveness. Evaluation of soft tissue and articular structures should include pain, irritation, and inflammation status. The functioning of soft tissue and joint structures as a synergistic pattern should be noted.
- **Basic postural and functional movement evaluations** include sit-to-stand and return, sit-to-supine and return, rolling to supine, side lying and return, overhead reach. Evaluation of functional positions and assuming positions, including the quality of movement as well as any centralization or peripheralization of pain, signs, and symptoms.
- Other palpation skills include muscle play, restriction, guarding, reflex contractions, soft tissue restrictions, trigger point, and/or referred pain. **Intervertebral movement evaluation** is based on a numerical scale set between 0–6, with 0 being anklylosed and 6 being unstable, and with 3/6 being normal. The intervertebral movement can also be classified as hypomobile, hypermobile, and painful. The general evaluation can be broad or specific.

Work Capacity Assessment (WCA) and Functional Capacity Assessment (FCA)

The terms *work capacity assessment* and *functional capacity assessment* are sometimes used synonymously. They can also be more definitive, with WCA being an evaluation used for base line of work capacities. The FCA would involve a more direct study of basic, functional activities of daily living (ADLs) with the potential of also evaluating work-related activities. The WCA/FCA can be done at the beginning, middle, and/or end of any treatment evaluation process, or as part of a total perspective of life care planning depending on what is needed. There can also be varying degrees of specific details in the WCA, since the parameters are determined by the physical therapist's understanding of the goals of the evaluation process. The WCA/FCA can occur during the initial stages of the life care planning process or can be extended throughout the span of the life care plan. Follow-up assessments are to upgrade and adjust the goals and plans for the patient, as well as to update the base line data for reevaluation. All physical therapy evaluations are done in coordination with other professionals and their evaluations. Integrating the results of other health professional's assessments into the physical therapy plan allows for a more holistic approach in achieving the goals for the individual patient.

There are a number of evaluative techniques in the areas of WCA and FCA that are effective and appropriate for any given situation in the life care planning process. According to Blankenship (1989, p.122), "the WCA or the FCA is an evaluation of physical capabilities and limitations as they relate to work, recreation, and ADL. It describes the optimum and maximal capabilities in terms of strength, endurance, related joint problems, fine and gross motor coordination, limiting factors and methods of functional and task performance." Therefore, in order to make a more accurate assessment, the WCA/FCA should involve measurements of different activities.

General areas tested in basic functioning are:

1. Lifting, which includes level lift, floor to table, and carrying;
2. Pushing to maximum tolerance;
3. Pulling to maximum tolerance;
4. Standing, sitting, and kneeling tolerance;
5. Bending, stooping, and squatting;
6. Walking, climbing, and balance;
7. Coordination activities, including the upper and lower extremity with gait analysis and gait function.

Activities of Daily Living (ADL)

Establishment of proper body ergonomics and posture during functional ADL, as well as work-related activities, is important not only in establishing and facilitating present health, but also in preventing further dysfunction and injury. It is important that ergonomics be applied in the evaluation process as a tool to determine the patient's capabilities (physically and mentally) in comprehending the issues of proper body mechanics. In the evaluative functional capacity/work capacity arena, proper ergonomics and posture will need modifications based on equipment handling capabilities and/or the use of adaptive equipment.

Functional aspects of ADL, such as personal grooming, hygiene, and dressing, are issues that are often considered in the FCA (also see Chapter 7). Areas of nutrition and speech can also be evaluated by a qualified physical therapist with appropriate training. Some aspects of the FCA, as well as other aspects of WCA, are often overlapped in the expertise area with the occupational therapist, speech therapist, recreational therapist, ergonomic specialist, and appropriate physician specialist. In any evaluative process, standard body mechanics are to be evaluated by the therapist during the lifting task portion, as well as basic functional activities task, in order to ensure the most advantageous body mechanics for handling basic ADL functions and work functions.

Evaluation for sports and other specific recreational skills need to be considered in the evaluative process. There is a correlation between functional skills, work skills, and sports or recreation skills. Collating these concepts provides for efficiency of movement, as well as promoting correct body function and health, within the parameters of the given dynamics of the patient's physical challenges.

Evaluation of body mechanics is crucial to determine potential for "wear and tear" on the patient. Appropriate alternatives, suggestions, and varying procedures and skills for handling any given dysfunction should be understood. Full comprehension of these procedures and skills will enhance the development of proper use of strength, as well as minimize irritation and pain. Also, with proper evaluation of the patient's present knowledge and skill, the need for further training or education can be developed. The role of the physical therapist from the basic evaluative process or WCA/FCA can essentially be refined or specified for any catastrophic impairment.

When performing the evaluative process and listing objective findings, substantial data are important to assist the delivery of health care to the patient. Gathering of data and information in the objective format also plays an important role in defending the patient's present situation and in presenting the plan for future services. Skilled assessment is vital in giving direction for the best possible outcome for the patient's return to health, as well as providing long-term care. It is appropriate to develop parameters allowing for changes in the patient's function and health and in the patient's environmental situation and basic home lifestyle. Adaptability and changes in preparing the patient for return to work or work activities is crucial in understanding the format for performing the evaluative FCA or WCA.

Isokinetic Testing

Isokinetic testing provides a technologically advanced approach to human performance testing, rehabilitation, and exercise. The test allows all major joints of the body including the upper extremities, lower extremities, and trunk to be evaluated and compared. Bilateral testing, as well as comparative testing, can differentiate between muscle groups in the isokinetic test. Isokinetic exercise is performed at constant speed throughout the range of motion. As the muscle applies force, it is resisted by appropriate proportional opposing force. Therefore, the speed of movement is kept constant. The isokinetic evaluation process and/or exercise provides an excellent means of qualifying many aspects of movement and function, including muscle torque, work, fatigue, ROM, and peak torque levels. As the sophistication of technology improves, more accurate and appropriate measuring devices will allow for basic data and parameters in which to assess body function. Again, the isokinetic test can be used in a cross correlation with functional measurements being taken, as well as manual muscle testing and basic lifting capabilities. This cross correlation can help define the patient's present level of activity and assist in determining symptom magnification and inappropriate illness behavior parameters.

Neurological Evaluation

As in the general evaluation given earlier, the neurological examination can be an expanded appraisal involving specific parameters. It involves specific emphasis on neurological and neuromuscular mechanisms of the body, including: muscle test and evaluations; sensory tests; functional and neuromuscular developmental sequencing and evaluations; and specific injury evaluations to the central nervous system or peripheral nervous system. Associated dysfunction as in gait, transfers, dressing, grooming, hygiene, sports, and work can also be neurologically evaluated.

Cardiovascular Fitness Evaluation

Cardiovascular fitness evaluations incorporate a range of specifically applied stress testing under the supervision of the physician and appropriate professionals, including a physical therapist. The cardiovascular appraisal is often involved in the FCA/WCA, which establishes a minimal level of conditioning protocol that could include treadmill, bicycle ergometer, and/or step climbing evaluations. All these tests have basic guideline parameters. Often a cardiovascular clearance evaluation is needed before other evaluations, WCA, and FCA can be performed. The pertinent physician or professional may give appropriate parameters under which the cardiovascular system may be stressed or tested.

Neuromuscular, Balance, and Coordination Evaluations

The neuromuscular skeletal function is evaluated in specific areas or systems and/or holistic body systems and functions. This evaluation can involve the study of the balance system of the body in relationship to gait and functional activities. Proper consideration for a proprioceptive feedback system in static and dynamic functional activities is measured. This evaluation can involve specific job activities, sports activities, and ADL with coordination, balance, and skill being integrated into foundation data. The criteria involve general standardized tests, as well as specific tests designed by the physical therapist to the given situation based on age, developmental sequencing, and specific goals of the functional or life care demands.

Gait Evaluation

Gait evaluation involves specific general evaluation of the patient's ambulatory status in a variety of environment situations. Consideration for adaptive equipment, tools, and prosthetics are part of this evaluative process.

Evaluation Recommendations

The role of the physical therapist as a facilitator in health care is to treat, train, condition, and assist in the direct structure and setting of goals for the patient. Basic communication to the patient, family, professionals, and financial parties serves as a primary directive of achieving the life care planning process. It should be understood from the physical therapist's point of view that his or her establishment of feedback into the life care planning process is crucial in developing a long-term solution for the patient's care. Proper structured treatment, evaluation, follow-up physical therapy, and training involves clear communications among the professionals involved so that all forms of facilitation are utilized.

The Lifelong Physical Therapy Plan

An attitude of openness and understanding should be the goal while preparing the patient for the highest level of independence. This same directive should be applied when providing options for those who will need long-term and/or lifelong physical therapy. Examples of this attitude and structure are as follows: a patient who is in need of a wheelchair and is dependent upon the wheelchair for most of his or her life will develop other dysfunctions. Sometimes there is greater wear and tear on the upper extremities, cervical, neck, thoracic, and spine, due to having to handle a greater load of total body function in the upper extremities and upper trunk and neck areas. It is important to understand that lower extremities that are not functioning do not provide support and therefore cannot be used in functional skills. This greater demand of activity and function is placed on the remaining working cardiovascular, neuromuscular, and skeletal systems. Patients or clients are susceptible to greater breakdown of all involved systems and/or structures. Effective planning involves addressing the immediate dysfunction in preparing the patient to develop a higher level of independence and future preparation. It should also be understood that the patient would in all probability have an increased ratio of wear and tear factors and greater susceptibility to further lesions and insult in their remaining systems and structures.

The dysfunctional areas of the body and mind will still need suitable care and support. These would include areas of strength, ROM, hygiene, wound care, tissue function, and basic vascular and neurological functional considerations. Sometimes injured areas become hypersensitive, even though not functional. Phantom and referred pain can occur in the dysfunctional area.

As in any treatment and/or evaluation process, the therapist should be open-minded and aware of any new studies and/or opportunities to increase the function and promote the facilitation of health in the injured area. This especially applies for adaptive equipment. The progressive use of equipment, awareness of advanced technology, and the foresight to predict need are essential. For example, a lower-level tetraplegic patient would require a primary electric wheelchair for basic ambulating. However, there are occasions in which an additional manual wheelchair would provide the patient with a variety of sitting postures, back-up to the power chair, and an opportunity for the wheelchair to be used as a piece of exercise equipment. The manual wheelchair provides an excellent source of exercise potential and/or opportunity for the patient to develop some control and direction in ambulating.

Thoughtful modifications and supplements to the patient and the given situation, with appropriate equipment, should be considered for both short-term and long-term care. This allows the physical therapist and the life care planning team to develop a "full" perspective in returning the patient to the highest level of independence and an appropriate, dignified lifestyle. Motivating, encouraging, and challenging the patient to use equipment and supportive devices is part of the evaluative, training, and treatment process.

Financial considerations include original equipment, maintenance, modifications, and replacement equipment. All these factors are to be considered over the patient's life span. As the patient changes and various challenges are presented, considerations for equipment should be appropriate to the life care plan and goals. Financial support for equipment and the evaluative process should be based on the highest goals and principles presented.

Physical Therapy Treatment

In the life care planning process, an evaluation establishes the base line for treatment throughout the process. In many situations, specific treatment by the physical therapist is required and involves not only therapy, but also ongoing evaluation. Physical therapy treatment may involve seven basic categories:

1. Education
2. Conditioning
3. Physical medicine treatment
4. Function-specific and ADL-specific treatment
5. Occupational and industrial physical therapy
6. Sports physical therapy
7. Total life relationship skills and integration treatment

Education involves an emphasis on ergonomic principles applied to posture, body mechanics, and essential principles for carrying out assisted or independent programs of conditioning, strengthening, ROM, and functional care. Education in ADL, functional, sports, and work-related skills is delivered to all parties involved. It is important that these skills are developed in the patient's real world setting and that there is ample opportunity to implement them in an appropriate manner — with supervision, leading toward independence as base-line goals. The appropriate support of professionals and family members in the real world setting will require adaptive thinking.

Establishment of specific patient potential in any given area needs to be determined and understood by the patient and team members. An understanding of the patient's situational lifestyle, critical work demands, task analysis, functional activities, and recreational plans is important. The patient's understanding of educational information presented and the development of a functional delivery by the patient in handling basic nonmaterial ergonomics and/or essential material handling ergonomics should be considered. Material handling and nonmaterial handling ergonomics is not just a matter of work-related issues, but also of functional ADL and the total environment.

Integration into the whole aspect of the patient's life care with the life care planning team on an as-needed and program-developmental basis will be required. This will probably require the physical therapist to coordinate with the patient/client, other professionals, and family members to follow through with essential concepts of physical therapy education.

Conditioning involves aerobics, cardiovascular, and physiological conditioning. It should be noted that in conditioning, appropriate adaptations to the patient's/client's needs will be made and evaluated, as well as developed into a working solution by the physical therapist. Strengthening, which will incorporate specific muscle dynamics, will be used to increase strength levels for performing functional activities, work activities, sports activities, and ADL. Specific areas of strengthening can involve techniques in cardinal and diagonal planes, which can involve singular movements and/or multidirectional movements. The physical therapist has at his or her disposal the use of many strengthening techniques, including isometrics, isotonics, isokinetics, plyometrics, and proprioceptive neuromuscular facilitation (PNF). Strengthening could involve rotational, multidirectional facets to prepare the patient for a variety of lifestyle situations. Mobility, stretching, and flexibility categories are used synonymously to describe appropriate mobility exercises to ensure basic principles of full functional ROM in both physiological and accessory patterns. Using balanced concepts of strengthening without strain or further injury is of vital importance in designing a program specific to the individual patient and situation.

The integration of all conditioning factors with functional skills, ADL skills, work skills, and sports skills should be considered and integrated into life care planning. Specific neuromuscular, balance, and coordination activities allow the integration of the central nervous system and the peripheral nervous system to handle ADL, functional, work, and sports activities. Ballistic and dynamics are stresses to be applied to prepare the patient to handle a variety of velocity forces and changes that occur in any lifestyle situation. This can involve specificity of training at various speeds and various levels of physical performance.

Physical medicine treatment includes the use of appropriate medications, modalities, manual therapy, and specific exercises. Physical therapy medicine is used for basic signs and symptoms, which may include pain management, wound care, and improving function. Physical medicine includes the areas of specialized program development or treatment that could include relaxation techniques, weight control, and appropriate uses of supportive devices, equipment, and braces.

Function-specific and ADL-specific treatment are specific treatment programs the physical therapist can use to encourage increased functional capabilities, such as in gait, transfers, personal hygiene and grooming, speech, and general ADL.

Occupational and industrial physical therapy involves the process of creating a situation in which a patient/client may progress from a beginning level of handling any job task to the actual performance of the job. The job-specific program can involve a program starting in the clinic and being transferred to the on-site job location. Work hardening, work conditioning, and work start are synonymous terms to describe this process.

Sports physical therapy involves the direct relationship of physical therapy in establishing appropriate conditioning and training, structure, and protocol. This skilled development of parameters and goals creates an atmosphere that develops independent training techniques, as well as independence to continue higher levels of sport or sports-specific performance.

Total life relationship skills and integration treatment involves the physical therapist working with the patient, family, and total environmental in developing a workable plan structured for assisting the patient in facilitating their full health at the highest level possible. This total life care integration involves a coordination of all previous physical therapy treatments and evaluations with the potential for upgrading, changing, and adapting any given treatment plan and program.

Exit Program and Care Resolution

Preparing the exit program involves a combination of compiling all previous evaluations, treatment, data, and observation processes in communication with the associated team members to arrive at a conclusion of the involvement process in the patient and/or client. During the exit program, appropriate recommendations and post-discharge plans are made from the physical therapist's point of view with preferred sequencing, as well as post-discharge plans for status to returning to full lifestyle situations. Options and variations of any program, as well as reentry into a program are open for consideration, as is proper application of newly found situations.

Follow-up care resolution is a broad category involved in interpreting the appropriateness and efficacy of the evaluative and treatment process from the patient's perspective. It also involves the physical therapist's perspective in the areas of physical ergonomic integration into basic life, concepts of preventative physical medicine, appropriate concerns for future update and recheck, and any issue of compliance. This involves a process of communication between the patient and all team members in restoring the patient to the highest level of function, and a dignified lifestyle.

Symptom Magnification

Symptom magnification or inappropriate illness behavior is an issue that is present in the life care process and involves many complications and issues. Physical therapists, as well as other professionals, have attempted to arrive at appropriate systems tests and evaluative procedures for giving appropriate feedback and baseline data to establish appropriate behavior in any given situation. General considerations for inappropriate illness behavior and symptom magnification are behaviors that are out of proportion to the impairment. It should be understood that symptom magnification is a behavior that is improper but does not implicate a reason or motive for that behavior. Furthermore, it should also be understood that there could be a psychosocial basis for some behaviors that do not necessarily originate from a physiological or organic basis.

In determining symptom magnification or inappropriate illness behavior it should be understood that there are often degrees and levels at which it is expressed. Some of these levels are extreme and can impede the appropriate fair process of assisting a person to achieve a healthy lifestyle. In addition, there are forms of symptom magnification that exist on a low level that are intrinsic to basic lifestyle teachings. Therefore, appropriate considerations for establishing objective information, as well as objective treatment, require skill and appropriate consultation from the team of life care planners and associated professionals.

If the physical therapist is involved in the identification of the type of symptom magnifier, which could be classified in the areas of an experimenter, a refugee, a game player, and psychogenic type of magnification, appropriate consultation with the appropriate professional should be performed and used (Blankenship, 1989). Appropriate test questionnaires and scales administered by the physical therapist, or previously by associated professionals, can be considered as part of the evaluative process. It should also be noted that in understanding, evaluating, and commenting on appropriate and inappropriate illness behavior one should have an open mind and be alert to cross correlation factors in the evaluative and the treatment processes.

An example of this would be a patient being asked to perform a cardinal plane ROM by lifting their arm over their head, but the patient states or demonstrates that they cannot lift their arm above 70° of shoulder flexion. Then when asked to take their shirt off, they are able to demonstrate taking their shirt off over their head, thus demonstrating their ability to flex their shoulders above 100° or more of shoulder flexion. Cross correlation of specific evaluative techniques and functional techniques assists in determining the reliability and validity of the patient's status. In communicating this information, the physical therapist should use the words "the data presents itself." Another way to express performance is to use the words "the patient demonstrated (this or that)." Therefore, the therapist avoids conjecture and judgment when communicating.

Physical Therapy Charges

Basic rates in physical therapy for services rendered are wide and varied. Each profession and professional has their requirements and their specific insights into delivery of any evaluation and/or treatment process. The following numbers are given as a broad perspective and are estimates for considering lifelong life care planning issues, and are subject to change with all basic life situational economics, as well as specific professional demands.

- Basic physical therapy treatment and conditioning range from $60 to $150 per hour.
- General evaluative techniques, depending on the extensiveness of the techniques, range from $60 to $700.

- These techniques could involve a beginning basic physical therapy evaluation of $60 (average charge) to more specific exams running $200.
- WCAs and FCAs range from a modified WCA/FCA costing $200 to a more extensive WCA-FCA costing $700.

Again, there is such a wide variety in pricing, it is best to be specific to the physical therapist involved in the analysis, evaluation, and treatment processes to determine the best life care planning situation. As in other life care planning areas, considerations for "how would I like to be treated" and what is fair should be a basis for appropriate structuring for financial reimbursement.

Establishing a Knowledge Base

The physical therapist should establish an appropriate information system in order to accomplish the following:

1. provide a means of examining the specific case issues as a professional;
2. establish appropriate correlations between injury and patient types;
3. establish appropriate protocol for returning the patient to their lifestyle and life situation;
4. establish appropriate modifications for further patient assistance and/or study.

CONCLUSION

The role of the physical therapist is vital in life care planning. There exists the opportunity to facilitate good health, to minimize suffering and pain, and to restore patients or clients to the highest functional level of life. The experienced physical therapist is capable of being an effective leader and director of life care planning. The physical therapist, as a responsible leader, accepts the challenges of encouraging responsibility in the patient and team members. When participating in the life care planning process, if the physical therapist seeks to apply the principles of "seek first to understand before you are understood" (Covey, 1989, p. 239) and "do unto others as you would have them do unto you" (Bible, p. 7), the outcome will be an integration of the spiritual and physical worlds. This philosophy offers an appropriate balance of structure, goals, and priorities to enhance the life care planning paradigm.

Acknowledgments

The author wishes to acknowledge all the educators, mentors, associates, and work professionals, as well as friends and family who have contributed in the past to my profession as a physical therapist. Some of the material in this chapter was based on readings from Polinsky Rehabilitation, Keith Blankenship's **Industrial Rehabilitation**, Health South's Rehabilitation, Gordon Cummings, Stanley Paris, and John Barnes. This chapter seeks to introduce the general population of professionals who are involved in life care planning with a general overview of insights to physical therapists and their role in the life care planning process. It encompasses information I have read and received from a variety of sources, integrating those ideas and resources with my experience and opportunities in providing life care planning in the past and present. There are many excellent sources of further specific details, evaluations, and treatments available to those concerned. It is of vital importance that we apply our skills, training, and knowledge with appropriate understanding balanced with growth.

REFERENCES

Barnes, J. (1989). **Myofascial Release Treatment.** (Available at Myofascial Release Treatment Center, Rt. 30-252, Suite 1, 10S Leopard Rd., Paoli, PA 19301.)

Blankenship, K. (1989). **Industrial Rehabilitation.** Athens, GA: American Therapeutic.

Covey, S. (1989). **The Seven Habits of Highly Effective People.** New York: Simon & Schuster.

Mathew. (1956). **Holy Bible**, King James Version. Cleveland, OH: World Publishing Company.

Polinsky Medical Rehabilitation Institute. (1983). **Functional Capacity Assessment.** (Available from Polinsky Medical Rehabilitation Institute, 530 East 2nd Street, Duluth, MN 55805.)

9

THE ROLE OF THE SPEECH-LANGUAGE PATHOLOGIST AND ASSISTIVE TECHNOLOGY IN LIFE CARE PLANNING

Carolyn W. Watkins

INTRODUCTION

Individuals with communication disorders present complex, confusing, and often frustrating challenges to the life care planner. Communication in itself is an abstract concept, defined by brain-monitoring technology, well-done differential diagnoses, and an ability to understand normal and dysfunctional human speech and language. The person who is best qualified to evaluate and make recommendations in this specific area of speech and language is the speech-language pathologist. The area of study is more accurately referred to as communication sciences and disorders, which includes speech-language pathology and audiology.

Although we are currently approaching the threshold of the second century of neuroscience, we have embarrassingly little information about how speech and language are created and comprehended in the normal human brain, and our understanding of how those processes can be disrupted is also extremely primitive. To a large extent, this predicament results from severe technological limitations on the study of human anatomy and physiology that have prevailed until fairly recently. Either techniques have been too invasive for use with human subjects, or, for those less invasive techniques (conventional electroencephalography), the information generated is difficult to interpret, particularly with regard to normal function.

Improvements in computers during the last two decades have significantly enhanced our ability to study aspects of human anatomy and physiology otherwise inaccessible (e.g., deep structures of living brains), and to consider sophisticated experimental questions (e.g., the temporal course of neural function and the

1-57444-075-6/99/$0.00+$.50

nature of individual differences). Thus, in many ways these techniques have placed us on the threshold of the first century of "human neuroscience."

This information is significant in the process of life care planning because it allows life care planners the critical, and now more measurable, information to make projections about disability related to the communication disorders, as well as in providing thoughtful input into the long-term medical, educational, clinical, rehabilitative, psychosocial, recreational, vocational, and technology needs of the individuals. This also mandates that the life care planner carefully identify the speech-language pathologist for the life care planning process to ensure that they demonstrate the basic knowledge and skills necessary to provide irrefutable information that will stand up under scrutiny from other team members in the life care planning process, as well as from other medical, legal, and funding sources.

This chapter will discuss the role of the speech-language pathologist and the areas of training and preparation needed to demonstrate the advanced level of knowledge and skills necessary in this area of communication sciences and disorders in life care planning. Qualifications and credentials of a speech-language pathologist are reviewed, along with the assessment process, funding and economic considerations that impact on the area of speech-language pathology. Neurolitigation considerations for the speech-language pathologist expert are discussed in the second half of the chapter. The whole concept of taking a role in the life care planning process is a newer consideration for the speech-language pathologist, who provides an integral part in the development of the life care plan for individuals with communication or swallowing deficits. The credibility and complexity of this area is just beginning to be recognized, as well as the impact that deficits in this area have on cognition, technology, future work and education, independence, and psychosocial issues.

The Role of Speech-Language Pathologist in Life Care Planning

The purpose of a life care plan is to identify the comprehensive and individualized needs of a person as it relates to a disability and/or chronic illness with relevant associated cost considerations. These "needs" are the operational components of a life care planning process. These needs should never be compromised or manipulated. The costs assigned to these needs are determined by the geographical consumer rate for the identified services and/or equipment. The costs can be developed through understanding the range of available funding streams, creative and innovative ways of negotiating and resources, and the cost projection analyses that accompany such planning.

The speech-language pathologist must be well-grounded in the theory of normal development in all ages, in any previous learning or developmental problems affecting the individual, and in the current status of the individual, and must be able to predict future functioning of the individual. Many times speech-language pathologists will practice in the treatment of either the pediatric or the adult population. This frequently precludes the speech-language pathologist from being able to look backward or beyond to make accurate recommendations about future functioning needs.

It is always useful for the speech-language pathologist who is consulting in the life care planning process to be able to be actively engaged in the clinical treatment of individuals and their families. This enhances their credibility, because the speech-language pathologist should have realistic estimates of current needs and prognostic predictions. However, it is also imperative that the consulting speech-language pathologist have a fluid understanding of the current literature and research that directly or indirectly impacts on the area of communication sciences and disorders. This includes a knowledge of cutting edge assessment procedures, state of the art assistive technology (Appendix 6), trends in pharmacology and medical care, and possible needs in the areas of residential and geriatric care.

The Intake

The speech-language pathologist must perform his or her own case intake, consisting of talking with the referral source, determining the time frames needed, arranging the financial and billing agreements, and arranging for a release of all pertinent information. Additional testing needed may be identified at this time or during the initial interview arrangements.

The speech-language pathologist will then review a copy of the medical records to include:

- Nursing notes
- Doctor's orders
- Other services' reports
- Educational information
- Vocational information
- Day-in-the-life videos
- Other relevant documentation, depending on the etiology and diagnosis

A thorough assessment battery is then administered, including gathering information from the spouse, family, or other relatives, including the clients themselves. This step may also include the opportunity for the speech-language pathologist to consult and interview other team members whose information may have a bearing on recommendations of the speech-language pathologist and on the final outcome. At this time, if additional medical, clinical, vocational, or educational information or evaluations are needed, requests for these additional information-gathering steps should be submitted to the referral source. A letter may be composed outlining the correct questions with supporting data to ensure that the speech-language pathologist has the opportunity for soliciting the needed information.

At this time the speech-language pathologist must be able to provide a written report, documenting the test results, observations, and conclusions with clear recommendations. These recommendations must be clear and detailed, including projection of future care costs, frequency of service or treatment, duration, base cost, source of information, and recognized vendors or manufacturers, current prices, collaborative sources, and categories of information. It is recommended that the consulting speech-language pathologist be knowledgeable about the local sources and costs of these recommendations, either through direct contact with suppliers or through catalog and desktop/computerized research. Recommendations from the speech-language pathologist should be discussed with the client and family, treatment team members, and other team members if they directly impact on the final recommendations and the cost analysis of the plan by the economist. Any coordination and agreement needed between team members including the economist should occur at this time. A draft of the communication sciences and disorders assessment and recommendations report should be written and distributed to the life care planner for review relative to the accuracy and completeness of the information. The speech-language pathologist must be able to explain, from a life care planning perspective, the reasons and rationales that are relative to their recommendations. These must be "lifelong" recommendations and objectives, developed in an integrated format. Once the document is correct and complete, a final draft should be compiled and distributed to the life care planner and the referral source. It should be determined, by these two parties, whether the written documentation should be sent to other internal (life care planning team members including the family and client) and external individuals (Appendix 1).

Training and Preparation

The competent speech-language pathologist (SLP) has received preparation in the following areas, as they relate to human communication, swallowing, and development across the life span. This is a person who is knowledgeable in the following areas:

- Theories and processes of normal development and aging, including motor, cognitive, social-emotional, and communication.
- Physiology of speech production and swallowing, including: respiration, phonation, articulation, resonance, and the vocal/aerodigestive tract.
- Embryological, genetic factors in development, including the development of craniofacial structures and nervous system.
- Anatomic structures, neuroanatomy, and neurophysiology supporting speech, language, hearing, swallowing, and respiration.
- Organic etiologies of disorders of communication and swallowing.
- Psychological and psychosocial influences on communication and swallowing.
- Neurolinguistic, linguistic, cultural, and social influences on communication.
- Theories of speech perception and production, language development, and cognition.
- Ethics related to diagnosis, treatment, and professional conduct.
- Basic computer theory and systems applications, including frequently used software and input and output devices, as they relate to evaluation and treatment of language and communication, augmentative and alternative communication (AAC), and swallowing.
- Interpersonal communication, human learning, counseling theories and practices; and family systems and systems theory.

The speech-language pathologist who is consulting on a life care plan may need to be able to demonstrate an advanced knowledge and understanding of health care and educational facility practices; the common diseases and conditions affecting human communication, swallowing, and development across the life span; and their medical, educational, surgical, and behavioral treatment, including knowledge of:

- Medical terminology
- Physicians' orders, confidentiality, legal issues in medical practices, and information and data systems management
- Elements of the physical examination and vital sign monitors
- Medical and laboratory tests and their purposes
- Medical record documentation practices
- Pharmacologic factors affecting communication and cognitive processes, development, and behavior
- Assistive technology, augmentative and alternative communication approaches, and the range of bioengineering adaptations used in medical settings
- Concepts of quality control and risk management
- Concepts in medical setting environmental safety (such as universal precautions procedures and infection control principles, radiation exposure precautions, and the Safe Medical Devices Act)
- Team processes
- Performance improvement processes
- Theories, concepts, and practices in outcomes measures
- Theories and concepts related to the impact of psychosocial and spiritual needs and the individual's cultural values on health care services
- Voice and laryngeal health and disorders
- Respiratory functions, tracheostomy tubes, and respiratory support requirements
- Neuroanatomy, neuropathology, and the neurophysiological support of swallowing, speech, language and related cognitive abilities, and the effects of diseases and disorders of the nervous system
- Concepts in human nutrition and hydration needs and their disorders
- Methods and interpretations in neuroimaging and other forms of anatomic imaging
- Esophageal, oropharyngeal, laryngeal, and neurologic tumors
- Concepts in neuropsychology and psychiatric and psychosocial disorders
- Common medical conditions
- Educational terminology
- Federal mandates related to education
- Broad understanding of curricula and literacy
- Educational philosophy of state education agencies
- Medical and surgical management of communication and swallowing

The speech-language pathologist should be able to demonstrate advanced skills and abilities in diagnostics, treatment, and service delivery. They should be able to review medical records and conduct succinct clinical case histories and interviews, gather relevant information related to communication and swallowing, and select and administer appropriate diagnostic tools and procedures and treatment for communication and swallowing disorders that are functionally relevant, family-centered, culturally sensitive, and theoretically grounded.

The SLP should be able to:

- Obtain a representative sample and describe articulation and voice production in meaningful, accurate, and reliable terminology that addresses intelligibility and the audio-perceptual judgments of quality, tension, pitch, loudness, variability, steadiness, oral and nasal resonance, and severity of the disorder.
- Interpret a range of acoustic and physiologic measures of voice production.
- Demonstrate skills in instrumental assessments (acoustic, aerodynamic, electroglottographic, electromyographic, manometric, and ultrasonic measures).
- Apply techniques that ensure validity of signal processing, analysis routines, and elimination of task or signal artifacts.
- Use one or more techniques for imaging the larynx, vocal tract, and nasopharynx, (flexible/rigid endoscopy, ultrasonography, or stroboscopy).
- Select and implement training and treatment procedures appropriate for speech prostheses and orthotics (tracheoesophageal puncture prosthesis, electrolarynges, speaking trachs and one-way valves, palatal lifts, voice amplifiers, voice output communication aids, obturators and palatal agumentation prostheses).
- Conduct an oropharyngeal swallow examination accurately identifying abnormal structures and functions, identify symptoms, medical conditions and medications pertinent to dysphagia; interpret and document examination findings; use instrumental techniques for screening and diagnosis of orpharyngeal dysphagia and for biofeedback in dysphagia management.
- Conduct reliable and accurate modified barium swallow procedures following a standard protocol that includes identification of structural abnormalities, swallowing motility disorders, presence, time and etiology of aspiration, and appropriate treatment techniques (posture, maneuvers, bolus modification).
- Determine patient management decisions regarding oral/nonoral intake, diet, risk precautions, candidacy for intervention, and treatment strategies.
- Select and appropriately apply aided and unaided communication including both linguistic and not linguistic modes and methods.
- Locate and access assistive technology, services, and funding sources.
- Work effectively with interpreters and translators and use assistive listening devices when needed for patient care.
- Communicate findings and treatment plans in a manner that is fitting and consistent with health care facility procedures.
- Counsel and educate patients and families and work within family systems to elicit participation in the treatment plan and work as a member of a health educational care team.

The speech-language pathologist will need to consider all of the following categories, regardless of the age of the individual, in the development of information for the life care plan. These categories include an oral and pharyngeal swallowing (dysphagia) assessment to include modified barium swallows, videostroboscopy evaluation, prostodontic intervention, and palatal prostheses, cognitive communication information, auditory processing information to include central auditory processing, augmentative communication assessment information, assistive technology assessment information, voice and vocal information including videostroboscopy, and botox assessment information, oral peripheral motor information, hearing acuity information, assistive listening device and/or cochlear implant information.

The critical information obtained from a thorough communication sciences and disorders assessment must be considered within all the parameters of the life care plan itself. In other words, any and all areas that are impacted upon by deficits in communication and swallowing, must be addressed with recommendations, if deemed appropriate by the evaluating speech-language pathologist. These parameters include projected evaluation, projected therapeutic modalities, diagnostic testing and educational assessment, mobility (including accessories and maintenance of mobility technology), aids for independent functioning, orthotics and prosthetics, home furnishing and accessories, pharmacology needs, home/facility care, future medical care, transportation, health and strength maintenance, architectural renovations, potential complications, orthopedic equipment needs, vocational/educational planning, assistive technology in the areas of sensory deficits, cognitive challenges, and communication disorders to include hearing and processing difficulties needing assistive listening devices (see Appendix 2).

Qualifications and Credentials of a Speech-Language Pathologist for Life Care Planning Purposes

The generally accepted national standard for practice in speech-language pathology (communication sciences and disorders) is the American Speech and Hearing Association (ASHA) Certificate of Clinical Competence in Speech-Language Pathology (CCC-SLP). The ASHA CCC-SLP requires a master's degree in speech-language pathology, completion of a one-year clinical fellowship experience, and passing the national examination. For states with licensure, the legal right to practice will vary with the individual licensing acts. Most licensure laws were modeled after the ASHA CCC standard. These individuals may hold additional credentials through their state education agency. Often, the state education agency requirements do not equate to the national standard, requiring only a bachelor's degree and education certification in that state to practice. Speech-language pathologists with specific interests may hold additional certifications determined by societies and organizations interested in developing credentials to define expertise in a particular area, such as RESNA, Special Interest Divisions of ASHA.

When funding is available, third party intermediaries in most instances require the ASHA CCC and licensure. The national certification standards are generally tied to the ASHA CCC for both funding by third party intermediaries and for service delivery while other certifications in existence such as the education agency certification, traditionally do not equate to the CCC. If you are not familiar with an individual and their credentials, it is wise to contact ASHA and the state licensing board to determine their credentials. It is also important to note that licensing laws usually relate to direct patient assessment and treatment in the state where the service is provided, but do not address review of records or expert testimony. The national certification is a generic certification whereby the individual has met the *minimum* entry level requirements across a broad spectrum of knowledge areas in communication sciences and disorders. When funding is available, third party intermediaries use as a guideline the requirements for service delivery established by Medicare and Medicaid (i.e., ASHA CCC-SLP), and where applicable, a current state license.

Speech-language pathologists who have the expertise to provide information in their area must also understand and participate in transdisciplinary integrated assessment and treatment models, have a knowledge of funding streams and creative funding, are knowledgeable about state and federal policy, laws, and changes in these laws and policies, and are knowledgeable of collaborative sources and how to build them. They must also be able to provide clear, concise, understandable documentation that is written in a defensible but understandable format with functional milestones and goals available. For a complete communication assessment and many of the services related to delivery of care for individuals exhibiting communication and swallowing difficulties described in this chapter, it is advisable that the consulting speech-language pathologist hold a doctoral level degree with emphasis in the areas of assistive technology.

Terminology in the Field of Communication Sciences and Disorders

The importance of terminology relative to our communication with other professionals and the general public, as well as the very special needs of international and transdisciplinary communication and development, has become increasingly apparent. In addition to improved consistency in the use of terms, there is the need to carefully examine what meanings the jargon that is developing may have to other individuals who rely primarily on a dictionary and common sense. Although many people in the field may know what is meant by a given term, others may not share the same meaning. Some terms used by many people in one country may not easily translate into other languages. Even more apparent, with the diversity of people in the world today, care must be exercised to consider multiple interpretations of a term, sometimes affected by the perspective of one's culture.

Because of the transdisciplinary nature of the medical-legal-clinical world, there are also problems of various disciplines using other jargon to describe essentially the same phenomenon, act, and/or characteristic. These problems reflect the need for an emerging field like life care planning to develop an internally consistent and logical terminology that will facilitate the international and transdisciplinary development of the field. It is important to actively educate individuals on the life care planning team concerning specific terminology that defines and describes areas of assessment and treatment within the field of communication sciences and disorders.

Assessment Process

There are four methods of gathering and interpreting quantitative and qualitative information about the client that should be used in the communication sciences and disorders assessment process by the speech-language pathologist. These four measures are a collection of the initial database, interview procedures, clinical assessment, and formal assessment procedures (Dunn, 1991). Often more than one method is used to gather information about the same aspect of a client's skills and abilities, the context, the activity, or the use of technology or equipment. Information collected should include the reason and need for referral, medical diagnosis, and educational and vocational background information. This information is collected during the referral and intake phase and its purpose is to provide preliminary data for planning the assessment. The interview takes place during the identification phase as a means of gathering information regarding the consumer and his or her needs. It is important that the consumer, family members, rehabilitation or education professionals, and other care providers be interviewed.

Formal assessment procedures are administered in a prescribed way and have set methods of scoring and interpretation. Therefore, they can be duplicated and analyzed. They may or may not be standardized. Clinical assessment techniques involved skilled observation of the consumer and are used throughout the assessment process. These techniques may be structured so that a series of steps is followed to determine specific skills or it may be intentionally left unstructured to see what takes place. Observation can be done during a simulated task in a clinic setting or in a context familiar to the consumer such as a classroom or workplace. Differential diagnosis is an ongoing and essential component of the assessment process and one that requires an advanced level of understanding and perspective about the trauma or injury.

Pediatric and Adolescent Assessments

Evaluating children (pediatric and adolescent) presents complex and challenging issues, complicated by the catastrophic nature of the disease, disability, or trauma and frequently challenged by the almost insurmountable task of planning a child's life. For these reasons, it is critical to make accurate and thorough projections and careful analysis of the disability; educate team members and caregivers about the pediatric disabilities; and develop a differential diagnostic therapeutic approach to service delivery to the child. The checklist of pediatric and adolescent considerations in the communication sciences and disorders assessment is lengthy, detailed, and can be complex. This author affirms that this list is not all inclusive, but rather changes as research and science give us additional opportunities and areas to address with children in being able to give prognostic predictions and a fluid plan for a growing child or adolescent.

There are areas that warrant consideration when performing a communication evaluation for a pediatric or adolescent individual that are not considered, or at least not in the same detail, when evaluating an adult. Chronological age and pretrauma development are used as the normal benchmarks against which to measure the disability issues. Routine medical needs must be addressed to the pediatric specialists who would provide the information that impacts on a child's communication development. These include pediatric physiatry, otolaryngology, pediatric neurology, developmental medicine, audiology, dental/orthodontic, prosthodontist, and pediatric neuroophthalmology and ophthalmology. It should be noted here that there is a trend in the medical specialty fields to identify specialists who work solely with adolescents. Additional cognitive and educational information is gathered from the following sources:

- Educational consultants to private and public educational programs,
- Personal caregivers and attendants,
- Pediatric neuropsychological assessment,
- Occupational and physical therapy,
- Vision and hearing specialists,
- Evaluators of driving,
- Programs for the development of social and pragmatic skills,
- Prevocational and vocational training programs.

Individuals with Disabilities Education Act (IDEA)

It is timely to discuss, at this point in the chapter, the Individuals with Disabilities Education Act (IDEA), which is the law that requires that all children with disabilities, birth to age 22, receive a free, appropriate public education (FAPE) including special education and related services. Because of its broad language, IDEA is often interpreted differently from state to state and district to district. Therefore, the Department of Education, Office of Special Education Programs (OSEP) often provides policy interpretations, guidance, and applications of IDEA's provisions. Many of these documents issued by OSEP providing guidance and policy interpretation are directly related to the provision of assistive technology services and devices.

Recently, OSEP has issued several letters reflecting policy interpretations and guidance that included affirmation for schools to provide assistive technology services and devices, including hearing aids (01/13/95, 12/22/94, 11/19/93, and 08/10/90) and permitting assistive technology devices purchased by schools to be used at home (11/27/91). In these interpretations OSEP states that when an IEP team meets and determines that a student requires assistive technology to receive FAPE, and the use of such device or service is written into the student's IEP, then the device, according to IDEA, must be provided at no cost to the student, and the device may be taken home if necessary. In another letter providing clarification on a school's liability for a family-owned device (08/09/94), OSEP determined that in many cases it is reasonable for public agencies to assume liability for family-owned assistive technology devices used by students.

In its policy interpretations, OSEP has made it clear that assistive technology devices and services are to be provided to students at no cost if written on their IEP in order to meet the requirements of FAPE. However, there has been some confusion among consumers about the provision of technology services or devices. IDEA requires the provision of "appropriate" devices and services and the term "appropriate" does not necessarily equate to the most costly or advanced piece of technology. Therefore, when considering technology services and devices, audiologists and speech-language pathologists must consider costs, features, flexibility, compatibility, the functional needs of the student, and so forth. Then, with supporting documentation, the speech-language pathologist will make technology device and service recommendations. It is important for speech-language pathologists who enter into the life care planning process to understand key provisions and policy interpretations, as well as how those may or should impact on their recommendations. It is also important to understand the rules and regulations of the federal and the state mandates and initiatives, to be able to effectively draw up these mandates to develop support and cohesive recommendations that are fiscally and economically sound.

Funding and Economic Issues

There are a variety of financing and funding options for services and technology needs that a qualified speech-language pathologist would recommend for support in the life care planning process. It is the consulting speech-language pathologist's responsibility to understand where and how to access this information on collateral funding sources. These include public programs such as maternal and child health, education, vocational rehabilitation, developmental disability programs, department of veterans affairs programs, and older Americans act programs. There are alternative funding sources such as loans, libraries, foundations, and charitable organizations, as well as understanding options under the U.S. tax code, and the issues of civil rights, universal access, and telecommunications (Appendix 3).

Information on current initiatives and emerging promising best practices related to the funding and the acquisition of technology and services is also available and should be considered in the development of the life care plan for the areas of speech-language pathology and assistive technology. Knowledge of policy and funding information adds credibility and strength to this portion of the life care planning process. Frequently, recommended technology and services in the areas of communication sciences and disorders/speech-language pathology are costly and require a lengthier and more complex plan of treatment than some other areas of the plan. If the consultant in this area can show his or her ability to understand and develop funding options and plans, the success of this portion of the plan is strengthened. The speech-language pathologist who is involved in the life care planning process must have a current and accurate analysis of the marketplace with regard to the cost of services and technology or other goods needed in their portion of recommendations in the life care process. This also directly relates to potential policy changes in health care and education that may directly affect specific recommendations in the areas of communication sciences and disorders.

Neurolitigation

Following the development of the complete life care plan by the life care planner, it is possible that the plan will become part of neurolitigation. Success in neurolitigation frequently depends on the quality and quantity of expert evidence, which directly relates to the presentation of the life care plan, especially during medical malpractice cases, and traumatic brain injury and spinal cord injury cases. Courts may admit the life care plan into evidence and rely on those plans as the predicate for compensatory damage awards when a well-qualified rehabilitation specialist prepares those plans. Included should be a list of treatment interventions that are reasonable and necessary and that show the real need for the individual to incur the expenses noted in the plan, and accurate, reasonable, and conservative costs for future care. Speech-language pathologists participating in the life care planning process need to appreciate these requirements and understand their possible role in neurolitigation. It is possible that the consulting speech-language pathologist will have to give testimony in a deposition concerning their areas within the life care plan, or may be considered as expert witness if the case goes to trial. The speech-language pathologist will be responsible for answering questions and explaining his or her portions of the life care plan.

Regardless of particular knowledge, skills, experience, training, or education, the expert who is able to clearly articulate his opinions and conclusions, who understands the dynamics of the litigation process, and who comports with common sense techniques for presenting testimony is the expert the attorney wishes to use to advance his or her client's cause. Obviously, the expert must be both professional and knowledgeable in their demeanor and appearance, must be familiar with the various types of rehabilitation programs and therapeutic services available, must possess an in-depth knowledge of the current literature, and understand and be able to explain intervention strategies employed at all levels of treatment. Being able to explain the complexities involved in extremely specialized fields of expertise, without appearing to condescend to lay jurors, is particularly important.

The following is a list of general considerations that speech-language pathologists who function as experts for the purpose of explaining their part of the life care planning process should espouse.

1. Tell the truth. Then you will not have to remember what you said.
2. Phrase your answers with care. Be conscious of what they will look like in black and white.
3. Answer only the question asked; do not volunteer information.
4. Do not answer a question that you do not understand. It is not up to you to educate the examiner, and if he misuses words common in your profession, do not explain distinctions or ask questions as to what he means; it is up to him to formulate an intelligible question.
5. Do not guess, speculate, or assume anything. You only "know" what you have seen or heard; there is a difference between what you "know" and whether you "have information" concerning a particular subject.
6. Do not be positive about a subject unless you are; it is no crime to fail to remember or to be vague if that is the truth.
7. Do not adopt the examiner's phraseology or conclusions. If the question contains a false assumption ("Isn't it true that all communication tests are conducted in this manner?"), or terms that are not precisely correct ("So you *frequently* performed this treatment for this patient?"), point out the language you do not wish to accept and stick to the facts. Beware of questions that start with "Isn't it fair to say…", or that attempt to paraphrase or summarize your previous testimony on a particular point.

8. Do not explain the manner in which you reached your answer, because such invariably involves other facts concerning which you have not been asked.
9. Do not testify concerning a document that is an exhibit until you have read it over thoroughly. Do not discuss documents that are not exhibits unless specifically asked about them, and then do not be positive about their content unless you are certain of your answer. Make no assumptions about documents.
10. Never get upset, explain, or argue with the examiner. You are liable to say things that are not correct, and in any event, it is not your duty to help him in this task.
11. If an objection to a question is made by counsel who retains you, listen very carefully, as it may provide information as to some underlying snare.
12. Avoid small talk, levity, ethnic or derogatory slurs of any kind, and even the mildest obscenity. Better to come across as formal than as a nonserious or offensive person.
13. If at any time during the deposition you realize you previously said something that was a mistake or incorrect, correct the error as soon as possible. Should this realization arrive after the deposition has been completed, you should make such correction on the errata sheet that will be supplied to you at the time you are asked to sign off on the deposition as transcribed.

Presentation of testimony by selected members of the rehabilitation team in litigation can be of immense benefit to counsel, the court, and lay jurors in furthering the understanding and costs associated with present and future needs, care and treatment, and in providing a framework on which an insurer or jury can justify a substantial settlement or award. One's abilities to be effective in this regard are aided by a clear understanding of one's role as an expert witness and the ability to interact with others and clearly articulate one's specialized knowledge in the areas at issue, placed in the context of a full understanding of the dynamics of the litigation process and an awareness of the techniques of proper presentation.

CASE STUDY

RE: Merrie Chrismoss

Disability

The client reportedly experienced asphyxia at birth and has cerebral palsy which mildly impairs her ability to control her extremities and possible mild brain dysfunction which may impair her ability to learn. At the time of the interview, she was 2 years and 9 months of age. She did not demonstrate a functional ability to speak but was alert and responsive to the environment.

A complete series of tests was administered including cognitive and oral-motor (results will not be included in this brief example) evaluations appropriate for her age and the child clearly appeared capable of participation in speech and language therapy. The rehabilitation plan below was part of a comprehensive life care plan; however, only the appropriate topics for the speech-language therapist are included.

Partial Rehabilitation Plan

Recommendation	*Dates*	*Frequency*	*Expected Cost*
		Medical Needs	
Swallow study with videofluoroscopy	1994–2014	Yearly to 10/97 then at age 16 and age 22	$400
Otolaryngologist	1994–1998	Yearly to 1998 then optional depending on complications	$200 (est.)
Nutrition consult	1994–2014	Yearly to age 6 then at ages 14 and 22.	$50 each
Drooling medication	1994 to life expectancy	Daily	$100/yr. (est.)
Optional pulmonology	Only if complications	Unknown	Unknown
		Home and Accessories	
Environmental control unit	1994 to life expectancy	Replace every 5 yrs.	$640 + $50/yr. maintenance and updates
		Assistive Technology Supplies/ Equipment	
Augmentative communications (AAC)	1994 to life expectancy	*Evaluation:* 1 X yr. through school and every 5 yrs. specialty evaluation begin 1997. *Devices:* Replace every 7 years from 1997 to life	$0 for school $1,500 evaluation $2,000 now $6,000–7,000 1997 and every 7 yrs. thereafter
Wheelchair mount and latching system for AAC	1994 to life expectancy	When power wheelchair is replaced	$1,200
Power pack for AAC	1994 to life expectancy	When wheelchair is replaced	$595 for power chair $400 for manual
Summer AAC camp in lieu of summer therapy	1995–2017	Yearly	$2,000 plus $1,000 (est.) for transportation
Speech and language therapy	1994–2014	Weekly	$0 provide by school system. Also see education.

Partial Rehabilitation Plan (continued)

Recommendation	*Dates*	*Frequency*	*Expected Cost*
		Education Related	
Adapted education program	1998–2014	Public school schedule	No additional cost
Work/study station in home (school to provide equipment and software for education program)	1998–2014	Update 2004, 2014	$1,000 (1998) $2,000 (2004) $8,000 (2014)
Computer, printer, oversized monitor, initial operating software and setup	1994 to life expectancy	Replace every 5 yrs.	$2,700 + $50/yr. switches
Specialized software	1994 to life expectancy	Yearly	$2,000 1994 then $500/yr.
Multiphone for AAC	2002	1 X only	$300
Technical support/engineer	1998–2014	1998, 2004, 2014	$1,200 (1998) then $300 in 2004 and $300 in 2014

CONCLUSION

The opportunity to participate in the life care planning process should not be taken lightly. It is one of the most rewarding parts of the profession of speech-language pathology for this author. It requires professionals who are respected among their peers for their hard work, diligent study, research, data collection and use, expert testimony, and even their ability to explain their results and information in written form. Standards must be placed on what the industry expects from its consultants when the consultants provided strong, useful assessments and recommendations. It is time for life care planners to set a level of accountability, responsibility, and recognition for the consultants that they use to develop the communication and swallowing areas of the life care plan, and it is time for speech-language pathologists to empower themselves for this process.

REFERENCES

American Speech–Language-Hearing Association. (Spring, 1996). Guidelines for the training, credentialing, use, and supervision of speech-language pathology assistants. **ASHA,** (Suppl. 16), 21-34.

American Speech-Language-Hearing Association. (1996). **Strategic Plan for Credentialing Speech-Language Pathology Assistants.** Rockville, MD.

American Speech-Language-Hearing Association. (1996). Scope of practice in speech-language pathology. **ASHA, 36** (Suppl.16), 12-15.

American Speech-Language-Hearing Association. (1994). Code of ethics. **ASHA, 36** (Supp. 13), 1-2.

American Speech-Language-Hearing Association. (1993). Preferred practice patterns for the professions of speech-language pathology and audiology. **ASHA, 35**, (Suppl. 11), 25-26, 27-28, 49-50, 51-52, 61-62, 87-88).

American Speech-Language-Hearing Association. (1991). Augmentative and alternative communication. **ASHA, 33,** (Suppl. 5), 8-12.

American Speech-Language-Hearing Association. (1989). Competencies for speech-language pathologists providing services in augmentative communication. **ASHA, 31,** 61-64, 107-110.

Dunn, L. & Dunn, L. (1991). **Peabody Picture Vocabulary Test** (revised ed.). Circle Pines, MN: American Guidance Service.

Venkatagiri, H. (1996). The quality of digitized and synthesized speech: What clinicians should know. **American Journal of Speech-Language Pathology, A Journal of Clinical Practice, 5**(4), 24-28.

Appendix 9.1 Communication Sciences and Disorders/SLP Assessment Process

1. ***WHO*** is a "qualified" speech-language pathologist for life care planning purposes?
   A. Training, licensure, certification, and practice settings
   B. Ability to network
   C. Integrated transdisciplinary model
   D. Knowledge of funding streams and creative funding
   E. Knowledge of state and federal policy, laws, and procedures
   F. Knowledge of the development of collaborative sources
2. ***WHAT*** will a "qualified" speech-language pathologist need?
   A. Review of all pertinent medical, vocational, educational, pharmacological, sociological information
   B. Differences between a staff speech-language pathology evaluation and the type of data needed to support a life care plan and to support the medical legal challenges
   C. Time needed to complete a communication sciences and disorders assessment
   D. Understanding of related professional information and how it impacts and affects the speech-language information and plans
   E. An ability to understand future trends and their application to the life care plan
3. ***COMPONENTS*** of a communication disorders assessment
   A. Oral and pharyngeal swallowing (dysphagia) assessment to include modified barium swallows, videostroboscopy evaluations, prostodontic intervention, and palatal prostheses
   B. Cognitive communication information
   C. Audiological information to include central auditory processing information
   D. Augmentative communication assessment information
   E. Assistive technology assessment information
   F. Voice (to include videostroboscopy, botox assessment information, etc.)
   G. Oral peripheral motor information
   H. Hearing acuity information
   I. Assistive listening device or cochlear implant information
4. ***WRITTEN*** documentation prepared in a defensible but understandable plan with functional milestones and goals
   A. Ability to determine lifelong goals and functional outcomes
   B. Ability to understand how to develop services and technology needs over time
   C. Ability to explain how decisions within other areas of the life care plan will impact on assessment, treatment, and technology needs within the communication sciences and disorders part of the plan
   D. Ability to explain present data in terms of future impact

Appendix 9.2 Communication Sciences and Disorders: Checklist for Life Care Planning

___1. Does the funding source understand the purpose and usefulness of a complete evaluation from a speech-language pathologist?

___2. Check qualifications, credentials, and areas of expertise of the speech-language pathologist you have selected to provide the information.

___3. Does the speech-language pathologist understand the concepts of the "life care planning" process, and how the information provided by them will be used?

___4. Is the speech-language pathologist aware of the professional content areas within communication sciences and disorders that must be included/considered in the report to the life care planner?

A. Expressive language
B. Receptive language
C. Cognitive communication
D. Oral and pharyngeal dysphagia
E. Augmentative communication
F. Assistive technology
G. Hearing and auditory processing as it relates to communication
H. Voice and voicing aspects
I. Fluency and rate

___5. Can the speech-language pathologist provide the results in a timely manner that meets deadlines?

___6. Has the speech-language pathologist been provided access to all available and necessary records including medicals, educational, vocational, and specialized testing?

___7. Is the client and family available for a thorough test battery? Are there access restrictions?

___8. Once information is gathered, is the speech-language pathologist able to provide thorough written documentation with clear recommendations?

___9. Have the questions in the following areas been considered during the communication sciences and disorders assessment?

Evaluations/assessments

____ Have all the necessary assessments in the areas of communication sciences and disorders (language, speech, swallowing, augmentative communication, assistive technology, hearing, central auditory processing, videostroboscopy, modified barium swallow studies) been considered?

____ When will reassessments be scheduled?

____ At what ages or levels of functioning will these reassessments (or additional assessments) be considered?

Therapy

____ How will necessary therapies be identified?

____ How will collaborative sources be used?

Assistive Technology

____ How will technology recommendations for augmentative communication be integrated with other assistive technology recommendations or other assistive technology that is already present?

____ Consider the use of low and high technology to include wheelchairs, environmental controls, vision equipment, hearing aids, computers, adaptive aids, assistive listening systems.

____ Have maintenance schedules, maintenance contracts, extended warranties, and replacement schedules been considered?
____ What is the range of assistive technology that is needed?
____ Have the following been considered: computers, means of access, size of screens, assisted listening, low technology communication needs, high technology communication needs, memory aids, swallowing program equipment, necessary software, ancillary battery power, systems to integrate augmentative communication with computers for complete system development, adapted phones, variety of synthetic and digitized voices, amount of memory needed in computerized systems, positional items for mounting and portability?

Home Furnishing/Accessories
____ How will assistive technology within the existing home and environment be included?
____ Have probable vs. potential environmental changes been considered?

Drug Supplies and Needs
____ Is there a need for medications for saliva control?
____ Have all pharmacological interventions been recommended for motor control (ataxia, tremors, etc.), for memory enhancement, for seizure control?
____ Have potential "side effects" of drugs or pharmacological intervention plans been considered in relationship to all areas of communication, swallowing, or auditory processing? These drug recommendations directly impact on treatment recommendations and must be aggressively considered in the plan.

Future Medical Care
____ What annual evaluations will be needed?
____ What specialties will need to repeat the evaluations for specific treatment needs and recommendations?

Potential Complications
____ What complications could potentially occur as a result of poor treatment or no treatment in the areas where recommendations have been made?
____ What complications in speech, language, swallowing, communication, cognitive communication, oral motor, hearing, processing, could occur with this etiology during the life span?

Vocational Planning
____ How will communication, hearing, and language/speech recommendations as well as augmentative communication and assistive technology recommendations integrate with vocational plans and needs at this time and in the future?

Educational Planning
____ How will communication, hearing, and language/speech recommendations as well as augmentative communication and assistive technology recommendations integrate with educational plans and needs at this time and in the future?
____ What systems and equipment are available within educational programs (primary, secondary, and post-secondary)?
____ Is the software appropriate for cognitive needs and projections in the future?
____ Have specialized camps, summer training programs, specialized preschools, and specialized short-term programs for upgrading and improvement as well as further training needs in the future been considered?

___10. Is the speech-language pathologist able to explain from a life care planning perspective, the reasons and rationales relative to the recommendations?

___11. Does the speech-language pathologist understand how to develop "lifelong" recommendations and objectives? an integrated plan?

___12. Is the speech-language pathologist able to give detailed specifications in the written documentation that allows the life care planner, the ability to develop life care plan specifics (i.e., vendors, dates, current prices, specific individuals, collaborative sources, categories of information)?

___13. Once the draft of the life care plan is complete, is the speech-language pathologist furnished a draft for careful review relative to the accuracy and completeness of the information?

___14. Is the speech-language pathologist aware that the data collection and analysis (evaluation) information may be presented to an insurance carrier, in testimony through deposition, or at a trial?

Appendix 9.3 Funding and Financing

Public Programs

Medicaid and Medicare

Required and Optional Services
Intermediate Care Facilities for Persons Who, are Mentally Retarded (ICFs/MR)
Early and Periodic Screening, Diagnosis and Treatment (EPSDT)
Section 2176 Home and Community Based (HCB) Waivers
Community-supported Living Arrangements

Maternal and Child Health

Maternal and Child Health Block Grant
Children with Special Health Care Needs
Special Projects of Regional and National Significance (SPRANS)

Education

Individuals with Disabilities Education Act (IDEA) State Grants (Part B)*
IDEA: Programs for Infants and Toddlers with Disabilities and Their Families (Part H)
State-operated Programs (89-313)
Vocational Education
Head Start

Vocational Rehabilitation

State Grants
Supported Employment
Independent Living Parts A, B, and C

Social Security Benefits

Title II: Social Security Disability Insurance (SSDI)
Title XVI: Supplemental Security Income (SSI)
Work Incentive Programs

Developmental disability programs

Department of veterans affairs programs

Older Americans Act programs

Alternative Financing

Revolving Loan Fund
Lending Library
Discount Program
Low-interest Loans
Private Foundations
Service Clubs
Special State Appropriations
State Bond Issues
Employee Accommodations Program
Equipment Loan Program
Corporate-sponsored Loans
Charitable Organizations

Funding Options through Private Insurance

Health Insurance
Workers' Compensation
Casualty Insurance
Disability Insurance

Funding Options through the U.S. tax code

Medical Care Expense Deduction
Business Deductions
Employee Business Deductions
ADA Credit for Small Business
Credit for Architectural and Transportation Barrier Removal
Targeted Jobs Tax Credit
Charitable Contributions Deduction

10

THE ROLE OF THE AUDIOLOGIST IN LIFE CARE PLANNING

Vic S. Gladstone, Larry Higdon, & Roger O. Weed

Audiology is the independent health profession that is involved with the study of hearing and disorders of hearing. An audiologist is the hearing health-care professional who is educated and trained to evaluate and treat individuals with hearing, balance, and related disorders. Within life care planning, the audiologist may be involved in a variety of pediatric and adult rehabilitation efforts. Although many clients are hard of hearing or deaf due to genetic or natural aging factors, there are occasions where services are needed due to undiagnosed meningitis, injuries to the brain, environmental noise, or reactions to medications.

Services provided by audiologists include the ability to:

- Test and diagnose hearing and balance disorders
- Select, fit, and dispense hearing aids and assistive devices
- Provide aural (re)habilitation services
- Educate consumers and professionals on prevention of hearing loss
- Participate in hearing conservation programs to help prevent workplace-related and recreational hearing loss
- Consult for federal, state, and local agencies in reducing community noise
- Conduct research

These services are available in the following work settings:

1. Colleges and universities
2. Public and private schools
3. Hospitals
4. Community-based hearing and speech centers
5. State and local health departments
6. Private practices
7. Rehabilitation centers
8. Nursing care facilities

1-57444-075-6/99/$0.00+$.50

9. Industry
10. State and federal governmental agencies
11. Military

Audiology can be categorized based on either the setting in which one practices or the population one serves. The various specialty areas of audiology have been described in the following manner (Bess & Humes, 1995). The **pediatric audiologist** concentrates on the audiologic management of children of all ages. The pediatric audiologist is often employed in a children's hospital or a health care facility primarily serving children. The **medical audiologist** works with patients of all ages and is more concerned with establishing the site and cause of a hearing problem. Medical audiologists are typically employed in hospitals as part of either a hearing and speech department or a department of otolaryngology (i.e., ear, nose, and throat). Some audiologists who work in a medical environment perform intraoperative monitoring, which involves monitoring central and peripheral nerve function during surgical procedures. The **rehabilitative/dispensing audiologist** focuses on the management of children or adults with hearing impairment. Rehabilitative audiologists are often seen in private practice and specialize in the direct dispensing of hearing aids. Rehabilitative audiologists are also employed by a variety of health care facilities (e.g., hospitals and nursing homes). The **industrial audiologist** provides consultative hearing conservation services to companies whose workers are exposed to high noise levels. The industrial audiologist may be in private practice or work on a part-time basis. The **forensic audiologist** is involved in legal issues related to audiology. The forensic audiologist may serve as an expert witness for the plaintiff or defense in compensation cases and may also serve as a consultant in community or environmental noise issues. Finally, the **educational audiologist** serves children in the schools and is employed or contracted by the educational system. Many audiologists, not just those in academic environments, engage in basic and applied research that is not only essential to understanding human auditory function but necessary in order to develop testing materials and procedures and improved amplification systems.

BASIC AUDIOLOGIC PROCEDURES

When you refer a patient to an audiologist you may expect certain basic procedures to be conducted. These include a pure tone hearing test, speech audiometry, and acoustic immittance procedures. Of course, these may be modified depending on the age or level of cooperation of the patient.

Pure Tone Testing

An audiologist using an electronic device called an audiometer measures hearing. An audiogram is a graphic representation of hearing. It relates intensity (loudness) as a function of frequency (pitch). Frequency, measured in Hertz (Hz), is plotted along the abscissa and intensity, measured in decibels (dB), is plotted along the ordinate. For a simplistic explanation of the various sounds and definitions of hearing loss, See Fig. 10.2.

A person wears earphones and the audiologist presents tones at varying frequencies and intensities for each ear. When the individual hears the tone, he or she

Figure 10.1 Audiology Specialties. Source: Bess, F. & Humes, L. (1995). Audiology: The Fundamentals (2nd ed.), p. 7. Baltimore, MD: Williams & Williams. Reprinted by permission.

responds by raising his or her hand. When the tone is heard at the lowest intensity level two out of three times, the audiologist records this intensity level for each frequency on the audiogram. This level is called threshold. Thresholds for the left ear are plotted with a blue **X** and thresholds for the right ear are plotted with a red **0**.

Normal hearing is considered to be between -10 dB HL and 15 dB HL. The example audiogram indicates normal hearing in the left ear and a hearing loss in the right ear.

The area enclosed by the two wavy lines is called the "speech banana." This area represents the frequencies and intensities of spoken English and assists the audiologist in explaining how a hearing loss may affect a person's ability to understand speech. In the example audiogram, the person will not be able to hear speech sounds above 1000 Hz in the right ear because their thresholds are out of the "speech banana." Were this person to have this degree of hearing loss in both ears, they may be expected to have difficulty understanding high-frequency speech sounds such as/*s, f, th, p, t, k, sh, ch*/, for example. In addition, they may be expected to have considerable difficulty understanding conversational speech in the presence of background noise such as in a cafeteria.

Audiograms are very important because they can indicate whether a person has a hearing loss and also the type and degree of loss they have. There are three types of hearing loss: conductive (a problem in the outer or middle ear), sensorineural (a problem in the inner ear or the 8th cranial nerve, which carries the auditory signals to the brain), and mixed conductive and sensorineural loss.

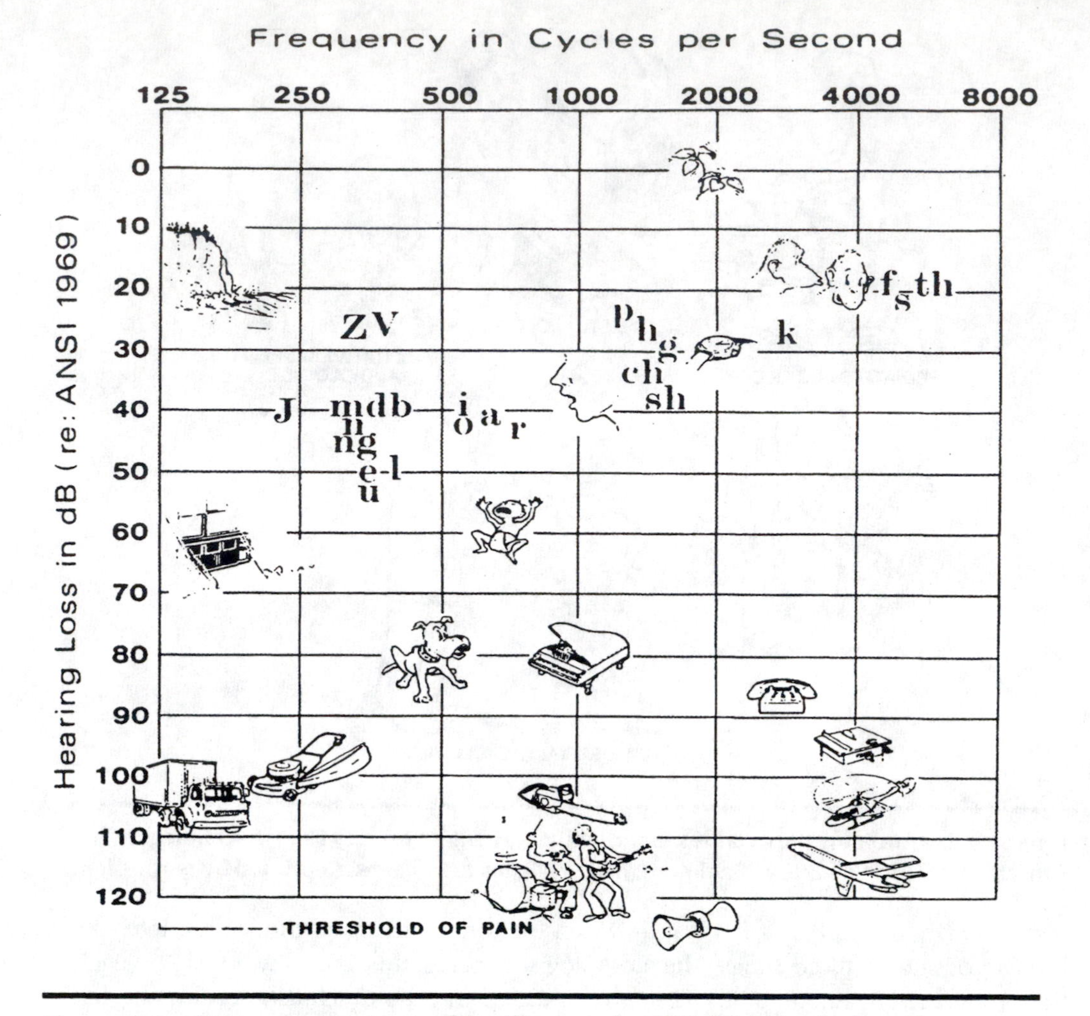

Figure 10.2 Frequency spectrum of familiar sounds plotted on standard audiogram. Source: Northern, J. & Downs, M. (1991). Hearing in Children (4th ed.), p. 17. Baltimore, MD: Williams & Williams. Reprinted by permission.

SPEECH AUDIOMETRY

Audiologists also test how well a person can hear and understand speech. This type of testing is called speech audiometry, which consists of speech threshold and word recognition or speech discrimination testing. Speech threshold testing determines how soft a speech sound a person can recognize, whereas word recognition testing tells the audiologist what percentage of conversational speech is correctly identified at a particular intensity level. One method of obtaining a word recognition/speech discrimination score is called the Articulation Gain Function (or Performance Intensity/Phonetic Balance Function). This method assures that the patient's maximum score possible will be identified.

Most people understand conversational speech excellently at approximately 40 dB above their speech threshold. The evaluator starts by presenting the speech level at 40 dB above the patient's speech threshold and reading a list of 50 single syllable words with the person instructed to repeat back each word.

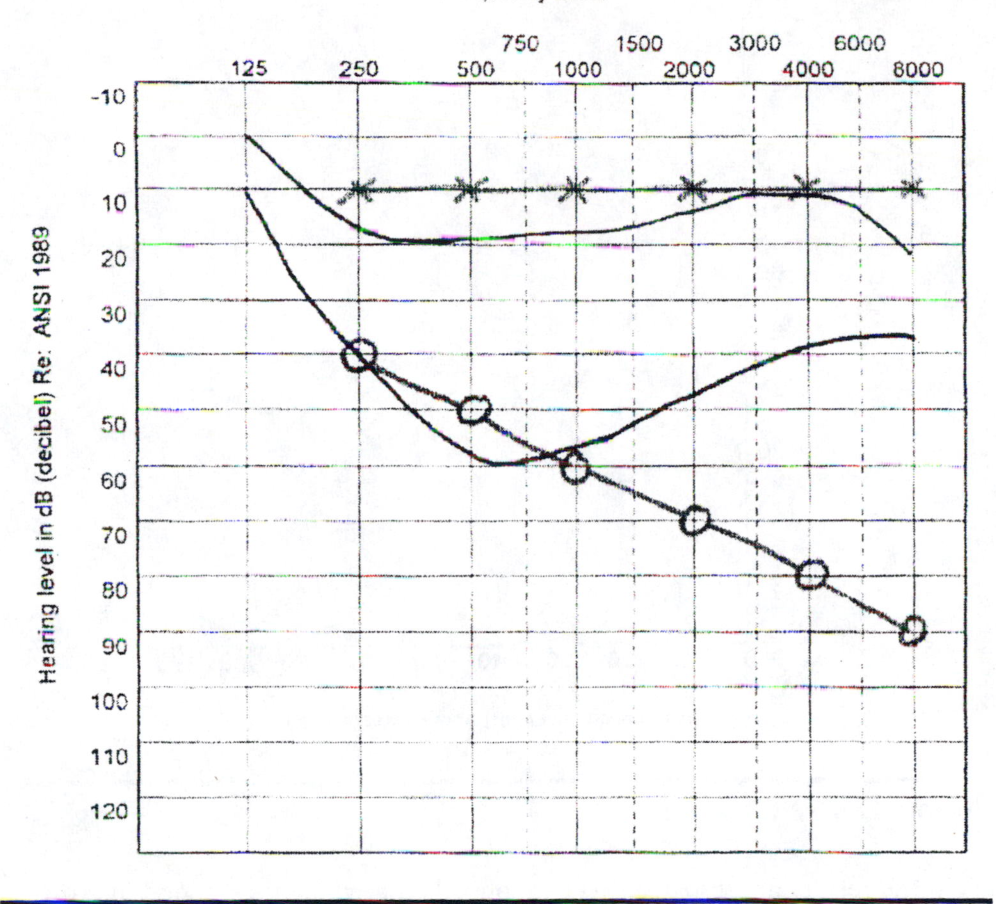

Figure 10.3

The percentage correct score at 40 dB above their threshold is then plotted. If 100% correct is not achieved, the test is repeated using a similar list of words at 50 dB above the person's threshold and that score is plotted. This procedure is repeated until their best score is obtained. The score in the example graph indicates that the person will understand speech 90% of the time as long as it is 60 dB above threshold.

Acoustic Immittance

Acoustic immittance measures tell an audiologist about the mobility of the middle ear system. The middle ear is basically a vibratory system consisting of the eardrum and the three middle ear bones: the malleus, incus, and stapes. The middle ear is responsible for transferring the acoustic energy (sound) from the outer ear to the fluids in the inner ear. The functioning of the middle ear affects the way people hear. Tympanometry is a measure of the mobility of the middle ear (compliance) as a function of middle ear pressure, measured in deka Pascals

ARTICULATION GAIN FUNCTION

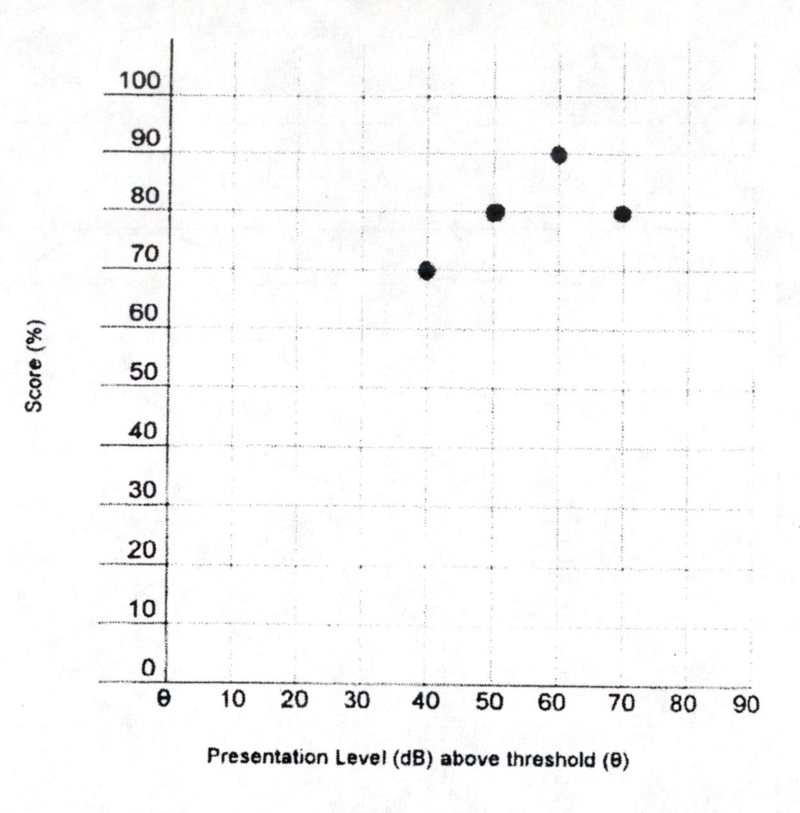

Figure 10.4

(dapa). The results are displayed on a graph called a tympanogram and interpretation of these results can help indicate what is causing a hearing loss.

An electroacoustic immittance meter is used to measure the middle ear function. A plug is inserted into the ear canal and the instrument takes the measurements and graphs the information.

There are five basic types of tympanograms:

Type A	Middle ear pressure is between +100 to −150 daPa. Compliance is normal.	
Type A_s	Middle ear pressure is normal. Compliance is reduced.	Otosclerosis
Type A_d	Middle ear pressure is normal. Compliance is increased.	Disarticulation
Type B	Middle ear pressure can't be measured due to fluid. Compliance is reduced.	Middle Ear Effusion
Type C	Middle ear pressure is reduced.	Eustachian Tube Dysfunction

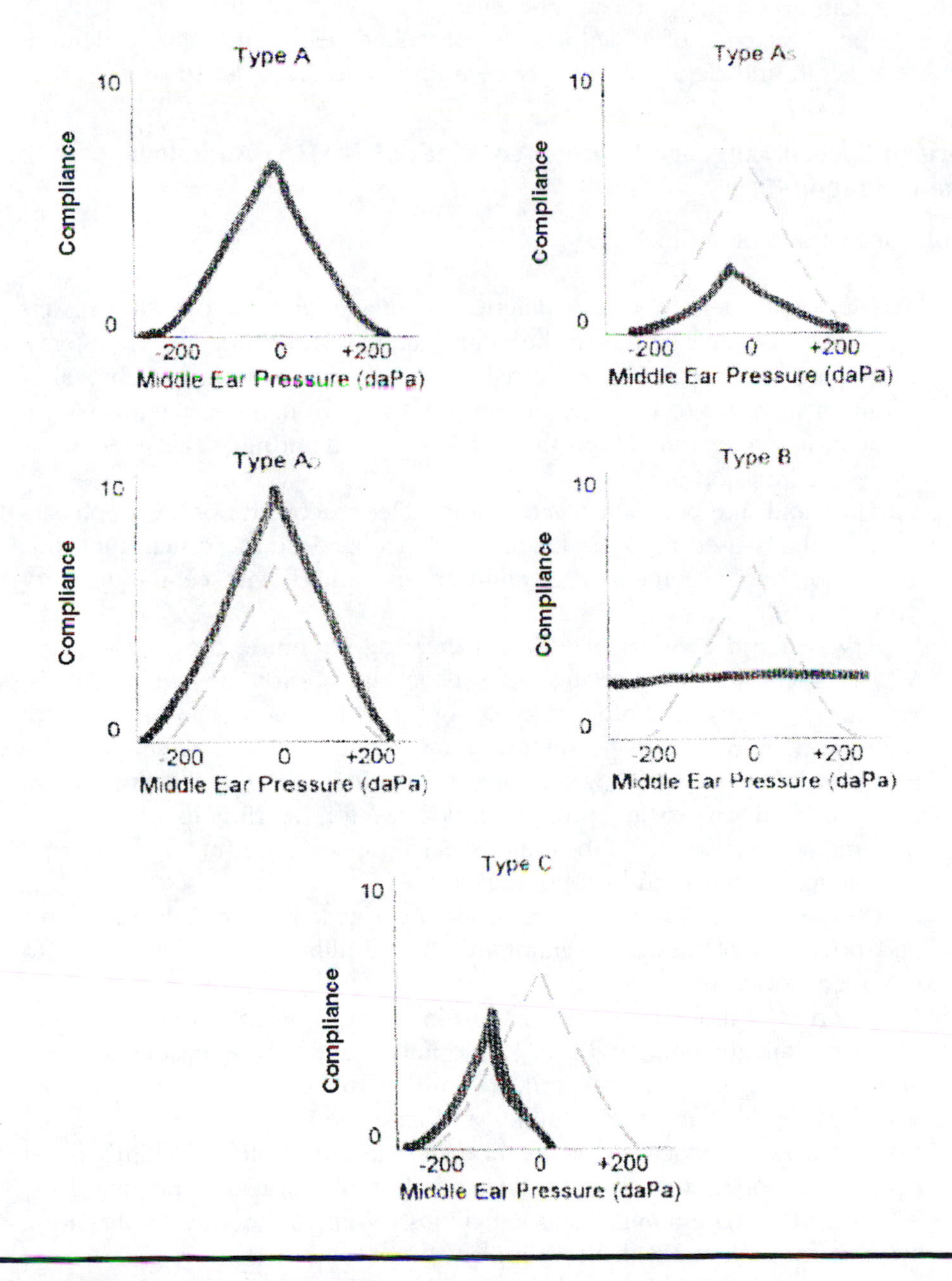

Figure 10.5

Although these procedures are typically conducted during an audiologic evaluation, they may be modified to meet the special needs of children and other difficult-to-test patients. For patients that cannot or will not tolerate earphones, test signals (tones and speech) can be presented through loudspeakers strategically placed within the sound attenuated test booth. The patient will either look toward the sound or be taught to place a peg in a board, ring on a peg, or block in a box, etc., in response to the sound. At that moment, the patient's positive response behavior will be reinforced. Successive trials will enable the audiologist to establish threshold or an acceptable estimate of hearing level.

The scope of practice of audiologists is described below and should demonstrate the breadth and depth of knowledge and skill audiologists possess.

American Speech-Language-Hearing Association* (ASHA) Audiology Scope of Practice

The practice of audiology includes:

1. Activities that identify, assess, diagnose, manage, and interpret test results related to disorders of human hearing, balance, and other neural systems.
2. Otoscopic examination and external ear canal management for removal of cerumen in order to evaluate hearing or balance, make ear impressions, fit hearing protection or prosthetic devices, and monitor the continuous use of hearing aids.
3. Conduct and interpretation of behavioral, electroacoustic, or electrophysiologic methods used to assess hearing, balance, and neural system function.
4. Evaluation and management of children and adults with central auditory processing disorders.
5. Supervision and conduct of newborn hearing screening programs.
6. Measurement and interpretation of sensory and motor evoked potentials, electromyography, and other electrodiagnostic tests for purposes of neurophysiologic intraoperative monitoring and cranial nerve assessment.
7. Provision of hearing care by selecting, evaluating, fitting, facilitating adjustment to, and dispensing prosthetic devices for hearing loss, including hearing aids, sensory aids, hearing assistive devices, alerting and telecommunication systems, and captioning devices.
8. Assessment of candidacy of persons with hearing loss for cochlear implants and provision of fitting, programming, and audiological rehabilitation to optimize device use.
9. Provision of audiological rehabilitation including speech reading, communication management, language development, auditory skill development, and counseling for psychosocial adjustment to hearing loss for persons with hearing loss and their families and caregivers.
10. Consultation to educators as members of interdisciplinary teams about communication management, educational implications of hearing loss, educational programming, classroom acoustics, and large-area amplification systems for children with hearing loss.
11. Prevention of hearing loss and conservation of hearing function by designing, implementing, and coordinating occupational, school, and community hearing conservation and identification programs.

---

* See resources section for address and phone number.

12. Consultation and provision of rehabilitation to persons with balance disorders using habituation, exercise therapy, and balance retraining.
13. Design and conduct of basic and applied audiologic research to increase the knowledge base, to develop new methods and programs, and to determine the efficacy of assessment and treatment paradigms; dissemination of research findings to other professionals and to the public.
14. Education and administration in audiology graduate and professional education programs.
15. Measurement of functional outcomes, consumer satisfaction, effectiveness, efficiency, and cost-benefit of practices and programs to maintain and improve the quality of audiological services.
16. Administration and supervision of professional and technical personnel who provide support functions to the practice of audiology.
17. Screening of speech-language, use of sign language (e.g., American Sign Language and cued speech), and other factors affecting communication function for the purposes of an audiologic evaluation and/or initial identification of individuals with other communication disorders.
18. Consultation about accessibility for persons with hearing loss in public and private buildings, programs, and services.
19. Assessment and nonmedical management of tinnitus using biofeedback, masking, hearing aids, education, and counseling.
20. Consultation to individuals, public and private agencies, and governmental bodies, or as an expert witness regarding legal interpretations of audiology findings, effects of hearing loss and balance system disorders, and relevant noise-related considerations.
21. Case management and service as a liaison for the consumer, family, and agencies in order to monitor audiologic status and management and to make recommendations about educational and vocational programming.
22. Consultation to industry on the development of products and instrumentation related to the measurement and management of auditory or balance function.
23. Participation in the development of professional and technical standards.

Credentials Held by Audiologists

As health professionals concerned with the welfare of the patients they serve, audiologists must possess certain credentials in order to practice audiology. These credentials signify a specific level of education and competence that serve to protect consumers. Certification and licensure are the two most common credentials possessed by audiologists. The following table delineates the characteristics of certification and licensure.

In order to be certified by the American Speech-Language-Hearing Association (ASHA) and licensed/registered/certified by a particular state regulatory board or agency to practice audiology, one must possess either a master's or doctoral degree earned from an accredited college or university audiology graduate program. College and university graduate audiology programs seek accreditation from the Council on Academic Accreditation of the American Speech-Language-Hearing

Table 10.1 Characteristics of Certification and Licensure

CHARACTERISTICS	CERTIFICATION	STATE LICENSURE
Purpose:	grants recognition to practitioners who have met certain qualifications	protects the public's life, health safety or economic well being
Function:	restricts the use of the designated title to individuals who choose to meet the qualifications	restricts scope of practice so that it is illegal for unlicensed individuals to provide the services
Qualifications:	formal education, experience, personal characteristics, and completion of examination	may piggy-back on qualifications required for certification
Establishment of Regulations:	developed and approved by members of the association	developed by regulatory body and approved according to the state's Administrative Procedures Act
Provider:	usually a private association	state agency
Status:	voluntary	mandatory
Penalties for Violation:	• rescind membership • rescind certification	• admonishment • monetary fine • incarceration • license revocation • restrictions on practice • license suspension
Continuing Education:	certifying entity may sponsor continuing education opportunities for members; may be required for recertification	may be required for licensees to renew

ASHA State Policy Division
10/10/95-aew

Association. This ensures that graduates of these programs are eligible for the Certificate of Clinical Competence (CCC) issued by the Clinical Certification Board of ASHA. The United States Department of Education and the Council on Recognition of Postsecondary Accreditation have approved ASHA as a credentialing agency. ASHA-certified audiologists possess specific knowledge and competencies and must pass a national examination as well as maintain currency through continuing education.

Additionally, most states require audiologists to be licensed, registered, or certified in order to practice audiology in that particular state. Each state's licensing or regulatory board has specific educational and competency requirements, which are assessed through examination. Renewal of state credentials usually requires maintenance of currency through continuing education.

Referral Considerations

Referrals to audiologists can be made directly by contacting the office, center, hospital, or facility in which the audiologist is employed. The American Speech-Language-Hearing Association (301-897-5700) or a state speech-language-hearing association can provide the names of audiologists practicing in specific geographic areas.

It is important and helpful to be aware of the types of test procedures and terminology used by audiologists. This will assist the case manager in making appropriate referrals and in conversing knowledgeably with the audiologist. The following is a listing of some of the test procedures and terminology used by audiologists:

Types of Hearing Loss

Conductive — Abnormalities of the outer and/or middle ear
Sensorineural — Abnormalities of the inner ear
Mixed — Combination of conductive and sensorineural
Central — Abnormalities of the central auditory nervous system

Assessment Procedures

Behavioral Observation Audiometry (BOA) — Controlled observation of responses (i.e., changes in behavior such as quieting, arousal from sleep, eye shift, eye widening, eyebrow raising, body movement and head turn) to acoustic stimuli

Visual Reinforcement Audiometry (VRA) — Reinforcement with lighted toys when the child turns toward the sound source

Conditioned Play Audiometry (CPA) — Conditioning the child to respond to the stimulus through game playing

Conventional Audiometry — Hand-raising or button-pushing response to stimulus

Auditory Evoked Potentials (AEPs) — Measurement of changes in electrical activity of the auditory nervous system in response to acoustic stimuli

Otoacoustic Emissions (OAEs) — Measurement of sound generated by motion of the outer hair cells

Central Auditory Processing Evaluation — Assessment of the central auditory system to process complex auditory stimuli

Mode of Presentation

Soundfield — Testing via loudspeakers; does not allow a unilateral or asymmetrical hearing loss to be ruled out.

Air conduction — Testing via earphones; allows each ear to be evaluated in isolation.

Bone conduction — Testing via a bone vibrator; directly stimulates "better" cochlea.

Test Battery

Frequency-specific information — Absolute vs. minimum response.

Speech Awareness Threshold (SAT) — Lowest intensity level at which there is awareness of speech.

Speech Reception Threshold (SRT) — Lowest intensity level at which a spondee word can be repeated 50% of the time.

Word Recognition Ability — Percentage of monosyllabic words repeated correctly when presented at a comfortable listening level.

Acoustic Immittance — Previously explained.

Tympanometry — Measurement of the mobility of the tympanic membrane/middle ear system as a function of varying degrees of air pressure in the external ear canal.

a. *Static compliance* — Mobility of the tympanic membrane/middle ear system.

b. *Equivalent volume* — Ear canal volume.

Acoustic Reflex Measurements — Observation of the contraction of the muscles of the middle ear in response to loud sounds.

Outcomes of Audiology Services

Outcomes of audiology services may be measured to determine treatment effectiveness, efficiency, cost-benefit analysis, and consumer satisfaction. Specific outcome data may assist consumers to make decisions about audiology service delivery. The following listing describes the types of outcomes that consumers may expect to receive from an audiologist.

1. Interpretation of otoscopic examination for appropriate management or referral.
2. Identification of populations and individuals with or at risk for hearing loss or related auditory disorders:
   a. With normal hearing or no related auditory disorders.
   b. With communication disorders associated with hearing loss.
   c. With or at risk of balance disorders, and tinnitus.

3. Professional interpretation of the results of audiological findings.
4. Referrals to other professions, agencies, and/or consumer organizations.
5. Counseling for personal adjustment and discussion of the effects of hearing loss and the potential benefits to be gained from audiological rehabilitation, sensory aids including hearing and tactile aids, hearing assistive devices, cochlear implants, captioning devices, and signal/warning devices.
6. Counseling regarding the effects of balance system dysfunction.
7. Selection, monitoring, dispensing, and maintenance of hearing aids and large-area amplification systems.
8. Development of culturally appropriate, audiologic, rehabilitative management plans including, when appropriate:
   a. Fitting and dispensing recommendations, and educating the consumer and family/caregivers in the use of and adjustment to sensory aids, hearing assistive devices, alerting systems, and captioning devices.
   b. Counseling relating to psychosocial aspects of hearing loss and processes to enhance communication competence.
   c. Skills training and consultation concerning environmental modifications to facilitate development of receptive and expressive communication.
   d. Evaluation and modification of the audiologic management plan.
9. Preparation of a report summarizing findings, interpretation, recommendations, and audiologic management plan.
10. Consultation in development of an Individual Education Program (IEP) for school-age children or an Individual Family Service Plan (IFSP) for children from birth to 36 months old.
11. Provision of in-service programs for personnel, and advising school districts in planning educational programs and accessibility for students with hearing loss.
12. Planning, development, implementation, and evaluation of hearing conservation programs.

Impact of Hearing Loss on Communication

Case managers and other individuals should be aware of the impact hearing loss can have on communication. Generally speaking, a conductive (outer or middle ear) hearing loss, which cannot be medically remediated, can be adequately benefited through amplification. It must be cautioned that young children commonly experience conductive hearing loss due to ear and/or upper respiratory infections. Although these episodes are usually self-limiting or respond to medical intervention when necessary, some children persist with conductive hearing loss, which may affect their speech and language development. These children should be referred to an audiologist as well as a speech-language pathologist.

An individual with a sensorineural (inner ear) hearing loss, however, can be expected to experience some degree of difficulty ***understanding*** speech particularly when the listening environment is less than ideal. This means that when a person with a sensorineural hearing loss is greater than 3 to 4 feet from the source of the sound or when there is noise in the background (there almost always is ***some*** noise in the background!) that person will likely misunderstand some of what is being said. This is because the pattern of hearing with a sensorineural hearing loss is typically worse in the high frequencies or pitches and better in the low frequencies or pitches. In order to understand speech clearly we must hear all the pitches equally well. As the following graph depicts, the vowels are generally low in pitch (and loud) compared to consonants, which are high in pitch (and soft).

A properly fitted hearing aid can be extremely beneficial. However, it is important for all to recognize that even with appropriate amplification, individuals with sensorineural hearing loss might still have difficulty understanding what is being said, particularly with noise in the background.

How to Communicate with Hard of Hearing People

The following suggestions are examples of effective strategies for communicating with individuals with hearing impairment.

1. *Positioning:*
   a. Be sure the light, whether natural or artificial, falls on your face. Do not stand with the sun to your back or in front of a window.
   b. If you are aware that the hard of hearing person has a better ear, stand or sit on that side.
   c. Avoid background noise to the extent possible.
2. *Method:*
   a. Get the person's attention before you start talking. You may need to touch the person to attract attention.
   b. Speak to the hard of hearing person from an ideal distance of 3 to 6 feet in face-to-face visual contact.
   c. Speak as clearly as possible in a natural way.
   d. Speak more slowly to the hard of hearing person. Pausing between sentences will assist the listener.
   e. Do not shout! Shouting often results in distortion of speech and it displays a negative visual signal to the listener. Do not drop your voice at the end of the sentence.
   f. If the person does not understand what you said, rephrase it.
   g. When changing the subject, indicate the new topic with a word or two or a phrase.
3. *Physical:*
   a. Do not obscure your mouth with your hands. Do not chew or smoke while talking.
   b. Facial expressions and lip movements are important clues to the hard of hearing person. Feelings are more often expressed by nonverbal communication than through words.
4. *Attitude:*
   a. Do not become impatient.
   b. Stay positive and relaxed.
   c. Never talk about a hard of hearing person in his or her presence. Talk *to* them, not *about* them.
   d. Ask what you can do to facilitate communication.

First Aid For Hearing Aids

The following are some suggestions for troubleshooting minor hearing aid difficulties.

For These Symptoms	*Read Paragraphs*
Hearing aid dead	1,2,3,4,5,9
Working, but weak	1,2,3,4,5,6,7,8,9,12
Works intermittently	3,4,5,9
Whistles	6,8,10,11
Sounds noisy, raspy, shrill	3,4,5,8,10,11
Sounds hollow or mushy	1,2,7

*Causes, Tests, and Remedies**

1. Cause — Dead or rundown battery. Test–Substitute new battery. Remedy — Replace worn-out battery.
2. Cause — Battery reversed in holder so that + end is where – end should be. Test — Examine. Remedy — Insert battery correctly.
3. Cause — Poor contacts at cord receptacle of battery holder due to dirty pins or springs. Test — With hearing aid turned on, wiggle plugs in receptacles and withdraw and reinsert each plug and the battery. Remedy — Rub accessible contacts briskly with lead pencil eraser, then wipe with clean cloth moistened with dry-cleaning liquid. Inaccessible contacts usually can be cleaned with a broom straw dipped in cleaning fluid.
4. Cause — Internal break or near-break inside receiver cord. Test — While listening, flex all parts of cords by running fingers along entire length and wiggle cords at terminals. Intermittent or raspy sounds indicate broken wires. Remedy — Replace cords with new ones. Worn ones cannot be repaired satisfactorily.
5. Cause — Plugs not fully or firmly inserted in receptacles. Test — While listening, withdraw and firmly reinsert each plug in turn. Remedy — Insert correctly.
6. Cause — Ear tip not properly seated in ear. Test — With the fingers, press the receiver firmly into the ear and twist back and forth slightly to make sure that the ear tip in properly positioned. Remedy — Position correctly.
7. Cause — Ear tip plugged with wax, or with drop of water from cleaning. Test examine ear tip visually and blow through it to determine whether passage is open. Remedy — Disconnect ear tip from receiver, then wash ear tip in lukewarm water and soap, using pipe cleaner or long-bristle brush to reach down into the canal. Rinse with clear water and dry. A dry pipe cleaner may be used to dry out the canal; blowing through the canal will remove surplus water.

* Adapted from Sonotone Corporation

8. Cause — Insufficient pressure of bone receiver on mastoid. Test — While listening, press the bone receiver more tightly against the head with the fingers. Remedy — Bend the receiver headband to provide greater pressure. Your audiologist who is more skilled in maintaining conformation with the head preferably does this.
9. Cause — Battery leakage (resulting in poor battery connections). Test — Examine battery and battery holder for evidence of leakage or corrosion. Remedy — Discard the battery and wipe the holder terminals carefully with cloth dampened (not wet) in warm water.
10. Cause — Receiver close to wall or other sound-reflecting surfaces. Test — Examine. Remedy — Avoid sitting with the fitted side of the head near a wall or other surfaces. Such surfaces tend to reflect the sound from the receiver so that it is more readily picked up by the microphone, thus causing whistling.
11. Cause — Microphone worn too close to receiver. Test — Try moving instrument to provide wider separation between it and the receiver. Remedy — Avoid wearing microphone and receiver on same side of body, or close together.
12. Cause — Plastic tubing not firmly seated at hearing aid or ear tip ends, or tubing so sharply bent as to block the passage of sound through it. Test — Examine and check for tightness at ends. Remedy — Push tubing ends firmly onto nubs. See that there is no kink or sharp bend. Replace the tubing if necessary.

Behaviors of Children at Risk for Auditory Disorders*

Certain characteristic behaviors by children should alert parents and/or teachers to be concerned about their hearing. Some of the signs are:

1. Often misunderstands what is said.
2. Constantly requests that information be repeated.
3. Has difficulty following oral instructions.
4. Gives inconsistent responses to auditory stimuli.
5. Turns up the volume of the television, radio, or stereo.
6. Gives slow or delayed response to verbal stimuli.
7. Has poor auditory attention.
8. Has poor auditory memory (span and sequence).
9. Is easily distracted.
10. Has difficulty listening in the presence of background noise.
11. Has poor receptive and expressive language.
12. Has difficulty with phonics and speech sound discrimination.
13. Learns poorly through the auditory channel.
14. Has reading, spelling, and other learning problems.
15. Exhibits behavior problems.
16. Says “huh” or “what” frequently.

* Adapted from the Fisher's Auditory Problems Checklist.

Indicators Associated with Hearing Loss*

Some common indicators associated with hearing loss include:

1. Family history of hearing loss.
2. *In utero* infection (e.g., cytomegalovirus, rubella, syphilis, toxoplasmosis).
3. Craniofacial anomalies including those with morphological abnormalities of the pinna and ear canal.
4. Birthweight less than 1500 grams (3.3 lbs.).
5. Hyperbilirubinemia at a serum level requiring exchange transfusion.
6. Ototoxic medications including, but not limited to, chemotherapeutic agents, or aminoglycocides used in multiple courses or in combination with loop diuretics.
7. Bacterial meningitis and other infections associated with sensorineural hearing loss.
8. Severe depression at birth with Apgar scores of 0–4 at one minute or 0–6 at five minutes.
9. Prolonged mechanical ventilation 5 days or longer (e.g., persistent pulmonary hypertension).
10. Stigmata or other findings associated with a syndrome known to include a sensorineural and/or conductive hearing loss.
11. Parent/caregiver concern regarding hearing, speech, language, and/or developmental delay.
12. Head trauma associated with loss of consciousness or skull fracture.
13. Recurrent or persistent otitis media with effusion for at least 3 months.
14. Neurofibromatosis Type II and neurodegenerative disorders.
15. Anatomic deformities and other disorders, which affect eustachian tube, function.

Costs Related to Amplification:

The cost of *hearing aids* varies from approximately $500 to $2500 per instrument depending upon type and options. A single behind-the-ear instrument may be as little as $500, while a digital instrument will typically cost $2100 to $2500. Many patients with disabilities may need manufacturer support to ensure they are capable of operating the volume control and other instrument options. Digital hearing aids often have an external control much like a television remote control. Care must be given to obtaining appropriate fitting and follow-up services. Pitfalls that must be avoided are indiscriminate fitting of patients with amplification not appropriate for their loss, and insufficient follow-up and aural rehabilitation.

- A hearing aid should be effective for three to five years before *replacement* is necessary. It is wise to purchase replacement and repair warranties.
- A standard factory *warranty* will be one to two years.
- *Battery costs* may vary dependent upon the severity of the hearing loss and the power required of the hearing aid. A package of six batteries will

* Adapted from the Draft Joint Committee on Infant Hearing 1993 Position Statement

cost $4.00 to $5.00. The average life expectancy for a battery is approximately ten days to two weeks when the instrument is worn during waking hours. If an instrument is out of warranty the cost of repair is approximately $150 with a one-year warranty.

Funding Issues Related to Audiological Services

Obviously, anyone with the financial resource to pay privately for these devices and services will be able to obtain what they need. However, most rely upon alternative funding and specific issues are revealed below.

- Medicaid: States must cover hearing aids for children through the Early and Periodic Screening, Diagnosis, and Treatment Program. Coverage for adults is optional.
- Medicare: Medicare does not cover hearing aids or tests related to hearing aids. Social health maintenance organizations (SHMOs) are part of a demonstration project that includes some long-term care. All SHMOs cover hearing aids. As risk HMOs enter the Medicare market, many are providing partial coverage of hearing aids. For example, the Medicare HMO might cover $500 of a hearing aid.
- Private Health Plans: Most do not cover hearing aids unless there is a labor union contract such as the United Automobile Workers (UAW), which covers the costs related to one hearing aid every three years. The benefit is not limited to automobile workers but is found in many contracts negotiated by the UAW. Another example of a union contract is the California Public Employees Retirement System which offers a hearing benefit to retirees enrolled in Medicare managed care plans. Some private plans such as Blue Cross and Blue Shield may cover a hearing aid if the need is related to an accident or illness.

Special Issue — Cochlear Implant

As referenced above, the audiologist may evaluate clients for the cochlear implant (telephone 303-790-9010). This device is implanted in nearly 10,000 children and adults who are profoundly hearing impaired or deaf due to genetic factors, ototoxic drugs, meningitis, rubella, and head trauma. A criterion for candidacy primarily requires that the auditory nerve must not be destroyed. General guidelines include:

- Be at least 2 years of age.
- Have profound bilateral sensorineural deafness.
- Demonstrate no significant benefit from amplification.
- Strong family support.
- No medical contraindications to surgery.
- For children, a supportive school system.
- For adults, appropriate expectations.
- Have the ability to pay for the device and services. The total cost of an implant, in 1995, was more than $40,000, not including replacements (see example care below).

With regard to children, there appears to be a controversy regarding the device. Although promoters report that a child can more effectively learn language with the implant, they are neither a "normal" hearing person nor deaf. The child may not fit in the deaf subculture and may experience ridicule from others that can aversely affect social development. On the other hand, adults who became deaf before learning language commonly do not read higher than the third or fourth grade level. This barrier, of course, can significantly affect their vocational outlook.

Example Case

Below is an example *portion* of a plan for a 6-year-old child, profoundly hearing impaired due to meningitis at the age of 1, who met the criteria for evaluation. His parents were very bright based on educational achievements and testing. Both were employed by the school system. The child and an older sibling were both judged intellectually gifted.

Recommendation	*Dates*	*Frequency*	*Expected Cost*
Speech-language therapy and assistive technology prescriptions	1996–2014 (25 y.o.)	3 X week avg. during school year and 2 X week for 10 weeks during summer. Then 1X/wk age 20 to 25.	$0 provided by school system under IDEA for sch. year. If private pay, during summers, and age 22-25 expected cost $100/hr.
Education	1996 – 2007	School year	$0 Provided under IDEA
TTY text telephone unit. Recommend Superprint 4425 (includes printer, auto answer, ring flasher, etc.)	1999 (10 y.o.) to life	Every 10 years	$387–$500 (includes 1 year warranty)
TTY unit uses regular phone line; however, units are unable to distinguish between incoming TTY call or voice call. A separate phone line dedicated for the TTY unit may be appropriate. Cost for additional phone line installation estimated between $100–$110 plus monthly charge of approximately $35 per month. Does not include long distance charges which are usually higher due to length of time to transmit written words rather than spoken words. Cost cannot be projected. Internet access cost is $19.95 per month.			
Portable TTY with printer	1999 (10 y.o.)	Every 5 years (est.)	$500 (includes 1 year warranty)
TTY refill paper 3/pack of 2 1/4" thermal paper	1999 (10 y.o.)	Every 3 mos. or as needed depending on use	$3–$4 pkg. $12–$16/year (est.)
TTY Batteries (6)		Yearly or more depending on use	$19.50 @ $6.50 for 2/pkg.

Recommendation	*Dates*	*Frequency*	*Expected Cost*
Sonic Alert or Silent Call Alerting System, including receiver, transmitters, and rechargeable battery	1996	Sonic Alert: 1 X only Silent Call: Every 10 years or more (est.)	Sonic Alert: $259.80 w/1 yr. warranty Silent Call: $539.80 w/vibrating unit and 2 yr. warranty
Door Knock Signaler with light	1996	Every 10 years	$29.95–$34.95 each
Portable Smoke Detector w/Strobe	1996	Every 10 years	$166
Allowance for batteries, light bulbs, etc.	1996	Batteries: monthly Bulbs: yearly depending on use	$50/yr. (est.)
OPTIONAL Baby Cry Alerter (assumes marriage and child)	Est. 2019 (30 y.o.)	1 X only (assumes marriage and family)	Sonic Alert: $39.95 (may also be used as smoke detector)
OPTIONAL Silent Call Sleep Alert Charger Unit	1996	Every 10 years or more (est.)	$106.95
OPTIONAL Cochlear Implant (1)	1996	One replacement over life	$40,744 (includes all costs for first year)
Follow-up for Cochlear implant	1997 or 1 year after implant performed	1 per year	$300/visit for 3 hrs. @ $100/hr.
Hearing/Auditory Therapy	1996 to age 22	4–5 hrs/wk avg thru high school then 1–2 hrs/wk to age 22	$85/hr.
Speech Therapy	1996 to age 22	4–5 hrs/wk avg. thru high school then 1–2 hrs/wk to age 22	$100/hr.
Service contract for external speech processor and headset. (Internal device has 99 yr. warranty)	1996 to life	Every two years	$595 for 2 years (after 3 year manuf. warranty expires)
Programming, map adjustment and tuning, general maintenance	1996 to life	1 X/wk for 1st 2 mos. then 1 X every other week for 2 mos. then 1 X/mo for 3 months then every 3 mos. to age 16 (2005) then ev. 6 mos. thereafter	1996: $0 included in cost of implant 1997-2005: $400/yr. 2006+: $200/yr. @ $100/hr

Recommendation	Dates	Frequency	Expected Cost
Replacement cords & batteries	1996 to life	Every 3 mos for 2 cords @ $10 ea. 1 X/yr for 2 pk batteries. @ $10/yr	$90/year
Replacement headset	1999 (after 3 yr. warranty) to life	Project 3–4 upgrades over lifetime	$500 (est.) every 3 years
Upgrade external processor	2001 (est.)	1 x only	$5,500 (est.) each upgrade
Note 1: No provision for technology advances.			
Note 2: Economist to determine present value.			
Interpreter	1996 to lifetime	6 hrs/day, 5 days/week during school (Aug-June) to 2007. Then expect 2–4 hrs/week avg. to lifetime.	$0 provided through school system through age 18. Then expect 2–4 hrs/wk avg. @ $15/hr for medical, dental, contracts, legal, and other non-education related activities.

Resources

Selected resources for information, services, and products are:

Information:

American Speech-Language-Hearing Association
10801 Rockville Pike
Rockville, MD 20852
301-897-5700

National Information Center on Deafness
Gallaudet University
800 Florida Ave., NE
Washington, D.C., 20002
202-651-5051 (Voice)
202-651-5052 (TTY)

Alexander Graham Bell Assoc. for the Deaf
3417 Volta Place, NW
Washington, D.C., 20007
202-337-5220 (Voice/TTY)

American Assoc. for the Deaf-Blind
814 Thayer Ave., Room 302
Silver Spring, MD, 20910
301-588-6545 (Voice/TTY)

American Athletic Association for the Deaf
3607 Washington Blvd., #4
Ogdon, UT 84403
801-393-5710 (Voice)
801-393-7916 (TTY)

American Association for Deaf Children
10th and Tahlequah Streets
Sulphur, OK 73086
800-942-ASDC

Helen Keller National Center for Deaf-Blind Youths and Adults
111 Middle Neck Road
Sands Point, NY 11050
516-944-8900 Voice
516-944-8637 (TTY)

National Association for the Deaf
814 Thayer Ave., Room 302
Silver Spring, MD, 20910
301-587-1788 (Voice)
301-587-1789 (TTY)

Products/Services:

Canines
Paws with a Cause
1235 100th Street, SE
Byron Center, MI 49315
800-253-PAWS

Cochlear Implant
Cochlear Corporation
Suite 200
61 Inverness Drive East
Englewood, CO 80112
800-523-5798

Interpreters
Registry of Interpreters for the Deaf
9719 Colesville, Road, Suite 310
Silver Spring, MD 20910
301-608-0050 (Voice/TTY)

General Products
LS&S Group
P. O. Box 6783
Northbrook, IL 60065
800-317-8533
E-mail: lssgrp@aol.com

General Products
NFSS Communications
8120 Fenton Street
Silver Spring, MD 20910
888-589-6671 (Voice)
888-589-6670 (TTY)
E-mail: sales@nfss.com

General Products
HARC Mercantile, LTD.
1111 West Centre Ave.
P. O. Box 3055
Kalamazoo, MI 49003
800-445-9968 (Voice)
800-413-5245 (TTY)

General Products
Potomac Technology
One Church Street, Suite 402
Rockville, MD 20850
301-762-4005 (Voice)
301-762-0851 (TTY)

Tactile Aids
Audiological Engineering Corporation
35 Medford Street
Somerville, MA 02143
800-283-4601 (Voice)
800-955-7204 (TTY)

Conclusion

In many life care plans audiological services can be a critical component. In personal injury litigation common sequelae from head trauma can destroy or reduce hearing, disrupt balance, and produce serious ringing in the ears (tinnitus). In medical illness, malpractice, or mistakes the audiologist is commonly an important member for diagnosis and treatment of hearing dysfunction. Of particular interest is the role the audiologist can play with regard to children. Hearing deficits can seriously hamper educational achievement that can lead to poor social adjustment and a poor vocational outlook. Indeed, many deaf children are initially diagnosed mentally retarded and miss services during critical developmental periods. This chapter assists the life care planner with information related to the roles and responsibilities of the audiologist and provides resources for information, services, and products.

REFERENCES

American Speech-Language-Hearing Association. (March 1993). Preferred practice patterns for the professions of speech-language pathology and audiology. **ASHA, 35**(11), 1-102.

American Speech-Language-Hearing Association. (March 1994). Code of ethics. **ASHA, 36** (13), 1-2.

American Speech-Language-Hearing Association. (March 1995). Reference list of position statements, guidelines, definitions, and relevant papers. **ASHA, 37**(14), 36-37.

Bess, F. H. & Humes, L.E. (1995). **Audiology: The Fundamentals**. Baltimore, MD: Williams & Wilkins.

Fisher, L. I. (no date). **Fisher Auditory Problems Checklist** Cedar Rapids, IA: Grant Wood Area Education Agency.

Joint Committee on Infant Hearing (1993). Position Statement. **ASHA, 36**, 38-41.

11

THE ROLE OF THE ECONOMIST IN LIFE CARE PLANNING

Everett G. Dillman

INTRODUCTION

An economist is frequently called upon to compute the present value of the future medical and care costs set forth in a life care plan prepared by a specialist. Although the economist generally will have little or no input in the development of the plan, he or she does have an interest in how the plan is structured and what it contains. This chapter examines the content of life care plans from the point of view of an economist and identifies some areas of potential concern.

The structure of the life care plan, including what elements are covered, will differ to some extent from author to author. Experience has shown, however, that there are a number of consistent patterns that emerge, some of which will cause difficulty for economic analysis. The areas of concern, from an economic point-of-view include, (1) cost categories, (2) items that should be included, (3) timing of the items, (4) the use of actual or annual averages, and (5) the emphasis placed on trivial items. Each of these elements is discussed in more detail.

Categories of Costs

In making the economic evaluation the economist must consider the fact that the costs of the various items included in the plan will not remain static over time but can be expected to increase with inflation. The historical rates of increase will differ depending upon the particular item, as the prices of some things tend to increase faster than others. For instance, the inflation of doctors' fees and hospital costs have historically been much greater than the inflation for such items as bandages, hospital beds, and other commodities.

In considering future inflation, the economist generally looks at the past inflation of the type of good being evaluated. Although it may be possible to develop data series for many individualized items, the economic analysis will

1-57444-075-6/99/$0.00+$.50

generally place the items into the broad classifications of medical services, nonmedical services, medical commodities, and nonmedical commodities.

Two of the categories, medical services and medical commodities, are subsets of the Consumer Price Index (CPI) and are defined by the Bureau of Labor Statistics. These definitions, as well as those for the other two categories, follow.

Medical Services

This category involves professional and hospital services. Included are payments for physicians, dentists, and other professionals such as optometrists, ophthalmologists, opticians, psychologists, and therapists. Chiropractors and nurse practitioners are also included. The category of hospital services includes nursing home care. Hospital services for inpatients, such as pharmacy, laboratory tests, radiology, short stay units, ambulatory surgery, physical therapy, and emergency room fees billed by the hospital, also fall into this category.

Medical Commodities

The medical commodities classification includes:

1. Prescription drugs and medical supplies. This includes all drugs and medical supplies dispensed by prescriptions. Also included are all prescription-dispensed over-the-counter drugs, i.e., those drugs that are obtained over-the-counter but are prescribed by the doctor and dispensed by the pharmacist.
2. Internal and respiratory over-the-counter drugs. This includes all nonprescription medication taken by swallowing or inhaling, as well as suppositories or enemas.
3. Topicals and dressings. Includes all nonprescription medicines and dressings used externally.
4. Medical equipment for general use. Includes nonprescription medical equipment not worn or not used for supporting the body. Included in this group are nonprescription male and female contraceptives. Whirlpools and vaporizers are also included.
5. Supportive and convalescent medical equipment. This category includes all supportive and convalescent medical equipment and auxiliaries to such equipment. Also included are prostheses, crutches, wheelchairs, and associated accessories.
6. Hearing Aids. Includes all types of hearing aids and the cost of testing and fitting of the hearing aid.

Nonmedical Services

The nonmedical services category is concerned with all personal services that are not included in Medical Services. Examples would include services such as lawn care and auto repair. Some services which are medical-related will fall into this group, such as wheelchair repair and maintenance of a van wheelchair lift.

Nonprofessional attendant care (when not provided through a health care provider) can be classified as a nonmedical service.

Since the long-term inflation rate of nonmedical services is less than that for medical services, when there is a doubt as to the correct classification, the conservative approach would be to place the service item in the nonmedical services category.

Nonmedical Commodities

The nonmedical commodities category includes all the commodity (i.e., nonservices) items that do not fall under medical commodities. Such items might be specialty foods, housing and alterations to housing, automobiles, games, bedding, and computers.

The historical inflation rates of each of these categories are given by the appropriate subseries of the Consumer Price Index (CPI) or, in the case of the nonmedical services, the average increase in hourly wages in the private nonagricultural economy. These are shown in Tables 11.1 to 11.6.

What Should Be Included

The life care plan should include all of the medical and care items (both services and commodities) that will be, or should be, incurred because of the incident in question. Which specific items to include is usually not a question for the economist. The economist needs to make sure that only marginal costs are considered. In addition, the value of the items or services should be evaluated even if provided at no cost by family members, significant others, or some other collateral source. Each of these concepts will be briefly discussed.

Marginal Costs

A marginal cost can be defined as an additional or extra cost that is incurred because, and only because of, the injury in question. For instance, the entire cost of a new car (every three years or so) would generally **not** be considered a marginal cost. The individual would normally need transportation even if not injured. What would be appropriate, however, is the additional cost required by the nature of the limitations. A van rather than a regular car might be necessary to transport a client in a wheelchair. If so, the additional cost of a van or a regular car would be appropriate. Any special modifications such as a lift or special controls would also qualify as a marginal cost. To obtain the marginal cost one would subtract the cost of a "normal item" (for instance, a compact car) from the cost of the recommended item.

Items such as television sets, radios, and books are often set forth in life care plans. In some cases, the inclusion of such items may be justified because of the specifics of the case, but often the items are duplications of what the individual would normally have purchased without the injury and therefore are not a marginal cost and should not be included.

Table 11.1 Consumer Price Index Medical Components All Urban Consumers

Year	All Items CPI 1982–1984 = 100.0	Medical Care 1982–1984 = 100.0
1935	13.7	10.2
1936	13.9	10.2
1937	14.4	10.3
1938	14.1	10.3
1939	13.9	10.3
1940	14.0	10.4
1941	14.7	10.4
1942	16.3	10.7
1943	17.3	11.2
1944	17.6	11.6
1945	18.0	11.9
1946	19.5	12.5
1947	22.3	13.5
1948	24.1	14.4
1949	23.8	14.8
1950	24.1	15.1
1951	26.0	15.9
1952	26.5	16.7
1953	26.7	17.3
1954	26.9	17.8
1955	26.8	18.2
1956	27.2	18.9
1957	28.1	19.7
1958	28.9	20.6
1959	29.1	21.5
1960	29.6	22.3
1961	29.9	22.9
1962	30.2	23.5
1963	30.8	24.1
1964	31.0	24.6
1965	31.5	25.2
1966	32.4	26.3
1967	33.4	28.2
1968	34.8	29.9
1969	36.7	31.9
1970	38.8	34.0
1971	40.5	36.1
1972	41.8	37.3
1973	44.4	38.8
1974	49.3	42.4
1975	53.8	47.5
1976	56.9	52.0
1977	60.6	57.0
1978	65.2	61.8
1979	72.6	67.5
1980	82.4	74.9

Table 11.1 (continued) Consumer Price Index Medical Components All Urban Consumers

Year	All Items CPI 1982–1984 = 100.0	Medical Care 1982–1984 = 100.0
1981	90.9	82.9
1982	96.5	92.5
1983	99.6	100.6
1984	103.9	106.8
1985	107.6	113.5
1986	109.6	122.0
1987	113.6	130.1
1988	118.3	138.6
1989	124.0	149.3
1990	130.7	162.8
1991	136.2	177.0
1992	140.3	190.1
1993	144.5	201.4
1994	148.2	211.0
1995	152.4	220.5

Source: U.S. Department of Labor. Bureau of Labor Statistics

Table 11.2 Consumer Price Index Medical Commodities All Urban Consumers

Year	Medical Commodities 1982–1984 = 100.0	Prescription Drugs 1982–1984 = 100.0	Nonprescription Drugs and Medical Supplies Dec. 86 = 100.0	Internal and Respiratory Over-the-Counter Drugs 1984–1986 = 100.0	Nonprescription Medical Equipment and Supplies 1982–1984 = 100.0
1935	31.7	30.6			
1936	31.6	30.6			
1937	31.8	30.8			
1938	32.0	31.0			
1939	31.9	31.0			
1940	31.8	31.0			
1941	32.0	31.4			
1942	32.8	32.2			
1943	33.0	32.5			
1944	33.3	33.1			
1945	33.6	33.5			
1946	34.2	34.6			
1947	36.7	38.1			
1948	38.6	41.2			
1949	39.2	42.2			
1950	39.7	43.4			
1951	40.8	45.5			
1952	41.2	46.0			
1953	41.5	46.0			

Table 11.2 (continued) Consumer Price Index Medical Commodities All Urban Consumers

Year	Medical Commodities 1982–1984 = 100.0	Prescription Drugs 1982–1984 = 100.0	Nonprescription Drugs and Medical Supplies Dec. 86 = 100.0	Internal and Respiratory Over-the-Counter Drugs 1984–1986 = 100.0	Nonprescription Medical Equipment and Supplies 1982–1984 = 100.0
1954	42.0	46.9			
1955	42.5	47.6			
1956	43.4	49.0			
1957	44.6	50.7			
1958	46.1	53.0			
1959	46.8	54.2			
1960	46.9	54.0			
1961	46.3	52.2			
1962	45.6	50.1			
1963	45.2	48.9			
1964	45.1	48.3		38.8	
1965	45.0	47.8		39.0	
1966	45.1	47.7		39.4	
1967	44.9	46.8		39.8	
1968	45.0	46.0		40.8	
1969	45.4	46.6		41.2	
1970	46.5	47.4		42.3	
1971	47.3	47.4		43.9	
1972	47.4	47.2		44.3	
1973	47.5	47.1		44.8	
1974	49.2	48.2		46.8	
1975	53.3	51.2		51.8	
1976	56.5	53.9		55.3	
1977	60.2	57.2		59.1	
1978	64.4	61.6		63.3	69.1
1979	69.0	66.4		68.0	73.3
1980	75.4	72.5		74.9	79.2
1981	83.7	80.8		84.2	86.5
1982	92.3	90.2		93.3	94.5
1983	100.2	100.1		100.3	100.4
1984	107.5	109.7		106.5	105.1
1985	115.2	120.1		112.2	109.6
1986	122.8	130.4		117.7	115.0
1987	131.0	140.8	103.1	123.9	119.6
1988	139.9	152.0	108.1	130.8	123.9
1989	150.8	165.2	114.6	138.8	131.1
1990	163.4	181.7	120.6	145.9	138.0
1991	176.8	199.7	126.3	152.4	145.0
1992	188.1	214.7	131.2	158.2	150.9
1993	195.0	223.0	135.2	163.5	155.9
1994	200.7	230.6	138.1	165.9	160.0
1995	204.5				

Source: U.S. Department of Labor. Bureau of Labor Statistics

Table 11.3 Consumer Price Index Medical Services All Urban Consumers

Year	Medical Care Services 1982–1984 = 100.0	Professional Medical Services 1982–1984 = 100.0	Physician's Services 1982–1984 = 100.0	Dental Services 1984–1986 = 100.0	Eye Care 1982–1984 = 100.0	Professional Services Dec. 1986 = 100.0
1935	8.3		11.1	13.4		
1936	8.3		11.2	13.4		
1937	8.4		11.2	13.7		
1938	8.4		11.2	13.8		
1939	8.5		11.2	13.8		
1940	8.5		11.2	13.8		
1941	8.5		11.3	13.8		
1942	8.8		11.5	14.2		
1943	9.2		12.3	14.8		
1944	9.6		12.8	15.6		
1945	9.9		13.1	16.3		
1946	10.4		13.7	17.2		
1947	11.3		14.6	18.7		
1948	12.1		15.2	19.7		
1949	12.5		15.5	20.5		
1950	12.8		15.7	21.0		
1951	13.4		16.3	21.8		
1952	14.3		17.0	22.3		
1953	14.8		17.4	23.0		
1954	15.3		18.0	23.7		
1955	15.7		18.6	24.0		
1956	16.3		19.1	24.4		
1957	17.0		20.0	25.0		
1958	17.9		20.6	25.8		
1959	18.7		21.3	26.4		
1960	19.5		21.9	27.0		
1961	20.2		22.4	27.1		
1962	20.9		23.1	27.8		
1963	21.5		23.6	28.6		
1964	22.0		24.2	29.4		
1965	22.7		25.1	30.3		
1966	23.9		26.5	31.3		
1967	26.0	30.9	28.4	32.8		
1968	27.9	32.5	30.0	34.6		
1969	30.2	34.7	32.1	37.1		
1970	32.3	37.0	34.5	39.2		
1971	34.7	39.4	36.9	41.7		
1972	35.9	40.8	38.0	43.4		
1973	37.5	42.2	39.3	44.8		
1974	41.4	45.8	42.9	48.2		
1975	46.6	50.8	48.1	53.2		
1976	51.3	55.5	53.5	56.5		
1977	56.4	60.0	58.5	60.8		
1978	61.2	64.5	63.4	65.1		
1979	67.2	70.1	69.2	70.5		

Table 11.3 (continued) Consumer Price Index Medical Services All Urban Consumers

Year	Medical Care Services 1982–1984 = 100.0	Professional Medical Services 1982–1984 = 100.0	Physician's Services 1982–1984 = 100.0	Dental Services 1984–1986 = 100.0	Eye Care 1982–1984 = 100.0	Professional Services Dec. 1986 = 100.0
1980	74.8	77.9	76.5	78.9		
1981	82.8	85.9	84.9	86.5		
1982	92.6	93.2	92.9	93.1		
1983	100.7	99.8	100.1	99.4		
1984	106.7	107.0	107.0	107.5		
1985	113.2	113.5	113.5	114.2		
1986	121.9	120.8	121.5	120.6		
1987	130.0	128.8	130.4	128.8	103.5	102.4
1988	138.3	137.5	139.8	137.5	108.7	108.3
1989	148.9	146.4	150.1	146.1	112.4	114.2
1990	162.7	156.1	160.8	155.8	117.3	120.2
1991	177.1	165.7	170.5	167.4	121.9	126.6
1992	190.5	175.8	181.2	178.7	127.0	131.7
1993	202.9	184.7	191.3	188.1	130.4	135.9
1994	213.4	192.5	199.8	197.1	133.0	141.3
1995	224.2	201.0				

Source: U.S. Department of Labor. Bureau of Labor Statistics

Table 11.4 Consumer Price Index Hospital Services All Urban Consumers

Year	Hospital and Related Services 1982–1984 = 100.0	Hospital Room 1982–1984 = 100.0	Other Inpatient Hospital Services Dec. 1986 = 100.0	Outpatient Services Dec. 1986 = 100.0
1935		2.1		
1936		2.1		
1937		2.1		
1938		2.2		
1939		2.2		
1940		2.2		
1941		2.3		
1942		2.5		
1943		2.6		
1944		2.7		
1945		2.9		
1946		3.2		
1947		3.8		
1948		4.4		
1949		4.8		
1950		4.9		
1951		5.4		

Table 11.4 (continued) Consumer Price Index Hospital Services All Urban Consumers

Year	Hospital and Related Services 1982–1984 = 100.0	Hospital Room 1982–1984 = 100.0	Other Inpatient Hospital Services Dec. 1986 = 100.0	Outpatient Services Dec. 1986 = 100.0
1952		5.9		
1953		6.3		
1954		6.6		
1955		6.9		
1956		7.3		
1957		7.9		
1958		8.3		
1959		8.7		
1960		9.3		
1961		9.9		
1962		10.6		
1963		11.1		
1964		11.7		
1965		12.3		
1966		13.6		
1967		16.2		
1968		18.4		
1969		20.9		
1970		23.6		
1971		26.5		
1972		28.2		
1973		29.6		
1974		32.7		
1975		38.3		
1976		43.6		
1977		48.6		
1978	55.1	54.0		
1979	61.0	60.1		
1980	69.2	68.0		
1981	79.1	78.1		
1982	90.3	90.4		
1983	100.5	100.6		
1984	109.2	109.0		
1985	116.1	115.4		
1986	123.1	122.3		
1987	131.6	131.1	103.9	103.3
1988	143.9	143.3	114.0	112.5
1989	160.5	158.1	128.9	124.7
1990	178.0	175.4	142.7	138.7
1991	196.1	191.9	158.0	153.4
1992	214.0	208.7	172.3	168.7
1993	231.9	226.4	185.7	184.3
1994	245.6	239.2	197.1	195.0
1995	257.8			

Source: U.S. Department of Labor. Bureau of Labor Statistics

Table 11.5 Historical Hourly Earnings Non-Agricultural Wage and Salary Employees 1947–1995

Year	Hourly Wages
1947	1.13
1948	1.23
1949	1.28
1950	1.34
1951	1.45
1952	1.52
1953	1.61
1954	1.65
1955	1.71
1956	1.80
1957	1.89
1958	1.95
1959	2.02
1960	2.09
1961	2.14
1962	2.22
1963	2.28
1964	2.36
1965	2.46
1966	2.56
1967	2.68
1968	2.85
1969	3.04
1970	3.23
1971	3.45
1972	3.70
1973	3.94
1974	4.24
1975	4.53
1976	4.86
1977	5.25
1978	5.69
1979	6.16
1980	6.66
1981	7.25
1982	7.68
1983	8.02
1984	8.32
1985	8.57
1986	8.76
1987	8.98
1988	9.28
1989	9.66
1990	10.02
1991	10.34
1992	10.59

Table 11.5 (continued) Historical Hourly Earnings Non-Agricultural Wage and Salary Employees 1947–1995

Year	Hourly Wages
1993	10.83
1994	11.13
1995	11.46

Source: Economic Report of the President, 1996.

Table 11.6 Average Annual Increases Medical and Care Costs

Cost Category	*Data Series*	*Average Annual Rate of Increase (1947–1995)*
Medical Services	Medical Care Services CPI	6.42%
Medical Commodities	Medical Care Commodities CPI	3.64%
Nonmedical Services	Average Hourly Earnings	4.94%
Nonmedical Commodities	All Items (CPI)	4.09%

Source: Tables 11.1–11.5.

Value of the Items

Care must be taken to include the type and extent of all additional commodities and services necessitated by the injury even if these have been, or are expected to be, provided without direct out-of-pocket cost to the client. For example, an injured party may require 24-hour-per-day attendant care, which has been provided in the past by family members. Even if the family members are able and willing to continue to provide the services, from an economic point-of-view the value of the services should be estimated and included as a part of the life care plan. In economics, this is called the "opportunity cost."

The concept of marginal cost may also come into play when assigning a value to some of the services provided. That is, some of the services provided by the family member would have been provided even without the injury and consequently should not be double counted. For instance, if the injured party is a young child who requires constant care, only the additional care necessitated by the injury should be considered. The normal and customary care a mother and other family members would provide the child should not be considered as an additional cost necessitated by the injury.

In some life care plans an attendant or aide is priced at the "going rate" as if one were to directly hire and become the employer. In other plans the service is considered to be provided by a home care provider. If the direct hire approach is to be recommended, consideration must be given to the following:

1. The hourly wage must be at least the Federal minimum wage.
2. The employer (i.e., the client) will be responsible for the withholding and payment of all Social Security taxes. Arrangements must be made for the filing of all reports in a timely fashion.
3. Provision must be made for vacations, sickness, or otherwise unavailability of the employee.
4. The client will be responsible for hiring and training. The turnover of such employees can be expected to be very high.

The administrative tasks necessary when an "employee" is used may prove too burdensome for the client, who is, after all, injured or at least in need of assistance. Although family members may assume the responsibility for these administrative matters, it is not incumbent upon them to do so. In most cases, the preferred treatment would be to assume that attendant costs would be provided by a home care agency.

Delivery Period and Amount

In computing the present value of the life care plan the economist must know the timing of each cost element as well as the length of time the element will be needed. There are two separate considerations concerning the delivery period — that is, **when** the element will be needed (including replacements) and for **how long** it will be needed.

The life care planner should attempt to be as specific as possible as to exactly when a procedure or item will be required. Estimates such as "when needed" or "as required" are often seen in life care plans but cannot be evaluated by the economist.

Statements such as "two operations will be required over his lifetime" are less precise than the economist would prefer but can be used and evaluated. In such a case, the economist may make the estimate by assuming that the procedures will occur at equal time intervals over the life expectancy. As an alternative the economist may total the costs for all like procedures and divide by the number of years of life expectancy to give an "annual amortized cost." This would represent the average annual cost for the procedures. If the delivery times are given as a range (e.g., every 3 to 5 years) the economist may space the delivery at the mean (e.g., 4 years) or, again, compute an annual average. Using an average per year is slightly less accurate than using given amounts in specific years, however. The problem is, however, that in many cases the exact timing is not known.

Statements such as "an operation will be needed within the next ten years" is very imprecise but still may be evaluated. The most conservative evaluation would place the timing at the beginning of the period if the inflation rate is expected to exceed the discount rate, or at the end of the period if the interest is expected to exceed inflation. A compromise evaluation may be made by timing the procedure at the midpoint of the stated duration or by averaging the cost over this period and using an annual average.

The duration of the delivery period is also a very important consideration. The life care plan should note when the element is to start (usually identified by age) and when it is to end. Statements such as "These costs will continue until he reaches adulthood" provide little information.

Many of the elements identified in the life care plan will be delivered over the life expectancy of the injured party. The question may arise as to what is the life expectancy of the client given the medical condition. Changes to the life expectancies set forth in the typical mortality table are not an economic determination but rather a medical one. The economist should be made aware of any modifications to a normal life expectancy made by a specialist. It should be emphasized that the client's life expectancy should be based on the assumption of the provision of first class care as set forth in the life care plan. For this reason, data from studies of the mortality rates of patients with like conditions but who did not have the advantages of first class care should not be used, uncritically, as evidence of a changed life expectancy for the client.

Actual or Average Annual

The costs of the various items may be stated in terms of a specific value in one or more years or may be stated in terms of an average cost per year. For instance, assume a medical item costs $12,000 and will have to be replaced every four years. The life care planner may opt to average the expenditures as $3,000 per year. The present value of items listed in these two ways will differ slightly because of the math involved. If the initial costs and the replacement periods are known exactly, then analyzing the data based on a specific amount in a given year will be slightly more accurate than using the average per year. The problem in most cases, however, is that both the initial costs and the length of the replacement periods are estimates, averages, or ranges. When this is the case, little accuracy will be lost by allocating the costs on an average basis.

Economy of Effort

A comprehensive life care plan will contain a large number of items, some of which cost little and some of which cost a great deal. Experience has shown that most of the costs are concentrated in just a relatively few items — usually those elements associated with care, such as the costs of doctors, hospitals, nurses, LPNs or attendants. The total value of the commodity items generally represents only a small proportion of the total costs.

Many life care plans set forth trivial commodity items in minute detail. Some go as far as to estimate the number of additional boxes of facial tissue that will be used annually. On the other hand, the same plan may set forth two or more care options that differ by many thousands (or even hundreds of thousands) of dollars per year. In many cases, the care options will be assigned a cost, but detailed discussion as to the relative benefits of each option will not be given. The reader of the plan will have little or no idea of the relative advantages or disadvantages of the various care options.

The life care plan would be strengthened if the major research, development, and discussion were concentrated on those items that make the greatest impact on total costs. That is, the important items should be emphasized. In many cases, even if the marginal costs of the trivial items (such as facial tissue) were eliminated from the analysis there would be little difference in the final total cost of the life care plan.

Total Lifetime Values

The only important total cost, over the life expectancy, that needs to be considered in a life care plan is the total present value. This is the number the jury will be asked to consider to provide for the lifetime medical and care needs of the client. Present value considers the rates of price inflation as well as the earning power of money (i.e., interest).

When a life care planner gives a total lifetime value of the recommended items by adding all of the items over life expectancy, the results may be confusing and even misleading. If such a total is intended to represent present value, the implicit assumption is that inflation and interest will cancel out. Unless the economist uses “the total offset” discounting method, the present value calculation will always differ from the “lifetime total.” These differences will invariably cause confusion.

Conclusions

When an economist is called upon to compute the present value of the future medical and care costs set forth in a life care plan prepared by a specialist, he or she must rely on the accuracy of data, including the need, the dollar values, the timing, and the duration. Since the life care plan is the foundation for the economic analysis, the economist has an interest in how the plan is presented. This chapter has looked at life care plans from the economist's point of view and has made a number of recommendations.

REFERENCES

Dillman, E. (1987). The necessary economic and vocational interface in personal injury cases. **Journal of Private Sector Rehabilitation**, 2, 3, 121-142.

Dillman, E. (1988). **Economic Damages and Discounting Methods**. Athens, GA: Elliott & Fizpatrick.

II

SELECTED DISABILITIES: TOPICS AND ISSUES

12

LIFE CARE PLANNING FOR THE AMPUTEE

Robert H. Meier, III

INTRODUCTION

The physiatrist has been trained in the team approach to provide rehabilitative care to persons with simple and complex disabilities. The physiatrist should serve as an ally with the life care planner in determining the ideal outcome of rehabilitative care. In addition, if the physiatrist has been the care provider throughout the active rehabilitation treatment phase, they also will have insights into the psychosocial issues of the person with the disability that will enhance the life care plan. The physiatrist can also medically case manage the variety of health professionals and treatments that are necessary, especially in cases of catastrophic disability. The physiatrist is an excellent resource to provide rehabilitative care and determine equipment costs.

For the person with an amputation, the physiatrist should have the ability to provide meaningful information for the life care plan, especially in the following areas:

1. Point of maximum medical improvement
2. Life expectancy
3. Expected functional outcomes
4. Costs of prosthetic service
5. Frequency of prosthetic replacement
6. Adaptive equipment needs and costs
7. Architectural modifications for function
8. Attendant care hours and level of service
9. Psychosocial needs
10. Vocational and avocational expectations and modifications
11. Future medical needs
12. Future surgical needs

If the local physiatrist is unable to provide useful life care planning information, there is a network of specialized physiatrists who have years of experience in working with the rehabilitation of specific areas of disability. These

1-57444-075-6/99/$0.00+$.50

physiatric specialists can be located through the life care planner network. They should have extensive experience in providing health care for a person with an amputation. The physiatrist can be of great service to the life care planner in indicating the appropriate level of function and future needs for the amputee, as well as which phase of amputation rehabilitation the person has already achieved.

Phases of Amputation Rehabilitation

The loss of a body part(s) is an emotionally traumatic experience. Yet most persons who sustain an amputation can look forward to a fulfilling life of meaningful function using contemporary prosthetic designs. The key to successful prosthetic rehabilitation is understanding the desired functional outcome and the process of achieving that outcome. In addition, the physiatrist should provide a time framework for the achievement of the ideal outcome. The physiatrist can also outline the most cost efficient array of rehabilitative services to achieve the desired rehabilitation goals.

To understand the rehabilitative process for a person with an amputation, it is best to consider the following phases of amputation rehabilitation. These phases, while somewhat artificial, do interweave and flow from one to the next. By knowing the phase of the amputation rehabilitative process, the life care planner can identify the issues to be considered in each phase and assist the amputee toward the next phase. The hallmarks of each phase can be used to determine if the amputee is successfully moving through the phases or is delayed in a phase. Being delayed in a phase of rehabilitative care can detract from the best functional or psychosocial outcome and will also add to the costs of health care.

The phases for amputation rehabilitation staging are:

1. Preoperative
2. Surgical
3. Acute postsurgical
4. Preprosthetic
5. Prosthetic prescription and fabrication
6. Prosthetic training
7. Community reentry
8. Vocational/avocational
9. Follow-up

Hallmarks of each phase have been assigned to measure the progress of the person with an amputation from one phase to the next (Table 12.1). There is usually some overlap from one phase to the next and the person may move more quickly through one phase than another (Meier, 1994). The focus throughout all these phases is on the needs and desires of the amputee. The person's ability to adapt to an altered body image and in some cases, an altered lifestyle, is essential for achieving the idealized outcome. Paying attention to and providing service for their psychosocial well being is paramount to successful rehabilitative outcomes.

Table 12.1 Medical and Rehabilitation Progression of Amputation

Phase	*Hallmarks*
1. Preoperative	Assess body condition, patient education; discuss surgical level, postoperative rehabilitation, and prosthetic plans
2. Amputation surgery	Length, myoplastic closure, soft tissue coverage, nerve reconstruction handling, rigid dressing
3. Acute postoperative	Wound healing, pain control, proximal body motion, emotional support
4. Preprosthetic	Shaping and shrinking amputation stump, increasing muscle strength, restoring patient locus of control
5. Prosthetic fabrication	Team consensus on prosthetic prescription, experienced prosthetic fabrication
6. Prosthetic training	Increase wearing of prosthesis, mobility, and ADL skills
7. Community reintegration	Resume roles in family and community activities; regain emotional equilibrium and healthy coping strategies; pursue recreational activities
8. Vocational rehabilitation	Assess and plan vocational activities for future. May need further education, training, or job modification
9. Follow-up	Provide lifelong prosthetic, functional, medical, and emotional support; provide regular assessment of functional level and prosthetic problem solving

Preoperative

On a few occasions, the patient is delayed in the decision for an amputation. This is an ideal time for the rehabilitation team to assess and begin a treatment plan focusing on function of the remaining extremities. This is also an appropriate time to practice preventive care to maintain full range of motion and strength in the proximal limb muscles of the side to be amputated and also in the intact limb. An aerobic conditioning program should be provided during this phase since this type of exercise will hasten the postoperative functional recovery.

Amputation Surgery and Reconstruction Phase

Amputation surgery should proceed as a reconstructive surgery that will provide a residual limb with the best function, whether or not a prosthesis is likely to be prescribed. A reconstructive philosophy of amputation is best accomplished by a surgeon who has performed a number of amputations and understands contemporary prosthetic options and functional outcomes.

Acute Postoperative Phase

This is a time for wound healing and pain control. Usually there is wound care necessary until the sutures are removed. The rehabilitation focus is on the remaining limbs and instructing the amputee in preventive exercise for the amputated limb and the opposite limb. Psychosocial support is essential during this period of loss for the individual.

Preprosthetic Phase

This period is usually accomplished on an outpatient basis. Once the sutures are removed, attention is paid to shaping and shrinking the residual limb in preparation for prosthetic casting. This is a good time to educate the amputee and the family regarding the prosthetic options available, and to develop and review the rehabilitation plan, if it has not previously been accomplished. At this time careful therapeutic attention should be paid to aerobic conditioning and strength training. Emotional stresses should be anticipated that surround change in body image, function, family roles, and income. Helping the amputee regain the locus of control in their life is important during this phase.

Prosthetic Fabrication

At this phase, the team, including the amputee, should decide on a prosthetic prescription that best meets the person's needs and desires (Meier, 1995). More and more, the prosthetic prescription is also dependent on what a third-party payer will sponsor. It is preferable that a prosthetist who is frequently experienced in fitting the specific level of amputation be used to fabricate the prosthesis. The time framework from prosthetic casting until final fitting should be presented to the amputee and the rehabilitation team for planning purposes.

As a general rule, the lower limb amputee should be fitted within eight weeks of amputation and the arm amputee fitted within four to six weeks of amputation surgery. If the upper limb amputee is delayed in fitting, their chances of using a prosthesis for bimanual activities decreases significantly. They become accustomed to performing activities in a one-handed manner and, therefore, do not find the prosthesis to be of much assistance in performing their daily activities.

Prosthetic Training

This phase is best accomplished in an outpatient therapy setting by therapists who have trained many amputees with similar levels and types of prostheses. This phase should continue until the expected level of functional outcome has been achieved. The length of treatment time will vary depending on the level of amputation, the amputee's health, level of function prior to the amputation, associated injuries, and medical problems. The rehabilitation team should proceed with gradual prosthetic wearing and functional training with the goal of achieving the idealized functional outcomes listed in Tables 12.2, 12.3, and 12.4. The rehabilitation treatment plan should focus on the level of function necessary for community reintegration, vocational and avocational outcomes.

Community Reintegration

The person with the amputation should begin to resume their roles in the family and the community as quickly as possible following the amputation. Prosthetic

Table 12.2 Functional Expectations for the Below-Knee Amputee

1.	Wears the prosthesis during all waking hours
2.	Walks on level and uneven surfaces
3.	Climbs stairs step over step
4.	Drives a car (if desired)
5.	Can fall safely and arise from the floor
6.	Can run (if cardiovascular status permits)
7.	Can hop without the prosthesis
8.	Participates in avocational interests
9.	Has returned to same or modified work
10.	Does not use any gait aid
11.	Performs aerobic conditioning exercise (if cardiovascular system permits)
12.	Knows how to inspect skin of the amputated and nonamputated legs and foot
13.	Knows how to change stump socks to accommodate for soft tissue changes
14.	Knows how to buy a correctly fitting shoe for the remaining foot
15.	Independent in ADL
16.	Understands the necessity of follow-up

training can assist with community reintegration by providing meaningful function. A psychologist or social worker should assist the amputee in developing productive social interactions with their family, friends, peers, and other persons in their community.

Vocational Rehabilitation

The physiatrist should be closely involved during this phase of amputee rehabilitation. The physiatrist is most knowledgeable in the expected level of prosthetic use in a variety of vocational settings. The physiatrist is also best suited to place the work restrictions in relationship to the level of amputation and functional outcome. Working as a team, the case manager, the physiatrist, and the vocational rehabilitation specialist can provide an excellent support system for the amputee and enhance their successful return to the workplace.

While vocational rehabilitation should begin shortly following the amputation, return to the workplace may require a functional capacity evaluation, worksite evaluation, and perhaps worksite modification. Generally, it is ill advised to provide a vocational prognosis until the person has achieved maximum functional outcome with or without the prosthesis.

Follow-Up

In order to ensure the most appropriate level of prosthetic function, prevent prosthetic problems, and address emotional adjustment to amputation, a regular and periodic program of rehabilitation follow-up should be provided for the amputee. Once the ideal level of function has been achieved and the amputee is wearing a definitive prosthesis, the person should be seen in regular follow-up on an annual or every-other-year basis. This schedule permits measurement

Table 12.3 Functional Expectations for the Above-Knee Amputee

(Greater energy expenditure than for below-knee prosthetic use)

1. Wears the prosthesis during all waking hours
2. Walks on level and uneven surfaces
3. Climbs stairs step over step (some may do one step at a time)
4. Drives a car (if desired)
5. Can fall safely and arise from the floor
6. Can hop without the prosthesis
7. Participates in avocational interests
8. Has returned to same or modified work
9. Does not use any gait aid (some may need a cane)
10. Performs aerobic conditioning exercise (if cardiovascular system permits)
11. Knows how to inspect skin of the amputated and nonamputated legs and foot
12. Knows how to buy a correctly fitting shoe for the remaining foot
13. Independent in ADL
14. Understands the necessity of follow-up
15. A few can run with high-level training

Table 12.4 Functional Expectations for the Above- and Below-Elbow Amputee

1. Independent in donning and doffing the prosthesis
2. Independent in activities of daily living
3. Can write legibly with remaining hand
4. Has successfully switched dominance (if necessary)
5. Drives (if desired)
6. Has returned to work (same or modified job)
7. Can tie laces with one hand or with the remaining hand and the prosthesis
8. Uses a button hook easily
9. Has prepared a meal in the kitchen
10. Has been shown adaptive equipment for the kitchen and ADL
11. Has performed carpentry and automotive maintenance (if desired)
12. Wears prosthesis during all waking hours
13. Uses the prosthesis for bimanual activities
14. Understands the necessity of follow-up

of the functional outcomes of amputation rehabilitation. It also serves to enhance the education of the amputee regarding preventive care and further prosthetic needs.

Demographics of Limb Amputation

Amputation of the leg is more common than amputation of the arm and occurs in a 3:1 ratio. The leg amputee is usually a person in the sixth or seventh decade of life who sustains the amputation because of occlusive arterial vascular disease. Often this person also has associated diabetes mellitus. In addition to the vascular disease in the legs, there is often accompanying arterial disease in the coronary and cerebral arteries. With associated diabetes, the complications can include peripheral neuropathy, renal disease, and diminished eyesight. All of these comorbid factors can diminish the functional outcomes in prosthetic rehabilitation.

The arm amputee is usually a young man who has sustained a work-related injury. The amputation most frequently involves the right arm and most often results in a below-elbow amputation of the dominant arm. The arm amputee, unlike the leg amputee, can function independently with the use of one arm. Functional prosthetic restoration in the arm amputee is less successful than in the leg amputee.

Phantom and Residual Limb Pain

This phenomenon occurs in most patients immediately following the amputation surgery and subsides during the first 4 to 6 weeks after the amputation. In only a few amputees does phantom limb pain become so problematic that it interferes with the quality of life. It should not be treated with narcotics other than during the acute postoperative period. Today, a variety of medications can be used to alleviate this pain. Popular at this time are tricyclic antidepressants, gabapentin, and carbamazepine (Davis, 1993). These medications affect the way the body processes pain messages in the peripheral and central nervous systems. Other physical modalities have been utilized but have met with varied success depending on the individual amputee. If the phantom pain interferes greatly with the quality of life and/or prosthetic function, an amputee pain specialist should be consulted.

Pain in the residual limb should be differentiated from phantom pain. Often, residual limb pain is caused by a poorly fitting prosthesis and can be alleviated with socket modifications. Residual limb pain may also be caused by the development of a neuroma from a peripheral nerve that was severed at the time of the amputation. There are a variety of conservative and surgical methods to attempt to decrease the pain from a neuroma (Sherman, Sherman, & Gail, 1980).

Levels of Limb Amputation

In general, the longer the length of the residual limb, the better the prosthetic function that can be expected. In the leg, amputation below the knee provides for lower energy expenditure than the use of an above-knee prosthesis. Salvaging the leg at a below-knee level is now the goal of leg amputation surgery in the United States (Moore & Malone, 1989). Disarticulation levels for the arm and leg have certain relative contraindications and should be carefully considered on an individual basis. Full thickness skin and soft tissue coverage are also helpful in achieving ideal prosthetic functional outcomes. However, with the new gel interfaces, scarred skin and poor soft tissue coverage can be dealt with in a more satisfactory manner than in the past.

Prosthetic Prescription

There has been an explosion of available prosthetic components in the past ten years and it is hard to keep up with the constant barrage of new options for the amputee. Most of the new components have added to the expense of the prosthesis without scientific demonstration that they have enhanced the functional outcome. Many of the new components are lighter weight and therefore more comfortable to wear. New prosthetic foot designs have added the ability to run and jump that were not previously possible with the older component designs (Esquenazi & Torres, 1991). The use of electric components for the arm amputee has not been universally applied in the United States. This technology remains less frequently prescribed than the conventional body-powered designs. The prices of prostheses, especially those using the new socket designs and components, have risen dramatically. A "high tech" above-knee prosthesis frequently will cost $17,000 to $20,000, while an above-elbow myoelectric arm can cost $60,000 and more. With costs at these levels, it is imperative that the amputee be treated in a comprehensive interdisciplinary center of amputee rehabilitative excellence.

The usual components required for a prosthetic leg include the socket, a foot/ankle complex, and a means of suspension. Of course, for the above-knee prosthesis, a knee component is also prescribed.

For the arm amputee, there is a socket that fits onto the residual limb and for the below-elbow amputee, a wrist joint, a terminal device, and a suspension system are required elements of the prescription. Terminal devices can be a hook or a hand (Sears, 1991). The hand can be passive or it can move. For the above-elbow amputee, an elbow joint is prescribed. In considering the arm prosthetic prescription, the team needs to consider the three basic prosthetic designs available. They are a passive prosthesis that provides mainly cosmetic restoration, one that is cable controlled by body power, or one that has electric moving parts. A comparison of these types of arm prostheses is presented in Table 12.5 (Esquenazi, Leonard, Meier, et al., 1989).

Partial Hand

This level of amputation can be handled in several ways. Many partial hand amputees choose to not wear any prosthetic restoration. However, if cosmesis is desired, a cosmetic glove can be fabricated. This is usually made from a mold taken of the residual hand. A custom-made silicone glove that is hand-colored can provide excellent cosmesis and is reasonably durable. However, if it is worn at work, a protective glove should be worn. Another manner to prosthetically handle this level is to make an opposition bar that can provide improved prehension between the prosthetic bar and the residual moving parts of the hand. If the thumb has been amputated, an excellent prosthetic thumb can be fabricated. The functional and cosmetic results from this prosthesis often decrease the need for surgical reconstruction of the amputated thumb.

Wrist Disarticulation/Below Elbow

The below-elbow prosthesis is usually composed of a double-walled plastic laminate socket that fits intimately over the residual limb. A locking, quick-change wrist unit is commonly prescribed through which the terminal device is attached to the forearm shell. This wrist unit permits ease of change of various terminal devices and locks the terminal device in a position of function when handling heavier objects. For most men who will return to heavy-duty work, a body-powered

Table 12.5 Advantages and Disadvantages of Various Upper-Limb Prostheses

Type	*Pros*	*Cons*
Cosmetic (passive)	Most lightweight Best cosmesis Least harnessing	High cost if custom made Least functional Low-cost gloves stain easily
Body powered	Moderate cost Moderately lightweight Most durable Highest sensory feedback	Most body movement to operate Most harnessing Least satisfactory appearance
Externally powered (myoelectric and switch control)	Moderate or no harnessing Least body movement to operate Moderate cosmesis More function-proximal levels	Heaviest Most expensive Most maintenance Limited sensory feedback
Hybrid (cable elbow/ electric TD)	All cable excursion to elbow Increased TD pinch	Electric TD weights forearm (harder to lift) Good for elbow disarticulation (or long above elbow)
Hybrid (electric elbow/ cable TD)	All cable excursion to TD Low effort to position TD Low maintenance TD	Least cosmesis Lower pinch force for TD

Esquenazi, Leonard & Meier, 1989

prosthesis will be useful. For the businessman or white-collar worker, a myoelectric or a passive cosmetic prosthesis may be preferable (Meier, 1996).

Elbow Disarticulation/Above Elbow

The prosthetic options at this level of restoration are body-powered or electric control. The electric prosthesis is many times the expense of the body-powered arm. For a very short above-elbow level of amputation, an electric prosthesis may be the only functional restoration that is reasonable.

Shoulder Disarticulation

This level can be fitted with a lighter weight endoskeletal design with a passive elbow joint and a moving terminal device. At this proximal level of amputation, an electric prosthesis will permit more functional motion of the component parts. However, it is extremely heavy to wear and very expensive.

Partial/Hindfoot

Often this level of amputation can be fitted with a full-length insole with toe filler that fits inside the shoe. This insole can usually be interchanged between various shoes. The bottom of the shoe may need to be modified to provide a more normal gait pattern.

Below Knee

The prosthesis that is currently used for this level of amputation was popularized in the mid-1950s. It is called a patellar tendon bearing (PTB) design. It was originally designed to place superincumbent body weight on the remaining anatomic landmarks that were pressure tolerant. It relieves pressure from the pressure-intolerant areas of the residual stump. For this level, the prosthetic prescription includes the design of the prosthetic socket, a foot/ankle complex, and a means of suspending the prosthesis on the residual leg. A current popular suspension design is called the triple "S" system or the silicone sleeve suspension. A silicone sleeve is worn against the skin and a knurled pin extends from the distal end. This pin locks inside a coupling in the distal end of the prosthetic socket. The silicone sleeve provides additional padding to the inside of the socket against the skin. Other types of gel liners are in vogue today and have made prosthetic leg wearing more comfortable. These liners reduce the number of skin problems seen with prosthetic wear and function.

Knee Disarticulation/Above Knee

The contemporary socket design for the above-knee amputee has changed in the 1980s and 1990s (Leonard & Meier, 1993). There are a number of designs available but the one in greatest use is a narrow mediolateral, ischial containment design. New socket designs also include thermoplastic inner liners that have improved the comfort of prosthetic wearing. Gel liners are also available for this level of amputation. A variety of knee units are also available that provide differing degrees of knee stability and cosmesis with gait.

Hip Disarticulation

This is a difficult level to fit comfortably and to have the amputee walk successfully with the prosthesis. This level of amputation should be handled by a prosthetist who makes ten or more of this type of prosthesis a year. More important, for best success, this amputee should have their rehabilitation in a center that has trained a number of amputees to wear this type of prosthesis with good results.

Prosthetic Complications

A well-fitted prosthesis is in intimate contact with the skin of the residual limb. There are shearing forces applied to the skin in arm and leg prostheses. In the leg amputee, there are also direct pressures applied from the prosthesis to the skin of the residual leg. These forces can create skin pressure problems. These issues are usually addressed with prosthetic socket modifications or the use of gel-skin interfaces. A differing socket design may also be necessary to change the forces applied to the skin.

Prosthetic Costs

Because of the high cost of prosthetics, a team of experienced amputee rehabilitation specialists should develop a prescription. To have the prosthetist develop the prescription in a vacuum is almost a conflict of interest and should be avoided.

Prosthetic Replacement

Within the first two years following the amputation, several socket changes are usually necessary to accommodate the rapid soft tissue changes that occur. These changes improve the prosthetic fit and comfort of wearing. Usually after this time, a prosthesis should last the amputee from three to five years before a replacement prosthesis is prescribed. Certainly, the level of activity in using the prosthesis will affect the frequency with which these replacements are needed. Modifications to the prosthesis are usually needed once every six months on average.

Life Care Planning with the Physiatrist

There are three differing scenarios for physiatric involvement with life care planning. The best scenario is when the physiatrist to be involved with the life care plan has been the treating physiatrist throughout the individual's rehabilitation process. In this scenario, the physiatrist has become quite involved with directing the amputee's rehabilitation treatment goals and plan. Having worked with the amputee through the phases of amputation rehabilitation, they can give the best prognostic information. The physiatrist will have a clear picture of the amputee's psychosocial support system and their needs and desires, as well as the amputee's preamputation lifestyle and how likely it will be to achieve that quality of life post-amputation.

Another scenario is the physiatrist who has been asked to participate in a life care plan but has never been involved with the amputee's rehabilitation program. This physiatrist has agreed to evaluate the individual to provide meaningful information for a life care plan. Often, this requires a visit from the amputee to the physiatrist for a thorough assessment. This may be accomplished over a one to several day process, depending on the complexity of the case. Almost always, this evaluation will be performed during an outpatient visit. The evaluation usually includes the physiatric assessment and visits with an occupational therapist, a physical therapist, a psychologist, and a prosthetist. Other rehabilitation professionals and consultants may be included in this evaluation depending on other areas of disability or comorbid factors. The product of this evaluation should be a report that provides all the information that a life care planner will include in the final plan. For this reason, it is essential that the life care planner pose all of the important questions they wish the physician to address before the evaluation process begins.

The evaluation process by the physiatrist should include the following elements that are clearly delineated during the evaluation and the physiatrist's opinions that are to be included in the life care document.

These items should include:

1. History
2. Past medical history
3. Review of systems
4. Medications
5. Psychosocial history
6. Activity status

7. Vocational history
8. Avocational history
9. Prosthetic history
10. Adaptive equipment used
11. Achievement of maximum medical improvement
12. Future needs
    - prosthetic
    - emotional
    - rehabilitative
    - medical
    - surgical
    - equipment
    - architectural modifications
    - attendant care
    - vocational options
    - follow-up plan
    - health maintenance and preventive care

A third manner for physiatric involvement in life care planning is the "curbside consultation." In this instance, the physiatrist does not have the advantage of evaluating the amputee but instead reviews the case records and provides input into the life care plan based on the physiatrist's experience with similar patients. This manner of physiatric involvement can be very useful to the life care planner in helping to assure that important life care planning issues for a person with an amputation are not overlooked.

Potential Complications

Potential complications are dependent on the reason for the amputation (trauma, electrocution, diabetes, cancer, cadiovascular disease, etc.), fit of prosthesis (if one is used), work demands, living environment, quality of medical treatment, and other factors. However, common considerations include (Weed & Sluis, 1990):

1. Some of the most common complications are psychological. In many cases, psychological counseling will be provided while the client is an inpatient and may be continued following discharge from acute care. If psychological counseling is offered, the costs for this should be placed on the "Projected Therapeutic Modalities" page. In the example case, the client experienced significant depression, was hospitalized for suicidal ideation, and had undergone a significant amount of psychological counseling following discharge. In this case, the family unit fell apart and a number of family counseling issues were raised.
2. In the event of amputations where the client wears a prosthesis, one would expect the probability of occasional skin breakdown. In one case, the client suffered amputations as a result of an electrocution injury. In this situation, the skin loses its integrity due to the burn. The client may require surgical intervention in order to repair skin breakdown.
3. Bone spurs occasionally become a problem and may require surgery.

4. Phantom pain or sensations are very common, at least during acute recovery, and may need some sort of treatment.
5. Other complications include osteoarthritis, which may be experienced in the knees and lower back, as well as back pain that may be experienced due to an abnormal gait. Fit of the prostheses is of paramount importance to avoid these kinds of complications. In addition to proper fit, specific gait training to educate the client as to proper body mechanics will be important.
6. Another often overlooked complication has to do with weight gain. Weight gain affects the fit of the prostheses, requiring either adjustment or a complete refabrication of the socket.
7. Complicated recoveries from other injuries may be a result of the inability of the client to manage self-care during periods of injury or illness. For example, an individual who is a triple amputee (bilateral below knee and dominant arm at the shoulder) may be unable to take care of himself for even bowel and bladder care or other survival needs should he injure his other arm.
8. Knee problems when not wearing the prosthesis is often a complication for bilateral below-knee amputees. It is sometimes much easier to avoid the time it takes to put on a prosthesis by simple walking on one's knees in order to get around the house, such as going to the bathroom at night or trying to get out of the house in case of an emergency. After years of using this method to move around, it is not uncommon for clients to experience knee problems.
9. While working in hot environments or having to exert considerable effort to walk or engage in physical activity with a prosthesis, sweating can become an irritating problem. Prostheses tend to feel heavy and awkward and will require an approximate 10% increase in energy for a single below-knee amputation and much more energy expenditure with multiple amputations (Friedmann, 1981). It does not take an educated observer to understand that a bilateral above-knee amputee will expend considerable energy simply getting from one place to another. In fact, many amputees may prefer to use a wheelchair to do things quicker. In addition, an upper-extremity amputee, such as a shoulder disarticulation, requires the addition of a mechanical arm or a Utah arm, which also requires considerable effort. This may result in excessive sweating and irritation as well. In addition, working in a hot environment, such as outdoors in the summertime in the south or in a boiler room indoors, may become intolerable.
10. Neuromas are also fairly frequent and can be quite irritating if the prosthesis impacts on the area where the neuroma resides. Often surgery is the treatment of choice.

CONCLUSION

The physiatrist should play a valuable role in assisting in the development of the life care plan for the person who has sustained an amputation. An emphasis should be placed on the amputee achieving the ideal level of function with an appropriate rehabilitation program. Just providing a prosthesis is not the same as providing an integrated rehabilitation program that includes a prosthesis. The emphasis should be placed on the amputee's needs and desires. Measuring the functional outcome, the success of community reintegration, and the individual's emotional adaptation to the changes in their life are important in developing an accurate life care plan. The physiatrist should serve as an invaluable collaborator with the life care planner in order to develop the most accurate and comprehensive life care plan.

REFERENCES

Davis, R. (1993). Phantom sensation, phantom pain and stump pain. **Archives of Physical Medicine Rehabilitation, 74 (70),** 79-84.

Esquenazi, A., Leonard, J. A., & Meier, R. H. (1989). Prosthetics. **Archives of Physical Medicine Rehabilitation, 70** (suppl.), 207.

Esquenazi, A. & Torres, M. M. (1991). In L. W. Friedmann (Ed.), **Physical Medicine and Rehabilitation Clinics of North America.** Philadelphia: W.B. Saunders.

Friedmann, L. (1981). Amputation. In W. Stolov & M. Clowers (Eds.), **Handbook of Severe Disability**. Washington, D.C.: U.S. Department of Education, Rehabilitation Services Administration.

Leonard, J. A. and Meier, R. H. (1993). Upper and lower extremity prosthetics. In J. A. DeLisa (Ed.), **Rehabilitation Medicine: Principles and Practices.** Philadelphia: J.B. Lippincott.

Meier, R. H. (1994). Upper limb amputee rehabilitation. In A. Esquenazi (Ed.), **Prosthetics: State of the Art Reviews.** Philadelphia: Hanley & Belfus.

Meier, R. H. (1995). Rehabilitation of the person with an amputation. In R. B. Rutherford (Ed.), **Vascular Surgery.** Philadelphia: W.B. Saunders.

Meier, R. H. (1996). Upper limb prosthetics: design, prescription and application. In C. A. Peimer (Ed.), **Surgery of the Hand and Upper Extremity.** New York: McGraw-Hill.

Moore, W. S. & Malone, J. M. (Eds.). (1989). **Lower Extremity Amputation.** Philadelphia: W.B. Saunders.

Sear, H. H. (1991). Approaches to prescription of body-powered and myoelectric prosthetics. In L. W. Friedmann (Ed.), **Prosthetics: Physical Medicine and Rehabilitation Clinics of North America.** Philadelphia: W.B. Saunders.

Sherman, R. A., Sherman, C. J., & Gail, N. A. (1980). Survey of current phantom limb treatment in the United States. **Pain, 8,** 85-99.

Weed, R. & Sluis, A. (1990). **Life Care Plans for the Amputee: A Step by Step Guide**. Boca Raton, FL: CRC Press.

13

LIFE CARE PLANNING ISSUES FOR PEOPLE WITH CHRONIC PAIN

Thomas M. Ward & Roger O. Weed

INTRODUCTION

Significant pain can be experienced as a result of a multitude of medical problems. The most common is associated with low back pain, an affliction experienced by 80% of the population sometime during their lifetime (Cailliet & Helberg, 1981). Objective definitions of pain have eluded researchers (Weed, 1987). No pain literature available to these writers has been able satisfactorily to define pain objectively. Pain appears to be a subjective experience measured by self-report (Sternbach, 1968; Sternbach, 1974; Shealy, 1976; Fordyce, 1976; Melzak, 1973; Merskey, 1964; Merskey, 1972; Skinner, 1974; Loeser, 1980; Bresler, 1979; Ramsey, 1979; Engel, MacBryde, & Blacklow, 1970; I.A.S.P., 1979). Research indicates that the pain threshold is similar from person to person and culture to culture, but pain tolerance can vary dramatically (Shealy, 1976). Sternbach has simply stated that "pain is a hurt we feel" (1968, p. l).

Sternbach (1974) has also identified more than l00 words that people use to describe their pain, revealing how difficult it is to objectively quantify. Pain seems clearly not merely a neurophysiological event, but a combination of variables complicated by evidence that pain is not simply what a patient says it is (Fordyce, 1976). Most patients can describe how intense their pain is, but attempts to describe the quality has led to the development of the McGill-Melzack Pain Questionnaire in an effort to standardize treatment approaches (Meissner, 1982).

For purposes of this chapter, chronic pain can be described as pain that has lasted anywhere from six months to one year after the original pain incident. Although there is controversy regarding definitions, most physicians agree that *acute pain* is from the date of onset to one month, *subacute pain* is defined as pain lasting from one month to six months, and *chronic pain* can thereafter be defined as lasting six months or longer.

Chronic pain and the subsequent costs to society, however, do not necessarily include all individuals who have had pain of some type or another for longer than a year. In general, the diagnosis of chronic pain becomes broader as it includes the psychological stress and disruption to the everyday quality of life of

1-57444-075-6/99/$0.00+$.50

individuals who suffer from it. There are an estimated 34 million people in this country who suffer from chronic pain (Brownlee & Schaf, 1997). Each year millions of people seek relief at hospitals or pain clinics. The overall cost in lost work days, medical treatment, and additional psychological counseling can be enormous. Counting back pain, migraine and headache pain, osteoarthritis, rheumatoid arthritis, fibromyalgia, failed surgical fusion lumbar or cervical spine, reflex sympathetic dystrophy, causalgia, diabetic neuropathy, and cancer pain, estimates exceed over $40 billion annually. Of the workforce, complaints of pain and related complications of pain result in one quarter of all the sick days taken or, to put it in another way, over 50 million lost work days per year are due to pain (Brownlee & Schaf, 1997).

The history of pain management actually probably dates back to the first known practicing doctors. It has been said that 80% of patient problems prompting a visit to a physician are the direct result of some form of pain, acute, subacute, or chronic. However, most recently with the advent of chronic pain management programs, more comprehensive multidisciplinary team management for chronic pain and the associated disability/psychological stress/depression and subsequent functional loss have sprung up. Now there are pain management centers in nearly every major metropolitan area in the United States. Pain management has become a subspecialty recognized by the American Medical Association, and numerous societies offer continuing medical education, seminars, legislative lobbying assistance, and national boards of directors to oversee the problems associated with the disease state now classified as chronic pain. Beginning in 1911, workers compensation laws were enacted to require employers to assume the cost of occupational disability without regard to fault (Weed & Field, 1994). These laws have dramatically altered the recovery of the individual injured in the workforce since that time. However, additional aspects involving litigation have become more prevalent in the last 20 to 30 years. Because of litigation an adversarial role between the workplace and the injured worker often develops.

Also of interest are the recent efforts to reduce health care costs by any and all means. Thus, again, injured workers suffering chronic pain ailments are often given little, if any, direct assistance, and legal assistance through litigation has become necessary to allow the patient to pursue more comprehensive treatment of their chronic pain condition. It can be said that if a patient truly has significant chronic pain it will disrupt every aspect of their lives. This includes vocational, as well as avocational pursuits, sleep, routine daily activities such as dressing, bathing, hygiene, and self-care. Exercise, relationships, sexual relationships, and financial stresses will all ensue. In this way, a comprehensive approach to the treatment of the chronic pain patient embodies all the aforementioned areas as it focuses attention on restoring the patient to a level of independence to the extent that it is possible. The long-range goal is to achieve a degree of independence of the patient from the health provider. Recent studies seem to indicate that those individuals suffering from chronic pain who are not seeing physicians or receiving constant medical attention may do better overall than those individuals who do seek chronic pain management for years at a time (Ernonoff, 1997).

Diagnostic Efforts in Work-Up

The first thing necessary for any patient suffering from pain of six months duration or longer is to review what medical attention he or she has been receiving from the standpoint of diagnostic evaluations, medical consultations, laboratory and X-ray, and surgical intervention. Before any comprehensive management addressing the other areas mentioned above can be initiated, it should be ascertained that the patient does not have a remedial or correctable cause for his or her chronic pain. The scope of diagnostic evaluations of the patient with chronic pain is quite numerous. Magnetic resonance imaging of the affected area, CT scanning, plain film X-rays, myelograms, electromyographic muscle examinations and nerve conduction velocity, and invasive procedures such as laparoscopic surgical evaluation, epidural steroid injections and differential blocks, and diskograms are all helpful in the diagnosis of axial skeletal related cervical, thoracic, or lumbar spine pain resulting from disk injuries or fractures.

Occasionally, multiple specialty consultations are required to achieve such thorough evaluations in our present era of medical specialties. Inclusive of this would be a psychologist for determination via psychological testing, Minnesota Multiphasic Personality Inventory — 2 (MMPI-2) or other assistive testing to determine a patient's psychological status as it pertains to his or her pain complaints. Benefits of having several specialists evaluate the patient will be that significant overlap of observations, including questionable symptom magnification with litigious patients with secondary gain in mind, will be noted from a variety of clinicians' vantage points. Despite being a suspicious point of view to include in an evaluation of the patient with pain, it is nonetheless necessary as certainly questions will arise later on regarding the authenticity of the patient's symptoms. Occasionally it will be difficult to show from the objective testing standpoint that pain has an organic cause that is immediately observable with the aforementioned testing. In these instances, chronic pain management specialists can add a further backdrop from which to define and further assess the patient's pain complaints. There are a number of sensory feedback loops to the central nervous system, including the sympathetic nervous system, bones, joints, ligaments, muscles, and, ultimately, the dermatomes of the peripheral nervous system. Despite the insurance company's desire to be shown where the pain is coming from, many times pain resulting from trauma does not reveal the presence of a herniated disk, fracture, or ruptured ligaments. In these instances, additional documentation or proof as to the nature of the patient's pain complaints will be required.

Approaches to Management of Pain

Following a complete evaluation of the work-up requiring the aforementioned tests, consultation with the psychologist or psychiatrist and subsequent psychological testing batteries, differential nerve blocks, and MRI scans, etc., the patient may be placed in a number of different settings for continued pain management and treatment.

Of recent prevalence is the anesthesiologist-based pain management clinic. The majority of these function in an outpatient surgical setting or in the confines of a local hospital. The anesthesiologist in this case has been trained through specialty residency training for the performance of injections of anesthetic agents and narcotics into different regions, thereby blocking the local neuroanatomy and allowing for the cessation of the pain symptom complex. Depending upon the nature of the pain and its subsequent causes, the patient may require surgical intervention. The most common surgeon involved in spine ailments, including cervical and lumbar spine pain, is the neurosurgeon and the orthopedic surgeon. Specialists in these areas in most major metropolitan regions are familiar with causes and treatment of pain, and will offer surgical remedies for their relief.

Another resource for treatment for pain would be the less aggressive, more conservative outpatient rehabilitation or physiatrist office. In this setting the comprehensive nature of the pain is addressed from a number of areas, including medications, sleep restoration, diet and exercise, orthotics, therapy, electrical stimulation devices, and other neurological diagnostic work-ups. The decision as to which resource to employ is often made by the patient.

The majority of patients in the physician author's outpatient clinic have typically been injured for over a year and have already been evaluated by either a neurosurgeon or orthopedic surgeon. Many of them have already undergone surgical intervention and have subsequently been referred to an anesthesiologist where additional aggressive management is pursued through injection therapy with narcotics or local anesthetics. At that juncture, the anesthesiologist also employs a number of medications and usually initiates a psychological evaluation including biofeedback and stress management. Depending upon the benefits of those measures, an additional referral is made to other physicians such as physiatrists where exercise programs, further medication adjustments, orthotics, diet, sleep restoration, stress management, and family counseling are usually initiated. Outpatient physical therapy may be employed on a number of different occasions throughout the chronological time frame from the original injury, surgical intervention, anesthesiological intervention, and, ultimately, for rehabilitation and restorative functional gains.

If an individual has already undergone a number of surgeries and has already undergone a number of injections, then a physician may be reluctant to send them back for more surgery. It should be remembered that each patient needs to have a thorough evaluation of their present condition to determine the etiology of their pain. If a patient's pain has not been evaluated for two or more years, despite a thorough documentation of the presence of a nonoperative lesion from the past, then it is quite possible that further evaluation and diagnostic X-ray information may need to be obtained.

Life Care Planning and Chronic Pain

Individual types of pain are very variable and are almost beyond the scope of this short chapter. A listing of types of injuries that can result in chronic pain requiring lifetime medical care would include the following:

- Spinal cord injury — cervical, thoracic, lumbar with paraplegia, quadriplegia, or tetraplegia
- Lumbar, cervical, or thoracic spine injury

- Herniated disk
- Spinal cord infarctions
- Spinal cord fractures or axial spine fractures
- Neuropathy
- Causalgia
- Reflex sympathetic dystrophy
- Multiple orthopedic fractures and subsequent claudication injuries
- Cancer of any organ or any tissue type
- Traumatic head injury
- Abdominal problems
- Genital/urinary problems
- Pulmonary problems
- Osteoarthritis
- Rheumatoid arthritis
- Systemic lupus erythematosus
- Fibromyalgia
- Trigeminal neuralgia
- Motor vehicle accidents
- Failed spinal surgeries
- Orthopedic joint replacement surgery including hip and knee surgeries
- Vascular injuries including angina
- Peripheral vascular injuries
- Peripheral vascular ischemia with crush injuries
- Headaches, including migraine, cluster, and tension headaches
- Brachial plexus injuries
- Pelvic inflammatory disease
- Environmental toxins and exposures

The medical needs and future care for these conditions run the gamut and require a coordinated effort of services that are individually determined. Some of the considerations include the following.

Psychological Considerations

In the comprehensive management of chronic pain, psychological testing and treatment for depression, anxiety, and stress are all components required for maximum improvement. All chronic pain patients should have psychological counseling and psychological testing somewhere in the course of their pain management. The family will also require assistance in coping with the patient's pain problems as it is very disruptive to the normal activities of family life following an injury or illness that causes chronic pain. Depending upon when the life care planner becomes involved in the case, an evaluation by a psychologist and subsequent further recommendations of biofeedback and stress management on a weekly basis for at least one year to improve on the patient's ability to initiate and maintain a program that will benefit him for the lifetime of his complaint is commonly recommended.

There are numerous additional resources from which the chronic pain patient can draw. Self-help groups and certain newsletters are available for individual diseases that the patient can access through the Internet. Local chapters of the larger disease diagnoses that cause chronic pain may be available. These include rheumatoid arthritis foundation groups, fibromyalgia groups, spinal cord injury and recovery groups, brain injury recovery groups, multiple sclerosis groups, local diabetes foundations, and others.

It should be noted that self-treatment through alcohol or illicit drug use is a common feature of our society, which probably increases with the advent of chronic pain. Recently additional guidelines have been released by the American Academy of Chronic Pain, the World Institute of Pain, and the American Academy of Pain Management. All entities now recognize the therapeutic use of chronic narcotic analgesia for chronic pain. However, medical societies in local as well as state medical boards are concerned about the use of chronic narcotic analgesia for chronic pain. This view seems to reflect our fears of addiction and the subsequent costs and problems that addiction has caused in our society. As this may be a national resource book for life care planning, it is likely that the reader may find in his or her locality a remaining bias toward the avoidance of use of chronic narcotic analgesia for the treatment of chronic pain. Multidisciplinary pain programs that employ psychologists, social workers, anesthesiologists, orthopedic surgeons, neurosurgeons, neuropsychologists, physiatrists, and allied health professionals are often quite familiar with the local political flavor of the area, and will be one of the better resources in determining what a patient's needs are in general, as well as giving him or her an understanding of what the trends throughout the nation are at that time.

Additional Considerations for Chronic Pain Management

As mentioned above, a multidisciplinary team is the best resource for thorough and comprehensive management of chronic pain. Typically the needs of the patient will require five or six comprehensive measures to maximize the outcome of the patient's ability to manage his own condition after a period of six months to a year. Most outpatient treatment of a chronic pain patient will result in a very brief one to two month period of intense evaluation and management followed by a middle period of three to six months of continued weekly monitoring or monthly monitoring and establishing of a management program that will fit the patient's needs. Biofeedback, stress management, counseling, psychological testing, and family counseling will be included. Additional areas for maximizing the patient's independence will include diet, weight loss, and exercise. Normally, most patients with chronic pain have a hard time functioning in the upright position and the normal gravity environment. For that reason exercise programs, especially ones employing a pool, are very popular and quite prevalent and seem to best suit the needs of the chronic pain exercise program prescription.

The physician author of this chapter prescribes a six-step comprehensive program in the treatment of chronic pain patients. Note that this occurs in the rehabilitation setting, since the majority of the patients seen in this setting have already undergone anesthesia and surgery. A comprehensive, conservative chronic pain management program would consist of the following areas:

1. *Exercise.* A program including a pool for both strength conditioning and checking the effects of the central nervous system related to exercise with serotonin and norepinephrine release. Additional cardiovascular and pulmonary conditioning for weight loss assistance is also a key element of this.
2. *Diet.* A thorough review is usually achieved with a dietary journal kept by the patient for two weeks. After the journal is reviewed, recommendations are made with specific restrictions of foods that are clearly harmful to the patient's diet. For additional help with diet, reading materials and instruction are added for food selection, and a basic understanding of carbohydrates, fats, and protein is taught. Subsequently, the patient's weight is taken on a weekly basis for their next several visits and further assistance and encouragement is given.
3. *Sleep restoration.* Patients cannot handle the daily stress of chronic pain without adequate sleep. Sleep achieves a degree of relaxation and resets the "thermostat" of the central nervous system. The sleep-deprived patient will have more difficulty responding to minute-to-minute changes in his or her day and thereby be much less adaptable to their chronic pain condition than those who are sleeping through the night. Pharmacological agents for this are often needed to restore the patient to a restful night's sleep. Additional concerns would be for patients who have sleep apnea or other obstructive forms of sleep disturbance. Sleep centers are usually run and directed by a pulmonologist or neurologist and are available in most metropolitan areas. I have used these clinics as an assistive consultation in helping the patient to return to a more restful night's sleep.
4. *Pharmacological agents.* Here again, the recitation of all medications that are prescribed and used in current pain management would be beyond the scope of this short chapter. Mainly they would fall into five categories:
   - 4.1. Anti-depressants consisting of Prozac, serotonin, and in general, tricyclic antidepressants, and anxiolytics.
   - 4.2. Medications for the resolution of nerve pain, which consist of Tegretol, Dilantin, Phenobarbital, Neurontin, and Depakote.
   - 4.3. Muscle relaxants, consisting of Soma, Skelaxin, Robaxin, Flexeril, Baclofen, Parafonforte, and occasionally Valium or anxiolytics which would fit into this category as well.
   - 4.4. Nonsteroidal antiinflammatory agents or other nonnarcotic analgesics that also assist with the reduction in inflammatory joint changes. These would consist of Advil, Motrin, Releve, Relafen, Oravail, and others.
   - 4.5. Narcotic analgesia. This would depend on efforts of resolving the pain from all other measures. Examples include methadone, Percodan, morphine, and Duragesec patches, and others.
5. *Physical therapy and outpatient modalities.* Usually patients who have chronic pain also have a sedentary lifestyle as a consequence of trying to avoid pain. A brief burst of physical therapy for two to four weeks following the intake of a new patient may prove useful. This is usually aimed at providing the modality that may have already been used in other efforts of physical therapy. The difference with the use of physical therapy at this

time is to try other physical therapy prescriptions and also to allow patients the use of a TENS (transcutaneous electric nerve stimulation) unit or other locally available stimulation unit to attempt to decrease their pain. Further sessions of physical therapy throughout the course of the patient's lifetime may also be necessary depending upon brief or prolonged periods of inactivity, which will result in a loss of strength and function. In general, the nature of the comprehensive, conservative measures implemented for chronic pain management attempts to keep the patient from losing significant degrees of function for prolonged periods of time by instituting an exercise program. Nonetheless, a once per year physical therapy evaluation may be necessary to forestall more remedial forms of functional loss.

6. *Orthotics and other adaptive equipment.* These products can usually be procured at the local orthotist or prosthetist or durable medical equipment supplier. There are a number of self-care adaptive aids, such as long-handled reachers, button hooks, assistive devices for eating, grooming, and daily household tasks. In addition, under this heading would fall the grouping of spinal orthoses such as cervical pillows or orthopedic braces for sleeping and comfort in sitting, driving, walking, and moving about. From this standpoint electric mobility devices, power chairs, assistive bathing devices, and personalized aids could all be considered for prescription. Throughout this it should be mentioned that the patient's condition is not presumed to be static. Occasional retesting, obtaining X-rays and, in some cases, other surgical, neurosurgical, or orthopedic surgery interventions may be required.

Determining Patient's Functioning Level

The patient's needs, at the time of intake as a chronic pain patient and throughout life, can be ascertained most effectively through an outside source of local physical therapy where functional capacity evaluations are performed. A functional capacity evaluation is usually an eight-hour assessment that is performed over a two-day period. During this assessment the patient's autonomic functions are evaluated, including heart rate, respiratory rate, and skin temperature. Other measurements, such as a visual analog scale of pain may also be performed.

The majority of the testing includes performance of a number of different tasks that are observed and are also repeated in a number of different fashions to ascertain the patient's reliability from one task to the next. Typically, insurance companies and other health care providers will request these as will workplaces at the time of a patient's disability. They are useful for disability determination, but are typically not adequate for disability rating. Disability ratings would come under a different evaluation. Many times the consultants who have been working with the patient throughout the months are not capable or are not interested in performing disability evaluations. Determining individuals who are willing and capable and will perform these assessments can be the source of difficulty in bringing the patient's legal problems to a close.

Life Care Planning and Chronic Pain and Future Concerns

In making preparations in the life care plan for the needs of a patient with chronic pain, it becomes necessary to take into consideration all of the measures listed above. To this end, identifying someone who will follow the patient and participate in a comprehensive chronic pain management multidisciplinary team approach is preferred. If, however, that is not possible, then the needs from a chronic pain future life care plan would include all of the steps mentioned in the evaluation and treatment of a chronic pain patient at the initial intake. It should be noted that from a chronic pain standpoint efforts are directed at making the individual with chronic pain self-reliant and avoiding of constant medical intervention. Although this is the desired outcome, it is very time consuming to achieve this goal, and as with any long-term disease problem, it becomes necessary for routine reevaluations and upgrades in the individual program. Cost estimates for chronic pain include medication costs, equipment repair and replacement, and one to two year reevaluations with X-rays, blood work, and consultations of the individual specialists will be necessary. It may also be necessary to include physical therapy and psychological counseling reevaluations. As the patient with chronic pain ages additional evaluations and treatments with upgrades in equipment and possible surgical interventions may also be required. It once again becomes necessary to include in an exhaustive fashion a comprehensive listing of the patient's problems and some future prognosis as to the deterioration of these diagnostic considerations.

Case Study

The following life care plan was prepared for a patient who fell on stairs at her home, resulting in a back injury. After attempts at conservative treatment, back surgery was accomplished on two occasions with poor results. The client was referred to a specialist for a dorsal column stimulator, which failed to provide long-term relief. Following the surgery, she was referred to a pain clinic and the attending psychiatrist diagnosed her with multiple personality disorder. Her history included intestinal bypass for obesity. She had also been hospitalized on occasion for psychiatric reasons. At the time of the plan she remained essentially nonfunctional and did not drive, work, or clean her home. Her bed was relocated to the living room to avoid stairs or excessive movement. Her husband was supportive and actively assisted in her rehabilitation efforts.

CONCLUSION

Chronic pain has the ability as a diagnostic entity to cause as much disruption in patient care as do the functional, psychological, and social losses involved in the original injury. It should be noted that as a specialty chronic pain is developing and should be available in its broadest sense from the multidisciplinary approach nearly everywhere in the United States. A carefully arranged initial intake with subsequent development of the six categories outlined should place the life care

Roger O. Weed, PhD, CRC, CDMS, CLCP, FNRCA

2728 Irene Circle

Duluth, Georgia 30096

LIFE CARE PLAN

Projected Therapeutic Modalities

Client Name: Roberta Melvins

Date of Birth: 4/11/48

Date of Accident: 6/7/89

Date Prepared: August 27, 1991

Therapy	Age/Year at Which Initiated	Age/Year at Which Suspended	Treatment Frequency	Base Cost Per Year	Growth Trend	Recommended By:
Pain support group, individual, couples & crisis therapy, medication supervision	43/1992	Life expectancy	Group @ $50/wk Individ @ $125 1 to 2 X week for 2 ½ yrs, then 25 sessions per year (ave) to 1997	$2400 (group) $6,000-12,000 (individ) to 6/94, then $3,125 to 12/31/97	To be determined by economist	Dr. Hertz
Occupational therapy Included as part of inpatient pain program. See page 6.	43/1992	3 to 4 months	2 times per week, one hour per session as part of P.A.I.N. program (see p. 6)	See page 8.		Dr. Hertz
Physical therapy	43/1992	3 to 4 months	2 times per week, one hour per session following P.A.I.N. program (see p. 6)	$1,920-3,200 @ $80-100/hour	To be determined by economist	Dr. Hertz

Format reproduced with permission of Dr. Paul M. Deutsch. Adapted from the *Guide to Rehabilitation*. LCARE_2.DOC

Roger O. Weed, PhD, CRC, CDMS, CLCP, FNRCA

2728 Irene Circle

Duluth, Georgia 30096

Client Name: Roberta Melvins

Date of Birth: 4/11/48

LIFE CARE PLAN

Diagnostic Testing/Educational Assessment

Date of Accident: 6/7/89

Date Prepared: August 27, 1991

Diagnostic Recommendation	Age/Year at Which Initiated	Age/Year at Which Suspended	Per Year Frequency	Base Cost Per Year	Growth Trend	Recommended By:
Psychological testing, IQ and psychological status testing	43/1992	43/1992	One time only	$500-600	To be determined by economist	Dr. Hertz

Format reproduced with permission of Dr. Paul M. Deutsch. Adapted from the *Guide to Rehabilitation*. LCARE_3.DOC

2

Roger O. Weed, PhD, CRC, CDMS, CLCP, FNRCA
2728 Irene Circle
Duluth, Georgia 30096

Client Name: Roberta Melvins
Date of Birth: 4/11/48
Date of Accident: 6/7/89
Date Prepared: August 27, 1991

LIFE CARE PLAN

Wheelchair Needs

Wheelchair Type	Age/Year at Which Purchased	Replacement Schedule	Purpose of Equipment	Base Cost	Growth Trend	Catalog or Supplier Reference
3 wheel power chair rear wheel drive (e.g. Pride)	43/1992	Every 5 years	Mobility, independence and avoid complications Maintenance: Expect $150/year after 1st year warranty.	$2,000-2,500 $150/year, 4 out of 5 yrs.	To be determined by economist	Adaptive Equipment Specialists

Format reproduced with permission of Dr. Paul M. Deutsch. Adapted from the *Guide to Rehabilitation*. LCARE_4.DOC

3

Roger O. Weed, PhD, CRC, CDMS, CLCP, FNRCA
2728 Irene Circle
Duluth, Georgia 30096

Client Name: Roberta Melvins
Date of Birth: 4/11/48
Date of Accident: 6/7/89
Date Prepared: August 27, 1991

LIFE CARE PLAN

Orthotics/Prosthetics

Equipment Description	Age/Year at Which Purchased	Replacement Schedule	Equipment Purpose	Base Cost	Growth Trend	Supplier
Right leg ankle/ foot orthosis	Sept. 1989	Every 3 yrs.	Support body weight, avoid falls, reduce complications.	406.64	To be determined by economist	Butte Limb & Brace
Straps	Sept. 1989	Every 8 -12 mos.	Attach AFO to leg	$10.00		
Left leg ankle/ foot orthosis	Sept. 1989	Every 3 yrs.	Support body weight, avoid falls, reduce complications.	406.64	To be determined by economist	Butte Limb & Brace
Straps	Sept. 1989	Every 8 -12 mos.	Attach AFO to leg	$10.00		

Format reproduced with permission of Dr. Paul M. Deutsch. Adapted from the *Guide to Rehabilitation*. LCARE_7.DOC

4

Roger O. Weed, PhD, CRC, CDMS, CLCP, FNRCA
2728 Irene Circle
Duluth, Georgia 30096

LIFE CARE PLAN
Drug/Supply Needs

Client Name: Roberta Melvins
Date of Birth: 4/11/48
Date of Accident: 6/7/89
Date Prepared: August 27, 1991

Supply Description	Drug (Prescription)	Purpose	Per Unit Cost	Per Year Cost	Growth Trend	Recommended By:
	Methadone, 10 mg 3 X per day	Pain control	$9.76/30	$356.00	To be determined by economist	Dr. Hertz
	Ativan, 2 mg 3 X per day	Anti-anxiety	$12.62/90	$153.00		
	Note: Medications listed are representative of current and future need. Specific prescriptions may change.				TOTAL = $509.00	

Format reproduced with permission of Dr. Paul M. Deutsch. Adapted from the *Guide to Rehabilitation*. LCARE_9.DOC

5

Roger O. Weed, PhD, CRC, CDMS, CLCP, FNRCA
2728 Irene Circle
Duluth, Georgia 30096

LIFE CARE PLAN

Home/Facility Care

Client Name: Roberta Melvins
Date of Birth: 4/11/48
Date of Accident: 6/7/89
Date Prepared: August 27, 1991

Facility Recommendation	Home Care/Service Recommendations	Age/Year at Which Initiated	Age/Year at Which Suspended	Hours/Shifts/Days of Attendance or Care	Base Cost Per Year	Growth Trends
P.A.I.N. Pain Management Program		43/ 1-1-92	3 1/2 weeks		$7,000-8,000	To be determined by economist
	Companion, psycho-logical support, aide, and house maintenance	1991	Life expectancy	Husband performs these functions. Expect 2 days/wk @ $36/day if hired.	$0 if continued marriage or $3,744 if hired.	To be determined by economist

Format reproduced with permission of Dr. Paul M. Deutsch. Adapted from the *Guide to Rehabilitation*. LCARE_10.DOC

6

Roger O. Weed, PhD, CRC, CDMS, CLCP, FNRCA
2728 Irene Circle
Duluth, Georgia 30096

Client Name: Roberta Melvins
Date of Birth: 4/11/48
Date of Accident: 6/7/89
Date Prepared: August 27, 1991

LIFE CARE PLAN

Future Medical Care - Routine

Routine Medical Care Description	Frequency Of Visits	Purpose	Cost Per Visit	Cost Per Year	Growth Trends	Recommended By:
Psychiatrist follow-up	As needed	Review of medications	See page 1.	N/A		Dr. Hertz
Neurological/ Orthopedic follow-up (not including X-ray, lab or other diagnostic costs. e.g., MRI = $800-1,000)	1 X year to life expectancy	Prescribe braces, follow-up to back surgery, and prevent complications.	$75	$75	To be determined by economist	Standard of Care

Format reproduced with permission of Dr. Paul M. Deutsch. Adapted from the *Guide to Rehabilitation*. LCARE_11.DOC

7

Roger O. Weed, PhD, CRC, CDMS, CLCP, FNRCA
2728 Irene Circle
Duluth, Georgia 30096

LIFE CARE PLAN

Transportation

Client Name: Roberta Melvins
Date of Birth: 4/11/48
Date of Accident: 6/7/89
Date Prepared: August 27, 1991

Equipment Description	Age/Year at Which Purchased	Replacement Schedule	Equipment Purpose	Base Cost	Growth Trend	Catalog or Supplier Reference
Option 1 Handicap accessible van with lift and hand controls	43/1992	Every 5-7 years (Trade-in value to be determined by economist)	Mobility and independence	$22,000-24,000	To be determined by economist	Handicapped Services, Inc.
Option 2 Car with trunk lift and hand controls	43/1992	Every 5-7 years	Mobility and independence	$1,200 - $1,750 ($400-550 hand controls. $800-1,200 trunk lift. Car must be equiped with power steering and brakes.)	To be determined by economist	Adaptive Equipment Specialists

Format reproduced with permission of Dr. Paul M. Deutsch. Adapted from the *Guide to Rehabilitation*. LCARE_12.DOC

Roger O. Weed, PhD, CRC, CDMS, CLCP, FNRCA
2728 Irene Circle
Duluth, Georgia 30096

LIFE CARE PLAN

Health and Strength Maintenance

Client Name: Roberta Melvins
Date of Birth: 4/11/48
Date of Accident: 6/7/89
Date Prepared August 27, 1991

Equipment Description	Special Camps or Programs	Age/Year of Purchase or Attendance	Replacement or Attendance Schedule	Base Cost	Growth Trend	Catalog or Supplier Reference
Universal gym with physical conditioning components/stationary bike/weights		1992	1 X only	$500-1,500	To be determined by economist	Sports Town

Format reproduced with permission of Dr. Paul M. Deutsch. Adapted from the *Guide to Rehabilitation*. LCARE_13.DOC

Roger O. Weed, PhD, CRC, CDMS, CLCP, FNRCA
2728 Irene Circle
Duluth, Georgia 30096

LIFE CARE PLAN

Architectural Renovations

Client Name: Roberta Melvins
Date of Birth: 4/11/48
Date of Accident: 6/7/89
Date Prepared: August 27, 1991

Accessibility Needs		Accessibility Needs		Costs
Ramping	X	Bathroom		No house can be assessed, therefore no cost estimate is possible. Cost is dependent on client's ability to located suitable accessible housing.
Light/Environmental Controls	X	Sink	X	
Floor Coverings (if wheelchair is used inside)	X	Cabinets	X	
Hallways	X	Roll-in Shower	X	
Doorways	X	Temperature Control Guards		
Covered Parking	X	Heater		
Kitchen		Fixtures		
Sinks/Fixtures		Door Handles		
Cabinets		Additional Electrical Outlets		
Appliances		Central Heat/Air		
Windows		Therapy/Equipment Storage	?	
Electric Safety Doors		Attendant Bedroom		
Fire Alarm	X	Single story home. No steps.	X	
Smoke Detectors	X			
Intercom System				

Format reproduced with permission of Dr. Paul M. Deutsch. Adapted from the *Guide to Rehabilitation*. LCARE_14.DOC

10

Roger O. Weed, PhD, CRC, CDMS, CLCP, FNRCA
2728 Irene Circle
Duluth, Georgia 30096

Client Name: Roberta Melvins
Date of Birth: 4/11/48
Date of Accident: 6/7/89
Date Prepared August 27, 1991

LIFE CARE PLAN

Potential Complications

Complication	Estimated Costs	Growth Trend
Rehospitalized for psychological/psychiatric care care and crises management. Electro-convulsive therapy costs approximately $1,000 each treatment.	No duration or frequency available. Costs not included in plan.	
Failed back with additional surgery required.		
Falls and re-injury.		
Adverse reactions to medications.		

Format reproduced with permission of Dr. Paul M. Deutsch. Adapted from the *Guide to Rehabilitation*. LCARE_15.DOC

11

LIFE CARE PLAN

Roger O. Weed, PhD, CRC, CDMS, CLCP, FNRCA

2728 Irene Circle

Duluth, Georgia 30096

Future Medical Care

Surgical Intervention or Aggressive Treatment Plan

Client Name: Roberta Melvins

Date of Birth: 4/11/48

Date of Accident: 6/7/89

Date Prepared: August 27, 1991

Recommendation (Description)	Age/Year Initiated	Frequency of Procedure	Per Procedure Cost	Per Year Cost	Growth Trend	Recommended By:
Based on history, client likely to be re-hospitalized for psychological reactions to disability.	Unknown	Unknown	Unknown	Unknown	Unknown	Dr. Hertz

Format reproduced with permission of Dr. Paul M. Deutsch. Adapted from the *Guide to Rehabilitation*. LCARE_17.DOC

12

planner in the position to expertly assess and recommend the appropriate level of care for patients with chronic pain. However, as with all diseases, individuals with chronic pain will suffer variable outcomes based upon their individual application of the programs outlined for them. It is not unlike that of a diabetic, who, although having undergone a comprehensive study and treatment program, nonetheless is left on daily basis to provide the right type of treatment for their own condition. The responsibility of the patient in chronic pain is much the same. It is incumbent upon the patient to adopt new lifestyle measures, restrict their activities, and habituate certain aspects such as biofeedback and relaxation and not just do the easy thing, which is to take a pill or apply a TENS unit. Patient compliance in this regard is key, and assistance through psychological counseling and frequent monitoring is often the best hope for achieving some degree of success in modifying a patient's former lifestyle to include measures necessary for chronic pain management program. The goal of chronic pain planning, therefore, is not to reduce the pain to the level it was before the injury, but to modify the pain such that the patient can enjoy an enhanced quality of life and maintain a reasonable degree of function. It is also pertinent to note that a comprehensive treatment plan that uses all six outlined areas mentioned above will offer the best chance of success rather than a patient selectively using two or three modalities. The goal is to get the patient's pain down to a level where certain activities that were prohibitive or restrictive are now possible. Clearly this does not necessarily mean that the patient will be able to perform all activities. It is along these lines that the compromise between where the patient was and where the patient is now needs to be identified. In this context, the patient can be encouraged to achieve some degree of compromise with the condition of chronic pain and the future activity level that is beyond where they have been functioning. In light of these issues, the life care plan can be a valuable adjunct to assist the chronic pain patient.

REFERENCES

Aronoff, G. and Wilson, R. (1978). How to teach your patients to control chronic pain. **Behavioral Medicine, July,** 29-35.

Beecher, H. (1959). **Measurement of Subjective Responses**. New York: Oxford University Press.

Bowsher, D. (Jan., 1989) Assessment of the chronic pain sufferer. **Journal of Surgical Rounds for Orthopedics**, **2**, 70-73.

Bresler, D. (1979). **Free yourself from pain**. New York: Simon & Schuster.

Brownlee, S. & Schaf, J. (March 17, 1997). Quality of Life. **U.S. News and World Report**, 54-62.

Cailliet, R. & Helberg, L. (1981). Organic musculoskeletal back disorders. In W. Stolov and M. Clowers (Eds.). **Handbook of Severe Disability**. Washington, D.C.: U.S. Department of Education, Rehabilitation Services Administration.

Davis, R. (Oct. 1975). **Clinic Orthopedics and Related Research, 112,** 76-80.

Ernonoff, W. (1997). **Current Review of Pain**, **1**(4), 320-324.

Engel, G., MacBryde, C. & Blacklow, R. (1970). **Signs and Symptoms** (Fifth ed.). Philadelphia: J. P. Lippincott.

Ericson, J. C. (1996). Pain. In David Green (Ed.), **Medical Management of Long Term Disability**, (2nd edition), 303-312. Boston: Butterworth-Heinmann.

Fibromyalgia. **Post Graduate Medicine,** (Nov. 15, 1985), 80(7), 47-69.

Fordyce, W. E. (1976). **Behavioral Methods for Chronic Pain and Illness**. St. Louis: C. V. Mosby.

Heddox, J.D. (1997). Consensus statement. **Clinical Journal of Pain, 13**(1), 6-8.

IASP (1979). International association for studies on pain, subcommittee on taxonomy. **Pain, 6**, 249-252.

Kotkey, F., Stillwell, G., & Lehmann, J. (1982). In Krusen's (Ed.), **Handbook of Physical Medicine and Rehabilitation**, (3rd. ed.) Philadelphia: W. S. Saunders.

Loeser, J. (1980). **Underlying components of chronic pain**. [Seminar].

Meissner, J. (Sept.-Oct. 1982). McGill-Melzack Paion Questionnaire. **ASHP Signal**, 24-37.

Melzak, R. (1973). **The Puzzle of Pain**. New York: Basic Books.

Merskey, H. (1964). **An Investigation of Pain in Psychological Illness**. Unpublished doctoral dissertation. Oxford, England.

Merskey, H. (1972). Personality traits of psychiatric patients with pain. **Journal of Psychosomatic Research, 16,** 163-166.

National Institute of Disability and Rehabilitation Research (1993). Chronic back pain. **Rehab Brief, 15**(7).

Ramsey, R. (1979). The understanding and teaching of reaction to pain. **Bibliotheca Psychiatrica, 159,** 114-140.

Rasch, J. (1985). **Rehabilitation of Workers' Compensation and Other Insurance Claimants**. Springfield, IL: Charles C Thomas.

Shealy, C. (1976). **The Pain Game**. Los Angeles, California: Celestial Arts.

Skinner, B. F. (1938). **Behavior of Organisms**. New York: Appleton-Century-Crofts.

Skinner, B. F. (1974). **About Behaviorism**. New York: Random House.

Spengler, D., Loeser, J., & Murphy, T., **Orthopedic Aspects of Chronic Pain Syndrome**. Unpublished manuscript.

Sternbach, R. A. (1968). **Pain: A Psychophysiological Analysis**. New York: Academic Press.

Sternbach, R. A. (1974). **Pain Patients: Traits and Treatment**. New York: Academic Press.

Supernaw, R. (Ed.) (July 1997). Review article. **American Journal of Pain Management, 7**(3), 104-115.

Walsh, M.E. & Dumit, D. (1988). The treatment of the patient with chronic pain. In Joe L. Delisa (Ed.), **Rehabilitation Principles and Practice**, 707-725, Philadelphia: J. B. Lippincott.

Weed, R. (1987). Pain basics. **Journal of Private Sector Rehabilitation, 2**(2), 65-71.

Weed, R. & Field, T. (1994). **The Rehabilitation Consultant's Handbook** (2nd ed.). Athens, GA: E & F Vocational Services.

14

LIFE CARE PLANNING FOR ACQUIRED BRAIN INJURY

James A. Young & Roger O. Weed

INTRODUCTION

Acquired brain injury (ABI), also known as traumatic brain injury (TBI), is perhaps the most complicated and least understood problem in all of medicine. Patients present to treating physicians in only a limited number of ways, but their outcomes vary greatly. Unfortunately, despite our increasing understanding of neuroanatomy, neurophysiology, and neuropsychology, and enormous advantage of MRIs, CTs, EEGs, and other means of evaluation, our ability to make an accurate prognosis is limited and such prediction can easily be partly or completely wrong.

Due to the complexities of the brain, many aspects of central nervous system injury, and more importantly, its recovery, are unknown. Why does one individual not improve to the extent expected after falling "just" six feet, where others, after a gunshot wound to the head, make a good recovery? Why, after a seemingly mild injury, does one just fail to wake up? Frequently, the tests do not tell the whole story. Additionally, information from the patient can be incorrect or distorted.

ABI has a recovery profile that changes over time. Patients progress though multiple cognitive states before reaching a more stable level (the Rancho Los Amigos Cognitive Scale, Table 14.1). Each level has its own particular set of gains and difficulties, understandings and mishaps. With every ABI survivor, it is never known if the patient will continue to improve and work "up the scale" or not. To assist in the formulation of a life care plan, one needs an awareness of the injury itself, the apparent prognosis, and potential problems faced by the patient at his or her level of function. Many in the medical community understand acute needs, surgical approaches, medicines, and even some of the future complications. However, once the patient leaves the hospital or clinic, a great number of practitioners are unaware of the behavioral, psychological, and vocational problems that lie ahead. The life care plan can outline and educate the patient, family, caregivers, legal profession, trust officers, and others about future needs. A clearer comprehension of ABI will protect the patient and his or her environment, and assure proper benefits and care. Due to the enormous costs of such injury ($25 billion per year in the United States, not including legal costs), ABI remains one of the most important and controversial rehabilitation issues today.

1-57444-075-6/99/$0.00+$.50

Table 14.1 Rancho Los Amigos Scale of Cognitive Functioning

Variable outcomes dependent on nature and severity of injury

I.	*No Response:* Unresponsive to any stimulus.
II.	*Generalized Response:* Limited, inconsistent, non-purposeful responses, often to pain only.
III.	*Localized Response:* Purposeful responses; may follow simple commands; may focus on presented object.
IV.	*Confused, Agitated:* Heightened state of activity; confusion, disorientation, aggressive behavior.
V.	*Confused, Inappropriate, Non-Agitated:* Appears alert; responds to commands; distractible; does not concentrate on task.
VI.	*Confused, Appropriate:* Good directed behavior, needs cueing; can relearn old skills; serious memory problems; some awareness of self and others.
VII.	*Automatic, Appropriate:* Robot-like appropriate behavior, minimal confusion; shallow recall, poor insight into condition; initiates tasks, but needs structure; poor judgment, problem-solving and planning skills.
VIII.	*Purposeful, Appropriate:* Alert, oriented; recalls and integrates past events; learns new activities and can continue without supervision; independent in home and living skills; capable of driving; defects in stress tolerance, judgment, abstract reasoning persist; many functions at reduced levels in society.

Types of Brain Injury

It is a misnomer to use the term "traumatic" to describe the entire range of the patients included within this category. Individuals who have sustained central nervous complications from ruptured aneurysms or arteriovenous malformations (AVM), tumors, or perinatal injuries are also included in this grouping. In addition, the generic term "head injury," may not refer to an insult to the central nervous system. Any injury to the face (lacerations, eye injuries, etc.) could also fall into this category. It is for these many reasons that estimates of the number of brain injuries may be inaccurate. For the sake of this chapter, we will use the term "acquired" or "traumatic" brain injury to refer to any central nervous system insult, whether traumatic, vascular, congenital, degenerative, infectious, or other, in origin.

ABI is typically classified into one of five major categories: focal, diffuse axonal injury (DAI), hypoxic, penetrating, or vascular. (Tumors would be a focal mechanical disruption of neurologic function, and cerebral vascular accidents or bleeding from aneurysms or AVMs would be vascular).

- **Focal injuries** can occur at any site, usually resulting from accelerations/decelerations and can vary from a slight concussion to a subdural or epidural hematoma. Causes include falls, assaults, or motor vehicle accidents. Focal injuries are also seen accompanying other types of ABI, such as vascular or penetrating injuries.
- **Diffuse axonal injuries** of ABI, unlike focal injuries with mostly limited periods of loss of consciousness, can result in hours, days, or even longer

periods of unconsciousness. The twisting and turning of the brain (usually from motor vehicle accidents) tears the axons, causing large fields of injury. CT studies significantly underestimate the DAI, as opposed to the readings on localized focal insults. The MRI is much more sensitive to see DAI lesions and can correlate with neuropsychological outcomes.

- **Hypoxic injuries** accompany other forms of ABI and are seen in about one third of severe injuries. Also in cases of cardiopulmonary arrests or drownings, hypoxia is the main cause of damage. Like the aforementioned, a careful inspection of the emergency room and paramedic report is required to appreciate the degree of injury from hypoxia. The diffuse nature of hypoxia can result in some of the most severe injuries to the brain, with poorer prospects of recovery.
- **Penetrating brain injuries** (e.g., gunshot wounds) often cause both diffuse and focal injuries, without axonal damage. Widespread perivascular damage is seen. Patients surviving the wound can show "moderate" or "good" recoveries, but with significant motor, sensory, and cognitive difficulties. Note that "severe" indicates 24-hour dependency, moderate, significant injury, and disability, but with the ability to take public transportation, and good (the most confusing), implying some recovery but *without* restoration of normal function (Byron & Teasdale, 1981).
- **Vascular damage,** (i.e., strokes, AVMs, and aneurysms) unlike the above-listed groups, is more predictable in its recovery, due to the readily identifiable blood vessel involved. Knowledge of the function of the area involved makes it is easier to predict future problems. These focal neurologic insults are limited to the distribution of the blood vessel involved. This is in contrast to the diffuse and focal injuries of the hypoxic, diffuse axonal penetrating, or focal injuries listed. For example, the speed of the car, the degree of turning or twisting at impact, or the amount of damage on the side of the injury or to the opposite cerebral hemisphere, all complicate prognostication in ABI.

Several observations and measures are helpful in predicting outcomes. These include the Glasgow Coma Scale (a scoring system based on eye openings, motor and verbal responses during the first two to three days, with scores less than 7 out of 15 being more ominous (Table 14.2); intracranial pressures (more than 20 mmHg portends a worse outcome); age (those older than 40 do significantly worse); post-traumatic amnesia (loss of consciousness longer than two weeks show a rapid decline in good recoveries); and initial cranial nerve and motor evaluations.

Although manifestations of brain injury can vary significantly, the location of the injury in the brain can predict certain functional sequela. Generally, the effects of brain injury on functioning are as follows (Handler & Sample, 1994):

Brainstem Consciousness, alertness, and basic body functions such as breathing, respiration, and pulse.

Cerebellum Coordination of movement.

Table 14.2 Glasgow Coma Scale

	Examiner's Test	*Patient's Response*	*Assigned Score*
Eye Opening:	Spontaneous	Opens eyes on own	4
	Speech	Opens eyes when asked to in a loud voice	3
	Pain	Opens eyes when pinched	2
	Pain	Does not open eyes	1
Best Motor Response:	Commands	Follows simple commands	6
	Pain	Pulls examiner's hand away when pinched	5
	Pain	Pulls part of body away when examiner pinches patient	4
	Pain	Flexes body inappropriately to pain (decorticate posturing)	3
	Pain	Body becomes rigid in an extended position when examiner pinches victim (decerebrate posturing)	2
	Pain	Has no motor response to pinch	1
Verbal Response (Talking):	Speech	Carries on a conversation correctly and tells examiner where he is, who he is, and the month and year	5
	Speech	Seems confused or disoriented	4
	Speech	Talks so examiner can understand victim but makes no sense	3
	Speech	Makes sounds that examiner can't understand	2
	Speech	Makes no noise	I

Cerebral Cortex *Frontal Lobe* controls emotion, motivation, and social functioning, as well as expressive language, inhibition of impulses, motor integration, and voluntary movement.

Temporal Lobe is the source of memory, receptive language, sequencing, and musical awareness.

Parietal Lobe is responsible for sensation, academic skills such as reading, and awareness of spatial relationships.

Occipital Lobe is the area responsible for visual perception.

Medical Complications

In the acute and subacute stages of ABI, every organ system is involved. Going through the medical chart and listing every complication helps to organize and correctly formulate an LCP. Knowing the patient had a tibial plateau fracture assists in requesting orthopedic assistance in the future. Being aware of severe dysautonomias in the acute stage (episodes of abnormal blood pressure or heart readings, or excessive sweating) may prod one to ask about similar problems later. Knowing the sites of injury, the types of acute complications incurred, and the present problems, all assist the life care planners in their job.

An overall perspective involves the following systems and problems:

1. The nervous system for seizures, chronic subdural hygromas or hematomas, hydrocephalus
2. Peripheral nerve injuries
3. Spasticity
4. Depression and behavioral disturbances
5. The gastrointestinal system for injuries to the liver, bowel, or stomach
6. Genitourinary system complications include the neurogenic bladder or changes in sexuality
7. Respiratory problems involve complications of the tracheostomy, vocal cord changes, and infection
8. Cardiovascular complications of hypertension and arrhythmias
9. Nutritional difficulties of the gastrostomy tubes and eating disorders
10. Musculoskeletal changes due to fractures, contractures, and heterotopic ossification
11. Dermatologic difficulties due to decubiti
12. Cranial nerve problems of vision, hearing, swallowing, dizziness and vertigo, and articulation

Other nonsystemic problems involve sleep disturbances and pain. The latter two are grossly underestimated and hence undertreated.

Spasticity and Behavior Problems

Some of the most common problems for an LCP involve **spasticity** and behavioral disturbances. Spasticity is a constant nemesis that has yet to be tackled consistently. Patients who have shown a moderate or severe level of spasticity are bound to have future problems. Reasons to treat this include functional considerations (ADLs and mobility), hygiene, compression neuropathies, and pain. Some of the factors in the persistence of significant spasticity include the recovery level of the patient, infections, skin breakdown, behavioral changes, or pain. Thus, a strong reason to request "appropriate care" (e.g., either in the form of attendant care or therapy) would be to prevent the above complications.

One complication begets another. For example, inadequate respiratory therapy may result in pulmonic infiltrates leading to antibiotic treatment, increased spasticity, less activity out of bed, more skin breakdown, more behavioral disturbances, a loss of functional gains, a need for additional therapy time, and possibly surgery for the decubiti. Understanding the interdependence of each organ system helps to validate the need for cares. Treatments for spasticity include medicines, castings, and ranging by therapy, phenol or alcohol blockade, botulinum injections, intrathecal pumps (of baclofen), selective posterior rhizotomy (cutting nerve roots), or other surgical interventions. It is helpful to discuss these issues with the rehabilitation, orthopedic, and neurosurgical specialists.

Behavioral problems are the major disturbance recorded at all levels of ABI. Having a working knowledge how ABI affects behavior is essential. One must be familiar with the problems seen with frontal, temporal, and limbic lobe dysfunction to both educate and defend one's plan. Due to the fact that ABI is an evolving disability over the first few months, it is difficult to accurately predict future behaviors at this time. However, after this initial period and when the patient has stabilized, predictions can be more accurate.

Behaviors after ABI are a result of several factors: the severity and site of injury in the brain; the discharge location, and the education level of those living with the patient; secondary influences including pain, physical impairments, and medications. Since every major personality profile is possible after ABI (from anger, through psychosis, to withdrawal), understanding and focusing on these determinants strongly influences discharge success, and long-term attendant needs. Is the patient safe by himself or herself, do they need supervision (constantly, daily, weekly, never), is violence toward self or others a concern? One must carefully consider the patient's understanding of their disability, the family and their educational level, and availability and experience of local health care providers (professional and paraprofessional alike).

Limited alertness and rapid fatigue, memory problems, poor attention selectivity, confusion, disorientation, and overstimulation are but a few of the factors contributing to behavioral problems. Finding the proper personnel to help can be difficult. Psychologists, neuropsychologists, behavioral specialists, and social workers may all be employed. One must use one's experience, judgment, and the assistance of the caregivers and healthcare providers to anticipate needs. Due to the toll behavioral disturbances (especially) impact on the family, respite care is regularly added to many plans. Finally, the LCP must try at all costs to *prevent* a second head injury. Understanding potential behavioral and situational conflicts is preventative, and one of the most important purposes of the written plan.

Other Neurological Problems

Other neurological complications to be aware of, but more likely occurring in the first few months after the injury, include endocrinologic disturbances (thyroid, cortisol, and for pediatrics, growth hormone levels), arachnoid or leptomeningeal cysts, movement disorders, AVMs, aneurysms, and cerebrospinal fluid leaks. The syndrome of inappropriate antidiuretic hormone (SIADH) and posterior pituitary failures can be seen early in the care.

Related Problems

Important **gastrointestinal** medical concerns include the need to change the gastrostomy or jejunostomy tubes (once or twice a year), gastritis (irritation of the stomach due to ulcerations or a hiatal hernia), or liver-function test aberrations. Ongoing discussions with the treating internist or specialist is essential for total healthcare.

Genitourinary problems after ABI can be as high as 45% with bladder infections occurring in over a third of patients. The prevention of infections and treatment of the neurogenic bladder are the most important concerns here. There are several ways to empty the patient's bladder. After injury to the central nervous system (brain or spinal cord), there can be a disruption in the coordination between the nervous system and the bladder. The dyscoordination can cause the urine not to empty, backward pressures on the kidneys, or to spastically empty without control. The results can lead to infection, injury to the kidney, and incontinence. A genitourinary specialist is required to diagnose the problem and to provide recommendations on the proper use of medicines and techniques for drainage; self-catheterization (intermittent catheterization); an indwelling catheter (Foley or suprapubic catheter); or surgery (electric stimulation, "sling procedures," pouches, or artificial sphincters to name a few). Bladder training in the hospital and/or at home needs to be considered to ensure success.

Another need is for **sexual** counseling after ABI. This can take the form of medicines, penile injections, surgery, or artificial insemination. Again, genitourinary consultation (or gynecological assistance) is urged.

Many of the severely injured or vegetative individuals spend considerable time on a respirator. Overall rate of **respiratory** problems is approximately one third with 32% due to long-term tracheotomy use. As noted above, one complication frequently leads to another. Patients who are immobile or relatively immobile are at high risk to incur pulmonary infections. Due to limited movements, parts of the lung are less than optimally inflated and prone to bacterial overgrowth and later infection. The collapse of that portion of the lung (with the bacterial collection) is called atelectasis. Passive treatments are usually inadequate to help clear these sites. Aggressive respiratory therapy, in the form of chest physiotherapy (percussion and postural drainage) and nebulization (pressurized volumes with or without medicine traveling to the more distal bronchi) promote the mechanical expectoration of lung. In addition, chest physiotherapy requires the therapist to turn the patient over, thus permitting an additional skin check. Depending on the patient's needs, regular respiratory therapy is strongly urged to prevent infection, costly antibiotics, increased spasticity, prolonged functional losses, and unnecessary hospitalizations. Again, the LCP is promoting a prophylactic approach to the patient's well being.

Noted in almost one half of patients with ABI (especially the more severely injured) is **heterotopic ossification**. The formation of bone islands in muscles and joint spaces begins six weeks to four years after the injury (most commonly two to four months afterward). Its onset can lead to "frozen" joints, preventing movement and functional gains for over a year. This is seen less often in children (5%–20%) and is more likely to reasorb spontaneously in this age group. Medicines (Etidronate, Disodium, Indomethacin), radiation therapy, and finally surgical removal are used to combat this terrible affliction. Even with surgical excision, the problem can recur.

Another **musculoskeletal** complication involves contractures. This muscle fibrosis (scarring) leads to limited ranging of the affected limb. Ranging, splinting, medicines, injections (similar to those used in spasticity) and finally surgical lengthenings are commonly used. Regular physical and occupational therapy evaluations and treatment sessions are recommended to prevent such events. Educating the family or caregivers is recommended. However, this needs to be balanced with their educational levels, motivation, availability, and proper demonstration of the techniques. Again, the consequences can lead to days, weeks, months, or more of functional losses, a diminution of quality of life, or loss of independence.

Injury to the **cranial nerves** can result in some of the most disturbing findings. Loss of smell is a common occurrence after ABI. Visual complications and difficulties impede driving, work opportunities, and independence. (As an aside, visual perception, so common after ABI, is extremely difficult to test, and is not appreciated by the public and legal system.) The resolution of third and seventh cranial nerve palsies appear better in the pediatric population. One should wait at least six to nine months before surgically correcting the third nerve. Dysarthria should be aggressively addressed by the speech-language pathologist. Improvements in communication, cognition, and swallowing are vital to one's quality of life. In addition, after ABI, aphasia is known to show improvement as far out as five years (the present limit of longitudinal studies). Continuation is urged if the patient is deemed capable of participating, especially with the newer augmentative systems using as little as a blink response. Many children show dramatic physical improvements after ABI. Because they *appear* better, it can be terribly misleading especially where their language is concerned. Their language and cognitive skills can lag far behind, especially since it is being developed through their preschool and school-age years. Thus, they fall behind scholastically and socially, which often affects their behaviors. These problems only widen as they age and responsibilities and pressures change.

Common in the moderate and mild head injury groups (probably because they can discuss the difficulty better) is **dizziness** and **vertigo**. In addition to being uncomfortable and disconcerting, driving, recreational activities, and independence are disturbed. Finally, those with any dysphagia would benefit from a video fluoroscopic evaluation. One cannot accurately diagnose all three phases of the swallowing mechanism by external observation. If one has a gastrostomy tube or a prior history of dysphagia, it is reasonable to anticipate this need.

Medicines

Medicines to be considered during the lifetime of the traumatically brain injured include drugs for seizures, agitation, "alertness," sleep, depression, pain, and (rarely) psychosis. Accompanying drug levels and possible side effects should be included. Those with physical limitations, and at higher risks for seizures, plain X-rays are recommended (for falls or painful sites), as are several CTs or MRIs, and a limited number of EEGs. The more severe the injury, the higher the number requested. Discussing this with the neurologist or neurosurgeon is suggested.

Probably the most underestimated problem (beyond behavioral disturbances) is **pain**. Many sites can be missed in the acute setting, and biomechanical changes can begin during the patient's convalescence. Even those without paralysis or fractured bones can sustain significant and disabling pain syndromes. Simple musculoskeletal pain can be a major source of neck and back discomfort and headaches, leading to problems with concentration, depression, and loss of work time. In the "Minor" ABI category (Glasgow Coma Scale 13–15 out of 15, and loss of consciousness less than 24 hours), pain can be one of the primary reasons patients progress from the postconcussive states to the more permanent or persistent postconcussive syndromes.

Minor ABI

Because they "don't look injured," the sympathy, understanding, and patience usually afforded the injured never materializes for those with minor (or mild) ABI. The psychotherapy frequently prescribed for the family and individual after a moderate to severe ABI is commonly neglected for those without external disfigurement. Because 75% of all ABI is minor, and so many attempt to return quickly to their former lives and jobs, it is imperative that a carefully considered counseling program is written into the plan. In addition, the family has to be interviewed separately (or be present during the exam to correct responses by the patient) to determine the severity of marital, parental, or sibling discord or violence. Without this important data, overall success is unlikely. It is strongly urged that the life care planner push for adequate and prolonged psychological assistance. Treatments can be frequent initially, with as needed sessions reserved for the future. The number of sessions (or even medical specialist visits) can be averaged out over time. Thus, one may need more concentrated help over one or two stretches (over several weeks or months). Later the number of sessions may average out.

Vocational Assessment

A vocational assessment is urged at the moderate or better level of recovery. Unfortunately, employability and stability in the ABI population is poor. Vocational assessment, planning, and placement assistance can be recommended twice especially in the pediatric population, possibly at age 18 or 21, then may be repeated several years later. Very common functional limitations include memory impairments that can prevent or significantly reduce efficiency for new learning, and fatigue that hampers working a full day. Many are incapable of maintaining their positions due to cognitive impairments, adynamia or disinhibition, a lack of awareness of the implications of their injury, unrealistic expectations of their abilities, ambiguous instruction at work, time pressures, supervisor criticism (and misperceptions), and a change in work demands. Some also have serious physical limitations involving motivity, balance, and general motor control. Having on-site job coaching and the cooperation and understanding of the employer are probably the strongest allies to facilitate a successful return to work.

One way to determine the vocational impact of an injury is to include an evaluation by a neuropsychologist (Weed, 1994). Specific questions will assist the vocational counselor with effective planning (Table 14.3). For example, the brain impairment may adversely affect the client's ability to understand visual stimuli. Therefore, teaching driving with the aid of maps, or how to make hamburgers with photos of the steps could end in failure. Also, some have difficulty listening and comprehending verbal instructions. It may be appropriate to include social modeling or visual aids to help with education or training in these cases. Also, assistive technology as well as seating and positioning may be needed. These issues could involve speech and language pathologists and occupational therapists. In summary, vocational planning for brain-injured clients usually requires comprehensive assessments by a variety of professionals in order to successfully place them in the work force (Weed, 1996).

Table 14.3 Neuropsychologist Questions

In addition to the standard evaluation report, add the following as appropriate.

1. Please describe, in layman terms, the damage to the brain.
2. Please describe the effects of the accident on the client's ability to function.
3. Please provide an opinion to the following topics:
   a. Intelligence level? (include pre- vs. post-incident if able)
   b. Personality style with regard to the workplace and home?
   c. Stamina level?
   d. Functional limitations and assets?
   e. Ability for education/training?
   f. Vocational implications — style of learning?
   g. Level of insight into present functioning?
   h. Ability to compensate for deficits?
   i. Ability to initiate action?
   j. Memory impairments (short-term, long-term, auditory, visual, etc.)?
   k. Ability to identify and correct errors?
   l. Recommendations for compensation strategies?
   m. Need for companion or attendant care?
4. What is the proposed treatment plan?
   a. Counseling? (individual and family)
   b. Cognitive therapy?
   c. Reevaluations?
   d. Referral to others? (e.g., physicians)
   e. Other?
5. How much and how long? (Include the cost per session or hour and reevaluations.)

General Considerations

Other general considerations are a *Driver's Evaluation* (an extended behind-the-wheel evaluation, driving simulation, and a written test), transportation requirements, and the living environment. This physician author requires a Driver's Evaluation for all cases (even minor ABI). This one-time "insurance policy" protects the patient, family, and society. One needs to be realistic about transportation needs. Can, how, or will the injured emergently or leisurely travel to the hospital, store, or next door? Is it reasonable to expect the patient, family, or caregiver to help, supervise, or participate in this function, which may define one's independence in the world? A home visit is recommended to accurately assess the patient's living environment. Does the patient require simple renovations to accommodate a wheelchair or walker, or limited arm or back functioning? Or are more elaborate aids, including environmental controls, even a fully accessible home, needed? Will the home devices considered operate from the wheelchair or an augmentative communication system? Obviously, knowing the patient's cognitive, physical, and behavioral disabilities helps determine each phase of the plan.

In developing any life care plan prior *educational, vocational, medical, family, and social histories* are recommended. There is nowhere this is more true than with those who have suffered a brain injury. Due to the complexities of ABI, case management is virtually always necessary (except for the very independent). Case management helps orchestrate and prevent complications, and allows the life care plan to function as the dynamic entity it was intended.

Case Study

Brain injury cases will vary dramatically from individual to individual based on the location and extent of damage. The selected case is a pediatric case where vocational issues are a relevant part of the plan.

Description of Injury

According to the client's mother, she and the 2½-year-old child were waiting in line at the pick-up area of a local toy store. Reportedly, the child was pulling on a chain when the counter to which the chain was attached fell on him. The mother states the counter weighed between 200 and 300 pounds and required two men to pull it off. The child was unconscious and had blood coming from his ears, mouth, and nose. He was transported by ambulance to the Emergency Room and diagnosed with severe closed head injury with multiple skull fractures and facial lacerations.

The child arrived in ER via ambulance. He was unresponsive, but no seizure activity was noted. He was paralyzed and sedated. A CT scan revealed a fracture over the vertex from right to left, numerous valvular skull fractures, right occiput extending forward, cerebral contusion on left parietal area and possibly right temporal area, no significant midline shift, no hydrocephalus. Initial impression was closed head injury, multiple skull fractures and cerebral contusion; basilar skull fracture.

Further evaluation revealed severe brain injury with multiple intracranial fractures/contusions. Major cerebral contusion on the left parietal region causing significant right hemiparesis and right homonomous hemianopsia. Evidence of bicerebral injury, question hearing loss, excess drooling/motor dysfunction, right facial weakness, feeding difficulties, regressed toileting skills, history of strabismus was also noted. The discharge summary included the following diagnoses:

1. Closed head injury
2. Status post right cerebellar infarction
3. Cerebral contusion, left deep temporal lobe/left posterior parietal lobe
4. Basal skull fracture
5. Forehead laceration
6. Ringworm
7. Second degree burns of right palm
8. Left frontal ventriculostomy
9. Right frontal intracranial pressure monitor

The child was seizure free with no evidence of neurological deficit of peripheral vision. His ocular motility was intact, central vision good, but he had esotropia aggravated by the closed head injury. Deficits were noted in visual perception, mild right hemiparesis, upper extremity more than lower extremity, but he was able to walk independently with wide-based gait and balance/coordination problems. He had memory deficits, especially with presentation and retention of new material. The MRI showed injury to right cerebellar hemisphere, injury to left temporal lobe and left posterior parietal lobe.

Neuropsychological Evaluation results included:

Early Learning Accomplishment Profile (E-LAP): Cognitive functioning equivalent to 27- to 30-month-old child (at risk).
Pediatric Rancho Los Amigos Level I
Attention/Concentration: Mildly to moderately impaired.
Woodcock-Johnson Test of Cognitive Ability-Revised (WJTCA-R) Low average for immediate recall for verbal information; ability to acquire new information mildly impaired; difficulty learning new basic concepts; memory relative weakness; above-average auditory integration; severely impaired visual integration; scanning difficulties; expressive vocabulary at risk.
Kaufman Assessment Battery for Children (K-ABC):
Sequential Processing Standard Score (SS) = 97
Simultaneous Processing SS = 72
Mental Processing Composite SS = 79 (well below avg. to below avg.)
Achievement SS = 95
Profile consistent with perceptual-based learning disability, suggestive of difficulty learning to recognize shapes of letters, in addition to math skills and handwriting skills. Sequential Processing Scale may be better estimate of current intellectual functioning. Intellectual performance is weak.
Receptive/Expressive language skills: Age appropriate.
Preschool Language Scale (PLS): Age equivalent 3–6 years.
Rossetti Infant-Toddler Language Scale: Age 33–36 months.
Peabody Picture Vocabulary Test-Revised (PPVT-R): Age equivalent 2–5 years.
Speech Skills: Appropriate with mild errors, articulate noted. Quality of oral motor movements mildly impaired, vocal quality mildly hoarse.
Play skills: Roughly age appropriate.
Pragmatic skill: Attention deficits, delayed response/reaction times.
Early Learning Adaptive Program: Fine motor skills at 27-month level. Decreased strength, speed, skill with right hand, decreased proprioception/sensory awareness on right, visual perceptual deficits. Child uses left hand though was right-handed prior to injury.
Gross Motor Skills: Active/passive range of motion within normal limits, proprioception, ambulation, balance problems, independent on level surfaces but often fell due to loss of balance.
Activities of Daily Living: Minimal assistance.
Recommendations: Neuropsychology evaluation within 4–6 months, annual developmental evaluation, comprehensive neuropsychology evaluation prior to beginning school. OT 2x/week up to 5 years old with evaluations at developmental milestones. Speech/lang. pathologist 1x/week, 6 month evaluations for first 2 years, then yearly. PT 2x/week up to 2–3 years. Home program.

A follow-up developmental assessment revealed the following:

Stanford Binet: Average range.
Kaufman Assessment Battery for Children: Score was substantially lower, reflective of fact that less emphasis is put on verbal abilities. He had problems with sequential processing.

Language Functioning: Strength area, receptive vocabulary in low avg. range but may be due more to difficulty with visual scanning and perceptual difficulties.

Visual Perceptual Functioning: Ongoing difficulty, attentional difficulties especially attending to material in right visual field.

Fine Motor: Difficulty holding pencil.

Behavioral Observations: Very distractible, short attention span, difficult with sustained visual attention and scanning.

Summary: Good ability to master new information, esp. language related information. Attentional, visual, and motor deficits. Recommends reevaluation in 6 months.

A review of systems at one year post-injury revealed the child was medically stable and was taking no current medications.

Cognitive status: Attention/concentration span significantly improved.

Mobility/Physical: Attends gym class and swims weekly. Child is more motivated to work on coordination and balance with peers than in individual PT. Has difficulty throwing, jumping, and other balance/coordination activities.

Activities of Daily Living: Able to dress self, do most fasteners, cut with scissors. Difficulty with visual-motor tasks, right UE use, and grading his motions.

Nutrition: Currently weighs 39.5 lbs., 75th percentile for height and 80th percentile for weight. Child has improved ability to attend to eating during mealtimes.

Psychological: Some behavioral problems at home.

Recommendations: Comprehensive neuropsychological evaluation at age 5, outpatient PT eval. on 6-month basis, outpatient OT evaluation within next few months, and follow-up OT visits on 6-month basis.

Recommendations:

1. Comprehensive neuropsychological evaluation at age 5.
2. Continue with occupational therapy 1–2 times per week until age 5 then reevaluate.
3. Physical therapy reevaluation in 6 months. If no improvement, may need P.T. intervention.
4. Continue group activities with peers to enhance gross motor activities.
5. Once enters school, may need adaptive P.E. consultation.
6. Follow-up with physician in 1 year.
7. Speech/language reevaluation in 6–12 months.

Table 14.4 Rehabilitation Plan

Anticipated Length of Rehabilitation Program:
Through childhood and potentially lifetime follow-up.

Recommendation	*Dates*	*Frequency*	*Expected Cost*
Comprehensive neuropsychological evaluation	1994 (age 5) through 2007	1 X 1994, then yearly through 2000 (age 11), 3003, 2007 (age 18)	$600 (1994) then $1,000 each
Psychological			
a. Individual or couples therapy	1993–1995	Expect 1 X per week for 6–8 mos.	$90–110 per hour
b. Family and individual counseling	Begin 1995	1 X per week for one year, 2 X per week from age 12–14, 2 X per week from age 16–18, 1 X per week from age 18–21	$90–110 per hour
Physiatric evaluation	1993–2007	Yearly	$75–100 each
Occupational therapy	To 1994 (age 5)	1–2 X per week	$100 each visit
Physical therapy evaluation	Est. September 1993	1 X only (also see comprehensive eval.)	$100
Neurological evaluation	1993–2001	Yearly	$80 each (does not include EEG or CT scans or other diagnostic studies, if needed)
Ophthalmologic evaluation for strabismus	June 1993 to life expectancy	Yearly	$35–55 each (does not include dilation or corrective lenses, if necessary)
Speech/language evaluation	1993 and 1994 at age 5 (included in comprehensive evaluation)	1 X in 1993, 1994	$100 (1993) 1994 cost included in comp. eval.
Comprehensive team evaluation (include medical, P.T., O.T., speech/language, etc.)	1994 (age 5)	1 X only	$1,800

Table 14.4 (continued) Rehabilitation Plan

Anticipated Length of Rehabilitation Program:
Through childhood and potentially lifetime follow-up.

Recommendation	*Dates*	*Frequency*	*Expected Cost*
Special Education *Option 1:* Private school for children with disabilities. Also consider summer education or camp.	1993–2007	36 weeks per year (40 weeks per year if summer school)	$10,000 per school year (recommended for max. outcome by Devel. Psych.) 4 weeks @ $350–$1,000 per week (summer)
Option 2: Public school system covered by the Individuals with Disabilities Education Act (IDEA). Include 13 years of learning disability consulting, 3 days per week for school year and summer school.			$0 for public school. $40/hour learning disability consulting 36 weeks per year regular school or 40 weeks per year with summer school
Neurobehavior development consultant	1993–2007	3 contacts with school and client per year to enhance educational achievement	Expect 2 hours per occasion at $100/hour (total 6 hours per year)
Health and Strength Maintenance (including pool therapy, walking, and recreational activities to encourage motor coordination, perceptual training and strengthening)	1993 through entrance into school, 1994 (age 5)		No additional expected cost.

Table 14.4 (continued) Rehabilitation Plan

Anticipated Length of Rehabilitation Program:
Through childhood and potentially lifetime follow-up.

Recommendation	*Dates*	*Frequency*	*Expected Cost*
Driving evaluation	2004 (age 15)	1 X only	$400
Vocational			
a. Prevocational evaluation	2005 (age 16)	1 X only	$600
b. Vocational evaluation	2007 (age 18)	1 X only	$600
c. Vocational counseling, guidance, placement assistance, and follow-up. (Note: Costs for job coaching and supported employment, which may be appropriate, are not included.)	2006–2009	150 hours over three years	$65/hour
d. Post-high school education or vocational-technical training			Unknown

Potential Complications

Potential complications include, but are not limited to:

1. Seizure disorder.
2. Risk of reinjury due to reduced judgment, intelligence, physical skills, and visual perception.
3. More significant psychological reaction to injury than expected.
4. Poorer educational/vocational achievement than expected.
5. Medical treatment and follow-up which is more extensive than expected.

Access to the Labor Market

VOCATIONAL CONSIDERATIONS
The limitations listed below are consistent with the U.S. Department of Labor definitions:

Physical Demands

Jobs which require significant amounts of functioning in following categories:

Standing	Balancing
Reaching upward	Stooping
Crouching	Fingering
Sitting	Visual perception

Eye/hand/foot coordination
Operating controls with right hand/arm or right foot/leg

Cognitive

Significant visual-spatial perception disturbance
Problems with attention, concentration, memory
Reduced frustration tolerance
Difficulties following through on tasks
Slowed thought process
Trouble following directions
Distractibility
Reduced intelligence
Reduced ability to be educated/trained (auditory learning recommended)

Emotional

No current significant emotional difficulties noted. Expect moderate emotional difficulties upon entrance into formal education program (1994, age 5) and various developmental periods to adulthood.

Conclusion

The client has experienced a mild to moderate impact on the range of job alternatives available to him. The client has reduced ability to be educated or trained. His loss of access to the *competitive* labor market is expected to be in excess of 98%.

Placeability

The client has experienced an impact on his ability to be placed in a job. Cognitive retraining and special educational services will be needed. Additionally, guidance/career counseling, job skills training, and selective placement is expected to decrease the impact of the injury on the client's ability to be placed in the *competitive* labor market. Job placement will depend to a large extent on the success of the client's rehabilitation program and his ability to complete a minimum of a high school education. Employment should maximize the client's strength in auditory skills.

Earnings Capacity

Pre-Incident	A review of the client's family history suggests the capacity for college education or master's level education. Earnings potential to be determined by economist.
Post-Incident	High school or its equivalent and possibly technical school training. Earnings potential to be determined by economist.

Diminution of earnings capacity: To be computed by an economist.

Labor Force Participation (Work Life Expectancy)

Although clearly not employable in the manner as before the accident, the client will have no reduction in labor force participation assuming no complications and excellent rehabilitation/education program. Expect entry into labor force at age 20 (2009).

CONCLUSION

Traumatic Brain Injury is a lifetime disability that affects almost every organ system of the body, but most importantly, attacks the very core of the person's personality and prior life. By trying to understand what happened, and the daily experience of the individual, the planner is in a better position to outline what the present and future cares will be. Each life care plan requires creativity and compassion, and the realization that lives have changed forever. The life care plan may be the best and only opportunity to put some of the broken pieces back together and offer hope for the future.

REFERENCES

Alexander, M. (1995). Mild traumatic brain injury: pathophysiology, natural history and clinical management. **Neurology, 45**(7), 1253.

Ben-Yishay, Y. & Silver, S.L. (1987). Relationships between employability and vocational outcome after intensive holistic cognitive rehabilitation. **Journal of Head Trauma Rehabilitation, 2**(1), 35-48.

Byron, J. & Teasdale, G. (1981). **Management of head injuries.** Philadelphia: F.A. Davis.

Handler, B. & Sample, P. (1994). **Beyond brain injury.** Athens, GA: Elliott & Fitpatrick.

Wilson, J. T., Wiedman, K. D., Hadley, D. M., Condon, B., Teasdale, G., & Brooks, D. N. (1988). Early and late magnetic imaging and neuropsychological outcome after head injury. **Journal of Neurology, Neurosurgery and Psychiatry, 51,** 391-396.

Weed, R. (1994). Evaluating the earnings capacity of clients with mild to moderate acquired brain injury. In C. Simkins (Ed.), **Analysis, understanding and presentation of cases involving traumatic brain injury,** 213-228. Washington, D.C.: National Head Injury Foundation.

Weed, R. (1996). Life care planning and earnings capacity analysis for brain injured clients involved in personal injury litigation utilizing the RAPEL method. **Journal of Neurorehabilitation, 7**(2), 119-135.

15

LIFE CARE PLANNING FOR THE BURN PATIENT

Melissa A. Brown & Phala A. Helm

INTRODUCTION

The development of the life care plan for the burn patient is best begun immediately following the injury to ensure provision of adequate medical, emotional, social, and financial support for the patient and family. There is an enormous investment of health care manpower, time, money, and facilities in the acute treatment of burn patients and in restoring them to health (Feck, Baptiste, & Tate, 1978). The treatment process is long, arduous, demanding, complex, and expensive (Fisher & Helm, 1984; Helm & Fisher, 1988). The rehabilitation process begins as soon after initial hospital admission as possible. The end point of rehabilitation is not easily defined, but can continue for up to two years after discharge (Helm & Cromes, 1995).

A basic knowledge of the incidence, classification, and pathophysiology of burn injury is essential to the medical case manager. In the United States 1.5 to 2.0 million persons per year sustain burn injuries, 6,000 to 12,000 of which result in death. Approximately 55,000 to 100,000 injuries require hospitalization and of those 50% will develop either temporary or permanent disability (Fisher & Helm, 1984; Committee on Trauma Research, 1985; Rice & MacKenzie, 1989). Those at greatest risk for burn injuries are young children (2-4 years) and young adult males (17-25 years). The upper extremity is the most commonly involved body part in burn injury, followed by the neck and head. Injury to these areas obviously affects function and appearance and can result in disability (Demling, 1989).

Classification of Burns

Burn injuries are usually classified by the extent of body surface area (BSA) of skin involved and the depth of the burn. Traditionally, burn depth was classified as first, second, and third degree. Today burn depth has been reclassified as superficial (first degree), partial (second degree), full (third degree), and deep full thickness (fourth degree). The depth of burn injury refers to the skin layers that have been destroyed.

1-57444-075-6/99/$0.00+$.50

- *Superficial* burns involve only the superficial epidermis and usually require 3 to 7 days for healing with no scarring.
- *Superficial partial thickness* burns involve the epidermis and the dermis excluding hair follicles, sweat glands, and sebaceous glands and should heal in less than 21 days with minimal scarring.
- *Deep partial thickness* burns involve the epidermis and most of the dermis, requiring more than 21 days for healing and may develop severe hypertrophic scarring.
- *Full thickness* burns result in total destruction of the skin, both epidermis and dermis, and may involve additional tissue. Full thickness burns of any significant size require skin grafting.
- *Deep full thickness* burns involve muscle and/or bone and are usually a result of prolonged contact with heat or an electrical injury and may require flap coverage or amputation (Fisher & Helm, 1984).

Burn injuries are also classified in terms of the percentage of total body surface area (TBSA) involved. The percentage of partial and full thickness burns should be indicated separately. The American Burn Association (ABA) classifies burn injuries as mild, moderate, and major. Moderate and major burns require hospitalization.

- Minor burns are defined as those less than 15% TBSA partial thickness (10% for children) and less than 2% full thickness unless the eyes, ears, face, or perineum are involved.
- Moderate burns include 15%–25% TBSA (10%–20% for children) regardless of depth, and 2%–10% full-thickness burns unless the eyes, ears, face, or perineum are involved.
- Major burns include greater than 25% partial-thickness burns (20% for children); greater than 10% full thickness burns; all burns involving the face, eyes, ears, feet, and perineum; all burns that are electrical or involve inhalation injury; all burns with ancillary injury (fracture, tissue trauma, etc.); and all burns involving a person with factors that suggest poor risk secondary to age or illness (Cromes & Helm, 1993).

The Skin: Consequences of Burns

Skin is the largest organ system in the human body and the tissue most affected by burn injury. The purpose of skin is to keep body fluids inside, regulate body temperature by controlling perspiration, prevent infection, and decrease the effect of radiation from the sun. The skin is composed of two layers: the epidermis (or outer layer) and the dermis (or inner layer). The epidermis contains cells that produce skin color and form the outer protective layer of skin. The dermis lies below the epidermis and is composed of connective tissue, capillaries, collagen, and elastic fibers. It provides structural and nutritional support to the epidermis and the skin appendages (i.e., hair follicles, sweat glands, and sebaceous glands) and contributes to the skin elasticity. Full thickness burns that involve both the epidermis and dermis will result in hair loss, sweat gland and sebaceous gland loss. Beneath the dermis is a layer of fat and connective tissue. Muscle, bone, and tendons lie below this layer. Sensory nerve endings are distributed throughout the skin and subcutaneous layer. Therefore, depending on the depth, a burn injury may result in altered ability to sense pain, touch, and temperature (Fisher & Helm, 1984).

Rehabilitation

Rehabilitation of the burn patient begins during acute hospitalization and may last for several months post-discharge (Choctaw, Eisner, & Wachtel, 1987). Upon discharge it is likely that some wounds are not completely healed. Wound care is one focus of the outpatient rehabilitation program, along with positioning, splinting, range of motion (ROM), exercise, and conditioning. After discharge the rehabilitation process increasingly focuses on independence in daily activities, increased physical conditioning, and psychological adaptation to burn sequelae (Buschbacher, 1996; Cromes & Helm, 1993).

A prolonged rehabilitation course is inherent to a burn injury. A large burn may require a year or more of rehab intervention. Treatment should be initiated in a timely manner before burn scar maturation; otherwise, complications can occur, resulting in more prolonged treatment and increased cost of care. The burn scar takes 6 to 18 months to mature, and it is during this time that the scar can be successfully mobilized to prevent contractures, deformities, and hypertrophic banding. After the scar matures, correction of most deformities and cosmetic abnormalities require expensive surgical procedures with rehabilitation follow-up afterward to maintain functional gains (Cromes & Helm, 1993).

Outpatient Services

In order to provide appropriate outpatient rehabilitation services, it may be necessary to temporarily relocate the patient and perhaps a family member near a recognized burn center. A comprehensive outpatient burn rehabilitation program may entail six hours per day for five days per week, with a gradual decrease in frequency of treatment to three times per week (TIW), and then two times per week (BIW). Initially the patient may require 24-hour attendant care from a family member or health care provider for assistance with activities of daily living. A severe burn may require several weeks or even months of assistive care. If spouses or family members are providing attendant care or transportation, reimbursement for their time and services should be considered.

Physician follow-up visits are needed approximately every one to two weeks in the initial outpatient stage, with frequency decreasing to once or twice per month as long as the patient is on physical therapy and/or occupational therapy treatment, and for the first few weeks after treatment is stopped. To make sure the patient is maintaining function after therapy has stopped, physician follow-up should continue but gradually decrease to once every three months, biannual, and annual visits, unless unforeseen complications arise.

Psychological Evaluation

Psychological intervention begins in the acute hospitalization phase and may continue on a weekly basis for several months post-discharge, depending in part on the preinjury emotional stability of the individual. Because of pain, disrupted sleep, rigors of treatment, slowness of progress, interruption of lifestyle patterns, concern about physical and cosmetic outcomes, and not being able to work as well as host of other possibilities, the patient may display emotional difficulties (Cromes & Helm, 1993). Disfigurement can affect self-concept, body image, comfort in interpersonal situations, and acceptance in the workplace (Sheffield et al., 1988). Psychological services should be available to spouses, caregivers, and families. Individual and family counseling interventions may be more pertinent after discharge. Severe burns are more likely to result in long-term quality-of-life problems with both physical and psychosocial aspects (Cobb, Maxwell, & Silverstein, 1990).

Vocational Rehabilitation

Vocational rehabilitation issues should be addressed early in the outpatient phase of the rehabilitation process. Frequent communication with employers should be encouraged to maintain a positive work relationship and to allay fears of loss of employment. Acquisition of a detailed job description can be used to focus therapy plans and concentrate on job-related skills. When job modifications and/or returning to a former job is unrealistic, vocational evaluation and training can be initiated in the latter stages of medical rehabilitation and reconstructive procedures. Burn patients are frequently able to return to work before scars are mature. Options for part time employment or light duty should be explored with the employer to help alleviate financial stress and the establishment of dependency patterns.

Complications

Burn complications can be extensive and involve every part of the body. In addition, vocational, psychological, and family functioning can be significantly altered. The following burn sequelae (Table 15.1) have been arranged according to body systems with suggestions for rehabilitation intervention, frequency and duration of treatment, and surgical options. Although these lists are not all-inclusive, the most significant and common burn injury related complications and treatment options have been listed.

Resources

In addition to the references associated with this chapter, information regarding burn rehabilitation is available from the American Burn Association and its professional journal.

American Burn Association
Jeffrey Saffle, MD
Secretary
Dept. of Surgery, Room 3B306
Univ. of Utah Medical Center
50 N. Medical Drive
Salt Lake City, UT 84132
jsaffle@msscc.med.utah.edu
fax 801-585-2435
800-548-2876

American Burn Association Journal
Charles Baxter, MD
Editor-in-Chief
Burn Care and Rehabilitation
6516 Forest Park Road
Dallas, TX 75235

Table 15.1 Complications Associated with Burn Injury

Problem	*When/Where Occurred*	*Results in*	*Dx Tests*	*Rehab Intervention*	*Duration of Treatment*	*Surgical Options*
			Musculoskeletal			
Heterotopic ossification	Usually occurs in large joints such as elbows, knees, & hips.	Severely limited ROM & loss of function.	X-ray, Bone scan	PT/OT to provide ROM w/in functional limits, splinting, Continuous Passive Motion (CPM) unit.	6 mos from dx.	If HO does not absorb on its own, surgical intervention is indicated followed by therapy for wound care & ROM and/or CPM 5x/wk to TIW for 6–12 wks to obtain max results.
Joint ankylosis	Usually occurs in small joints of fingers & toes. May occur in other joints.	Frozen or locked joint often leaving digit in an awkward position.	X-ray	No rehab intervention.		Consider surgical pinning of joint or digit in a more functional position.
Osteomyelitis	Usually occurs from a very deep burn w/exposed bone, resulting in a long-term chronic open wound, may occur mos after date of injury.	Chronic open wound.	X-ray, Bone scan	Requires extended wound care & possible hospitalization for IV antibiotics.	Can occur intermittently for years.	Surgical debridement of dead tissue. Amputation may be required.
Scoliosis	Usually occurs in children w/unilateral (asymmetric) hip, trunk, & shoulder burns.	Spinal curvature. If child hits a growth spurt, structural spinal deformity can occur w/wedging of vertebrae.	X-ray to r/o structural deformity	Functional scoliosis will respond to therapy using paraffin, sustained stretch, & ROM of trunk.	Monitor semi-annually until age 18.	May require surgery for early release of hip or axillary contracture &/or z-plasty, or skin grafting down sides of trunk to release tight skin.
Reflex Sympathetic Dystrophy — RSD — Shoulder/Hand syndrome	Usually begins in acute phase of burn before wound closure — questionable etiology but seems to be related to immobility for long periods of time. Occurs in both partial and full thickness burns, primarily in the hands.	Hypersensitive hand with painful swollen joints, tapered, shiny fingers, and moist skin. If not treated immediately and aggressively, can result in permanent contracture deformities.	X-ray, Clinical exam	Stellate block immediately followed by vigorous physical therapy modalities of paraffin and sustained stretch, ultrasound, ROM and exercise, and desensitization. Splinting may be indicated to prevent contracture. A one week trial of steroids may reduce pain and swelling.	Early dx and tx are the key to successful intervention. Treatment time varies.	None. Sympathectomy — rare.
Kyphotic deformity	Occurs in children and thin adults with anterior chest and shoulder burns.	Decreased respiratory function, spinal deformity.	X-ray	Physical therapy for paraffin and sustained stretch, ROM, exercise and serial casting of the trunk, clavicular strap for shoulders.	Until scar matures at 6-12 mos. post burn if no surgery.	Axillary contracture releases and/or release of skin of anterior chest with skin grafting for adequate chest expansion.

Table 15.1 (continued) Complications Associated with Burn Injury

Problem	*When/Where Occurred*	*Results in*	*Dx Tests*	*Rehab Intervention*	*Duration of Treatment*	*Surgical Options*
Joint subluxation	Can occur before wound healing is complete or as a result of tight scar tissue. Usually occurs in small joints such as finger MPs, thumb, and toes.	Permanent ankylosis or deformity.	X-ray	Anticipate and treat early with splinting or casting to prevent.	Until scar matures at 6–12 mos post-injury.	Surgical release of scar tissue will sometimes correct.
Boutonniere finger deformity	Occurs in deep burns to the dorsal aspect of the fingers and hand, resulting in exposed or burned extensor tendons.	Permanent deformities severely compromising hand function.	Clinical exam, X-ray	Prevention is the key. Requires specific treatment protocol for positioning, hand therapy, wound care, and finger casting.	6 weeks or until tendon is covered.	None.
Swan neck deformity	Contracture of intrinsic muscles of the hands and/or volar plate rupture.	Permanent finger deformity severely compromising hand function.	X-ray, Clinical exam	Stretching of intrinsic muscles, splinting of hand.	Until ROM plateaus.	None. If problematic, reconstructive procedures for better positioning of finger.
Mallet finger deformity	Usually occurs in full thickness burns of dorsal fingers and involves the insertion of the extensor tendon.	Inability to extend the DIP joint of the finger.	Clinical exam	Splint 24 hours/day for reattachment of ruptured extensor tendon.	24 hours/day for 6 weeks.	None. If no reattachment, pin in extension.
Muscle contracture	Develops from protective posturing to decrease pain, may occur without skin involvement.	Loss of ROM.	Clinical exam	Physical therapy for stretching program and serial casting.	3–4 mos.	Surgical release is rarely required.
Joint capsule contracture	Secondary to skin contracture, primarily in shoulder and fingers.	Loss of ROM, may result in permanent deformity.	Clinical exam	PT/OT for stretching program, ultrasound.	3–4 mos. trial.	Surgical release.
Exposed bone	Occurs in deep full thickness burns.	Prolonged open wound.	R/O Osteomyelitis	Intense wound care protocol including burr hole stimulation to promote growth of granulation tissue.	Daily wound care until wound bed is ready for grafting.	Skin graft or flap procedure.
Exposed tendons	Occurs in deep full thickness burns.	Prolonged wound care and permanent deformities if not treated appropriately. May result in tendon rupture.	Clinical exam	Intense wound care program to stimulate granulation tissue and prepare wound for surgery. Splinting, casting, and orthotics may be needed for positioning and protection of tendon.	Daily wound care and 24 hour splinting until tendon is covered.	Surgical procedures for tissue flap and/or skin graft.
Septic arthritis	May occur in joints associated w/open wounds and/or joints w/out open wounds.	Warm, painful, swollen joints and possible joint fusion.	X-ray	ROM within pain limitation; oral or IV antibiotics.	Condition can last for several weeks.	May require surgical incision and drainage.

Post-ischemic hand syndrome	Can occur from prolonged application of pneumatic tourniquet during grafting procedure.	Numb, stiff, swollen hand.	Clinical exam	OT program of massage, coban wraps, and compression gloves to reduce swelling.	5x/wk to TIW until problem resolves.	None.
Residual joint pain	Occurs primarily in hands and knees after wound healing and into the rehab program, perhaps from micro trauma to joints secondary to exercise program.	Results in aching joints in absence of redness, warmth, or swelling and with negative X-rays.	Clinical exam, X-ray	Usually controlled with over-the-counter analgesics or antiinflammatory medications.	Condition can persist for years.	None.
Limb amputation	Occurs with full thickness and deep full thickness burns, and electrical injuries.	Loss of extremity.		Prior to prosthetic fitting, ROM, strengthening and stump conditioning to prepare the limb for prosthesis; prosthetic fitting, gait training and activities of daily living.	TIW for 6–8 weeks. Mobility aids such as wheelchair or crutches may be needed. A replacement schedule for the prosthesis should be considered.	Surgical modification of the stump may be required to improve skin integrity and padding for the prosthesis.
Shortened extremity	Occurs in the growing child when scar tissue crosses a joint and inhibits bone growth.	Permanent shortened extremity.	Clinical exam, extremity measurements	Child should be followed semi-annually for extremity measurements and spinal screening.	Follow until adult or bone maturity; 18–girls, 24–boys.	Surgical release of scar tissue may be necessary to prevent permanent deformity.
			Neurological			
Generalized peripheral neuropathy	Occurs during the first 3–6 weeks post-injury.	Sensory loss and distal weakness of upper and lower extremities. Although improvement is generally seen, some weakness can be permanent.	EMG, NVC, muscle test	Therapy program consisting of muscle reeducation, strengthening, and electrical stim. Weekly muscle test to monitor progress. Assistive devices for ADLs. Splints and AFOs for positioning to prevent contracture.	Generally plateaus within 3–6 months.	None.
Mononeuropathy	Occurs anytime during the initial hospitalization. Commonly affected nerves include the median, ulnar, peroneal, radial, and brachial plexus.	Residual weakness and sensory loss extending down from the level of lesion.	EMG, NVC, muscle test	Therapy program consists of muscle reeducation, strengthening, electrical stimulation, ROM, and specialized splinting. Weekly muscle test to monitor return of function.	Duration of treatment and recovery rate varies depending on the level of lesion. The more proximal the level of the lesion, the longer the intervention. 3 mos to 2 years.	None.
Neuroma	A hypersensitive nerve ending or nerve bundle that occurs when an injured nerve tries to repair itself, generally after a surgical procedure.	Localized hypersensitive, painful area.	Clinical exam	Therapy program of desensitization techniques such as tapping, vibration, and massage; steroid injection.	TIW from 6–8 weeks.	A persistent neuroma may require surgical removal.

Table 15.1 (continued) Complications Associated with Burn Injury

Problem	*When/Where Occurred*	*Results in*	*Dx Tests*	*Rehab Intervention*	*Duration of Treatment*	*Surgical Options*
			Skin			
Open wounds	Occurs with partial and full thickness burns.	Painful wounds. (Prolonged wound healing usually results in worse scarring.)	Clinical exam	Hydrotherapy, debridement, and wound care by an experienced rehab professional at a burn center.	Wound care should be done by a professional 3–5 times/week and by a trained family member or caregiver on the other days. Partial thickness burns without complications heal in approx 21 days. Full thickness burns, depending on the size, can take months to heal.	Full and/or split thickness skin grafts for deep partial and full thickness burns will decrease pain and healing time.
Chronic open wounds	Occurs with infection as MRSA, scratching, fragile skin, pressure, shearing, or blistering.	Prolonged wound care, cellulitis, multiple hospitalizations.	Wound culture to R/O MRSA	Oral and/or IV antibiotics may be indicated. Hydrotherapy, debridement, and wound care.	Wounds can heal and then reopen for years, especially when MRSA is the cause. Treatment is required intermittently for several weeks depending on wound size.	Surgical excision of the wound and debridement; skin grafting.
Blistering	Generally occurs in early stages of wound healing from shearing of new skin.	Open wounds on previously healed skin.	Clinical exam	Requires a specific wound care protocol. May require oral antibiotics.	The blistering stage generally lasts from 2–6 weeks.	Occasionally skin grafting.
Depigmentation/ hyperpigmentation	Noticed in newly healed skin.	Uneven skin tones.		May want to try camouflage make-up to improve cosmesis. Vendors of camouflage make-up are often difficult to identify and locate. The make-up is expensive and uncomfortable for some patients.	Skin tones can continue to change and improve for 6 mos. to 2 years, but will never totally return to normal.	Pigmentation procedures.

Hypertrophic scars	Generally occurs in nongrafted areas of deep partial and/or full thickness burns with prolonged wound healing. Usually occurs more often in children and individuals with darker pigmented skin or very fair skin. If a burn wound loses its redness in 3 mos, hypertrophic scarring usually does not occur. Chances for hypertrophic scarring decrease if full thickness or deep partial thickness burns are grafted early.	Red and/or purple, thick, lumpy, firm scar tissue that is warm to touch, hypersensitive, and may be painful.	Clinical exam	Compression garments are worn for scar flattening, to decrease itching, and control pain. Intermediate compression garments, such as isotoner gloves and Elastic net, should be worn 23 hours/day for 2–4 weeks post-healing. These should be followed with custom made compression garments that should be worn for 23 hrs/day. Two sets of garments should be ordered each time and will need to be replaced every 2–3 months.	Compression garments are worn for 6–24 months or until scars are mature. Mature scars are pliable, softer, flatter, cool to the touch, and lighter in color.	After the scars mature, surgical reconstructive procedures, such as scar excision or tissue expanders, may be an option. This is often a time consuming process as reconstructive procedures are often done in stages requiring wound care and therapy between surgeries to obtain maximum benefit.
				Silicone sheets can be worn over scars for at least 12 hrs/day for 4 weeks to facilitate flattening and scar maturation. May cause maceration of skin.	Worn 23 hrs/day for 6–24 mos. May require periodic revisions.	
				Clear plastic face masks and neck collars for optional methods of pressure.	May require multiple or alternating splints to be worn for several mos. Splints will be revised periodically as scar tissue band softens and stretches.	
				Splints for scar banding. Worn over compression garments to apply additional pressure. Web spacers or otoform may be worn under garments for additional pressure.		
				Camouflage make-up.	Indefinite.	
Painful scars	Usually occur over the lateral chest wall and medial arm.	Sensitive, painful scars. Can interfere with sleep.	Scar palpation	Treat with silicone gel sheets underneath compression garments. Ice massage, vibrator, ultrasound scar massage or desensitization can offer some relief, as well as steroid injections.	Can last for up to 2 years.	In severe painful cases, can be surgically removed.

Table 15.1 (continued) Complications Associated with Burn Injury

Problem	*When/Where Occurred*	*Results in*	*Dx Tests*	*Rehab Intervention*	*Duration of Treatment*	*Surgical Options*
Skin contracture	Can occur anywhere in the burned area, causing bands of scar tissue that limit motion.	Decreased ROM and function.	Clinical exam, ROM measurements	Aggressive therapy protocol including paraffin and sustained stretch, scar massage, portable vibrator to break up scar tissue, fluidotherapy, ROM, and exercise program. Serial splinting and casting to prevent further loss of ROM and hopefully gain ROM. Different joints require specific splinting protocols which may involve alternating splints and/or multiple splint changes.	Therapy is recommended 3–5 times/wk for several months. Frequent cast changes and splint revisions can be expected. Often the role of therapy is to keep the contracture from worsening until a surgical release can be performed.	Surgical contracture releases are often done in stages in order to obtain maximum range. Wound care and therapy are required between surgical procedures.
Microstomia (small mouth)	Occurs with facial and lip burns.	Decreased mouth opening resulting in compromised dental hygiene and poor nutritional status.	Clinical exam, Mouth opening measurements	Therapy protocol including scar massage, mouth exercises with cones and appliances, or mouth stretchers. Plastic face mask and cervical collars may also be indicated.	Therapy 3–5 times/wk until problem resolves.	In severe cases surgical releases may be indicated.
Ectropion (contraction of scar tissue of the eyelid or eversion of the eyelid caused by contraction of facial skin)	Occurs with deep facial burns and or burns to the eye area. Usually becomes obvious during acute hospitalization.	Inability to close the eyes, thereby causing corneal damage due to drying.	Clinical exam, Ophthalmology consult	Therapy including scar massage and stretching.	Daily therapy until problem resolves.	Surgical intervention for release and skin grafting is usually indicated.
Skin infection	Occurs when healed burned skin develops pustules from clogged pores and/or ingrown hair follicles. Infection secondary to MRSA.	Skin irritations characterized by weeping pustules and open wounds. Requires prolonged wound care.	R/O MRSA	Antibiotics and wound care. Severe cases may require hospitalization and IV antibiotics. If MRSA is diagnosed, Bactroban ointment and extended wound care may be indicated.	May occur intermittently for years.	Wound excision and grafting in severe cases of MRSA.
Fingernail burns	Occurs with deep hand burns.	Deformed nails with ragged sharp edges that catch on clothing, etc.	Clinical exam	Therapist can trim and grind nails. Scar tissue massage over fingers to decrease pull at base of nail.	Continue therapy until problem resolves.	May require surgical removal and/or modification. Reconstructive procedures to graft from toenails has been successful.

Hair follicle loss	Most disfiguring with full thickness burns to the scalp and forehead involving the eyebrows.	Permanent hair loss and poor cosmesis.	Clinical exam	Wigs or hairpieces, as well as hats and glasses, can be used to improve appearance.	Items will be needed indefinitely without reconstructive procedures.	Reconstructive procedures using tissue expanders have been successful with scalp burns; however, it often requires multiple procedures over several years depending on the size of the burn. Eyebrows may be reconstructed with hair transplants or tattooing.
Ingrown hairs	Usually occurs on men's faces and necks with thick scarring.	Local infection.	Clinical exam	Treat local infection with wound care and antibiotics.	May occur intermittently for years.	Surgical intervention to remove ingrown hairs may be required when large areas are involved.
Loss of sebaceous glands	Occurs in full thickness burns or with hypertrophic scarring.	Dry, cracked skin and/or itching.	Clinical exam	Requires lubrication of skin 2–3 times/day	Permanent.	None.
Loss of skin innervation	Occurs in full thickness burns and in areas of thick hypertrophic scars.	Easily traumatized skin.	Test for sensory loss	Patient education. Protective clothing such as gloves and knee pads, fleece lined shoes and custom insoles can help decrease traumatization. May require occupational modifications or vocational change.	Permanent.	None.
Decubitus ulcer	Generally associated with long-term ICU hospitalization. Most commonly occurs over bony prominences such as heels and sacrum.	Prolonged rehab process, adherent scar tissue over the defect.	Clinical exam	Prevention is the key. Roho mattresses are preferred over constant air flow beds due to the poor positioning associated with air flow beds. Requires an extensive wound care protocol, including hydrotherapy, debridement, packing, and bandaging.	Can take several months to heal.	May require surgical flap procedure.
Marjolin's ulcer (Squamous Cell Carcinoma)	Develops from chronic open wounds. (Wounds that close and reopen over a prolonged period of time.) (Rare — occurs in .1 of .01% of burns.)	Malignancy.	Wound biopsy	Awareness of complication.		Requires surgical procedure and wound closure.
Allergic reactions	Healed skin becomes irritated due to lubricants, pressure garments, soaps, detergents, etc. It is difficult to identify the irritating agent.	Weeping wounds, burning and itching. Prolongs healing time and can interfere with return to work.	Clinical exam	Discontinue use of topical agents, lotions, garments, and soaps for 2–4 days. Begin substituting with alternative products, adding one at a time. May need short course of topical or oral steroids.	Once the irritating product is discontinued, the problem resolves in 1–2 weeks.	None.
Itching	Can occur in any burned area after burn is healed.	Open wounds from scratching.	Clinical exam	Skin lubrications and antihistamine.	Possibly years.	None.

Table 15.1 (continued) Complications Associated with Burn Injury

Problem	*When/Where Occurred*	*Results in*	*Dx Tests*	*Rehab Intervention*	*Duration of Treatment*	*Surgical Options*
			Psychological, Social, Vocational			
Psychosocial problems	Psychosocial and/or emotional difficulties manifest at any time during the burn recovery and rehab process; and are often related to the etiology of the burn.	Poor body image and decreased self-esteem; sexuality problems; increased dependency or sick role; anxiety related to loss of control; depression; fear of dying; anxiety over the future; post-traumatic stress syndrome; discomfort in interpersonal situations and lack of acceptance in the workplace &/or fear of workplace.	Psychiatric consult on all inpatients, rehab psychological eval for outpatients	Psychotropic medication if indicated; individual therapy sessions; support group participation; training in relaxation techniques; give patient appropriate options regarding treatment schedule, etc.	Psychological intervention may be prolonged or periodic in nature.	Long-term emotional problems in burn patients appear to be the exception. Some reports suggest that more severe burns are more likely to result in long-term quality-of-life problems with both physical and psychological aspects. Others indicate that emotional problems may be more frequent in persons with more than 30% TBSA burns or if visible areas, such as the face and hands, are involved.
	Spouses and caregivers may also experience emotional distress.	Anxiety and distress related to fear of losing a loved one or material possessions. Anxiety regarding ability to provide care for patient. Concern for the future and economic issues.		Participation in individual therapy sessions and spousal support group. Adequate family training.		

Vocational problems	Vocational concerns usually begin to surface as the physical rehab process comes to an end, particularly if the burn was work related. Both physical and psychological factors can impair function in the work place, i.e., intolerance for heat and cold extremes, skin sensitivity to exposure to the sun or chemical agents, fatigability and reduced stamina, poor concentration, fear of workplace, decreased functional ROM and strength, and psychological adaptation.	Delayed return to work.	Functional capacity eval, comprehensive medical eval identifying functional limitations, vocational evaluation	Initiate formal vocational rehabilitation program as soon as patient is medically stable. Encourage open and frequent communication with employer. Obtain a comprehensive job description or complete job site eval. Consider physical modification of job site &/or job tasks. Participation in a formal work hardening program. Identify a modified work schedule, or light duty, and encourage progressive return to full time and regular duties.	Approximately 90% of persons admitted to burn centers return to their pre-burn functional levels within 1 year. Size, depth, and location (hands) are factors that influence time to return to work. Surgical reconstructive procedures may also delay return to work.	If return to one's pre-burn job is not feasible, consideration must given to modifying that job, changing to a new job that might require retraining, or accepting permanent disability. Decreased earning potential is a concern as are difficulties in qualifying for SSDI.
Return to school problems	Can occur in any school child who receives a burn injury, but is usually a bigger problem when the child has had a lengthy absence from school. Children may be concerned about appearance, discomfort due to compression garments and splints, and acceptance of peers.	Post-traumatic stress syndrome, anxiety, depression.	Psychological evaluation	Prepare teachers and students for the burned child's return by having a therapist, social worker, or nurse give a special presentation of the ABack to School@ program allowing students and teachers to see garments and splints and ask questions about burn injuries; individual therapy sessions.		
Sleep disturbances	Generally occurs after hospital discharge. Can be secondary to pain and discomfort from burn wounds and/or splints. May also result from fear related to injury or anxiety relative to the future.	Nightmares or night terrors, decreased energy and coping skills, or depression due to inadequate rest and sleep.	Psychological eval may be indicated	Psychological intervention and desensitization and relaxation techniques. Sleep medication.	Usually improves with time and improved physical health. May require sleep medication up to 1 year post-injury.	
			Other			
Visual impairment	May occur with facial burns or electrical injuries.	Burned or damaged corneas. May result in permanent partial loss of vision or blindness or cataracts in electrical injuries.	Ophthalmology exam and follow-up	After wound healing or in conjunction with wound healing and burn rehab program, patient will need to participate in a rehab program for blind/visually impaired for ADL, mobility training, etc.	Several months depending on degree of visual loss.	Corneal transplant.

Table 15.1 (continued) Complications Associated with Burn Injury

Problem	*When/Where Occurred*	*Results in*	*Dx Tests*	*Rehab Intervention*	*Duration of Treatment*	*Surgical Options*
Hearing loss	Probably secondary to antibiotics.	Hearing loss that may be permanent.	ENT consult and audiological eval	In severe cases, training in sign language and lip reading may be indicated; hearing aids.	Several months depending on degree of hearing loss.	Cochlea implants offer limited improvement.
Amputation of body parts	Deep full thickness burns to ears, noses, fingers, and/or toes can result in amputations.	Deformity and disfigurement, impaired body image, and emotional difficulties.		Although it is very expensive, excellent prostheses are available from one who specializes in cosmetic prostheses.	Replacement schedule for prostheses is 5–7 years.	Reconstructive plastic surgery.
				Psychiatric/psychological intervention may be indicated.	Psychological support may be indicated periodically or continuously for several months.	
Speech impairment	Occurs with prolonged intubation with endotracheal tube and when severe inhalation injuries are associated with burn injury.	Hoarseness and decreased volume.	ENT consultation	Speech therapy.	Generally resolves or improves over extended time.	None.
Deconditioning	1–1.5% loss of strength per day of bed rest. Loss of strength and muscle mass plateaus after 2 weeks of continuous bed rest, but can result in an overall strength loss of 25–40%.	Decreased strength, endurance.	Depending on individual's age and medical hx, a stress test to evaluate cardiac status is indicated.	Formal conditioning program under the supervision of a therapist. Activities utilizing treadmill and life cycle or similar equipment, and weight training are indicated in a progressive program.	Formal conditioning program can last 10–12 weeks, after which the individual can be placed on a home program using home exercise equipment or through a health club. This should be a lifetime commitment.	None.
Poor dental hygiene	Occurs with prolonged intubation and ICU stays.	Tooth decay, chipping of teeth.	Dental exam	Cooperate with dentist to improve dental hygiene.		None.

Abbreviation Key

ADL	Activities of daily living	MRSA	Methicillin Resistant Staph Aureus
AFO	Ankle foot orthosis	NVC	Nerve velocity conduction
BIW	2 times/week	OT	Occupational therapy
DIP	Distal interphalangeal	PT	Physical therapy
dx	Diagnosis	R/O	Rule out
EMG	Electromyography	ROM	Range of motion
ENT	Ear, nose, & throat	TBSA	Total body surface area
HO	Heterotopic ossification	TIW	3 times/week
hx	History	tx	Treatment
ICU	Intensive care unit		

CONCLUSION

It is unrealistic to think that the total rehabilitation of the burn patient is dependent on the actual therapy treatment experience. Carryover and consistent follow through by the patient for splinting regimens and home exercise programs must be stressed for maximum recovery. Giving patients control of appropriate options (type of medication, dressing change schedule, treatment schedule, etc.) can facilitate the process of their becoming more responsible and independent in their care. Nonetheless, the rehab process for a burn patient can totally overwhelm the patient's life, as well as the life of the patient's family. Therefore, the identification and attention to psychological problems is necessary throughout the rehabilitation process to address the impact of emotional difficulties on compliance and successful community reentry (Helm & Cromes, 1995). Overall, burn rehabilitation is complex, expensive, and involves considerable time and effort on the part of the patient. This chapter outlines many of the concerns and goals regarding treatment. Compliance and effective treatment can maximize the ultimate outcome and reduce complications.

REFERENCES

Buschbacher, R. M. (1996). Deconditioning, conditioning, and the benefits of exercise. In R. L. Braddom (Ed.), **Physical medicine & rehabilitation** (pp. 687-708). Philadelphia: W. B. Saunders.

Choctaw, W. F., Eisner, M. E., & Wachtel, T. L. (1987). Courses, prevention, prehospital case, evaluation, emergency treatment, and prognosis. In B. M. Achover (Ed.), **Management of the Burn Patient** (pp. 4-5). Los Altos, CA: Appleton & Lange.

Cobb, N., Maxwell, G., & Silverstein, P. (1990). Patient perception of quality of life after burn injury — results of an eleven year survey. **Journal of Burn Care & Rehabilitation, 10**, 251-257.

Committee on Trauma Research. (1985). **Injury in America: A Continuing Public Problem**. Washington, D.C.: National Academic Press.

Cromes, G. H., Jr. & Helm, P. A. (1993). In M. Eisenberg, R. Glueckauf, & H. Zaretsky (Eds.), **Medical Aspects of Disability** (pp. 92-104). New York: Springer Publishing Company.

Demling, R. H. (1989). In I. C. LaLonde (Ed.), **Burn Trauma** (p. X). New York: Thieme Medical Publishers.

Feck, G., Baptiste, M. S., & Tate, C. L., Jr. (1978). **An Epidemiological Study of Burn Injuries & Strategies for Prevention.** Washington, D.C.: U.S. Department Health, Education, and Welfare, Public Health Services.

Fisher, S. V. & Helm, P. A. (1984). **Comprehensive Rehabilitation of Burns**. Baltimore: Williams & Wilkins.

Helm, P. A. & Cromes, G. F., Jr. (1995). Burn injury rehabilitation. In The National Rehabilitation Hospital Research Center (Ed.) **The State-of-the-Science in Medical Rehabilitation** (pp. IV1-IV22). Falls Church, VA: Birch & Davis Associates.

Helm, P. A. & Fisher, S. V. (1988). Rehabilitation of the patient with burns. In J. A. DeLisa (Ed.). **Rehabilitation Medicine Principles & Practice** (pp. 821-839). Philadelphia: J. B. Lippincott.

Rice, D. P. & MacKenzie, E. J. (1989). **Cost of Injury in the United States: A Report to Congress**. Atlanta, GA: Centers for Disease Control.

Sheffield, C. G., Irons, G. B., Muehal, P., Jr., Malie, J. F., Ilstrup, D. M., & Stonnington, H. H. (1988). Physical & psychological outcome after burn. **Journal of Burn Care & Rehabilitation, 9**, 172-177.

16

LIFE CARE PLANNING FOR THE HIV/AIDS PATIENT

Julie A. Kitchen

INTRODUCTION

Acquired immunodeficiency syndrome (AIDS) was first recognized more than 15 years ago and since that time it has continued to spread at an incredible rate throughout the world. Despite new medications that are showing some promise of slowing down the spread of this disease, acceleration continues in Southeast Asia, South America, and Eastern Europe. There are even subtypes of the human immunodeficiency virus (HIV) that are different from those commonly studied in the United States and Europe (Kitchen, 1995). The result of this is a massive disease process that appears to have no vaccine available in the near future, which translates into continued spread and devastating infection of more of the population. In the United States alone, heterosexual sex is the fastest growing method of transmission, particularly among women in minority populations. Crack cocaine use (often resulting in prostitution) appears to be an important factor in the transmission of HIV, just as it is for other sexually transmitted diseases. This suggests that aggressive STD control programs can reduce HIV transmission; however, there appears to be little evidence that major support for these efforts will be forthcoming. There are also increasing trends of HIV infection seen in the transmission of the disease in young gay men. Interestingly, there also appears to be an increase in the numbers of AIDS cases reported in homosexual males over the age of 50. This reportedly is in part due to unprotected sex and the fact that many of these individuals first contracted the HIV infection approximately 10 years earlier and are now showing signs of the AIDS virus.

The approval in the early part of 1996 of several new antiretroviral drugs and tests for quantifying viral load has made a major impact on the care of HIV patients. These new drugs appear at this time to have the potential to significantly slow the progression of HIV infection and prolong survival. The impact of these drugs and the resultant prolonging of survival have a significant impact on the case management responsibilities in our society. Case management strategies in the past primarily dealt with cost effective means of treatment over what was a relatively short period of time. Now, however, significant other variables have been introduced that require case management strategies to be broadened in

1-57444-075-6/99/$0.00+$.50

scope and direction and responsibilities. In addition, the psychosocial adaptations and considerations that must be taken into account are also staggering. This not only includes the psychological health of persons with HIV/AIDS and their families, caregivers, and health related professionals, but the financial and job-market considerations too, which are immense.

Brief History

Acquired immune deficiency syndrome (AIDS) was first defined in 1981. At that time the U.S. Centers for Disease Control (CDC) (Now known as the Centers for Disease Control and Prevention) reported unusually high outbreaks of Pneumocystis carinii pneumonia (PCP) and a virulent form of Kaposi's sarcoma among small numbers of young male homosexuals in New York City and San Francisco. At that time, AIDS was initially considered almost exclusively a male "homosexual disease." Subsequently, the number of cases increased rapidly and was reported among persons with Hemophilia A and certain high-risk communities such as intravenous drug users. Then another "group" of victims emerged that did not fit into either of the aforementioned categories: blood transfusion recipients. Mortality was quite clear-cut at that time–imminent death, the cause and prevention of which were unknown. There was also an abundance of misinformation, hysteria, and lack of information that created great anxiety for health care workers and the general population at large. New insights, research, medication breakthroughs, and educational awareness have all worked together for the common good, which provides a reasonably accurate picture of the HIV/AIDS disease epidemic. This increased awareness allows a more commonsense approach to be instituted, rather than a "knee-jerk" response to the situation.

Epidemiology/Classification

The classification and reporting of AIDS is based on standard definitions for adults and children under the age of 13 that have been developed by the CDC and state and local health departments. The AIDS surveillance case definition was revised in 1985, 1987, and 1993 to incorporate additional severe illnesses that were found to be associated with HIV infection. Additionally, changes were made in the definition to reflect changes in medical management of persons with AIDS. The most recent revision (1993) included HIV-infected adults and adolescents with CD4+ T-lymphocyte counts of less than 200 cells or a percentage of total lymphocytes of less than 14. Immunologic criteria such as the above resulted in almost half of the AIDS cases reported in 1993 and 1994 (Sande & Volberding, 1997).

In 1993, the number of AIDS cases reported increased over 100% compared to those reported in 1992. In 1994, slightly fewer cases were reported, which reflected a slightly decreasing effect of the expansion of the AIDS surveillance criteria. (Typically, AIDS cases reported based only on the immunologic criteria represented persons less immunosuppressed than persons with AIDS-defining opportunistic illnesses (OIs), and are now reported at an earlier stage of HIV illness. Following the broadening of the disease definition, some increases in AIDS cases included HIV-infected persons who would only later have been reported to be AIDS-OIs in later years).

Once a person is HIV positive, they may remain asymptomatic or show persistent generalized lymphadenopathy. As the disease process continues, but before an "AIDS indicator" condition has been duly diagnosed, these individuals may experience various symptoms, such as fever of unknown etiology, night sweats, weight loss, fatigue, and diarrhea. The immune system is progressively being impaired by viral replication, which leads to dysfunction and ultimately to a serious depletion of CD4 lymphocytes. When the CD4 cell count falls to between 200 and 400, HIV-positive individuals may begin to experience minor opportunistic infections (OIs), including such conditions as candidiasis (thrush), herpes-zoster (shingles), tinea pedis (athlete's foot), and chronic skin conditions such as dermatitis (seborrheic) and oral hairy leukoplakia.

With continued dysfunction of the immune system, more severe opportunistic infections, such as Pneumocystis carinii pneumonia, may occur, but this usually requires that the CD4 count fall to less than 200. Other opportunistic infections such as cytomegalovirus (CMV) or mycobacterium avium complex (MAC) occur with CD4 counts of less than 50. Additional indicators of disease progress include Kaposi's sarcoma or lymphoma, central nervous system disease, and severe wasting.

An expansion of the definition for AIDS will classify patients according to their clinical condition and CD4 count. Clinical conditions are classified as (1) asymptomatic, (2) symptomatic, and (3) AIDS-indicator conditions. The symptomatic and AIDS-indicator conditions have been expanded to include recurrent bacterial pneumonia, and vulvovaginal candidiasis, cervical cancer, and tuberculosis, in addition to tumors and opportunistic infections. CD4 counts are classified as category 1, more than or equal to 500; category 2, CD4 counts of 200–499; and category 3, less than 200.

From 1990 through 1994, the diagnosis of all AIDS-related OIs increased 40%. In 1993 and 1994, however, the annual increase slowed to approximately 5%, suggesting that the national epidemic was approaching a plateau. Further analyses indicated the plateau was largely the result of decreasing AIDS incidence among white homosexual/bisexual men, particularly in large cities. This white homosexual/bisexual male trend has resulted in a smaller increase in the incidence of AIDS-OIs among all homosexual/bisexual men than among male intravenous (injecting) drug users (IDUs) and men with heterosexually acquired AIDS. For women, however, AIDS-OIs are increasing fastest among those with heterosexually acquired disease, and the number of women in this category has far outpaced the number related to injecting drug use.

Morbidity and Mortality

Of those HIV-infected persons in clinical care, over 95% will develop OIs (opportunistic infections) before their death. The five leading opportunistic infections are: Pneumcystis carinii pneumonia; Kaposi's sarcoma; disseminated mycobacterium avium; Esophageal candidiasis, and wasting syndrome. Cytomegalovirus retinitis/disease; HIV encephalopathy; extrapulmonary cryptococcosis; toxoplasmosis of the brain; chronic cryptosporidiosis; and extrapulmonary tuberculosis round out the list of the 12 most common opportunistic infections. (Sande & Volberding, 1997).

National vital statistics data are insightful measures of HIV-related mortality and how HIV-related deaths have increased over the course of the HIV epidemic. HIV is the fourth leading cause of years of potential life lost among all Americans under 65 years of age and is the leading cause of death for Americans between the ages of 25 and 44. Racial minorities share a high burden of HIV-related deaths. In 1994 HIV was the cause of death for 32% of Black men and 22% of Black women ages 25–44. For this age group, HIV was also the leading cause of death for Caucasian men (47 per 100,000) and was the fifth leading cause for white women (6 per 100,000). It is important to note that not all death certificates clearly indicate the cause of death as HIV-related; thus the magnitude of HIV mortality in the United States is even greater than is indicated by vital statistics data.

HIV-I Infection/AIDS and the Ongoing War

Human immunodeficiency virus type I (HIV-I) has been clearly identified as the primary cause of the acquired immunodeficiency syndrome (AIDS), which terminates in the near complete destruction of the CD4+ T-lymphocyte population. In June 1995, over 470,000 cases were reported to the CDC. The World Health Organization (WHO) reports that an estimated 18+ million adults and 1.5+ million children worldwide have been infected with HIV. Conservative estimates show 38 million people being infected by HIV by the year 2000. This translates into substantial healthcare costs, loss of work time and resources, and significant case management responsibilities over time.

The range and severity of symptoms in primary HIV-I infection vary considerably, with an acute mononucleosis-like viral syndrome developing in about 40% of patients. Generally, the individual will have fever, sore throat, swollen lymph nodes (lymphadenopathy), arthralgia, myalgia, lethargy/malaise, and anorexia/weight loss. Neuropathic manifestations include headache, meningoencephalitis, peripheral neuropathy, radiculopathy, brachial neuritis, Guillain-Barré syndrome, and cognitive/affective impairment. They may have dermatologic manifestations of rash, diffuse urticaria, desquamation, hair loss (alopecia), and mucocutaneous ulceration. Gastrointestinal manifestations include oral/oropharyngeal candidiasis; nausea/vomiting and diarrhea; and respiratory cough.) Once the symptoms of primary infection subside and an antiviral immune response appears, patients usually enter a chronic, clinically asymptomatic, or usually minimally symptomatic state that may last for 7 to 11 years before the development of overt immunodeficiency.

During early study of the disease, it was speculated that an almost dormant period occurred after initial infection before "something happened" to encourage the virus to seek out and destroy all the other healthy T-cells, reproducing multitudes of copies of itself, damaging the immune system in the process and rendering it host to all sorts of opportunistic infections. Now, however, scientists have discovered that the body and the virus were involved in a fierce battle from the very beginning of the primary infection. The viral intruder produces billions of copies of itself every day, whose main goal is destruction. Every day the infected host (person with the primary infection) would fight back by producing a billion new immune cells in an effort to stop the battle, which primarily took place in the lymph nodes, not in the bloodstream as was initially thought. New research believes the "best bet" is to try to defeat HIV early on, when it is residing in the lymph nodes and before it has a chance to infiltrate structures such as the brain. In an effort to "corner the offending party," researchers developed (and are still developing) the use of several different antiviral drugs in combination (cocktails). As recently as December 1995, the FDA approved a new medication called Saquinavir, a protease inhibitor, to attack the virus at a previously untargeted stage in its reproductive cycle. This cocktail, made up of Saquinavir, AZT, and 3TC (a chemical cousin to AZT), in a number of cases seemed to force the disease into remission. Strikingly, even the most sophisticated tests could not find a trace of the disease (virus) anywhere in patients' bodies. At the present time, the antiviral cocktails appear as if they can prolong the lives of thousands of sick people for several months and maybe years. Research continues, of course, as there is a possibility that the drugs will prove too toxic to be used long-term, or that HIV may find another hiding place in the body from which to deploy its armies. The overall goal in research, of course, is to create a cocktail of drugs that can prevent the virus from making a billion copies a day, so the host's immune systems will not have to waste a billion cells a day in defense.

Antiretroviral Therapy/Protease Inhibitors

At the present time, there are at least ten HIV antiretroviral and protease inhibitors being used in clinical trials, or ready to enter clinical development. These include the following:

Zidovudine (AZT, Azidothymidine, Retrovir)
Didanosine (ddl, Dideoxyinosine, Videx)
Zalcitabine (ddc, Dideoxycytidine, HIVID)
Staduvine (d4T, Zerit)
Lamivudine (3TC, Epivir)
Neveripine
Saquinavir (Invirase)
Ritonavir (Norvir)
Indinavir (Crixivan)
Nelfinavir (Viracept)
Delavirdine (Rescriptor)
Nevirapine (Viramune)
Acyclovir

Case management/medical issues associated with the use of these drugs include routine follow-up with general chemistry and hematologic evaluations on a schedule established by the physician. Usually, the frequency of follow-ups decreases once the user is stable.

Zidovudine

This is a nucleoside analog that inhibits HIV reverse transcriptase. It is primarily used for people with AIDS or those infected with HIV who have CD4 counts of less than 200, or for people with CD4 counts between 200–500 with symptomatic HIV infection. Current dosing is about 100 mg five times per day, which causes some megaloblastic anemia, but severe cases are not significantly found. This drug has been shown to decrease maternal–fetal transmission. Major toxicities are hematologic, myopathy, and gastrointestinal.

Didanosine

This medication works similar to Zidovudine. Indicators are intolerance to Zidovudine at 500mg/day or lower; or progression of clinical disease despite Zidovudine treatment, and CD4 count of less than 200. (This medication can be used in combination with Zidovudine). Using this medication can cause painful chronic peripheral neuropathies that produce a mild stocking-and-glove pattern of discomfort. This causes about 20% to 30% of individual users to discontinue this therapy. It can also cause pancreatitis and diarrhea.

Zalcitabine

This is similar to ddl (Didanosine), but it is more easily tolerated, and is approved as a combination therapy with Zidovudine when CD4 counts are less than 300. Side effects include pancreatitis (if IV pentamidine is administered); peripheral neuropathy, rash, fever, stomatitis, and esophageal ulceration.

Staduvine

This is another HIV reverse transcriptase inhibitor that is approved for treatment of individuals intolerant of other nucleoside analogs, or those who have disease progression while on other treatments, or those who have received prolonged prior Zidovudine therapy. A dose-related peripheral neuropathy occurs in 19% to 24% of individuals with advanced disease and 14% of those with less advanced HIV disease.

Lamividine

This is an HIV reverse transcriptase inhibitor that can develop a rapid resistance if used alone (monotherapy). It has been approved for use with Zidovudine for those with advanced HIV disease and for previously untreated patients with CD4 counts of less than or equal to 300. Major side effects include nausea, diarrhea, anemia, low white blood cell count, and pancreatitis (especially in children). Renal failure would require the dosage to be decreased.

Nevirapine

This is a non-nucleoside reverse transcriptase inhibitor (NNRTI) recently approved for use only in combination with a reverse transcriptase inhibitor and maybe a second agent such as a protease inhibitor. This drug (and others in its class) is characterized by rapid emergence of HIV resistance when used as monotherapy.

Saquinavir

This is one of a new class of drugs that inhibit HIV protease activity and are effective against viral strains resistant to nucleoside analogs. It is used in combination with other retrovirals for treatment of those people with advanced disease and no prior Zidovudine use. Adverse effects are generally mild and include diarrhea, nausea, and abdominal discomfort.

Ritonavir

This is an HIV protease inhibitor that has been approved in combination with nucleoside analogs or as monotherapy for the treatment of HIV when therapy is warranted. In advanced disease, this drug treatment shows a reduction in mortality and disease progression over six months. Side effects are gastrointestinal (nausea, diarrhea, vomiting, anorexia, abdominal pain, and taste perversion).

Indinavir

Indinavir is an HIV protease inhibitor approved for the treatment of HIV infection when antiretroviral therapy is warranted. This alone, or in combination with other drugs, led to sustained decreased viral RNA load and increased CD4 counts compared to Zidovudine monotherapy. Adverse effects that are noteworthy includes nephrolithiasis, which occurs infrequently and requires a temporary interruption of treatment for one to three days. Adequate hydration is critical.

Acyclovir

The use of this pharmacological agent is primarily for treatment of herpes simplex and varicella zoster viral infection. This is the antiviral agent of significance for most HSV infections in AIDS patients. Nausea, headache, and gastrointestinal complaints are typical side effects.

It is critical to remain optimistic about the progress medical science has made in its effort to find a cure for HIV/AIDS, but it must also be understood that these protease inhibitors and antiretroviral agents cannot be considered a cure. They do, however, represent viable, potent supplements to the war on this disease and show promise. Continuing study must be accomplished in order for any side effects and limitations to be understood and documented. Additionally, the medical follow-up of individuals on any pharmacological therapy must be maintained, as well as diligent case management, in order to closely monitor the patient's progress and changing needs. Underdosing or erratic prescription maintenance could lead to resistance of the protease inhibitors, which would certainly delay study results and cloud the issues.

Opportunistic Infections: Treatment and Prophylaxis

Pulmonary disease is a major source of morbidity and mortality in HIV-infected individuals. The number one opportunistic infection is **pneumocystis carinii pneumonia (PCP),** which is preventable with the prophylactic use of Bactrim. One double-strength Bactrim a day is over 95% effective at preventing PCP. (Bactrim is also a prophylaxis against Toxoplasma gondii encephalitis.) PCP is the leading life-threatening infection among women with AIDS and the fourth leading life-threatening infection among men. It is critical that all individuals with HIV infection receive pneumococcal vaccine every five years. The earlier the pneumococcal vaccine is given, the more effective the immune response. TB testing is also highly recommended, as HIV infection alters the natural history of tuberculosis so that those who are HIV positive are more likely to contract TB. Annual chest x-rays may be required. Fungal infections mainly affect persons who live or have lived in the various endemic areas, such as in developing countries, where, for example, tuberculosis (TB) is by far the most important AIDS-associated indicator disease. AIDS-related Kaposi's sarcoma and lymphoma generally do not involve the lungs until the malignancies are advanced.

The second most common opportunistic infection is **Mycobacterium avium complex (MAC),** which occurs in profound immunosuppression, with advanced AIDS. MAC bacteremia is associated with fever, progressive anemia, hepatic involvement manifested by an elevated alkaline phosphatase, and wasting. Prophylactic Rifabutin reduces the incidence of mycobacteremia by half. The Public Health Service Task Force has recommended lifetime prophylaxis with Rifabutin (or Clarithromycin) for all HIV-infected patients with less than 100 CD4 counts.

AIDS-associated malignancies such as **Kaposi's sarcoma, non-Hodgkin's lymphomas (NHLs),** and **invasive cervical cancer** (added in 1993 to the CDC list of AIDS-defining conditions) are all considered to be diseases indicative of AIDS in HIV-infected individuals (Krown, 1996). Both males and females with HIV infection have been noted to have a high frequency of noninvasive intraepithelial lesions of the anogenital squamous epithelium that may be precursors to invasive cancer. AIDS-associated malignancies are seen in approximately 40% of HIV-infected individuals at some point in their clinical course. These AIDS-associated malignancies may increase in frequency as survival is prolonged, especially in view of the new antiretroviral and protease inhibitor drug therapy; and are especially prone to occur as greater numbers of HIV infections occur in women. Children born with HIV infection also show longer survival and increased cancer rates.

Fungal infections, which are commonly seen in patients with AIDS, are now routinely being treated topically with Ketoconazole, for example, used for treating thrush, reserving the more expensive systemic drugs (Fluconazole) for more serious cases. Most fungal infections occur in the oral cavity and esophageal area.

Vaginal candidiasis, followed by oropharyngeal and esophageal candidal infections, is usually the order of presentation of this manifestation. Cryptococcal disease is less common than candidiasis, but is considered the most common life-threatening fungal infection. Cryptococcus neoformans occurs in 2% to 6% of patients with AIDS, most often occurring as disseminated disease, with meningitis being the most common manifestation. Pulmonary manifestations of disseminated cryptococcoses have been seen as well.

Mycobacterium avium-Intracellulare (MAI) bacterium and disease is a common complication seen in individuals with CD4 counts of less than 100. Rifabutin is licensed for the prevention of MAI, but this has been limited because of concerns about costs, toxicity, resistance, and efficacy (there was found a reduction in bacteremia rate but no survival benefit). There is a suggestion that MAI disease is predictive of cytomegalovirus disease and vice versa.

Cytomegalovirus (CMV) infections are a serious HIV-related infection, particularly in those with CD4 counts of less than 50. CMV is the most common virus causing life-threatening infections in patients with AIDS. Several clinical illnesses, including chorioretinitis, esophagitis, colitis, pneumonia, and several neurologic disorders are associated with CMV infection. Retinitis occurs in up to 40% of AIDS patients, whereas gastrointestinal disease occurs in 5% to 10%. CMV accounts for at least 90% of HIV-related infectious retinopathies. Retinal detachment may occur in later stages as the necrotic retina scars and thins.

Oral Ganciclovir was nearly as effective as IV Ganciclovir at delaying reactivation of CMV retinitis; and prophylactically, oral Ganciclovir reduced the rate of CMV disease by nearly 50%. Maintenance therapy throughout the life of the patient is critical for CMV retinitis because the virus is only suppressed by Ganciclovir and not eliminated. The primary problems associated with oral Ganciclovir include its cost (up to $20,000 per year) (Sande & Volberding, 1997) and its toxicity (particularly hematologic).

Toxoplasmosis (a parasitic infection) is the second most common opportunistic infection of the eye. It is associated with cerebral toxoplasmosis in the majority of patients. (Syphilis, herpes simplex, varicella-zoster virus (VZV), and TB are other infections but these rarely involve the retina.) Toxoplasma gondii is one of the most common tissue parasites found in humans and is hosted by the domestic cat as well as many other mammals and bird species. Humans can come in contact and become infected by coincidental exposure to cat feces or by eating raw or undercooked meat. In a non-immunosuppressed individual, the parasite is usually dormant, causing no signs or symptoms. However, in the patient with depressed cellular immunity, the parasite may become reactivated and cause full-blown disease. In the United States 16% to 68% of adults have latent tissue infection with T. gondii. In some European countries such as France and Germany, more than 90% of adults have positive serologic findings for toxoplasmosis. Among individuals with AIDS 3% to 40% develop toxoplasmic encephalitis and it may be the primary initial opportunistic infection in up to 38% of these patients (Smith, G. H., 1994). Persons with T. gondii are at risk for developing toxoplasmosis, which is most commonly manifested as encephalitis, but may also cause pneumonia.

Cryptosporidiosis is present in patients with AIDS at about the 10% to 15% rate in the United States and up to 50% in developing countries. This is another parasitic infection, causing profuse, watery diarrhea with crampy abdominal pain, fatigue, anorexia, and nausea and vomiting. No specific therapy has been shown to be effective, therefore necessitating reliance on antidiarrheal agents, fluid replacement, and nutrition.

Radiculopathy is the most characteristic neurologic syndrome caused by CMV in AIDS patients. This occurs as a spinal cord syndrome with lower extremity weakness, spasticity, areflexia, urinary retention, and hypoesthesia. Subacute encephalitis caused by CMV also occurs in AIDS patients. Personality changes, difficulty concentrating, headaches, and sleepiness frequently are present.

CMV Colitis occurs in at least 5% to 10% of AIDS patients. Diarrhea, weight loss, anorexia, and fever are usually present. Esophagitis can also occur in the AIDS patient and is most commonly due to either Candida albicans or herpes simplex virus (HSV) or CMV. Those individuals with CMV esophagitis are prone to having pain on swallowing and large distal ulceration.

Life Care Planning Considerations for the HIV/AIDS Patient

Life care planning for the individual with AIDS or symptomatic HIV can cover a vast array of needs. In order to be as comprehensive as possible in outlining the potential areas of needs, a checklist may prove helpful. The following will outline potential need areas that must be considered, i.e., it is a checklist for planning purposes. In the interest of space, not each and every possible consideration has been outlined. However, this will guide the interested party in the thought process needed to systematically and comprehensively cover all the need areas.

Physical impairment/considerations, to include:

- Hemiplegia
- Loss of balance
- Loss of strength
- Paralysis
- Coordination
- Fatigue
- Weakness
- Clumsiness
- Ataxia
- Reduced functional capacity
- Pain
- Visual acuity
- Physical stamina and endurance
- Loss of bowel control
- Arthralgia
- Arthritis
- Fibromyalgia

Cognitive Impairment/Neuropsychological Considerations, to include:

- Depression
- Dementia
- Intellectual impairment

Inattention
Forgetfulness
Reduced concentration
Expressive/receptive speech
Aphasia
Dysarthria
Adjustment disorder
Apathy
Disorientation
Social isolation
Delirium
Manic disorder
Psychotic disorder
Anxiety disorder
Adjustment disorder

Respiratory Considerations, to include:
Bacterial infection
Lymphoma
Fungi
Mycobacteria
Pneumocystis
Kaposi's sarcoma
Viral infections
Tuberculosis

Gastrointestinal Considerations, to include:
Abdominal pain
Painful elimination
Hepatomegaly
Cholecystitis
Colitis
Enteritis
Megacolon/colon perforations
Pancreatitis
Intestinal obstruction
Mucosal biopsy

Neurological Considerations, to include:
Meningitis
Focal CNS lesions
Encephalitis
Headache
Myelopathy
Cranial nerve palsies
Seizures
Peripheral neuropathy
Demyelinating neuropathy

General Health Considerations, to include:

Diarrhea
Painful elimination
Apathy
Anorexia
Dysphagia
Poor intake (painful mouth/throat)
Medication reaction/interaction
Adverse drug reactions
Chronic pain
Esophageal disease
Fever
Malnutrition
Weight loss
Malabsorption
Wasting syndrome
Candida (oral/esophageal/vaginal)
Sleep disorder

Hematologic Considerations, to include:

Anemia
Leukemia
Bone marrow disorders
Leukopenia
Thrombocytopenia

Cardiovascular Considerations, to include:

Pericarditis
Pulmonary hypertension
Myocardial involvement
Vascular abnormalities
Arrhythmias
Venous thrombosis and pulmonary embolism

Endrocinologic Considerations, to include:

Hypothalamic-pituitary
Adrenal
Glucocorticoid hormones (Cortisol)
Mineralocorticoid hormone deficiency (Renal sodium wasting, hypotension, hypokalemia, metabolic acidosis)
Thyroid
Gonad
Pancreas
Mineral homeostasis
Lipid metabolism
Wasting syndrome

Renal Considerations, to include:

Fluid imbalance
Electrolyte imbalance
Acid-base disturbance
Acute tubular necrosis
Metabolic acidosis
HIV-associated nephropathy
Hemolytic uremic syndrome
Dialysis

Dermatologic Considerations, to include:

Infections
Shingles
Herpes virus infection
Hairy leukoplakia
Neoplastic disease
Seborrheic dermatitis
Hypersensitivity rashes

Oral Considerations, to include:

Candidiasis
Gingivitis
Periodontitis
Herpes simplex
Herpes zoster
Bacterial lesions
Cytomegalovirus ulcers
Hairy leukoplakia
Warts

Neoplastic Disease

Kaposi's Sarcoma
Lymphoma
Carcinoma
Recurrent aphthous ulcers

Life Care Planning: Recommendations, to Include

Evaluations:

Physical therapy
Occupational therapy
Speech therapy
Respiratory therapy
Recreational therapy
Psychology
Neuropsychology

- Vocational/educational
- Financial planning
- Seating/mobility
- Adaptive driving
- Medical (Evaluations and follow-up)
  - Physiatry
  - General medicine
  - Dental
  - Podiatry
  - Oncology
  - Dermatology
  - Neurology
  - Rheumatology
  - Anesthesiology (pain control)
  - Nutritional
  - Routine laboratory (CBC, CD4+ lymphocyte count, blood chemistry, etc.)
  - Gynecological
  - Gastroenterology
  - Urological
  - Plastic/reconstruction
  - Pulmonary
  - Cardiology
  - Ophthalmology
  - Diagnostics (such as TB testing, MRI, CT scans, pap smear, etc.)
  - Routine preventative immunizations (i.e., pneumonia vaccine; hepatitis B)

Therapeutic Modalities:

- Physical therapy
- Occupational therapy
- Speech therapy
- Respiratory therapy
- Recreational therapy
- Therapy/counseling (group-individual)
- Career guidance/counseling
- Staff training
- Family counseling
- Family education
- Patient education
- Driver's education (with adaptations)
- Legal/financial counseling
- Spiritual support/counseling
- Caregiver support
- Case management
- Leisure pursuits

Equipment Considerations:

- Mobility equipment (wheelchairs/scooters, etc., manual/power)
- Equipment repairs/maintenance

Emergency call equipment (Wander guard/cell phone, Call Alert & other safety systems)
Home furnishings (to conserve physical energy)
Lift recliner
Accessible setting
Mobile stools
Reachers
Environmental control devices/maintenance and repair
Ramping
Stair-glide
Elevator
Hospital bed/mattress
Special sized linens/blankets
Washer/dryer
(for excess laundry requirements)
Feeding pumps
(parenteral/enteral feeding)
Scale
Hand-held shower
Shower bench
Hand rails

Medical Equipment:
Suction machine
Apnea monitor
Oxygen concentrator
Liquid oxygen
Ventilator
Humidifier

Miscellaneous:
Supplies (Medical)
Catheters
Feeding bags
Suction catheters
Syringes
Diapers
Bed pads
Gloves
Creams/powders
Gauze/tapes
Masks
Thermometers
Blood pressure monitors
Garbage bags
Wipes
Paper towels
Anti-bacterial soaps

Architectural Renovations/Medical Retrofitting

Barrier free design
Grab bars in bathroom
Temperature guards
Call system

Orthotics

(as prescribed)

Orthopedic Equipment

(for strength maintenance and mobility)
Walkers
Parallel bars
Canes
Crutches
Bath seat

Aids for Independent Function

Built-up plates/utensils
One-handed equipment
Voice activated computer/software
Adaptive clothing

Infection Control Devices

Sharps/needle/contaminant storage and destruction
Decontaminant cleaners

Medications:

Antiretrovirals
Protease inhibitors
Palliative care
Pain treatment
Oral
IV
Feeding supplements
Dietary supplements
Vitamin therapy

Attendant/Nursing Care:

Respite care
Caregiver support
Hospice care
Home health aide
Driver
Nursing care
Home maintenance (interior/exterior)

Surgical/Aggressive Intervention:

Ports for TPN access
Plastic surgical repairs
Pain control devices (implanted)
Surgical treatment of complications
Tumor removal

Complications:

Hospital care
Clinic care
Secondary infections
Falls
Accidents
Medical complications (myriad)
Financial

Costs of Care

There is one certainty when considering the costs of care for the HIV-positive/AIDS patient: there is no way to accurately predict the costs of care. There is such a rapidly changing sphere of medications alone, which are in a constant state of rearrangement and priority. There is just no reasonable way to outline a treatment course and provide those costs and feel comfortable that adequate funding or services will have been identified. Also, there is no accurate way to predict the frequency and occurrence of opportunistic infections, which can substantially influence the total sphere of costs. For example, the routine use of Diflucan for persons with CD4 counts of less than 100 would cost almost $100,000 for each major infection prevented. Another example to consider is the medication for CMV (cytomegalovirus infections). Oral Ganciclovir has been found to be as nearly effective as IV Ganciclovir at delaying reactivation of CMV retinitis. Oral Ganciclovir as a prophylaxis of CMV disease reduced the rate of CMV disease by nearly 50%; however, oral Ganciclovir costs approximately up to $20,000 per year.

Information is available on approximate costs of care for medical/pharmacological care, given certain parameters. For example, an article in the *Missoulian* (newspaper of Missoula, MT), of Tuesday, August 20, 1996, Section C-3, by Heather Lalley of Knight-Ridder Newspapers, provided "One-Man's Story" about the costs of an individual's medications per month. These included:

Crixivan — to prevent virus replication:	$900
Retrovir — antiviral drug	$245
Epivir — antiviral drug	$197
Tegretol — to control shaking	$14
Biaxin — antibiotic	$170
Diazepam — sleep aid	$6
Zovirax — antibiotic	$104
Dapsone — antibiotic	$9
Triazolam — sleep aid	$20
Diflucan — antifungal drug	$182
Peridex — mouthwash to control receding gums	$13
Retin-a — skin cream to treat lesions	$66
Elocon — skin cream to treat inflammation	$29
Percocet — pain medication	$9
Total:	**$1,964**

Many patients can spend $12,000 to $14,000 per year for just a two-drug combination, requiring 12 to 16 pills per day. Studies are continuing to determine the best combo-therapy drugs to use for best results and to avoid the possibility of drug-resistance being developed.

Pharmaceutical costs are certainly not the only consideration. Opportunistic infections, which generally occur in the later disease stages, can be significant, especially if one factors in the ongoing prophylactic treatment after the initial acute infection has subsided. For example, annual costs (in 1995 dollars) for treatment for specific opportunistic infections (Gable et al., 1996) are as follows:

Esophageal candidiasis	$2,194
Tuberculosis	$2,924
Kaposi's sarcoma (mild/moderate)	$5,902
Kaposi's sarcoma (severe)	$10,744
CM (cytomegalovirus)	$17,264
Toxoplasmosis	$17,631
MAC (Mycobacterium avium complex)	$20,153
Non-Hodgkin's lymphoma	$22,329
Wasting syndrome	$26,676
CNS lymphoma	$27,333
PCP (mild)	$3,545
PCP (moderate)	$4,889
PCP (severe)	$32,609
(Weighted average of PCP)	$11,483
(Weighted average of Kaposi's)	$6,870
CMV retinitis	$100,337

It is important to note that at higher CD4+ counts, treatment costs are primarily due to primary therapy, and not opportunistic infections. The primary treatment therapy does remain the most expensive cost consideration, however; monitoring for complications and prophylaxis costs do increase as the CD4+ counts decrease.

These costs quoted above certainly *do not include* treatment with any of the new antiretroviral (ARV) pharmaceuticals or the protease inhibitors, which can be substantial, as indicated in the illustration aforementioned. Typical cost studies assume the individual was identified early as an HIV/AIDS patient, and therefore treated early on, which translates to reduced therapy time and hence reduced costs. Additionally, most of the studies do not consider social services, palliative treatment (i.e., pain management); psychological intervention; and certainly not home health requirements. Home health requirements can include services provided and arranged through an agency (home health agency), private home health hires, friends, family services, community or church volunteers, and local service programs.

This discussion of costs also leads to a consideration of the availability of funding for the proper treatment of early intervention and prophylaxis. As is typical in the general population, funded health care has been proven to reduce overall costs of health care since preventative steps can be taken that reduce actual costs per incidence of medical need. That is true in the HIV/AIDS population as well. If there is no funding for preventative treatment or for the new and highly costly antiretroviral/protease inhibitor medications, costs can skyrocket due to complications and opportunistic infections, resulting in more hospital stays and a shorter life expectancy.

Also, not considered in this discussion of costs, is the economic impact on the individual through loss of productivity, quality of life issues, and loss of self-esteem and will to live. Services must be provided to assist in empowering the HIV+/AIDS individual in all spheres.

In Table 16.1 is a sample cost presentation of healthcare resource use in 1995 dollars (Gable et al., 1996).

Table 16.1 Cost Of HIV*/AIDS. Health Care Resource Use Costs (1995 dollars)

Resource Use	*Unit of Treatment*	*Cost per Unit ($)*
Amikacin levels	Tests	$150
Barium swallow	Procedure	$232
Blood chemistries	Test	$35
Blood culture	Test	$175
Blood gas	Test	$59
Bone marrow biopsy	Procedure, physician, laboratory tests	$1,160
Bone marrow	Test	$214
Bone marrow and culture (MAC)	Test	$472
Brain biopsy	Procedure, hospital (3 days), laboratory tests, physician	$11,599
Bronchoscope	Procedure	$1,624
Catheter placement	Procedure	$2,320
CD4* cell count	Test	$157
Chest radiograph	Test	$116
Colonoscopy (biopsy)	Procedure	$536
Complete blood count test	Test	$2
Consultation (oncologist)	Visit	$173
Cryptococcal antigen titer	Test	$66
CT scan/CAT	Procedure	$696
CT scan (noncontrast)	Procedure	$348
CT chest, abdomen, head	Procedure, contrast material	$2088
Dermatologic biopsy	Procedure	$291
Detached retina	Treatment, hospitalization	$3,480
Dilantin level	Test	$52
Electroencephalogram	Test	$580
Endoscopy (biopsy)	Procedure	$580
Emergency room visit	Visit	$291
Foscarnet administration induction	Treatment	$7,160
Foscarnet administration maintenance	Treatment	$11,364
Foscarnet induction monitoring	Test/cycle	$566
Foscarnet maintenance monitoring	Test/cycle	$680
Ganciclovir administration induction	Treatment	$4,658
Ganciclovir administration maintenance	Treatment	$10,607

Table 16.1 (continued) Cost Of HIV*/AIDS. Health Care Resource Use Costs (1995 dollars)

Resource Use	*Unit of Treatment*	*Cost per Unit ($)*
Ganciclovir induction monitoring	Test/cycle	$104
Ganciclovir maintenance	Test/cycle	$207
Home (drug) administration	Visit	$116
Home care	Visit	$261
Hospital physician visit	Visit	$145
Hospitalization	Day	$1,150
Intensive care unit	Day	$2,299
Induced sputum	Procedure	$407
Indwelling catheter	Procedure	$2,299
Infected catheter	Treatment and replacement	$2,784
Intralesional injections	Procedure	$116
Lipase and triglycerides	Test	$41
Lumbar puncture	Procedure, laboratory tests	$546
Lumbar puncture	Associated tests	$255
Lymphoma biopsy	Procedure, hospital (1 day), physician, laboratory tests	$2,900
Magnesium test	Test	$23
Magnetic resonance imaging	Procedure	$1,392
Office visit (physician)	Visit	$59
Ophthalmology examination	Test	$232
Ophthalmology examination (follow-up)	Test	$175
PPD skin test	Test	$11
Pulmonary function test	Test	$53
Radiation therapy 2 to 3 weeks		$12,758
Serum amylase	Test	$18
Specialized test battery	Tests	$1,160
Sputum smear and culture sensitivities	Test	$243
Toxoplasmosis titer	Test	$41
TPN	TPN material and home infusion charges (9 days)	$430
TPN laboratory work	Test	$93
Transfusion	Each	$580
Wasting syndrome diagnostic workup	Clinical tests	$2,320

CT, computerized tomography: TPN, total parenteral nutrition

Reprinted with permission: Costs of HIV+/AIDS at CD4 + Counts Disease Stages Based on Treatment Protocols. *Journal of Acquired Deficiency Syndromes and Human Retrovirology,* Volume 12:413-420, 1996, Lippincott–Raven Publishers, Philadelphia.

Viatical Settlements

There is available to individuals facing a life-threatening illness a unique financial resource — viatical settlements, which allows individuals to sell their life insurance policy for cash. This process is called "viaticating" — and is quite simple. It requires no invasive process, just a single application form, which the patient (client) completes. These settlements, which provide valuable financial resources, can help patients restore control over their lives and make choices they might not otherwise have, such as paying for medical treatments, keeping their home, and even meeting day-to-day living expenses.

Viatical settlement is not a new concept. The term comes from "viaticum" — Latin for "provisions for a journey." Viaticum were the supplies that Roman soldiers were given in preparation for their journeys into battle (presumably journeys from which they might not return). In essence, viaticum were the supplies soldiers needed for the closing phase of their lives. The parallel here, of course, is that a person wishing to "viaticate" is preparing for the closing phase of their lives.

Initially, the viatical settlement industry was comprised of an informal network of small companies primarily serving the AIDS community. Now, however, persons with other life-threatening illnesses such as cancer or Alzheimer's disease can benefit from the financial resources available to individuals through the viatical settlement process to go toward the cost of hospitalization, treatment, home care, or other expenses, including day-to-day living expenses.

Viatical settlements are available in all 50 states. There are no restrictions on how the funds can be used, which restores some control to the patient for making decisions he or she feels necessary. Almost any kind of insurance policy — including term, whole life, universal life, or group (employer paid) policies — from any company can be used. Policies from values of just $10,000 to well over $1 million have been purchased. The entire viatication process usually takes about three to six weeks to complete.

The value (the amount paid to the patient) of the insurance policy is determined by several factors, including prevailing interest rates, premium obligations, and projected life expectancy. The National Association of Insurance Commissioners (NAIC) has established pricing guidelines. Viators (patients) generally receive between 50% to 80% of the face value of the insurance policy. Generally, the longer the life expectancy, the less the viatical settlement company is likely to pay for that individual's policy because the company must assume responsibility for maintaining the policy for a longer period of time. (The proceeds from a viatical settlement may, however, impact certain means-based entitlement programs such as Medicaid.)

Under current law, the proceeds from a viatical settlement are taxable as income for federal tax purposes. However, several states have adopted or are considering specific regulations or provisions, which may include:

1. State and city tax free treatment of viatical settlement proceeds to encourage the use of these settlements;
2. Preventing the "brokering" of life insurance policies to individual investors who are looking for speculative returns without due regard for the policy owner's welfare;
3. Requiring viatical companies to maintain a minimum level of capital or surety bond to fund the purchase of life insurance policies as part of the viatical settlement process (this helps ensure that companies can fund

settlements and prevents the involvement of viatical settlement companies that may put people at financial risk);

4. Requiring licenses and other strictly enforced reporting mechanisms for viatical settlement companies and limiting licenses to companies with well-established operations. (For more information, contact The Viatical Association of America, 800-390-1390.)

Case Management: A Critical Component

Certainly case management of individuals with HIV+/AIDS is extremely critical. Not only in managing the case from a direct economic standpoint, but also from managing the case from an early intervention/prevention standpoint. It is critical that case managers keep themselves informed on the total scope of knowledge available on HIV+/AIDS and on new drug treatment modalities and their uses, resistance issues, and side effects. In addition, the case manager must be able to communicate effectively with physicians who may not be so familiar with the rapidly changing trends; must be able to address nutritional issues, compliance of patients, psychological issues, payment issues, and loss of identify/self-esteem issues.

Since data are changing so rapidly, it is critical that the effective case manager subscribe to professional journals that are dedicated to the subject (e.g., the *Journal of Acquired Immune Deficiency Syndromes and Human Retrovirology,* Lippincott–Raven Publishers, Philadelphia), and, of course, learn to use the Internet wisely. Suggested trials include National Health HOTLINES (see Appendices), then to government agencies and professional organizations; private sector AIDS services, information and advocacy groups; AIDS lobby/watchdog groups; and other AIDS-related information sources. Information from the Centers for Disease Control and Prevention (CDC) is also available on the Internet. Additional good sources of information are the GMHC Treatment Issues (Gay Men's Health Crisis) — *Newsletter of Experimental AIDS Therapies,* New York, NY 10011; and the Agency for Health Care Policy and Research (AHCPR) — specifically the AHCPR Publications Catalogue, U.S. Department of Health and Human Services, Public Health Service; Agency for Health Care Policy and Research, 800-358-9295.

When case managing an HIV+/AIDS client, the health professional should encourage patients to become advocates for themselves. This will empower the person with HIV+/AIDS to become involved with the treatment of the disease, rather than simply being a victim of the disease. Delays in treatment are not only costly, but could be life-threatening as well. Some **suggested activities** (for both the case management professional and the patient) are:

1. Join the local AIDS organization, the county AIDS consortium, and the State Board;
2. Attend conferences on AIDS, arming oneself with information to share;
3. Call local health departments or HIV/AIDS organizations for information;
4. Seek out pharmacists who have taken the time to become familiar with the new treatment modalities; and,
5. Become involved in local support groups.

There are a multitude of state and federal programs that can be of assistance if one is willing to invest the time and energy required for its acquisition.

Resources for additional information are listed in Appendices A–G. These include AIDS hotline numbers (national and state level); government health agencies and professional societies; private sector service and advocacy groups; AIDS lobby/advocacy/watchdog groups; other AIDS-related information sources; Patient Assistance Programs — through pharmaceutical companies; and pharmaceutical information.

CONCLUSION

The AIDS epidemic continues to present unrelenting challenges to the medical profession. Billions of dollars have been spent for medical care and research, and countless lives have been lost to this disease. Medical science has made headway by reducing the frequency and duration of complications as well as improving longevity and the quality of life of those affected. This disease is very unpredictable, which presents significant obstacles to the life care planner, since, unlike most diseases, complications and the course of the ailment cannot be accurately anticipated. The care plan will rely heavily on the individual's physician and relevant research. The life care planner who chooses to practice in this industry must be aware of the myriad of complications and must strive to maintain currency in AIDS medical research. As such, they must also be prepared to regularly update the plan based on the client's ever-changing scenarios and information.

RESOURCES

AIDS Hotline Numbers

http://www.critpath.org/aric/pwarg-03.htm#statehot
National Health Hotlines

AIDS Clinical Trials Information Services/CDC (ACTIS):
800-T*R*I*A*L*S-A (800-847-2572)
TDD/Deaf Access: 800-243-7012

AIDS Treatment Information Services/CDC (ATIS):
800-H*I*V-0440 (800-480-0440)

National AIDS HOTLINE/CDC:
800-342-A*I*D*S (800-342-2437) (*24 hours a day, every day*)
ALSO: Spanish: 800-334-7432
TDD/Deaf: 800-243-7889
International: 301-217-0023

National AIDS Information Clearinghouse:
800-458-5231 (Information and publication orders)

National Association of People with AIDS HOTLINE:
202-898-0414 (+TTY/TDD)

National Clearinghouse for Alcohol and Drug Information's Center for Substance Abuse Prevention (CSAP):

National Indian AIDS Hotline:
800-283-2437

National Sexually Transmitted Diseases HOTLINE/CDC:
800-227-8922

Herpes Resource Center HOTLINE:
919-361-8488 (M-F, 9-6)

NY State Gay/Lesbian Task Force AIDS Information HOTLINE:
800-221-7044
(Founded by Gay/Lesbian Task Force, New York: 212-807-6016)

Substance Abuse and Mental Health Services Administration's (SAMHSA) Drug Abuse Information and Treatment Referrals Hotline:
800-662-HELP

State AIDS Info Hotline

Alabama:	800-228-0469
Alaska:	800-478-AIDS
Nationwide:	907-276-4880
Arizona:	520-326-2437
Arkansas:	800-364-2437
California	
Northern California:	800-367-2437
Nationwide:	415-863-2437
TTY/TDD:	415-864-6606
Southern California:	800-922-2437
In Los Angeles:	213-876-2437
TTY/TDD:	800-553-2437
Colorado:	800-252-AIDS
Denver only:	303-782-5186
Connecticut:	800-342-AIDS
Delaware:	800-422-0429
District of Columbia:	202-332-AIDS
Within metro DC & VA:	800-332-7432
Florida:	800-352-AIDS
In Haitian Creole:	800-243-7101
In Spanish:	800-545-SIDA

Administration

Rockville, MD USPHS Public Affairs Office	202-245-6867
U.S. Agency for International Development (USAID) Washington, D.C.	703-875-4494
Visual AIDS (U.S. Government effort to increase AIDS awareness through image, video, etc.)	212-206-6758
131 West 21st St., 3rd floor New York, NY 10011	

Government Health Agencies and Professional Societies

American Medical Association (AMA) Chicago, IL	312-645-5000
American Public Health Association (APHA) Washington, D.C.	202-789-5600
American Red Cross Washington, D.C.	202-973-6025
(American Red Cross AIDS Education Offices)	202-737-8300
American Social Health Association (ASHA) Triangle Park, NC Atlanta, GA	800-227-8922
Department of Health and Human Services Washington, D.C.	202-245-6296
Food and Drug Administration (FDA) Rockville, MD	301-443-2894
(FDA Center for Drug Research)	301-443-2894
Hemophilia and AIDS/HIV Network for the Dissemination of Information (HANDI) New York, NY	212-431-8541
Intergovernmental Health Policy Project (IHPP) Washington, D.C.	202-872-1445
National Adoption Information Clearinghouse	301-231-6512
National AIDS Information Clearinghouse Rockville, MD	301-763-5111
National Institutes of Health (NIH) Bethesda, MD	301-496-4000
National Library of Medicine (NLM)	800-638-8480
National Institute of Allergy and Infectious Disease (NIAID)	301-496-5717
National Cancer Institute	301-496-4000

National Hemophilia Foundation (NHF)	212-219-8180
National Minority AIDS Council (NMAC) Washington, D.C.	202-843-6622
National Native American AIDS Prevention Center Oakland, CA	510-444-2051
National Pediatric HIV Resource Center (NPHRC) Newark, NJ	201-268-8251
Rural AIDS Network (RAN) Santa Fe, NM	505-986-8337
US Public Health Service (PHS) Washington, D.C.	202-472-4248
Health Resources and Services Administration	301-443-4588
Substance Abuse and Mental Health Service Administration	301-443-5305
USPHS Public Affairs Office	202-245-6867
U.S. Agency for International Development (USAID) Washington, D.C.	703-875-4494
Visual AIDS (U.S. Government effort to increase AIDS Awareness through image, video, etc.) New York, NY	212-206-6758

Private Sector Service and Advocacy Groups

AIDS Project Los Angeles (APLA) Los Angeles, CA	213-962-1600
Baltimore, MD	410-342-ARIC
AIDS Treatment Data NETWORK New York, NY National, toll-free	212-260-8868 800-734-7104
American Foundation for AIDS Research (AmFAR)	212-682-7440 800-764-9346
New York, NY	
AIDS/HIV Treatment Directory	800-764-9346
TxLINK	800-764-9346
AIDS/HIV Clinical Trial Handbook	800-764-9346
AIDS Targeted Information (ATIN)	212-682-7440
American Lung Association (of South Alleghenies) Johnstown, PA	814-536-7345
Carl Vogel Foundation Washington, D.C.	202-289-4898
Center for Natural and Traditional Medicine Washington, D.C.	202-387-3645

Community Research Initiative on AIDS (CRIA) New York, NY	212-924-3934
Direct AIDS Alternative Information Resources	212-689-8140
Drug Reform Coordination Network (DRCNet) Washington, D.C.	202-362-0030
Gay Men's Health Crisis (GMHC) New York, NY	212-807-6664
National Association of People W/AIDS Washington, D.C.	202-898-0414
National AIDS Network Washington, D.C.	
National Council of Churches/AIDS Task Force New York, NY	212-870-2421
N.C.C./Minority Task Force on AIDS New York, NY	212-749-1214
National Gay/Lesbian Health Foundation Washington, D.C.	202-797-3708
National Women's Health Network Washington, D.C.	202-347-1140
Parents and Friends of Lesbians and Gays (P-FLAG) Washington, D.C.	202-638-4200
Pharmaceutical Research and Manufacturer's Association Washington, D.C.	202-835-3400
Project Inform San Francisco, CA	415-558-9051 800-334-7422
PWA Health Group New York, NY	212-532-0289
Women and Aids Resource Network (WARN)	718-596-6007
Women's AIDS Resource Movement (WARM) Tampa, FL	813-237-6455
Women Organized to Respond to Life Threatening Diseases (WORLD) Oakland, CA	510-658-6930

AIDS Lobby/Advocacy/Watchdog Groups

AIDS Action Council Washington, D.C.	202-986-1300 (ext. 47)

Direct Action for Treatment Access (DATA) Palo Alto, CA	415-321-6670
Human Rights Campaign Fund Washington, D.C.	202-628-4160
National AIDS Treatment Advocacy Project Brooklyn, NY	718-624-8541
National Association of People with AIDS (NAPWA) Washington, D.C.	202-898-0414 (ext. 11)
National Gay and Lesbian Task Force (NGLTF) Washington, D.C.	202-332-6483
National Minority AIDS Council (NMAC) Washington, D.C.	202-544-1076
Mobilization Against AIDS (MAA)	415-862-4676
The Sheridan Group Washington, D.C.	202-462-7288
Treatment Action Group New York, NY	212-260-0300
Treatment Action Network New York, NY	415-558-8669

Other AIDS-Related Information Sources

Palliation (relief of pain/discomfort/symptoms):

American Chronic Pain Foundation Rocklin, CA	
International Pain Foundation Seattle, WA	
Roxanne Pain Institute	800-335-9100

Patient Assistance Programs

http://www.critpath.org/aric/pwarg-10.htm#TOP

Drug Company	Contact Information
Abbott	800-659-9050 for ritonavir (Norvir); 800-688-9118 for clarithromycin (Biaxin)
Adria	800-795-9759 for rifabutin (Mycobutin)
Alza	800-321-3130 for testosterone patch (Testoderm)

Amgen	800-272-9376 for filgrastim (G-CSF/Neupogen) erythropoietin (Epongen)
Astra	800-488-3276 for foscarnet (Foscavir)
Agouron	800-621-7111 for nelfinavir (Viracept)
Bio-Technology General	800-741-2698 for oxandrolone (Oxandrin)
Bristol-Myers Squibb	800-272-4878 for Stavudine (d4T/Zerit), didanosine (ddI/ Videx), megestrol acetate(Megace)
Chiron Vision	800-843-1137 for ganciclovir implants(Vitrasert)
Ciba	800-257-3273 for clofazimine (Lamprene)
Eli Lilly	317-276-2950 for vancomycin (Vancocin)
Fujisawa	800-888-7740 (x8604/8607) for Aerosolized pentamidine (Nebupent)
Glaxo-Wellcome	800-722-9294 (X54418) for acyclovir (Zovirax), atovaquone (Mepron), AZT (zidovudine/ Retrovir), pyrimethamine (Daraprim), TMP/SMZ (Septra), lamivudine (3TC/Epivir), and others; previous number (Glaxo): 800-248-9757
Hoffmann-La Roche	800-282-7780 for saquinavir (Invirase) 800-285-4484 for zalcitibine (ddC/HIVID) 800-526-6367 for TMP/SMX (Bactrim) 800-443-6676 for interferon-alpha
Immunex	800-334-6273 for sargramostim (GM-CSF/Leukine)
Janssen	800-544-2987 for itraconazole (Sporanox) and ketoconazole (Nizoral)

Lederle	800-533-2273 for ethambutol (Myambutol)
Merck	800-850-3430 for indinavir (Crixivan)
Miles	800-468-0894 (x 5170) for ciprofloxacin (Cipro)
Ortho Biotech	800-553-3851 for erythropoeitin (Procrit)
Parke-Davis	800-223-0432 for paromomycin (Humatin)
Pfizer	800-646-4455 for fluconazole (Diflucan) 800-742-3029 for azithromycin (Zithromax) 800-221-3033 for additional info; other numbers: 606-225-7442; 212-573-3954
Pharmacia/Upjohn	800-779-0070 for delavirdine (Rescriptor) also: 616-329-8244
Roche Molecular Diagnostic Systems	800-526-6367 for info. on Amplicor viral load tests
Roxane Labs	800-274-8651 for dronabinol (Marinol) and various narcotics
Sandoz	800-447-6376 for octeotide
Schering-Plough	800-521-7157 for interferon Alpha (Intron-A)
Sequus	800-375-1658 for liposomal doxirubicin (Doxil)
Syntex	800-444-4200 for ganciclovir (Cytovene IV) 800-596-4630 for oral ganciclovir (Cytovene oral)
Univax	800-789-2099 for IV gamma-(IVIG)/WinRho)
US Bioscience	800-887-2467 for trimetrexate (Neutrexin)
Vestar	800-247-3303 for liposomal daunorubicin (Daunoxome)

Pharmaceutical Information

http://www.mediconsult.com/frames/aids/drugs/content.html

Brand Name	Generic Name	General Category
Videx	Didanosine	Didanosine (Systemic)
ddI	Didanosine	Didanosine (Systemic)
Apo-Sulfatrim	Trimethoprim/ Sulfamethoxazole	Sulfonamides and Trimethoprim (Systemic)
Apo-Sulfatrim DS	Trimethoprim/ Sulfamethoxazole	Sulfonamides and Trimethoprim (Systemic)
Bactrim	Trimethoprim/ Sulfamethoxazole	Sulfonamides and Trimethoprim (Systemic)
Bactrim DS	Trimethoprim/ Sulfamethoxazole	Sulfonamides and Trimethoprim (Systemic)
Bactrim I.V.	Trimethoprim/ Sulfamethoxazole	Sulfonamides and Trimethoprim (Systemic)
Bactrim Pediatric	Trimethoprim/ Sulfamethoxazole	Sulfonamides and Trimethoprim (Systemic)
Cofatrim Forte	Trimethoprim/ Sulfamethoxazole	Sulfonamides and Trimethoprim (Systemic)
Coptin	Trimethoprim/ Sulfamethoxazole	Sulfonamides and Trimethoprim (Systemic)
Coptin I	Trimethoprim/ Sulfamethoxazole	Sulfonamides and Trimethoprim (Systemic)
Cotrim	Trimethoprim/ Sulfamethoxazole	Sulfonamides and Trimethoprim (Systemic)
Cortrim DS	Trimethoprim/ Sulfamethoxazole	Sulfonamides and Trimethoprim (Systemic)
Cotrim Pediatric	Trimethoprim/ Sulfamethoxazole	Sulfonamides and Trimethoprim (Systemic)
Novo-Trimel	Trimethoprim/ Sulfamethoxazole	Sulfonamides and Trimethoprim (Systemic)
Novo-Trimel D.S.	Trimethoprim/ Sulfamethoxazole	Sulfonamides and Trimethoprim (Systemic)
Nu-Cotrimox	Trimethoprim/ Sulfamethoxazole	Sulfonamides and Trimethoprim (Systemic)
Nu-Cotrimox DS	Trimethoprim/ Sulfamethoxazole	Sulfonamides and Trimethoprim (Systemic)
Roubac	Trimethoprim/ Sulfamethoxazole	Sulfonamides and Trimethoprim (Systemic)
Septra	Trimethoprim/ Sulfamethoxazole	Sulfonamides and Trimethoprim (Systemic)
Septra DS	Trimethoprim/ Sulfamethoxazole	Sulfonamides and Trimethoprim (Systemic)
Septra I.V.	Trimethoprim/ Sulfamethoxazole	Sulfonamides and Trimethoprim (Systemic)

Septra Pediatric	Trimethoprim/ Sulfamethoxazole	Sulfonamides and Trimethoprim (Systemic)
Sulfatrim	Trimethoprim/ Sulfamethoxazole	Sulfonamides and Trimethoprim (Systemic)
Sulfatrim Pediatric	Trimethoprim/ Sulfamethoxazole	Sulfonamides and Trimethoprim (Systemic)
Sulfatrim S/S	Trimethoprim/ Sulfamethoxazole	Sulfonamides and Trimethoprim (Systemic)
Sulfatrim Suspension	Trimethoprim/ Sulfamethoxazole	Sulfonamides and Trimethoprim (Systemic)
Sulfatrim-DS	Trimethoprim/ Sulfamethoxazole	Sulfonamides and Trimethoprim (Systemic)
Hivid	Zalcitabine	Zalcitabine (Systemic)
ddC	Zalcitabine	Zalcitabine (Systemic)
AZT	Zidovudine	Zidovudine (Systemic)
Apo-Zidovudine	Zidovudine	Zidovudine (Systemic)
Novo-AZT	Zidovudine	Zidovudine (Systemic)
Retrovir	Zidovudine	Zidovudine (Systemic)

REFERENCES

AIDS education series debuts on world wide web (Announcement, 1996, November/December). **The Case Manager,** 20.

Alexander-Israel, D. & Ireton-Jones, C. (December 1996). Incorporating dietitian services into your home care practice. **Infusion,** 24-29.

AMA notes MD pay decrease. (Announcement, 1996, November/December). **The Case Manager**, 6.

AMA program offers database on physicians (Announcement, November/December, 1996). **The Case Manager**, 20.

Baker, D. (1994). Management of the female HIV-infected patient. **AIDS Research and Human Retroviruses, 10**(8), 935-938.

BCB federal employee program announces disease management program (Announcement, November/December, 1996). **The Case Manager**, 6.

Brady, M. (1995). Management of children with human immunodeficiency virus infection. **Comprehensive Therapy (Pediatrics), 21**(3), 139-147.

Culhane, C. (1993). AIDS costs-one more reason for health reform. **American Medical News, 36**(2), 3 & 35.

The drug scene (Announcement, November/December, 1996). **The Case Manager**, 22.

The drug scene (Announcement, September/October, 1996). **The Case Manager,** 26.

Fanning, M. (1997). **HIV infection: A Clinical Approach**, Philadelphia: W.B. Saunders.

Flanigan, T., CuUvin, S., Rich, J., Mileno, M., Vigilante, K., & Tashima, K. (1996). Update of HIV and AIDS in North America. **Medicine and Health/Rhode Island, 79**(5), 180-187.

Freeman, W. (1996). New developments in the treatment of CMV retinitis. **Ophthalmology, 103**(7), 999-1000.

Gable, C., Tierce, J., Simison, D., Ward, D., & Motte, K. (1996). Costs of HIV+/AIDS at CD4+ counts disease stages based on treatment protocols. **Journal of Acquired Immune Deficiency Syndromes and Human Retrovirology, 12**(4), 413-420.

Gerson, V., (May/June, 1996). AIDS issues for case managers.**The Case Manager**, 91-94.

GMHC treatment issues: Newsletter of experimental aids therapies (all Issues up to June/July 1996).

Gorman, C. (Fall, 1996). The exorcists. **Time, 148**(14), 64-66.

Harindra, V. (1995). Neurologic manifestations of HIV infection. **Annals of Internal Medicine, 122**(11), 883-884.

Hellinger, F. (1993). The lifetime cost of treating a person with HIV. **Journal of American Medical Association, 270**(4), 474-478.

Henry, K. (1995). Management of HIV infection: A 1995-96 overview for the clinician. **Minnesota Medicine, 78,** 17-24.

Hospitalization costs rise sharply for AIDS patients in months before death. (Announcement, July/August, 1996). **The Case Manager,** 22.

Hurley, P., Ungvarski, P., & Rottner, J. (October 1996). Predictors of home care service costs in adults living with HIV/AIDS in New York City. **The Journal of Care Management, 2**(5), 48-64.

Kitchen, J. (1995) Acquired Imune Deficiency Syndrome. In P. Deutsch & H. Sawyer (Eds.), **A Guide to Rehabilitation**. (Vol. 2), 31.1-31.99. White Plains, NY: Ahab Press.

Krown, S. (1996). Cancer chemotherapy and biological response modifiers, Annual 16. **Elsevier Science**, Chap. 19, "AIDS-associated malignancies," pp. 441-461.

Lalley, H. (August 20, 1996). AIDS sufferers are struggling with finances of fighting disease. **Missoulian**, C-3.

Marks, S., Upadhyay, S., & Crane, L. (1996). Cytomegalovirus sinusitis: A new manifestation of AIDS. **Archives of Otolaryngology Head Neck Surgery, 122,** 789-791.

Martone, W., Mellors, J., Flesnor, C., Phair, J., Markowitz, M., Collier, A., & Dobkin, J. **Infections in Medicine** (supplement) (1996). New York, NY: SCP Communications.

McCloskey, W. & Stofko, J. (December 1996). Interferons in clinical practice: An update, **Infusion,** 31-37.

Murray, J. (1996). Pulmonary complications of HIV infection. **Annual Review of Medicine, 47**, 117-126.

Nickel, J., Salsbury, P., Caswell, R., Keller, M., Long, T., & O'Connell, M. (1996). Quality of life in nurse case management of persons with AIDS receiving home care. **Research in Nursing & Health, 19,** 91-99.

Ottery, F. (September 1996). Nutritional screening & assessment in home care. **Infusilon**, 36-45.

Polis, M. & Masur, H. (1995). Promising new treatments for cytomegalovirus retinitis. **Journal of American Medical Association, 273**(18),1457-1459.

Rahhal, F., Arvalo, F., Munguia, D., Taskintuna, I., Chavez de la Paz, E., Azen, S., & Freeman, W. (1996). Intravitreal cidofovir for the maintenance treatment of cytomegalovirus retinitis. **Ophthalmology, 103**(7), 1078-1083.

Sande, M. & Volberding, P. (1997). **The Medical Management of AIDS**, 5th ed., p. 384, Philadelphia: W.B. Saunders.

Seage, G., III, Landers, S., Lamb, G., & Epstein, A. (1990). Effect of changing patterns of care and duration of survival on the cost of treating the acquired immunodeficiency syndrome (AIDS). **American Journal of Public Health, 80**(7), 835-839.

Smith, G. (1994). Treatment of infections in the patient with acquired immunodeficiency syndrome. **Archives of Internal Medicine, 154**, 949-973.

Study notes major changes in catastrophic comprehensive management, (Announcement, November/December, 1996), **The Case Manager**, 16.

U.S. Department of Health and Human Services, Agency for Health Care Policy and Research Publications Catalog 1995/96. (AHCPR Publication). Rockville, MD.

Wachter, R., Luce, J., Safrin, S. Berrios, D., Charlebois, E., & Scitovsky, A. (1995). Cost and outcome of intensive care for patients with AIDS, pneumocystis carinii pneumonia, and severe respiratory failure. **Journal of American Medical Association, 273**(3), 230-235.

Ward, D. & Brown, M. A. (1994). Labor and cost in AIDS family caregiving. **Western Journal of Nursing Research, 16**(1), 10-25.

17

LIFE CARE PLANNING FOR SPINAL CORD INJURY

Terry Winkler and Roger O. Weed

INTRODUCTION

Spinal cord injury historically has been described by physicians as one of the most catastrophic conditions in medicine (Kennedy, 1986). In ancient Egyptian times, it was considered a condition not to be treated since patients died and the demise reflected on the physician's ability if attempts to cure them failed. Clinical features were first described in great detail by Hippocrates around 400 B.C. Paraplegia and neurogenic bowel and bladder were observed. However, since complications were poorly understood and modern medications were unavailable, an early death was the common result. It was not until this century that significant strides were made based on medical research begun particularly in England in 1944 at the Stoke Mandeville Hospital. In the United States the first federally funded research program was established in Arizona in 1970. Since its early beginnings, the research center has been moved to the University of Alabama with contributing support by 16 spinal cord rehabilitation programs throughout the United States. Research data is now available regarding a plethora of issues, and life expectancy as well as quality of life have significantly improved. Fortunately, there have been many positive changes in health care and in society for spinal cord injured patients. Technology is rapidly changing and continues to provide positive changes in life expectancy and quality of life for the spinal cord injured. However, there are a number of physicians and health care providers who continue to hold a somewhat pessimistic view of spinal cord injury. Indeed, as late as 1947, Dr. William Asher described the paralyzed patient as follows:

> Picture the pathetic patient lying longabed, the urine leaking from his distended bladder, the lime draining from his bones, the blood clotting in his veins, the flesh rotting from his seat, the scybala stacking up in his colon, and the spirit draining from his soul (Asher, 1947, p. 967).

One goal of this chapter is to provide the background information that life care planners need to prevent the above portrait from developing in a spinal cord injured person's life. The rehabilitation professional should become involved with

1-57444-075-6/99/$0.00+$.50

the spinal cord injury patient immediately after the acute hospital care (Winkler, 1997). The life care planner must have a thorough working knowledge of the physiological effects, the most common side effects, and proper medical interventions of spinal cord injury. He or she must work with other health professionals to provide counseling for the patient and the family, and offer suggestions for environmental modifications, equipment, and services for the patient that offer greater mobility and independence. This chapter is intended to provide a foundation of basic medical knowledge of spinal cord injury, vocational information, functional abilities of people with spinal cord injury, future medical and nonmedical needs, and serve as an introduction to life care planning and spinal cord injury. It is imperative that the life care planner go beyond this chapter to the references cited to develop a deeper understanding of the issues that have impact on life care planning in spinal cord injury.

Prevalence of Spinal Cord Injury

The most current discussion of epidemiological factors of spinal cord injury can be found in Bette Go (Go, Devivo, & Richards, 1995). The model systems data provide good information on general trends in spinal cord injury. It should, however, be pointed out that the model systems data perhaps are skewed toward individuals who have a higher level of lesion and an adequate funding source. Individuals who have lower level or incomplete spinal cord injuries or who do not have adequate funding for extended hospital stays tend to be treated locally rather than referred to the model systems. Krause and colleagues found an incidence of spinal cord injury of 32 cases per million per year who survived or reached a hospital with an additional 21 cases per million per year dying prior to reaching the hospital (Krause, Frantice, Riggins, et al., 1975). Griffin and colleagues describe an incidence that approached 55 per million with 35 cases per million surviving to reach the hospital (Griffin, Opitz, Kurland, et al., 1985).

The incidence of spinal cord injury has been reported as low as 29 cases per million to a high of 60 cases per million in various studies. There appears to be some variability from state to state regarding the exact rate of spinal cord injury. However, overall the annual rate of hospitalized individuals with spinal cord injury is between 30 and 40 cases per million. This would correspond with between 7,000 and 10,000 new cases of spinal cord injury per year in the United States. The prevalence of individuals with spinal cord injury at any one given time in the United States is between 180,000 and 230,000 persons (Go, Devivo, & Richards, 1995).

Causes of Spinal Cord Injury

Gibson (1992) has described the four leading causes of spinal cord injury as motor vehicle accidents, falls, violence, and sports injuries (Table 18.1).

Automobile accidents remain the number one cause of traumatic spinal cord injury, but there has been a recent decline reported (Go, Devivo, & Richards, 1995). The peak incidence occurred between 1978 and 1980 at 47% and has recently dropped to as low as 38% reported in 1990. This reduction in motor vehicle accidents and spinal cord injury may be attributed in part to the improved

Table 18.1 Causes of Spinal Cord Injury

Injury Source	*Percent of Total Injuries*
Motor Vehicle Accidents	45%
Falls	20%
Violence	15%
Sports	15%
Other	5%

safety features of some automobiles. Another interesting trend is the reduction of sports related spinal cord injuries that has occurred over the last 15 years. Spinal cord injuries as a result of falls has increased by 5% in the same period of time, and spinal cord injury as a result of violence has almost doubled from 1978 to 1990. In some areas, violence is the number two cause of spinal cord injury. Louisiana ranks it as the number two cause, resulting in 32% of its reported cases of spinal cord injury (Lawrence, Bayakly, & Mathison, 1992).

Go et al. (1995) pointed out that the etiology of spinal cord injury differs substantially by age, gender, and race. The most common age of injury is 19 years, with a range of 16 to 30. Males account for 80% of all spinal cord injuries. The mean age at the time of spinal cord injury from 1973 through 1992 has increased by 4.9 years, with the mean age of 28.5 years increasing to a mean age of 33.4 years. This trend has important implications. Since older persons with spinal cord injury tend to have more preexisting major medical conditions and are more likely to have tetraplegia (previously known as quadriplegia), they therefore develop a higher rate of secondary complications and more frequent hospitalizations than their counterparts (Go, Devivo & Richards, 1995; Roth, Lovell, Heinemann, et al., 1992).

As perhaps expected, there are seasonal variations, with the lowest number of spinal cord injuries occurring during the winter months, particularly February. The highest number of spinal cord injuries occurs during the summer months, with July having the highest incidence. Half of all spinal cord injuries occur on a weekend day, with 20% occurring on Saturday, which is nearly double the rate of spinal cord injury occurring during weekdays.

Of all spinal cord injured people 55% have tetraplegia with the remainder having paraplegia. Tetraplegia is defined as paralysis or partial paralysis in four extremities, with paraplegia being paralysis or partial paralysis in two extremities. Between 50% and 55% of all spinal cord injuries have some sensory sparing and can be classified as incomplete.

Functions of the Spinal Cord

Spinal cord injury is a traumatic insult to the spinal cord that can result in alterations of normal motor, sensory, and autonomic function (Staas, Formal, & Gershkof, 1993). The discussion will be confined to traumatic spinal cord injury; however, the principles will apply to spinal cord injury of all etiologies.

The spinal cord has three basic functions:

1. It serves as a conduit to bring sensory messages from the body and internal organs to the brain, where the brain can monitor activities of all structures and act as a central processing unit to interpret messages from the body.
2. In a similar fashion, it carries messages from the brain to the effector organs or structures in the body. In this regard, the spinal cord can be viewed as a series of cables or connections between the brain and the body.
3. It provides protective and coordination function where by reflex mechanisms protect the body (e.g., withdrawal reflexes) and other centers facilitate or coordinate some bodily functions, such as urination, which is controlled by the micturition center in the sacral cord.

This is, of course, a simplification of the spinal cord. The spinal cord is a tremendously complex structure with literally hundreds, if not thousands, of functions being performed. Many of the body's autonomic functions are coordinated and regulated at least in part in the spinal cord, and we have learned that the modulation and control of pain is in part based in the spinal cord. There is a very complicated group of interneurons and proprioneurons in the spinal cord whose roles are to facilitate or inhibit the activity of other neurons in the spinal cord. There is virtually no bodily function occurring below the level of the foramen magnum that is not influenced in some way by the integrity of the spinal cord. Therefore, the number of complications and problems that occur as a direct result of spinal cord injury are enormous, with implications for almost every body system (Schoenen, 1991).

The Spinal Column: Basic Anatomy

The spinal column consists of 33 vertebrae, intervertebral disks, and ligaments. The vertebrae provide a weight-bearing structure or spinal column to house the spinal cord and protect it. In addition, the vertebral column allows a great deal of flexibility in the cervical and lumbar spines. There is a relatively high degree of rigidity in the thoracic spine, easily identified by the rib cage, which provides support and protection for the internal organs.

The vertebrae are divided into five segments:

- 7 cervical vertebrae (Neck): These support the head and provide a great deal of mobility. There are eight spinal nerves, C1 through C8. This is accomplished by the first cervical vertebra having a spinal nerve exiting above and below it, with each vertebral body from that level down having a spinal nerve exiting below the vertebra.
- 12 thoracic vertebrae support the ribs.
- 5 lumbar vertebrae (lower back) allow flexion and extension, some rotation and side bending.
- 5 sacral vertebrae provide a base of support and attachment for the pelvis.
- 4 coccygeal vertebrae are fused together and form the "tailbone."

Each vertebral body is separated by an intervertebral disk that is made of cartilage and acts as a shock absorber and cushion for the spinal column. The intervertebral disks make up one-fourth of the total height of the spinal column and allow a great deal of flexibility between vertebral bodies. The vertebral disks have the ability to herniate and can cause injury to the spinal cord or nerve root in cases of severe herniation.

Numerous ligaments are responsible for maintaining the integrity of the spinal column and its alignment. Two of the most important are the anterior longitudinal ligaments on the front of the vertebral bodies and the posterior longitudinal ligaments on the back of the vertebral bodies. If either of these ligaments is torn, the column is said to be unstable and this greatly increases the likelihood of spinal cord injury or damage.

The central nervous system is made up of the brain and the spinal cord. It is completely encased in a very protective membrane, the dura mater and is bathed in cerebrospinal fluid. The spinal cord begins at the base of the skull, the foramen magnum, and extends to the L1 or L2 vertebral level, ending in the shape of a cone called the conus medullaris. From the conus medullaris down, nerve roots continue down through the spinal canal to exit at their proper levels. These nerve roots are referred to as the cauda equina.

It is important to note that there is a disparity between the bony level and the neurological level. For example, the nervous segments that are adjacent to the L1 vertebral body in the spinal canal are S2, S3, and S4. Therefore, an injury to the L1 vertebral body would result in damage to S2, S3, and S4 nerves. This is a very important concept in life care planning. When developing a life care plan, it is extremely important that the life care plan be developed for the neurological level of injury, not the bony level of injury.

Spinal Cord Damage

Spinal cord damage can occur in several ways, some of which include

1. Overstretching or tearing of the nervous tissue of the spinal cord.
2. Direct pressure on the spinal cord from bony fragments, bulging disks, or hematoma.
3. Swelling and edema can produce increased pressure and decreased blood flow in the area of the spinal cord injury, leading to further damage.

The initial spinal cord injury usually does not result in a complete disruption of the cord and it is generally felt that high dose steroids, such as methylprednisolone, given within four hours after the spinal cord injury may have some beneficial effect, although there are conflicting reports in this regard. Intense research in spinal cord injury treatment and intervention may hold the most promise of providing some relief from the effects of injury. However, to date there is no cure for spinal cord injury and none foreseeable in the near future.

It is possible to determine the mechanism of injury in spinal cord injury by reviewing X-rays and CT scans. Axial compression alone, such as from a diving accident, will result in a burst-type fracture. Rotation combined with flexion is the most damaging type of force on a spinal column and it will result in disruption of the posterior ligamentous structure (Staas, Formal, & Gershkof, 1993). Central cord syndromes are the result of a hyperextension injury. Injury to the thoracic spine requires much greater forces due to the protective effect of the rib cage and the stability of the spine. These are usually only involved in very high speed vehicular type traumas or accidents that involve very high forces. They also can occur when the occupant is ejected from the vehicle (Zigler & Field, 1992).

Distraction forces placed at a vertebral body can result in a Chance fracture. This type of injury is observed in motor vehicle accidents where only a lap belt is worn. This can be prevented with the use of a shoulder harness belt in addition to the lap belt. A similar injury occurs in automobiles that are provided with passive restraints in which the shoulders are restrained but the hips are not. A collision can result in the person's hips moving forward, causing a hyperflexion of the neck and resultant spinal cord injury at a higher level. Another recent reported phenomenon is high tetraplegia to children and smaller adults as a result of air bag deployment.

The stability of the spinal column is determined by the intactness of the anterior and posterior longitudinal ligaments as well as the vertebral body and will dictate whether or not surgery is needed. Surgical decompression even a number of years after the spinal cord injury can result in improvement. This issue is of the utmost importance in cervical spinal cord injury where, for example, a late decompression can result in a person with C5 motor function having an improvement in C6 motor function, which would make a tremendous difference in their functional outcome. In general, for the lower level spinal cord injury, decompression is not as crucial. Spinal cord management may include traction, halos, bracing, Harrington or similar rods, and/or fusion.

Spinal Cord Injury Classifications

It is important to establish a worldwide standard for the nomenclature and classification of spinal cord injury. Without this, it is impossible to perform meaningful spinal cord injury research from center to center or country to country. Likewise, it is impossible to view spinal cord injury in terms of life care planning and to critique and review and make recommendations in life care planning without a standardized classification system.

In response to this need, the American Spinal Injury Association (ASIA) and the International Medical Society of Paraplegia developed a worldwide nomenclature system (American Spinal Injury Association/International Medical Society of Paraplegia, 1992)*. This system of classification gives key sensory levels to identify dermatomes of injury and key muscle levels to identify the levels of muscle functions. Spinal cord injuries may be *complete* or *incomplete* with partial sparing. The ASIA classification system includes a level for the sensory impairment and a level for the motor impairment, as well as a letter designation for the degree of completeness.

* Copies of booklet can be obtained from Ms. Leslie Hudson, Shepherd Center, Atlanta, GA, 404/352-2020.

The selected scale, known as the modified Frankel classification system, is used to describe completeness, with five classes being recognized.

Class A: Complete spinal cord injury: All motor and sensory function is absent below the zone of partial preservation.

Class B: Incomplete spinal cord injury: Sensation preserved below the level of injury, but no voluntary motor activity preserved.

Class C: Incomplete spinal cord injury: There may be some minimal motor activity below the level of the lesions, such as moving a foot or extremity, but it is nonfunctional.

Class D: Incomplete spinal cord injury: Some motor activity preserved below the level of lesion that is useful. This is a level of motor strength that is graded at 3 or more. The person may be able to use the motor function, for example, for a brief transfer.

Class E: Complete return of all motor and sensory function below the level of the lesion, but may have abnormal reflexes.

Examples of Incomplete Syndromes

The following are specific types of incomplete syndromes:

1. Central cord syndrome. Central cord syndrome is said to be present when the individual has paralysis greater in the upper extremity than the lower extremities.
2. Brown-Sequard syndrome. Brown-Sequard syndrome is a hemisection of the spinal cord and is characterized by ipsilateral paralysis with contralateral sensory loss from the level of the lesion down.
3. Cauda equina syndrome. Cauda equina syndrome is an injury to the lumbosacral nerve roots within the neural canal below the conus medullaris resulting in a loss of bowel and bladder control and weakness of the lower extremities or paralysis.
4. Conus medullaris syndrome. An injury to the sacrospinal cord at the level of the conus and the lumbosacral nerve roots, which results in areflexic bladder and bowels, and lower limb paralysis.
5. Anterior cord syndrome. A lesion that produces variable loss of motor function and of sensitivity to pinprick and temperature while preserving proprioception.

Functional Effects

Spinal cord injury is considered to be a permanent condition with very few people experiencing significant long-term recovery from the disability. Individuals with complete spinal cord injury have very little improvement in general; only 2% will improve to a Frankel's Class D. Of those who present with a Frankel's Class B, 20% will improve to a Frankel's Class D or E. For Frankel's Class C, 50% will improve to a Frankel's Class D or E. The length of time since spinal cord injury is also a factor in prognosis. Individuals who have had no improvement within the first six months to one year are considered to have permanent injury with no likelihood for significant functional improvement.

Upper motor neuron (UMN) lesions in general refer to a lesion in the spinal cord that occurs at the T11 or T12 level or higher. Most tetraplegics have a UMN lesion. UMN lesions are characterized by increased spasticity with intact reflex bladder and bowel functioning and sexual functioning, in general.

Lower motor neuron (LMN) injuries occur at T12 or below, usually seen in paraplegics, especially cauda equina syndromes. In general, LMN lesions have impairment of the reflex arcs that control bowel and bladder functioning and sexual functioning. These individuals will have flaccid bowel and bladder functioning, which results in much greater difficulty controlling bowel and bladder incontinence. In general, erectile function in the male is impaired.

Individuals with intact reflex voiding mechanisms of the bladder and the bowel may experience less complications, infections, and incontinent episodes.

Potential Complications of Spinal Cord Injury

Numerous physiological changes occur in almost every system of the body as a result of spinal cord injury. In addition, there are a host of complications that occur as a result of spinal cord injury. A comprehensive discussion of these factors and issues is beyond the scope of this chapter. However, an introduction to the topic is useful and necessary to understand the implications for life care planning. At the conclusion of this chapter, several references for more in-depth discussion of these issues are offered.

Cardiovascular: Normal physiological control of the arteriovenous system and the heart are lost in spinal cord injury from the injured vertebral level down. The portion of the spinal cord that controls the heart directly ranges from T1 to T7. Injuries at this level or above result in altered cardiovascular physiology, not only of the vasculature, but of the heart proper.

Loss of blood pressure control is a very common problem in spinal cord injury. Higher level spinal cord injuries result in orthostatic hypotension in which the individual experiences a drop in blood pressure and an elevating heart rest in response to attempting to sit up. These episodes tend to improve with time; however, a select group of individuals may continue to have this throughout the remainder of their lives and require very aggressive management in order to tolerate a sitting posture. Orthostatic hypotension is most commonly seen in individuals with a spinal cord injury at T6 or above. It can be quite severe and result in a patient having a fainting episode or loss of consciousness. Numerous techniques to assist in the management of this are available, including TED hose, abdominal binders, reclining chairs, elevating leg rests. Physical therapists address this complication by progressive elevation with a tilt table. Medications useful in the management of orthostatic hypotension include ephedrine, tyramine, steroids, and ergotamine. The orthostasis will interfere with the number of hours a person can be in a wheelchair and with their ability to be out in the community for vocational or social activities.

High level spinal cord injuries can result in bradyarrhythmias that can lead to cardiac arrest and standstill during tracheal suction. Patients at risk for this may require atropine or possibly placement of a pacemaker. A highly skilled caregiver who is capable of responding to such emergencies should be available.

Deep vein thrombus (DVT) has been recognized as a significant cause of morbidity and mortality in spinal cord injury. The incidence of DVT is likely to occur in well over 80% of cases (Waring & Karunas, 1991). The use of heparin has been demonstrated to be effective in reducing the incidence of DVT. Spasticity and its effects on the development of DVT have been studied. There are varying reports in the literature; however, overall, it is felt that increased spasticity may result in a decreased incidence of DVT in the acute sitting (Bors, Conrad & Massell, 1954). Chin (personal communication, 1997) has studied DVT and the use of Lovonox (a low molecular weight heparin) in the prevention of DVT and has documented that Lovonox is extremely effective in reducing the acute incidence of DVT.

Of those individuals who develop DVT, approximately one third can develop pulmonary embolus. Pulmonary embolus can be a life threatening condition and result in death in a number of individuals. Venous Doppler studies and/or venograms are necessary to follow the DVT as are serial laboratory studies, such as Protimes. Once a DVT has developed, an individual will be treated for six months to one year, depending on clinical response. A small number of spinal cord injured people will develop a chronic DVT and require lifelong management with anticoagulation therapy. Some individuals with DVT and other comorbidities or injuries may require the placement of a vena cava filter to protect them from risk of pulmonary embolus. Of those individuals who do not develop DVT during the acute hospital stay, there is approximately 14% to 20% risk of developing a DVT at some point during their lifetime. The period of greatest risk for development of deep vein thrombosis (DVT) seems to occur within the first three months after injury (Staas, Formal & Gershkof, 1993). If the person is one year out from the development of DVT and experiences increased swelling and temperature when Coumadin (a blood thinner) is stopped, this likely represents a permanent condition and will require lifelong anticoagulation treatment.

Individuals who have experienced a DVT are twice as likely to develop a blood clot again in the same extremity at some point later in their life (Wyngaarden, Smith, & Saunders, 1988).

Autonomic dysreflexia (AD) is a life-threatening complication. It most commonly occurs in individuals who have a spinal cord injury at T6 or above. The complication is characterized by one or more of the following:

- Flushing or redness of the skin that develops above the level of the spinal cord injury
- General malaise
- Severe headache
- Elevated blood pressure
- Increased heart rate
- Occasionally, slowed heart rate

While AD commonly occurs at T6 or above, with the right type of stimulus (such as giving birth) it can occur at lower levels of spinal cord injury. This condition is extremely uncomfortable and can be life-threatening. The patient may feel as if they are dying and the sequela can cause an extreme and diffuse malaise. Individuals that have frequent and recurring autonomic dysreflexia or who tend to have alarmingly high blood pressures, i.e., diastolic pressure over 120 mmHg or systolic pressure over 200 mmHg, require ongoing use of medications such as Dibenzyline and Procardia. In addition, they will require a failproof emergency response system to ensure that they obtain required urgent care. The danger lies in the elevated blood pressure that can result in stroke and death. The life care plan should be designed in such a fashion as to make every effort to prevent the episodes by providing adequate supplies for frequent catheterization and bowel programs and ensuring that the personal care attendants have been trained to the proper level to assist in preventing the autonomic dysreflexia, recognizing and treating it.

In incomplete spinal cord injuries, AD is generally not a significant problem. AD occurs as a result of some noxious stimulus, the most common being distended bowel or bladder. Other causes may be occult fractures, decubitus ulcers, infections, and abdominal lesions (ulcers or cholelithiasis). Improper positioning in the chair as well as tight clothing or wrinkles in the clothing have been reported to cause episodes of AD. In individuals who are experiencing increasing autonomic dysreflexia, a complete and thorough medical work-up is indicated to determine the etiology of the AD.

AD is treated by identifying and relieving the noxious stimulus. In the case of bowel and bladder, the complication can be reduced or eliminated by emptying the bowel or bladder. In refractory cases of AD, medications such as Dibenzyline may be required. In acute episodes of AD, calcium channel blockers such as Procardia are indicated to gain control of the blood pressure while the underlying etiology is determined.

The spinal cord injured patient is also at higher risk for developing peripheral vascular disease, both arterial and venous disease (Lee, 1991).

Pulmonary: Individuals with spinal cord injuries below T12 have virtually no impairment of their pulmonary system. As the spinal cord injury levels rise from T12 to T5, there is a progressive loss of abdominal motor function and chest wall function that impairs expiration and cough. As the level rises further from T5 to T1, intercostal function is impaired and inspiratory function as well as expiratory function is impaired (ref 14). Jackson and Groomes have reported that approximately 70% of new spinal cord injured persons experience respiratory complications, with one third developing pneumonia (Jackson & Groomes, 1991).

The most critical level for pulmonary function is C3, C4, and C5, the neural segments that supply the phrenic nerve and the diaphragm. With injuries at this level and above, the individual is at high risk for relying upon a ventilator for pulmonary function. Spinal cord injury at levels C3 and above will result in total dependency on ventilators. These individuals require a whole host of support to maintain them, including high-level attendant care and frequent physician follow-up visits. In a select group of these individuals, phrenic pacers (although expensive) may be indicated and will result in a more physiological breathing mechanism. It can be expected that individuals with phrenic pacers will experience fewer respiratory complications, have an improved quality of life, and improved longevity. In high levels of spinal cord injury, careful monitoring of the pulmonary status is absolutely essential and problems must be reported immediately to the treating physicians.

Upper respiratory tract infections and pneumonias can be expected to occur at a higher frequency and require aggressive preventive care in order to limit morbidity and mortality. Tetraplegics should receive annual influenza vaccinations and a pneumococcal vaccination. The winter months are likely to be the most troublesome and may require daily respiratory therapy treatments in order to prevent complications.

Individuals with high level spinal cord injury will require a host of equipment including ventilators, respiratory monitors, suctioning equipment, and pulse oxymetry. Additional emergency equipment will include a backup ventilator, a home generator system in the event of prolonged power failure, and an Ambu bag.

Additional factors that can complicate respiratory status in spinal cord injury is a progressing scoliosis, increasing spasticity, and syringomyelia. High spinal cord injury in females who become pregnant may also experience a worsening pulmonary status and require additional support during pregnancy.

Sleep Disturbances: Braun and colleagues have reported an increased incidence of sleep apnea in spinal cord injured patients (Braun, Giovanni, & Levin, 1982). Consideration of monitoring of their condition is required in patients with symptoms of sleep apnea, particularly in patients who are overweight.

Gastrointestinal (GI): Individuals with spinal cord injury experience a number of physiological changes in the function of their GI tract. There is a slowing of transient time through the GI system and gastric acid secretion may increase. GI bleeding is a very common early complication in spinal cord injury with the incidence of ulcers being reported around 20%. The risk for GI bleeds and ulceration are higher in individuals with spinal cord injury at T6 and above. Prophylactic use of H2 blockers is common and medically appropriate. The GI bleeds frequently result in anemia after spinal cord injury.

Cholelithiasis is a common complication of spinal cord injury and may occur three times more often than in able bodied populations (Apstein & Dalecki-Chipperfield, 1987). Possible causes for this may include decreased GI tract motility, gallbladder motility, and abnormal bowel secretion.

Individuals with UMN lesions may have an unaltered defecation reflex and respond to digital stimulation of the rectum with a reflex defecation. Individuals who do not have an intact anorectal reflex for defecation have a much more difficult time controlling bowel incontinence.

Dietary factors are used to assist in controlling bowel incontinence by maintaining a proper consistency of the stool. In addition, rectal suppositories such as Dulcolax, Therevac, Mini Enemas, and Magic Bullet may be necessary. Oral medications such as Metamucil, Colace, or Peri-Colace also may assist in bowel management.

Individuals with spinal cord injuries experience a high rate of hemorrhoids and rectal fissures that will require the assistance of gastroenterologists and/or colorectal surgeons. Spinal cord injured patients who have intractable diarrhea and difficulty controlling their incontinence may be candidates for a colostomy. Bowel incontinence poses serious social, recreational, and vocational limitations for the spinal cord injured patient. Individuals with high-level spinal cord injuries are dependent on others for assistance and management of their bowel incontinence.

In addition, individuals with low level spinal cord injury or paraplegias will require the assistance of an attendant during times of illness for management of their bowel program, and a personal care attendant will be required during times of illness that result in GI upset or diarrhea. Management of the neurogenic bowel can be quite time consuming and require from 30 minutes to three hours or more for each event.

Urinary Complications: Spinal cord injury results in a neurogenic bladder (urinary incontinence) in most people. The management program required depends on the level of spinal cord injury and the patient's unique bladder function or dysfunction. Upper motor neuron lesions may be managed with an external catheter if an intact reflex voiding mechanism is present. This technique is by far the most desirable if it is functional for the patient. It should be recognized that as a patient ages or changes occur with the spinal cord injury, the external condom catheter may not continue to be an effective method of urinary control.

Most patients with spinal cord injury will require intermittent catheterization performed four to six times daily. Spinal cord injured males with low level lesions are the best suited for intermittent catheterization. Intermittent catheterization becomes increasingly more difficult in females, obese individuals, and individuals with high-level lesions. Indwelling Foley or suprapubic catheters may be required to manage the neurogenic bladder for these patients.

Individuals with spinal cord injury experience an increased rate of urinary tract infections and urosepsis and will require urinalysis urine and intermittent antibiotics. Some individuals may require lifelong use of prophylactic antibiotics to reduce the incidence of urinary tract infections. Bladder and renal calculi are a common complication of spinal cord injury that should be screened annually and will require a urologist to manage. Urinary incontinence may lead to skin breakdown in the perineal area and result in decubitus ulcers that require expensive surgery. High-level spinal cord injury will mandate the assistance of a personal care attendant.

The individual with spinal cord injury will likely require catheters, leg drainage bags, night drainage bags, gloves, tape, Betadine, and other supplies. Follow-up evaluations will require renal ultrasounds, intravenous pyelograms (IVPs), urinalysis, urine cultures and sensitivities, urology visit, and urodynamic studies.

Goals of neurogenic bladder management including preserving renal function and reducing morbidity may require a change in management of the system during the patient's lifetime (Cardenas, 1992).

Musculoskeletal: A host of physiological changes occur after spinal cord injury, including body composition, lipid metabolism, energy expenditure, nutritional parameters, glucose and calcium metabolism, thermoregulation, and soft tissue changes (Yarkony, 1996). All of these affect the musculoskeletal system.

Approximately 40% of the spinal cord injured will have multiple fractures below the level of the injury. In addition, due to the extensive osteoporosis from the level of the lesion down, it can be anticipated that many spinal cord injured individuals will experience at least one long bone fracture during their lifetime. Long bone fractures below the level of the lesion are slow to heal or may not heal at all, resulting in a nonunion. Such fractures have to be evaluated carefully; they may require future surgical interventions or prolonged care and treatment. These fractures can be a source of ongoing pain and can produce autonomic dysreflexia symptoms in a patient. Fractures below the level of the spinal cord injury can result in the development of heterotopic ossification and require extended periods of treatment.

Fractures above the level of the lesion or in the upper extremities can interfere with rehabilitation care and make the patient more dependent for personal care services until the fracture and the resulting sequelae have resolved.

Spinal cord injury can result in altered nutritional requirements, hypercholesterolemia, and dyslipidemia. Nutritional counseling and changes in the diet may be required to assist the patient with learning how to manage these complications. Exercise has been demonstrated to be beneficial in assisting and restoring a desirable HDL to LDL ratio.

Glucose metabolism is altered in spinal cord injured patients and there is an increased incidence of adult-onset diabetes mellitus. It appears that insulin resistance is a factor that contributes to the development of abnormal glucose metabolism (Duckworth, Jallepalli, & Solomon, 1983).

Heterotopic ossification (HO) is a common complication of spinal cord injury by which the body begins making ectopic bone in an area where bone should not exist. Typically, this bone is formed in the soft tissues around a joint, most commonly in the hips, knees, shoulders, elbows, and ankles. The condition rarely occurs in small joints of the hands or feet. It is reported to occur in as many as 20% to 30% spinal cord injured patients and can result in limited range of motion of a joint. HO can lead to complications such as repeated skin breakdown, or it interferes with positioning and ADL activities. Triple phase bone scan is the earliest and most sensitive test to diagnose HO. Additional useful tests include serum alkaline phosphatase and X-rays.

HO must be treated by a physical therapist with range of motion to prevent ankylosing of a joint. Medications that are useful include Indocin and Didronel and may require from six months to one year of treatment. When active HO is present, frequent follow-ups with a physiatrist, serial bone scans and/or X-rays, and serum phosphorus levels are required.

After HO has "matured" and has no longer been active for at least one year, and if the HO is causing interference with activities of daily living, positioning, or skin breakdown, it can be surgically removed. Refractory HO that is not responsive to medication may benefit from radiation treatment, although there are conflicting reports in the literature regarding the efficacy of radiation treatment.

Once spinal cord injured patients have experienced HO, they have approximately a 50% chance of reactivating the disease sometime during their lifetime. Factors that will result in reactivation of the HO include fractures, infection, kidney stones, decubitus ulcers, and surgeries. Reactivated HO is treated the same as the original episode of HO, requiring Indocin, Didronel, physical therapy, and possibly radiation treatment. It also requires physician follow-up, bone scans, X-rays, and frequent laboratory evaluation.

Poikilothermia is related to a decreased ability to maintain body temperature. In an able bodied person, body heat is generated through shivering and vasoconstriction and body heat is reduced through sweating and vasodilation. These mechanisms are impaired in the patient with a spinal cord injury. The higher the level of injury, the more significant the poikilothermia. This loss of ability to regulate body temperature can be life-threatening in individuals with spinal cord injury and require adequate safeguards to assist in maintaining body temperature. This includes central heating and air systems in their homes as well as good functioning air conditioning systems in their vehicles. Cellular telephones are required so that in the event the vehicle breaks down, the person can summon help. Spinal cord injured people are at risk for skin injury from exposure to extreme heat or cold and may, in fact, suffer life-threatening complications if exposed to the extremes of either temperature for longer than a brief period of time.

Osteoporosis is a common complication of spinal cord injury because as much as 50% of the bone mineralization may be lost within the first few months of the injury. This poses the patient at greater risk of fractures below the level of the lesion. In addition, it has been reported that fractures below the level of the lesion are much slower to heal or may not heal at all. Bone mineralization loss continues with aging, raising the risk of skeletal complications with the length of time from spinal cord injury onset.

Musculoskeletal complications such as overuse syndrome and chronic pain of the upper extremities, shoulders, elbows, and wrists are common sequelae of spinal cord injury and can result in a decreased functional status of the patient. Up to 75% of patients may experience the development of peripheral nerve entrapment such as carpal tunnel syndrome and ulnar nerve entrapments at the wrists and elbow. Davidoff has reported the incidents to be as high as 86% (Davidoff, Werner, & Waring, 1991). Decreased shoulder functioning and increasing pain has been reported with aging. Rotator cuff impairment and tendonitis of the shoulders are common problems associated with spinal cord injury. At least one study reports upper extremity complications occur earlier in females (Pentland & Twomey, 1991).

Spasticity, an involuntary rhythmic contraction of a muscle, can result in increased disability by interfering with transfers, activities of daily living, and positioning in the chair, as well as interrupting sleep and causing pain. However, there also are some beneficial effects of spasticity such as assisting with weight shifts, improving circulation, helping to reduce skin breakdown, and at times may be used for functional purposes, such as a transfer.

Increasing spasticity can result from sitting on a foreign object, skin breakdown, infections, kidney stones, ingrown toenails, bony fractures, or other painful stimuli. Syringomyelia, a cyst in the spinal canal that can raise the level of injury if not treated, is a diagnosis that must be excluded when no other source of the increasing spasticity can be found.

Spasticity is treated by providing full range of motion to all involved joints at least twice a day with prolonged terminal stretch by the therapist. Standing in a standing frame or tilt table can help reduce spasticity. Avoiding extreme temperature changes, whirlpool treatments, preventing bladder infections, constipation, and skin breakdown will also help.

Medications that are commonly useful in the treatment of spasticity include Baclofen, Dantrium, and Valium. Xanaflex is a newer antispasticity medication that is an alpha blocker and can be helpful in cases not responding to other oral agents. In severe cases, the patient may require an intrathecal Baclofen pump. Surgery such as a rhizotomy may be considered. The patient may require motor point blocks or nerve blocks using phenol, alcohol, or Botox. Spasticity has been reported to increase with aging in spinal cord injury (Menter, 1995).

Fleming reported an incident of neck and shoulder pain at 80% for tetraplegics. Upper extremity pains are commonly reported to exist in 75% of the spinal cord injured. Females seem to have greater difficulty with upper extremity and shoulder pain than males.

The result of increased tone and decreased range of motion (ROM) are well-known complications of spinal cord injury. They can require surgical intervention, treatment with physical therapists, range of motion, standing frames, whirlpool treatments, peripheral nerve or motor point blocks, and splinting.

Decubitus ulcers are a common and perhaps most costly complication of spinal cord injury. It is reported that most spinal cord injured patients will experience at least one decubitus ulcer. Ulcers may be classified according to their level of involvement.

- *Grade I* is redness and induration of the skin.
- *Grade II* is superficial breakdown of the dermis.
- *Grade III* extends through the entire subcutaneous tissue but not into the muscle.
- *Grade IV* involves deep ulceration that extends into muscle tissue and to underlying bone.
- *Grade V* results in widespread extension of the ulcer into adjacent body joints or cavities.

The best management for decubitus ulcer is prevention; however, this is not always possible. Given the very best level of care individuals can still develop decubitus ulcers. It particularly becomes a problem as the individual with spinal cord injury ages. Adequate seating systems and positioning in the chair with proper cushions are crucial in maintaining skin integrity and reducing the incidence of decubitus ulcers. In addition, adequate personal care attendants for hygiene and to assist in transfers and positionings are also necessary. Nutritional support is beneficial at reducing the risk of decubitus ulcers and at helping decubitus ulcers to heal.

Once decubitus ulcers have developed, a variety of treatments may be appropriate, including antibiotic ointments, debridement preparations, whirlpool treatments, and surgery. A scar is left in the area of a decubitus ulcer after healing and predisposes this area to further breakdown in the future. This complication can be a very expensive and time-consuming event. One model spinal cord injury treatment center reported that the average cost of treatment for decubitus where hospitalization was required was $63,000.

Infections are common complications that may be a direct result of skin breakdown, be it from virulent organisms transmitted to the patient by others via poor sterilization procedures or from common diseases. Review of the past medical records to determine the number of infections and the types of infections that the patient has suffered will serve as a useful guide for making projections about the future rates and types of infections the person is most likely to experience. In addition, the severity of the infections should be assessed to determine the level of care that will likely be required. For example, a patient who has had numerous infections with highly resistant organisms requiring hospitalizations and IV antibiotics is likely to continue to require that level of care.

Sexual Functioning: Spinal cord injury has a significant impact on sexual functioning in males and females. Sipski & Alexander (1992) reported that in males with UMN injuries, reflex erections are present in 70% to 90%. Ejaculation occurs in only 4% of these patients. In males with LMN lesions, approximately 20% achieve an erection, with 20% of these achieving ejaculation. Females with spinal cord injury have reported higher levels of reflex lubrication and psychogenic lubrication with 50% to 75% reporting orgasm.

Male fertility is impaired in spinal cord injury. Techniques such as vibratory stimulation and electroejaculation may be used to harvest sperm for artificial insemination. Success rates vary from center to center but may approach 50%. In general, it is felt that the earlier the sperm is harvested after spinal cord injury, the greater the likelihood of successful pregnancy. Repeated urinary tract infections and development of scar tissue in the male reproductive system reduces the viability of sperm as a function of time.

Spinal cord injured males may require assistive techniques for erectile dysfunctions such as prostaglandin penile injections, vacuum tumescence pumps, or penile implants. In general, penile implants are discouraged in the spinal cord injury population since they can lead to erosion and skin breakdown in the perineum. A newer treatment for erectile dysfunction is MUSE, an intraurethal suppository. An oral agent is in clinical trials and may be available in 1998.

In spinal cord injured females, half will not miss a menstrual cycle. Of those who have a delayed menses, all will begin normal menstruation within a three to six month period. The spinal cord injured female has no change in her fertility. Birth control becomes a major problem since the female is at high risk for development of deep vein thrombosis (DVT) and birth control pills are known to increase the risk of DVT. It is generally recommended that birth control pills not be utilized. The Norplant implant is not recommnended if there has been a preexisting history of DVT. Condom usage may be the method of choice for prevention of pregnancy in the spinal cord injured female.

Women with spinal cord injuries who become pregnant have a higher incidence of premature and low birth weight infants (Sipski & Alexander, 1992). In addition, females during the last trimester of pregnancy may experience more difficulty with urinary tract infections, decubitus ulcers, edema, autonomic dysreflexia, transfers, and self-care. Due to these complications, admission to the hospital during the thirty second week of pregnancy may be required. Breast-feeding in the tetraplegic female may be difficult due to positioning or due to its triggering autonomic dysreflexia. SCI mothers may require assistance with child rearing.

Individuals with spinal cord injury should have access to counseling regarding their sexuality and relationships with others. Counseling can provide sex education to assist the couple in resuming sexual activity and to teach alternate techniques for giving and receiving sexual pleasure with the presence of a spinal cord injury.

Anemia after spinal cord injury develops early. It was originally generally believed to represent only an acute incidence of blood loss and acute gastrointestinal problems. There are, however, individuals who continue to have ongoing difficulty with anemia that is clearly related to their injury. The exact etiology of the anemia remains elusive although there are reports that there is decreased erythropoietin produced at the kidneys. It is clear that persistent anemia is likely a multifactorial problem (Hirsch, Menard, & Anton, 1990).

There is evidence that individuals with spinal cord injuries experience a greater rate of **coronary artery disease** and **myocardial infarction**. When all other risk factors are controlled for, such as sex, age, family history, and lifestyle, the individual with a spinal cord injury is twice as likely to develop coronary artery disease as the able-bodied counterpart (Yehutil, 1989; Kesseler, 1986; Duckworth, 1983; Bauman, Razam, Spungen, & Machac, 1994). Schmitt has pointed out that the leading cause of death for persons with neurologically incomplete paraplegia is ischemic heart disease (Schmitt, Midha, & McKenzie, 1995).

Diabetes mellitus (adult onset) is clearly related to spinal cord injury. Several studies have well established the glucose intolerance of individuals with spinal cord injury. There may be a relative insulin resistance present. Other factors may also include the decreased ability of the spinal cord injury patient to exercise and maintain fitness and the tendency to gain weight due to decreased activity (Duckworth, 1983; Bauman & Spungen, 1984).

Cholelithiasis: Individuals with spinal cord injury have an increased risk and rate of development of gallstones. Reports have suggested an increased rate from three to eleven times more likely to develop gallstones than the able-bodied population. It is generally believed that this may be related to a relative stasis in the gastrointestinal tract and/or an overproduction of bile by the gallbladder (Apstein & Dalecki-Chipperfield, 1987; Stone, Nino-Murciam, Wolfe, & Perkash, 1990).

Peptic Ulcer Disease: There is an increased risk and rate of development of peptic ulcer disease connected with a spinal cord injury. Almost all acute spinal cord injured people will have gastritis or peptic ulcer disease (Epstein, 1981; Kewalramani, 1979).

Factors to Consider in Life Care Planning

A thorough and comprehensive review of the medical records from the acute care hospital stay and the initial rehabilitation stay should be performed to obtain the most accurate information available regarding the complications the patient has experienced that can have an impact on future medical needs. In addition, a thorough review of the most recent records from physical therapy and occupational therapy will provide valuable clues to the person's current functional status, equipment needs, and, occasionally, reveal complications. When reviewing the medical records, there are key items that should be searched for, since they can and do alter the future medical needs of the patient. In addition to the complications noted above, the list below is intended to be a partial list of important topics and issues to glean from records that can have an effect on life care plan entries.

Neurological Level

Knowing the neurological level of the patient is crucial as a starting point to determine future medical needs. Therefore, careful review of the records should be performed to determine the exact neurological level and completeness of the spinal cord injury. If this cannot be determined from the records, then the life care planner must obtain an accurate neurological level from a knowledgeable physician. In addition, knowing and describing accurately the neurological level of the patient serves as a baseline in the event that there is a change in the person's neurological status so that it can easily be determined by the caregivers.

Comorbidities

Comorbidities and other medical complications and problems of the patients are extremely important and can impact upon the life care plan. Such complications as coronary artery disease, peripheral vascular disease, preexisting renal disease, chronic obstructive lung disease, or diabetes mellitus have a significant interplay with the effects of spinal cord injury. Preexisting conditions can become much worse when combined with spinal cord injury and dictate that a higher level of care be provided. Some conditions, although not related to the traumatic spinal cord injury, are seriously complicated by the traumatic spinal cord injury and therefore mandate that the life care plan provide a higher level of care as a result of the spinal cord injury. For example, the insulin-dependent diabetic who becomes tetraplegic requires an increased level of attendant care in part to monitor blood sugar and give insulin injections, even though diabetes is not directly related to the spinal cord injury.

Preexisting disabilities combined with spinal cord injury can have a synergistic effect and require higher levels of care than would be required by the presence of either disability alone. For example, the blind individual who becomes paraplegic will require a much higher level of attendant care than the average paraplegic.

Functional Independent Measures (FIM)

FIM scores are used to communicate the level of independence of the patient in many areas. The scale ranges from a Level 7, fully independent, to a Level 1, which requires total assistance. The rehabilitation record will reflect FIM scores in several areas, including dressing, bathing, grooming, transfers, medications, bowel and bladder, and mobility. If the FIM score is 5 or less in any category, then attendant care is needed to assist the patient in that area. While FIM scores are not the only way to determine what personal care services are needed by the individual, they are an excellent way to establish a baseline and provide objective documentation of the need.

Equipment

Review of the records can also determine in part what equipment needs the patient has and what equipment needs have been met at that point. It is not necessary to recommend the exact same type and style of equipment that was recommended by the hospital, but it is important to review what has been provided to the patient and when it was provided prior to making any future recommendations.

Psychological and Social Adjustment

The rehabilitation and acute care record should provide information on family support and the patient's psychological adjustment to the disability. Patients who cope poorly or fail to complete initial rehabilitation are at much higher risk for experiencing complications and problems and will require a more intensive level of service in the life care plan. In addition, identifying social activities that were important to the patient prior to the spinal cord injury and establishing alternative ways to participate in these activities for the newly injured person is an important goal of a life care plan.

Future Needs

Functional Outcomes

The functional status of the patient is crucial in projecting future equipment needs and, specifically, personal care attendant (PCA) needs. Careful consideration to the needs of a patient must be given and every attempt made to accurately represent the number of personal care attendant hours that are required. PCA needs can represent the single most expensive part of the plan for higher-level injuries. For example, ventilator-dependent tetraplegics require 24-hour awake care. If PCA services are purchased through an agency, at least licensed practical nurse (LPN) level care will be provided. In many cases, there are no LPNs trained in ventilator care, in which case an RN will be required (check with the agency within each state with regard to their policies on this topic). At the other extreme, a lower-level paraplegic may be self-sufficient with a few hours of homemaker services. Underrepresentation of attendant care needs will result in the patient not having adequate services to maintain them throughout their lifetime and will likely lead to a higher rate of complications and hospitalization, and in extreme cases can reduce life expectancy. Overestimating the PCA needs will result in an inaccurate, unjustifiable, and more expensive plan that is unfair to all parties involved.

There are a number of tables that can be used to provide a starting point on what a person's functional level is anticipated to be given their neurological level of spinal cord injury. There are several very comprehensive tables that are available, including those published in Blackwell, Weed, & Powers (1994), Staas, Formal, & Gershkof (1993), and Braddom (1995).

The above references and tables are intended to serve as a guide only in making projections about the types of support an individual will need. There are patients who will function with less care and others who will require much greater care, given their unique set of circumstances, and each person must be evaluated individually. Failure of a patient to meet the projected level of independence does not necessarily mean the patient is not trying, is poorly motivated, or is malingering.

The tables referred to above are general starting points. However, there are specific areas in each of these tables that these authors have serious disagreements with and we do not, by noting them here, suggest that we agree wholeheartedly with the recommendations in these publications.

Psychological and Vocational Rehabilitation Issues

Adjustment to disability and community reintegration are crucial factors that have an effect on quality of life and longevity. Sufficient attention must be provided in this area in the life care plan to ensure that an adequate adjustment to disability is achieved by the patient, and that they can reassume a functional role in their community.

Vocational goals should be assessed when appropriate and require the expertise of a vocational counselor who is knowledgeable in spinal cord injury. Rehabilitation engineering or assistive technology may be very useful to the spinal cord injured patient's successful return to productivity.* Recreational activities have an important impact not only on the patient but on their family as well. Attempts should be made to assess the person's important preincident recreational activities and to reintegrate into these activities to the extent possible and appropriate given their injury level. For example, an outdoor enthusiast who hunted frequently may be accommodated with an all-terrain vehicle and appropriate hunting-assisted devices. Some activities may have specific benefits. For example, a tetraplegic may exercise the pulmonary system with blow darts.

As previously noted, sexual adjustment and marital relationship issues must be considered in the life care plan. Appropriate counseling should be provided to both the individual with the spinal cord injury and the spouse or significant other. This may require consideration for family adjustment, which is frequently an issue after spinal cord injury. All members of the family, including the children, have suffered losses and may need to have available some level of support and counseling to assist with their readjustment.

The life care plan must ensure that the patient's highest functional level is achieved and maintained throughout their lifetime. The support services that are provided have the major impact in this area. The patient should have adequate access to individuals who can assist in improving and maintaining strength, endurance, and range of motion. They should be given the opportunity to learn advanced wheelchair skills and improved community mobility. Equipment should be provided to allow the individual to maintain an active exercise program. Higher-level spinal cord injured who are unable to voluntarily move the muscles may be appropriate for functional electrical stimulation units to perform this activity for them.**

Various durable medical equipment will be required, although the amount and style depends on the level of injury, funding available, and the competence of the patient. A life care plan should address wheelchair needs, home and ramp modifications, environmental control systems, equipment maintenance, security systems, transportation needs, cellular phones, and other appropriate equipment.

Medical Follow-Up

The spinal cord injured patient will require physician evaluations and treatment. The required physician specialties and evaluations will depend on the patient's

---

* A resource for accommodations is the Center for Rehabilitation Technology, Georgia Institute of Technology, Atlanta, Georgia, 800/726-9119

** As a resource for functional electrical stimulation programs, contact FES Information Center, 11000 Cedar Avenue, Cleveland, OH 44106-3052, *http://www.fes.cwru.edu*, 216-231-3257

level of injury and unique situation. In general, every spinal cord injured person should have a physiatrist if one is available in the local community. Additional physicians that often are required will include urology, internal medicine, neurosurgery, orthopedist, pulmonary medicine, podiatry, and plastic surgery. Laboratory evaluations will include complete blood counts (CBCs), sequential multiple analysis (SMAs), urinalysis (UAs), urine cultures and sensitivities, renal ultrasounds, intravenous pylograms (IVPs), electrocardiograms (EKGs), X-rays, and magnetic resonance imaging (MRIs).

In most cases physical therapy and occupational therapy evaluations will be required. Additional support services may include respiratory therapy, particularly with a higher-level injury. Annual or semiannual spinal cord injury evaluations by a team of experts should be provided in order to reassess the patient's functional status, evaluate medication needs, train new caregivers, introduce new equipment and technology to the patient, reduce the likelihood of complications, and improve the level of overall care provided to the patient. These evaluations can be provided in a specialty spinal cord treatment center or by a local team that is particularly knowledgeable and expert in providing these services.

Transportation

Transportation to medical appointments, work, recreation, or shopping can be a significant issue for patients with spinal cord injuries. Lower-level paraplegics may do well with an automobile and hand controls initially. A Braun car topper may be adequate for wheelchair storage or a patient may be able to store the wheelchair behind the driver's seat. Tetraplegics or aging paraplegics may require an accessible van with a wheelchair lift. In general, parking should be covered since protection from the elements is important. Some vans are designed to fit into a standard garage. However, most have a raised roof that may prevent the use of standard carports or garages.

Supplies/Medications

As the life care planner probably expects, supplies can be a major part of the life care plan. Catheters and bladder management related materials, chux, bowel program supplies, skin care products, dilitation sticks, latex gloves, sanitation supplies, etc., will be required. A strategy to assess this need is to obtain a list of suppliers and request a printout of the products obtained over the past six months. This list will usually provide a complete picture, including amount, size, usage, and cost. Often lists of medications from the pharmacist will reveal forgotten complications that should be considered in the life care plan. The plan should include provisions for changes for additional supplies in the future.

Vocational Considerations

Many individuals with a spinal cord injury will be able to enter the labor market (Devivo, Whiteneck, & Charles, 1995; Krause & Anson, 1996; Krause 1996). The number one factor for successful employment is amount of education. As one may expect, the higher the education level, the more likely the spinal cord injured is able to find employment (Kause & Anson, 1996; Krause 1996). Other influences include level of injury, with paraplegics more likely to be employed than tetraplegics. Race also seems to play a role, with Caucasians finding employment more often than minorities. With regard to race, it is interesting to note that current research reports that minority women are more likely to be employed than minority men, but Caucasian men are more likely to be employed than Caucasian women (Krause & Anson, 1996). With regard to age spinal cord injured people in the age group of 41–50 were more likely to be employed than cohorts who were younger or older. One study reports that people working at the time of their injury had a better chance of finding employment than people who were not working (Devivo, Whiteneck, & Charles, 1995). Of interest, only 74% of the participants in one study were working at the time of their injury (Krause & Anson, 1996). Their employment rate was 25% at the time of the study. However, even if they were not currently working, 42% of Caucasians and 23% of minorities reported working at some point since their injury. It is also noted that it may take several years to adequately recover from their injury and obtain employment skills. The employment rate continued to rise for more than eight years post-injury. Krause also notes that clients who are socially active have a better chance of employment (Krause, 1996).

Earning capacity is another related issue. Even though the client may be employed, they may not be working full-time. In addition, their ability to choose jobs, ascend up the promotion ladder, and otherwise maximize their earning potential is likely compromised. Berkowitz reported that the average annual loss of earnings and benefits for people ages 18–64 were $25,097 per year (adjusted to 1992 dollars) (Devivo, Whiteneck, & Charles, 1995).

The life care plan should address the costs for assisting clients with preparing for employment if this work is a reasonable option. Potential costs could include:

- Tuition and fees
- Books and supplies
- Computer technology designed to reduce physical effort (such as IBM voice type, Dragon Dictate, Kurzweil, Voice Master, smaller keyboards, keyboard panel, head points, etc.)
- Work stations (such as AbleOffice produced by the Center for Rehabilitation Technology, Georgia Institute of Technology, Atlanta, Georgia)
- Vocational evaluation, vocational counseling, job placement assistance, job coaching, and related costs

Many life care planners are not vocational experts and may easily overlook or fail to include costs for this important quality-of-life issue. It is suggested that the life care planner include a vocational expert as a part of the team.

Aging with Spinal Cord Injury

Numerous changes occur as an individual ages, and people with spinal cord injury are no exception. In fact, there is evidence that the spinal cord injured tend to "age faster" or experience some of the changes commonly associated with aging earlier. This phenomenon is both a function of the absolute age of the individual and the number of years the individual has had the disability. As a result, the patient has changing needs throughout the course of their lifetime. The life care plan should reflect this change in needs by incorporating appropriate services and equipment to meet the anticipated need as the individual ages. For example, it can be anticipated that an individual who has had a spinal cord injury for 20 to 25 years and has been using a manual wheelchair will have more difficulty with upper extremity pain and complications and may consider switching to a power wheelchair. Similarly, the patient may have more difficulty with transfers and self-care needs and require a higher level of attendant care.

For research regarding aging and spinal cord injury, excellent sources include Menter (1995), Stover (1995), Whiteneck, Mentor, Charlifue, et al. (1991), and Yarkony, Roth, Heinemann, et al. (1988). Menter has described general physiological changes that occur with aging, such as:

- Loss of muscle mass
- Decreased strength
- Decreased range of motion
- Increasing osteoarthritis
- Increasing problems with urinary and bowel management

These aging related risks combined together can lead to increased pain and decreased functional status. When these effects occur in the spinal cord injured, they are additive and accelerate the decline of the person's functional status. Menter's model of aging predicts a functional decline that will begin between 15 and 20 years post-injury for the average spinal cord injured patient. Some of the specific problems associated with aging include:

1. Pain has been reported to occur in over 90% of individuals with a spinal cord injury (Melzack, 1978). There are several types of pain that can increase with time. One is musculoskeletal pain from overuse of the upper extremities, osteoarthritic changes, and other causes. Two is a central pain from the spinal cord injury that is usually described as a burning dysesthetic type pain that has been reported to increase with aging. A neurological pain can develop due to poor posture, arthritic changes at the spinal column, or peripheral nerve entrapments that will further deteriorate the patient's functional status. Woozly & Young (1995) have reported pain is frequently a major lifelong management issue in patients with traumatic myelopathy. Potential sources of the pain include bones, ligaments, spinal meninges, cauda equina, and the spinal cord itself (Schmitt, Midha, & Mckenzie, 1995). Local pain at the level of the spinal cord injury may be addressed with surgical procedures even after having been present for a number of years (Bohlman, Kirkpatrick, Delamarter, et al., 1994). Pain control techniques such as physical therapy, transcutaneous electrical stimulation (TENS) unit, electrical stimulation, and whirlpool therapy should be considered. In some cases, the individual may require an inpatient pain management program.
2. Spasticity has been reported to increase with time and can become quite problematic and difficult to control. As an individual ages, they may no longer tolerate the medications to treat the spasticity and require the

placement of an intrathecal Baclofen pump. Spasticity may require additional physical therapy, whirlpool treatments, or electrical stimulation to control.

3. Because as a person ages, they have a decline in strength and increasing weakness, it is not surprising that fatigue has been reported as one of the most common problems affecting lifestyle and quality of life and is a difficult problem to treat. Fatigue can best be addressed by providing more assistive equipment reducing the level of activity or providing additional personal care services.
4. There is mounting evidence that there are physiological and hormonal changes in the spinal cord injured population that contribute to aging at a faster rate than the "abled" population. Tsitouras and colleagues have documented abnormally low levels of serum testosterone, growth hormone, and insulin-like growth factors in individuals with spinal cord injuries that predisposes the individual to age-related changes (Tsitouras, Zhong, Spungen, & Bauman, 1995). Over time there is little doubt that other changes will be discovered that correlate with Menter's theory that the spinal cord injured person ages at a faster rate.

Spinal Cord Injury and Life Expectancy

A common question asked of the physician is related to the effect of the injury on life expectancy. Although treatment for complications have improved dramatically over time, available statistics continue to reflect a reduced life expectancy. However, life expectancy is clearly improving as care improves and complications are effectively managed. In general, research demonstrates that the higher the injury, the more the loss. For example, a 40-year-old male tetraplegic who is ventilator dependent will statistically die sooner than a similar tetraplegic who is not on a ventilator, and a 40-year-old male paraplegic will statistically have a longer life expectancy than both tetraplegic patients noted above. For generalized information based on research by Devivo and Stover (1989).

General Considerations

It is difficult to rely on statistics for specific clients since many elements can effect longevity. There are several factors to consider including such general issues as:

- Diagnosis: The type and level of injury has the most obvious impact.
- Intelligence: The ability to comprehend and participate in the management of their injury directly affects quality of care. A severely retarded or brain-injured patient with a spinal cord injury is less able to assist in their care or recognize complications than someone who is cognitively unimpaired.
- Education: This probably is related to intelligence and refers to understanding the educational value of learning about their situation to prevent complications or accommodate to the disability.
- Quality of care: Poor quality of care can lead to unobserved complications that can be life threatening. Good medical follow-up can intervene in complications before they become expensive or life threatening.

- Compliance: Compliance in medicine is a well-known problem. For example, a poor weight shift schedule can lead to serious and expensive skin breakdown care.
- Personality and/or psychological state: Also related to compliance is the person's ability to train and "get along" with caregivers. Good and assertive communicators are better able to convey their needs than shy, ineffective patients. Also, clients with a poor psychological adjustment may be harmful to themselves.
- Family support: Another well-known and researched attribute is the client's family support system. Overall, the better the support, the better the recovery and adjustment.
- Home vs. Institution: The client's place of residence can have an effect by subjecting the patient to virulent diseases if they are in a nursing home. Also, staff who work for the facility are often less responsive to patients than staff whose paychecks come directly from the client. In addition, staff who work for a facility may have several patients to manage, whereas clients at home usually are the attendant's only responsibility.

Risk Factors

As with the general population there are risk factors that the physician must consider when opining about the patient's life expectancy.

- Age: As noted above, aging leaves patients with reduced ability to rebound from illness and complications.
- Sex: Males generally are expected to have a shorter life span.
- History of complications: Some patients have a history of problems that can be serious with regard to life expectancy. Upper respiratory infections, skin breakdown, serious spasticity are just a few examples.
- Diseases: As noted previously, patients with diabetes pose greater problems than patients without this disease. Preexisting cancer, cardiovascular disease, or other diseases may be a factor.
- Smoking: Smoking is a well-known life-reducing activity. Tetraplegics with already impaired respiration may be at even more risk.
- Substance abuse: Alcoholism or drug addiction can significantly affect the patient's basic physical well-being as well as detrimentally affect their judgment. For example, one patient who became a paraplegic from an automobile accident after drinking was rendered a tetraplegic when he had another motor vehicle accident after drinking.
- Good or bad genetics: Family history has been linked to longevity.

In summary, to project the patient's life expectancy, the life care planner should consult a physician with regard to this topic in order to consider the individual's factors. A strong caution must be given on attempting to apply generalized statistics to a specific person with a spinal cord injury. Deutsch & Sawyer (1996) have an excellent discussion on the problems of "mindless use of data." The available information must be reviewed and interpreted by a physician experienced and knowledgeable in the field of spinal cord injury. Currently available data, in all likelihood, underrepresents true life expectancy of spinal cord inured individuals.

In patients who appear to have higher risk factors for shortened life expectancy, the life care planner should make fair and reasonable attempts to provide a level of care in the plan to reduce the risk to the extent possible.

CONCLUSION

Spinal cord injury represents a complex array of medical challenges to the life care planner. Fortunately, enough research exists to effectively plan for the patient's needs with regard to care, products, supplies, and equipment. A detailed analysis of the patient's situation, review of medical records, and knowledge of the available literature, as well as the participation of a qualified physician will assist the life care planner with a quality and effective road map of care that will enhance the patient's life.

REFERENCES

American Spinal Injury Association/International Medical Society of Paraplegia. (1992). **International Standards for Neurological and Functional Classification of Spinal Cord Injury** (rev. ed.). Chicago: American Spinal Injury Association

Apstein M. & Dalecki-Chipperfield, K. (1987). Spinal cord injury is a risk factor for gallstone disease. **Gastroenterology, 92**, 666-668.

Asher, R. (December 1947). On dangers of going to bed. **British Medical Journal, 13**, 967-968.

Bauman W.A., Razam, M., Spungen A.M., & Machac J. (September 1994). Cardiac stress testing with thallium-201 imaging reveals silent ischemia in individuals with paraplegia. **Archives of Physical Medicine and Rehabilitation, 75**(9), 946-950.

Bauman W.A. & Spungen A.M. (1994). Disorders of carbohydrate and lipid metabolism in veterans with paraplegia or quadriplegia: A model for premature aging. **Metabolism, 43** (6), 749-756.

Blackwell T., Weed R., & Powers A. (1994). **Life Care Planning for Spinal Cord Injury**. Athens, GA: Elliott and Fitzpatrick.

Bohlman H.H., Kirkpatrick, J.S., Delamarter R.B., et al. (1994). Anterior decompression for late pain and paralysis following fractures of the thoracal lumbar spine. **Clinical Orthopedics, 300**, 24-29.

Bors, E., Conrad C.A., & Massell T.B. (1954). Venous occlusion of the lower extremities in paraplegic patients. **Surgery, Gynecology and Obstetrics, 99,** 451-454.

Braddom, L.R. (Ed.). (1995). **Physical Medicine and Rehabilitation**. Philadelphia: W.B. Saunders.

Braun S.R., Giovannoni R., Levin A.B., et al. (1982). Oxygen saturation during sleep in patients with SCI. **American Journal of Physical Medicine, 61**, 302-309.

Cardenas D.D. (November 1992). Neurogenic bladder evaluation and management. **Physical Medicine & Rehabilitation Clinics of North America, Traumatic Spinal Cord Injury. 3**, 4.

Davidoff G., Werner R., & Waring W. (1991). Compressive mononeuropathies and chronic paraplegia. **Paraplegia 29**, 17-24.

Deutsch, P. & Sawyer, H. (1996). **Guide to Rehabilitation**. White Plains, NY: Ahab Press.

Devivo M. (1989). Causes of death in spinal cord injury. **Archives of Internal Medicine, 149,** 1761-1766.

Devivo, M., Whiteneck, G., & Charles, E. (1995). The economic impact of spinal cord injury. In S. Stover, J. DeLisa, & G. Whiteneck (Eds.). **Spinal Cord Injury Clinical Outcomes from the Model Systems,** 234-288. Gaithersburg, MD: Aspen.

Drory, L.N. (1990). Coronary artery disease. **Archives of Physical Medicine & Rehabilitation, 71**, 389-392.

Duckworth, W.C. (1983). Glucose intolerance in spinal injury. **Archives of Physical Medicine & Rehabilitation, 64**, 107-110.

Duckworth W.C., Jallepalli P., & Solomon S.S. (1983). Glucose intolerance in spinal cord injury. **Archives of Physical Medicine & Rehabilitation, 64**, 107-110.

Epstein, N. (1981). GI bleeds in Spinal Cord Injury. **Journal of Neurosurgery, 54**, 16.

Formal, C. (November 1992). Metabolic and neurological changes after spinal cord injury. **Physical Medicine & Rehabilitation Clinics of North America, Traumatic Spinal Cord Injury. 3**(4), 1002.

Gibson C.J. (1992). Overview of spinal cord injury**. Physical Medicine and Rehabilitation Clinics of North America, 3,** 699-709.

Go, B., Devivo, M., & Richards, J. (1995). The epidemiology of spinal cord injury. In S. L. Stover, J. A. DeLisa, & G. G. Whiteneck (Eds.) **Spinal Cord Injury Clinical Outcomes from the Model Systems**. Gaithersburg, MD: Aspen.

Gore R., Mintzer R., & Calenoff L. (1991). Gastrointestinal complications of spinal cord injury, **Spine, 6**(6), 538–544.

Griffin M. R., Opitz J. L., Kurland L. T., et al. (1985). Traumatic spinal cord injury in Omstead County, Minnesota, 1935 through 1981. **American Journal of Epidemiology, 121**, 884.

Hirsch, G.N., Menard, M.R., & Anton, H.A. (1990). Anemia after Spinal Cord Injury. **Archives of Physical Medicine & Rehabilitation, 71**, 3-7.

Jackson A.B. & Groomes T.E. (1991). Incidents of respiratory complications following spinal cord injury. **Journal of American Paraplegia Society, 14**, 87.

Kennedy, E. (1986). **Spinal Cord Injury: Facts and Figures**. Birmingham, AL: University of Alabama.

Kesseler, B.I. (1986). Coronary artery disease in spinal cord injury. **The American Journal of Cardiology,**

Kewalramani, L.S. (1979). Neurogenic ulcers in spinal cord injury**. Journal of Trauma, 19**, 259-265.

Krause, J. (1996). Employment after spinal cord injury: Transition and life adjustment. **Rehabilitation Counseling Bulletin, 38**(4), 244-255.

Krause, J. & Anson, C. (1996). Employment after spinal cord injury: Relation to selected participant charaterisitcs. **Archives of Physical Medicine and Rehabilitation, 77** (8), 737-743

Krause, J. F., Frantice, P.T., Riggins R. S., et al. (1975). Incidence of spinal cord lesion. **Journal of Chronic Disease, 28**, 471.

Lanis I. & Lammertse D., (November 1992). The respiratory system and spinal cord injury. **Physical Medicine & Rehabilitation Clinics of North America, 34**, 725-740.

Lawrence D. W., Bayakly A.R., & Mathison J.B. (1992). Traumatic spinal cord injury in Louisiana: 1990. **Annual Report**. New Orleans, LA: Louisiana Office of Public Health.

Lee, B. (1991). Management of peripheral vascular disease in the spinal cord injured patient. **The Spinal Cord Injured Patient Comprehensive Management** Philadelphia: W.B. Saunders.

Melzack, R. (1978). Pain and spinal cord injury. **Pain, 4,** 195-210.

Menter R. (1995). The effects of age at injury and on aging and the aging process. **Spinal Cord Injury Clinical Outcomes From the Model Systems**. Gaithersburg, MD: Aspen.

Pentland, W.E. & Twoney, L.T. (1991). The weight bearing extremity in women with long term paraplegia. **Paraplegia, 29** (8), 521.

Roth, E.J., Lovell N.L., Heinemann A.W. et al. (1992). The older adult with a spinal cord injury. **Paraplegia, 30**, 520 -526.

Schmitt J., Midha M., & McKenzie, N. (1995). **Diagnosis and Management of Disorders of the Spinal Cord**. Philadelphia: W.B. Saunders.

Schoenen, J. (1991). Clinical anatomy of the spinal cord. In Robert M. Woozly and Robert R. Young (Eds). **Disorders of the Spinal Cord, Neurological Clinics, 9**(3), Philadelphia: W.B. Saunders.

Sipski M.L. & Alexander C.J. (November 1992). Sexual function and dysfunction after spinal cord injury. **Physical Medicine and Rehabilitation Clinics of North America, 34**, 811-828.

Staas, W., Jr., Christopher, S., Formal, A.M., & Gershkof, G. (1993). **Rehabilitation Medicines, Principles and Practice**, (2nd ed.) Philadelphia: J.B. Lippincott.

Stone J.M., Nino-Murciam, Wolfe V.A & Perkash I. (1990). Chronic GI problems in spinal cord injury. **American Journal of Gastroenterology, 85**(9), 1114-1119.

Stover, S. (1995). **Spinal Cord Injury, Clinical Outcomes of Model Systems**. Gaithersburg, MD: Aspen.

Tsitouras, P.D., Zhong, Y.G., Spungen, A.M. & Bauman, W.A. (1995). Hormone levels in patients with spinal cord injury. **Hormone and Metabolic Research, 27**, 287-292.

Waring, W.P. & Karunas, R.S. (1991). Acute spinal cord injuries and the incidence of clinically occurring thromboembolic disease. **Paraplegia, 29**, 8-16.

Whiteneck, G., Menter, R., Charlifue, S., et al., (1991). Impairment, disability, handicap, and medical expenses of persons aging with spinal cord injury. **Paraplegia, 29**, 613-619.

Winkler, T. (1997). Spinal cord injury and life care planning. In P. Deutsch & H. Sawyer (Eds.). **A Guide to Rehabilitation**, White Plains, NY: Ahab Press.

Woozly, R.M. & Young, R.R. (1995). **Diagnosis and Management of Disorders of the Spinal Cord.** Philadelphia: W.B. Saunders.

Wyngaarden, J.B. & Smith, L.H. (1988). **Cecil's Textbook of Medicine** (18th ed.). pp. 384-387, Philadelphia: W.B. Saunders.

Yarkony G.N. (1996). Rehabilitation of patients with spinal cord injury. In Randall L. Braddom (Ed.). **Physical Medicine & Rehabilitation**. Philadelphia: W.B. Saunders.

Yarkony G.N., Roth E.J., Heinemann A.W., et al. (1988). Spinal cord injury in rehabilitation outcome: The impact of aging. **Journal of Clinical Epidemiology 41,** 173-177.

Yehutil, Y. (1989). Prevalence of heart disease in spinal cord injury. **Paraplegia, 27**, 58-62.

Zigler, J. & Field, B. (1992). Surgical procedures for spinal cord injury. **Physical Medicine & Rehabilitation Clinics of North America. 3(4)**.

18

LIFE CARE PLANNING FOR TRANSPLANTATION PATIENTS

Gloria Lane & Roger O. Weed

INTRODUCTION

Transplantation involves the transfer of living tissues or cells from one person to another with the intention of continuing the functional integrity of the transferred tissue in the receiver (Russell, 1997). According to data from the United Network for Organ Sharing (UNOS, 1997) 19,145 transplants were performed in 1995. The most common transplant was kidney (10,892), with liver second (3,925), heart third (2,361), kidney-pancreas fourth (918), lung fifth (871), pancreas sixth (110), and heart-lung the seventh most common (68). However, there were more than 50,000 people on waiting lists. As of 1997, 281 transplant centers were listed. The most common transplant center was for kidney (255) followed by heart (164), pancreas (124), liver (121), heart-lung (99), and lung (94). A few smaller programs are available for pancreas (18) and intestine (29). (The numbers add up to more than 281 because some perform more than one kind of transplant.)

The greatest challenge for the successful transplantation continues to be the rejection reaction, which destroys the tissue shortly after the transplant (Brinker, 1996).

Transplants are categorized according to the site of the transplant:

1. Orthotopic is a tissue or organ graft transferred to an anatomically normal site; an example is a liver transplant.
2. Heterotopic is a transplant to an anatomically abnormal site; an example is a kidney into the iliac fossa of the recipient.

There are four types of transplants currently performed and they are categorized according to the genetic relationship between the donor and recipient (Roche, 1994).

1. Allograft — graft between genetically different member of the same species, the most common type.
2. Autograft — tissue from one location to another in the same individual for events such as skin grafting due to burns.
3. Isograft — tissue between identical twins such as a kidney transplant.

1-57444-075-6/99/$0.00+$.50

4. Heterograft — (xenograft) graft between members of different species such as a baboons heart to a human.

Typical transplants are allografts from living relatives or cadaveric donors. The living related donor (LRD) is becoming more common as immunosuppressants and technology improve. Due to the need for organs and the urgent supply problem the availability of an LRD should always be a consideration in the life care plan. It appears that seat belt laws and the AIDS epidemic have reduced the number of potential donors. A person of normal health can be an LRD and there usually is no cost associated with being a *donor* (National Kidney Foundation of Georgia, 1997). Cost for transplants (see below) can be an enormous burden if the patient does not have access to insurance. Live donors have been used for heart, lung, liver, kidney, pancreas, and bone marrow transplants. Live donors for heart and lung transplant can be used when an individual receives a heart-lung transplant and then donates their own healthy heart or lung to another transplant recipient (Haubolt, 1996).

Transplantable Organs

The human tissue and organs presently considered for transplantation are heart, lung, heart/lung, kidney, simultaneous kidney/pancreas, liver, and small intestines (Russell, 1987; Young, Frost, & Short, 1996). All of these transplants require a lifetime of immunosuppressant therapy and could necessitate a life care plan to adequately assess the future care costs.

Tissues that are transplantable but do not require long-term immunosuppressive drugs include bone, corneas, and skin. These transplants would probably not on their own necessitate a life care plan since long-term care, and therefore costs, should be negligible.

Potential transplant patients include people with:

- Hematological cancers
- High-dose chemotherapy with bone marrow transplant (BMT) may be a treatment for breast cancer, neuroblastoma, ovarian cancer, germ cell tumors, multiple myeloma, leukemias, and congenital agranulocytosis
- Congenital metabolic disorders
- Immunologic disorders
- Solid tumors
- End-stage organ failure
- Congenital abnormalities
- Aplastic anemia

Common Contraindications for Transplant

Although many patients may be in need of a "new" organ, there are occasions when the transplant is not appropriate. Examples are:

- Prior history of poor medical compliance
- Active infection
- Unstable psychosocial profile

- Over 50 years of age for heart (Roche, 1994) or over 60 years of age (generally) for other
- Peptic ulcer disease
- Systemic inflammatory diseases
- Severe osteoporosis
- Active diverticulosis/diverticulitis
- Acute pulmonary embolism with infarction
- Irreversible pulmonary hypertension
- Positive for HIV and/or hepatitis B
- Body weight more than 15% of ideal
- Severe peripheral and cerebral vascular obstructive disease
- Presence of metastatic disease (except for bone marrow transplants)
- Various organ specific contraindications

While this is not an exhaustive list, as technology and medications advance the contraindications will continue to change and many of these guideline will become more flexible.

Transplant Centers

To develop a credible transplant life care plan, it is preferable to have a transplant center designated prior to preparing the life care plan. As noted above, at the time of this writing there were 281 centers listed with UNOS. As one may expect, medical outcome and cost may vary significantly between transplant centers. When a client is registered with a *Center of Excellence* transplant program, the likelihood of optimum results increases with the total transplant process. Distinct qualities of a *Center of Excellence* include:

1. Established protocols for the selection of potential patients.
2. Active participation with procedures established for the distribution of transplant organs by United Network of Organ Sharing.
3. Board certified, experienced physicians.
4. The length of time the present transplant team has been together (has the head of the team recently changed?)
5. The center has at least five years transplant-specific experience.
6. The quantity of transplants is of adequate numbers to be considered expert.
7. A reliable, but not primary, guide of quality for a facility is the approval by Medicare for the transplant program.
8. The facility should have adequate support services available, including social services, discharge planning, blood bank, physical therapy.
9. There should be evidence of ongoing evaluation of the transplant program and also the sharing of their outcomes.

Pretransplant Issues

Before receiving a transplant the patient will be expected to accomplish certain tasks and responsibilities. The facility-based transplant coordinator will be extremely helpful in the extensive work-up prior to the acceptance of the patient into the transplant program. There are numerous medical evaluations, in addition to psychological and social evaluations. There may be a prolonged hospital stay prior to the transplant depending on the medical deterioration of the patient prior to acquisition of the appropriate organ. Consideration should also be given to housing costs at the transplant center location, of the patient and/or family, if the patient lives out of the transplant center vicinity.

Transportation costs will need to be considered, particularly if airline travel is required, for pretransplant check-ups prior to relocation to the transplant center vicinity. Transportation costs should also be included for the caregiver. The patient will need support physically and emotionally.

The transplant procedure and acute follow-up may require an extensive hospital stay. The average length of hospital stay is *organ*-specific. The possibility of a complication, which can dramatically affect their stay, should always be considered. However, the facility transplant coordinator may be able to give a *patient*-specific estimate regarding potential complications particularly after the medical work-up is completed. Frequently the transplant coordinator will be able to give a projected, reasonably accurate, estimate of the length of time the patient will be on the waiting list after approval for transplant. This estimate is very helpful in determining the pretransplant costs.

If an LRD is used, there will also be an extensive work-up on them. Initially the use of an LRD is typically more costly than a cadaveric donor; however, the rate of rejection is lower in the LRD, thus causing overall costs to be lower. Psychological considerations should be given to the LRD, especially in the event of a post-transplant organ failure, rejection, or adverse complications by the recipient. This may be especially true if the donor is a family member.

Post-Transplant Issues

Following the transplant, frequent (one to three visits per week) physician office visits in the immediate hospital discharge period will be required. Home care visits should be considered, especially for bone marrow transplant recipients. Follow-up organ biopsies, the best indicator for determining rejection, will often be expected at regular intervals (frequency of organ biopsy is transplant center specific.). The patient will be expected to reside in the transplant center vicinity for approximately three months post-transplant. The patient can expect immunosuppressant therapy for the remainder of his or her life. It should be noted that the immunosuppressant therapy may differ widely between centers of excellence. In addition, a physical reconditioning program should be initiated in the hospital and continue post-transplant. Should rejection reaction occur, the following should be considered (Evans, 1993):

1. Rehospitalization
2. Anti-rejection rescue therapy
3. Loss of graft (organ) with retransplantation
   - retransplantation is more costly than the original transplant
   - retransplant recipients report a lower quality of life

Long-term general implications for the life care plan for most transplantation patients include provision for physician follow-up visits, which may include transportation expenses and attendant care for children, costs of drugs and medications, and planning for expected complications such as rejection or side effects to the medications (see below). In many cases a need for counseling the individual and/or family is appropriate. In addition, a case manager knowledgeable in transplantation is a valuable resource for encouraging compliance and trouble-shooting various problems.

Complications Unique to Transplantation

Due to the unique nature of an organ transplant, one should be vigilant for complications. In most cases some degree of rejection will be observed and, left untreated, can lead to organ failure. Common examples include:

- Infection, particularly CMV (cytomegalovirus)
- Graft rejection/graft failure
- Chronic rejection
- Lipid abnormalities
- Hypertension
- Complications of immune suppression
  1. Acute bacterial infection
  2. Infectious mononucleosis
  3. Severe mycobacterium or fungal disease
  4. Development of malignancies
  5. Recurrence of malignancies
  6. Sarcoidosis
  7. Neutropenia
  8. Hypocalcemia
  9. Renal failure
- Death

Various situations listed above may require retransplantation.

In order to control the rejection process, medications are used to suppress the immune system. Examples are:

- Azathiopine (Imuran)
- Cyclosporine (Sandimmune)
- Antithymocyte globulin (ATG or ATGAM)
- Muromonab-CD3 or OKT-3 (Orthoclone)
- Tacrolimus or FK-506 (Prograf)

These medications are glucocorticoid steroids that work by decreasing circulating lymphocytes; inhibiting Il-1, a cytokine responsible for T-cell proliferation; and inhibiting complications associated with the use of drugs. Since immunosuppressed patients lack common responses to infection, such as fever and inflammation, it is

Table 18.1 Summary of Estimated Charges per Human Organ/Tissue Transplantation (1996 Dollars)

Organ/Tissue	*First Year Charge*	*Estimated Annual Follow-up Charge**	*Estimated Total Charge for First Five Years Adjusted for Survival**
Heart	$253,200	$21,200	$316,600
Liver	314,500	29,100	393,900
Kidney	116,100	15,900	171,700
Pancreas	125,800	6,900	148,700
Heart-Lung	271,400	25,100	317,000
Lung	265,900	25,100	312,200
Bone Marrow	217,000	29,300	287,300

* Includes cost of immunosuppressants

Table 18.2 Average Billed Charges Per Transplantation First Year Following Transplant* (1996 Dollars)

Charge Category	*Heart*	*Liver*	*Kidney*	*Kidney-Pancreas*	*Pancreas*	*Heart-Lung*	*Lung*	*Cornea*	*Bone Marrow*
Evaluation	$11,000	$11,000	$11,000	$11,000	$11,000	$11,000	$11,000	$0	$8,300
Candidacy (per mo.)	10,600	10,600	0	0	0	10,600	10,600	0	10,600
Procurement	25,200	24,700	22,400	26,000	16,200	24,800	24,800	0	20,600
Hospital	155,800	188,900	50,600	67,300	76,200	160,400	160,400	4,000	134,500
Physician	21,800	42,600	8,900	12,600	12,600	31,800	26,300	4,000	4,900
Follow-up	18,500	26,400	11,900	11,900	4,700	22,500	22,500	0	34,000
Immuno-suppressants	10,300	10,300	11,300	12,500	5,100	10,300	10,300	0	4,100
Total	$253,200	$314,500	$116,100	$141,300	$125,800	$271,400	$265,900	$8,000	$217,000

* First year immunosuppressant charges were based on Medicare data and on research by Battelle Human Affairs Research Centers.

difficult to determine if they have had an infection. Regular checkups with laboratory assessments will be critical (Roche, 1994). Obviously, the patient should avoid persons with contagious infections such as colds or flu. They should avoid sharing drinks or food, and cleanliness is a requirement.

Costs

In general, surgical costs for these procedures are very expensive due to the complexity, length of treatment, cost of current technology, number of health care professionals involved, and the expertise of the team for this highly specialized area. As one may expect transplant costs vary widely between transplant centers and the cost does not necessarily reflect the quality of the program proportionally. See Tables 18.1 and 18.2 for a summary of national average costs for selected transplants (Haubolt, 1996).

Vocational Issues

The potential for employment depends on several factors. Some recipients have never worked and others may be retired. Their outlook may also depend on the kind of transplant. In summary, the vocational assessment will depend on the individual and their unique situation. If the patient was working, it is difficult to determine pretransplant if the patient will be able to return to the previous employment. However, there should be consideration given to graduated return to work or abbreviated work schedules, shortened total length of time in the work force, and the type of work able to be performed. Clearly there is an increased probability the patient will require post-transplant vocational assistance.

Pediatric Considerations

Transplantation recipients who are children present unique challenges (Russell, 1987). There may be mental and physical developmental delay due to the pretransplant physical condition. There is a strong psychological component concerning the chronically or terminally ill child who may need professional support post-transplant. The concerns relate primarily to family dynamics, self-image issues, and stress on the family unit. Decreased physical activity will necessitate creative therapies to ensure maximum bone and muscle development. Retaining the services of a qualified recreational therapist may be necessary. Also, contact with the local association for the particular disability (e.g., kidney disease) may reveal special camps or services for children. Provision will also be necessary for teachers for homebound school-age children. Also, there may be a need for two caregivers to accompany the pediatric patient to the transplant center.

Miscellaneous Considerations

There are special medical rules with regard to the end stage renal disease (ESRD) patient. They become Medicare Primary eighteen months after beginning renal dialysis. The ESRD status with Medicare is current for three years post-renal transplant. Medicare does not approve pancreas transplants, although renal transplant is more cost effective in the treatment of ESRD than renal or peritoneal dialysis.

Being approved and placed on a transplant list does not assure a patient of the transplant. Patients may have psychological reactions to the unknown nature of their destiny and this will affect the family also. The stress level for the transplant patient and family usually is very high, as they will be asked to tolerate living away from home, endure undetermined hospitalizations, take new medication with unpleasant side effects, and generally experience a much different lifestyle than that normally anticipated. The transplant *will* affect the quality of life for the patient and family.

Conclusion

Multiple economic, case management, psychological, and family decisions are involved in transplantation. Most recipients have little or no knowledge about what to expect, yet their lives are irrevocably changed. They must adhere to a lifelong regimen of medical care that will effect every aspect of their existence. The qualified life care planner offers a service that will provide a road map of care. Complications are of particular interest in this specialized area since one can often plan on problems. In general, health care organizations and insurance companies are not yet utilizing the life care plan as a mechanism for managing care or controlling costs of transplantations. Indeed, transplantation planning is a complex need that is "ripe" as a new business opportunity for the entrepreneurial life care planner.

Resources and Organizations

American Council on Transplantation
700 North Fairfax St., Suite 505
Alexandria, VA 22314
703-863-4301

American Kidney Foundation
800-638-8299

American Organ Transplant Association
281-261-2682

Bone Marrow Transplant Newsletter
708-831-1913

International Bone Marrow Transplant Registry
P.O. Box 2650
Milwaukee, WI 52336
414-456-8325

Leukemia Society of America
733 Third Ave.
New York, NY 10017

National Marrow Donor Program
National Coordinating Center
3433 Broadway St., NE, Suite 400
Minneapolis, MN 55413
800-526-7809

Transplant Recipients Inter Organization
244 North Bellfield Ave.
Pittsburgh, PA 15213
412-687-2210

United Network of Organ Sharing (UNOS)
1100 Boulders Parkway, #500
Box 13770
Richmond, VA 23225
800-330-8500
www.unos.org.

Transplant Centers (Sampling)

Albert Einstein Medical Center (Philadelphia, PA)
Brigham and Women's Hospital's Lung Transplant Program (Chestnut Hill, MA)
Cliniques Universitaires St-Luc (Belgium)
Emory University, Division of Transplantation (Atlanta, GA)
Jewish Hospital (Louisville, KY)
Loma Linda University Medical Center — International Heart Institute (California)
Loma Linda University — Transplantation Institute (California)
London Health Sciences Centre — Transplant Program (London)
Medical College of Ohio (Toledo, OH)
The Methodist Hospital/Baylor College of Medicine — Multi-Organ Transplant Center (Houston,TX)
Rush Heart Transplant Program (Chicago, IL)
Stanford University Medical Center — Liver Transplant Program (Palo Alto, CA)
Stony Brook University Hospital and Medical Center — Transplant Services (Stony Brook, NY)
Toronto Hospital/University of Toronto — Multi Organ Transplant Program
University of Arizona Medical Center — Transplant Program (Tucson, AR)
UCLA — Transplant Program (Los Angeles, CA)
University of Colorado School of Medicine — Transplant Program (Denver, CO)
University of Florida Health Sciences Center at Jacksonville
University of Kentucky Medical Center — Transplant Services (Lexington, KY)
University of Michigan — Transplant Center (Lansing, MI)
University of Pittsburgh Medical Center (UPMC) (Pittsburgh, PA)
University of Texas — Division of Immunology and Transplantation (Houston, TX)
University of Washington School of Medicine — Transplant Program (Seattle, WA)
University of Wisconsin Medical School — Transplant Program (Madison, WI)

REFERENCES

Brinker, K. (September, 1996). Chronic Rejection — Where Are We? **Forum on Current Issues in Organ Transplantation**, Dallas, TX: Dallas Transplant Institute/Methodist Medical Center.

Evans, R. (1993). A cost-outcome analysis of retransplantation: The need for Accountability. **Transplantation Reviews, 7** (4), 163-175.

Jenkinson, S. G. (1993). Lung transplantation: An update. **Respiratory Care, 38** (5), 278-281.

National Kidney Foundation of Georgia (1997). **Myths and Facts about Organ Donation** (brochure). Atlanta, GA.

Miller, C. L. & Swanson, Susan R. (1996). The latest on treating cystic fibrosis, Part 2. **Nursing and Allied Healthweek-Dallas/Ft. Worth, 1** (23), 12-13.

Haubolt, R. (1996). **Research Report, Cost Implications of Human Organ Transplantations, An Update: 1993**. Milwaukee, WI: Milliman & Robertson, Inc.

Roche (1994). **Overview of Solid Organ Transplantation**. Paramus, NJ.

Russell, P. (1987) Transplantation. In R. Berkow (Ed.). **The Merck Manual of Diagnosis and Therapy,** 322-336. Rahway, NJ: Merck & Co.

St. Coeur, M. (1996). Transplant case management guideline. **Case Management Practice Guideline**. St. Louis, MO: Mosby-Yearbook.

UNOS (1997). United Network for Organ Sharing Facts and Statistics [Online] www.ew3.att.net/unos.

Young, J., Frost, A., & Short, H. (1996). A clinical perspective of heart and lung transplantation. **Immunology and Allergy Clinics of North America, 16** (2), 265-290.

19

LIFE CARE PLANNING FOR THE VISUALLY IMPAIRED

Terry Winkler

INTRODUCTION

Visual impairment can have a devastating effect on an individual, personally, emotionally, socially, and vocationally. Younger & Sardegna (1994) have pointed out that an individual's personality, past experiences with blindness, education, social and financial factors, mobility, occupation, cultural background, general physical condition, psychological readiness, and family support system will affect how they are able to deal with vision loss. The consequences of vision loss or impairment are all-encompassing, impacting every area of an individual's life. This demands that the rehabilitation professional develop a carefully thought out life care plan that meets the needs of the individual over a lifetime through all of the various areas affected. In addition, vision impairment encompasses a continuum of problems from low vision to total blindness. The level of preserved vision will affect the recommendations of the life care plan. Technology is rapidly changing and continues to provide interventions that have a tremendously positive effect on a visually impaired person's life and vocation.

The goal of this chapter is to provide background information that the life care planner will need to initiate a life care plan for visually impaired individuals. In addition and perhaps more important, the chapter provides references to assist in locating resources for the visually impaired. The life care planner must have a thorough working knowledge of visual impairment, its effect and impact, and expertise regarding the types of equipment and technological advances for the visually impaired.

Definitions

Visual impairment may be divided into two main categories — low vision and blindness. Low vision is much more common than total blindness. From an educational standpoint, blindness is defined as visual acuity in both eyes of less than 20/200 or visual field of less than 20° despite the best correction with glasses (Deutsch & Sawyer, 1996). Low vision is defined as visual acuity better than 20/200 but worse than 20/70 with correction (PL101-476, The Individuals with Disabilities

1-57444-075-6/99/$0.00+$.50

Education Act). Additional important terminology distinctions are "severe visual impairment" and "legally blind." Severe visual impairment is defined by Nelson as the self or proxy reported inability to read ordinary newspaper print even with the best correction of glasses or contact lenses. In other words, severe visual impairment is not based on test of visual acuity. Rather, it measures perceived visual problems. "Legally blind" is used to indicate entitlement to certain government and private agency services. Low vision is defined by the American Academy of Ophthalmology (1995) to exist if ordinary eyeglasses, contact lenses, or lens implants do not give clear vision. People with low vision still have useful vision; however, this vision can be improved with visual aid devices.

Epidemiology

A variety of estimates are available at various sources regarding the numbers of individuals with low vision or blindness. Definitions of blindness and low vision vary with different authors or sponsoring organizations. This results in some variability of the numbers that are reported. The Prevention of Blindness Database estimates that in 1990 38 million people worldwide met the definition of blind (Tielsch, Sommer & Witt, 1990). This was more than double the population reported in 1972 of 10 to 15 million. Thylefors et al. (1995) reported that 4.6% of the U.S. population met the definition for blindness and 14.4% met the definition of low vision. Nelson & Dimitrova (1993) reported a total number of U.S. citizens with blindness among civilian noninstitutionalized population of 4,300,000. They went on to say that they believed this number represented approximately one-half of all the individuals with visual impairments in the United States. Nelson & Dimitrova's discussion of severe visual impairment revealed that the five states with the highest number of individuals meeting the definition were California, New York, Texas, Pennsylvania, and Florida. Florida had the highest rate of severe visual impairment at 22.6 persons per 1000. It was estimated that approximately 1,000,000 to 1,250,000 were of working age between 18 and 64. In the national picture in 1990, more than 17 out of every 1000 persons in the civilian noninstitutionalized population of the United States were severely visually impaired. Slightly over half a million met the definition of blindness in both eyes, with approximately 100,000 children meeting the definition of severely visually impaired. The National Information Center for Children and Youth with Disabilities estimates that for individuals under the age of 18, 12.2 per 1000 have visual impairments and 0.06 per 1000 have severe visual impairments, i.e., either legally or totally blind (Teplin, 1995). Some studies indicate that visual problems are strongly linked to race. For example, Tielsch et al. (1990) reported legal blindness is much more common among black Americans than whites.

Etiology

A variety of conditions can lead to visual impairment. The most common causes of visual impairment vary with the age of the individual. Deutsch and Sawyer (1996) pointed out that the leading cause for children under the age of 5 include retrolental fibroplasia, neoplasm, infections, and injuries. The same is true for individuals of age 5 to 19. Over age 20, cataracts become the most common cause. During the 1970s, glaucoma was the second leading cause of blindness. However, recent data indicates that as of 1992, the most common causes of blindness in the United States are cataract, trauma, amblyopia, and macular degeneration, respectively. This likely reflects a greater awareness, early detection, and treatment of glaucoma.

Low vision may occur from a variety of causes, which include birth defects, inherited diseases, injuries, diabetes, dacryoma, and cataracts. The most common cause is macular degeneration, which is a disease of the retina and causes damage to the central vision. Peripheral vision, however, is not affected. There are different types of low vision according to the American Academy of Ophthalmology (1995). Reduced central or reading vision is the most common; however, decreased peripheral vision may occur, or a loss of color vision, or the ability to adjust to light, contrast, or glare. The different types of low vision may require different kinds of assistance.

Traumatic etiology of eye injuries occurs in a variety of ways. They may be the result of chemical or ultraviolet burns, direct penetrating wounds, abrasions, lacerations, or from violent shaking type injuries, which can damage the retina. Burns to the eye, lacerations, and corneal abrasions can result in significant visual impairment. However, later scar tissue development can also be a complicating factor that leads to deteriorating vision. Detached retina can lead to blurred or altered vision, flashes of light, or total blindness in an eye.

Some medical conditions that are undiagnosed or not treated properly can lead to severe visual impairment. These include eye infections, glaucoma, cataracts, hydrocephalus, and vascular disease. The central causes of visual impairment would include stroke, traumatic brain injury, hydrocephalus, and tumors. A significant limitation to vision can occur from ocular motor injuries.

Functional Outcomes

The degree of visual loss may vary significantly with the more severe visual impairments leading to the most profound types of functional deficits. The age of onset and level of development before loss of sight occurs are critical factors in a person's ability to acquire skills and concepts. Vision may actually fluctuate or be temporarily influenced by factors such as fatigue, light glare, or inappropriate lighting. An understanding of the types of visual impairment is important, but generalizations about a person's visual functioning cannot be made solely on the basis of a diagnosis. Assessment of functional and vocational implications must be conducted on an individual basis, which in turn affects the nature of the final life care plan (Bristow, 1996; LaPlant, Hendershot, & Moss, 1992).

The types of interventions that are required vary, depending on the nature of the visual impairment. For example, if peripheral vision is damaged, the person has tunnel vision and requires different interventions than an individual with macular degeneration, which would result in the loss of central vision with relative sparing of the peripheral vision. Or an individual may have night blindness where they have very little vision in dimly lit areas such as in retinitis pigmentosa, or they may have photosensitivity where their vision is severely impaired in the bright sunlight.

Special issues occur in very young children with visual impairment (Dodson-Burk & Hill, 1989; Mathews, 1996; Teplin, 1995). In fact, the child's development depends upon the severity of the visual impairment, type of visual loss, and age at onset of the vision deficit. The National Information Center for Children and Youth with Disabilities reports that a young child with visual impairment has little reason to explore interesting objects in the environment and misses opportunities to have experiences to learn. This lack of exploring will continue until learning becomes motivating or until intervention begins. Children with visual impairment may be unable to imitate social behavior and understand nonverbal cues because they are unable to see peers or parents. This creates obstacles to a growing child's independence. It is imperative that children with visual impairment be assessed early and receive appropriate interventions. They will require ongoing assessment as they grow and develop. An interdisciplinary approach will be beneficial in teaching self-care and daily living skills as well as approaching educational and vocational issues. Deutsch and Sawyer (1996) have pointed out that even relatively minor impairment can result in vocational handicaps that limit the range of job alternatives available to an individual and reduce earning capacity. An example is color blindness, which can reduce the range of job opportunities that would otherwise be available. The degree to which total blindness results in permanent impairment and loss of earning capacity varies with the individual and depends on many personal and vocational factors.

Psychological Impact

Few conditions are as feared as blindness. As stated in the introduction, an individual's reaction is affected by personality, past experience, education, social and financial factors, mobility, occupation, cultural background, general physical condition, psychological readiness, and family support. Common psychological reactions include anxiety, depression, anger, and perhaps the most limiting of all, fear. The individual may experience the five emotional stages of a loss as defined by Dr. Elizabeth Kuebler-Ross — denial, anger, bargaining, depression, and finally acceptance (1975). While all individuals will not experience each of the stages, and the length of time per stage may vary a great deal, some part or all of these reactions may occur.

Deutsch and Sawyer (1996) described a variety of sensory distortions that can occur early on, including a loss of position sense such as a sensation of floating. This disorientation is often exacerbated by the psychological problems that accompany visual impairments. In addition, an individual who has a sudden onset of total visual impairment may have more acute or severe psychological reactions than an individual who has had a slow onset of blindness and has had time to adjust along the way. Varying degrees of independence will be lost, with some individuals experiencing a high degree of dependence on others. This cannot be viewed as a lack of motivation on an individual's part. It should be recognized, as previously stated, that there are multiple factors involved that dictate the ultimate functional outcome from visual impairment. Most will experience a great deal of social isolation, frequently having difficulty in establishing relationships. Some individuals have a substantial difficulty in communicating with sighted people after the onset of their visual impairments. If the visual impairment occurs at a very young age, certain concepts such as visual spatial arrangements can be extremely difficult to grasp.

Psychological counseling will be crucial for individuals with visual impairment to assist in dealing with the impact of the disability. In addition, a variety of specialized training and equipment can be utilized to help improve the person's independence, which will have a positive psychological effect.

Aids to Independent Function and/or Durable Medical Equipment for the Visually Impaired

This need can be divided into two broad general categories — high-technology and low-technology devices. Devices exist to help individuals with low vision and individuals with total blindness. A low vision device is an apparatus that improves vision. The American Academy of Ophthalmology (1995) cautions that no one device restores normal vision in all circumstances, so that different devices may be required for different purposes. Bristow (1996) reports that a rehabilitation professional should consider three types of aids for the visually impaired — tactile, auditory, and visual aids. Low-vision devices can be divided into optical and nonoptical devices. Optical devices use a lens or combination of lenses to produce magnification. There are five categories — magnifying spectacles, hand magnifiers, stand magnifiers, telescopes, and closed circuit television. Nonoptical low-vision devices include large print books, check writing guides, large playing cards, large telephone dials, high contrast watch faces, talking clocks and calculators, and machines that can scan print and read out loud.

Lighting is extremely important to individuals with low vision. As you age, your need for light to perform a task increases. On average, a 60-year-old person will need twice as much illumination as he or she needed when they were 20. A visually impaired person may require complete renovation or modification of the entire lighting system in their home or office in order to best accommodate their disability. In some cases having light sources that can be portable or move close to the work area, such as high-intensity lights on adjustable arms, are beneficial. Hat brims or visors can be useful in blocking annoying overhead light, and absorptive lenses, which can help control glare, should be considered.

Gail Pickering, an Assisted Technology Specialist, has published an excellent chapter regarding assisted technology for the visually impaired in the 1996 edition of *A Guide to Rehabilitation* by Deutsch and Sawyer*. This article provides a comprehensive discussion of low-technology and high-technology devices and concludes with an exhaustive list of resources for obtaining the devices and/or information about their cost and use.

Examples of low-technology devices that should be included in a life care plan include check writing guides, watches that can indicate time by voice, tactile clues or feeling, Braille, tape recorders, labels, timers, cooking cups, measuring cups, cooking devices, rulers, large dial telephones, etc. High-Marks is a liquid paste that hardens to make colored fluorescent raised lettering for writing notes or labeling items that can be easily seen or appreciated tactilely. Label makers can make labels that are large print, Braille, or talking labels that will allow a

* Available from Ahab Press, 1-914-696-0708.

person to organize their closets and wardrobes, among other uses. Pill splitters and liquid medication guides and measuring spoons are available. Individuals with diabetes and visual impairment will benefit from insulin measuring devices that are accessible or perhaps a computerized insulin pump. Numerous kitchen devices are available such as liquid level indicators, elbow length oven mitts to prevent burns, vegetable and meat slicing guides. There are self-threading needles, magnetic padlocks (that do not require a combination or a key to open but use a magnetic sensor), typewriters, and letter writing templates.

High-technology devices include portable money handling, accounting, and identification machines, portable Braille note takers, refreshable Braille displays that can integrate with TDD devices, optical character reader devices such as the Optacon — this device will scan printed material and convert it to a tactile display. Similar devices can be obtained that will convert the printed material to a computer file or voice synthesizer. Descriptive video services are available that will allow a visually impaired person to receive narrative descriptions of the visual portions of a television program. In order to receive this service, the person must have stereo VCR or TV and a second audio program channel to receive the descriptive video service. These devices should be considered in every life care plan for a visually impaired person. Computers can be modified or adapted, such as utilizing a screen reader, a speech synthesizer to allow a visually impaired or blind person to access computer programs. Screen readers are available from Microsoft that will read the graphical portion of a computer program. Electromagnetic ovens can be used to heat food without flames or heating elements to reduce the risk of burns. Kurzweil readers, a computerized camera that scans print media and converts it to voice synthesized output, are available.

Closed-circuit TV will allow the visually impaired person to modify printed text to an enlarged image or to an image that has enhanced contrast so that it may be easier read. Software programs are available that will scan books on disk for individual words or combinations of words.

Mobility devices are the most common aid and the simplest is a cane. The proper length is important. The individual should flex the shoulder until the upper limb is parallel with the floor. The distance from the hand to the floor is the proper length for the cane. The cane should be lightweight, flexible, easily collapsible, and the end of the cane is painted red to indicate to others that the individual has a visual impairment. High-technology mobility devices include a laser cane — examples are the Pathsounder, the SonicGuide, and the Mowat Sensor. These devices operate either by sonar or by light beams. Walkmate is an electronic mobility device that vibrates to indicate when an obstacle is in the path. Some individuals will benefit from the Night Vision Aid, which will provide improved vision by amplifying available light. Aids are available that will help to orient an individual or familiarize a person with the environment that they are in (Galvin & Caves, 1996). Examples would be three-dimensional maps or tactile aids, verbal recordings, and sight descriptions of travel routes. A new high-technology device for mobility is a GPS — Global Positioning Systems device — which can literally help a person locate their position on the earth accurate to within a few feet. These devices are now being modified to provide verbal directions and are available in models that can be installed in cars or be handheld. If the individual has turned the wrong way, the device will alert you to this fact.

Digitized compasses are available also. Some areas or cities have transmitters in public areas such as telephones, restrooms, street signs, ATM machines, elevators, etc., which transmit information about the location.

Guide dog services are extremely beneficial for some visually impaired individuals. Most organizations provide a guide dog at no out-of-pocket cost to the person with a visual impairment. These organizations often have long waiting lists and fairly stringent criteria as to who may qualify to receive the animal. Although there may be no direct cost, there clearly are numerous expenses associated with a guide dog, including the cost of transportation to obtain the guide dog, receive training on how to use the animal, and lost wages if the individual is employed. The training varies from a couple of weeks to six to eight weeks in length. Once the guide dog has been obtained, there are costs associated with maintaining the animal's health, tick and flea control, food costs, cost of grooming, veterinarian charges, and kennel fees. In addition, there may be some increased costs to maintaining the home. Appropriate modifications such as a fenced-in yard to allow the guide dog the opportunity to be out of the home during times when not working is essential. Periodic replacement of the guide dog's harness will also be required. The individual with visual impairment may choose not to own a private vehicle and utilize public transportation or taxicab services for community mobility. Such costs must be included in the life care plan. If a private vehicle is maintained, then the cost of hiring a driver should be determined.

There are times and situations where the visually impaired individual's community mobility is best assisted by using a sighted companion as a guide. Some individuals do not adapt well to canine guides or the use of assistive mobility devices. There may be emotional or cognitive factors that demand a companion assist the visually impaired person with their community mobility. Indeed, in many cases, dependent on the activity level of the person, career choice, environment, etc., all of the mobility aids mentioned will be required or used.

PERSONAL CARE AND HOME MAKER SERVICES

There are numerous activities that are required to maintain a home or to live with a measure of independence in the community. The life care planner must carefully evaluate the individual's unique situation and functional abilities and keep foremost in mind the safety of the person for whom the plan is being developed. In addition, it is important to recognize that marked changes in the person's functional status can occur with what would be otherwise relatively minor illnesses for sighted people. The life care plan should have adequate funding for personal care services and/or homemaker services to cover this eventuality. The visually impaired individual will benefit from some assistance in areas such as personal banking, identifying and marking bills for payments, labeling clothing, food shopping and storage, marking settings on the furnace, washing machine, microwave, and stove, some housecleaning, maintaining the home, lawn, and yard, and many other tasks.

When attending school, college, or seminars, note takers and readers may be required and should be considered in the life care plan (Hazekamp & Huebner, 1989). In many school settings, these services may be provided by the school system with funding from the Individuals with Disabilities Education Act (IDEA).

There are also funding sources available through state, federal, and nonprofit resources if the person qualifies (Mendelson, 1987). Such funding can vary with jurisdiction and congressional funding.

Mobility training is essential for the visually impaired and requires a time-intensive initial training period and then updates on an annual or as needed basis. Mobility instructors will be required when there are any changes in the individual's life such as a new home or home modifications, a new or change in job, move to a new city, or orientation to new stores and businesses that develop in the community. Changes in public transportation systems or bus routes may also require an additional training period. This is separate from orientation training that is required on an ongoing basis. For example, a visually impaired person will have times when strangers are required to be in the home, such as for home repairs, servicing for utilities, deliveries, etc. Having a trusted sighted companion present in the home during these times provides an extra measure of safety for the visually impaired person and their personal belongings.

Formal Rehabilitation

For the newly blind or severely visually impaired, a formal rehabilitation program should be undertaken. Topics that should be addressed at a minimum include communication with the sighted world, training in personal management and household tasks, accessing printed material, meal preparation and consumption, in-home and community mobility, and other activities of daily living. Mobility training should be refreshed at least on an annual or as-needed basis and is somewhat dependent on changes in the person's life. Additional areas to be addressed would include Braille instructions, typing lessons, vocational training, and psychological counseling or adjustment.

Case Study

The following excerpts of a life care plan are for a 49-year-old woman injured in a motor vehicle accident. She experienced a mild brain injury as well as blindness from a blood clot on her brain. The following is for illustration purposes only and does not constitute the complete life care plan.

CONCLUSION

Visual impairments can be caused by disease, injury to the eye or brain, or by the natural process of aging. Although total blindness is relatively rare, low vision or vision disturbance (such as neglect or field cuts) can adversely affect the person's ability to live independently or work. This chapter is designed to suggest life care planner topics and services that need to be considered when developing a comprehensive plan. Since the cause of the person's visual impairment are varied and specific functional limitations and medical care are very individual, the life care planner should either have education or training in this specialized area, or associate with someone who does. Fortunately, many resources and adaptive aids (see below) have been developed for enhancing the person's quality of life as well as productive functioning.

Recommendation	Dates	Frequency	Expected Cost
Aids for Independent Function			
Arctic Business Vision software	1997–2027	Replace every 5 years	$1,895.00
Arctic transport synthesizer	1997–2027	Replace every 5 years	$1,295.00
Braille & Speak portable note taker	1997 2027	Replace every 3 years	$1,794.00
Braille printer	1997–2027	Replace every 3 years	$3,995.00
Duxbury Braille Translator	1997–2027	Replace every 5 years	$495.00
DUXWP Translator	1997–2027	Replace every 3 years	$295.00
Optic scanner	1997–2027	Replace every 5 years	$4,500.00
Personal computer with voice control	1997–2027	Replace every 5 years	$2,500.00
Refreshable Braille display	1997–2027	Replace every 5 years	$14,495.00
Talking money identifier	1997–2027	Replace every 5 years	$685.00
Maintenance for above equipment	1998–2027	Yearly with deduction for warranty	$500/year average
Mobility training	1997–1998	1 × only	$45,000
Seeing eye dog	1997–2027	Every 12 years	$0 for dog $1,500 year food, grooming, vet., flea and tick treatments
Allowance for aids such as canes, talking clock, watch, kitchen timer, blood pressure cuff, travel alarm, scale, yard stick, writing guide, garment labeler, talking books, etc.	1997–2027	Yearly	$300/year
Home Care			
Housekeeper	1997–2027	Weekly	$2,080.00/yr.
Handyman	1997–2027	Weekly	$2,080.00/yr.
Lawn maintenance	1997–2027	Seasonally weekly	$700/year
Personal assistance for shopping, etc.	1997–2027	10 hrs/week	$6,240.00
Home security	1997–2027	1 x only	$1,500 + $25/month maintenance and monitoring
Future Medical Care–Routine			
Physiatrist	1997–2027	3 × per year	$204.00/year
Neurologist	1997–2027	1 × per year	$54.00/year
Ophthalmologist	1997–2027	2 × per year	$224.00/year
Lab tests inc. UA, Tegretol, & blood	1997–2027	2 × per year	$156–$578/year
Transportation			
Taxi	1997–2027	As needed	$600 per month avg. Economist to deduct avg. cost of car expense.

SELECTED RESOURCES

Reading material

Books On Tape, Inc.
P.O. Box 7900
Newport Beach, CA 92658-7900
800-626-3333

Choice Magazine Listening
85 Channel Drive
Port Washington, NY 11050-2216
516-883-8280

American Printing House for the Blind
P.O. Box 6085
Louisville, KY 40206-0085
800-233-1839

Associated Services for the Blind
919 Walnut Street
Philadelphia, PA 19107
800-876-5456

Library of Congress
National Library Service for the Blind
1291 Taylor Street, N.W.
Washington, D.C. 20542
800-424-8567

General Information Referral Services
The American Foundation of the Blind
11 Penn Plaza, Suite 300
New York, NY 10001
800-232-5463

American Academy of Ophthalmology
P.O. Box 7424
San Francisco, CA 94120-7424

The Lighthouse National Center for Education
111 East 59th Street
New York, NY 10022
800-334-5497

The National Association for Visually Handicapped
22 West 21st Street
New York, NY 10010

National Federation of the Blind
1800 Johnson Street
Baltimore, MD 21230

Hadley School for the Blind
700 Elm Street
Winnetka, IL 60093
800-323-4238

Helen Keller National Center for Deaf, Blind Youths and Adults
111 Middleneck Road
Sands Point, NY 11050
516-944-8900

Perkins School for the Blind
175 N. Beacon Street
Watertown, MA 02172
617-926-4443

Adaptive Equipment
Catalogs

LSS Group
P. O. Box 673
Northbrook, IL 60065
800-468-4789

American Federation for the Blind
Product Center
3342 Melrose Avenue
Roanoke, VA 24017
800-829-0500

Maxi-Aids
P. O. Box 3209
Farmingdale, NY 11735
800-522-6294

Other

Abledata
c/o Newington's Children's Hospital
181 East Cedar Street
Newington, CT 06111
800-344-5405

Descriptive Video Service
125 Western Avenue
Boston, MA 02134
617-492-2277

Washington Ear, Inc.
35 University Boulevard East
Silver Spring, MD 20901
301-681-6636

Arkenstone, Inc.
1185 Bordeaux Drive, #D
Sunnyvale, CA 94089-1210
408-752-2200

Artic Technologies
55 Park Street
Troy, MI 48083-2753
313-588-7370

Enabling Technologies Company
3102 Southeast Jay Street
Stuart, FL 34997
561-283-4817

Human Ware, Inc.
6245 King Road
Loomis, CA 95650
916-652-7253

Talking Computers
140 Lills Road
Falls Church, VA 22046

Ann Morris Enterprises
890 Fams Court
East Meadow, NY 11554-5101
516-292-9232

Duxbury Systems
P.O. Box 1504
Littleton, MA 01460
508-486-9766

Easier Ways, Inc.
1101 North Calvert Street, Suite 405
Baltimore, MD 21202-3840
410-659-0232

Dragon Systems, Inc.
320 Nevada Street
Newton, MA 02160
800-825-5897

Kurzweil Applied Intelligence
411 Waverly Oaks Road
Waltham, MA 02154
800-380-1234

Local State Rehabilitation Services — Can be assessed in each state generally by contacting the state division of vocational rehabilitation

Dog Guide Resources

Eye Dog Foundation for the Blind
512 North Larchmont Boulevard
Los Angeles, CA 90004
213-626-3370

Fidelco Guide Dog Foundation
P.O. Box 142
Bloomfield, CT 06002
203-243-5200

Leader Dogs for the Blind
1039 Rochester Road
Rochester, MN 48063
313-651-9011

Pilot Dogs, Inc.
625 West Town Street
Columbus, OH 43215
614-221-6367

Seeing Eye, Inc.
P.O. Box 375
Morristown, NJ 07960
973-539-4425

Southeast Guide Dogs, Inc.
4210 77th Street East
Palmetto, FL 33561
813-729-5665

Recreation

Sports and Recreation Access to Art
15 West 16th Street
New York, NY 10011

American Alliance for Health, Physical Education, and Recreation for the Handicapped
1201 16th Street, N.W.
Washington, D.C. 20036

American Blind Bowling Association
150 North Bellair Avenue
Louisville, KY 40206

American Blind Skiing Foundation
610 South William Street
Mount Prospect, IL 60056

REFERENCES

Bristow, D.C. (1996). Assistive technology. In P. Deutsch and H. Sawyer. (Eds.) **A Guide to Rehabilitation**. White Plains, NY: Ahab Press.

Deutsch, P.M. & Sawyer, H.W. (1996). **A Guide to Rehabilitation**. White Plains, NY: Ahab Press.

Dodson-Burk, B. & Hill, E.W. (1989). **An Orientation and Mobility Primer for Families and Young Children**. New York: American Foundation of the Blind.

Galvin, J.C. & Caves, K.M. (1996) Computer assisted devices and environmental controls. In R. Braddom (Ed.). **Physical Medicine and Rehabilitation.** Philadelphia: W. B. Saunders.

Hazekamp, J. & Huebner, K.M. (1989). **Program Planning and Evaluation for Blind and Visually Impaired Students: National Guidelines for Educational Excellence** New York: American Foundation for the Blind.

Kuebler-Ross, E. (1975). **Death: The Final Stage of Growth** Englewood Cliffs, NJ: Prentice-Hall.

LaPlante, M.P., Hendershot, G.E., & Moss, A.J. (1992). Assisted technology devices and home accessibility features: Prevalence, payment, needs and trends. **Advanced Data from the Vital Health Statistics, #217**. Hyattsville, MD: National Center for Health Statistics.

The American Academy of Ophthalmology (1997). **Low Vision Facts, Questions and Answers**. [Online] http://www.eyenet.org/.

Matthews, D.J. (1996). Examination of the pediatric patient. In R. Braddom (Ed.), **Physical Medicine and Rehabilitation**. Philadelphia: W. B. Saunders.

Mendelson, S. (1987). **Financing Adaptive Technology: A Guide to Sources and Strategies for Blind and Visually Impaired Users**. New York: Smiling Interface.

Nelson, K.A. & Dimitrova, E. (March 1993). Severe visual impairment in the United States and each state. **Journal of Visual Impairment and Blindness, 87**(3), 80-85.

Teplin, S. W. (1995). Visual impairment in infants and young children. **Infant Young Children 1995 8**(1), 18-51.

Thylefors, V., Negrel, A., Pararajasegaram, R., & Dedzieky, K.Y. (1995). Available data on blindness update, 1994. **Ophthalmic Epidemiology, 2**(1), 5-39.

Tielsch, J.M., Sommer, A., & Witt, K. (1990). Blindness and visual impairment in an american urban population. **Archives of Ophthalmology, 108**, 236-241.

Younger, V. & Sardegna, J. (1994). **A Guide to Independence for the Visually Impaired and Their Families**. New York: Demos Publications.

III

FORENSIC CONSIDERATIONS

20

FORENSIC ISSUES FOR LIFE CARE PLANNERS

Roger O. Weed

INTRODUCTION

This chapter will summarize some of the issues that the life care planner must consider in order to practice in the area of forensic rehabilitation that may offer a somewhat different perspective than that offered in the chapters authored by attorneys. Clearly, the life care plan is used for more than litigation (Deutsch & Sawyer, 1996; Riddick & Weed, 1996; Weed, 1994). Historically the care plan has been used in setting reserves for insurance companies, assisting workers' compensation companies with assessing future care costs associated with work-related disabilities, estimating the cost of future care for health care insurance companies, and providing the client and/or family with an outline of future care. In the event that inadequate funding is available, the life care plan can become the road map for care. On many occasions the future care plan is not fully funded; therefore, the life care plan can be used to prioritize treatment so that available funding is used most appropriately. In a simplistic way, the life care plan is used to develop a budget so that the most important items are given the highest priority.

Since life care plans are used in a variety of jurisdictions, the appropriate rules must be considered. Probably the most comprehensive setting is in personal injury litigation. In the litigation arena, the life care plan must consider the entire person and their situation. Only items that have economic value are included. For example, hedonic damages, such as the loss of pleasure of life or choice, are not included in this format. This chapter is not intended to provide a comprehensive analysis for items and issues that do not lend themselves to economic projections; the reader is referred to Brookshire and Smith (1990) for a more detailed discussion of this specialized area. It must also be recognized that many states have different legal rules with regard to evidence and testimony. Indeed, federal rules are interpreted differently across the United States. This chapter is intended to address common issues and topics associated with civil litigation.

According to *Black's Law Dictionary* (1990), forensic rehabilitation refers to the practice of rehabilitation principles in legal settings. This short dissertation will discuss the relationship between rehabilitation and the courts, expert witness roles, and selected terms that may be important to the rehabilitation consultant within the legal system.

1-57444-075-6/99/$0.00+$.50

Rehabilitation experts are relatively new to the courtroom. Indeed, rehabilitation "counselors" historically were trained specifically to work in public agencies and were often shielded from acting as expert witnesses in personal injury litigation. The first entry into the rehabilitation private sector, which involved nurses, was initiated on a larger scale in the late 1960s, when International Rehabilitation Associates, now Intracorp, was formed by an insurance company to help process and manage insurance claims. By the 1990s, private sector rehabilitation has extended into almost all areas of disability care, including workers' compensation, long-term disability, Social Security disability insurance, health insurance, railroad (Federal Employee's Liability Act), longshore workers, Jones Act, as well as personal injury litigation (Weed & Field, 1994). Although there is considerable similarity across jurisdictions, there are a number of differences the rehabilitation expert should know about before stepping into court.

For example, the word "disability" is defined differently in various systems. In public rehabilitation, "disability" usually refers to the medical condition, which establishes eligibility for services, indicating that the client is able to perform work and benefit from rehabilitation services (Weed & Field, 1994). When Social Security determines a person is "disabled," the person is deemed unable to perform "substantial gainful activity" and may qualify for government support. In workers' compensation systems, some states have provision for disability that may be permanent or temporary, as well as partial or total. As with the word disability, terminology can make a significant difference and it is important for the rehabilitation expert to understand the words used in the courtroom.

Although generally recommended, it is not necessary for the rehabilitation professional to be certified or possess a certain level of education to be considered an expert. According to legal precedence (*Kim Manufacturing v. Superior Metal Treating,* 1976), an "expert witness is one who by reason of education or specialized experience possesses superior knowledge respecting a subject about which persons having no particular training are incapable of forming an accurate opinion or deducing correct conclusion." Therefore, an attorney may retain someone who would not be considered an expert in some states for workers' compensation or as a vocational expert (VE) for the Social Security system.

Earnings Capacity Analysis

Often one element of damages is the loss of earnings capacity. If the life care planner is not independently qualified to opine about this aspect of the case, they may associate with a vocational expert. In order to provide an "expert" opinion regarding the loss of potential earnings, the "expert" must be prepared to provide an assessment of the person's earnings capacity. Although a separate chapter addresses the details for what must be evaluated to arrive at a vocational opinion, generally accepted methods for determining loss of earnings capacity include the following:

1. The most common method assumes the client has a work history. The rehabilitation professional scrutinizes vocational and medical records, perhaps supplemented by testing, and provides a professional opinion regarding

pre-incident and post-incident earnings capacity. Obviously, this is not useful for a client with limited or no work history.

2. The Labor Market Access method, developed by Field and Field (1992), uses federal data regarding worker traits and the *Dictionary of Occupational Titles* (United States Department of Labor, 1991). A computer program (Labor Market Access 1992) can be used to help sort through more than 70 worker traits for 12,741 job titles pre-incident vs. post-incident. This process identifies the number of pre-incident vs. post-incident jobs, pre-incident and post-incident average earnings, the top 20 pre-incident and post-earnings capacity, and other information that can be used as a basis for the expert opinion. It may be useful to be aware of the new World Wide Web O-Net developed by the federal government, which in the near future is expected to replace the *Dictionary of Occupational Titles*.
3. *To determine earnings capacity* for children and others who may not have ample work history, an extensive review of the client's background is useful. This may include school records, scrutiny of the parents and extended family with regard to work and/or education, and educational or neuropsychological testing. In acquired brain injury pediatric cases, pre-incident vs. post-incident ability to be educated can be applied.
4. Another method, known as L-P-E, identifies the client's probability of life (L), the probability of labor force participation (P), and probability of employment (E). For more information on this method, the professional is directed to *Economic/Hedonic Damages: The Practice Book for Plaintiff and Defense Attorneys* by Brookshire and Smith (1990).

A more detailed explanation of these areas can be found in *The Rehabilitation Consultant's Handbook* (Weed & Field, 1994), the *Encyclopedia of Disability and Rehabilitation* (Weed, 1995), and Chapter 11.

Hedonic Damages

Another domain that some rehabilitation experts address is the loss of pleasures or choices in life, known as "hedonic damages." Methods include describing to the jury the client's situation regarding pain, loss of access to the labor market, psychological effects, loss of consortium and other factors, or using a chart developed by Drs. Brookshire and Smith (see above reference) to provide the jury with guidelines.

Life Care Plan

Regardless of the topic, the expert must be able to quantify damages in a way that provides the economist, if one is used, or the jury with the necessary information to project costs over time. These data are used to help determine the amount of award to the client, if the party against whom the suit is lodged is found at fault. To ascertain the costs of future care, particularly for serious medical conditions and catastrophic injuries, the life care plan was originally published by Deutsch and Raffa in *Damages in Tort Action* in 1981. This method organizes

Table 20.1 Elements for Future Care Damages

- When does treatment start?
- What is the frequency of sessions?
- What is cost per session (if relevant)?
- When does treatment stop?
- Additional costs such as evaluations, test, laboratory, or medications?
- Any other costs?

Table 20.2 Example Entry for Future Care Damages

- Psychological evaluation in June, 1997 @ $600
- Expect counseling to begin in July, 1997 at 1X/week, 1 hour session for 26 weeks @ $100/hour, then expect group counseling for 2 years (48 sessions per year) @ $40/session.
- Expect medication, Prozac, 1 tab of 20 mg per day for life expectancy, @ $53.86 per month.
- Expect psychiatrist follow-up for medication 4X/year beginning 1/98 @ $150 initial visit, then $75 each visit to life.

topics according to various categories (see Chapter 1 for an overview and Tables 20.1 and 20.2 above) that outline expected treatment, start and stop dates, costs, and other information that will provide the jury with an understanding of the treatment plan. The format is designed to develop a comprehensive rehabilitation plan that includes the necessary information to project the expense, usually with the help of an economist, in order to arrive at a "bottom line figure."

Report Writing

Some general report writing issues were discussed in the chapters written by the attorneys. Of special interest in this author's view is the 1993 ruling known as the Daubert decision (*Daubert v. Merrell Dow*). This decision implied that any testimony offered by an expert must be founded on a methodology or underlying reasoning that is scientifically valid and can be properly applied to the facts of the issue. Considerations included whether the theory or technique has been subjected to peer review and publication. Although this topic has been addressed in preceding chapters, it is important to emphasize that proper foundations must be provided to a plan. Since many "Life Care Planners" either have failed to undergo specific training or do not follow published guidelines, it underscores the importance of continuing education, developing standards and methodologies, and publishing guidelines specific to our industry (Feldbaum, 1997).

One important aspect of the report is inclusion of appropriate details for the jury to determine the cost of future care and effects on vocational opportunities including earnings capacity. Assuming that an expert has developed all of the necessary data and opinions relative to damages in a personal injury case, it is appropriate to offer a rationale to encompass the issues that should be addressed in a written report. The **RAPEL** method (Table 20.3) is designed to address the topics in a rational and commonsense way as well as a format for displaying the information to the jury.

Table 20.3 The RAPEL Method: A Commonsense Approach to Life Care Planning and Earnings Capacity Analysis

REHABILITATION PLAN Determine the rehabilitation plan based on the client's vocational and functional limitations, vocational strengths, emotional functioning, and cognitive capabilities. This may include testing, counseling, training fees, rehab technology, job analysis, job coaching, placement, and other needs for increasing employment potential. Also consider reasonable accommodation. A life care plan may be needed for catastrophic injuries.
ACCESS TO THE LABOR MARKET Determine the client's access to the labor market. Methods include the LMA92 computer program, transferability of skills (or worker trait) analysis, disability statistics, and experience. This may also represent the client's loss of choice and is particularly relevant if earnings potential is based on very few positions.
PLACEABILITY This represents the likelihood that the client could be successfully placed in a job. This is where the "rubber meets the road." Consider the employment statistics for people with disabilities, employment data for the specific medical condition (if available), economic situation of the community (may include a labor market survey), availability (not just existence) of jobs in chosen occupations. Note that the client's attitude, personality, and other factors will influence the ultimate outcome.
EARNINGS CAPACITY Based on the above, what is the pre-incident capacity to earn compared to the post-incident capacity to earn. Methods include analysis of the specific job titles or class of jobs that a person could have engaged in pre- vs. post-incident, the ability to be educated (sometimes useful for people with acquired brain injury), family history for pediatric injuries, and LMA92 computer analysis based on the individual's worker traits. Special consideration applies to children, women with limited or no work history, people who choose to work below their capacity (e.g., highly educated who are farmers), and military trained.
LABOR FORCE PARTICIPATION This represents the client's work life expectancy. Determine the amount of time that is lost, if any, from the labor force as a result of the disability. Issues include longer time to find employment, part-time vs. full-time employment, medical treatment or follow up, earlier retirement, etc. Display data using specific dates or percentages. For example, an average of four hours a day may represent a 50% loss.

R = Rehabilitation Plan. This section includes the life care plan that comprehensively outlines the expected future care of the client (see previous chapters for topics). This section may include, as applicable, the following: additional future testing, counseling, training fees, rehabilitation technology, job analysis, job coaching, placement, and other needs for improving the client's potential for employment.

A = Access to Labor Market (Employability). In many of these cases, an individual may very well be able to return to a job that is custom-designed around their disability or with an employer who is interested in helping an employee with mild to moderate cognitive deficits. However, the client may not have access to the same level of vocational choices he or she did prior to the incident. In essence, the client might appear to have no particular loss of earnings capacity but at the same time be at high risk for losing a job and then having a significant problem locating suitable employment. The access to labor market can be determined through a variety of means. The Labor Market Access 92 computer program

(Field & Field, 1992) is one tool used to assist in determining, based on worker traits, the client's ability to choose in the labor market. For example, one client may have a 50% loss of access to the labor market and another individual may have a loss of access of 95% to the labor market. Obviously, an individual who has access to 5% of the labor market should be employable or placeable; however, the difficulty factor for suitable or sustained employment has increased significantly. By placing a loss of access percentage to the labor market, one can sensitize the reader to the potential difficulty for placement. Generally, this is described in a particular percentage loss of access to the client's **personal** labor market rather than to the national labor market. Few unimpaired people have access to 100% of the labor market.

P = Placeability. This represents the likelihood that the client will be successfully placed in a job with or without rehabilitation support or rehabilitation consultant assistance. One may need to conduct labor market surveys, job analyses, or, in pediatric cases, rely upon statistical data to opine about ultimate placeability. The economic condition of the community may also be a factor. It is important that the rehabilitation consultant recognize that the client's personality, cognitive limitations, and other factors certainly influence the ultimate outcome. For adults, the rehabilitationist may find that is it is useful to include an opinion about jobs that are available (actual openings) in addition to jobs that exist but are not currently available to the client — if it is likely that the client will have worker traits that match various job titles. Matching to a job title does not suggest that the person can indeed be placed in a particular occupation. Other factors, such as location, experience, education, personality, can adversely impact placement. Also, many jobs, which may be appropriate for the client, are difficult to obtain. The vocational opportunity may be highly competitive or there may be very few positions available.

E = Earnings Capacity. Based on the rehabilitation plan, access to the labor market, and placeability factors, the client may or may not be employable in the labor market. If employment is likely, an estimate of the earnings potential is important. In general, the difference between wage loss and earnings capacity analysis for an individual is that which they can reasonably attain and hold. For example, consider a 17-year-old who delivers papers for an income when he is catastrophically impaired and is never able to work again. Certainly, the earnings history from the paper delivery does not represent the individual's capacity. On the other hand, a 55-year-old union truck driver may exhibit earnings history that is consistent with his capacity. The considerations include whether the individual is a child or an adult and, if an adult, the industry for which they are best suited. For example, a drywall hanger of marginal intelligence may have very well reached their earnings potential by the time they reach their late 20s or early 30s. On the other hand, an attorney may not reach their potential until late in their career.

L = Labor Force Participation. This category represents an opinion about the client's expected work life expectancy. Usually an individual who has a reduced life expectancy will also be expected to have a reduced work life expectancy. At the other end of the spectrum, the client's participation in the labor force may be unchanged. An individual may also be expected to work six hours per day rather than eight hours per day, which represents a 25% loss of normal work life expectancy. Some clients have demonstrated consistent extra income by working overtime and this situation can be considered in this arena as well. Generally speaking, the counselor will express the opinion of loss by percentage or perhaps a number of years. It is usually the economist who makes the actual projections. This particular area is quite complicated and most vocational counselors are not prepared to address the subtleties and the complexities of economic projections. However, for additional information, the counselor can review work life estimates in **Worklife Estimates: Effects of Race and Education** (Bulletin # 2254, USDOL, 1986).

CONCLUSION

This chapter has outlined many of the topics and issues that the life care planner must consider when developing opinions for civil litigation cases. The expert is in an excellent position to assist in resolving litigation by soliciting information that addresses almost all of the damage aspects of the case. Knowing the health care industry and effectively researching the future care and costs associated with a complex injury is a specialized service that offers a true enhancement to the profession. When completed objectively and professionally, the care plan will assist the jury with a clear understanding of the needs of the client as well as providing "the road map of care" for the client and family.

REFERENCES

Black, H. (1990). **Black's Law Dictionary,** (6th ed.). St. Paul, MN: West Publishing.

Brookshire, M. & Smith, S. (1990). **Economic/Hedonic Damages: The Practice Book for Plaintiff and Defense Attorneys.** Cincinnati, OH: Anderson Publishing.

Daubert vs. Merrell Dow (1993), 125 L Ed 2d 469.

Deutsch, P. & Raffa, F. (1981). **Damages in Tort Action,** Vols. 8 & 9. New York: Matthew Bender.

Deutsch, P. & Sawyer, H. (1996). **Guide to Rehabilitation**. New York: Matthew Bender.

Dillman, E. (1987). The necessary economic and vocational interface in personal injury cases. **Journal of Private Sector Rehabilitation, 2**(3), 121-142.

Feldbaum, C. (1997). The Daubert decision and its interaction with the federal rules. **Journal of Forensic Vocational Assessment**, **1**(1), 49-73.

Field, T. & Field, J. (1992). **Labor market access plus 1992** (computer program). Athens, GA: Elliott & Fitzpatrick.

Field, T. & Weed, R. (1988). **Transferability of Work Skills.** Athens, GA: Georgia Southern.

Kim Manufacturing, Inc. vs. Superior Metal Treating, Inc. 537 S W Reporter, 2d. 424 (1976).

Riddick, S. & Weed, R. (1996). The life care planning process for managing catastrophically impaired patients. **Case Studies in Nursing Case Management,** 61-91. Gaithersburg, MD: Aspen.

Weed, R. (1988). Earnings vs. earnings capacity: The labor market access method. **Journal of Private Sector Rehabilitation, 3** (2), 57-64.

Weed, R. (1994). Life care plans: Expanding the horizons. **Journal of Private Sector, Rehabilitation, 9** (2 & 3), 47-50.

Weed, R. (1995). Forensic rehabilitation. In A. E. Dell Orto & R. P. Marinelle (Eds.). **Encyclopedia of Disability and Rehabilitation**, 326-330. New York: Macmillan.

Weed, R. & Field, T. (1994). **The Rehabilitation Consultant's Handbook** (2nd ed.). Athens, GA: E & F Vocational Services.

Weed, R. & Sluis, A. (1990). **Life Care Planning for the Amputee: A Step by Step Guide.** Orlando, FL: Paul M. Deutsch Press.

21

A PERSONAL PERSPECTIVE OF LIFE CARE PLANNING

Raymond L. Arrona and Mamie Walters as told to Anna N. Herrington

INTRODUCTION

This chapter is a brief telling of Anita Arrona's "story." On September 7, 1987, Anita was returning home from visiting her boyfriend when a drunk driver hit her. Her injuries were profound and included open brain trauma, severe brain contusion of the left and right frontal lobes, supraorbital fractures of her left and right eyes, multiple blunt trauma to the chest, hydrocephalus, pleural effusion of the left lung, fractured right clavicle, and severe spasticity with minimal control of bodily functions. By October 5, 1987, infected frontal lobe brain tissue was removed and a shunt was inserted to drain off excess fluid. Her left eye was unsalvageable. After three months and multiple surgeries, it became evident that Anita would never achieve independence, and the family's attorney retained the services of a life care planner to develop an outline of future expected care. Over the years, although severely brain injured, hemiparetic, and blind in the left eye, her medical situation has stabilized and she has learned to speak a few words. She resides in a wheelchair, which requires attendant's service to move her. She is totally dependent on others for her well-being.

Anita's journey since her injury in 1987 has involved many factors: family and friends, high moral standards and strong values, and a solid plan. First, Anita's father, Ray Arrona, has been and continues to be her warrior in the many battles that must be fought to obtain what she needs. Mamie Walters, a family friend who has turned professional caregiver, has been devoted to seeking out creative therapeutic methods to enhance Anita's abilities and is committed to her growth. Second, Anita and Ray have had strong coping resources based on deep-rooted beliefs in optimism, honesty, perseverance, stubbornness, hard work, and faith in God. Last, on Anita's journey, has been the pragmatic vehicle — the life care plan. Anita's life care plan has been the essential road map, though detours are sometimes taken, of her often arduous journey.

1-57444-075-6/99/$0.00+$.50

RAY ARRONA: MY DAUGHTER'S STORY

Let me begin with one of the codes by which I live my life: *be responsive.* A story I heard at a recent conference illustrates this well. There was a first mate that came to his captain advising him that the ship was going to be under attack and inquiring as to what to do. The captain told the first mate to run and get his (the captain's) red shirt. So he got the red shirt, they engaged in battle, and they won. About a week or two passed and the first mate returned to the captain and warned him of a pending battle with pirates. Once again the first mate asked, "What do you advise?" Again the captain replied, "I want you to bring my red shirt." So, they engaged in battle and wiped out all the pirates. When putting everything away the first mate was curious and asked the captain, "Can you please tell me about this red shirt? Every time you put this red shirt on we seem to do well. I wonder if there is some point in this." The captain told him that it "was the leadership thing." The captained explained that if he happens to get stabbed while under attack or is hit by a volley, "I don't want the men to see me get hurt and bleed so I can continue to lead them through the battle." That's pretty wise. Another month passes and the first mate rushed to the captain shouting, "Captain, Captain I have news of yet another battle. There are pirates on starboard, on the bow, and they are on the port side! What shall I do?" So the captain says, "Will you please get me my brown pants?"

I tell this story to express the importance of a quick and smart response. I have found that "being ready" for the battle has been of immense importance in my life. I was born and raised in Miami, Arizona, a copper mining community about 80 miles east of Phoenix. Being Hispanic, I grew up in a strict and disciplined home. At home I learned the importance of a good attitude. I learned about making good choices and taking responsibility for those choices. I learned to believe strongly in myself. Now, I am 50 years old and I know these early lessons have assisted me through my life. I worked while attending college at Arizona State University and had plans to pursue a pre-med curriculum. That was in 1964. However, my plans changed when I met Anita's mother in 1965. Soon we were married and a year later, in November 1966, Anita was born.

I continued to work with my college employer, Wear-Ever, Inc., the first subsidiary of Alcoa, and later transferred to another subsidiary, Cutco. I have been associated with these the two companies for nearly 30 years though many changes have occurred. Our second child was another daughter, Andrea, who was born just about 11 months after Anita. Little did we know how short a time we would have with Andrea. Andrea, at 11 months, drowned in the bathtub. It was terrible. This tragedy was our first to experience as a family. I am not sure whether it prepared us for the future, but it certainly tightened the family.

Then there was the aftermath and our struggles. We had a son, my namesake, who was born on Christmas Day. You may remember the Apollo moonshot; it was somewhere around that time in 1968. Ray, Jr. was 18 at the time of Anita's accident. (Ray is now married and has two children. He is in the Navy and lives in Seattle, Washington.) For many, many different reasons our marriage did not work and we were divorced in 1971.

I later met and married (October 1974) Sheri, the love of my life. We just recently celebrated 22 years of marriage. At the time of Anita's accident Sheri was 38 years of age. My employer offered me a promotion to a position that required transferring all the way across the country in Atlanta, Georgia. We moved in 1976. Alyson was born to Sheri and me a year later in May, 1977. Alyson, Anita's younger sister, was 10 years old and was in 5th grade at the time of the accident. Alyson probably has the most anger in the family about Anita's accident, even to this day. Ryan, whom Anita used to take care of often, was born four years later in October 1981. At the time of the accident he was 5 and not really aware of what was happening.

It was during this period of time (1979) that Anita moved in with my parents in Miami, Arizona, because of difficulties she was having with her mother. However, Anita didn't realize how strict her grandparents would be and we soon realized that it might be best for her to move to Atlanta to be with me. Anita moved in with us and enrolled as a junior at North Cobb High School in Kennesaw, Georgia. She graduated in May 1984. Anita is a very determined person — she has not lost this trait. She is a hard worker and has not lost that drive either. After school she worked several jobs with the goal of eventually attending court-reporting school. During this time she saved enough money to buy her dream car: a new, red, 1986 Toyota GT. Anita would not let anyone else drive or even touch that car. She loved that car.

It was Labor Day, 1987, and, since I am a football fanatic, I was glued to the television. At the end of the evening the news came on detailing Labor Day highway accidents. According to the report the number of accidents was less than predicted. I thought — this is really great. Then the phone rang. The phone call was very similar to the one I received when I was working in Tucson and heard the news from an official at a local hospital about my second daughter, Andrea's accident. Although they wouldn't say what was going on, I knew that something was terribly wrong. Anita had been visiting with her boyfriend, Dan, that evening of Labor Day and was on her way home. I called Dan and asked him what was going on. He did not know. Dan lived about ½ mile from the hospital and I asked him if he would please join me there. Upon arrival at the hospital, I was escorted into a private conference room and as I walked in I saw Dan talking with two professional men dressed in white. Later, I learned those were the neurosurgeons who were preparing for a lengthy, all-night operation on Anita. They informed me that Anita had been involved in a terrible auto accident that had crushed her skull. They said she was critical and was given only about a 20% chance to survive.

I felt all numb inside, as if I was living through a bad dream. That night was spent making emergency phone calls trying to find out what was happening because there was no information. I had a lot of support from Dan and his family; we prayed the rosary all night long together. We prayed that God would take care of Anita. The next morning the doctors came in and they told us Anita had made it through the evening but it was still touch-and-go. I was shocked when I went into the room. Tubes were inside of her, IV's, multiple machines that I had no idea what they were for, lights, monitors. I could barely find Anita because her body was very swollen. I felt a feeling of helplessness, not knowing what to do. I was overcome with feelings of despair, feelings of sorrow. As fate would have it, my mother had passed away the year before and Anita was planning to take a trip on that Labor Day to see my father. But the trip was postponed because of an American Legion conference that my dad, a veteran and an avid American legion member, wanted to attend. So, there was this anger about why things could not have been different. There was a lot of grief.

During the next few weeks, I was not really aware of what was taking place. There were many visitors and everyone was trying to understand what happened. I can recall staying up all night, sleeping on the floor, and waiting to be awakened for any news that we would have of Anita. There were many, many life-threatening decisions on Anita's behalf that needed to be made. I don't know if you are familiar with edema. I had no idea what that was. There was pressure that was being caused by the cerebral spinal fluid because it was not draining properly. So we learned what edema was. It was to plague us throughout the next several months. There were several needed operations that required removing part of the brain to relieve building pressure. We learned what a shunt was. That is something that was where the fluid needs to drain back and we learned what operation that was going to take. We learned what the left brain does and what the right brain does. Throughout several months we were just hoping that all parts of her body would work. We were hopeful that she would have movement in the right side of her body. We did see that and it gave us a lot of hope that things were going to be alright and that Anita could return, by the grace of God, to the original Anita. However, many, many problems continued to appear. So, the hope for survival was in and out, in and out, and the prognosis changed day by day. She had good days and she had bad days.

Many people told us that quite often in a crisis, your emotions and your intelligence do not work together. All I know is that we learned to measure gains in inches and seconds and minutes. Anita was in the hospital ICU for nine months. Everyone was distraught; there was a lot of sadness, but the family pulled together. The many prayers and visits from my extended family were invaluable. I believe in prayer. It brought hope to our family. We had so much support: from our family, church, friends, and business associates sending cards and making visits, calls, and saying prayers. The hospital staff was supportive, especially the ICU nurses and the physicians. We had legal and financial support. We were truly blessed.

However, our family was under tremendous stress. Our family had changed. Most of the attention was on Anita. All talk was Anita. Being a husband had to go by the wayside. Though I did the best that I could, being a father to all my children was sacrificed. I really didn't have any idea how it would affect the other children. There was a different schedule that was imposed upon us. New schedules, new decisions, emotions we hadn't experienced before. As parents, we were obligated to take care of Anita, even though she was an adult. We had a lot of bills to pay, unaware of where the money would come from. My business is commission-based and, therefore, dependent on my being "in the field" to produce. Because I had become an independent contractor, I no longer had health insurance with the company. Our private-pay insurance did not cover Anita since she was not a full-time student. There were going to be a lot of things that were unclear to me. There were increased workloads for everyone in the family; we were stressed to the limit. We had no idea of what was ahead of us.

So what caused the accident? I can recall the second night that I was in ICU and a police officer came and talked to me. I thought he was very considerate to come up and find out how Anita was doing. However, that was not his intention at all. The purpose of his visit was to serve me with a ticket, intended for Anita, for running a red light. Fortunately, there was an eyewitness who revealed the truth: Anita was broadsided by a young, college-age, drunk driver who had run a red light. He was also on drugs at the time and, unfortunately, this was his third DUI offense.

I had no idea what was going to take place as far as Anita's litigation. The physician who had done the operation asked me if I had someone in mind, and I said no. He recommended an attorney who is very good with personal injury cases. However, I didn't know he was good, I had never heard of him. My mind went through many things. I was unsure who to select and what to do so I did what I was accustomed to doing and I sought out other attorneys to see what their prices would be. I was told it would not cost me anything; however, it would be one-third of whatever was awarded on a contingency basis. That blew my mind. I thought Anita needs all of this money. I certainly can have an appreciation in retrospect. I did look for another attorney. I described the situation and he was willing to do it for a fixed cost and a certain percentage that was lower. However, as I talked with him he thought we could make the records look like Anita was going to school at the time and work out something with the insurance. There was a part of me that was tempted to listen to that because I was desperate to find a way to preserve as many funds as I could. Thank God, I did not hire that individual. I found a good attorney and it has worked out well in our case.

I learned how our courts work. There was to be a criminal trial and a civil trial. The criminal trial came first and I don't know what effect the criminal trial would have on our civil trial but it was an ordeal. I came to the conclusion that our court system was not a justice system but an injustice system. Eyewitnesses had to be sought out to put together the actual scene of the accident and we soon discovered the drunken driver who hit Anita was out of town on a vacation. He was out on bail. He never even spent one night in jail.

It was really hard for our family to sit in a courtroom with the man who hit Anita. He showed no remorse and neither did his family. That made it hard. Not once did they come and say they were sorry or anything at all. There were so many coincidental things that happened that would literally blow me away. One of the things is the attorney that represented the defendant was a close friend of Anita's boyfriend. He did not know that Anita was the girl who had been hit so he took the case. He happened to be an excellent attorney and I could not believe how things could be done in a way to make the innocent look guilty. There was a young lady in ICU who really gave a lot of care to our daughter. She worked in another hospital and she was a close friend of Dan's family. She transferred to Kennestone. As fate would have it, her brother was working for the defendant. It was very, very emotional and distressing. After about a week of trial, the defendant decided to plead guilty. We never had a civil trial. That was settled out of court. The young man was sentenced to 5 years for a third offense and we heard later he was given 2 years to serve and after about 18 months he was up for parole. We took an active role to ensure he served his full 2 years.

Based on the life care plan, a settlement was reached with the defendant and I was made Anita's legal guardian. I opted to select an irrevocable trust. The reason I did so is that if something happened to me I could pretty much dictate who would be in charge of the financial affairs for Anita, and, also, to avoid temptations either by myself or anyone else to misuse those funds. I have used the trust, my attorney, and the professional rehabilitation consultant as my second conscience. The professional rehabilitation consultant/professional expert was very involved in the life care plan. It is amazing how many things he was right on target with and how important that was in supporting Anita's case.

Would Anita be better off now if she had not lived through the accident? What is her life going to be like? That almost seems unfair. There was a lot of anger in dealing with this situation and probably always will be. Will we ever totally recover from the catastrophic effects to our family, let alone Anita? Since the accident, my daughter, Alyson, has had to deal with much residual anger. A positive aspect is that time and being vocal has helped to dissolve much of that anger. My dad is from the old school and wanted to be a vigilante and come and shoot the drunk driver. Many times the emotions speak instead of the intelligence. Occasionally I pop in and out of that anger. Dealing with the resentment is hard, too. Why Anita? A beautiful person, a bright future, why us? My Alyson cries for the sister she lost and I grieve for my daughter.

It was becoming evident that Anita was coming to the end of her hospital stay. The people at the hospital were telling me to look for a long-term facility. That is when I started doing research and making trips. I have a whole bunch of files on everything. I went to Tennessee to Rebound and was impressed. I went to Florida to see a program they had there. I had heard about Peachtree Re-entry here in Atlanta, but I was told they would not take her. I visited Texas but that was too far away. We settled on a facility near Birmingham, Alabama.

Because of Anita's condition at the time of transfer, she went into a Birmingham hospital and was later transferred to the Alabama facility. The quality of care went down. My gut feeling after awhile was that she wasn't getting the care we wanted. The people seemed to be superficial. That was the feeling I got. I was advised to get a case manager. I would offer the same advice. If you are ever in a similar situation I urge you to hire an independent person or case manager that is your advocate and not use the facility's advocate.

Our case manager expressed dissatisfaction with the treatment that Anita was receiving and she suggested we visit a brain injury program in Louisiana. We asked our initial life care planer to go with us and give us his professional opinion. We liked what we saw, so we moved Anita to Louisiana. Anita made many gains at the treatment facility. In fact, the first thing she ate since her accident was a communion, which was a great sign. A minister who worked at the facility administered this holy food. That is when Anita started eating.

A new facility had opened in Atlanta and I began to investigate the possibility of Anita returning "home." With the assistance of the initial life care planner, I obtained another case manager to study this possibility. When she was in Louisiana it seemed as though the accident did not happen because she was a long distance away. Although I made trips, they could only be occasional and we had to rely on and trust the quality of care of the facility. The family visitations were strained and the family seemed to be embarrassed of being with Anita in public. The involvement was guarded, and still is, though it is gradually getting better. A lot of it has to do with each family member maturing in their process of acceptance, as well as everyone remembering how much fun it is to be around Anita.

I have been very pleased with the things that I have obtained in the institutional setting but I wanted something better for our daughter. We decided Anita's quality of life would improve if she lived in her own home. We tried to work with the doctors to set up a facility. There were many conflicts of interest that came about here in Georgia with doctors recommending clients to their own facilities and we were hopeful that there would be a home environment. In trying to check out all our options, our life care planner and I made some more investigative trips. As it happened (God does work in mysterious ways) I was aware of a friend from work who had recently been "outsourced" (due to corporate downsizing). In fact, I was sending her resumes out throughout Atlanta trying to help her find a position because I was so convinced of her capabilities. Lightning struck my brain: what if I could convince our friend, Mamie Walters, to come to Atlanta and help us start a new program? Have Anita come out of Meadowbrook and go into her own home? Could we do this? Could we afford paying her? I confirmed the financial feasibility. We approached Mamie with the concept and she was interested. She came to Atlanta and I will tell you it has made a phenomenal difference.

There is hope for the future. One of the things we do in our business is to make measurable gains in a reasonable amount of time. That is by charting things, to chart the sales. We look for behavior that is going to enhance that increase. It requires positive thinking. Mamie and Anita have positive attitudes and it is evident by the progress Anita has made. She is tipping her chart.

So what about the future? Our long-term plans include the establishment of a licensed home with a home environment. However, as one might expect, there are obstacles (or a more positive interpretation is challenges). We want a home with a family atmosphere, a high quality of life, a healthy, natural nutritional diet for the occupants. We are trying new ideas and approaches. I always laugh when I see Mamie coming up with something new and natural and noninvasive. I am so often humbled when her alternative therapies produce great results. Certainly there are going to be changes that are going to take place as time goes on. There are also many challenges that remain.

In conclusion, I would like to emphasize how much we all have learned from Anita during this whole ordeal. She has brought deeper meaning to perseverance, faith, determination, and love. One of the things that I always have done in my life is target areas in which there is control and in which there is potential for progress. I can look and find possibilities anywhere. I also like to identify areas in which there is no control and learn how to make adjustments or accept this lack of control. This concept is captured so well in the prayer of serenity.

> God grant me the serenity to accept the things that I cannot change,
> The courage to change the things that I can, and
> The wisdom to know the difference.
>
> Saint Francis of Assisi

It is this prayer that has guided me throughout this ordeal and continues to be a source of comfort to me on my journey as Anita's dad.

MAMIE WALTERS: MY JOURNEY WITH ANITA

I remember one day a contractor was building a ramp at my home for Anita and he made the comment to me that if this accident had happened to him that he would just want to be dead. He couldn't see himself in this position, going through what Anita goes through, and having people do for her what has to be done. My answer to him was "You don't get to be dead. You just deal with this every day. You just live with it. You have to adjust to it because you did survive." And that is what I have seen Anita do. What an inspiration she has been to me.

My children's father had passed away (1994), and it was our first holiday (Thanksgiving) without their Dad. Ray's family, being the dear family that they are, invited us to their home. We had a wonderful time. It was about 11:00 on Thanksgiving evening and just out of the blue, Ray started discussing the possibility of me moving to Atlanta and working with Anita. Even though I had never worked with this type of client before, I had worked with Ray for many years and I knew that we have had great success in the past in what we tried to achieve. I decided if he was willing so was I. If it didn't work out, we would both know we gave Anita our best effort and that was what really counted.

Once I made this decision, I returned to Orlando. One of the assignments Ray and I had given ourselves was to set our goals and objectives for the program and for Anita. At our next meeting, in January, we compared notes. As it turned out, our goals and objectives were almost identical, including the time frames. That was really exciting. Our original plan was to have Anita in her own home by the end of the year — 1995. We actually had her home in 6 months.

I had experience in corporate forecasting for a number of years and Ray is one of these math wizards. He also had been doing forecasting for about 30 years. We knew what we were doing. However, I believe the key to our progress was being of the same mindset. Our singular vision allowed us to focus our energies and to be expedient in the pursuit of our goals.

One of the first things we did was to arrange for me to come to Meadowbrook and work with Anita. I did so for six weeks. I wanted to observe Anita's care and have some supervised hands-on experience. This observation and experience was vital in preparing for Anita's weekend visits with me. When I first began working with Anita, and the facility staff was in agreement, I noticed that Anita was very depressed. She had no initiative. Her arms were always folded and her head stayed down unless she was watching television. If she liked you, she smiled.

This was the Anita that I met. Her speech therapist said she just did not try to do any work. Her interpretation was that Anita felt like there was no reason to bother. There was not a lot of progress at Meadowbrook. We believed that there were many things that are possible in a home environment that are either not possible or practical or just not done in an institution. Ray and I were very excited about the possibilities.

In March 1995, I brought Anita home two days a week; in April we increased to three days a week, and we continued this schedule through the end of June. I would bring her home from Friday night until Monday morning. In March, I was doing the care, the meals, everything. In April, I realized with the increase of three days that I might not be able to handle the care alone. My 17-year-old daughter, Ana, helped out and soon became very interested in assisting with

Anita's care. Anita's total transition time from institutional care, including her hospital stay, was 7½ years. She has been back at home for almost two years now (Fall, 1996).

My first objective for Anita, once she was home, was to increase her self-esteem. Without high self-esteem, she had little confidence. Without confidence she had no initiative and so it goes. I began by giving her control. Anytime I could give her control, I did. I bought different colored sheets so she could choose what color she wanted on her bed. I gave her a TV remote and CDs to choose for music. With more choice and independence she began to have some self-respect and self-dignity. I let her know she was loved. As we worked together she gained trust and she knew the things we were doing were for her own good (even the range of motion, which she hated).

One of the challenges that Anita had was to drink enough fluids. She did not drink fluids. As a result, problems occurred. We wanted to increase her fluids. She drank V-8 juice but refused water and all other drinks except sometimes a little pineapple juice. Currently Anita is drinking approximately 30 ounces of fluid a day and she has been doing that for quite some time, and most of this is water. She has really come a long way with positive reinforcement and increased control. We took shopping trips so she could pick out some special drinking glasses for her water. Her favorite color is green so we went on a shopping trip for green glasses. So simple, yet so effective.

Since Anita had a brain injury, I really did not know what she was capable of doing. I knew what I had been told. I knew that there was, supposedly, no place for her to go in her rehabilitation and progress. Her dad had taught her the word "Hi" and that was all she could say for about a year. Anita had not learned how to tap into her real voice so her voice sounded really breathy. I would take her to the computer and she enjoyed it. I experimented and knew she could read. We made it fun. She has learned to type some words strictly from memory. This was a major accomplishment for Anita.

I believe this learning became possible with self-control, self-confidence, and the initiative to work. Once she started working and saw she could actually do things she became more confident and more enthused about continuing to work. At this time she is reading a large number of words. We have organization skills activity where she will group flash cards using the words in categories. Her proficiency is about 85% to 90%. Sometimes better. Anita presently has a vocabulary of about 20 different words and syllables that she speaks with her true voice. This is something I felt could happen. She has worked very, very hard.

Her grandfather was coming for a visit from Arizona and Anita dearly loves her grandfather. She is crazy about him. I asked her if she would like to greet her grandfather when he arrives. She nodded her head yes that she would work with me. In working with Anita I have learned how much she loves Elvis. We would practice to Elvis music. I didn't know what I was going to get. We were having fun and we were working at it. She started getting the "Pa pa pa pa." From this we put a short sentence together. This was a giant step for Anita because of her severe apraxia. She eventually could say "Hi Papa" and "Bye Papa." I wondered if she would remember this when she saw her grandfather. A few weeks went by and we kept practicing. Her grandfather arrived and she said "Hi Papa" and when he got ready to leave she said "Bye Papa." There are some things money can't buy because they are priceless and that moment was one of them.

One of her words she learned was "Hi." We were working on the pie sound and I told her if she learned the word "pie" I would take her and we would go out and get some pie. I let her order it from the waitress. Her most current word is "sly." That is because she is in love with Sylvester Stallone. Sometimes motivation gets easier and easier. Elvis is her romantic guy and Sylvester is her macho, hero guy. I told her if she could learn "Sly" I would take her to the movies. She worked and she said it, and so we went. I think it is important that if you do offer a reward that it is given quickly. In her case, it has kept her going.

We have a Christian home where Anita lives. I believe that the mind, spirit, and body are intricately joined to make up the human being. In working with Anita I felt like the ball had been dropped in her spirituality. This is something Ray and I wanted to address. Today she enjoys Mass. She truly gets very excited about going to Mass. She loves gospel music. We try to address the spiritual side of Anita as a holistic approach to her care. Anita is very strong in her spirit and she is a survivor. I don't require my staff to go around saying Hail Marys all day. They don't walk around with rosaries. We only provide for spiritual requests if the client wishes. I do ask the staff to play a Rosary audiotape at nighttime for Anita because this is what she likes to hear. She likes gospel music so they put in the tapes so she can hear that. These are the ways we are addressing her spiritual life. It is the belief in the importance of balancing the mental, the physical, and the spiritual.

When Anita came back to a home environment, her family visits increased. She dearly loves her family. Her strongest bonds are with her dad and with her grandfather, her aunt and her former boyfriend, Dan, who still comes to see her. Anita is quite social now and loves their visits. She also enjoys our emphasis on games, recreational outings, and community involvement.

Our home promotes prevention. One of the strongest results of our prevention approach has been the vast improvement in Anita's health through our nutritional program. Anita was plagued with upper respiratory infections, urinary tract infections, chronic conjunctivitis, and such. Now Anita experiences very few infections. Basically, we use only real food. There are no canned goods, no processed foods; our kitchen is stocked with fresh fruits and vegetables. We have eliminated meats, dairy products, and sugars from Anita's diet. Anita doesn't have a problem with swelling, her circulation is good, and she has had no skin breakdown since her return home. Her attention span has increased, her energy level has increased, and her stamina has improved. This has really helped with her therapy sessions.

If I had to select one aspect of the program that is essential, it would have to be teamwork. Teamwork started with the life care plan. That was our road map for Anita. When I came on board, it was essential that I have the life care plan available because my expertise is not in the medical field. I am not a certified case manager, rehabilitation specialist, or a nurse. The life care plan was and is a main reference for Anita's life care. Also, the life care plan has been key in our financial success. We provide excellent care for minimal funds. The type of care we are providing costs approximately $250 to $300 per day. This does not include doctor visits, supplies, or medications. It does include 24-hour nursing care, bed pads and briefs, personal care for the individual, housekeeping duties, recreational and occupational reinforcement, and scheduled outings. We provide better care than the larger institutions with less money for this type and level of client.

Another vital aspect of our program is staff education and staff appreciation. If I explain to the staff the importance of why things need to be done, I find the job performance is good and their attitude is positive. I believe in staff recognition. The attitude at the home and the attitude of the staff is one of respect. We respect each other, we respect the clients, and we respect the guests coming into the home. We show a lot of dignity. The staff takes pride in what they are doing because they can see the results. We try to encourage each other, we try to encourage the client and not criticize.

We find that this attitude permeates the home and affects Anita's spirit. Although she continues to receive "therapies" and improvements are observed, the bottom line is that Anita is home — where she belongs.

EDITOR'S NOTE

This story underscores the value of a dedicated and supportive family. The family, particularly the father, was thrown into a complex arena with little preparation. The event has irrevocably changed the family's, and Anita's, lives. Without the caring and unwavering problem-solving dedication as well as diligent pursuit for improving Anita's life, it is unlikely that progress in her situation would have occurred.

22

A PLAINTIFF'S ATTORNEY'S PERSPECTIVE ON LIFE CARE PLANNING

Tyron C. Elliott

INTRODUCTION

It is better to judge a man by his questions than by his answers.

♦ Voltaire

Plaintiff's attorneys define themselves by their ability to ask the right questions, not only of their opposition, but also of themselves and their own clients. In the catastrophic case, the plaintiff's attorney understands that a myriad of questions may and should be asked about the future. Yet, that same attorney is buffeted by thoughts that no real answers can be given. He fears that all his attempts to probe the future or assist the "trier" of fact in probing the future will slide into that murky realm of "the possible" and away from the safe ground of "the probable" where he must remain if he is to prove his case. The attorney also knows that the more specific the questions become the more difficult they are to answer. The safe thing to do then seems to be to generalize about future care and future needs and thus avoid these pitfalls.

Following this course leaves the attorney and his client ill-equipped to stand before the trier of fact and ask for specific compensation for the special damages for future medical and rehabilitation needs. He knows the judge or jury will be asking the next obvious question. What will those needs be, and how much can we expect that they will reasonably cost? The modern plaintiff's attorney must and should provide the judge or jury with all the evidence that exists on those issues.

As plaintiff's attorneys, we are accustomed to marshalling all our own evidence, tracking down its sources, and shaping our cases so that it can be fairly and clearly presented to the judge or jury. We are reluctant to say that in the catastrophic case the medical and rehabilitation needs are too complex for us to attempt that marshalling of evidence. We do not know where to begin. We do not know what questions to ask.

1-57444-075-6/99/$0.00+$.50

Fortunately, we now have the life care plan and qualified persons able to prepare it. This specialization is being followed more and more by various rehabilitation professionals and nurses who, using their background training, become proficient at the business of working out a plan for the future medical and rehabilitation needs of the client. In working with the professional life care planner the attorney does not abdicate the attorney's traditional role as the one who asks the critical questions and who "marshals" the evidence to prove a point. The attorney joins with the life care planner to make sure the right questions are asked. The skilled plaintiff's attorney recognizes that he needs the assistance of an equally skilled life care planner to identify those questions.

Roles of the Forensic Expert

There are generally two areas that the attorney must address in litigation: liability and damages. When a party is found liable, that party is determined to be at fault. The next task is to prove damages, or the costs associated with the incident. The rehabilitation professional may act as a "consultant," which implies that he or she will work behind the scenes to assist the attorney with developing a case or reviewing the work of others (Riddick & Weed, 1996; Weed, 1995). Although psychologists, rehabilitation counselors, neuropsychologists, physicians, therapists, and others offer these services, this seems to be a unique role for rehabilitation nurses and life care planners. Indeed, many larger law firms employ consultants on staff to conduct medical research, locate experts, develop deposition and trial questions, summarize medical records and depositions, and provide other litigation support services.

A more common role for the rehabilitation professional is to act as the "expert" and develop opinions, which will be offered as testimony. The rehabilitation expert will generally participate in the damages portion of litigation by assisting in establishing the cost of future care and the significance of the incident with regard to the person's ability to perform work (earnings capacity). Most life care planners are not qualified to offer opinions in these two areas: future medical care costs and earnings capacity loss. Therefore, two experts will usually be retained to opine about these separate damages.

Life Care Plans in the Catastrophic Case

There are other very specific reasons why the plaintiff's attorney should use a life care plan in the catastrophic or neurolegal setting. It is an essential tool for settlement and trial preparation since it gives the insurance company and their counsel a clear look at what will be presented to the jury (Elliott, 1993; Taylor, 1996). It gives the plaintiff's attorney the comfort of knowing that those things that could be addressed have not been left to chance and uncovers items of damages that were not thought of by the attorney (Sbordone & Shepherd, 1991).

Potential Problems

Life care plans are becoming more and more acceptable to different courts, and they are increasingly required in specialized situations such as pediatric neurolitigation

(Sellars, 1996). There are pitfalls, however, which must be watched for by the plaintiff's attorney. The attorney cannot assume that the life care planner in every instance understands the legal system to the extent that the planner can know what will or will not be properly received into evidence. It is tempting to assume that because you have found the life care planner, as a trial attorney, your job is over in that area. Nothing could be further from the truth.

The attorney must make sure that the life care planner understands the need for a medical evidentiary foundation for each item in the plan. There have been cases where the entire plan was thrown out and the award with it, because the attorney, and perhaps later the initial trier of fact, took the life care plan as the word of the life care planner and did not show or prove that the various items in the plan were there because they were authorized by medical personnel. In the case of *Diamond R. Fertilizer, et al. v. Jimmy L. Davis,* 567 So.2d 451 (1990), the court found that the lower court had approved a treatment plan that allowed the rehabilitation company that prepared the plan to determine the treatment needed. The court held that the authority for the plan must rest with the physicians, and it disallowed the plan. With no showing of medical necessity or physicians' orders, the plan provided for a TV, a VCR, a specially equipped van, a whirlpool, a hydraulic lift, and an environmental control unit for the client. The court found no justification and denied all of these items.

Insurance Concerns

Another area of care in crafting life care plans that the attorney must follow is in those cases where the funding is structured in dependence upon a specific health care policy and not upon general medical necessity. In the case of *Dempsey v. United States of America,* 32 F.3d 1490 (1994), the plan provided for daily attendant home care. The lower court had mistakenly assumed that such care had been provided by the existing CHAMPUS policy that had to be offset. A close scrutiny by the appeals court showed that such care was not provided and the life care plan with that provision was approved. Not only must the attorney see that the plan provides necessary care but also must often prove that it is covered by insurance.

Logical Consistency of Life Care Plan

The attorney must also assume that the plan he or she uses may be scrutinized by the opposition or by the court for logical consistency. If there is illogic in its premises and if it is inconsistent, the plan may be considered flawed and not adopted at all. The plaintiff's attorney does not have to be a life care planner to read the plan in light of its logical underpinnings. For example, if a therapy, such as speech therapy, is proposed to terminate at a certain age and yet speech evaluations are proposed to continue beyond that age, there should be a very logical reason why the evaluations continue after the therapy is discontinued. This also applies to areas such as physical therapy and particularly applies to pediatric issues. If a child is to receive certain therapy only through childhood, evaluations that are pediatric in nature should not continue under the plan past childhood without specific explanation.

In the case of *Brewer v. Secretary of Health and Human Services,* Case No. 93-0092V, U.S. Court of Claims (1996), the court applied just such a fine-tooth comb to the plan. Among other things, the court found that all parties and their life care planners had misread and miscalculated the dosage and amount of anti-seizure medication. The court took it upon itself to research the issue and to determine the dosage of medication and the proper cost. The court also found that the replacement of assistive communicative devices was not coordinated to their useful life and that no proof was given for the number and type of devices. Finally, the court approved an award for counseling for siblings and parents, citing reasons of well-being for the patient, not the family itself, which the court based on an article from the *Journal of Head Trauma Rehabilitation*. None of these reasons had been advanced by the plaintiff.

The Role of the Plaintiff Attorney in the Life Care Plan

From the plaintiff's perspective, the life care plan is an integral tool in the proof of damages in neurolitigation or any other catastrophic injury. The attorney must continue to play an active role in making sure the plan fits the parameters for admission into evidence and that the plan meets the test of logic. The life care planner and the attorney must work as a team in reaching this goal. The plan cannot simply be drafted by the life care planner and then handed to the attorney, who, in turn, tenders it into evidence. It is not a chain letter to be passed on. It is a part of the mosaic of the case and must be viewed as such.

The life care planner also brings a new analysis and a fresh look to the legal case. If the plaintiff's attorney is open to examining new perspective, new things are discovered about the damages aspect of the case. Some may be good for the case, such as an element of damages that should be sought but has been overlooked. Some may be bad for the case, such as the discovery of some exaggeration of an aspect of damages by the client, well intentioned or not. The life care planner is searching for different information than the attorney and in reviewing the same material will shed a new light on it for the attorney.

The level of objectivity of the life care planner is, therefore, very important. It is essential that the person doing the life care plan give the information to the attorney without sugar coating and without bias so that the attorney can adjust the theory of the case to the facts that are developed and not vice versa. This is particularly true in the area of employability. By using devices such as the functional capacities assessment and other tools, the vocational assessment as a component of the life care plan becomes the foundation for credibility. The jury can see what jobs the plaintiff may reasonably expect to perform in the future, how they are suited to the client, and why he or she cannot perform the tasks that would allow other employment. All this is integral to the solid life care plan. It shows thoroughness on the part of the plaintiff's team in bringing the facts to the decision maker on the other side, be that person an adjuster or a juror. The pitch that the plaintiff has compensation neuroses fades before the plain facts of what he or she can do, what he or she cannot do, and how this will affect life in the future.

Table 22.1 Reducing Hearsay Challenges

- Are you qualified as an expert?
- Are you offering opinions that are in your area of expertise?
- Are you relying on facts and data that you and others in your professional field commonly rely upon?
- Are people employed or retained by you working under your direction and supervision?
- Have you provided a foundation for medical opinions by utilizing physicians for medical diagnosis?

Special Forensic Considerations

It is useful for the rehabilitation expert to be sensitive to special rules and issues related to civil litigation. A few are listed below.

Hearsay

The ethical rehabilitation professional who practices in forensic settings provides a valuable contribution by establishing a reasonable treatment plan, helping to settle personal injury litigation, and/or providing the jury with information on which to base an award. Offering testimony is fraught with obstacles such as (1) introducing "hearsay" evidence, and (2) developing appropriate exhibits for the courtroom. In general, hearsay refers to relying on information from another person that may be unreliable or inappropriate. Hearsay taken to the extreme can be applied to your personal identity. For example, you are likely to know your name because someone (your parent) told you your name many years ago. Rules of Evidence have been developed to address this problem (see Table 22.1).

Although the discussion below is based on Federal Rules, most states have either adopted these rules in some form or precedent has been established through previous legal cases. Rule 702 states that a witness qualified as an expert by knowledge, skill, experience, training, or education may testify by offering an expert opinion. Rule 703 allows the expert to rely on facts or data, which is not entered as "evidence" if the information is commonly relied upon by experts in the field. Practically, this is demonstrated in two ways. First, the consultant may hire a subcontractor or use an employee to develop research, assist in report writing, and summarize medical records. As long as these professionals are qualified and they work under direction and supervision by the lead consultant, the information should be allowed in the courtroom. Second, it is common for life care planners to rely upon physicians for treatment plans, vendors or catalogs for costs, and other sources for the foundation of the plan. The key issue is related to what the consultant, and others in the field, commonly "do" to conduct business (see Weed & Field, 1994 for more Federal Rules of Evidence information).

Written Opinions

In most rehabilitation settings, it is expected that consultants will provide written reports with conclusions and opinions. The same standard should apply to the role of the expert witness. Attorneys may occasionally ask the expert to act as an expert but not provide a written report. Although narratives may be optional, conclusions, recommendations, and opinions should be provided in writing. In this author's opinion, failure to follow the standards of the "expert's" industry reflects badly and ultimately damages the profession as a whole. Experts who play the "game" of challenging the attorney to guess what they will say at trial through depositions are shortsighted. This has become enough of an issue that some jurisdictions now require a written report.

Disclosing Prior Expert Testimony

A recent rule has been added to federal and other cases that may require revealing cases in which the consultant testified in deposition or trial during the previous four years. Data should include the case caption, the date of the deposition and/or trial and the state in which the case was filed. This disclosure does not apply to cases where the life care planner was acting as a consultant or the expert did not testify.

Collateral Source

Collateral source rules vary from state to state and jurisdiction to jurisdiction (i.e., federal vs. state cases). In practical terms, collateral sources refer to rules that require that a personal injury award be offset by reasonable available services and products. Generally, this is represented in pediatric cases by including the "free" services that are available in the school system through the Individuals with Disabilities Education Act (IDEA). This may include special education, occupational therapy, physical therapy, speech and language therapy, aide services, and specialized equipment and supplies. Other options may include offsets for Medicaid or Medicare. The consultant is advised to discuss this issue with the attorney prior to rendering an opinion.

Interrogatory

An interrogatory is a list of questions that is submitted through an attorney usually to the client but sometimes to an expert. A series of questions is asked that is expected to elucidate the reason you were called as an expert. This is usually a prelude to a deposition. Generally the "other side" is attempting to discover what will be entered as evidence at a trial. This is a formal procedure that should not be taken lightly.

Deposition

The rehabilitation consultant's role at the deposition is similar to their role at a trial. The primary difference is the location and the lack of the presence of a judge. The deposition can be conducted at the office of the expert, at a court reporter's office, in the office of the attorney, and occasionally by telephone. A judge is not present to preside or to rule on objections by the counsels for plaintiff or defense. While the client may attend, their presence is uncommon.

There are two types of deposition that the expert is likely to face. One is an "evidence" deposition. The evidence deposition generally is called by the "side" that retained the expert. In this situation either the attorney believes there is good reason to attempt to settle the case, or the expert will not appear "live" at trial. Both attorneys present their case similar to how it would be presented at trial. In some cases the expert may be videotaped although more often than not, the deposition will be transcribed from an audiotape or other court recording method. Many physicians utilize this method. Another type of deposition is the "discovery" deposition. In this case the "other" side is attempting to uncover, or discover, what evidence is expected to be offered at trial. Usually the attorney that retains the expert being deposed does not ask questions of the specialist since the attorney does not want to give away any more information than necessary.

The attorney who requested the deposition initiates direct examination. Cross, redirect, and recross examination may follow. A certified court recorder records (and later transcribes) the entire testimony. Since a judge is not present to control the proceedings, objections by either side are stated. The rationale for such objections are given and discussed. The judge, prior to the submission of the testimony, will make a ruling on each objection into evidence at a trial. The rehabilitation expert should be aware that although the deposition appears to be a much more informal process, its content is equally important to that of the formal courtroom testimony. The entire deposition, or selected portions of its contents, may be read at the formal hearing or trial.

Note that some professionals find themselves in awkward positions. Many times opposing attorneys ask questions of experts that would not be allowed in trial when a judge is present. The experienced expert can usually set boundaries, but professionals new to the industry may not know what is proper. Seeking training in this specialized area is recommended in order to avoid compromising your reputation or offering opinions contrary to forensic rules. There may also be occasions where the expert is bordering on saying something that documents malpractice such as incorrectly disclosing records, which have been subpoenaed, or providing confidential information about other clients. Remember, the attorney that retains the expert is NOT representing the expert. An expert should not expect personal legal advice from the attorney who hired them; if an expert makes this assumption, they are treading on dangerous legal territory. The expert is advised to consult *their* attorney if there are legal questions.

Subpoena

A subpoena is a formal "legal" request for records or appearance at a deposition or trial. It may or may not be a proper request. For example, the expert receives a subpoena for confidential records of a client. It happens to be a difficult client who is involved in litigation. Should the records be sent? The expert may decide that they must comply with the threatening warrant. However, the expert must first be clear on confidentiality. The expert should know that a judge does not usually review a subpoena for records. If the client has not signed a release, the expert should check with their own attorney before releasing the records. Recently, this author had a personal injury defense attorney subpoena him for a deposition. The expert was to appear at a specific date and time, but if he submitted records, the deposition would be canceled. The author contacted the attorney to tell him records would be released when a release of information was received. Ultimately, the deposition and the requested records were canceled when it was disclosed to the client's attorney since the expert was not being called to testify. Another example involves a rehabilitation counselor who received a subpoena for her records on a client from a defense attorney. She felt compelled to send the records only to learn that the client's attorney was furious since she had also provided the "other side" with "attorney work product," which was privileged communication. Generally, it is best for the rehabilitation professional to agree to provide information once the appropriateness is determined. This is accomplished by writing to the attorney who requested or subpoenaed the information and explaining that as soon as proper releases or a judge's order is received, the information will be provided promptly.

On the other hand, a subpoena for appearing in court as a witness carries a different expectation. If the individual is to appear as a witness to the event or accident, then it is expected that he or she appear or suffer possible warrant for arrest. On the other hand, if the individual is to appear as an expert witness, it is generally accepted that one can not be forced to provide an expert opinion even though you may be required to appear.

Trial by Jury

The primary difference in a jury trial and other settings is the courtroom. At the jury trial, the expert is called to testify at the time the attorney deems to be the most critical time for such testimony. The life care planner most frequently testifies without the benefit of hearing live testimony (referred to as "sequestering"), although in some courts the expert is allowed to sit in and to listen to others testify.

The presence of a jury and the necessity to sit in the witness chair adds an air of sophistication and formality that matches no other legal setting. It becomes very easy to do those things, which one should not and forget to do those things one should do. The consultant should realize that the jury will not remember most of the testimony presented. What is remembered is the impression they held of the expert. Therefore, it is very important to avoid confrontation with the cross-examining attorney and become an advocate for one side over another. Remaining as objective as possible is vital but very difficult in the heat of the "battle."

One more suggestion is to speak to the jury since the lawyer probably already knows the answer to the question. This is harder than it sounds. However, many juries have been sitting for days in a boring (usually) courtroom and may "doze off" at times. Speaking directly to the jury will help keep them on task and perhaps leave them with a better impression. There are several ways to display evidence to a jury to help convey your opinion in a more interesting way. For example, you may choose to write figures on a flip chart, blow up the life care plan or vocational opinions on a large chart that can be seen by the jury and others, use transparencies, make slides of the evidence, and, more recently, utilize computer-based displays. In general, it is recommended to use an educational approach by teaching the jury. This will be more interesting to the jury and allow the expert to stand up and move around.

CONCLUSION

In the final analysis, the person receiving the life care plan for review or hearing it in testimony will filter that information through his or her own life experiences. If it contains items that just simply do not seem reasonable and necessary, those items will not be accepted. It will create an aura of skepticism about the entire plan. It is the job of the attorney working with the life care planner to analyze the plan and to search for items that may be perceived in this fashion. In many instances, the remedy is simply a matter of giving a proper explanation of why the item is needed, rather than an oblique reference to the source. Some items speak for themselves. Some require explanation if they are esoteric or very technical. It must be remembered by everyone involved in the process that communication is primary and essential.

The plaintiff's attorney in every case is sending a message in two parts: (1) the attorney must convince the opposing side of their obligation to pay money for damages, and (2) then must convince the opposing side how much they should pay. If the attorney is not certain about the future needs of the client, the attorney cannot maintain ardor in seeking that amount. To be effective, the attorney must first be convinced of the truth of the case and then must convince the opposing side. The life care plan is indispensable to that process. Properly done, the life care plan convinces the attorney. Properly presented, the life care plan convinces the jury. When the file is closed, the attorney will have to reflect on whether what was done was all that could be done to see that the client's life, all of the remainder of that life, was cared for in the best possible manner. It is often the life care plan that makes that reflection a source of satisfaction rather than regret.

REFERENCES

Elliott, T. (1993). Life Care Plans: The legal perspective. **The Neurolaw Letter, 2**(11) 1, 3.

Riddick, S. & Weed, R. (1996). The life care planning process for managing catastrophically impaired patients. **Case Studies in Nursing Case Management,** 61-91. Gaithersburg, MD: Aspen.

Sbordone, R. & Shepherd, J. (1991). The role of the neuropsychologist and life care planner in evaluating brain damage cases. **The Neurolaw Letter, 1**(5), 5.

Sellars, C. (1996). Life Care Planning for young children with brain injuries. The **Neurolaw Letter, 6**(4), 101, 106-107.

Taylor, S. (1996). Life Care Plans in court. **The Neurolaw Letter, 5**(5), 25, 28.

Weed. R. (1995). Forensic rehabilitation. In A.E. Dell Orto & R. P. Marinelle (Eds.). **Encyclopedia of Disability and Rehabilitation,** 326-330. New York: Macmillan.

Weed, R. & Field, T. (1994). **The Rehabilitation Consultant's Handbook** (2nd ed). Athens, GA: E & F Vocational Services.

23

A DEFENSE ATTORNEY'S PERSPECTIVE ON LIFE CARE PLANNING

Lee D. Gunn, IV & Tracy Raffles Gunn

INTRODUCTION

Counsel defending against serious injuries is likely to confront a life care plan presented by the plaintiff's attorney in an effort to quantify the various impacts upon the injured party's activities of daily living and quality of life.[1] A defendant must prepare early and thoroughly to rebut the plaintiff's various claims and identify areas of overreaching or weakness in the plan. This chapter will address the defense perspective on life care planning both in terms of attacking the plaintiff's life care plan and in terms of retaining a defense life care planning expert, either as a non-testifying consultant or to testify at trial.

Attacking the Plaintiff's Life Care Plan

Qualifications

The first step in attacking the plaintiff's life care plan is to determine whether the plaintiff's life care planner is, in fact, "qualified" to present the plan. This is a critical issue because an unqualified witness will not be accepted as an expert and will not be permitted to testify at trial. Thus, a successful attack on the plaintiff's life care planner's qualifications will result in the planner's entire testimony, and the plan itself, being kept from the jury's consideration.

There are two levels of qualification that will be required of a life care expert presenting a life care plan. First, the expert must be qualified generally in the area of life care planning. Second, the expert must be qualified to substantiate,

---

[1] Life care planning testimony may be relevant and helpful in cases other than personal injury cases. See, e.g., *Urbanek v. Urbanek*, 484 So. 2d 597 (Fla. 4th DCA 1986) (using life care testimony in a marital dissolution case to analyze the wife's changed circumstances in setting alimony amounts). Life care plans are often used to establish reserves in worker's compensation claims.

1-57444-075-6/99/$0.00+$.50

to the degree required under the particular jurisdiction's substantive law, the need for each element of care provided in the plan.

Qualifications as a Life Care Planning Expert Generally

Under the Federal Rules of Evidence,[2] a witness may establish his or her qualification as an expert by reason of "knowledge, skill, experience, training, or education."[3] The use of the disjunctive "or" in this list of the grounds for determining a proposed expert's qualification has been consistently held to permit qualification as an expert based on any one of these five factors. Thus, a properly qualified expert may have no practical experience in the particular area about which he or she testifies.[4] Similarly, a witness may qualify as an expert in an area in which he or she has no formal training, education, degree, or certification. In fact, at least one court has held that a skilled witness on a medical subject need not be duly licensed to practice medicine.[5]

The determination of whether an individual qualifies as an expert is a decision for the trial court pursuant to Federal Rule of Evidence 104(a). This determination is left to the sound discretion of the trial court and will not be reversed on appeal absent an abuse of that discretion.[6]

Because life care planning is a relatively new profession, there are few written court decisions addressing the degree of experience, education, or other qualification required to properly establish a proposed witness as an "expert" life care planner. At least one court has held that attending two seminars on life care planning and compiling 25 life care plans is not sufficient to qualify an individual

---

[2] The Federal Rules of Evidence apply only in federal courts, and different requirements may apply in certain state courts. However, the majority of states have patterned their rules of evidence after the federal rules and have adopted the case law interpreting the federal rules as persuasive in their respective jurisdictions.

[3] Federal Rule of Evidence 702, which governs the admissibility of expert testimony, provides as follows:

> If scientific, technical or other specialized knowledge will assist the trier of fact to understand the evidence or to determine a fact in issue, a witness qualified as an expert by knowledge, skill, experience, training, or education, may testify thereto in the form of an opinion or otherwise.

Rule 702 serves several distinct functions. It establishes the authority to use expert testimony in general, sets forth the standard for admissibility of expert testimony in a given case, and addresses the qualifications necessary to accord a witness status as an expert. See generally *Coleman v. Parkline Corp.*, 844 F.2d 863, 865 (D.C. Cir. 1988); *Sterling v. Velsicol Chemical Corp.*, 855 F.2d 1188, 1208 (6th Cir. 1988).

[4] See *Gardner v. General Motors Corporation*, 507 F.2d 525, 528 (10th Cir. 1974); *United States v. Viglia*, 549 F.2d 335 (5th Cir. 1977), cert. denied, 434 U.S. 834, 98 S.Ct. 121, 54 L.Ed.2d 95 (1977); *Friendship Heights Association v. Vlastimil Koubek*, 785 F.2d 1154, 1160 (4th Cir. 1986); *Exum v. General Electric Company*, 819 F.2d 1158 (D.C. Cir. 1987).

[5] *Jenkins v. United States*, 307 F.2d 637, 644 (D.C. Cir. 1962).

[6] *Salem v. United States Lines Co.*, 370 U.S. 31, 35, 82 S.Ct. 1119, 1122, 8 L.Ed.2d 313 (1962); *Grindstaff v. Coleman*, 681 F.2d 740, 743 (11th Cir. 1982); *Dunn v. Sears, Roebuck and Company*, 639 F.2d 1171, 1174 (5th Cir. 1981), *modified on other grounds*, 645 F.2d 511 (5th Cir. 1981); *Mannino v. International Mfg. Co.*, 650 F.2d 846 (6th Cir. 1981).

as an expert in life care planning.[7] Another court has determined that a rehabilitation consultant who prepared 200 to 225 life care plans per year and held a bachelor's degree in psychology, a master's degree in rehabilitation counseling with a minor in behavioral psychology, and a Ph.D. in counseling psychology and a minor in rehabilitation counseling with a subspecialty in severe orthopedic disabilities was qualified by both his education and practical experience to testify as a life care planning expert.[8,9]

Between these two extremes, the lack of case law precedent on the issue leaves a gray area that will give rise to debate concerning the qualifications of a proposed life care planning expert. A life care planner seeking to testify for the plaintiff should be prepared to establish his or her qualifications by relevant training, education, or experience. A defense life care planning consultant can assist his or her client not only in analyzing the elements of the life care plan, but also in determining whether the plaintiff's proposed life care planning expert is in fact qualified as such.

Qualification to Present the Particular Life Care Plan

Rule 702 was written as a grant of authority for the use of expert testimony and is therefore permissive in nature.[10] Therefore, in many applications of the expert witness rule, the threshold issue is whether the field of expertise is proper for expert testimony in court. Expert testimony is generally proper in any scientific field that has reached a level of general acceptance. Most courts have at least impliedly recognized that life care planning has reached such a degree of general acceptance as to be the proper subject of expert testimony. Thus, there should not usually be any question that expert testimony is permitted in conjunction with a life care plan.

However, it also has been recognized that the particular substantive law controlling a given case may *require* expert testimony regarding a certain issue. In these cases, expert testimony is not only permitted by Rule 702 but is, in fact, required by the relevant substantive law.[11] In cases involving claims of personal injury, courts around the country generally hold that expert testimony is required

---

7 See *Fairchild v. United States*, 769 F.Supp. 964, 968 (W.D. La. 1991).

8 *Midway National Bank v. Estate of Bollmeyer*, 504 N.W.2d 59, 65 (Minn. App. 1993).

9 Recently, the Commission on Disability Examiner Certification (CDEC) has created a program for the certified Life Care Planner Certification (CLPC). Such a certification assures a threshold of knowledge and experience. Failure to be certified will not likely preclude the expert from testifying, but will serve as an important factor in arguing the respective weight to be given competing life care plans. The CDEC may be contacted for more information at 13325 Queensgate Road, Midlothian, Virginia 23113, phone: (804) 359-3463. Also see chapter on credentialing.

10 This perspective derives from the fact that expert testimony is treated as an exception to the general rule requiring witnesses to testify as to facts instead of opinions. See generally *McCormick*, EVIDENCE 12, at 30 (3d ed. 1984).

11 See generally *International Brotherhood of Teamsters v. United States*, 431 U.S. 324, 97 S.Ct. 1843, 1851, 52 L.Ed.2d 396, 407 (1977) (recognizing that expert testimony is required in medical malpractice cases); *Randolph v. Collectramatic, Inc.*, 590 F.2d 844, 848 (10th Cir. 1979); *Huddell v. Levin*, 537 F.2d 726, 726 (3d Cir. 1976).

on the issue of whether treatment claimed as damages is "medically necessary." Under this rule, many elements of a life care plan will often require qualified medical expert testimony in order to be properly presented to the jury as a claimed element of damages.

In many cases, plaintiffs seek to present a life care plan to the jury supported only by the testimony of a rehabilitation consultant or certified life care planner. The defense will likely take the position, and several courts have held, that each element of the life care plan must also be independently supported by a separately qualified expert's testimony as to that element's reasonableness and necessity in the given case. As one court stated, "[t]he responsibility for establishing a treatment plan rests with a claimant's authorized physicians."[12]

Unless such requirements are enforced, the use of the life care planning expert will enable the plaintiff to circumvent the threshold for admissibility of each claimed element of damages in the plan. Thus, once the life care planner is properly qualified as an expert in the field of life care planning generally, the court will next consider whether the proposed expert is qualified as an expert in the relevant field for each element of the life care plan that is not supported by other evidence or another expert's testimony.

Failure by the plaintiff to properly limit the scope of the life care planner's proposed expertise may result in the entire plan and the planner's entire testimony being precluded or stricken.[13] A life care planner testifying for the plaintiff must therefore ensure not only that he or she is qualified to testify as a life care planner generally, but that he or she is qualified to testify concerning the necessity of any individual elements of the plan that are not independently supported by appropriate

---

[12] *Diamond R. Fertilizer v. Davis*, 567 So. 2d 451, 455 (Fla. 1st DCA 1990). In *Diamond Fertilizer*, the court held that it was reversible error to adopt a life care plan that was established by a rehabilitation counselor and that gave the counselor the discretion to oversee and supervise the claimant's medical and nursing home care, where the plan was supported solely by the counselor's own testimony without the testimony of any treating physician. The court emphasized that each element of a life care plan must be "medically necessary," and that in most cases medical expert testimony is required to establish medical necessity (567 So. 2d at 455).

[13] See *Fairchild v. United States*, 769 F.Supp. 964, 968 (W.D. La. 1991) (recognizing that each treatment element recommended by the life care planner must have independent record support); *First National Bank v. Kansas City Southern Railway Company*, 865 S.W.2d 719, 738 (Mo. App. 1993) (holding that a life care planner's testimony regarding the need for and costs of future attendant care should have been excluded due to the lack of a medical doctor's testimony establishing the need for such care on a medical basis) (analyzing the issue in terms of impermissible speculation on the question of damages). But see *Midway National Bank v. Estate of Bollmeyer*, 504 N.W.2d 59, 65 (Minn. App. 1993) (holding that a qualified life care planner who has reviewed the Plaintiff's medical records can testify as to the Plaintiff's need for future personal care services, and rejecting the argument that a medical doctor must testify regarding such need; the court did not state whether the medical evidence relied on by the life care planner established the Plaintiff's need from a medical standpoint in the first instance).

It should be noted that an appellate court may permit a trial court less discretion in determining the scope of the life care planner's expertise than in permitting the expert to testify in the first instance. See, e.g., *First National Bank v. Kansas City Southern Railway Company*, 865 S.W.2d 719 (Mo. App. 1993) (allowing the trial court broad discretion in qualifying the expert but holding that the trial court committed reversible error in permitting the qualified life care planner to testify to matters requiring medical expertise).

medical or other expert testimony.[14] In many cases the plaintiff's life care planner can best serve his client by enlisting the services of the proper medical experts, rather than by attempting to support the plan based on his testimony alone.[15] A defendant's life care planning consultant can be of great assistance in helping defense counsel to identify any weaknesses in the plaintiff's proposed expert's qualifications to testify regarding the need for any given treatment element in the plan.

In general, a rehabilitation or habilitation expert will attempt to translate the physical or mental "impairment" into a "disability" in order to assess the effect upon the injured party's ability to participate in activities of daily living. It is the role of the physician to establish the existence of a physical or mental impairment, and it is inappropriate for a rehabilitation consultant to present opinion testimony as to the existence of a medical condition or its likely progression. Rather, the foundation for the impairment must be laid by a physician, including any expected complications or progression. This medical opinion can then be translated by the rehabilitation consultant into the disabling effects.

---

[14] From a legal perspective, this issue of specific qualification to testify regarding each aspect of the life care plan can also be analyzed in terms of a foundational objection. In addition to the fact that a vocational rehabilitation expert or certified life care planner is likely not qualified to testify as to the necessity of many elements of the life care plan, the need for qualified expert testimony on the necessity of each component part of the life care plan is also mandated by the general evidentiary rule requiring that there be a proper foundation for an expert's testimony. Even where there is no question regarding the expert's qualification, an expert's opinion must be supported by an adequate foundation. *Randolph v. Laeisz*, 896 F.2d 964, 968 (5th Cir. 1990). The lack of an adequate foundation, as the lack of proper qualification, requires that the expert's testimony be stricken as based on speculation. *American Bearing Co., Inc. v. Litton Industries, Inc.*, 729 F.2d 943, 947 (3d Cir. 1984), cert. denied, 469 U.S. 854, 105 S.Ct. 178, 83 L.Ed.2d 112 (1984); *Twin City Plaza, Inc. v. Central Surety and Insurance Corporation*, 409 F.2d 1195, 1200 (8th Cir. 1969)("When basic foundational conditions are themselves conjecturally premised, it behooves a court to remove the answer from one of admissible opinion to one of excludable speculation."); *Polk v. Ford Motor Company*, 529 F.2d 259, 271 (8th Cir. 1976), cert. denied, 426 U.S. 907, 96 S.Ct. 2229, 48 L.Ed.2d 832 (1976) (an expert's opinion must be based on matters sufficient "to take such testimony out of the realm of guesswork and speculation").

In *Randolph v. Laeisz*, 896 F.2d 964, 968 (5th Cir. 1990), for example, the court held that a properly qualified economist's testimony was improper where the testimony was based on insufficient foundation. The economist had testified that a certain percentage reduction in lost wages was proper based on market conditions. The court held that because such "market conditions" did not appear in the record, there was insufficient foundation for the expert's testimony. The court found that the testimony was improperly admitted because "the expert's testimony served as substantive evidence rather than opinion interpreting facts in evidence."

[15] See *Reddish v. Secretary of the Department of Health and Human Services*, 18 Cl. Ct. 366, 375 (U.S. Claims Court 1991) (noting that life care plan incorporated needs outlined by treating physicians); *Neher v. Secretary of the Department of Health and Human Services*, 23 Cl. Ct. 508 (U.S. Claims Court 1991) (damage award reversed because elements of life care plan were speculative and were duplicated by other award); *Ainos' Custom Slip Covers v. DeLucia*, 533 So. 2d 862 (Fla. 1st DCA 1988), review denied, 544 So. 2d 199 (Fla. 1989) (reversing an order awarding the medical and nursing home services outlined in a life care plan where the testimony of the rehabilitation consultant was the sole support for the award and the medical witnesses testified that the claimant's current care was sufficient).

It should be noted that there may also be limitations on the authority of a life care planner to oversee and supervise the Plaintiff's treatment. In one case, the court reversed an award that placed a rehabilitation counselor in charge of supervising the claimant's medical and nursing home care where there was insufficient independent medical evidence to support the award:

> The award is patently erroneous insofar as it purports to give a rehabilitation company authority to oversee and supervise claimant's medical and nursing care. Such responsibility rests with a claimant's treating physicians. Further more, although [the rehabilitation expert] was apparently competent to testify concerning his rehabilitation services, his testimony was not sufficiently substantial to provide the sole support for such a far-reaching award of rehabilitative oversight and authority.[16]

Cross Examination of the Plaintiff's Expert

As courts increasingly relax the formal requirements for qualifications of expert testimony, it may not be possible to completely exclude the expert from testifying.[17] Where the threshold requirements for qualification are met, any deficiency in the witness's knowledge, education, training, or experience is relevant only to the weight to be given his or her testimony, and not the admissibility of that testimony. Courts will often hold that a proposed expert of marginal qualification should be permitted to testify and the opposing party required to elicit the defects in their qualifications on cross-examination, rather than barring the testimony completely. Thus, when a life care expert is permitted to testify over defense objection, the expert should expect any weaknesses in their qualifications to be explored in detail on cross-examination.

Defense counsel will determine whether the plaintiff's expert is state certified in rehabilitation, habilitation,[18] vocational rehabilitation, workers' compensation, or other form of counseling. A defendant will also find it helpful to determine whether the plaintiff's expert is a medical case manager. Oftentimes, plaintiffs will retain vocational rehabilitation consultants who have expanded their forensic practice into life care planning. Many plaintiffs' experts have never actively served as a patient advocate or coordinator of health services on behalf of an injured party. Establishing that the plaintiff's expert has done nothing more than read books and look at other life care plans in order to present a particular life care

---

[16] *Ainos' Custom Slip Covers v. DeLucia*, 533 So. 2d 862, 864 (Fla. 1st DCA 1988), review denied, 544 So. 2d 199 (Fla. 1989). See also *Alpha Resins Corp. v. Townsend*, 606 So. 2d 506 (Fla. 1st DCA 1992) (court retained jurisdiction to determine which elements of the life care were medically necessary).

[17] See, e.g., *First National Bank v. Kansas City Southern Railway Company*, 865 S.W.2d 719 (Mo. App. 1993).

[18] In the instance of rehabilitation, an individual has a known ability that is lost due to the impairment creating a disabling affect. In the art of habilitation, the counselor is seeking to develop skills unknown to the injured party prior to the impairment. Accordingly, the techniques required to rehabilitate persons differ from those to habilitate individuals. In this paper the term *rehabilitation counselor* refers to both rehabilitative and habilitative counseling, unless noted to the contrary.

plan can be crippling to plaintiff's case, even if the court finds the expert qualified to testify. A life care expert hired by the defendant to assist in preparing the defense case can assist their client by being familiar with all available training or education in the field, and making defense counsel aware of any such training or education that does not appear on the Plaintiff's life care expert's resume.

Financial Bias

After the plaintiff's life care planner has overcome any qualification issues, the planner must avoid additional potential pitfalls. Financial bias is a common ground for defense efforts to discredit the plaintiff's experts, including the life care planner. The obvious financial bias of any expert is that they are being paid to present opinion testimony on behalf of the plaintiff.[19] Beyond the bias that all retained experts have, defense counsel will likely inquire of the amount of money received by the expert for litigation support services generally. Many jurisdictions require that the expert give a best estimate of the amount of money or percent of income received from litigation services. Under the Federal Rules, the expert must disclose publications for the last ten years, compensation paid for the study and testimony, and a listing of cases in which testimony was given in the last four years. Prior retention by the plaintiff's law firm is often a fruitful source of showing an ongoing business relationship that the life care planner presumably would not want to jeopardize by presenting conservative plans.

Another source of financial bias impeachment is the appearance of impropriety created by recommended self-referral. Some life care planners are involved in owned and operated rehabilitation centers. Where the life care plan is centered around such a program, this creates the appearance of a financial incentive on the part of the life care planner. In some egregious cases, defense counsel can successfully establish that the life care planner has engaged in self-referral of prior plaintiffs who have received settlements or judgment awards and entered into the life care planner's own facility programs. It can be devastating to plaintiff's case for the jury to learn that the life care planner may receive a substantial amount of the life care plan funding by payment to a medical facility in which he owns a substantial interest.

Purpose of Retention

It is useful to establish why the rehabilitation consultant was retained by plaintiff's counsel. The obvious purpose is to support the plaintiff's litigation by providing

[19] It should be noted that even where the relevant substantive law would permit compensation to the Plaintiff for the fees of persons whose services were enlisted to obtain the award, a life care planner's fees may not be compensable. See *Southern Industries v. Chumey*, 613 So. 2d 74 (Fla. 1st DCA 1993) (holding in a worker's compensation context that the life care planning services of a rehabilitation counselor and psychologist were not reasonably necessary to the procurement of benefits and therefore were not compensable expenses); *Frederick Electronics v. Pettijohn*, 619 So. 2d 14 (Fla. 1st DCA 1993) (rehabilitation counselor and psychologist who developed life care plan did not qualify as a "health care provider," and his services were therefore not reimbursable expenses in worker's compensation case).

a life care plan that can be used by an economist as a foundation to support a present value of economic loss.

Rather than sharing such candor, some rehabilitation consultants will attempt to present themselves as an advocate for the client who is seeking advice regarding his future care needs and how they can be met. Defense counsel will establish carefully the extent to which the rehabilitation consultant has furthered advocacy of the client beyond obtaining the information necessary to prepare plaintiff's life care plan. In the usual instance, nothing has been done to advocate on behalf of the client beyond the preparation of the life care plan report. For example, rarely will plaintiff's expert have contacted an insurer or public assistance program in order to qualify the client for services. Such a line of inquiry can be most effective in instances where an insurer, the public school system, or other resource has provided a medical case manager who has not recommended the various therapies or other aspects of the plaintiff's life care plan.

Another area of recent aggressive attack is the failure of the life care planner to look at the injured party's circumstances in any "real world" sense. Defense counsel are increasingly inquiring of the history of the life care planner's clients who actually follow through with the life care plan after a court recovery or large settlement. Oftentimes, the catastrophic case takes several years to resolve. Life care planners need to be prepared to respond to defense counsel inquiry as to how the injured party is being presently cared for and the current economic cost for that level of care. Obviously, the life care planner must be prepared to explain why the proposed life care plan markedly differs from the current care plan and thereby justify the increased costs of the more intensive care.[20]

The Basis of the Opinions

The basis of any expert's opinions is another potential basis for criticism and cross-examination. In the discovery deposition, defense will establish the entirety of the work performed by the rehabilitation consultant in order to prepare the report and should determine that the work on the case is complete. Inquiry will be made regarding any interviews conducted and any authoritative text relied upon. Counsel should determine at the time of the deposition that the rehabilitation consultant is not attempting to interpret any of the medical, psychological, or therapeutic assessments made, unless the rehabilitation consultant is qualified to do so. If the inclusion of some therapy, medical examination, diagnostic testing, or other aspect of the plan requires the opinion of a physician, psychologist, or other expert, it must be determined whether such a person has been contacted

[20] Furthermore, the life care planner needs to be conversant with the stress being placed upon the current caregivers, especially when they are a spouse or parents, or some other family member. While the economist may talk about the economic cost to that caregiver, the role of the life care planner is to provide insight into the propriety of the care being given. In many instances, the life care planner will find that the parent or spouse is perfectly capable of giving adequate care with additional training and respite. In those situations, the life care planner should make that concession and remain objective. It is the role of economist to extrapolate the cost to the family member of this type of care. In most jurisdictions, the court will allow evidence of the value of these services being provided by the family member and the jury will thus be able to consider the dollar value of this care in making an award.

to validate those aspects of the life care plan. The more experienced rehabilitation consultant will have the life care plan reviewed by a physician in order to verify the inclusion of the various prescribed modalities. If this is not done, it can be a fertile source of cross-examination and perhaps striking of some elements of the plan for lack of proper predicate.

Base Costing and Duplication

In most instances, the plaintiff's life care planner will attempt to place a current cost for each aspect of the plan. Defense counsel will review the plan carefully to determine the reasonableness of each of the base cost assumptions. The defense rehabilitation consultant should also review the plan and point out any areas of weakness. Fertile ground for attack usually involves the failure of plaintiff's plan to recognize the availability of bulk purchasing and long-term contractual rates. Many plaintiffs' plans will set forth an hourly rate for home health aides, nursing services, and household services. Such hourly rates are then extrapolated by the plaintiff's economist, resulting in exorbitant annual costs. It is not unusual to be able to demonstrate that the annual cost of hourly services is more than double the cost of negotiated contract rates.

Plaintiffs' life care plans also commonly provide for many duplications of services and supportive items. Duplication is not only a basis for attack of the life care plan in argument to the jury, but may also result in the court striking all or part of the plan.[21] All costs of the life care plan should therefore be carefully assessed and a determination made of whether plaintiff is recognizing the fixed costs that would not be relatable to the injury event. For example, where a plaintiff's injury requires a special diet, the cost of the special diet should be offset by the normally expected food cost incurred by any individual. In instances of special transportation requirements, it is important to establish whether the plaintiff's plan has set off for those transportation expenses that would have been normally incurred. Where group home residency is being recommended, plaintiff's plan should set off for typical housing costs. The group home rate often includes laundry, food, and other expenses that may also be included in some other aspect of the plaintiff's economic analysis, such as lost earnings capacity.

Finally, defense counsel should explore with plaintiff's expert any consideration given to the availability of public programs or collateral sources.[22] It should be noted that the collateral source rules of the particular jurisdiction may impact the permissible scope of such evidence.[23] In most states, the collateral source rule has been modified to allow defendants to set off insurance benefits provided without lien rights and benefits provided or available under public assistance programs from the damages awarded. Defendant's rehabilitation consultant should

---

[21] *Neher v. Secretary of the Department of Health and Human Services*, 23 Cl. Ct. 508 (U.S. Claims Court 1991) (damage award reversed because elements of life care plan were speculative and were duplicated by other award).

[22] See generally *Cates v. Wilson*, 361 S.E.2d 734 (N.C. 1987) (noting that the Plaintiff's life care planner testified both in the Plaintiff's case in chief and on cross-examination by the defense regarding the availability of public facilities to meet the needs outlined in the life care plan).

[23] See generally *Cates v. Wilson*, 361 S.E.2d 734 (N.C. 1987).

assist defense counsel in pointing out those matters called for by plaintiff's plan for which there may be a government agency or other funding source not considered in plaintiff's economic analysis.

For example, states receiving federal funds are required to provide comparable education opportunities to severely handicapped children until age 18. The public school system also makes available those therapies that are required to further the educational opportunities of the student. Therefore, the public school program is an excellent resource for cases of catastrophic injury to infants and young children. Defense counsel should establish plaintiff's rehabilitation consultant's position with respect to the consideration of these public programs and be prepared to rebut plaintiff's expected contention that such programs are substandard and inappropriate for the particular client. The failure of a plaintiff's life care planner to recognize and take into account the availability and suitability of charitable and other publicly funded programs can cast doubt on an otherwise objectively prepared analysis.

Licensing Issues

To these authors' knowledge, no state has any specific licensing requirements for persons who author life care plans. As the majority of life care planning involves the medicolegal context, the lack of any standardized requirements and licensure makes the area fertile ground for those persons who wish to claim "expertise" for sale on the open market. Unlike recognized specialties that are subject to licensing requirements, the field is open to the unscrupulous expert who views the life care plan as a device to sell in the forensic marketplace. Without licensure, it is impossible to self-police those who are claiming to be life care planners. The long-term solution is the creation of a national standards organization that becomes recognized by the states and lobbies for enactment of statutory licensing.

In the absence of separate licensure, life care planners must be mindful of the limitations that are imposed by existing state licensure laws. In most states, persons are required to hold one or more licenses before they may prescribe or perform various therapies. For example, a licensed vocational rehabilitation counselor is not qualified in the State of Florida to prescribe or perform physical therapy. Moreover, therapists licensed to perform physical therapy may only do so subject to intermittent physician reviews. Life care planners must therefore be mindful not to misrepresent to the client or the jury the ability to "recommend" the various treatment modalities that the life care planner is not independently qualified to opine as reasonable and necessary.

Due to the minimal organization within the life care planning profession, a myriad of qualifications are typically seen on the life care planner's resume. The life care planner's formal training may be as a vocational rehabilitation counselor, nurse, certified case manager, mental health counselor, or some combination of these and other professions. Thus, the ability of the life care planner to give specific opinions for care will vary with the type of case presented. For example, a vocational rehabilitation counselor who has no training in case management or nursing is not qualified to render a life care plan assessing the needs of a child with catastrophic birth-related injuries. The same life care planner may, however, be perfectly qualified to render a life care plan in the case of a less catastrophically injured plaintiff who simply requires modality seeking to reasonably accommodate the client in the work force throughout his remaining work life. Conversely, a certified case manager with nursing experience in the long-term care of persons with impaired mobility would be well-suited to the evaluation of the life care needs of the catastrophically injured child and ill-equipped to assess the needs of the less catastrophically injured worker. Thus, the life care planner seeking to provide services in a medicolegal context should assess his or her own limitations and accept cases accordingly.

Moreover, a certified case manager may be very well qualified to opine as to future durable goods requirements and perhaps the nursing care coverage required for the type of injury presented. This same case manager would, however, be required to defer to a qualified physician the issue of future surgeries and attendant complications, prescription medication, and prescribed therapies. Similarly, this life care planner should defer to an orthotist for the type of orthopedic bracing required and the various therapists involved in the care for the form and frequency of therapy provided. As the clinical care of the catastrophically injured person involves a multidisciplinary approach, the life care planner should not be hesitant to interact with and gain insight from these disciplines when creating a plan. In fact, the greatest service the life care planner can provide to a retaining attorney is to express the limitations of the planner to give opinions and encourage the retaining party's use of other experts so as to assure a credible and legally sufficient foundation for the admission of the life care plan.

Many life care planners are unwilling to accept their own limitations for fear that it will erode the role of the life care planner. Such persons are encouraged to look at the other fields that are called upon to participate in the legal system. For example, economists were called upon to render opinions concerning future economic loss in catastrophically injured cases long before the assistance provided by life care planners today was available. In order to properly perform this assessment, the economist would frequently review the opinions of the health care providers, the costs provided therein, and the extrapolations required based upon this foundation of information.

The life care planner's role is to take this analysis to the next step and include a more holistic approach. The weakness of the economist's analysis historically was that it was incomplete in its scope. It is submitted that the life care planner is best able to assist the legal professional by using experience to dictate the probable needs that will be involved with a patient's future care. This assures that the life care planner and attorney will research and consider all aspects of care in creating the life care plan. Just as most of the economist's report of future economic losses is predicated by facts gained from others, there is no weakness in a life care planner relying upon information gained from other sources. Such reliance may make the difference between admissibility and inadmissibility of the life care planner's testimony.

THE DECISION TO RETAIN A DEFENSE REHABILITATION CONSULTANT

Because cases that are appropriate for plaintiff's use of a life care plan typically involve catastrophic physical injury and/or significant brain damage, the defense counsel is well advised to retain a defense rehabilitation consultant early in the case. Oftentimes courts do not require disclosure of experts'opinions until the months immediately preceding the trial.[24] As such, much of the discovery will be completed before the defendant has an opportunity to receive plaintiff's life care plan.

In order to be properly prepared to rebut the plaintiff's plan and to determine whether to present a defense plan, it is vital that much of the groundwork be laid in the early portions of the case discovery. A defense rehabilitation consultant can provide early assistance by suggesting the various records that should be requested and identifying persons to be deposed in order to make the determinations necessary to evaluate the injured party's life care needs. In most cases, the defense consultant rehabilitation consultant will not need to spend a significant amount of time or money in order to provide this initial assistance. Moreover, the dividends returned on this initial investment are paid in the form of easing the inevitably compressed final preparation toward trial.

The actual selection of a particular rehabilitation consultant requires a basic understanding of the types of injuries involved in the case and an investigation of those experts available and qualified to support the defense. The qualifications of any proposed rehabilitation consultant should be reviewed carefully by defense counsel. Most defense counsel will want to review the potential rehabilitation consultant's current curriculum vitae and rate sheet. Defense counsel will likely request referrals from other attorneys who have hired the counselor, in order to confirm both the expert's qualifications and his abilities as a witness.

Ultimately, defense counsel must exercise judgment in determining the practical interplay of the retained rehabilitation expert with the overall theme of the defense and the other experts. For example, if the plaintiff has no in-state experts, then defendant's theme may be to retain only local experts on all issues in order to point out the need for plaintiff to go to other jurisdictions to get experts to support the case. As with the selection of any expert, the overall picture of the case must not be lost and the rehabilitation expert must make a good fit.

THE TESTIFYING DEFENDANT REHABILITATION CONSULTANT

The initial scope of retention is usually limited to service as a consulting expert to assist defense counsel in the rebuttal of plaintiff's life care plan. In some cases, the defendant may want to take the next step and hire his or her own life care planning expert to testify at trial. The decision of whether to call a defense rehabilitation consultant at trial is troublesome and must be made on a case by case basis. Several factors affect this decision. First, a credible life care planner, even though testifying for the defense, will likely validate at least some of the plaintiff's plan. Defense counsel must weigh the price of validation of some or all of the plaintiff's plan with the benefit of attacking the credibility of those portions with which the defense rehabilitation consultant has substantial disagreement. Just as a defendant intends to elicit substantial concessions from plaintiff's

---

[24] Life care plans are subject to the same requirements for pretrial disclosure as are applied to other evidence in the particular jurisdiction, and the life care plan may be stricken for failure to comply with such pretrial discovery requirements. See *Department of Health and Rehabilitative Services v. Spivak*, 675 So. 2d 241 (Fla. 4th DCA 1996).

rehabilitation consultant on cross-examination, so too plaintiff's counsel anticipates being able to reinforce much of the plaintiff's theory of the case through cross-examination of the defense expert.

A second and perhaps more important factor in deciding whether to call a defense rehabilitation consultant as a testifying expert is the impact of this decision on the discoverability of the expert's work and opinions. In most jurisdictions, the contributions of consulting experts who do not testify at trial are protected by the work-product privilege. For example, under the federal rules, a party can discover facts known or opinions held by another party's consulting experts only upon a showing of "exceptional circumstances under which it is impracticable for the party seeking discovery to obtain facts or opinions on the same subject by other means."[25] Absent such a showing of exceptional circumstances, which is extremely rare, the expert's work is protected from discovery.

However, such protection is usually not afforded to experts expected to testify at trial. Thus, in instances where the rehabilitation consultant may be called upon to testify, both defense counsel and the life care expert should be aware that matters that would have been protected as work product if prepared by a consulting expert may be stripped of that protection. Notes, memorandums, research, and other matters held by the consulting expert may, by the decision to have the expert testify at trial, be transformed into the discoverable file materials of a testifying expert.[26] These materials may outline a great deal of the defense theory of the case. The cost of disclosing these materials to the plaintiff prior to trial may outweigh the benefit of having a defense life care planner testify at trial.

Furthermore, under the *federal* rules, a party must automatically disclose the identity of all testifying experts, and each testifying expert must provide the opposing party with a report that contains "a complete statement of all opinions to be expressed and the basis and reasons therefor; the data or other information considered by the witness in forming the opinions; any exhibits to be used as a summary of or support for the opinions; the qualifications of the witness, including a list of all publications authored by the witness within the preceding ten years; the compensation to be paid for the study and the testimony; and a listing of any other cases in which the witness has testified as an expert at trial or by deposition within the preceding four years."[27] This report must be provided 90 days prior to the trial date or at such other time as the court requires.[28] Additionally, the opposing party may depose any testifying expert, and the opposing party is entitled to take that deposition after the disclosure of the expert's report.[29] Such disclosure requirements and discovery opportunities are a substantial consideration in determining whether to retain a testifying life care expert for the defense.

In instances where the defense rehabilitation consultant will testify, it is imperative that a physical examination of the injured party occur, or that the court be requested to allow such an examination. Otherwise, the plaintiff will make the often persuasive argument that the defense expert has not even seen his

[25] See *Federal Rule of Civil Procedure* 26(b)(4)(B).
[26] See *Federal Rule of Civil Procedure* 26(b)(4)(A).
[27] See *Federal Rule of Civil Procedure* 26(a)(2)(A),(B).
[28] See *Federal Rule of Civil Procedure* 26(a)(2)(C).
[29] See *Federal Rule of Civil Procedure* 26(b)(4)(A).

client. As the provision of care to severely injured persons continues to become more complex and specialized, it is essential to recognize a multidisciplinary approach and to allow the defense rehabilitation consultant access to the depositions and, if possible, the actual persons involved in the care and treatment of the injured party.

In catastrophic injury cases, it is advisable for defense counsel to work with the rehabilitation consultant to engage the services of the specialized physicians and therapists necessary for the overall assessment of a life care plan. However, many jurisdictions have patient-physician or other privileges that preclude defense-retained experts from meeting with the plaintiff's physicians and therapists.[30] Additionally, many treating physicians and therapists do not want to become involved in litigation and therefore refuse to be informally interviewed by a defense-retained rehabilitation consultant. In such situations, compiling a defense team is the only approach that will assure a complete evidentiary foundation for a defense life care plan. Plaintiffs obviously have a distinct advantage in having access to treating physicians. The defense must minimize this advantage by putting together its own team of experts and, if permitted under the laws of the relevant jurisdiction, explaining to the jury why such assembly was necessary.

PRACTICAL CONSIDERATIONS: THE EFFECT ON THE JURY

It must be remembered by both plaintiff and defendant that the life care plan will not be presented in a vacuum. Issues of liability and causation can be affected by the credibility of the plaintiff's life care plan. Both plaintiff and defendant must be certain that they retain a well qualified, knowledgeable rehabilitation or habilitation expert who will present an objective life care plan. Although the economic incentive to prepare an overreaching life care plan can be tempting to plaintiff, the presentation of such a plan to the jury will often have a spillover effect on the overall view of the case. It may offend the jury and thereby swing a close liability case in favor of the defense. Defense counsel must therefore be prepared to take full advantage of the overreaching life care planner.

Conversely, the requirements of care for the injured party that are set forth in the life care plan directly affect the economic costs of the injury and indirectly affect the non-economic losses by the life care plan's efforts at improving the quality of life. Defense counsel must therefore be cognizant that an attack on any aspect of the plan may be viewed as insensitive to the efforts at improving the plaintiff's quality of life. Just as the overreaching plaintiff can alienate a jury, the insensitive attack on elements of a plan that appear not "reasonable and necessary" for the benefit of the injured party can offend juries.

CONCLUSION

Defense counsel involved in the catastrophic injury case in which the plaintiff relies upon a life care plan is advised to aggressively attack damages. This attack begins with early retention of defense experts, including a rehabilitation consultant.

[30] See McCormick, *EVIDENCE*, 98 at 244 n.5 (noting that more than 40 states recognize a physician-patient privilege).

At a minimum, the defense rehabilitation consultant will be instrumental in preparation of early discovery and effective cross-examination of plaintiff's expert. In instances where plaintiff's life care plan warrants the presentation of an alternative defense life care plan, the early involvement and careful presentation of the defense rehabilitation consultant as a testifying expert can enhance the overall credibility of the defendant's case and provide the jury with a more reasonable economic alternative.

IV

GENERAL ISSUES

24

ETHICAL ISSUES IN LIFE CARE PLANNING

Terry L. Blackwell

INTRODUCTION

Ethics and ethical responsibilities are issues that life care planners confront often during the course of their practice, especially during this time of rapid change in social and professional values and priorities. With this increasing complexity, professionals are more frequently being faced with dilemmas that require familiarity and skill in the areas of ethics and ethical decision making (Swartz, Martin, & Blackwell, 1996). The provision of competent and beneficial services for people with catastrophic injuries requires a keen awareness of ethical issues and standards at all times throughout the development and implementation phases of a life care plan. In essence, ethics provide an essential guide for the work of life care planning and are the process through which life care planners enhance, inform, expand, and improve their ability to work effectively with individuals with catastrophic injury.

The term *ethics* generally refers to a system of moral principles of conduct that guide the behavior of an individual or profession. These are principles that are considered to be fundamental in that they are proven to have enduring, permanent value (Beauchamp & Childress, 1994; Corey, Corey, & Callanan, 1993; Covey, 1989). From a professional perspective these principles can be viewed as a level of moral justification and described as a method of reflection on moral issues that focus on the goals of (1) solving a particular ethical dilemma or set of dilemmas, and (2) establishing a framework to guide future ethical thinking and behavior (Meara, Schmidt, & Day, 1996).

There are four principles — autonomy, beneficence, nonmaleficence, and justice — that are considered to be relatively well-established, broad standards that provide the foundation for ethical choices in health care and rehabilitation (Beauchamp & Childress, 1994; Blackwell, 1995a; Blackwell, Martin, & Scalia, 1994; Rubin, Wilson, Fischer, & Vaughn, 1992). In reviewing these principles, however, it must be noted that none is paramount over the others, nor are they arranged in any hierarchial order. Further, while these principles do not provide a one-to-one correspondence to action, they do provide a practical and commonsensical set of concepts that can be applied effectively to a variety of ethical issues that might be encountered during the life care planning process.

1-57444-075-6/99/$0.00+$.50

Ethical Foundations

Autonomy

The principle of autonomy refers to deciding what course of action maximizes the client's right of self-determination and acting in a manner that enables rather than hinders the person's exercise of this right. Basically, the actions of the life care planner, and, ultimately, the plan itself, should be to assist clients in gaining greater self-dependence and control over their lives. Consequently, it is important, where the rules allow, that the client and family be included as much as possible throughout the plan development process to enable them to make informed choices on the recommendations that will subsequently be offered for the benefit of the client (Blackwell, 1995b). Within the context of autonomy underlies the issue of informed consent and the obligation on the part of the life care planner to give the client and/or family a clear understanding of the life care planner's role and function, the areas that will be addressed, and goals and benefits of the life care plan, as well as the limits of confidentiality, prior to the onset of services (Bersoff, 1995; Haas, 1993).

Beneficence

Beneficence can be defined as deciding what is good as opposed to what is harmful to the individual and then taking positive steps that promote the growth and well-being of that person. The principle of beneficence is central to the life care planning process, which places a heavy focus on the preventive nature of many of the goods and services recommended to address the individual's long-term health care needs. Beneficence, however, can become complicated at times for a life care planner when there is a difference of opinion among the client, family members, professionals, or third party involvement about what should be considered in the best interests of the client or about what constitutes a good quality of life (Haas, 1993). This difference often requires a careful balancing of the principles of autonomy and beneficence on the part of the life care planner in addressing issues related to respecting client's choices and acting in the their best interests.

Nonmaleficence

The principle of nonmaleficence obligates professionals to take reasonable steps to avoid intentionally harming others with whom they work. Nonmaleficence, or the obligation not to harm others, can be viewed as separate from the principle of beneficence, which focuses on the professional's responsibility to promote the client's welfare (Kitchener, 1984). Although the life care planner needs to always avoid any improper and potentially harmful dual relationships with a client, a major area that is often overlooked in causing harm can be incompetence. Thus, nonmaleficence can be directly related to how competent the professional is in working with individuals with catastrophic injury (Meara, Schmidt, & Day, 1996). As such, practitioners who do life care planning need to be knowledgeable and skillful in addressing the long-term needs of persons with specific disability types. Competency also extends to skills and knowledge in working with clients who differ in terms of race, ethnicity, and other characteristics from those of the professional.

Justice

Justice refers to decisions that promote the fair treatment of people with disabilities and support an equitable distribution of benefits. This principle requires that practitioners not knowingly participate in or condone unfair discrimination practices in addressing the needs of individuals with disabilities. For example, for many life care planners the principle of justice generally applies to advocating the fair allocation of monies and resources so clients have access to the opportunities and services required as a consequence of injury. This obligates the life care planner to use a consistent methodology to determine the needs dictated by the onset of a disability and for subsequent plan development to be needs driven with the goods and services then prioritized according to entitlement, resources, and monies that may be available (Deutsch, 1996). The principle of justice further requires that in addition to developing the knowledge and skills necessary to work with these special populations the professional must also be able to deal fairly and sensitively with diversity.

Ethical Dilemmas

Typically, relevant state and federal laws and respective professional codes regulate ethical issues in life care planning. While both the laws and codes can provide broad guidelines, neither offers exact answers to many of the specific questions the practitioner may face during the planning process (Blackwell, Martin, & Scalia, 1994). Although ethical principles are basically aspirational in nature and the codes provide guides for best practice, the responsibility for competent practice still rests on the life care planner. As a minimum, it is important practitioners keep current on legislation affecting life care planning, the professional's respective ethics codes, and the organizational/institutional regulations under which they work. However, more important, the life care planner needs to be adept at recognizing the ethical issues surrounding a situation, analyzing the situation in terms of its relation to established laws and codes, and implementing a strategy based on an ethical and moral decision (Blackwell, Martin, & Scalia, 1994; Swartz, Martin, & Blackwell, 1996).

While many of the decisions made by the life care planner will be fairly clear-cut and easily made based on broad moral principles and ethical standards, there will be occasions or situations when the professional is faced with an ethical dilemma and needs to apply independent judgment and reasoning. An ethical dilemma can be described as a situation where a choice must be made between two courses of action, both of which are supported by an ethical code or principle. There are significant consequences for following either course of action and choosing one course of action will compromise the principles underlying the course of action not chosen (Rubin, Wilson, Fisher, & Vaughn, 1992; Swartz, Martin, & Blackwell, 1996). Although ethical dilemmas may be clear violations of specific codes, more often the analysis of ethical dilemmas requires careful consideration of the moral principles underlying the ethical codes (Blackwell, Martin, & Scalia, 1994; Kitchener, 1984; Swartz, Martin, & Blackwell, 1996; Wong

& Millard, 1992). Specifically, ethical dilemmas often present as conflicts between two or more of the four fundamental principles of autonomy, beneficence, nonmaleficence, and justice. In reaching a decision on an ethical dilemma, the life care planner needs to think in terms of both professional codes and guidelines as well as respond to personal values and practical considerations, and develop a systematic approach for dealing with these ethical issues.

Ethical Decision Making Model

An approach that readily lends itself to the life care planning process is the seven-step model for use in ethical decision making suggested by Corey, Corey, & Callanan (1993). By utilizing this seven-step model, the life care planner can, through use of systematic, consistent methodology, think through and reach decisions in situations that involve clear-cut ethical violations as well as ethical dilemmas. The seven steps in this model are summarized as follows:

1. Identify the problem or dilemma: This step requires the life care planner to compile data such as who is involved in the situation, what precisely occurred (i.e., a clear behavioral description of the situation), and whether the concern is a violation of legal, ethical, and/or moral principles.
2. Identify the potential issues involved: Based on assessment data gathered in the first step, the life care planning professional should identify any critical issues and evaluate the rights, welfare, and responsibilities of participants. Additionally, at this step, the life care planner examines the concern in relation to the ethical virtues.
3. Review relevant ethical guidelines: At this step, the life care planner should identify the ethical principles being violated and whether the ethical principles can provide guidance in resolving the concern.
4. Obtain consultation: In cases of ethical dilemmas, particularly with the continuing trend toward litigation, it is particularly important to be certain that professional judgment has not been clouded by involvement in the situation and that no details have been overlooked. In this way, consultation with colleagues allows the life care planning professional to ensure that the resolution is justified and arrived at through sound reasoning.
5. Consider the possible courses of action: At this step, it is useful for the life care planner to identify several different potential courses of action and choose among them. Again, consultation with colleagues is both helpful and suggested.
6. Enumerate the consequences of various decisions: In determining the best course of action to take, it is important that the life care planner examine the potential implications involved. The life care planning professional should evaluate the effects of the course of action on the individual(s) involved, those involved with the individual(s), and the life care planner.
7. Decide what appears to be the best course of action: In the final step, the life care planning professional reevaluates the findings from the first six steps to arrive at a resolution of the concern. Corey et al. (1993) maintain that the more subtle the dilemma, the more difficult it will be to determine the resolution.

ETHICAL RESPONSIBILITIES

Along with the ethical obligations of professionals who do life care planning come certain responsibilities. Practitioners who function as life care planners need to be aware of their dual responsibilities. Not only are they responsible for the judgments and ethics of their professional activities, but also for the real-life effect these activities have on the individual, family, and others involved in the long-term planning and decision-making process. Underlying this responsibility is the need for life care planners to maintain integrity, objectivity, independence, and competency in their work and conclusions. Life care planners' ethical responsibilities also extend to protecting client welfare and treating colleagues and professionals with respect and courtesy.

Integrity

Practitioners who do life care planning need to perform all aspects of their professional responsibilities with the highest degree of integrity, including the dissemination of findings and conclusions. Life care planners often work in an environment in which adversarial and advocatorial pressures exist and where there is often an absence of specific rules, standards, and guidelines. To meet these challenges, life care planners must frequently call on integrity and conscience. Integrity can tolerate an occasional error and the honest difference of opinion, but it cannot tolerate deceit or subordination of judgment or principles.

Objectivity and Independence

Objectivity is critical for life care planners in all professional dealings. In developing a life care plan they need to be free from conflicts of interest and to possess an independence that will not jeopardize their objectivity. Life care planners need to keep in mind that they are not advocates for the preconceived agendas of either client or third-party interests. Their role is to use their knowledge to develop and then advocate for a life care plan that is reasonable, responsible, and comprehensive in nature and meets the client's long-term needs. Objectivity and independence are never static. These qualities evolve with constant assessment of the needs of the client and the responsibilities of the life care planner.

Professional Care and Competence

Technical standards of the profession — whether written or implied — need to be observed at all times by practitioners providing life care planning services. Life care planners should continually strive to improve the competence and quality of their expertise in the field of life care planning and discharge that expertise to the best of their ability. Competence is not only the recognition of one's knowledge, it is also the recognition and affirmation of the limitations and range of that knowledge. Consequently, life care planners should accept only cases they can handle with technical competence.

Protecting Client Welfare

It is essential that life care planners be continually cognizant that the client is the person with disability and the practitioner is responsible for upholding the highest professional standards in promoting and protecting client welfare. This responsibility to individuals with disabilities obligates practitioners to be aware of various situations that could jeopardize client welfare and take steps necessary to alleviate the situation. Life care planners need to clarify their professional relationship with each client from the onset of services and avoid any other kind of relationship that would prevent that clarity and place the client at risk for harm (Pope & Vasquez, 1991). This need to clarify the nature and responsibilities of the professional relationship with the client is especially critical in settings involving third-party requests for services (Banja & Johnson, 1994; Canter, Bennett, Jones, & Nagy, 1994). Further, in conceptualizing their role as life care planners, practitioners need to emphasize they are first and foremost educators. They teach the client, family, insurance companies, and other interested parties about disability and educate them about rehabilitation and long-term care options to help them appreciate the available aids, equipment, and support care services appropriate for the client's best interests (Deutsch, 1996).

Confidentiality

Practitioners of life care planning are responsible for ensuring the client's rights to privacy are protected. Personal or confidential information is communicated to others only with the written consent of the client or legal guardian, or in those circumstances where there is a clear and imminent danger to the client, to others, or to society. Confidentiality also requires professionals to make sure the client is aware of limits of confidentiality, such as when a third party is involved, from the onset of services. Further, life care planners need to consistently review adopted standards, guidelines, and laws relating to the issue of confidentiality to protect the client's right to privacy.

Respectfulness

As life care planning involves a multidisciplinary team effort, each professional is consequently affected by and shares responsibility for the broader context. Professional courtesy and respect therefore become a basic element in the team approach. This collaborative process requires the life care planner to respect and understand the areas of competence of other professionals involved in the process and to work in full cooperation with other disciplines in order to meet the long-term needs of clients. Respect and cooperation in professional relationships consequently enable the practitioner to contribute to the common goal of fostering maximum self-development opportunities for each client. Professional courtesy and respect also extend to the prerogatives and obligations of the institutions or organizations with which the life care planner may be associated. Further, practitioners should not degrade individuals who hold differing opinions such as when reviewing another professional's report or life care plan. This suggestion does not imply that professionals should not challenge the opinions of others or their conclusions. It does mean that the life care planner should always respect the right of others to hold their professional opinion and refrain from any comments or statements that are demeaning or personally critical (Blackwell, Havranek, & Field, 1996; Deutsch, 1996).

Maintaining an Ethical Awareness

Although applying the previous standards is not as simple as it may seem, it is nonetheless necessary if the life care planning process is to further the best interests of the client as well as those of the larger society. In essence, sound ethical behavior on the part of the life care planner is the hallmark of a sound life care plan.

The following is list of activities that can assist life care planners in maintaining an ethical awareness and guiding their behavior and in making sound ethical decisions during the course of their practice.

- Practitioners should be familiar with and periodically review the ethics code of their disciplines.
- Practitioners should be well informed about current relevant state and federal laws and regulations relating to their respective disciplines and the provision of life care planning services.
- Practitioners should keep abreast of the current rules and regulations of the institutions, organizations, or groups in which they work.
- Practitioners should engage in continuing education in ethics by attending seminars or workshops on ethics or reading professional publications pertaining to ethics.
- Practitioners need to begin to develop a mindset whereby they start to identify where a potential ethical problem exists.
- Practitioners further need to develop a method for analyzing ethical obligations in complex situations.
- Because the various codes and published materials often provide insufficient guidance for a particular set of circumstances that might be involved in a life care plan, it will be extremely important for practitioners to begin to develop a network of professionals who are knowledgeable about ethics and whom they can consult in these situations.

CONCLUSION

Presently life care planning is being practiced in a time of rapid change in both social and professional values and priorities. Professionals need to consider a variety of approaches in dealing with ethics and ethical responsibilities in their practice if they are to enhance, inform, expand, and improve their ability to work effectively with individuals who have catastrophic injuries. Practitioners need to think in terms of both their respective professional codes and guidelines as well as respond to personal values and practical considerations in providing life care planning services. Sound ethical decision making involves a continual awareness and preventive posture on the part of the practitioner and an incorporation of this decision making process throughout the development and implementation of the life care plan.

REFERENCES

Banja, J. & Johnson, M. (1994). Part III: Ethical perspective and social policy. **Archives of Physical Medicine and Rehabilitation, 75,** 19-26.

Beauchamp, T.L. & Childress, J.F. (1994). **Principles of Biomedical Ethics** (4th ed.). New York: Oxford University Press.

Bersoff, D.N. (1995). **Ethical Conflicts in Psychology**. Washington, D.C.: American Psychological Association.

Blackwell, T.L. (1995a). Ethical principles for life care planners. **Inside Life Care Planning 1**(2), 2,9.

Blackwell, T.L. (1995b). An ethical decision making model for life care planners. **The Rehabilitation Professional, 3**(6), 18, 28.

Blackwell, T.L., Havranek, J.E., & Field, T.F. (1996). Ethical foundations for rehabilitation professionals. **NARPPS Journal, 11**(3), 7-12.

Blackwell, T.L., Martin, W.E., & Scalia, V.A. (1994). **Ethics in Rehabilitation: A Guide for Rehabilitation Professionals.** Athens, GA: Elliott & Fitzpatrick.

Canter, M.B., Bennett, B.E., Jones, S.E., & Nagy, T.F. (1994). **Ethics for Psychologists: A Commentary on the APA Ethics Code**. Washington, D.C.: American Psychological Association.

Corey, G., Corey, M.S., & Callanan, P. (1993). **Issues and Ethics in the Helping Professions** (4th ed.). Pacific Grove, CA: Brooks/Cole.

Covey, S.R. (1989). **The Seven Habits of Highly Effective People**. New York: Simon & Schuster.

Deutsch, P.M. (1996). **Ethics and Life Care Planning**. Unpublished manuscript.

Haas, J.F. (1993). Ethical issues in rehabilitation medicine. In J.A. DeLisa (Ed.), **Rehabilitation Medicine: Principles and Practice** (2nd ed.) (pp. 28-39), Philadelphia: J.P. Lippincott.

Kitchener, K.S. (1984). Intuition, critical evaluation and ethical principles. **The Counseling Psychologist, 12**(3), 43-55.

Meara, N.M., Schmidt, L.D., & Day, J.D. (1996). Principles and virtues: A foundation for ethical decisions, policies, and character. **The Counseling Psychologist, 24**(1), 4-77.

Pope, K.S. & Vasquez, M.J. (1991). **Ethics in Psychotherapy and Counseling: A Practical Guide for Psychologists**. San Francisco: Jossey-Bass.

Rubin, S.E., Wilson, C.A., Fischer, J., & Vaughn, B. (1992). **Ethical Practices in Rehabilitation**. Carbondale, IL: Southern Illinois University,Carbondale.

Swartz, J.L., Martin, W.E., & Blackwell, T.L. (1996). Maintaining an awareness of ethical standards in guiding professional behavior. **NARPPS Journal, 11**(3), 27-31.

Wong, H.D. & Millard, R.P. (1992). Ethical dilemmas encountered by independent living service providers. **Journal of Rehabilitation, 58**(4), 10-15.

25

TECHNOLOGY AND LIFE CARE PLANNING

Randall L. Thomas

INTRODUCTION

Integrating emerging technology with professional skills provides a powerful tool for a successful life care planning practice (Thomas, 1992, 1994; Weed, 1995, 1996a, 1996b, 1996c). Today, the life care planner can access a wider scope of available resources and information to ascertain the most appropriate recommendations for the client. Previously, the professional did not have access to all possible resources and the existing data usually required considerable time and effort to obtain. With today's technology, the professional can maximize efficiency and organization to produce a quality life care plan that best benefits the client's needs. This chapter presents guidelines for integrating today's emerging technology into a life care planning practice and provides practical information every life care planner should know.

Because of rapid changes in technology, especially computer processors, hard drive capacity, and the Internet, integration of technology can be confusing and problematic to the life care planner. For example, determining which computer system to purchase, selecting the appropriate software and/or network capability, training staff, and knowing how to maintain the integrity of the data on the computer system are only a few of the critical decisions in this often difficult process. Therefore, integrating computer technology into a life care planning practice is not easy and the temptation to avoid the transition may exist. Fortunately, emerging technology offers much more capability, convenience, and stronger computer hardware configurations that should remain functional and productive for the next two to five years. The professional can limit confusion and take advantage of this increased ability by identifying needs within the practice and simply obtaining a better understanding of today's technology.

Initial Steps

The life care planner must first determine the professional and business goals in the practice before purchasing computer equipment. If the goal is to complete a maximum of two or three life care plans a year, including narrative and tabular printing of recommendations with associated costs, many of the commercially available word processing, spreadsheet, and database programs will suffice. Simple

1-57444-075-6/99/$0.00+$.50

databases can be constructed by the life care planner to track information and resources. In fact, a 486 SX 33 megahertz (MHz) computer with 80 megabyte (MB) hard drive may be sufficient. However, this system will not allow the flexibility needed as life care plan referrals increase.

On the other hand, if life care planning is to comprise a significant part of the practice, upgrading the existing computer system will be necessary. Computer hardware and software are now available that can provide reliable and efficient processing. Access to this technology is essential because it allows production of a quality product that reflects current clinical knowledge and superior organization of information. This technology also enables the life care planner to create a summary table for costs during the client's lifetime, or on a year-by-year basis, while making the most productive use of staff time.

In short, technology impacts the life care planner in the following ways:

- Enhancing the ability to organize professional contacts and resources in a logical, easy-to-find method;
- Diminishing staff time for specialized reports or printouts;
- Allowing greater control over data integrity with less dependence upon external computer experts and resources;
- Increasing ability to customize reporting formats and invoicing to referral sources;
- Simplifying access to on-line services (such as America Online™, CompuServe™, and the Internet) for research;
- Enabling access to state and national databases;
- Accessing and distributing information via Home pages on the World Wide Web (WWW).

The successful life care planner should be prepared to incorporate the above changes in a proactive manner to reach optimal efficiency (Thomas, 1994). Following are useful concepts that will enable the professional to begin these "proactive" responses and take charge of integrating technology into the life care planning process.

Use of Computers in a Life Care Planning Practice

The impact of computers on life care planning will be very significant during the next three years. The new generation of computers, including PC processors, such as the Pentium™, and Macintosh® Power PC processors, will give increasingly significant power to the small or medium-sized business. This additional processing power will allow the small company or solo practitioner to execute very sophisticated programs that were beyond consideration a few years ago.

Now it is possible to use software programs to accumulate all case management information resources and easily identify specific vendors, recommendations, and costs for items in a life care plan. Once resources and vendors are identified in an informational database, a fax-equipped computer allows the professional to quickly contact potential vendors for current costs. Upon obtaining the specific descriptions with costs and other pertinent information, these items can be easily translated into the traditional life care plan tables or into a customized life care plan report, depending upon the professional's preference. Retyping redundant information such as the recommendation and vendor is minimized (Thomas, 1994).

Because there are a variety of report requests, the life care planner is able to provide a report that meets the standards of life care planning as well as the requests of the referral source. For example, a referral source may wish to have a summary of the items and, in some cases, a summary of costs over the lifetime of the client. In the past, the life care plan narrative may have been completed in a word processing program. If a cost summary involving mathematical calculations were required, it would likely be completed in a spreadsheet such as Excel™ or Lotus™, or all calculations would have been completed using a calculator. Now, all of this information can be completed at the same time in one software program.

Once appropriate software is installed, the professional will also become more familiar with resources available on the Internet, e-mail communication, and development of on-line databases to provide information in the life care planning process. By using the appropriate computer hardware and software, the life care planner will have a significant professional advantage. However, before the next purchase, review the following guidelines in order to make wise decisions.

*Computer Purchase Guidelines**

1. Purchase a Pentium 200 MHz processor or similar speed Power PC by Macintosh. If cost is not a significant factor, consider the fastest Pentium or Intel chip that is available. The MMX technology chip will increase the video quality of the computer.
2. Purchase a minimum hard drive capacity of 2.2 gigabytes (GB), preferably with 20 millisecond (ms) or faster hard drive access speed. The second figure is the speed at which information can be read from the hard drive. This can have a significant effect on the speed at which the computer operates, the screen refreshes, and information is printed. A typical access range is from 13 ms to 40 ms. The user will see a significant difference in the apparent operating speed of a program between a 20 ms hard drive (faster) and a 40 ms hard drive (slower).
3. Purchase a minimum RAM (Random Access Memory) of 32 megabytes.
4. Purchase a 15 inch (minimum) monitor with resolution of SVGA and/or .28 Dot Pitch or better.
5. If possible, purchase a laser printer instead of an ink jet printer.
6. Purchase a modem with a minimum transfer speed of 28.8 or 33.3 bytes-per-second (bps). This speed is fast enough for most applications.
7. Exercise caution when choosing network systems. Novell™, Lantastic™, or Windows NT™ are viable options.
8. The most popular operating system is Windows 95™, which is easier to use than Windows 3.x™. If you have not begun using Windows 95–compatible applications, do so as soon as possible. Have your staff trained on the Windows 95 operating system, even though Microsoft is releasing Windows 97™ in 1997. This "upgrade" of Windows 95 will have some improvements

* See Appendix A for terminology definitions.

over the current Windows 95 program. However, Windows 95 will reduce the learning curve for new Windows-compatible software programs.

9. Purchase an Uninterruptable Power Source (UPS) which usually costs between $100 and $200. The UPS prevents sudden power outages on the computer and the consequences of loss or corruption of data. It also serves as a surge protector.
10. Select a quality company from which to purchase computer and software products. Choose either (1) a reputable company, preferably one that will offer a 30-day, no-questions-asked, money back guarantee, or (2) mail order through a national company. Mail order companies such as Dell 800-424-1370, Gateway 800-846-2059, or Zeos 800-272-8993 have established reputations.
11. Select a good data backup system and have a thorough understanding of its use. Some users install this system with the hope it will never be used. Unfortunately, the user may not test the backup system until the dreaded hard drive crash occurs. One important quality of a backup system is that it is convenient and easy to use both for storing data and restoring data. The Iomega Zip Drive is an excellent example of a disk backup system.

The Iomega Zip Drive offers a 3.5-inch removable disk that holds approximately 100 megabytes of information. One of its advantages is that the disk and/or drive can be easily moved from one computer to another. This allows the user to save large files, then place the disk in a safe location. Also, the professional can use the 3.5-inch disk to mail data to other locations when it would not be practical to e-mail a 60- or 80-MB file. Another advantage to the removable disk is that it allows instant access to archived files. The Iomega Drive is compact and weighs approximately a pound, so it can be carried easily in a briefcase. The Iomega Zip Drive costs approximately $150 with 100 MB of storage on a 3.5 inch disk. Successful life care planners recognize the ongoing need to protect their investments with appropriate staff training and data back-up technologies.

Software

Software used to assist professionals is abundant in today's technology. Word processing programs such as Microsoft Word™ and Word Perfect™ are a necessity for any office. Database programs that allow the user to design templates are also becoming popular. Such database programs include Microsoft Access™ and Filemaker Pro™ (which is both PC- and Macintosh-compatible). The professional may also explore spreadsheet capability (Excel or Lotus previously mentioned) and presentation software such as Harvard Graphics™, Persuasion™, and PowerPoint™ if the practice needs these. In addition, software programs incorporating the Merck Manual on CD-ROM as well as other medically related software programs can be beneficial to the life care planner (see Weed, 1995 and 1996b for examples).

While much of the software currently available is designed for home health agencies, specific software for case management and life care planning will increase. Software programs such as LCPStat™ by TecSolutions, Inc.® and Life Care Creator™ by Objective Development, Inc.® should be considered for generating reports in a more efficient manner (Retzlaff, 1996). Such programs would also be a business advantage to those individuals using technology and life care planning.

Another type of software that would be advantageous for the life care professional is a voice recognition technology (VRT) program. Voice recognition technology is not a new concept; however it has only recently become popular because tremendous strides have been made in VRT and computer hardware and software are now available at a reasonable costs. VRT programs allow the professional to speak into a microphone and the computer will "type" at a rate of 50 to 125 words per minute with approximately 95% accuracy, increasing efficiency and reducing overhead in this "high technology" approach to office tasks. Most VRT products are compatible with the major word processing, spreadsheet, and database programs. The minimum recommended configuration for most VRT programs is a Pentium processor, 90 MHz speed, 16 MB of random access memory (RAM), and 30 MB available hard drive space, although some VRT programs will operate on a 486 DX 80MHz processor. There are a number of VRT products designed for Windows™ and DOS operating systems, and one program is available for the Macintosh™. Dragon Dictate offers the only "hands-free" VRT product. Initially, there is a period of two to four hours for installation and "teaching" the VRT software the user's voice. Another four to ten hours of practice and learning the software are necessary to maximize VRT productivity (Thomas, in press). There are a number of VRT products available, including programs by IBM and Kurzweil (see Appendix B for VRT vendors).

Also, Internet-related software includes a variety of possibilities such as Real Audio™, a software program that allows the user to listen to music or speech from various Internet sites. The audio capacity will become more important as continuing educational programs and "distance learning strategies" are introduced by professional associations and universities (see Appendix B for a complete listing of potential software vendors).

Computer Operating Systems

Most life care planners will be using the Windows 95™ operating system by Microsoft, Inc.® Some users have hesitated to upgrade to Windows 95 from Windows 3.x because of the increased RAM and additional hard drive space required to operate Windows 95 efficiently. However, Windows 3.x users should make plans to upgrade to Windows 95 because of its new features and easier-to-use interface. For example, the user can organize the Windows 95 screen and prioritize frequently used files with the "shortcut" icon. Then, after turning on the computer, the Windows 95 screen allows easy access to nearly all the activities the user wishes to execute. To take full advantage of Windows 95, the purchase of a new computer (or upgrade of your current hardware) may be necessary. If carefully chosen, however, a new computer system should give two to five years of satisfactory service.

Over 95% of the software used by life care planners can be used on either the Macintosh or the Windows operating systems. With any of the operating systems, the user can access the Internet, receive e-mail, download files, and research the various databases. Although there has been concern over the future of the Macintosh computer and Apple Corporation, it is probable that the Macintosh operating system will remain a viable operating system for many years to come. If the user is considering the purchase of a stand-alone computer system, and is a computer novice, the Macintosh computer is a feasible choice.

Other available operating systems include OS/2™ by IBM and UNIX. It is important to note life care planners seldom use these systems because of limited software choices and the popularity of Windows. However, they are powerful operating systems that are used by many large companies and experienced computer users.

Networking

Networking refers to the ability for several computers in an office to be connected together. The decision to network is complex and has no quick and easy rules. Windows 95 and Macintosh have peer-to-peer network capability built into their operating systems. For offices that have four or more people using the same life care planning databases, establishing a server and a "true" network should be seriously considered.

Once the decision to network is made, introducing the networking program into an office can create new challenges for any business. For example, there is a significant cost for the initial network software and associated hardware. There are also other costs involved such as ongoing maintenance and upgrades. Most successfully implemented network programs have a specific individual dedicated to the maintenance and supervision of the network programs. In addition to the costs for the initial technology purchase (i.e., specific hardware or software products), there is also a commitment to staff training and development in the use of the network. Networking may require three to six months to install and four to twelve hours of orientation and/or training to enable the user to successfully navigate the program.

Using the Internet as a Resource

The Internet continues to grow both in volume and quality of information. It has become a useful medium for life care planners to locate medical specialists and resources (Thomas, 1996b). In addition, most medical centers have "home pages" that allow users to learn of services offered by specific facilities and contact persons in these businesses. Data regarding specific medical costs are difficult to obtain over the Internet. For life care planners that have already attempted to find information on costs, there is a noticeable lack of printed materials. Materials that are available typically are expensive. Medical cost information is often proprietary and the publishers charge a premium price for the information in both printed form and access over the Internet. It is probable that databases with medical costs will become available on the Internet in the near future.

The Internet will continue to allow review of medical databases and legal databases. Some of these databases have excellent information that is free of charge, whereas other databases such as the Lexus system of legal research will continue to be proprietary and have an associated fee. A general rule of thumb is that any printed information requiring payment will also require payment when obtained over the Internet.

To successfully use the Internet, a modem and telephone line must be available that allow adequate speed of transmission of data. There are three alternative access mediums to the Internet to increase speed of transmission. One medium that is readily available is the higher speed ISDN telephone line for access to the Internet, which can be installed to a home or business for an extra cost. A second potential method that offers fast data transfer is the use of the "television cable." The third is PC Direct™.

ISDN Telephone Lines

Users/computers communicate over the Internet via telephone lines. Most telephone lines are composed of four copper wires (but only two wires are used) that convey information. The size of the copper wire (and the fact that only two are used) limits the amount of information that can be sent or received by the computer/modem. ISDN lines will become more prevalent and may become the minimum line speed for on-line users by 1998.

There are a number of considerations when choosing the ISDN telephone line. The cost of ISDN installation may vary from no charge to $300, depending on your local telephone provider. However, the monthly fee is approximately $100 per line compared to $25 to $45 per "normal" commercial line. The ISDN lines provide a cost-effective method for high-speed data transfer either for videoconference or conventional Internet connection. The ISDN telephone line allows approximately five to ten times the amount of data to be transferred compared to the traditional telephone line.

Television Cable

The television (TV) cable that is in your home or office has the capacity of transmitting significantly more data than the ISDN telephone line. A number of TV cable companies have plans to provide Internet access services via TV cable. Video conferencing and high-speed transmissions are also possible due to the tremendous bandwidth available with TV cable. Some TV cable companies are considering using the TV cable for local and long distance telephone access. This method is not readily available at this time although life care planners may wish to monitor its progress for future cost effectiveness in accessing the Internet and high-speed transmissions.

PC Direct™

PC Direct™ is similar to the small satellite dish for television except it is designed for digital transmission of computer data. This rather expensive option is much faster than the ISDN line and can be used in areas where phone lines are not available. Conceivably, this option could be used while traveling or camping.

Internet Browsers

A browser is a software program that allows the user to view and access information on the Internet. At present, there are a number of browsers. The most popular browser is Netscape™, which is a proprietary software program that can be purchased for approximately $75 (although often provided "free" with a subscription to an Internet service provider). It has an excellent interface for the user to "surf" the Internet. Another Internet browser is the Microsoft Network Browser™, which is included with Windows 95. However, Windows 95 and Netscape users still have to obtain Internet access via a local Internet access provider (Thomas, 1996a, 1996c).

Internet Access Providers or Internet Service Providers (ISP)

Internet access providers (IAP) and Internet Service Providers (ISP) are prevalent in nearly all areas of the United States. They typically provide unlimited access to the Internet for a monthly fee (usually $20 to $40). Most IAPs will supply an Internet browser, essential Internet access software, and an e-mail address. With a local IAP account, the life care planner can access the Internet from the office or home computer.

Internet Search Engines

Search engines are proprietary software programs that are accessed via the Internet and allow the user to list key words for topics to be researched on the Internet after entering "key" words. The search engine will review its database of Internet sites and provide the life care planner with specific names and locations of sites on the Internet that have information related to the key words. The life care planner can access a particular site by clicking on the site name. There is no charge to use the more popular search engines such as Yahoo™ and Excite™.

E-mail Communication

E-mail is another primary use of the Internet. E-mail means sending an electronic message to someone else who has an Internet or other e-mail address. This approach offers many advantages. For example, even though the United Stated Postal Service can deliver the same message, the exchange via e-mail occurs in a matter of minutes. Therefore, sending e-mail is essentially instantaneous and typically there is no per message charge for e-mail. Also, once an account with the Internet provider is established, the user can send unlimited messages (Thomas, 1996a).

There are software programs that will allow an Internet user to have a "telephone conversation" with another Internet user (Thomas, 1996b). These programs are in the early stages of development and quality of transmission varies but will continue to improve. The biggest advantage of this technology is that there will be no additional charge for an international phone call.

Videoconferencing

Videoconferencing will become a valuable tool during the next few years. As life care planners continue to purchase computers with faster processor and modem speeds, video compression programs are also becoming more effective. As a result, acceptable quality videoconferences will be available over the Internet. Video quality will not be that of a television, but video on the computer screen will provide acceptable viewing for communication.

Significant commercial value has been placed on videoconference software. Corporations (and life care planners) spend a significant amount of money for staff travels to "face-to-face" meetings. The value placed on the face-to-face meeting is so significant that the life care planner and others will pay premium prices for reliable videoconference software and hardware. Although the technology is currently available, software and hardware for a quality video are expensive. However, these prices will become more acceptable to most life care planners within the next two years.

CONCLUSION

In summary, technology has a significant impact on the life care planning process. Technology continues to evolve that will allow more efficient and accurate completion of life care plans for individuals with catastrophic injuries. Computer hardware and software will allow quicker processing of reports and locating appropriate resources. Use of software such as word processing, specialized programs for life care planning and case management, sources of information, and data on CD-ROM will continue to increase. Proprietary databases containing information valuable to life care planners will also become available. The life care planner will be able to purchase information on a per use basis, i.e., information related to a fee for various medical services will be purchased via the Internet instead of by the purchase of printed materials.

Implementing the use of computers and software into life care planning is more than simply buying a computer. There must also be an appropriate computer system including hard drive capacity, processor speed, software, backup system, software/hardware maintenance, and staff training. Since data that is becoming available is more comprehensive, additional computing power will be required to process this data at a speed acceptable to the life care planner. This chapter contains guidelines and other information to encourage the successful integration of technology and life care planning and provide the life care planner with necessary information.

REFERENCES

Retzlaff, K. (1996). Computerization makes its mark on case management. **Continuing Care, 5,** 16-17.

Thomas, R.L. (1992). The use of a computer in life care planning. **The Rehab Consultant, 3,** 4.

Thomas, R.L. (1994). Automation and life care planning. **The Case Manager, 5,** 77-82.

Thomas, R.L. (1996a). **The Internet and You!** Paper presented at the meeting of the National Association for Rehabilitation Professionals in the Private Sector, San Francisco, CA.

Thomas, R.L. (1996b). Research on the Internet. **The Case Manager,7,** 42-43.

Thomas, R.L. (1996c). Surfing the Internet, part two: Getting there on the world wide web. **Inside Case Management, 3,** 7-8.

Thomas, R.L. (in press). Is voice recognition technology for you? **The Case Manager.**

Weed, R. (1995). Samples of practical technology for the case manager. **The Case Manager, 6**(5), 67-74.

Weed, R. (1996a). More practical technology for the case manager, part 4. **The Case Manager 7**(3), 48-53.

Weed, R. (1996b). More practical technology for the case manager, part 3. **The Case Manager, 7**(2), 42,44.

Weed, R. (1996c). More practical technology for the case manager, part 2. **The Case Manager, 7**(1), 41, 43.

Appendix A

Selected Technological Definitions

E-Mail (Electronic Mail): Messages, usually text, sent from one person to another via computer. E-mail can also be sent automatically to a large number of addresses such as a mailing list.

FAQ (Frequently Asked Questions): Documents that list and answer the most common questions on a particular subject. There are hundreds of FAQs on subjects as diverse as pet grooming and cryptography. FAQs are usually written by people who are tired of answering the same question over and over.

FTP (File Transfer Protocol): A very common method of moving files between two Internet sites. FTP is a special way to log in to another Internet site for the purposes of retrieving and/or sending files. There are many Internet sites that have established publicly accessible repositories of material that can be obtained using FTP, by logging in using the account name "anonymous." Thus, these sites are called "anonymous FTP servers."

HTML (HyperText Markup Language): The coding language used to create Hypertext documents for use on the World Wide Web. HTML looks like old-fashioned typesetting codes, where the user surrounds a block of text with codes that indicate how it should appear. Additionally in HTML, the user can specify that a block of text, or a word, is "linked" to another file on the Internet. HTML files are designed to be viewed using a World Wide Web Client Program, such as Netscape.

HTTP (HyperText Transport Protocol): Used to move hypertext files across the Internet. It requires a HTTP client program on one end and an HTTP server program on the other end. HTTP is the most important protocol used in the World Wide Web (WWW).

Hypertext: Generally, any text that contains "links" to other documents — words or phrases in the document that can be chosen by a reader and that cause another document to be retrieved and displayed.

Internet (Upper case I): The vast collection of interconnected networks that all use the TCP/IP protocols and that evolved from the ARPANET of the late 1960s and early 1970s. The Internet now (February 1998) connects over 60,000 independent networks into a vast global internet.

internet (Lower case i): Occurs any time the user connects two or more networks together. The user has an internet — as in international or interstate.

IP Number: Sometimes called a "dotted quad." A unique number consisting of four parts separated by dots, e.g., 165.113.245.2. Every machine that is on the Internet has a unique IP number. If a machine does not have an IP number, it is not really on the Internet. Most machines also have one or more Domain Names that are easier for people to remember.

ISDN (Integrated Services Digital Network): Basically this is a way to move more data over existing regular phone lines. ISDN is rapidly becoming available to much of the U.S. and in most markets. It can provide speeds of roughly 128,000 bits-per-second over regular phone lines. In practice, most people will be limited to 56,000 or 64,000 bits-per-second.

ISP (Internet Service Provider): An institution/company that provides access to the Internet in some form, usually for money.

Netscape: This is a WWW browser and the name of a company. The Netscape™ browser was originally based on the Mosaic program developed at the National Center for Supercomputing Applications (NCSA). Netscape has grown in features rapidly and is widely recognized as the best and most popular web browser. Netscape corporation also produces web server software. Netscape provided major improvements in speed and interface over other browsers, and has also engendered debate by creating new elements for the HTML language used by Web pages. But the Netscape "extensions" to HTML are not universally supported. The main author of Netscape, Mark Andreessen, was hired away from the NCSA by Jim Clark. They founded a company called Mosaic Communications and soon changed the name to Netscape Communications Corporation.

POP: This term has two commonly used meanings: "Point of Presence" and "Post Office Protocol." A "Point of Presence" usually means a city or location that a network can be connected to, often with dial-up phone lines. So if an Internet company says they will soon have a POP in Belgrade, it means that they will soon have a local phone number in Belgrade and/or a place where leased lines can connect to their network. A second meaning, "Post Office Protocol" refers to the way e-mail software such as Eudora gets mail from a mail server. When a user obtains a SLIP, PPP, or shell account, one almost always get a POP account with it. This POP account is what the user tells the e-mail software to use to get e-mail.

PPP (Point to Point Protocol): Most well known one that allows a computer to use a regular telephone line and a modem to make TCP/IP connection and thus be really and truly on the Internet.

SLIP (Serial Line Internet Protocol): Standard for using a regular telephone line (a "serial line") and a modem to connect a computer as a real Internet site.

T-1: Leased-line connection capable of carrying data at 1,544,000 bits-per-second. At maximum theoretical capacity, a T-1 line could move a megabyte in less than 10 seconds. T-1 is the fastest speed commonly used to connect networks to the Internet.

T-3: Leased-line connection capable of carrying data at 44,736,000 bits-per-second. This is more than enough to perform full-screen, full-motion video.

TCP/IP (Transmission Control Protocol/Internet Protocol): This is the suite of protocols that defines the Internet. Originally designed for the UNIX operating system, TCP/IP software is now available for every major type of computer operating system. To be truly on the Internet, the user's computer must have TCP/IP software.

URL (Uniform Resource Locator): The standard way to give the address of any resource on the Internet that is part of the World Wide Web (WWW), i.e., http://www.matisse.net/seminars.html or telnet://well.sf.ca.us. The most common way to use a URL is to enter into a WWW browser program, such as Netscape, or Lynx and enter the URL address.

WWW (World Wide Web): Two meanings — First, the whole constellation of resources that can be accessed using Gopher, FTP, HTTP, telnet, Usenet, WAIS, and some other tools. (This meaning is loosely used.) Second, the universe of hypertext servers (HTTP servers) that are the servers that allow text, graphics, sound files, etc., to be mixed together.

Appendix B

Software Vendors

Association Management Services
Developers of STAFPAK Plus, software for home health care, hospice and supplemental staffing
800-636-2342
504-833-1741
504-833-6559 fax

Beyond Now Technologies
Software for both hospice and home health
913-385-0212
913-385-1735 fax

Capstone Computing. Inc.
Provides a modular business administration system for home health and medical staffing
800-803-5503
419-866-5503
419-866-9410 fax

CareWare Managed Care System
Provides managed care system software
800-766-1736
813-628-4108
813-622-8460 fax

Comprehensive Health Systems
Provides information management system to the home care industry
800-445-UNIX (8649)
305-599-9992
305-494-5652 fax

Decision Arts
Software for case management, rehabilitation, time billing and tracking, first report of injury, and imaging
610-296-7566
610-640-2107 fax

Elliott and Fitzpatrick
Passport to Data, LMA Plus 1992, DOT Lookup 1, DOT Lookup 2, Social Security Transferability, and Functional Capacity software
800-843-4977
706-548-8161
706-546-8417 fax

Graphix Zone
CD-ROM package for prescription and nonprescription drugs and guide to symptoms of illness and surgery
800-971-BEAR (2327)
714-833-3990 fax

HBO and Company
Home health affiliated software includes Documentation Plus
417-874-4010
417-874-4015 fax

Health Care Automation
Offers applications for alternate site infusion facilities and home health nursing agencies
401-272-6880
401-272-6883 fax

Home Care Information Systems
Modular software for home health agencies and hospices
201-338-2020
201-338-4946 fax

IMA Technologies, Inc.
Case management software such as CaseTrakker
800-458-1114
916-446-1157 fax

InfoMed
Integrated information system for health care industry
800-INFOMED (463-6633)
954-975-3906 fax

In Home Health
Software developed for home health care nurses including HomePac
800-968-3490

International Business Saveware, Inc.
Produces the Workers Compensation Consultant
604-873-2331
604-873-2467 fax

JobQuest
EZ DOT and Job Browser Pro (Windows based computerized Dictionary of Occupational Titles which includes Classification of Jobs and Occupational Handbook for 96-97)
800-541-5006
509-535-5000
509-535-1011 fax

LegalTech, Inc.
Lifestep for Windows
800-255-6945
770-643-9118
770-643-0455 fax

LINC
Software for case management including the Case Manager Assistant
800-424-LINC (5462)
818-585-4115 fax

Management by Information
Software for home infusion includes Home Manager 4.3
501-661-0386
501664-6761 fax

Medical Economics
Medically-related software such as Physician Desk Reference (PDR) on CD-ROM and The Merck Manual
800-232-7379
210-573-4956 fax

Nomis, Inc.
CaseMan Lite
800-266-4300
216-838-8200
216-838-4144 fax

Objective Development, Inc.
Life Plan Creator
813-734-4930

O'Net (Occupational Information Network), the automated on-line replacement for the Dictionary of Occupational Titles available in 1997. See web site http://www.doleta.gov/programs/onet for progress.

Professional Computer Consultants
Tracking and billing programs for home health
800-632-7045
310-578-7781 fax

Pro Services
Software for home health office automation includes HomePro
800-822-8050
414-226-6112
414-226-6033 fax

Medicode
Medical bill review software for worker's compensation
503-241-1841
503-223-6240 fax

TecSolutions
LCPSTAT — Case Management and Life Care Planning software for Windows and MacIntosh
800-733-9101
601-991-0551
601-952-0072 fax

TIMESLIPS Corporation
Time and billing software
800-285-0999
972-930-8938 fax

Voice Recognition Technology Companies

1. Kolvox Communications, Inc. offers OfficeTALK™ and LawTALK™. Please note Kolvox and PureData recently have merged to form a new company, WildCard Technologies Inc. Phone 905-731-6444 or web site www.kolvox.com and select "speech products" from the menu.
2. Dragon Dictate Systems offers Dragon Dictate™ for DOS and for Windows. Phone 800-825-5897 or web site www.dragonsys.com
3. Kurzweil Applied Intelligence offers the Kurzweil Voice for Windows™ and Kurzweil Clinical Reporter™ medical dictation systems. Phone 800-380-1234 or web site www.kurz-ai.com/
4. IBM offers IBM Voice Type for OS/2™, IBM Voice Type for Windows™, and the IBM continuous speech series. Phone 800-426-3333 or web site www.software.ibm.com/workgroup/voicetyp/index.html
5. Applied Language Technologies' SpeechWorks™. Phone 617-225-0012 or web site www.altech.inter.net/

Additional links to companies and VRT products can be located at HandiLinks™ web site at www.ahandyguide.com/cat1/s/s730.htm. Also see www.voicerecognition.com for an excellent discussion of various VRT software.

Appendix C

Internet Sites

Following is a listing of useful sites on the internet for life care planners. The http address is not provided for all sites; however, these sites can be accessed with the use of one of the popular search engines (i.e., Yahoo or Altavista). Simply enter the "site name" in the "key word" descriptor of the search engine. Then, review the "hits" obtained by the search engine. By using this search method, the life care planner will be able to identify not only the requested site, but related sites as well. Once located, use of the "bookmarks" in the web brower allows easy marking of the site location.

Clinical Resources

Alternative and Complementary Medicine
http://galen.med.virginia.edu/~pjb3s/ComplementaryHomePage.html

American Medical Association
http://www.ama-assn.org

Audiology
http://www.li.net/~sullivan/ears.htm

Biomedical Information
http://www.nnlm.nlm.nih.gov/index.html

British Medical Journal
http://www.bmj.com/bmj/

CDC's Morbidity and Mortality Weekly Report
http://www.cdc.gov/epo/mmwr/mmwr.html

Circulatory Resources
http://journals.at-home.com

Clinical Research Abstract
http://www.med.upenn.edu/cra/

Clinical Resource Listing
http://www.med.uni-muenchen.de/urls.htms

Columbia-Presbyterian Medical Center
http://cpmcnet.columbia.edu/health.sci/

Differential Diagnosis
http://www.ohsu.edu/intindx.html

Emergency and Primary Care Medicine
http://www.njnet.com/~embbs/

Heart Surgery Forum
http://www.hsforum.com/heartsurgery/hmchsf.html

Journal of Image Guided Surgery
http://www.igs.wiley.com

Interactive Patient
http://medicus.marshall.edu/medicus.htm

Interactive Patient Simulation
http://www.uchsc.edu/sm/pmb/medrounds/index.html

Lab Testing and Patient Evaluation
http://dgim.www.ucsf.edu:80/TestSearch.html

Levitt Institute
http://rpisun1.mda.uth.tmc.edu

Medical College of Wisconsin
http://www.intmed.mcw.edu

Medical References
http://www.tiac.net/users/jtward/index.html

National Institute of General Medical Sciences
http://www.nih.gov/nigms/

National Institutes of Health
http://www.nih.gov/

National Jewish Center for Immunology and Respiratory Medicine
http://www.njc.org

National Library of Medicine's "Visible Human Project"
http://www.nlm.nih.gov

Neuroscience on the Net
http://ivory.Im.com/~nab/

PaperChase
http://enterprise.bih.harvard.edu/paperchase/

Patient Encounter Simulation
http://www.sci.lib.uci.edu/~martindale/Medical.html

Penn Today
http://www.med.upenn.edu/penntoday/

Phantom Sleep Page
http://world.std.com/~halberst

Pharmaceuticals
http://www.rxlist.com

Pharmatech
http://www.henge.com/~ptech/

Physiology
http://www.physiol.arizona.edu/CELL/CELLHomePage.html

Prot-Web
http://www.gdb.org

Practice Guidelines
http://members.aol.com/sigalg3958/mypage.html

RuralNet
http://ruralnet.marshall.edu

Stanford Center for Tuberculosis Research
http://molepi.stanford.edu/tb.www.html

Transplantation and Donation
http://www.med.umich.edu/trans/transweb

Virtual Hospital
http://indy.radiology.uiowa.edu/

Virtual Medical Center
http://www-sci.lib.uci.edu.~martindale/Medical.html

World Health Organization
http://www.who.ch/

Disability-Related Sites

John Wobus re Autism
http://web.syr.edu/~jmwobus/autism/index.html

CeDRR U. of Arizona
http://wacky.ccit.arizona.edu/~cedrr/homepage.html

Deaf Magazine
http://www.deaf-magazine.org/tips/impn.html

Guillain-Barre Syndrome Disability Resources
http://www.adsnet.com/jsteinhi/html/gbs/gbsabel.html

Texas Commission for the Blind-Blindness Related Links
http://link.tsl.state.tx.us/.www/TCB.dir/blind.shtml

List of Disability Sites
http://www.nde.state.ne.us/ATP/listsites.html

Net Connections for Communication Disorders & Sciences 5.0
http://www.jmu.edu/libliaison/andersjl/commdis/cd-intro.html

Documents Related to Technology and Impairments

Americans with Disabilities Act Document Center
http://janweb.cdi.wvu.edu/kinder/

Assistive Technology for the Disabled
http://www.iat.unc.edu/guides/irg-20.html by Linda Wilson; Updated 11/94 by: Carolyn Kotlas and Michelle Martin. Institute for Academic Technology. (Information Resource Guides Series #IRG-20).

General Resources

Apple Computer's Newton in Guide
http://med-amsa.bu.edu/newton.medical/newton.medical.html

The Center for Advanced Medical Informatics at Stanford
http://camis.stanford.edu

Data Interchange Standards Association
http://www.disa.org

Healthcare Information and Management Systems Society
http://www.himss.org

Health Care Law
http://www.arentfox.com/telemedicine.html

Health Industry Business Communication Council
http://www.hibcc.org/

Health Informatics Standards
http://dumccss.mc.duke.edu/ftp/standards.html

Health Statistics
http://www.chas.uchicago.edu

Institute of Medicine
http://www.nas.edu/iom

Medical Records Institute
http://www.medrecinst.com/

Minnesota Health Data Institute
http://www.mhdi.com

National Clinical Surveys
http://ssdc.ucsd.edu/sdc/health.html

Wisconsin Health Information Network
vwww.fetch.com/whin/net.html

Health Care and Administration Resources

Australian Quality Management
http://www.hci.com.au/management/

Centers for Disease
http://www.cdc.gov

Clinical Surveys
http://ssdc.ucsd.edu/ssdc/health.html

Dysfunctional Doctors
http://http:/ww.wwma/com/kamt/kamt006.html

Healthcare Financial Management Association
http://www.hfma.org

HealthWeb
http://www.ghsI.nwu.edu/healthweb/

Hospital+Net
http://hospital.net/home.html

Medscape
http://www.medscape.com/

JCAHO Surveys
http://www.nnIm.nIm.nih.gov/nnIm/jcahorep/

Medical Transcription
http://www.wwma.com/kamt/

NCQA' s Quality Initiatives
http://www.ncqa.org

NHCSSP
http://www.fwl.org/nhcssp/health.htm

Stanford University Medical Center
http://med-www.stanford.edu/

State Medicaid Programs
http://www.geopages.com/WallStreet/1602

The American Medical Specialty Organization, Inc.
http://www.amso.com

Law Related Sites

AALLNET
http://www.aallnet.org/

About Elderlaw
http://www.naela.com/elderlaw.htm

Advertising Law Internet Site
http://wc2.webcrawler.com/select/law.27.html

Alan Gahtan's Canadian Legal Resources on the Internet
http://gahtan.com/lawlinks/master.htm

Appellate Counsellor Home Page
http://www.appellate-counsellor.com/

Askew School of Public Administration and Policy at FSU
http://www.pubadm.fsu.edu/

BigEar: Current Legal Resources on the Net
http://barratry.law.cornell.edu:5123/notify/buzz.html

Canadian Law Firms
http://www.acjnet.org/white/lawfirm.html

Department of Environmental Protection
http://www.dep.state.fl.us/

Duke University School of Law
http://www.law.duke.edu/

Florida Lawyers Conference Center
http://207.100.183.238/confer/conference/newthrd.cfm

Florida State University Law Review
http://barratry.law.cornell.edu:5123/notify/comments/1665.html

Law Links
http://www.globalserve.net/~aeford/links/links.html

U.S. COURT OF APPEALS (ALL CIRCUITS)
http://www.ljextra.com/public/daily/coaall.html

United States Court of Appeals, Tenth Circuit
http://www.law.emory.edu/10circuit

U.S. House of Representatives Internet Law Library (frames version)
http://law.house.gov/home.htm

United States Code and Code of Federal Regulations
http://www.pls.com:8001/his/usc.html

The World Wide Web Virtual Library: Law: Law Firms
http://www.law.indiana.edu/law/v-lib/lawfirms.html

West's Legal Directory
http://www.wld.com

Navigation Resources

Biomedical Resources
http://www.cc.emory.edu/WHSCL/medweb.html#toc

Carter Center
http://www.interaccess.com/ihpnet/health.html

Consultant Registry
http://lucky.innet.com/~rbb2/webbs/consult.html

Discussion Group Listing
http://www.liszt.com/

Doctor's Guide to the Internet
http://www.pslgroup.com/docguide.htm

Global Network Navigator
http://nearnet.gnn.com/gnn/GNNhome.html

Health Administration Resources
http://www.mercer.peachnet.edu/www/health/health.html

Health Information Resources & Services, Inc.
http:llwww.hirs.com/new.htm

HealthSeek
http://www.healthseek.com

Hospitals on the Net
http://dem0nmac.mgh.harvard.edu/hospitalweb.html

International Links
http://www.santeI.Iu/

Lycos
http://lycos.cs.cmu.edu

Medical Matrix
http://www.kumc.edu:80/mmatrix

Med Nexus
http://www.mednexus.com

MedWeb
http://www.mcs.com/~ablock/www/medweb.html

New Resources on the Net
http://rs.internic.net/scout_report-index.html

Nursing Index
http://www_son.hs.washington.edu/www-servers.html#index

Point Rated Web Sites
http://www.pointcom.com

Webcrawler
http://www.webcrawler.com/

The Weekly Bookmark
http://www.webcom.com/weekly/weekly.html

Yahoo
http://www.yahoo.com/Health/

U.S. Government Resources

Department of Health and Human Services
http://www.os.dhhs.gov

FEDWORLD
http://www.fedworld.gov/

Food and Drug Administration
http://www.fda.gov/fdahomepage.html

Government Accounting Office
http://ssdc.ucsd.edu/gpo/gao.html

Health Care Finance Administration
http://www.ssa.gov/hcfa/hcfahp2.html

Library of Congress' Thomas
http://thomas.loc.gov/

National Academy of Sciences
http://www.nas.edu

National Center for State Courts Home Page
http://www.ncsc.dni.us/ncsc.htm

RegLink
http://www.cybernetics.net/users/RAinfo/reglink1.htm

Statistics (wages and other government data)
http://www.fedstats.gov

United States Code and Code of Federal Regulations
http://www.pls.com:8001/his/usc.html

United States Disability Information Resources
http://www.contact.org/usdisa.htm

White House
http://www.whitehouse.gov/

Miscellaneous Resources

Apple Computer's Newton in Guide
http://med-amsa.bu.edu/newton.medical/newton.medical.html

ARC King
http://www.prostar.com/web/~the.arc/welcome.htm

Assistive Technology for the Disabled Computer User
http://www.iat.unc.edu/guides/irg-20.html

The Center for Advanced Medical Informatics at Stanford
http://camis.stanford.edu

Data Interchange Standards Association
http://www.disa.org

Disability Resources
http://www.valleyweb.com/krrc/resource.html

Electronic Disability Resources
http://www.gallaudet.edu/~cadsweb/disability.html

Healthcare Information and Management Systems Society
http://www.himss.org

Foreign Resources
http://www.dais.is.tohoku.ac.jp/~iwan/foreign_res.html

Health Care Law
http://www.arentfox.com/telemedicine.html

Health Industry Business Communication Council
http://www.hibcc.org/

Health Informatics Standards
http://dumccss.mc.duke.edu/ftp/standards.html

Health Statistics
http://www.chas.uchicago.edu

Institute of Medicine
http://www.nas.edu/iom

K.S.W.V.H. — Disability Sites
http://interpia.net/~kswvh/sites-e.html

Medical Records Institute
http://www.medrecinst.com/

Minnesota Health Data Institute
http://www.mhdi.com

National Clinical Surveys
http://ssdc.ucsd.edu/ssdc/health.html

National Technology Transfer Center Health, Assistive, and Rehabilitation Technology (HART) Gateway

Net Connections to Communication Disorders and Sciences
http://www.mankato.msus.edu/dept/comdis/kuster2/welcome.html

Special Education and Disabilities Resources
http://www.educ.drake.edu/rc/Sp_ed_top.html

Wisconsin Health Information Network
vwww.fetch.com/whin/net.html

Prevention Resources

Agency for Health Policy and Research
http://text.nlm.nih.gov/ahcpr/ahcprc.html

Centers for Disease Control and Prevention
http://www.cdc.gov

Compliance Control Center
http://users.aol.com/comcontrol/comply.htm

Department of Health and Human Services
http://www.os.dhhs.gov

Diabetes
http://www.nd.edu/~hhowisen/diabetes.html
see also: http://www.cdc.gov/nccdphp/ddt/ddthome.htm

Injury Control
http://www.hsc.wvu.edu/crem/crem.htm

Med Help
http://medhlp.netusa.net/index.html

The Medical Reporter
http://www.dash.com/netro/nwx/tmr/tmr.html

Medville
http://www.medville.com/

Patient Information
http://www.evansville.net/~wbbebout/

Physicians' Committee for Responsible Medicine
http://www.sai.com/pcrm/

Stress Management
http://www.webcom.com/~hrtmath/IHM/AboutIHM.html

Your Health Daily
http://www.nytsyn.com/medic

Professional Resources — World Wide Web

Boston University School of Medicine
http://med-www.bu.edu/cme/

Clinical Faculty Issues
http://www.biostat.wisc.edu/net_forum/clin/a/I

Community of Science
http://cos.gdb.org/maps/cos/exp/states/expstates.html

Consulting Subspecialists
http://www.coolware.com/health/pcp/pcphome.html

Interactive Medical Training
http://www.andromeda.co.uk/medical.html

International TeleNurses Association
http://www.his.tch.tmc.edu/ita.htm

Medical Schools
http://www.pisces.com/clients/pisces/elecpath.htm

Medical Students
http://med-amsa.bu.edu

Metronome Online Press, Inc.
http://www.metronome.com

Nurses' Call
http://www.npl.com/~nrs_cll/

Nurseweek
http://www.nurseweek.com/

Nursing Resources
http://www.lib.umich.edu/tml/nursing.html

On-Line Physician Referral
http://www.medsearch.com/pro

Physicians Assistants
http://www.halcyon.com/phyasst/

Quality
http://www.quality.org/qc

26

THE CERTIFICATION MOVEMENT IN REHABILITATION AND LIFE CARE PLANNING

V. Robert May, III

INTRODUCTION

The certification process in rehabilitation has a long history of development one that has evolved into a process with established reliability and validity under the Foundation for Rehabilitation Certification, Education, and Research. The concept of establishing accountability within the rehabilitation service delivery profession began as early as 1963 with a report from the Professional Standards Committee of the National Rehabilitation Counseling Association that proposed the development of a certifying agency for rehabilitation counselors (Leahy & Holt, 1993). Since this early proposal, numerous certifications have been established that address the practice standards of professionals engaged in some form of specialized service delivery for disabled persons and rehabilitation professionals who offer a myriad of similar services and who hold similar educational and training credentials. To date, there are certifications specific to case managers (Certified Case Manager — CCM), rehabilitation nurses (Certified Disability Management Specialist — CDMS and Certified Rehabilitation Registered Nurse — CRRN), vocational evaluators (Certified Vocational Evaluator — CVE), work adjustment specialists (Certified Work Adjustment Specialists — CWAS), and drug and alcohol counselors (Masters Addiction Counselor — MAC) (Eda Holt, personal communication, January 30, 1997). The newest and most recent addition to the rehabilitation certification credentialing process is the Certified Life Care Planner (CLCP) credential offered by the Commission on Disability Examiner Certification (CDEC).

This chapter explores the certification process in rehabilitation and, more specifically, details the development of certification in life care planning. The reader will note that this chapter reviews how the growth of the rehabilitation industry demanded that accountability be established both for the entity providing the services and the professional who coordinates and delivers the respective services. The credentialing process is reviewed and the four types of credentials are defined with applications. Finally, a detailed review and discussion of the following are included: Commission on Disability Examiner Certification process;

1-57444-075-6/99/$0.00+$.50

the development of the certification examination; the qualifications required of a rehabilitation professional to be approved as a certification candidate; and the examination content.

The Rise of Accountability

The rehabilitation service delivery system in this country has evolved from a basic monolithic vocational delivery service system as mandated by the Smith-Fess Act of 1920 (Bitter, 1979) to a complex, multidisciplinary service provider system boasting an array of services that are privately and/or publicly funded. The diversification and complexity of rehabilitation delivery systems over the years are best explained when one reviews the dramatic increase in the number of disabled persons surviving in response to advances in medical research and development, and the response to this need by the private insurance industry. The National Health Survey conducted by the United States Public Health Service in the winter of 1935–1936 revealed that for the year 1939 an estimated 7 million persons with disabilities were living in the United States (Shortley, 1947). The Social Security Administration updated this survey in 1978 and revealed that the number of persons with disabilities living in the United States had increased to approximately 21 million, or 16.5% of the population (Snook & Webster, 1987). Such a significant increase in citizens with disabilities had a profound effect on the traditional state/federal rehabilitation service delivery system: (1) it necessitated an expansion of service delivery from the public rehabilitation sector into a private, for-profit insurance-oriented rehabilitation sector, and (2) it led to an increase in demand for formally trained and educated rehabilitation field counselors and case managers.

The increase in the population of disabled persons in this country enlarged the range of rehabilitation services by expanding the specialties offered in the private sector more so than in the public sector. Rehabilitation service providers were no longer mandated to service delivery as defined by the federal and state systems under which their counterparts were employed, but gave them the freedom to explore other areas that suggested strong potential for revenue collection. Hotz, Maki, and Riggar (1984) noted that private service delivery systems have expanded to include, in addition to counseling and placement, vocational evaluation, case (medical) management, business ownership and management, and marketing. May (1983) further noted that the private sector opened a new field of expertise in our judicial system through expert testimony. It was the ruling in *Kerner v. Flemming,* 283 F 2d 916, in the United States Court of Appeals for the 2nd Circuit that mandated the use of vocational experts in the United States Office of Hearings and Appeals, and since this ruling in the early 1960s, expert witnessing has expanded to include cases involving product liability, workers' compensation, personal injury, and divorce (Anderson, 1979; Grenfell, 1980; Capshaw, Grenfell, & Savino, 1982).

Service expansion continued to evolve in the private sector through the 1970s as a result of the increased demand for rehabilitation expertise in personal injury, product liability, and work-related injury litigation. It was at this time that the concept of rehabilitation professionals developing plans that detailed a person's future medical and rehabilitation needs was readily accepted and demanded by the legal community; particularly cases that involved catastrophic injury and long-term, permanent disablement. However, it was not until 1981 that the term *life care plan* surfaced in the literature (legal publications). Approximately 4 years later Deutsch and Sawyer published their life care planning text, *A Guide to Rehabilitation* (Weed, 1994). For the first time, life care planning service delivery was offered a published protocol and guideline; a valuable resource given the many types of health care provider disciplines advertising this specialty service.

One issue that has plagued the various health care service fields through the years is accountability. With the growth of the rehabilitation industry so dramatic in this country, both in the number of trained professionals who have entered the field and the vast expansion of services offered, there is a concern regarding the quality of service delivery and the integrity and overall character of the case manager or case consultant who coordinates and/or provides the services directly. Accountability is applicable to both public and private sectors, but more so to the private sector given the profit incentive. The rehabilitation industry has responded with the development of credentialing agencies designed to hold service providers, as well as training, educational, and service agencies, accountable. Specifics of how accountability has been addressed to date are best explained through a review of the credentialing process and efforts of rehabilitation educators and leaders from both the public and private sectors.

Credentialing

Matkin (1985) noted that accountability operates on at least two levels; (1) the programs of service to be delivered and (2) the qualifications of practitioners providing those services. Credentialing refers to "…evidence that attests to and provides assurance of the [skills and/or knowledge] of a person or program to perform specific services (Matkin, 1985, p. 221)." When reference is made to a program rather than an individual, skills and knowledge become less of an issue, leading instead to the demonstration of program or service relevant to the specific occupation with which it is associated. There are fours areas of credentials that have strong applications in rehabilitation: (1) certification, (2) licensure, (3) accreditation, and (4) registration.

Certification

Certification is the nonstatutory process by which a governmental or nongovernmental association or agency grants recognition to an individual for having met certain predetermined professional qualifications (Fritz & Mills, 1980; Matkin, 1985). Its purpose is to establish professional standards of practice by which individuals with disabilities and the general public can evaluate the qualifications of individuals practicing or administering the services within the field in which they have been certified (Leahy & Holt, 1993). Theoretically, certification allows the general public, or the consumer of services, to request a review from the certifying agency under which the practitioner is certified for any transgressions the consumer alleges he or she may have experienced from the practitioner. By reviewing the standards of practice established by the particular certifying agency, the Administrative Board can determine if a violation has occurred, and thus proceed with appropriate action. Keep in mind, however, that no certification board has the administrative power to limit one's practice; the Board can only limit one's use of the "title" that the certifying agency awards and for which a set of professional activities are defined.

Licensure

Licensure is the statutory process by which governmental agencies (i.e., state or federal), grant permission to a person meeting predetermined qualifications to engage in a given occupation and/or use a particular title to perform specific functions (Fritz & Mills, 1980). Licensing represents the most restrictive form of occupational regulation, since the regulating licensing Board has the power to grant or withhold a license, thus potentially denying an individual the opportunity to earn a livelihood in their chosen occupation.

Unlike certification, licensing may be a requirement to practice. Approximately ten states require licensing for counselors, including Alabama, Arkansas, Florida, Georgia, Idaho, Ohio, South Carolina, Tennessee, Texas, and Virginia. However, certification may be a "selective" requirement among insurance carriers or third-party payers before reimbursement for services can be authorized to a practitioner. This concept is reviewed later in this chapter.

Registration

Registration is solely dependent on licensure and certification, for without either, registration does not exist (Gianforte, 1976). Matkin (1985) noted that once licensing or certification credentials have been issued, the professional is listed by name along with other pertinent information among other similarly designated members of a particular discipline. What is formed is a "registry," or a document, which assists the general public in identifying qualified practitioners to perform specific services. Some examples of registered professionals include Registered Nurses and Registered Rehabilitation Therapists.

Gianforte (1976) noted that registration could be administered on a state or national level. The difference is in territorial assignment; registering on a national level assures reciprocity and the legal ability to practice in any jurisdiction, whereas state registration is territorially restrictive (Matkin, 1985).

Accreditation

Accreditation defines the requisite knowledge and skills to be addressed by training and educational programs responsible for preparing individuals to enter a specific occupational discipline (Matkin, 1985). This definition also applies to service delivery programs responsible for providing a set of designated activities to consumers. To summarize, accreditation addresses programs or services within a specific entity that advertises and/or offers such services, and **not** the practitioners responsible for service delivery or for teaching a specific curriculum within an educational institution. However, Matkin (1985) noted that one of the criteria for accreditation might stipulate that a credentialed practitioner perform the specified service within a designated program.

Certification Development

Rehabilitation

Certification in the field of rehabilitation is the oldest certifying process among allied health care professions, beginning in 1963 with a proposal by the Professional Standards Committee of the National Rehabilitation Counseling Association that a certification system be designed to bring accountability to rehabilitation counseling (Leahy & Holt, 1993). Culminating from this early proposal was the establishment of the Commission on Rehabilitation Counselor Certification (CRCC), which was formally incorporated in January of 1974 (Leahy & Holt, 1993). The CRCC was designated as a nongovernmental body of the rehabilitation service delivery profession, authorized to conduct certification activities on a nationwide basis, and administered independent of any supporting organization. Between 1974 and 1976, the CRCC concentrated on administrative duties, which involved the appointment of a policy and governing body and the development of a certification examination. Representatives, or "Commissioners," were appointed from the original sponsoring organizations (American Rehabilitation Counseling Association and the National Rehabilitation Counseling Association), as well as other rehabilitation organizations, which included the Council of Rehabilitation Education (CORE, an accreditation body), Council of State Administrators of Vocational Rehabilitation (CSAVR), National Association of Rehabilitation Facilities (NARF), National Association of Non-White Rehabilitation Workers (NANWRW), National Council on Rehabilitation Education (NCRE), and a representative from a national consumer organization.

The grandfathering period began during this early development period in which individuals took the examination and rated each question for its relevance to the practice of rehabilitation counseling. During this period, all persons who took the examination were awarded the certification credential. Through this grandfathering process, the Commission was able to ensure the rehabilitation counseling profession that the certification examination focused on field-oriented content resulting in a criterion-referenced examination.

The first post-grandfathering certification examination was administered in April 1976, which preceded the development of the Commission's certification maintenance plan. The maintenance plan was adopted in September 1977 and went into effect in 1978. It required that each certified counselor attain 150 contact hours of continuing education during their five-year certification period or retake the certification examination. This figure has since been adjusted downward to 100 hours so that "...certified rehabilitation counselors (CRC) [could] focus their continuing educational activities on quality programs and increase their ability to achieve re-certification" (Leahy & Holt, 1993, p. 75).

The National Commission on Health Certifying Agencies accredited the CRCC as a certifying body in 1980, thus awarding the CRCC credibility to its mission and process. Rehabilitation in the private sector was gaining momentum and notoriety at this time as well, and yet there was not a methodology for determining and/or monitoring accountability within the private sector of rehabilitation practitioners. The National Association of Rehabilitation Professionals in the Private Sector (NARPPS) had established itself as the representative membership organization of private practitioners by 1980, complete with a rules committee, code of ethics, and behavioral review board. However, this professional organization had no means of determining who was accountable in the provision of services in private sector rehabilitation given the diversity of the practitioners' educational training and backgrounds. For the first time in its service delivery history, the rehabilitation field experienced the presence of a new group of practitioners whose roles and functions prior to this period were assigned to medical and hospital settings, the registered and/or rehabilitation nurse. It was the rehabilitation nursing population that was the first professional group to work in the private rehabilitation sector (Lewin, Ramseur, & Sink, 1979). Suttenfield (1983) noted that traditionally individuals practicing in the private rehabilitation sector came from one or the other of two primary educational and experiential backgrounds, nursing and vocational rehabilitation. The problem that the Commission on Rehabilitation Counselor Certification faced was that under its qualifying provisions of 1983, rehabilitation nurses could not qualify to become certified as rehabilitation service providers. To exclude nurses from certification meant excluding a whole specialty area from meeting accountability criteria. Thus, the Certified Insurance Rehabilitation Specialist (CIRS) was developed, which established criteria specific to nurses and formally trained vocational rehabilitation case managers and practitioners that would allow both groups to qualify for certification. In December 1983, the Board for Rehabilitation (BRC) was created to administer both the existing CRC and the new CIRS credentials. The CIRS credential has been upgraded and is now known as the Certified Disability Manager and Specialist (CDMS).

It was not until 1987 that the Code of Professional Ethics for Rehabilitation Counselors was adopted, which included nurse practitioners certified under the CIRS credential. A disciplinary code was established as well, whose purpose was to address ethical complaints received by the CRCC from consumers and fellow professionals (Leahy & Holt, 1993).

A comprehensive restructuring of the CRCC took place in 1990, which resulted in the abolition of the Board for Rehabilitation Certification in favor of a more flexible, autonomous administrative organization, which was titled the Foundation for Rehabilitation Certification, Education, and Research. Its primary mission is to support the Commission by staffing the administrative offices, conduct public relations activities, and conduct research and administer educational projects (Leahy & Holt, 1993).

The CRCC certification examination was initially researched in the early 1980s to ensure that some relevance and validity had been identified and achieved in terms of how the test related to field practice (Rubin, Matkin, Ashley, Beardsley, May, Onstott, & Puckett, 1984). To ensure constant monitoring of the relevance and the validity of the CRCC examination, the CRCC entered into a joint agreement with the Council on Rehabilitation Education (CORE) to conduct validation research of the examination process on a continuing schedule. With this joint effort, the CRCC established a research process that would provide ongoing validation of CRCC examination content and the curricular standards used in the accreditation of educational programs. Beginning in 1991, the first validation research from the joint CRCC and CORE agreement was completed by Szymanski, Linkowski, Leahy, Diamond, and Thoreson (1993), which "…supported the validity of the knowledge areas currently included in the standards for rehabilitation counselor certification or rehabilitation counselor accreditation" (p. 118).

The current structure of the Commission on Rehabilitation Counselor Certification (CRCC) consists of seventeen individuals appointed for five-year rotating terms who are representatives of the primary rehabilitation supporting organizations, which include the American Deafness and Rehabilitation Association (ADARA), the American Rehabilitation Counseling Association (ARCA), the Canadian Association of Rehabilitation Personnel (CARP), the Council on Rehabilitation Education (CORE), the Council of State Administrators of Vocational Rehabilitation (CSAVR), the National Association of Non-White Rehabilitation Workers (NANWRW), the National Association of Rehabilitation Facilities (NARF), the National Association of Rehabilitation Professionals in the Private Sector (NARPPS), the National Council on Rehabilitation Education (NCRE), and the National Rehabilitation Counseling Association (NRCA) (Leahy & Holt, 1993). These seventeen commissioners elect an executive committee that is organized around four standing committees: (1) Standards and Credentials, (2) Examinations and Research, (3) External Relations, and (4) Ethics. Outside consultants also are used to assist with activities such as item writing and participating in cut-score workshops (Leahy & Holt, 1993).

Life Care Planning

As noted previously, nurses and vocational rehabilitation case managers have had dominant roles in developing private sector rehabilitation, particularly in case management and life care planning. Just which group is best suited for what specialty area has yet to be empirically defined. Deutsch, Sawyer, Jenkins, & Kitchen (1986) noted that rehabilitation counselors are best suited for life care plan development because many of the skills and services provided by rehabilitation counselors are directly applicable to catastrophic disabilities and pediatric rehabilitation. Furthermore, rehabilitation counselors are uniquely qualified by definition; rehabilitation counselors often function as coordinators of interdisciplinary services and the care of the permanently injured patient.

Powers (1994) provided support for the rehabilitation nurse's role in life care planning by delineating the roles of the nurse both as a case manager and as a life care planner. Blackwell, Weed, and Powers (1994) and Blackwell, Powers, and Weed (1994) followed Suttenfield's (1983) contention that this specialty service belongs to two groups, nurses and rehabilitation counselors. Actually, who is best suited for predicting one's future medical and rehabilitative needs through life care planning is not important, nor does it have merit in the case for measuring accountability. What is important is that accountability be established, measured, and monitored with regard to all of the professionals who provide life care planning services.

As noted previously, measuring accountability is best established by:

- Defining the service to be monitored
- Identifying the service providers' roles and functions required to deliver the service
- Developing a field-tested certification examination
- Conducting validation research of the examination
- Establishing a Code of Ethics

The CRCC had experience in this process through its work in establishing accountability for rehabilitation counseling, though its work in researching the roles and functions of Certified Case Managers (e.g., nurses and rehabilitation counselors) is incomplete at this writing. In spite of its work in certification, however, the CRCC declined to get involved with life care planning certification in late 1995 because of the limited population of life care planners compared to rehabilitation counselors in the public and private sectors. Also, the expense involved in developing a certification process could not be justified given the potential for its return-on-investment (Taylor, personal communication, November 1995). The Commission on Disability Examiner Certification (CDEC), which had begun its work on developing a certification process in life care planning earlier in 1995, decided to proceed with total commitment in establishing a certification credential for life care planners once the CRCC withdrew its consideration.

The Commission on Disability Examiner Certification (CDEC) was incorporated in 1994 in response to the health care industry's need for certified clinical examiners in impairment rating and functional capacity evaluation practices (e.g., physicians, chiropractors, physical therapists, occupational therapists, and vocational evaluators). Though incorporated as a not-for-profit agency in 1994, the CDEC evolved in 1992 as a result of meetings with allied health care providers/practitioners around the country. Participants of the CDEC focused primarily on clinical examiner credentials, validity and reliability of rating protocol, and the establishment of a testing board to oversee the impairment rating and disability examining credentialing process. The resulting credential is the Certified Disability Examiner (CDE), with three levels that allow for the inclusion of all professionals who are involved in measuring functional performance of persons reporting impairment or disability. The Commission on Disability Examiner Certification awards the Certified Disability Examiner I, II, and III (CDE I, II, III) credential to persons who have satisfied the educational program requirements and training standards established by the National Association of Disability Evaluating Professionals (NADEP), with all classroom instruction currently offered at strategic cities and metropolitan areas around the country.

By the early 1990s, life care planning had made significant inroads in the field of rehabilitation (Deutsch, 1994). Comprehensive training programs in life care planning were developed through the National Association of Disability Evaluating Professionals (NADEP) and the National Association of Rehabilitation Professionals in the Private Sector (NARPPS). More significantly, life care planning had obtained formal academic recognition and acceptance through a joint venture, known as Intellicus, between the University of Florida and the Rehabilitation Training Institute from Ocoee, Florida. The CDEC recognized the need for accountability in this now-credible service delivery system, and in 1994 began its research and development for life care planning certification.

Goals and Objectives

The Commission on Disability Examined Certification was established for the development and administration of well-researched, standardized tests designed to measure the clinical examiner's working knowledge and demonstration of the NADEP work disability evaluation model and in life care plan development. The CDEC established several initial goals it considered relevant in developing and maintaining its mission. These goals are listed below in the context of how the CDEC was structured and with its current progress toward achieving these goals documented.

Goal 1: Develop a national test that measures the clinical practitioner's working knowledge of functional capacity and impairment rating practices as applied to the NADEP evaluation model. Because of the diversity of backgrounds, education, and training of persons who perform functional capacity evaluations and who conduct impairment ratings (e.g., medical doctors, chiropractors, physical therapists, occupational therapists, dental surgeons, etc.), the CDEC designed the test for all allied health care providers by grouping specialties by categories. This grouping is based on an educational/training focus and does not represent a ranking based on ability or status. The categories are:

Category I All physicians designated as primary care providers, subspecialists, or specialists in the administering of medical, dental, and/or chiropractic-related services. Specific physician groups include medical doctors (MD), osteopathic physicians (DO), dental surgeons (DDS), and chiropractors (DC).

Category II All persons who provide assistance to physicians in the treatment of injured persons, and/or whose practice is involved with providing symptom relief and function restoration through modality and therapeutic applications. These specialties include physical therapists, occupational therapists, speech pathologists, kinesiologists, physiologists, psychologists, and doctoral level vocational evaluators.

Category III All persons who are influential in the outcome of the injured person's disability litigation, including vocational evaluators, vocational case managers, rehabilitation nurses, and rehabilitation counselors. These individuals may assume various roles in the disability litigation process, such as performing functional capacity evaluations, labor market analyses, assisting in the placement of the injured worker back into the labor market, psychometric testing, and managing the medical care/costs associated with the respective disability case.

The examination is structured such that the examinee is required to demonstrate a working knowledge of research and resource utilization as well as to demonstrate one's examination skills applied to the NADEP model. The written examination consists of two case studies which are presented with varying orthopedic and psychological problems. The examinee is required to respond to a series of inquiries about different aspects of the cases, and a review of the literature is required for each inquiry response. Each of the categories identified above will have its own set of inquiries, with some crossover between categories since the material is directly related to the classroom content of the core courses. Thus, examinees are required to review the literature to respond to the inquiries, and apply their responses to fit the NADEP clinical examination protocol. All inquiries are developed by the Commissioners, and the Commissioners have the final approval of the examination content and list of inquiries before dissemination to the qualified certification candidates. Topics in which one's knowledge and expertise are measured on the written examination include:

- Medical Diagnoses/Correlates to Disability
- Psychological Disorders and Correlates to Disability
- Examination Tools, Instruments, and Work Sample Selection and Utilization
- Legislation Impacting Evaluation Protocol
- Report Writing and Results/Performance Interpretation
- Practice Theory and Concepts

Goal 2: Develop a national test that measures the life care planner's working knowledge of medical systems, associated disabilities, and treatment/maintenance protocols required to sustain life within an acceptable comfort level. Similar to the CRCC testing format, the CLCP test is comprised of multiple choice case scenarios that contain four distracters, one of which is considered the correct choice. All test answers are referenced within current professional literature from the medical, insurance, and rehabilitation professions. The certification candidate has two options for test administration:

1. Tests are administered within the certification candidate's local community college by proctor. The candidate is required to contact his or her local community college and arrange with the business office a date and time in which the candidate can secure a proctor and sit for the examination. The candidate is responsible for any proctor costs associated with this arrangement. This option is offered to the candidate as an attempt to minimize the expenses typically associated with travel and lodging when sitting for a certification examination administered at a national testing site. Once the candidate has notified CDEC of the community college site and proctor, the examination will be mailed to the proctor at the college address. All testing materials will remain with the proctor, who will be charged with the responsibility of returning all testing materials to the CDEC office. CDEC reserves the right to approve the recommended proctor or select an alternative proctor at the specified community college.
2. When possible, two national sites will be designated by CDEC for weekend test administration on an annual basis. Dates and locations of the national sites may be obtained from the CDEC office.

The certification test is under its second revision, which was released on March 1, 1997. This revised test is comprised of four categories and associated topical areas, which include the following (percentage of test content is designated beside each category):

Life Care Planner Certification Exam Categories

1. Medical Interventions and Complications Associated with Medical Conditions — 33%
   a. Traumatic brain injury (TBI)
   b. Amputations

   c. Low back chronic pain
   d. Burns
   e. Vocational worksheet information
   f. Vocational resources
   g. Vocational tests
2. Legislative Issues 11%
   a. Americans with Disabilities Act
   b. Home Health Practice Act
3. Measurement and Statistics 4%
4. Psychological Issues 4%
5. General Items 18%
   a. Terms and definitions
   b. Life care planning charts
   c. Miscellaneous items

The test results for the CLCP are scored at the corporate office of the Commission on Disability Examiner Certification. Passing cut-off criteria are determined statistically based on "t" and raw scores, as well as "mean" scores of each testing group and standard deviations applied to the bell curve. Anyone not meeting the passing criteria may take the examination a total of three (3) times. If the passing cut-off score is not achieved after the third trial, a Board Review by the Commissioners is undertaken to review the candidate's test performance and make recommendations regarding future certification arrangements (i.e., additional course work, recommended readings, etc.).

Goal 3: Conduct ongoing research in terms of test-item validity and reliability. Such research will ensure that both tests measure what they purport to measure and that the items are a fair representation of the knowledge required to measure impairment and disability and to develop life care plans.

The CDEC recognized early in its development phase that reliability needs to be established and validity research needs to be conducted to ensure that the test items are a fair representation of common knowledge regarding disability evaluation and life care plan development. The goal was that both tests should measure what they purport to measure. Currently, the Commission on Disability Examiner Certification is funding doctoral level research at Southern Illinois University, Department of Rehabilitation, Doctoral Program (Rh.D.) to conduct the reliability and validity research for both examinations. This endeavor includes a complete role and function study of persons engaged in the practice of determining disability and/or rating impairment and developing life care plans. The significance of these studies is that finally, specific roles and functions of persons in medical and rehabilitation settings engaged in impairment rating, disability evaluation, and life care plan development will be defined.

Regarding the CDE examination, the role and function study has been completed, which has resulted in the identification of the various categories of expertise, or specialty knowledge areas involved in clinical practice, and more specifically, the NADEP examination model (Washington, 1996). Because of Washington's research, the CDEC's three testing categories have been operationally defined and structured. The CLCP study has an expected completion date of May 1997. This study is designed to determine the roles and function of qualified professionals involved in providing life care planning services and related catastrophic care management.

Goal 4: Administer the examination within 6 weeks of (1) a clinical examiner completing the NADEP educational/training requirements necessary to sit for the CDE examination and (2) a life care planner completing the required and approved training necessary prior to sitting for the CLCP examination. This will ensure that minimal delays will incur for a qualified candidate to achieve certification status upon completion of required courses.

The CLCP certification is generic in the sense that it was developed without reference to specialty areas of training or a candidate's achieved degree level. The CDEC requires the following criteria to be met by all CLCP candidates in order to qualify to sit for the examination:

1. Each candidate must have a minimum of 120 hours of post-graduate or post-specialty degree training in life care planning and meet specific standards.
2. Each candidate must be certified or licensed within their respective profession by an accredited certifying agency or appropriate regulatory body.
3. Each candidate must have a minimum of one (1) year of work or professional experience in developing life care plans.
4. Each candidate must hold the entry level academic degree or certificate/diploma for their profession.

Goal 5: Procure qualified Commissioners to sit on the Board of Examiners to represent all CDE and CLCP candidates and certified professionals. Similar to the CRCC, the CDEC originally began with 12 Commissioners representing specialty field of practice in medicine and rehabilitation. In contrast to the CRCC, the CDEC opted to establish itself as a field-oriented, practical testing agency without input or representation from supportive field groups. In other words, the administration of the CDEC felt that being represented by supportive organizations would have the best interests of those organizations at the forefront rather than the interests of the clinical practitioner. The administration also felt that a political element would eventually surface that would impact any clinical-based decisions in a direction that would not be in the best interest of the field practitioner. However, the Commission has been approached by several supporting organizations in rehabilitation for representation on the Board, and consideration is underway for their inclusion.

Today, there are fourteen Commissioners representing fourteen different specialty groups within the fields of medicine and rehabilitation. These include rehabilitation nursing (Commissioner of Rehabilitation Nurses), kinesiology (Commissioner of Kinesiology and Physiology), case management

(Commissioner of Case Management), chiropractic (Commissioner of Chiropractic), chronic pain (Commissioner of Pain Medicine), occupational therapy (Commissioner of Occupational Therapy), physical medicine and rehabilitation (Commissioner of Physical Medicine and Rehabilitation), orthopaedic surgery (Commissioner of Orthopaedic Surgery), psychology (Commissioner of Psychology), research design and statistics (Commissioner of Research Design and Statistics), physical therapy (Commissioner of Physical Therapy), vocational evaluation (Commissioner of Vocational Evaluation), academia (Commissioner of University Studies), and life care plan education (Commissioner of Life Care Plan Education). The Commissioner of Rehabilitation Nurses and the Commissioner of Life Care Plan Education were added when the CDEC decided to fully commit to establishing a life care plan credential.

The CDEC was careful in its selection of commissioners, and established the following selection criteria to be applied to all commissioner candidates regardless of specialty:

1. Commissioners must hold a current license in their respective field. If licensure is not required within the specialty field, then the individual must hold certification common to the respective field of specialty.
2. Clinicians who have been asked to serve as Commissioners for the CDE credential must complete the mandatory courses offered by NADEP and pass the CDE certification exam. They must also have met the qualification standards for life care planning developed at the University of Florida and have taken and passed the CLCP examination.

Goal 6: Disseminate test scores within a six-week period after receiving the test from the respective Certified Disability Examiner (CDE) and Certified Life Care Planner (CLCP) candidates. To date, test scores have been disseminated on a timely basis for the CLCP credential. However, the dissemination record for the CDE credential is averaging between eight and twelve weeks due primarily to the essay style of the tests and the requirement of three reviewers (one of whom holds similar background, education, and training credentials of the certification candidate) to review each examination. The CDEC is actively pursuing a resolution to this dissemination problem.

Goal 7: Establish and monitor recertification policies to measure continued competence and/or to enhance the continued competence of the Certified Disability Examiner and Certified Life Care Planner. The CDEC contended that certified professionals should maintain a high level of skills and knowledge through professional development and continuing education. The CDEC certification maintenance program extends the status of a CDE I, II, or III and a CLCP at three-year intervals. The renewal requirement is a total of 60 clock hours for each three-year period of approved education/training. During the renewal process, documentation is required to validate that the education or training has been successfully completed. A second option for recertification is to retake the examination.

Education and training for maintaining certification as a CDE I, II, or III and as a CLCP must occur in specific areas relating to impairment rating and life care planning for each respective credential. Regarding CDE certification, these areas may include impairment rating, functional capacity evaluation, and any topic that may be reviewed in industrial rehabilitation and personal injury seminars. Topics may be specific to the clinician's area of specialty as well.

The topic areas for the CLCP credential may include various areas of the life care planning process, catastrophic disabilities and other disabilities requiring life care plans, case management related to catastrophic injuries and/or life care plans, resource development for life care plans, vocational issues related to life care plans, rehabilitation testimony, and other legal issues relating to life care plans, and professional/legal issues related to developing and maintaining life care plans.

Education and training for certification may be obtained from a number of potential sources, including in-service training programs, seminars and workshops, college and university courses, national and regional conferences, professional publications and presentations related to the above areas.

Certified Life Care Planner Expertise/Skill Standards

The CDEC acknowledged in its development of the CLCP credential that the life care planner is required to possess certain knowledge and skills that typify and that are required of the life care planning process. Practice standards were adopted from those established by the University of Florida — Gainesville, authored by Dr. Horace Sawyer, Chairperson, Department of Rehabilitation Counseling. Based on its interpretation of these standards with direct application to the field, the CDEC surmised that life care plan development involves data collection, resource development, and planning strategies in an interdisciplinary rehabilitation environment. It concluded that such an innovative, interdisciplinary approach allows for valid documentation of the needs of catastrophically injured individuals and projects the costs of needed services, treatment, and equipment over the individual's lifespan. To competently develop a life care plan, the CDEC mandated that those persons who provide this service should become certified in this specialty area, have expertise in research, development, coordination, integration, interpretation, and management of life care plans for catastrophic disabilities.

The CDEC adopted the training program standards established by the University of Florida when considering the approval of submitted maintenance hours by Certified Life Care Planners. The views of the CDEC were that not all training programs meet the standards for training necessary to minimize incompetence in the practice of life care planning; therefore, it adopted the following Standards for Training in life care planning:

I. Administrative/Faculty Content: The mission and objectives of the training program shall be made available to program applicants, consumers, public and private agencies, academic institutions, and the interested public. The title program shall maintain admission policies, procedures, and materials consistent with the mission of the program. The training ratio of students to faculty on-site shall be no greater than 25:1. Training faculty shall be sufficiently and appropriately qualified through preparation and experience in life care planning and related case management. Training facilities and environments are appropriate to maximize training value and accessible for individuals with disabilities.

II. Program Curriculum: The curriculum for the training program shall provide the essential skills and areas of expertise to effectively research, develop, coordinate, interpret, and manage life care plans for catastrophic disabilities. Training seminars would include, but are not limited to, the following minimal areas of knowledge, skills, and expertise:

1. Orientation of Life Care Planning and Case Management
   a. Definition and history of life care planning
   b. Overview of life care planning topics
   c. Role of medical, psychological, and rehabilitation professionals
   d. Issues of family dynamics
   e. Review of legislation relating to life care plans
   f. Issues and opportunities of case management
2. Assessment of Rehabilitation Potential
   a. Pediatric and early assessment
   b. Rehabilitation evaluation and special needs
   c. Interpretation of medical evaluations
   d. Personality and neuropsychological evaluation
   e. Physical and functional assessment
   f. Vocational assessment and earnings capacity analysis
3. Medical and Rehabilitation Aspects of Disability
   a. Medical records analysis
   b. Early medical intervention and acute rehabilitation
   c. Medical aspects: spinal cord injury, traumatic brain injury, amputations, burns, Psychiatric disabilities, chronic pain and back injuries, other catastrophic disabilities
   d. Behavioral aspects of disability
   e. Issues of neuropharmacology
   f. Long-term care considerations
   g. Issues of life expectancy
4. Development of Life Care Plans
   a. Systematic process of life care planning
   b. Planning strategies and resource development
   c. Interview procedures and data collection
   d. Computer applications of life care planning
   e. Rehabilitation technology and applications
   f. Utilization of collateral sources
   g. Areas of life care planning
      i. Planning for evaluation and treatment
      ii. Equipment and aids for independent function
      iii. Orthotics and prosthetics
      iv. Drug/supply needs
      v. Home/facility care

    vi. Medical-care routine/complications
    vii. Transportation
    viii. Architectural renovations
    ix. Leisure/recreational
5. Consultation in Life Care Planning
    a. Utilization of rehabilitation experts
    b. Analysis of established life care plans
    c. Medical/legal consultation
    d. Development of reports and reporting procedures
    e. Case preparation for consultation, mediation, settlement, conference, testimony
6. Professional and Operational Issues
    a. Process and issues of rehabilitation testimony
    b. Professional ethics and malpractice issues
    c. Operational and business practices
    d. Standard of practice in life care planning
    e. Public relations, marketing, and professional development
    f. Life care planning and research issues

More important for consideration are the underlying values related to the standard of practice for qualified professionals in life care planning. The CDEC supports and confirms the following value statements for life care plan development:

1. All individuals with catastrophic disabilities have worth and dignity.
2. Life care plans are designed to facilitate and maximize functional capacity and independence for persons with catastrophic disabilities.
3. The systematic process of life care planning and related catastrophic case management is conducted in an objective and fair manner within the context of family, community, and employment systems.
4. Comprehensive and integrated services are the focus of life care planning and are based on individual involvement, personal assets, and a sense of equal justice from all involved parties.

Board Structure

As noted previously, the Board consists of fourteen Commissioners representing backgrounds in all professions affiliated with impairment ratings, functional capacity evaluations, and life care planning. These Commissioners serve as advisors to the CDEC administration and serve on the other Boards that include the Board of Examiners, the Board for Ethics and Standards of Practice, and the Board of Test Development.

The Board of Examiners consists of three Commissioners who oversee the scoring of the examinations from both credential areas. The CDEC's bi-laws require that at least one Examiner on this Board carry the same background, education, and training as that of the certification candidate.

The Board of Ethics and Standards of Practice is in charge of writing the Ethical Standards of Practice for both credential areas. These standards consist of 10 canons which include:

1. Moral and legal standards
2. Disability examiners and life care planners/patient relationship
3. Patient advocacy
4. Professional relationships
5. Public statements/fees
6. Confidentiality
7. Assessment
8. Research activities
9. Competence
10. CDE, CLCP, and CAE credentials

The Board of Ethics and Standards of Practice also developed procedures for processing ethical complaints, but noted that the primary responsibility of investigating such complaints rests with the accused's own professional association under which he or she holds certification or licensure.

All Commissioners have input into these standards, and the CDEC included surveys from Certified Life Care Planners and Certified Disability Examiners I, II, and III for their input. The Board for Ethics and Standards of Practice has the final vote on which standards to include and editorial freedom in writing the final document for publication to the certified body of practitioners.

This Board serves as a review board for consumer/practitioner complaints and allegations that may have surfaced in the course of one's practice. The Board reviews each complaint and determines any penalties or fines that may be imposed on the certified practitioner. They have the power to remove one's certification status if the offense in question is proven to have occurred and thus merits such action.

The Board of Test Development oversees item writing for both tests. This is not to say that the CDEC does not accept input from certified field practitioners; it does. However, the Commissioners who staff this Board have the final say regarding the inclusion or exclusion of any test item.

National Compliance

Similar to the CRCC, the CDEC recognized the need to adhere to a national policy and standards regarding certification testing. The CDEC has applied to the National Commission for Certifying Agencies (NCCA) at this writing for consideration of review and compliance with this agency's certification standards. The CDEC concluded that such an affiliation would ensure that the highest quality of testing standards and development would be maintained for persons desiring CDEC certification. Areas under which the NCCA evaluates and monitors an agency include (1) administrative independence, (2) bias, (3) continuing competence, (4) discipline, (5) education and certification, (6) eligibility for certification, (7) public members, (8) reliability, and (9) validity.

In essence, the Commission on Disability Examiner Certification has attempted to cover all areas of certification in both fields of impairment rating/functional capacity evaluation and life care planning. Validity and reliability of its tests, or any tests for that matter, are essential ingredients of a credential that must withstand scrutiny at all professional levels, particularly when being scrutinized by the judicial system in which many of the CDEC's certified practitioners testify. More important, standards of practice have to be established to serve as guidelines when one's behavior has to be judged against another's complaint. Only through a committed effort on the part of the CDEC to define the roles of evaluators and life care planners can these services delivery systems be improved. The CDEC is young compared to the CRCC, as is its generic rehabilitation certification movement. The certification movement in life care planning is still in its infancy with much work ahead. Only through the continued recertification efforts and support of those who have completed the certification process in both areas of the CDEC will the credentialing movement establish a foothold in the rehabilitation profession.

Continuing Education Requirements

The CDEC certification maintenance program extends the CLCP status at three-year intervals if the life care planner completes a total of fortyeight clock hours of approved education/training. Failure to renew certification will result in revocation of certified status. Information submitted that is false or misleading may also result in certification revocation. As of 1997, the renewal fee was $90 for each three year period. A second recertification option is to retake the examination. The 1997 fee for this option was $180.

To Certify or Not to Certify: Discussion

Given the plethora of certifications in the rehabilitation industry, one may find justifying the obtaining of a certification in life care planning difficult at best. Matkin (1985) cited the seemingly redundant and/or ambiguous rehabilitation certification agencies that have surfaced over the past 15 years as a major contributing factor to one's trepidation. Multiple certifying agencies within one's profession appear to confuse both would-be consumers and rehabilitation professionals when attempting to select "appropriate" credentials/credentialing agencies for needed services. To exemplify his point, Matkin (1985) posed some interesting questions that address the core of the issue:

1. If counseling services are being offered by a rehabilitation practitioner, should that person be a Certified Rehabilitation Counselor, a National Certified Counselor, a Licensed Psychologist, a Licensed Employment Counselor, and so forth?
2. If a Rehabilitation Nurse provides patient care, should that person be certified by the Association of Rehabilitation Nurses, the Professional Rehabilitation Association, both organizations, or by neither group?
3. If rehabilitation practitioners are certified by their respective occupational disciplines, should they also seek additional certification as Certified Case Managers in order to offer their services to disabled clients receiving disability compensation insurance?
4. Should a rehabilitation service program be accredited by the Commission on Accreditation of Rehabilitation Facilities, the International Institute of Rehabilitation, by both organizations, or by neither group?

Thomas (1993) was more adverse in his surmise of the issue of whether or not one should pursue certification. He concluded that the primary purpose of professional credentialing in [rehabilitation] "…is not to protect the weak but rather to increase the power, authority, and [revenues] of the strong…none of the professional/traditional credentialing bodies in [rehabilitation] provide any protection whatsoever to clients…" (p. 187).

He expressed similar convictions toward the licensing movement, of which he noted that the primary proponents of licensure and credentialing in general are not the clients or consumers of services. Rather, the truth lies in the professionals striving to be credentialed so that they [can] enjoy the legal benefits accorded their profession and the exclusion of competitors whom they consider to be less qualified. In other words, the hidden agenda here is market share and revenues perpetuated by today's third-party reimbursement focus on capitation of fees and managed care.

Actually, both Matkin and Thomas have valid points for consideration. The private sector is highly competitive and rare is the occasion in which practitioners award praise and honor to colleagues for jobs well done. It stands to reason that current credentialed providers desire a limited or restricted marketplace so that their respective market share can be enhanced. The real concern appears not to be the consumer of services, but rather the solvency of the individual practitioner.

While it is true that there are ample rehabilitation certifications to confuse both consumers and rehabilitation professionals, resolution of this dilemma rests with the practitioner determining which certification will directly impact his or her practice. For example, in private sector settings that focus on litigation cases and subsequent deposition and court testimony, a rehabilitation nurse or case manager may do well holding certifications as Certified Rehabilitation Registered Nurse (CRRN) or Certified Rehabilitation Counselor (CRC). However, when the practice offers life care planning services that require additional training and postgraduate hours, the current certifications seem to hold little prominence when the opposing expert witness in the case has met the qualifying standards and criteria to hold the Certified Life Care Planner (CLCP) credential. It does not take the referring legal community much time before realizing the significance of one credential over another, especially when one is service-oriented and specific to the legal community.

Another practical aspect for support of certification and credentialing in rehabilitation is what was previously mentioned in this chapter: selective requirement. Currently, the CRC credential for rehabilitation counselors and the CCM credential for nurses and counselor-trained rehabilitation case managers are becoming mandatory credentials among third-party payers of private sector rehabilitation services. Although the respective states may not require the certification credentials, several major insurance companies have selected these two credentials as mandatory before payment for services can be authorized. Thus, the CRC and CCM are selectively required of practitioners in some states that do not require certification credentials.

A similar scenario is found in the negotiations the CDEC has had with several national insurance companies regarding their disability policies. The CDEC has proposed that functional capacity evaluators and impairment raters who carry the CDE I, II, and III credential perform the disability evaluations exclusively for the respective insurance company. The attraction of such an offer for these insurance companies is that the medical review officers located in the branch offices around the country will be assured of receiving a disability report that is consistent in content among all Certified Disability Examiners, consistent in its format, and that the protocol used to determine the disability outcome is research-based with established validity. The advantage of such an arrangement to the Certified Disability Examiner I, II, or III is simply an enhanced referral base for disability examinations, thus increasing the practitioners' overall revenue base. To summarize, the clinical practitioner needs to become credentialed and needs to select the credential that will best serve his or her practice.

Several arguments have been made that to become certified means nothing; there is no restriction of practice by the certifying agency, only the title can be removed, which is meaningless since the practice can continue under a different title. Secondly, there are no empirical research studies to support the notion that certified practitioners are more effective or competent in their practices than noncertified providers (Fritz & Mills, 1980). Regarding the first argument, imagine for a moment that a practitioner's certification title has been rescinded through an ethics review procedure. While it is true that the practitioner may legally continue practicing, there is no attraction for the private practitioner's insurance and legal referral sources to continue referring cases when this practitioner's blemish will appear continuously during every deposition and witness stand cross-examination. Second, this individual's referrals will discontinue from insurance companies who maintain a certification requirement policy.

Regarding the second argument, studies in specialty areas outside of rehabilitation have been conducted to establish the efficacy of credentialing. Slogoff, Hughes, Hug, Longnecker, & Saidman (1994) studied the competence of 1310 residents in anesthesiology. They concluded that board-certified physicians in anesthesiology were judged by their supervising physicians to be more competent in the performance of their medical duties than those residents who were not board certified. Hawk, Coble, & Swanson (1985) studied the effectiveness of certification on math teachers. They reviewed the competence of 36 teachers, half of whom were certified in mathematics and half of whom had no certification in math. Their results showed that students' achievement was greater in general mathematics and algebra when the students were taught by teachers certified in mathematics.

While it is true that there is a void regarding certification research in rehabilitation, studies in the above area have documented the efficacy of certification in those respective fields. The challenge that awaits the CRCC, the CDEC, and other certifying agencies in rehabilitation is to perform competency research of its certified professionals.

The answer to the question of whether to pursue certification or to leave the process to one's peers is clear given today's market trends and reimbursement policies. The profession is demanding closer scrutiny of service delivery and thus is requiring its practitioners to become credentialed. Life care planning has experienced significant growth over the past fifteen years, and the legal community demands credentialed experts in this field. The question of which credential to pursue is market driven and is best answered by the practitioner when considering which credential will best benefit his or her practice. If one's practice is engaged heavily in life care planning, then the CLCP credential is the obvious choice. On the other hand, third-party payers are demanding that case managers and rehabilitation consultants be certified even if state statutes do not require certification or licensure for rehabilitation practitioners.

We must not forget, however, the original intent of certification credentialing: (1) to define one's profession or in the case of life care planning, the service delivery system, and to provide some protection to the consumer through title regulation (Fritz & Mills, 1980). The latter is achieved by virtue of the third-party payment systems supporting the credentialing movement in rehabilitation and life care planning through the authorization of reimbursement contingent on one's certification status. The former is achieved through the respective credentialing agency's desire to produce a valid and reliable credential that is backed and supported by research from a university-level institution.

As stated previously, the rehabilitation profession has a plethora of credentials (certifications) from which the clinical provider can choose. When deciding on the certification credential that would best meet one's career goals, the reader is advised to review the integrity of the certifying agency through a thorough background review. Let us not be pretentious and think that because there is a complex application process, official looking forms, and letterhead from the certifying agency, which contains numerous, highly degreed and well trained professionals on the agency's Advisory Board that the respective agency delivers a valid credentialing process. This is simply not the case. The "proof in the pudding" rests with the effort the certifying agency has taken to ensure that the profession receives an unbiased credential without any conflicts of interest attached. The following checklist is designed to help the professional resolve this dilemma:

1. **Accreditation:** Choose the credential that has made an application to the National Commission on Certifying Agencies (NCCA). This is the prominent regulatory agency for health care certification agencies under which all of those in the field of rehabilitation would be categorized.
2. **Corporate Structure:** Choose the agency that is registered with the respective state corporate commission as a nonprofit entity. It is important that a profit-motive be eliminated from the daily business of a credentialing agency.
3. **Research Support**: Choose a credential that has been investigated for validity and reliability. This process involves extensive research from a university-backed institution that has a research-oriented human services department. What role research has in credentialing is to establish the examination's validity and reliability as the examination content is applied to the field.
4. **Training Conflict**: Avoid those certifications that are advertised through a training agency. In other words, some training agencies advertise that the participant will become certified or will receive notification of being

certified at the completion of the training program. These types of certifications usually do not require the participant to pass a certification test; just attend the training.

The other scenario to this situation is that the participant will attend the training and take a test to become certified at the conclusion of the class session. The certification is awarded by the very agency that provided the training, which is a direct conflict of interest. The motive is obvious; the more persons who become certified, the more other people will want to take the classes to obtain the certification, and the more the training/certification agency has invested to ensure that all students pass the certification test.

Finally, in this same genre, avoid agencies that mail out postcard announcements suggesting that the "grandfathering" period is about to expire, and that the professional needs to act promptly in order to ensure a place on the certification registry of that particular specialty area. The process usually requires the professional candidate to send in three letters of reference, complete the abbreviated application form, submit a curriculum vitae and, of course, a check. When one looks at the material closely, the credentialing agency is one that provides training as a primary function with certification as an added bonus. This practice is totally unacceptable and is what this author perceives to be criminal. However, there is nothing illegal with a credentialing agency to use this approach.

CERTIFICATION INFORMATION

For information about certification in life care planning contact:

V. Robert May, Rh.D.
Executive Director
Commission of Disability Examiner Certification
13325 Queensgate Road
Midlothian, VA 23113
fax 804-272-9257
804-272-9192

CONCLUSION

The integrity and future of credentialing in rehabilitation and life care planning rests with all rehabilitation practitioners and consumers of services (i.e., insurance carriers, attorneys, disabled persons, and employers). Our profession will not sustain itself without solid research-based credentialing, which in turn perpetuates a well-defined service industry. More practitioners need to support their respective specialty credentialing processes, and in turn these credentialing agencies need to respond readily to the needs of the consumer of services as well as the needs of those whom they certify.

REFERENCES

Anderson, R. (1979). Vocational expert testimony: The new frontier for the rehabilitation professional. **Journal of Rehabilitation, 45**(3), 39-40, 74.

Bitter, J. (1979). **Introduction to Rehabilitation**. St. Louis: C.V. Mosby.

Blackwell, T., Powers, A., & Weed, R. (1994). **Life Care Planning for Traumatic Brain Injury: A Resource Manual for Case Managers.** Athens, GA: Elliott & Fitzpatrick.

Blackwell, T., Weed, R., & Powers, A. (1994). **Life Care Planning for Spinal Cord Injury: A Resource Manual for Case Managers**. Athens, GA: Elliott & Fitzpatrick.

Capshaw, T., Grenfell, J., & Savino, W. (1982). **Practical Aspects of Handling Social Security Disability Claims.** Madison, WI: Professional Education Systems.

Deutsch, P. (1994). Life care planning: Into the future. **NARPPS Journal, 9**(2&3), 79-84.

Deutsch, P., Sawyer, H., Jenkins, W., & Kitchens, J. (1986). Life care planning in catastrophic case management. **Journal of Private Sector Rehabilitation, 1**(1), 13-27.

Fritz, B. & Mills, D. (1980). **Licensing and Certification of Psychologists and Counselors.** San Francisco: Jossey-Bass.

Gianforte, G. (1976). Certification: A challenge and a choice. **Journal of Rehabilitation, 42**(5), 15-17.

Grenfell, J. (1980). The attorney use of a vocational expert. In **How to Profitably Handle Social Security Cases.** Indianapolis: Indiana Continuing Legal Education Forum.

Hawk, P., Coble, C., & Swanson, M. (1985). Certification: It does matter. **Journal of Teacher Education, 35**(3), 13-15.

Hotz, J., Maki, D., & Riggar, T. (1984). Rehabilitation practice: An empirical examination. **Vocational Evaluation and Work Adjustment Bulletin, 17**(3), 113-118.

Leahy, M. & Holt, E. (1993). Certification in rehabilitation counseling: History and process. **Rehabilitation Counseling Bulletin, 37**(2), 71-80.

Lewin, S., Ramseur, J., & Sink, J. (1979). The role of private rehabilitation: Founder, catalyst, competitor. **Journal of Rehabilitation, 45**(3), 16-19.

Matkin, R.E. (1985). **Insurance Rehabilitation**. Austin, TX: Pro-Ed.

May, V.R. (1983). The vocational expert witness: Expanding the market place. **Vocational Evaluation and Work Adjustment Bulletin, 16**(3), 100-102.

Powers, A. S. (1994). Life care planning: The role of the legal nurse. **NARPPS Journal, 9**(2&3), 51-56.

Rubin, S., Matkin, R., Ashley, J., Beardsley, M., May, V., Onstott, K., & Puckett, F. (1984). Roles and functions of certified rehabilitation counselors. **Rehabilitation Counseling Bulletin, 27**(4), 199-224.

Shortley, M. (1947). Vocational rehabilitation. **Occupational Therapy Rehabilitation, 26**(4), 201-211

Slogoff, S., Hughes, F.P., Hug, C.C., Longnecker, D., & Saidman, L. (1994). A demonstration of validity for certification by the American Board of Anesthesiology. **Academic Medicine, 69**(9), 740-746.

Snook, S. & Webster, B. (1987). The cost of disability. **Clinical Orthopaedics and Related Research, 221**, 77-84.

Suttenfield, C. (1983). Credentialing for rehab practitioners. **The Claimsman, 7**(2), 38-39.

Szymanski, E., Linkowski, D., Leahy, M., Diamond, E., & Thoreson, R. (1993). Human resource development: An examination of perceived training needs of certified rehabilitation counselors. **Rehabilitation Counseling Bulletin, 37**(2), 163-181.

Thomas, K. (1993). Professional credentialing: A doomsday machine without failsafe. **Rehabilitation Counseling Bulletin, 37**(2), 187-193.

Washington, C. (1996). An investigation of the job roles of work disability evaluating professionals. Unpublished Dissertation. Southern Illinois University, Carbondale.

Weed, R. O. (1994). Life care plans: Expanding the horizons. **NARPPS Journal, 9**(2&3), 47-50.

27

LIFE CARE PLANNING RESOURCES

Julie A. Kitchen

A plethora of information has been written over the years about resources that can and should be used in life care planning. As life care planners, we know that "the person with the most accurate, accessible, and thorough resources is the winner" in the life care planning arena. Without proper resources — easily accessible, understandable, and updateable — the task of completing a competent, thorough, and accurate life care plan can be a formidable task. Most life care planners spend the majority of their time researching information for the plan, rather than actually formulating the specific components for the plan. Therefore, the life care planner with the competitive edge is the one who has a multitude of data — from a variety of sources, encompassing a large pool of information, rather than just the basics involved in setting up the outline for the recommendations for the life care plan.

There is an operative word that must be spoken and understood here — and that word is *"accessible"* resources. Just having the information available "somewhere in the office" is not enough. This will not help you during the stress of a deposition when asked to "pull that source," or during a telephone conference with a referral source, asking for specifics on something referenced in the life care plan. Additionally, there are many topics not specifically covered in the life care plan itself that must also be readily available — for conferencing, speaking, training, testifying, networking, and case managing. Remember, our role as life care planners is as educators — well-prepared, knowledgeable educators with an almost unlimited fund of knowledge and resources.

This chapter will outline some resources (and will in turn lead the reader to other resources) that will enable the life care planner to expand their horizons and base of information. This chapter is not designed to outline specific individual sources for a problem, but to globally outline information that will provide the life care planner/case manager with the ammunition needed to be well-rounded and knowledgeable in all facets of the life care planning industry and that will provide a basis on which to continually build upon your knowledge base.

Just as the key to comprehensive life care planning is to develop and maintain a consistent methodology to analyze and process catastrophic cases, the key to "resourcing" and maintaining a database is just as important, and a consistent

1-57444-075-6/99/$0.00+$.50

methodology must be used to obtain and maintain those sources. Otherwise, the professional will be mired in a deluge of information that is virtually useless if it is not accessible, updated, and maintained in such a fashion that the professional can have immediate access.

As professionals, we must keep abreast of technology available so as to benefit fully from what it can offer (see Chapter 25 on technology resources). This means being willing to investigate new technology, new data storage and retrieval systems. This is not to say that one cannot stay with a proven, successful method of data collection, retrieval, etc., but the professional must keep an open mind as to alternatives that are continually being made available. The professional is encouraged to seek out and evaluate a number of currently available software programs to determine which system (for case management, life care planning, and resource data storage and retrieval, etc.) will best fit specific needs.

The author currently uses LCPSTAT software as a life care planning tool. This enables maintenance of a consistent and easily retrievable record of all the life care plans amassed since the inception of the use of that program (as well as a storage device for resources — discussed further in this chapter). LCPSTAT, with some personal customization, enables the user to create, store, retrieve, and update sources easily and quickly. The main database is kept on one central computer in the office, with networking capabilities to all counselors. (A back-up is also kept off-site for safety reasons). There is a database manager assigned to the database system, with input from all counselors. This database is simply a means of data storage and retrieval. (Information on LCPSTAT can be obtained by contacting Lisa Busby, CLCP, TecSolutions, 601-991-0551, or E-Mail: TecSo196@AOL.com).

Our database enables us to do a "search." For example, to find home health aide costs/sources in Birmingham, AL, we would enter: *Nursing Services....Birmingham, Alabama*. The last time we did research in that area will appear, with names, addresses, telephone numbers, and costs. If we have not yet had the occasion to perform research in that area, no sources will be identified. This, then, requires the professional to begin a resource survey in that geographical area to determine the sources available. (The reader is referred to Appendix A — Nursing Research for a sample listing of the types of questions suggested to ask each and every home health agency when researching nursing costs in a particular area. This questionnaire is in response to the critical need for accurate information in this area. The nursing/attendant costs represent the single most expensive and valuable portion of a life care plan for a catastrophically injured individual.... Therefore, the numbers must be accurate and the definitions of terms understood prior to outlining cost projections in the plan. All too often there are terminology differences or geographical/cultural differences that must be clearly identified prior to outlining the costs. This questionnaire was designed to help the rehabilitation professional identify those questions and terminology definitions so consistency can be maintained).

It is extremely important to be well documented in your research, and to be thorough and 100% sure of the quality of information that was obtained. Make sure your definitions of job descriptions (live-in care, for example) are consistent with the agency's definition. Much anxiety and wasted time will be spared if you set up and follow a strict, structured methodology of information retrieval, collection, and storage.

Let us begin to examine an avenue of obtaining data and information and sources that can be extremely useful to the professional involved in life care planning/case management.

Acumyn™ Resource:

There is a source that can be used to supplement your research. **Acumyn Resource** is an interactive, voice response technology to case managers and life care planners that can be used to coordinate home health care (and equipment needs, IV, infusion requirements, etc.) for patients. The system contains thousands of home health care providers representing more than 150 service and equipment categories. (This system also provides home health care agencies, and equipment dealers, the edge on the competition by providing national exposure to their markets.) Acumyn Resource is the database that all case managers will be accessing in the future if they want to maintain their competitive edge in the marketplace. Those case managers and other health-related professionals "in the know" are already accessing this resource and reaping the benefits. This is the only currently available database of its kind. (Please see **Appendix B** for a sample listing of service codes available through Acumyn Resource, which can be accessed by the professional life care planner/case manager in their day-to-day work.)

Acumyn can be contacted by calling their toll-free number: **800-203-1514** and entering the patient's zip code along with the Acumyn code for the type of provider information needed. Acumyn then automatically locates providers matching the request and delivers the following information to the case manager/professional by phone or fax:

- Name, address, and phone number of the home health provider.
- Name, address, and phone number of the equipment provider.
- Name, address, and phone number of the IV/infusion provider.
- Current rates for services and rate negotiation policies.
- Details about the provider such as accreditation information.
- A contact name for further information.

Obviously, Acumyn is not the answer to *all* research required; however, it will provide the case manager with a starting point and increase professional productivity and billing time. The costs for accessing this service are extremely low, when one considers time spent in researching such items. Packages can be purchased that could make each search *as low as $5 or $10 per zip code accessed.* (Please contact Acumyn directly for current pricing.) So in essence, in the time it takes you to fix a cup of coffee in the morning, the research you need can be on your fax or available via the telephone. One phone call gives you pricing for providers nationwide. What could take up to two hours to research can be accomplished by Acumyn in a matter of minutes. Acumyn is daily adding new providers of services and has plans in the future to include the availability of physicians by specialty, rehabilitation facilities by specialty, hospital costs by procedure, etc. The future potential of this database is endless, as case managers continue to demand and require a database of this nature. Additionally, Acumyn guarantees to give the case manager better ancillary provider pricing than any national contracts that might be in force within any particular company.

Let us now consider some specific resource options that will undoubtedly assist the professional in day-to-day life care planning/case managment responsibilities.

Paralyzed Veterans Of America

PVA of America, Veterans Benefits Department, 801 Eighteenth Street, N.W., Washington, D.C. 20006, 202-872-1300, 800-232-1782, is another great source of information on a variety of topics related to long-term care planning/case management of catastrophic disabilities. PVA publishes guides for the benefit of veterans with disabilities to help them understand the requirements for receiving benefits, services, equipment, and so forth, from the United States Department of Veterans Affairs (VA). The guides explain who is eligible to receive services and equipment and the process of application. It also describes the number and kinds of equipment that are available to veterans, depending upon their entitlement status. This includes wheelchairs, prosthetic and sensory aids, automotive grants/allowances, clothing allowances, and a multitude of other benefits.

Section 38 of the Code of Federal Regulations (CFR) — Pensions, Bonuses, and Veterans' Relief will also provide the documentation needed to defend your recommendations for equipment replacement, values, length of service, eligibility, etc. This can be obtained through The Office of the Federal Register, National Archives and Records Administration (Special Edition of the Federal Register); U.S. Government Printing Office — Superintendent of Documents, Mail Stop: SSOP, Washington, D.C. 20402-9328. (*There are government bookstores available in many cities through which this book can be obtained as well.*)

Special Needs Trust

Special Needs Settlements Trusts (Trusts) have been in common usage for approximately ten years, and have been used on behalf of individuals with disabilities in litigation since 1978. The Trusts have received extensive attention lately and will continue to spark debate of changes over time.

Most Trusts are established by court order for settlement or judgment proceeds received on behalf of a litigating party who is severely disabled. The Trust's two basic purposes are: (1) to provide an ongoing management vehicle for the settlement proceeds to ensure that the funds allocated to the claimant with the disability are not subject to exploitation or wastage, and (2) to preserve the claimant's eligibility (when properly drafted and in the appropriate situation) for local, state, or federal benefit programs, including SSI — Supplemental Security Income, under Title XVI and Medicaid under Title XIX of the Social Security Act (42 U.S.C.). Congress amended the Medicaid statute in the 1993 Omnibus Budget Reconciliation Act (OBRA), now codified at 42 U.S.C. 396p(d)(4)(A) to expressly recognize the use of such Trusts as a means of preserving Medicaid eligibility if certain conditions are met.

Trusts are usually established by court order with funds that would otherwise pass into the possession of a disabled claimant/beneficiary. SSI eligibility must be determined pursuant to the Social Security Act (42 U.S.C.) and the Social Security Regulations (20 C.F.R., subsection 416). To be eligible for SSI, an applicant who otherwise meets the SSI disability and income standards must also meet a resource limitation of less than a cumulative total of $2,000 in resources actually "available" to them. In addition, the Social Security Administration (SSA) has begun the SSI Programs Operations Manual System (POMS), a set of internal guidelines and procedures to be used by local Social Security branch offices in interpreting and implementing the statute and regulations.

Part of the intrigue of a Trust is the Medicaid lien. The medical needs of an injured person are often funded by Medicaid after an accident and before the resolution of the case. Medicaid may be the only source of payment while liability is being contested. All attorneys should know that the Medicaid lien must be satisfied and discharged as part of the settlement process. Usually this process is left to the end of a suit, with the hopes that Medicaid will offer a substantial discount (often 30% to 50% or more of the actual lien). However, this discount may no longer be available. One can no longer leave the treatment of the Medicaid lien to the conclusion of a case. HCFA is taking a rather hard line of no compromise of the federal financial participation amount of Medicaid liens. Thus, to avoid the parties discovering at the end of a case that almost the entire recovery could go to the Medicaid lien, this lien must be examined at the front end of a case.

All of this may seem quite confusing…and it is. Each state is handled differently, so there is no blanket answer to questions often posed. The author suggests the case manager/life care planner obtain a subscription to: *The White Paper — A Journal Concerning Personal Injury Settlements and Public Assistance Benefits,* available by contacting one of the following four editors:

1. Roger M. Bernstein, Esq., 69 Merrick Way, Suite 201, Coral Gables, FL 33134 800-666-1366
2. Susan G. Haines, Esq., Law Offices of Susan G. Haines, 650 South Cherry Street, Suite 300, Denver, CO 80222, 303-321-0388
3. William L. Winslow, Goldfarb, Sturman & Averbach, 15760 Ventura Boulevard, 19th Floor, Encino, CA 91436-3012, 818-990-4414
4. William L. E. Dussault, Esq., William L. E. Dussault, P.P., Inc., 219 East Gales Street, Seattle, WA 98102, 206-324-4300.

University of Washington — Spinal Cord Injury Update

This newsletter is supported by a grant from the *National Institute of Disability and Rehabilitation Research, U.S. Department of Education, to the Northwest Regional Spinal Cord Injury System,* one of thirteen model SCI care systems nationwide. As of the date of this chapter, the project director is Diana D. Cardenas, M.D. The newsletter is issued several times per year and is packed full of information that is a MUST for all life care planners/case managers. Research-worthy articles abound, along with a Literature Review Section and SCI Forum Report. For example, the Summer 1996 issue, Volume 6, No. 1, includes in its SCI Forum Report the following topics: Quad Rugby; Summer Sports; Sex and SCI, and Parenting. In the Literature Review section, articles previewed are selected from a monthly screening of the National Library of Medicine database for articles on spinal cord injury. In the judgment of the editors, they include potentially useful information on the diagnosis or management of spinal cord injury. Articles reviewed in this newsletter can be obtained from the reader's local medical library, or obtained through University of Washington Health Sciences Library Document Delivery Service, 206-543-3436.

As a preview, some of the more interesting articles highlighted in the Summer 1996 newsletter include the following:

- Outcomes of tendon transfer surgery and OT in a child with tetraplegia secondary to spinal cord injury.
- Pulmonary function testing in spinal cord injury: correlation with vital capacity.
- Late-life SCI and aging with a long-term injury: characteristics of two emerging populations.
- The effect of aging and duration of disability on long-term health outcomes following spinal cord injury.
- Ambulation in children and adolescents with spinal cord injuries.

These articles are pertinent and can greatly add to the life care planner's experiential and educational base of knowledge. The newsletter also lists upcoming conferences and reference lists.

To obtain a subscription to the newsletter, contact: Anna Peekstok, Editor, University of Washington, *Rehabilitation Medicine,* Box 356490, Seattle, WA 98195-6490, 206-685-3999; e-mail: peekstok@u.washington.edu. The editors have been busy putting together a site on the World Wide Web that includes articles of interest from past issues of this newsletter; copies of patient education pamphlets on skin and bowel care, and links to other organizations and information sources related to spinal cord injury. The URL (Web address) is: http://weber.u.washington.edu/~rehab/sci.

National Council on Disability

The NCD Bulletin, a monthly publication of the National Council on Disability (NCD), is free of charge, and is also available in alternative formats and on the Internet (http://www.ncd.gov). It brings you the latest issues and news affecting people with disabilities. For example, the August 1996 issue includes such topics as the following:

- ADA/Civil Rights Update: H.R. 4017, The ADA, Amendment, was introduced on 8/2/96. The bill's official purpose is: "To amend ADA with respect to safety-sensitive employment functions and individuals who have a record or history of the habitual or regular use of illegal drugs or of the abuse of alcohol, or of clinical alcoholism, and for other purposes."
- The U.S. Bureau of the Census recently released encouraging data on employment trends for people with disabilities...employment population ratio for persons with disabilities increased from 23.3% in 1991 to 26.1%

in 1994. During that time, approximately 800,000 more individuals with severe disabilities were working, which represents a 27% increase.

- P.L. 104-121 eliminates Social Security Disability Insurance and Supplemental Security Income (SSI) payments and Medicare and Medicaid eligibility for individuals whose drug addiction or alcoholism is a contributing factor material to their disability.

To obtain this newsletter, contact: *NCD Bulletin,* 1331 F Street, N.W., Suite 1050, Washington, D.C. 20004-1107, 202-272-2004 voice; 202-272-2074 TT; or 202-272-2022 Fax.

Information from HEATH — National Clearinghouse on Postsecondary Education for Individuals with Disabilities

This newsletter is published three (3) times a year. Subscriptions are available in print, on disk, or on audiocassette free by request to: The HEATH Resource Center, One Dupont Circle, Suite 800, Washington, D.C. 20036-1193, 800-544-3284 or 202-939-9320 (both lines are voice/TT), 202-833-4760 (fax). The newsletter is prepared under a cooperative agreement awarded to the American Council on Education by the U.S. Department of Education.

Contents, for example — Volume 15, Numbers 2 and 3, June and July 1996, include the following:

- Students with Multiple Chemical Sensitivity/Environmental Illness: An Accommodation Challenge.
- National Clearinghouse on Disability and Exchange; New Publications and Resources.
- New from HEATH! (Information packets, for example to include): Vocational Rehabilitation Services: A Consumer Guide for Postsecondary Students.
- HEATH Tech Pack: A set of currently available HEATH materials on the topic of technology and disability. The summer 1996 newsletter contained the following: Adaptive Technology for Students with Learning Disabilities and Distance Learning and Adults with Disabilities; Computers, Technology and Disability; Electronic Communication; and Gopher/WWW; Computers, Technology, and People with Disabilities; College Students with Learning Disabilities; Section 504 — The Law and Its Impact on Postsecondary Education, etc.

Viatical Settlements

There is available a unique financial resource for individuals facing a life-threatening illness — viatical settlements. A viatical settlement allows individuals facing a life-threatening illness to sell their life insurance policy for cash. This process is called "viaticating" — and is quite simple. It requires a single application form that the patient (client) completes. These settlements, which provide valuable financial resources, can help the patients restore control over their lives and make choices they might not otherwise have, such as paying for medical treatments, keeping their home, and even meeting day-to-day living expenses.

Viatical settlement is not a new concept. The term *viatical settlement* comes from *"viaticum"* — Latin for "provisions for a journey". *Viaticum* were the supplies that Roman soldiers were given in preparation for their journeys into battle (presumably journeys from which they may not return). So, in essence, *viaticum* were the supplies soldiers needed for the closing phase of their lives. The parallel here, of course, is that a person wishing to viaticate is preparing for the closing phase in their lives.

Initially, the viatical settlement industry was comprised of an informal network of small companies primarily serving the AIDS community. Now, however, persons with other life-threatening illnesses such as cancer or Alzheimer's disease can benefit from the financial resources available to individuals through the viatical settlement process to go toward the cost of hospitalization, treatment, home care, or other expenses, including day-to-day living expenses.

Viatical settlements are available in all 50 states. There are no restrictions on how the funds can be used, which adds control to the patient to make the decisions he or she feels necessary. Almost any kind of insurance policy — including term, whole life, universal life, or group (employer paid) policies — from any company can be used. Policies from values of just $10,000 to well over $1 million have been purchased. The entire viatication process usually takes about three to six weeks to complete.

The value (the amount paid to the patient) of the insurance policy is determined by several factors, including prevailing interest rates, premium obligations, and projected life expectancy. The National Association of Insurance Commissioners (NAIC) has established pricing guidelines. Viators (the patients) generally receive between 50% and 80% of the face value of the insurance policy. Generally, the longer the life expectancy, the less the viatical settlement company is likely to pay for that individual's policy, because the company must assume responsibility for maintaining the policy for a longer period of time. (The proceeds from a viatical settlement may, however, impact certain means-based entitlement programs such as Medicaid.)

Under current law, the proceeds from a viatical settlement are taxable as income for federal tax purposes. However, several states have adopted or are considering specific regulations or provisions, which may include:

1. State and city tax-free treatment of viatical settlement proceeds to encourage the use of these settlements;
2. Preventing the "brokering" of life insurance policies to individual investors who are looking for speculative returns without due regard for the policy owner's welfare;
3. Requiring viatical companies to maintain a minimum level of capital or surety bond to fund the purchase of life insurance policies as part of the viatical settlement process (this helps ensure that companies can fund settlements and prevents the involvement of viatical settlement companies that may put people at financial risk);
4. Requiring licenses and other strictly enforced reporting mechanisms for viatical settlement companies and limiting licenses to companies with well-established operations. For more information, contact The Viatical Association of America, 800-390-1390.

The Testifying Expert

This newsletter is published monthly by LRP Publications, 747 Dresher Road, P.O. Box 980, Horsham, PA 19044-0980 215-784-0860, ext. 341. The purpose of the newsletter is to point out "Winning Strategies On and Off the Stand for the Expert Witness." There are some "pearls of wisdom" in this newsletter for those in forensic rehabilitation. As an example, the November 1996 issue (Volume 4, Issue 11) had the following articles:

- Expert's Testimony Fails Daubert Scrutiny
- Visualize Victory Through Effective Nonverbal Communication
- Maintaining Database Gives You an Edge for Getting Hired
- Knowing Your Rights Can Help You Survive Abusive Depositions
- Expert Found Himself Boxed in on the Stand
- Experts in the Courts
- Doctor's Specialty Doesn't Disqualify Him as an Expert
- Experts Can Testify in Malpractice Suit
- Testimony within Range of Common Knowledge
- Expert ID'd Just Before Trial Must Be Excluded, Judge Says
- Expert's Field Work Paid Off in McDonald's Coffee Spill Case
- Court Sides with Lawyer in Battle Over Expert's Fee
- Conference Calendar

Disability Compliance Bulletin

This bulletin is published biweekly by LRP Publications 747 Dresher Road, P. O. Box 980, Horsham, PA 19044-0980, 215-784-0860. This bulletin is a service of the National Disability Law Reporter. It contains information pertaining to ADA and a number of disability-related issues. For example, the November 21, 1996 issue contained the following:

- Update: The Latest on Litigation in Progress and Other News of Note
- Expenditures on Employment-Focused Programs for People with Disabilities
- EEOC Alters Charge Process in Effort to Reduce Backlog of Charges
- New Judicial Decisions
- Definition of Disability
- Practice and Procedure
- OCR Letters
- EEOC Policy Letters
- DOJ Policy Letters

Through the Looking Glass: Resources for Parents with Disabilities

Persons with disabilities still experience discrimination when it comes to everyday issues, even such basic issues as the human rights associated with reproduction. The ability of mothers with a disability to care for their babies is questioned by health care professionals and the general population. Through the Looking Glass is a nonprofit organization founded by Megan Kirschbaum in Berkeley, California in 1982. It focuses on preventative services, professional training, and research concerning families with a disability or medical issue for either parent or child. Contact: Through the Looking Glass, 2198 Sixth St., Suite 100, Berkeley, CA 94710-2204; 800-644-2666; or E-Mail: ThruGlass@aol.com.

Accessible Mortgages: CRA — Community Reinvestment Act

The Community Reinvestment Act (CRA) is a federal law that requires financial institutions to reinvest some of their profits in their communities. Banks, savings and loans, etc., must demonstrate that their lending programs serve local businesses and individuals, particularly in low-income areas. Usually these institutions kept track of loans applied for and granted to minorities. Rarely were the number of applicants with disabilities tracked, although many qualified for CRA reinvestment programs. In an attempt to correct and address this oversight, the Federal National Mortgage Association (Fannie Mae), recently launched a three year $50 million test program offering mortgages to people with disabilities. These loans, however, are currently available only in 11 states and Washington, D.C. The program, called HomeChoice, if deemed successful, may be extended to other states.

Under the plan, loans will be made for up to 95% of the purchase price of a home through financial institutions working with local disability and housing organizations. Applicants can include up to 50% of their income, including disability benefits paid by Social Security, toward their payments.

Provisions also have been made to provide counseling, both before and after home purchase, as well as financial assistance with down payments, closing costs, and accessibility modifications. States taking part in the program have to involve a coalition of disability agencies, housing development and finance agencies, consumer advocacy groups, and housing counseling organizations within the state.

Eligible borrowers include families that contain someone with a disability and households whose incomes do not exceed HUD-established medians. Since the per capita income of each state is different, the median income level is adjusted accordingly. (Contact Fannie Mae for more information on your state's median income requirement.)

Face-to-face counseling is required both before and after the loan is made, but this must be at an accessible location. Topics usually include homeownership responsibilities; mortgage terminology; personal financial management; move-in preparations; and property maintenance. The states chosen for the initial phase of the pilot program include: Alabama, California, Idaho, Massachusetts, Minnesota, Missouri, New Mexico, New York, Oregon, Texas, Washington, and the District of Columbia.

While this information may not be particularly useful during the development phase of a life care plan, it is certainly a case management tool that should be used to its fullest extent. For more information on Mortgage Resources contact:

1. Access Living. Alberto Barrera, 310 S. Peoria, Chicago, IL 60607, 312-226-5900.
2. Atlantis Community, Inc., Kathy Sandoval, Mortgage Counselor, 201 S. Cherokee Street, Denver, CO 80223, 303-733-9324.

3. Fannie Mae, Joy Horvath, Manager of Special Needs Housing, 3900 Wisconsin Avenue, N.W., Washington, D.C. 20016-2899, 202-752-4810.
4. National Home of Your Own Alliance, Institute on Disability/UAP, 7 Leavitt Lane, Suite 1201, Durham, NH 03824-3512, 603-862-0550.
5. Department of Veterans Affairs, 800-827-1000.
6. Venture, Inc./Oakland Livingston, Human Service Agency (OLHSA), Special Needs Housing Program (SNHP), 196 Oakland Avenue, P. O. Box 430598, Pontiac, MI 48343-0598, 800-482-9250; 810-858-5187.

Information for this resource was gathered from: *One Step Ahead— The Resource for Active, Healthy, Independent Living,* a monthly newspaper dedicated to providing the readers with resource information for independent living. Contact *One Step Ahead* at: P.O. Box 5163, Capitol Heights, MD 20791-5163.

Telecommunications — Accessibility

With the advent of the ADA, each state was required to implement a telecommunications system that is accessible to the disabled population. In Florida, for example, Florida Telecommunications Relay, Inc. (FTRI) is a not-for-profit organization that administers a statewide Specialized Telecommunications Equipment Distribution Program for hearing impaired, dual sensory impaired (hearing and vision), or speech impaired Florida citizens. The equipment provided through this program is loaned to *all* qualified citizens for as long as they need it, at no charge. (The FTRI Program provides basic access to the telecommunications network as mandated by the Telecommunications Access System Act of 1991 (TASA), Chapter 417, Sec. III, Florida Statutes.)

Every state must have some type of system in place to provide accessible telecommunications. Following is a listing of data available to date regarding equipment distribution programs nationwide. If your state is not listed, contact your local telephone service information system, usually located inside the front cover of your local telephone book.

EQUIPMENT DISTRIBUTION PROGRAMS

ALABAMA	2707 Artie St., Suite 18, Huntsville, AL 35805 (Institute for the Deaf and Blind) Provides TDDs free of charge.	205-539-7881 (Voice/TDD)
ALABAMA	P.O. Box 11586, Montgomery, AL (Division of Rehabilitative Services) Provides amplified phones, inline amplifiers, TDDs, braille TDDs, large display TDDs, light signalers, loud bells, tactile signaler, and large button phones free of charge.	800-441-6578 205-281-8780 (Voice/TDD)
ALASKA	501 N. Main St., Suite 200, Wasilla, AK 99654 (Relay Alaska) Provides TDDs free of charge.	800-770-6770 (Voice/TDD)
ARIZONA	1400 W. Washington St., Phoenix, AZ 85007 (Council for the Hearing Impaired/TTY Project) Provides TDDs, braille TDDs, large display TDDs, and light signalers free of charge.	800-352-8161 602-542-3323 (Voice/TDD)
ARKANSAS	P.O. Box 3781, Little Rock, AR 72203 (Rehabilitation Services Office for the Deaf and Hard of Hearing) Provides amplified phones, inline amplifiers, TDDs, braille TDDs, large display TDDs, light signalers, loud bells, tactile signalers, and large button phones free of charge.	501-682-6665 (Voice/TDD)
CALIFORNIA	1939 Harrison St., Suite 520, Oakland, CA 94612 (Deaf and Disabled Telecommunication Program) Provides amplified phones, inline amplifiers, TDDs, braille TDDs, large display TDDs, light signalers, loud bells, tactile signalers, large button phones, amplifiers (portable, cochlear implant), artificial larynxes, large number overlays, phones (handsfree, cordless, speaker, large button/picture), headsets, and one number dialers free of charge.	800-772-3140 (Pacific Bell V/T) 800-821-2585 (GTE)

CALIFORNIA	3140 Old Tunnel Rd., Lafayette, CA 94549 Attn. L.T. Maracci (Telephone Pioneers — George S. Ladd Chapter — Additional Equip.) Provides amplified phones, inline amplifiers, TDDs, light signalers, large button phones, phone (speaker, cordless, handsfree), and artificial larynxes free of charge.	510-934-4626 (Voice/TDD)
COLORADO	7346 S. Alton Way, Suite E, Englewood, CO 80112 (Assistive Communication Center) Equipment retailer with financial assistance program.	303-290-6227 800-743-1219 (Voice/TDD)
CONNECTICUT	Converse Communications, 34 Jerome Ave., Bloomfield, CT 06002 (Relay Connecticut) Provides TDDs and large display TDDs free of charge.	203-242-4974 800-743-1219 (Voice/TDD)
CONNECTICUT	141 N. Main St., West Hartford, CT 06107 (Connecticut Commission on the Deaf and Hearing Impaired.)	203-566-7414 (Voice/TDD)
DELAWARE	Delaware Elwyn Bldg., 321 E. 11th St., 4th Floor, Wilmington, DE 19801 (Division of Vocational Rehabilitation) Provides handset amplifiers, amplified phones, inline amplifiers, TDDs, braille TDDs, large display TDDs, light signalers, loud bells, tactile signalers, and large button phones.	302-577-2850 (Voice/TDD)
FLORIDA	Florida Relay Service 200 S. Biscayne Blvd. Suite 600, Miami, FL 33131 (There are Regional Distribution Centers in all of the major areas of Florida).	800-955-8013 800-222-3448 for Regional Distribution Centers.
ILLINOIS	527 E. Capitol Ave., Springfield, IL 62794 (Illinois Commerce Commission)	217-782-7663 (Voice) 217-524-5047 (TDD)

EQUIPMENT DISTRIBUTION PROGRAMS (continued)

ILLINOIS	P.O. Box 64509, Chicago, IL 60664 (Illinois Telecommunications Access Corporation)	(312) 419-4201 (Voice) (312) 419-4211 (TDD)
LOUISIANA	P.O. Box 94182, Baton Rouge, LA 70819 (Louisiana Commission for the Deaf)	504-925-4182 (Voice) 504-925-4177 (TDD) 800-256-1523
MAINE	35 Anthony Ave., Augusta, ME 04333 (Division of Deafness — Maine Bureau of Rehabilitation)	207-624-5318 (Voice) 207-624-5322 (TDD)
MASSACHUSETTS	125 High St., Boston, MA 02110 (New England Telephone Company)	617-743-9450 (Voice) 617-743-4108 (TDD)
MASSACHUSETTS	251 Lock Dr., Marlboro, MA 01752 (Customer Contact Center for Individuals with Disabilities)	508-624-1972 (Voice/TDD)
MASSACHUSETTS	600 Washington St., Boston, MA 02111 (Massachusetts Commission for the Deaf and Hard of Hearing)	617-727-5106 (Voice/TDD)
MINNESOTA	658 Cedar St., St. Paul, MN 55155-3814 (TACIP Board — State of Minnesota)	612-296-3293 (Voice) 612-282-2444 (TDD)
MINNESOTA	444 Lafayette Rd., St. Paul, MN 55155-3814	612-297-3639 (Voice) 612-296-9306 (TDD)
MONTANA	111 N. Last Chance Gulch, Helena, MT 59620 (Governor's Committee on Montana Telecommunications)	406-444-1486 (Voice/TDD)

NEVADA	505 E. King St., Carson City, NV 89710 (Nevada Rehabilitation Division — Dept. of Human Resources)	702-687-4452 (Voice) 702-687-3388 (TDD)
NEVADA	6200 W. Oakley, Las Vegas, NV 89102 (National Association for the Handicapped)	702-870-7050 (Voice/TDD)
NEVADA	624 E. 4th St., Reno, NV 89512 (Northern Nevada Center for Independent Living)	702-328-8000 (Voice) 702-328-8006 (TDD)
NEW HAMPSHIRE	c/o Division of Vocational Rehabilitation 78 Regional Dr., Bldg. #2, Concord, NH 03301 (New Hampshire Telecommunications Equipment Program)	603-271-3471 (Voice/TDD)
NEW YORK	(NYNEX) Provides weak speech handsets, impaired hearing handsets, visual signalers, audible tone signalers, tone ringers, and electronic artificial larynxes for lease or purchase at cost.	800-482-9020 (Voice) 800-482-9020 NEW YORK ONLY!
NORTH CAROLINA	P.O. Box 29532, Raleigh, NC 29626 (North Carolina Department of Services for the Deaf and Hard of Hearing)	919-733-5197 (Voice/TDD)
OKLAHOMA	RS 24, Oklahoma City, OK 73125 Services to the Deaf/Hearing Impaired, Telecommunications Relay/TDD Distribution, Vocational Rehabilitation	405-424-4311 (Voice) 405-424-2794 (TDD)
OREGON	550 Capitol St., Salem, OR 9731 (Oregon Public Utilities Commission-TDAP)	503-373-1282 (Voice) 503-373-1413 (TDD)

EQUIPMENT DISTRIBUTION PROGRAMS (continued)

RHODE ISLAND	100 Houghton St., Providence, RI 02904 (Vocational Resources, Inc.)	401-861-6677 (Voice/TDD)
RHODE ISLAND	40 Fountain St., Providence, RI 02903 (Rhode Island Office of Rehabilitative Services)	401-421-7005 (Voice) 401-421-7016 (TDD)
SOUTH DAKOTA	3520 Gateway Ln., Sioux Falls, SD 57106 (Communications Services for the Deaf)	605-339-6718 (Voice/TDD)
TENNESSEE	400 Deadrick St., Nashville, TN 37248-3600 (Tennessee Council for the Hearing Impaired)	615-741-5644 (Voice/TDD)
UTAH	P.O. Box 45585, Salt Lake City, UT 84145 (Utah Public Service Commission)	801-530-6781 (Voice/TDD)

The Directory for Exceptional Children

The Directory for Exceptional Children is an excellent resource that reflects the growing recognition of the multidimensional needs of exceptional children. Since its beginning in 1954, each subsequent edition has grown to include more than 3000 facilities and organizations. This is a resource for both families and professionals, with listings encompassing the entire range of developmental, organic, and emotional handicaps. Each listing conforms to a standardized format, making it convenient for referencing and easy comparison of programs. Directory listings include the following:

- Schools for the learning disabled
- Private facilities for the emotionally disturbed
- State and public facilities for the emotionally disturbed
- Psychiatric and guidance clinics
- Residential facilities for orthopedic and neurological disabilities
- Day facilities for orthopedic and neurological disabilities
- Private residential facilities for the mentally retarded
- Private day facilities for the mentally retarded
- State and public facilities for the mentally retarded
- Programs for the blind and partially sighted
- Schools for the deaf and hearing impaired
- Schools for the speech and language impaired
- Speech and hearing clinics
- Programs for the autistic
- Associations and agencies
- Associations, societies, and foundations
- Federal and state agencies

The *Directory* listings are all in alphabetical order, by state and type of facility.

To obtain the *Directory*: Porter Sargent Publishers, Inc., 11 Beacon Street, Suite 1400, Boston, MA 02108, 617-523-1670; Fax 617-523-1021.

Census Bureau

The U.S. Census Bureau is the nation's chief statistical collection agency. It has recently begun an Internet service that provides instant access to its reports and documents. The CenStats service contains 1000 reports and documents going back to the beginning of the year. Topics range from state government finances to homeownership in the United States.

The Census Bureau's reports are also available at government bookstores or through mail order from the U.S. Government Printing Office in Washington, D.C. Ordering a printed publication would involve calling the Census Bureau's customer service office to get the government document number and then calling the printing office to order the publication. CenStats eliminates that governmental two-step and provides almost instant access to the research. The Internet site also includes a cumulative catalog of census publications, their document numbers, and prices.

At the present time, and for a time not specified, the CenStats service is free to anyone with access to the Internet and an Adobe software program to decipher the information. Plans call for a $150 per year fee for access, but the Bureau is researching ways that would allow individual's to obtain and pay for specific documents without subscribing to the service year-round.

In addition to CenStats, the Bureau will distribute some of its shorter reports by fax. Users of the FastFax service call a 900 number to get a list of available documents or order a specific report. The only charge is for the time spent ordering the publication.

Important Numbers

CenStats Internet address: http://www.census.gov/prod/www/
Census Internet home page address: http://www.census.gov
Census Bureau Customer Service: 301-457-4100
FastFax phone number: 900-555-2329

Spinal Cord Injury/Brain Injury Information

Most professionals involved in life care planning/case management are quite familiar with a variety of magazines, newsletters, etc. pertaining to disability specific issues. Some of these include:

New Mobility — Disability Lifestyle, Culture and Resources. Published monthly by Miramar Communications, Inc. 23815 Stuart Ranch Road, Malibu, CA 90265, 310-317-4522; fax: 310-317-9644; E-Mail: sam@miramar.com. Web Site: http://www.newmobility.com. This is a division of The Disability Network. This group also publishes: *Spinal Network: The Total Wheelchair Book; Homecare; TeamRehab Report; Special Events Magazines; and Rental Equipment Register.*

PN — Paraplegia News. This is published monthly by Paralyzed Veterans of America, Inc., 2111 East Highland Avenue, Suite 180, Phoenix, AZ 85016-4702, 602-224-0500; fax: 602-224-0507; E-Mail:/pvapub@aol.com. This magazine is now in its fiftieth year of publication and is dedicated to the presentation of all news concerning paraplegics (civilians and veterans) and wheelchair living.

Topics in Spinal Cord Injury Rehabilitation. This journal is published quarterly by Aspen Publishers, Inc., 7201 McKinney Circle, Frederick, MD 21701, 800-234-1660, or 800-638-8437. This is a peer-reviewed topical journal devoted to multidisciplinary commentary on the management of persons with disability because of an insult to the spinal cord. The topics presented are current on the treatment of patients with spinal paralysis. Topics included, for example, in the Summer 1996 journal:

- Pressure Ulcers: Scope of Problem/Management
- Proactive Nursing Approach to Skin Management
- Role of Plastic Surgery in the Treatment of Pressure Ulcers

- Psychosocial Correlates of Pressure Ulcers
- Ethical Issues in Pressure Ulcer Management
- The Baclofen Pump for Treating Spasticity in SCI
- The Case Management Team

Exceptional Parent — The Magazine for Families and Professionals

This magazine is published 12 times per year by Psy-Ed Corp., dba Exceptional Parent Magazine, 209 Harvard St., Ste. 303, Brookline, MA 2146-5005, 800-562-1973 or 800-247-8080. E-Mail: http://www.familyeducation.com.

Departments include the following:

Editor's Desk
Letters
Search and Respond
Point of View
What's Happening
Ask the Doctor
Children's Health Notes
Health Insurance Troubleshooter
Directory of Private School and Residential Programs
Directory of Advertisers
Media
New Products
Exceptional Parent Library

Yearly Technology/Communication/Education issues are included. This magazine is a must for any professional working with pediatrics. Not only are the magazines stocked with informative articles, the resource sections alone are worth a subscription.

The Neurolaw Letter

This is a monthly HDI Publication for legal and health professionals for distribution to attorneys and professionals who provide services to survivors of brain injury and spinal cord injury and their families. Content, for example — the November 1966 issue — includes the following:

- Making the Best Use of Your Neuropsychology Expert: What Every Neurolawyer Should Know
- Recent Developments — Canadian TBI
- Chiropractic Malpractice
- Other Significant Cases
- PTSD and TBI

Newsletter available from: The Neurolaw Letter, P.O. Box 131401, Houston, TX 77219, 800-321-7037; 713-682-8700; fax 713-956-2288. HDI specializes in literature in brain injury for survivors, families, and professionals. A complete catalog is available through HDI.

Other Sources

The sources mentioned in this chapter are certainly not a complete list of all resources available. The author's goal was to present some sources of information that may not be commonly known among life care planning/case management professionals. Not mentioned, of course, are the vast resources available through the Internet. There have been entire books written on the sources that can be obtained through the Internet. The author's advice to the rehabilitation professional is to review the chapter on technology in this text and just "dive in" and begin "surfing the net" as they say. There are also short, informative classes taught at specific seminars by individuals such as Roger Weed and Randall Thomas on how to use and benefit from the Internet.

A chapter on sources would not be complete without mentioning some of the authoritative texts available on the market pertaining to life care planning/case management. Certainly, A *Guide to Rehabilitation,* by Paul M. Deutsch and Horace Sawyer cannot be overlooked. This book, formerly published by Matthew Bender, Inc., is now published by Ahab Press, Inc., 2 Gannett Drive, Suite 200, White Plains, NY 10604-3404, 914-696-0708; fax: 914-694-6856, or E-Mail: AHAB4@aol.com.

Several other texts that are filled with information and resources include *Life Care Planning for Traumatic Brain Injury,* and *Life Care Planning for Spinal Cord Injury— Resource Manuals for Case Managers,* by Terry L. Blackwell, Ph.D., Anne Sluis Powers, Ph.D., R.N.; and Roger O. Weed, Ph.d. Both are published by Elliott and Fitzpatrick, Inc. P.O. Box 1945, Athens, GA 30603, 706-548-8161; 800-843-4977.

Now What? Where Does the Life Care Planner Go from Here?

You, the professional, have just perused a mass of information available on specific disability topics; you have evaluated your client; and you are in the process of finalizing your life care plan. Where does one go for help, review, assistance, etc? As the author has indicated in seminars throughout the country for the past nine years, networking is a valuable asset. Discuss your recommendations and plan with a co-worker, friend, ally, or other interested party. If you are a single practitioner (or even if you are with a group), you have potential sources available through Rehabilitation Training Institute (RTI, also known as Intelicus), whose 1995 and forward graduates of the life care planning, two year program, are listed in the *Graduate Directory*— University of Florida/Rehabilitation Training Institute — Intelicus — 2710 Rew Circle, Ocoee, FL 34761, 800-431-6687; Fax: 407-656-7585; E-Mail: http://www.intelicus.ufl.edu.

Also available are individuals who perform life care plan mentoring or critiquing, where, for a fee, your plan can be reviewed by a competent professional to provide you a thorough review of your recommendations and communicated information. (It is imperative you select your mentor/critique professional wisely, with references, to be sure you have a qualified individual who will be able to constructively critique and guide you through the process.) This review provides you with feedback that subsequently will give you the comfort and assurance that your plan is thorough, defensible, and has been reviewed by an industry expert, knowledgeable in the life care planning process, and critical components of each disability. The "critique" will contain suggestions for improvement; areas not defined, overlooked components; overlaps and underfunding; and areas subject to scrutiny in the courtroom. (Please see **Appendix C** for a sample life care plan Critique form). For mentoring/critiquing, or life care plan preparation, suggested sources include the author and: National Life Care Institute (NLCI), William Goodrich, CRC, CLCP, ABVE, P.O. Box 8839, Missoula, MT 59807; Randall Thomas, Ph.D., 713 So. Pear Orchard Dr., Ste. 100, Ridgeland, MS 39157; and Susan Riddick-Grisham, P. O. Box 271827, Concord, CA 94520. There are also physical medicine and rehabilitation physicians who will consult with life care planners on medical issues pertinent to the life care plan. These include: Robert Meier, M.D. (303-779-8878), Denver, CO; Terry Winkler, M.D. (417-887-3293), Springfield, MO; Richard Bonfiglio, M.D. (412-826-2709), Erie, PA, and James Young, M.D. (312-791-3734), Chicago, IL.

Training/Certification in Life Care Planning

There is now a Certification for Life Care Planners — Certified Life Care Planner — CLCP, which issued its first certification in March 1996. The certification is through The Commission on Disability Examiner Certification — CDEC, which was established in 1994 in response to the health care industry's need for certified clinical examiners in impairment and disability rating practices (see Chapter 26 on credentialing for detailed information). Though established as a not-for-profit agency in 1994, the CDEC evolved in 1992 as a result of meetings with allied health care providers around the country in which issues were discussed that focused primarily on clinical examiner credentials, validity and reliability of rating protocol, and the establishment of a testing board to oversee the impairment rating and disability examining credentialling process.

The CDEC understands the required consistency of training among case managers and consultants who provide life care planning services. Therefore, the CDEC offers a generic certification without reference to specialty areas of training or a candidate's achieved degree level. The CDEC requires the following criteria to be met by all candidates in order to qualify to sit for the examination:

Minimum of 120 hours of postgraduate or post-specialty degree training in Life Care Planning and meeting specific standards.
Candidate must be certified or licensed within their respective profession by a certifying agency (accredited) or appropriate regulatory body.
Candidate must have a minimum of one (1) year of work or professional experience in developing Life Care Plans.
Each candidate must hold the entry level academic degree or certificate/diploma for their profession.

Specific training (curriculum) shall include the following:

Orientation of Life Care Planning and Case Management
Assessment of Rehabilitation Potential
Medical and Rehabilitation Aspects of Disability

Development of Life Care Plans
Consultation in Life Care Planning
Professional and Operational Issues

Specific information on the CDE and CLCP examinations can be obtained through: V. Robert May III, Rh.D., Commissioner of Research and Statistics, 9101 Midlothian Turnpike, Suite 200, Richmond, VA 23235, 804-272-9192.

Training can be through any approved agency or group such as NARPPS, RTI, NADEP. (For information on training through RTI/Intelicus/University of Florida, contact: Sheri Jasper, 800-431-6687.) Specific CEU opportunities such as the "correspondence CEU courses" contained within professional journals must be preapproved by CDEC prior to CLCP credits applying.

It is also interesting to note that university programs are addressing the need for training/education in life care planning. As noted above, the University of Florida, Gainesville, FL, has been involved for several years in bringing this training to the forefront, as has Georgia State University, Atlanta. LSU Medical Center, New Orleans, is also infusing this information into their curricula for the B.S. in Rehabilitation Services and the M.H.S. in Rehabilitation Counseling programs. There are other university programs that participate in this area, although not many address the value and importance of this planning concept within the private sector practice. The result of these introductory courses is that there is a continual stream of professionals seeking additional training and knowledge in this arena. To make sure quality is achieved, strict adherence to guidelines set forth by the certifying agency and parameters set forth through the ethics and planning committees must be adhered to.

CONCLUSION

This chapter on resources, training, and certification is designed to provide the life care planner with information needed to be continually prepared for the unexpected circumstances that occur in our profession. Preparedness is the key to a successful life care planning experience. Never discount information you may "run across" during your "travels through life"...there is a wealth of information available for the interested party. The goal will be to disseminate this information in a fashion that is easily understood, documented, and factual.

Appendix A

Paul M. Deutsch & Associates, P.A.
Julie A. Kitchen, CDMS, CCM, CLCP
407-898-7710

Nursing Research Format

PROVIDER: ____
____

Tele. #______________________ **Fax #**______________________

Contact: ______________________ **Title**______________________

Counties Served: ____
____.

Is there a mileage charge in addition to hourly? ___Yes ___No. If Yes: ____/Mile.

RATES: *(Private pay rate for all costs: ___Yes ___No)*

HHA/Hr: $_____
HHA/Visit: $_____

LPN/Hr: $_____
LPN/Visit: $_____

RN/Hr: $_____
RN/Visit: $_____

*Minimum # of hours per visit:*________.

Live-In: ___Yes ___No. **Daily Rate:** $_____

of "hands-on" care hours per day: _____.
of "uninterrupted sleep" hours per night: _____.

Definition: ____
____
____.

MSW/CASE MANAGER: $_____/Hr.

THERAPIES:

PT ___**Yes** ___**No $**_____**/Visit**
OT ___**Yes** ___**No $**_____**/Visit**
ST ___**Yes** ___**No $**_____**/Visit**

Recreational Therapy: ___**Yes**___**No $**_____**/Visit**

OTHER: ____
____.

TRANSPORTATION:

Can staff member transport patient? ___*Yes* ___*No*
Personal Car? ___*Yes* ___*No. Patient's Car:* ___*Yes* ___*No*

SKILL RESPONSIBILITIES:

Can Aide level:	*Administer Medications:*	___*Yes* ___*No*
	Perform Bowel Stim:	___*Yes* ___*No*
	G-Tube:	___*Yes* ___*No*
	Insert Catheter:	___*Yes* ___*No*
	Trim Finger/Toe Nails:	___*Yes* ___*No*
Can LPN level:	*Perform Trach Care:*	___*Yes* ___*No*
	Perform Vent Care:	___*Yes* ___*No*
	Trim Finger/Toe Nails:	___*Yes* ___*No*

RN SUPERVISION:

With Live-In or Aide Care: One visit per ________(Wk./Month/Qtr.)

With LPN Care: One visit per ________(Wk./Month/Qtr.)

Is there an EXTRA charge for the RN supervision visit? ___*Yes* ___*No.*
If Yes: $____/visit.

Comments: ____
____
____

Research By:________________ Date:________________

Appendix B
Acumyn Resource

Specialty Programs
150 Geriatric services
151 Pain management
152 Hospice
153 Ventilator management
154 HIV program
155 Pediatric programs
156 Pediatric respiratory services
157 Maternal/infant services
158 Rehab program
159 Home dialysis
160 Psychiatric home care
161 Mail order pharmacy
162 Chronic disease manag.
163 Patient education resources
164 Pediatric durable medical equipment
165 Pediatric specialty subacute
170 Non-invasive bone growth stimulator
171 Dynamic Splinting
172 Motorized Cryotherapy
180 Aeromedical services
181 Ground transportation

Nursing Services, Lic.
200 RN
201 High tech RN
202 LPN
203 High tech LPN
204 Psych RN
206 Stoma therapist

Nursing Services, Non-licensed
225 HHA
226 PCA
227 Homemakers
228 Companions
229 Sitters
230 Live-in

Specialty Professionals
250 Medical social worker
251 Dietician
252 Financial counselor

Therapy
275 Physical therapy
276 Occupational therapy
277 Speech therapy
278 Mental health therapy
279 Respiratory therapy

Maternal/Infant Services
300 Non-stress testing
301 Uterine monitoring
302 Phototherapy
303 Terbutaline therapy
304 Mag. sulfate therapy

Infusion/Nutrition Services
400 IV antibiotic therapy
401 Pain management therapy
402 IV hydration
403 TPN
404 Lipids — 10%
406 Chemotherapy
407 Epogen — 2000 units
411 Packed red blood cells
412 Enteral nutrition
413 Aerosolized Pentamadine
414 IV Pentamadine
415 Prolastin
416 Growth hormone
417 Heparin
418 Dobutamine
419 Immunoglobulins
420 Platelets
421 Neupogen

IV Supplies/Monitors
450 IV poles
451 Enteral feeding pumps
452 Home blood glucose monitor

Respiratory Treatment/Diagnostic
500 Nebulizer, ultrasonic
501 Nebulizer w/compressor & heater
502 Pulmoaide
503 Suction pump, home model
504 IPPB machine
506 Permanent humidifier
507 Compressor, bedside

Ventilators/Assisted Breathing
520 Volume ventilator, stationary
521 Volume ventilator, portable
523 BI-PAP
524 Percussor, elec or pneuma.
525 CPAP

Oxygen
540 Liquid 02 reservoir base
541 Liquid 02 portable system
542 02 contents, liquid, per lb
543 Oxygen concentrator

Compressed Gas
560 Portable gas oxygen system, E-tank and cart
561 Stationary compressed gas
562 E-tank 02 refill for portable gas system
563 H-tank 02 contents gas 240 cu ft
564 02 regulator

Sleep Monitors
580 Apnea monitor
581 Apnea monitor w/trend rec
582 Oximeter
583 Sleep studies

Beds
600 Hospital bed, manual, side rails
601 Hospital bed, fully electric
602 Hospital bed, semi-electric
630 Powered flotation bed, low air loss

Mattresses/Pads
625 Alt pressure pad, w/pump
626 Dry pressure mattress
627 Air pressure mattress
628 Synthetic sheepskin pad
629 Lambswool sheepskin pad
631 Dry pressure pad, egg crate

Bed Accessories
650 Heel or elbow protector
651 Bed board
652 Over bed table
653 Bed cradle

Traction Units
700 Traction frame, headboard, cervical traction
701 Traction frame, footboard, extremity traction
702 Traction frame, footboard, pelvic traction
703 Fracture frame, attach to bed, w/weights

Pneumatic Devices
725 Pneumatic compressor, non-segmental
726 Pneumatic compressor, segmental w/calib. press
727 Pneumatic appliance — arm
728 Pneumatic appliance — leg
729 Pneumatic appliance — foot

Misc. Orthopedic Devices
750 TENS, 4-lead
752 EMG, biofeedback device
754 Trapeze bar for bed
755 C.P.M. device

Canes/Crutches
800 Canes (all types)
801 Quad cane
803 Crutches, forearm—all types
804 Crutches, underarm—all types

Walkers
820 Rigid walker
821 Folding walker
822 Wheeled walker w/o seat
823 Rigid walker, wheeled, w/seat
824 Walker platform attachment
825 Standing frame

Wheelchairs
840 Wheelchair, standard adult, all types
841 Wheelchair, hemi, adult, all types
842 Wheelchair, lt. weight, adult, all types
843 Wheelchair, pediatric, all types
844 Wheelchair, hemi, pediatric, all types
845 Wheelchair, specialty, all types
846 3-wheeled powered vehicle
847 Geri-chair

Seating
860 Air pressure pad w/pump, w/c
861 Flotation pad, w/c
862 ROHO, high profile
863 ROHO, low profile
864 Jay seat cushion
865 Jay back cushion

Lift Devices
880 Seat lift chair, motorized
881 Sling seat lift
882 Patient lift, hydraulic, seat/swing
883 Transfer board

Toilet/Bathing
900 Toilet rail
901 Commode seat, raised
902 Portable commode
903 Commode, wide
904 Rehab commode
905 Stool or bench tub, w/back
906 Transfer tub rail attachment
907 Sitz bath, portable, fits over commode seat
908 Sitz bath chair
909 Padded tub transfer bench
910 Rehab shower chair

Specialty Products/Supplies
925 Ostomy supplies
926 Orthotics
927 Prosthetics
928 Diabetic supplies
929 Incontinence products

Appendix C

PAUL M. DEUTSCH & ASSOCIATES, P.A.

CRITIQUE CONSULTANT: JULIE A. KITCHEN
407-898-7710

Referred By:

Date Received:

Date Returned:

Type of Impairment:

I. REVIEW OF AREAS COVERED
   A. In relation to the type of disability involved, has the Life Care Planner analyzed all necessary areas?

II. REVIEW OF TERMINOLOGY
   A. Has the Life Care Planner used appropriate disability specific terminology?
   B. Does the use of this terminology reflect appropriately the Life Care Planner's knowledge of the disability?

III. ANALYSIS OF OVERLAPS
   A. Are the total number of hours involved in therapy within reasonable guidelines?
   B. Are the total number of weeks per year required to implement this plan within reasonable guidelines?
   C. Are the total number of days involved in implementing this plan per year within reasonable guidelines?
   D. Has the Life Care Planner avoided programmatic overlaps?

IV. ADDITIONAL RECOMMENDATIONS TO BE CONSIDERED BY THE LIFE CARE PLANNER
   A. Projected Evaluations:
      [ ] No Further Recommendations
      [ ] See Below For Recommendations
   B. Projected Therapeutic Modalities:
      [ ] No Further Recommendations
      [ ] See Below For Recommendations
   C. Diagnostic Testing/Educational Assessment:
      [ ] No Further Recommendations
      [ ] See Below For Recommendations
   D. Wheelchair Needs:
      [ ] No Further Recommendations
      [ ] See Below For Recommendations
   E. Wheelchair Accessories and Maintenance:
      [ ] No Further Recommendations
      [ ] See Below For Recommendations

F. Orthopedic Equipment Needs:
- [ ] No Further Recommendations
- [ ] See Below For Recommendations

G. Orthotics/Prosthetics:
- [ ] No Further Recommendations
- [ ] See Below For Recommendations

H. Aids For Independent Function:
- [ ] No Further Recommendations
- [ ] See Below For Recommendations

I. Home Furnishings and Accessories (Durable Medical Items):
- [ ] No Further Recommendations
- [ ] See Below For Recommendations

J. Drug/Supply Needs:
- [ ] No Further Recommendations
- [ ] See Below For Recommendations

K. Home/Facility Care:
- [ ] No Further Recommendations
- [ ] See Below For Recommendations

L. Future Medical Care — Routine:
- [ ] No Further Recommendations
- [ ] See Below For Recommendations

M. Future Medical Care Surgical Intervention or Aggressive Treatment Plan:
- [ ] No Further Recommendations
- [ ] See Below For Recommendations

N. Potential Complications:
- [ ] No Further Recommendations
- [ ] See Below For Recommendations

O. Transportation:
- [ ] No Further Recommendations
- [ ] See Below For Recommendations

P. Architectural Renovations:
- [ ] No Further Recommendations
- [ ] See Below For Recommendations

Q. Leisure Time and/or Recreational Equipment:
- [ ] No Further Recommendations
- [ ] See Below For Recommendations

R. Vocational/Educational Plan:
- [ ] No Further Recommendations
- [ ] See Below For Recommendations

V. IS THE PLAN EASY TO UNDERSTAND FOR ALL PARTIES CONCERNED (FAMILY, CLIENT, ATTORNEY, ECONOMIST, COUNSELOR)?

VI. OTHER COMMENTS

INDEX

INDEX

A

C

H

I

J

K

L

M

O

P

R

S

V

W

X

Z